No Aging in I

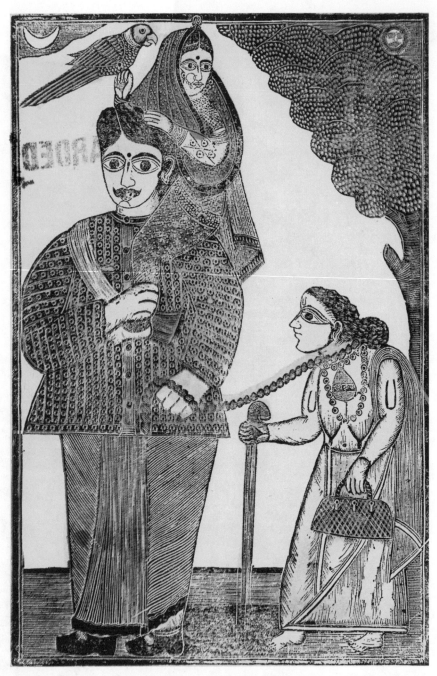

Ghar Kali satire. Woodblock print. Courtesy Victoria Memorial Hall, Calcutta.

No Aging in India

Alzheimer's, the Bad Family, and Other Modern Things

Lawrence Cohen

UNIVERSITY OF CALIFORNIA PRESS

Berkeley   Los Angeles   London

University of California Press
Berkeley and Los Angeles, California

University of California Press, Ltd.
London, England

First Paperback Printing 1999

Grateful acknowledgment is made for permission to quote James Merrill's "River Poem" from *Selected Poems 1946–1985* by James Merrill. Copyright © 1992 by James Merrill. Reprinted by permission of Alfred A. Knopf, Inc.
Thanks is also made for permission to quote the poetry of Ravi Das from *Songs of the Saints of India,* edited by John Stratton Hawley, translated by John Stratton Hawley & M. Juergensmeyer. Translation copyright © 1988 by Oxford University Press, Inc. Used by permission of Oxford University Press, Inc.
In addition, chapter 3 is reprinted in revised form from the author's "No Aging in India: The Uses of Gerontology," *Culture, Medicine and Psychiatry* 16(2), 1992, with kind permission from Kluwer Academic Publishers. Portions of other chapters appeared in an article by the author and are reprinted by permission of the American Anthropological Association from *Medical Anthropology Quarterly* 9(3), 1995. Not for further reproduction.

Library of Congress Cataloging-in-Publication Data
Cohen, Lawrence, 1961–
    No aging in India : Alzheimer's, the bad family, and other modern
things / Lawrence Cohen.
        p.   cm.
    Includes bibliographical references and index
    ISBN 0-520-22462-0 (pbk. : alk. paper)
    1. Aging—Anthropological aspects.   2. Ethnology—India—Vārānasi.
3. Aging—Anthropological apects—India—Vārānasi.   4. Senile
dementia—India—Vārānasi.   5. Alzheimer's disease—India—Vārānasi.
6. Vārānasi (India)—Social life and customs.   I. Title.
GN485.C64   1998
305.26—DC21
                                                            97-38659
                                                            CIP

Printed in the United States of America
9 8 7 6 5 4 3 2 1

This old man had lavender skin, a handkerchief
Toppling from his breastpocket like an iris.
We on the riverbank watched the gracing rowers
Leaving the shore and watched him watch them leave,
And Charles said: I wonder if they mean to him
As much as I can imagine they mean to him.

Charles was like that. But as evening became
A purple element we stayed there wondering
About the old man—talking of other things,
For although the old man by the time we all went home
Was gone, he kept in view, meandering
As with the current, thinking of rivery things

(We supposed) well into the twilight. We would never
Know, this we knew, how much it had meant to him—
Oars, violet water, laughter on the stream.
Though we knew, Charles said, just how much he meant to the river.
For he finally left us alone, the strange old man,
But the river stayed at our side, and shone, and ran.

JAMES MERRILL, "RIVER POEM"

When everyone is dead the Great Game is finished.
Not before.

RUDYARD KIPLING, KIM

For my grandparents
and especially in memory of my grandfather Joseph Glick

Yayāti said:
If my disdain for Gods, seers, and Gandharvas
Has brought these worlds to an end for me, Indra
Then, deprived of the world of the Gods, I hanker,
O king of the Gods, to fall with the honest.

MAHĀBHĀRATA

CONTENTS

LIST OF ILLUSTRATIONS   *xiii*

THE GROUND OF THE ARGUMENT   *xv*

ACKNOWLEDGMENTS   *xix*

NOTE ON TRANSCRIPTION, TRANSLATION, AND TRANSLITERATION   *xxv*

INTRODUCTION   *1*
    The Mad Old Woman of the Millennium   *1*
    The Age of Alzheimer's   *5*
    The View from the River   *9*

Dulari   *13*

1. ORIENTATIONS   *15*
    The Zagreb Tamasha   *15*
    What's Wrong with This Picture?   *18*
    The Better Brain   *18*
    Tropical Softening   *20*
    Embodying Probate   *24*
    A Medical Explanation   *25*
    The Senile Body   *32*
    An Anthropological Picaresque   *34*
    Of Varanasi   *39*

World Wide Web   *45*

2. ALZHEIMER'S HELL   *47*
    No Aging in America! Leading Scientists Reveal   *47*
    Alzheimer's, Subjectivity, and the Old West   *53*
    The Geriatric Paradox   *60*

Oublier *Postmodern Aging*   *70*
A Witch's Curse   *72*
The Senile Climacteric   *74*
Alzheimer's Family   *79*

Nuns and Doctors   *85*

3.   KNOWLEDGE, PRACTICE, AND THE BAD FAMILY   *87*
On Gerontological Objects   *87*
The "Aging in India" Series   *89*
Internationalist Science   *93*
The "Golden Isles"   *100*
Gerontology as Cultural Critique   *103*
BP Checks: The Volunteer Agency   *106*
Free Radical Exchange: The Geriatric Clinic   *109*
Into the Woods: The Retirement Ashram   *113*
Mothers versus Aunties: The Old Age Home   *116*

Aitaśa Pralāpa   *121*

4.   MEMORY BANKS   *123*
The Embodiment of Anxiety   *123*
The Promise of Rasāyana   *127*
The Marketing of Memory   *133*
Memory and Capital   *137*
Forgetting as a Path to Truth   *142*

Merī Latā Mahān   *149*

5.   THE ANGER OF THE RISHIS   *153*
Hot Brains   *153*
Sixtyishness and Seventy-twoness   *156*
Oedipus in India   *158*
Counting the Days and Hours   *166*
Old Women at the Polls   *171*
The Phenomenology of the Voice   *174*
The Familial Body   *177*
The Dying Space   *180*
Taking Voices Seriously   *183*

The Philosopher's Mother   *187*

6.   THE MALADJUSTMENT OF THE BOURGEOISIE   *189*
Civility and Contest   *189*
Balance and Adjustment   *193*
Senility and Madness   *199*
Loneliness and Menopause   *206*

Balance and Cartesian Possibility   211
The Dementia Clinic   214

The Way to the Indies, to the Fountain of Youth   *221*

7. CHAPATI BODIES   *223*
    Nagwa by Its Residents   223
    Weakness as Structure   229
    Muslims and Other Saints   235
    Generation and Weakness Revisited   241
    Jhaṇḍū and the Sound of Dying   248
    The Position of Repose   250

A Child Is Being Lifted   *257*

8. DOG LADIES AND THE BERIYA BABA   *263*
    Dogs and Old Women   263
    Old Women and Madwomen   266
    Madwomen and Witches   268
    Dogs and Old Men   274
    Old Men and Babas   277
    Babas and the State   281

The Age of the Anthropologist   *287*

9. THE BODY IN TIME   *291*
    My Grandmother's Letters   291
    No One Here Cares about Alzheimer's   297
    Lost at the Fair   302

A Last Few Trips up the River   *307*

NOTES   *309*
GLOSSARY   *327*
REFERENCES   *329*
INDEX   *353*

ILLUSTRATIONS

Ghar Kali satire   /   *ii*

The dying space, by Bishwanath Bhattacharya   /   *xiv*

Shravan Kumar carrying his parents   /   *152*

Elder's Day   /   *262*

Old woman voting   /   *290*

The dying space. Pen-and-ink drawing by Bishwanath Bhattacharya.
Collection of the author.

THE GROUND OF THE ARGUMENT

This book is about age, and about its appearance and disappearance in the making of knowledge. It is rooted in a sense that our practices of thinking about society, culture, the body, and the nature of our times would benefit from sustained attention to age as a kind of difference, one particularly relevant to how individuals, groups, and events are imagined and articulated as things in time. Age as difference has long been a dimension of certain kinds of contemporary critical and interpretive work, notably a philosophical concern with the relation of death to meaning and value and a psychoanalytic concern with the formation of subjects. But these are fairly singular narratives of age, defined through particular junctures, endpoints, or stages, and I have in mind a broader and more sparse conception.

I write as a medical anthropologist, and the way I will work toward such a conception of age is through a study that focuses on how people comprehend the body and its behavior in time. The focus will be on loss, and decay: decay of the body, its reason, and its voice, its ability to be heard as a speaking subject. The focus, in other words, is on *senility*, and by that I mean a process rooted in the material changes of physiology and political economy and in a diverse set of social practices that determine how generational and other sorts of difference come to matter. Language here is critical. To call things *dementia*, a clinical term, presumes a focus on the pathology of the individual. To call things *Alzheimer's*, a pathophysiologic term, presumes a focus on a particular set of cellular and subcellular processes resulting in a certain neuroanatomical picture. Calling things *senility* leaves open the hierarchy of relations between the varieties of material and social process at stake in understanding loss, voice, and the body in time.

Most philosophers and scientists are compelled by the nature of the questions they ask to choose between these varied processes, or at least to order and to rank them. Is senility best understood in terms of neuropathology and genetics; normative understandings and expectations of old age, dependency, and individualism; or the economics and politics of families, nations, and the world system? Put crudely, the choice is usually framed as being between biology and psychology, on the one hand, culture and language, on the other, and economy and society, on a third. Three-handed things are fairly monstrous, and most often one of these drops out of the explicit contest and lurks in the background, leaving the job of the scholar the resolution of what appears a weighty dualism. The anthropologist Marshall Sahlins once suggested that for the truly great divides there could be no fence-sitting.[1] Much of contemporary medical anthropology, with its iterative calls for *moral* inquiry, adopts a similar stance. One must choose, throwing one's lot in with medical rationality *or* its holistic or feminist critics, with cultural autonomy and distinctiveness *or* world systems theory and the deserving poor, with medicine as a resource *or* as an ideology.

For some kinds of critical inquiry, techniques of exaggeration and even parody that present the world as clearly dualistic and demanding a choice do indeed seem necessary if one is successfully to challenge received wisdom or practice. But my sense, for the inquiry on senility I have put forward, is that hierarchies of efficient causes—the fate of neurons *versus* the local knowledge of the person and the family *versus* the political economy of the aging body—offer false clarity. This sense comes first from my ethnographic practice itself, second from my graduate training in a program that set itself up at the uncomfortable border of medical practice and anthropological critique, and finally from the work of such scholars of science as Paul Rabinow, Donna Haraway, and Bruno Latour, who in different ways have investigated processes of reason and life so as to avoid either such easy dualisms or the usual alternative, romanticized and empirically vague nondualisms.[2]

In thinking about senility, and in using senility to think about the world, I have tried for the most part to stay away from formalizing such hierarchies of relevance, or my resistance to them, as "theory." My response to such grand theoretical debates has been a sort of thick analysis, to paraphrase Clifford Geertz by shifting the locus of ethnographic depth from "the field" to the process of inquiry. I have attempted a form of what social scientists call snowball sampling but on a different scale, continually adding different sites and methods of inquiry to my project until these juxtapositions ceased to produce interesting challenges to the main arguments.

This process has led to a book full of detail. Like the voices of some of the older people I write about here, it may seem to some to be *too* full, too stocked with unsolicited memories, opinions, and stories. For me, both the pleasures and the responsibilities of ethnography lie precisely in such excess, in a mode of writing and of engaging the world through continual juxtaposition and repetition. Kierkegaard called this kind of engagement *recollecting*, and he suggested that it was frequently utilized by the elderly and others for whom *remembering* had become difficult.[3] Recollection seems an appropriate mode of engagement for a book on senility.

Two broad questions have organized my recollection and writing. The first asks about the processes by which the age of a body comes to matter: specifically, *how are those practices constituted by which bodily decay is experienced, named, measured, treated, and drawn into law and history and science?* And when relevant, how do such practices differ across time, space, and the varieties of human difference we attempt to capture by terms like nation, class, and gender?

The second question emerged from my efforts to answer the first. *Why is it interesting to pose questions about senility in the first place?* This type of questioning has led to what will be the argument behind much of the book: that our understanding of the decay of the body is never only a matter of the techniques at hand. Again and again, I will suggest that the way senility marks a body as being irrevocably in time suggests a relationship between figures of the old body and temporal or political ruptures in the order of things. *Senility becomes a critical idiom through which collectivities imagine and articulate a consciousness of such rupture and of the possibility of some sort of recuperation.*

To ask about senility in India, as anywhere else, is therefore not only to pose some variant of the first question—which if isolated would degenerate into a set of neocolonial binaries or banalities—but to ground one's argument in what matters, at a given moment, in the figure of decay. An anthropology of senility must turn to the consciousness of particular social groups, of regions, and of an emerging colonized bourgeoisie. It cannot isolate the study of "old age" as a singular object awaiting scholarly appropriation and celebration and must avoid, to paraphrase the anthropologist Marilyn Strathern, "the manufacture of a subdiscipline."[4] I have tried, therefore, to think about age less through the solicitous elaboration of some category of "the old" and more through an examination of how age engages larger debates in and out of the academy, particularly those relevant to contemporary India and its political economy and public culture.

ACKNOWLEDGMENTS

ROOTS

I am grateful to my parents and sister for their love and support, and to my four grandparents, whose discussions with me were the genesis of the project. This book is dedicated to the memory of my grandfather Joseph Glick: a runaway at thirteen in search of modern things in the fleshpots of Poland and the Ukraine, a *maskil* and would-be Kabbalist, an immigrant to Quebec as one of two survivors of an extended family of some two dozen, and, among his many other avatars— from baker and fur trader to garment worker—a magician. His sense of growing older and his talks with me linking memory, doctors, religion, pleasure, and work shaped my eventual interests in gerontology and anthropology. He died when I was living in Varanasi; my landlady Mrs. Sharma watched my face come apart when she handed me the telegram and said in her particularly brusque form of deep concern: "Here we'd be happy because he lived so long. What are you crying over?"

TEACHERS AND COLLEAGUES

Arthur Kleinman, Byron Good, and Veena Das have been both distinguished mentors and friends, and it is from the discussions and ephemera of years together that this book has been fashioned. I am grateful for their guidance, and for that of Mary-Jo DelVecchio Good, Robert and Sarah LeVine, Sally Falk Moore, Leon Eisenberg, Jerry Avorn, Diana Eck, and John Carman. Paul Rabinow, Nancy Scheper-Hughes, and Sharon Kaufman—colleagues and friends but also very much mentors—have each in different ways had a great impact on how I have worked through the ideas here. They, and all my colleagues in anthropology at the University of California at Berkeley and in the Joint Program in Medical Anthropology, have been supportive of this work. My writing group—my colleagues Marianne Ferme and Liu Xin, and Janet Roitman—made many useful interventions. Other colleagues whose time and suggestions have been of great help include Aditya Behl, Robert Goldman, Linda Hess, and especially Tanya Luhrmann. My classmates in anthropology were the inspiration and touchstone for much of this book: in particular Rosemarie Bernard, Paul Farmer, Lindsay French, and Linda Hunt, and a few years ahead of me, Norbert Peabody.

Participants in graduate seminars in medical anthropology that I have facilitated over the past five years have helped me work through several of these ideas, and I am grateful in particular for the close readings of Joao Biehl, Liz Herskovits, and Cheryl Theis. There are a lot of remarkable graduate students at Berkeley, and consequently a lot of very smart people have pushed me to rethink parts of this book.

I have benefited from the work of others who have written on old age in India, in particular Sangeeta Chattoo, Marty Chen, Sarah Lamb, Baidyanath Saraswati, Sylvia Vatuk, and A. K. Venkoba Rao. I am grateful to other scholars, activists, and professionals I was fortunate to work with during this research, many of whom became my good friends: Bina Agarwal, Aniket Alam, Paola Bacchetta, Bettina Baumer, J. S. Bawa, P. B. Behere, Roma Chatterji, Uma and Ashin Das Gupta, Rohan D'Souza, Tara Doyle, Rita Gupta and the staff of the Nava Nir homes, Steven Harwood and his staff, Meena Khandelwal, Jamal Kidwai, N. L. Kumar, Nita Kumar, David Lawrence, Rachel and Scott McDermott, Rahul Mehrotra, Deepak Mehta, Diane Mines, Pankaj Mishra, Awadesh Misra, Aloka Mitra, D. N. Nandi, Ashis Nandy, Harish Naraindas, Sharda Nayak, Sudhir Nayer, R. K. Nehru, Michael Nunley, Tulsi Patel, Somita Pathak, Martha Selby, Sagaree Sengupta, Anuradha Shah, Gajendra Singh, R. H. Singh, Virendra Singh, Amrit Srinivasan, Eugene Thomas, Sarojini and Uma Varshney, and Shiv Visvanathan.

RESEARCH ASSOCIATES AND ASSISTANTS

I am grateful for the assistance of Rajesh Pathak, Swapan Chakraborty, Allison Yoh, Amanda Klang, Cheryl Roberts, and Hector Gandhi. Ratnesh Pathak's critical ideas and advice, as well as his research support, were invaluable.

MATERIAL SUPPORT

Periods of research and writing between 1983 and 1996 were funded through a variety of sources, principally the Fulbright-Hays Program, the American Institute of Indian Studies, the John D. and Catherine T. MacArthur Foundation, and the Mellon Foundation, with additional support from the Office of the Chancellor at the University of California at Berkeley, the Townsend Center for the Humanities at Berkeley, the Michael Rockefeller fellowship at Harvard College, the Smith-

Kline Beckmann Medical Perspectives fellowship and the Travellers'/National Council on Aging fellowship. The staff and scholars of both the Wellcome Library and the Indian Office Library in London were wonderfully helpful and gracious during a month I spent on archival work in 1994. The final draft of *No Aging in India* was written during a summer as a guest of the Indian Institute of Advanced Study in Simla; I am grateful to the IIAS director Mrinal Miri and his staff, as I am for the hospitality of the good friends and adopted families who guided and on many occasions housed and fed me during this work: Devraj and Devdatta Basu and their family, Chris Bhaskar, Bishwanath Bhattacharya, S. P. Bhattacharya and family, Ruskin Bond, the Dutt Thapliyar family, Amita Ganguli and her large and welcoming family, R. N. Mishra and his family, Neena and Mano Ranjan, Dewey and Caroline Weatherby, and the Zutshi family.

REVIEWERS AND EDITORS

Chapter 3 appeared in a somewhat different form as an article in *Culture, Medicine and Psychiatry* 16 (2): 123–61; portions of several chapters appeared as an article in *Medical Anthropology Quarterly* 9 (3): 314–34. I am grateful to the editors and reviewers of both journals for their suggestions. I am particularly grateful to Stan Holwitz of the University of California Press for his long and patient support, and to Sue Heinemann and Bonita Hurd for their editorial wisdom.

PEOPLE I INTERVIEWED

Over the past decade, in each of the Varanasi neighborhoods and institutions, in institutions in several other cities and towns across India, and in institutions in Boston, Montreal, and Miami I interviewed and hung out with several thousand persons in the name of research, for cumulative periods of time ranging from a few minutes to hundreds of hours. These exchanges represent several different sorts of debt. Many people were longtime acquaintances, some were close friends, and a few were relatives of mine. To all I iterate both my gratitude and my apologies for an insistence on translating life into fieldwork. In the neighborhoods at the heart of this study, I had fewer acquaintances or friends to begin with, and those that have since developed have usually been mediated by the fact that I came into the relationship writing a book. In one neighborhood, this mattered far more than the others.

There is a story I once heard, in the Varanasi slum of Nagwa Harijan Basti, where I worked from 1988 to 1990, about a young man wandering the neighborhood's lanes and asking too many questions. Some residents are fearful of the incursion; others get angry. Interrogation by the state or its self-appointed proxies might mean a redistribution or at the very least a contest over local resources. One worried resident finally approaches the stranger and demands to know who he is. "I'm a BHU student," comes the response, "preparing a thesis." The enormous campus of Banaras Hindu University lies a kilometer south of Nagwa. "Oh, a thesis," says the relieved resident. "I thought it was something important."

Theses abound, not only on Varanasi, paradigmatic space of Orientalist encounter, but nailed to the doors of Nagwa slum itself. Residents tell of many sociology theses from BHU, of enviable careers built on the enumeration of their own more marginal experience. On the road that leads from the university to the slum one can find several dissertation binding shops.

The flow of observers is not only from the university. International luminaries, from American presidential candidates to members of the Vatican curia, have wandered this untouchable slum's muddy lanes in search of a truer India, coming to view firsthand its poverty and the grassroots efforts of Father Paul, a Dutch priest, to create change. Bernard Cohn has described "the observational/travel modality"—India structured as points along a tour uncovering its varied and shifting essences—as an important form of the British construction of knowledge about its colonies.[1] Within the late twentieth century touristic, Nagwa is counterposed to the city's other indices of essential Indianness: the burning ghats, the narrow lanes, the "monkey temple," the mysterious yet filthy Ganges, and the peace of the Buddhist shrine of Sarnath. Amid this density of images, Nagwa points to the essences of caste and poverty and to the location of social change as external, in the person of the exemplary foreigner. Like a wizened peasant encountered amidst the wild in a Wordsworth poem, the untouchable Chamar of Nagwa slum are the icons of suffering and of the earthy rootedness of human experience that allow the transcendence of Varanasi to persevere, still one of the great sites of the Romantic for the European and American imagination. Recently, I discovered a Web site devoted to photographs of Varanasi slum Chamar.

My own research is not "about" Nagwa, nor is it the only neighborhood in which I worked. But it is here that I sense the ironies of my own practice most strongly. Books and theses are not that threatening in Nagwa, because they are "useless"; they do not seem to change anything. Like old people, they are called *jhaṇḍū*, a local word meaning "wasted" in the sense of a losing lottery ticket after the contest is over. Like old people and lottery tickets, they are full of strong-sounding but empty promises, so much *bakbak* or nonsense. They glide over the realities of the desiring body and the material world.

My earliest response to the ethics of what I call anthropological desire—the desire to spend time writing about both friends and strangers, often in vastly different and often more marginal circumstances than oneself, under the sign of realism—was to start training to become a physician. Arthur Kleinman, Byron Good, Mary-Jo DelVecchio Good, and Leon Eisenberg introduced me to new ways of thinking, through anthropology, about health and the roots of suffering. I began a Ph.D., and ultimately was "caught" by this new field enough to abandon a medical career. That particular decision made it still more difficult to deflect the accusations from Nagwa, imagined and real, of being *jhaṇḍū*. I wrote *No Aging in India* as an effort to participate in a critical medical anthropology in which the exigencies of the body and of material conditions inform as well as are informed by the powerful *bakbak* of what we sometimes still call culture. But so what? If cultural narratives, as I will suggest, are constructed and sustained as much against as for meaning, so my own theoretical project and moral posturing may be written against my lack of a good answer to the question of one woman in Nagwa slum: "What does writing do for us?"

Many of my colleagues in medical anthropology seem to be struggling with similar questions: a few have dedicated themselves to materializing through a locally driven and politically aware practice Nancy Scheper-Hughes's call for a "critically applied anthropology."[2] Such a path is certainly one of the most powerful and compelling examples of critical scholarly engagement in medical anthropology. But for those, myself included, who are committed to a different kind of engagement within the academy, the choice of how and what to write seems murkier. The language of the time is strewn with the best of intentions, reflexive articulations from the moral to the militant. I am somewhat uneasy about the usefulness of performative moralization in anthropology; still, I appreciate the sentiment. With the help of several thoughtful interlocutors, and in particular Veena Das and Niranjan Karnik, I have been working toward what Scheper-Hughes has called a "good enough" practice.[3] I am indebted to many people in Nagwa for talking to me at great length, without as of yet a good enough response on my part. Many others would not and did not, and here too I should acknowledge what I was taught. Ram Lakhan in particular straddled both camps, as mentor, harsh critic, and sometime friend. Among committed outsiders, the extraordinary and ubiquitous Om Prakash Sharma and the tireless community worker Frans Baartmans introduced me to many people in Nagwa and were unfailingly gracious with their time, insight, and example.

FRIENDSHIP

The love and support of many of these and other wonderful friends and family, and the occasional providential intervention of various mysterious strangers and tricks, have given possibility and shape to this work of the past decade. No list can begin to comprehend the friends whose caring has helped me write and finish this book, but I do want to remember two people who died recently, Tara Devi and Habib Khan. Memories: Tara making potato latkes using Linda Hess's recipe, while giving me advice on keeping things secret in Varanasi; Habib and his kids and I lying on the roof of his house looking at the stars and Habib lecturing me about the nature of love.

OF LOVE, THEN

Tom Boellstorff was my partner for most of the years I worked on this book; his integration of impassioned community service and rigorous intellectual practice remains a model, perhaps the best lesson with which to confront the practice of *jhaṇḍū* anthropology.

The years of this research and this writing have been rich and wonderful ones for me. Two friends, Punam Zutshi and Vimal Shankar, made this book and its author happen in unanticipated ways.

NOTE ON TRANSCRIPTION,
TRANSLATION, AND TRANSLITERATION

Unless otherwise noted, all reported conversations and statements come from field notes written in English a few minutes to several hours after an interview or encounter; thus, the wording frequently reflects an after-the-fact translation by a nonnative speaker and introduces a set of obvious biases. I found in most cases that discussions I initiated with notebook or tape at hand were less productive and less interesting. This finding is idiosyncratic and is not meant to convey any programmatic intent.

I have used the following guide to transliteration and diacritics: citations previously transliterated are printed as in the original, as are the titles of films and books. All quotations from interviews that I have transliterated are italicized and have diacritics. Hindi, Bhojpuri, Bengali, and Sanskrit words feature standard diacritics, and Urdu words are transliterated as they would be spoken by most Banarsis. The exceptions: (1) common nouns that have entered into English are neither italicized nor given diacritics; (2) anglicized spellings that do not follow standard diacritical usage have been retained in some cases, and I have tried to follow current convention on a case-by-case basis; (3) place, language, institutional, and personal names and proper nouns more generally are not written with diacritics (e.g., Varanasi not Vārāṇasī, Shankar not Śankar) unless they are part of a title or quotation. As the plural form of some Hindi words may confuse some readers, I have followed the trend toward hybrid "Hinglish" and used English plural endings when these seemed clearer.

Introduction

*in which river trips figure prominently, an old woman shakes her head,
and the author reflects upon losing his marbles*

THE MAD OLD WOMAN OF THE MILLENNIUM

She appears but for a moment, the mad old woman of the millennium, her presence noted because of a debate over whether times were hard enough that God
would take to writing letters. She appears—offering everything, demanding nothing—"giving up her food for five days and nights, during which period she sat shaking her head about." We know nothing else about her, save that this head-shaking,
food-resisting body of hers could at one point promise redemption, and that this
promise seems to have led (times being hard indeed) to bloodshed and misfortune.

Early in 1865 several boatmen returned westward from Calcutta, to their
homes along the Ganges River near the city of Varanasi, otherwise known as Banaras, Benares, or Kashi. They bore with them a letter from God. God in this case
was the goddess Kali, according to the Varanasi correspondent of the Allahabad
Pioneer, an English paper.[1] The boatmen in this case were Mallahs, members of a
community or caste of families whose hereditary work was boating and fishing. In
her letter the goddess called for the Mallahs to stop several low-status practices
with which they were identified: eating fish, eating meat, and selling fish for a
livelihood. The demand, which would have deprived many in the community of
their means of survival, seemed to presage a millennial change in which poor
communities like the Mallahs would no longer need to engage in difficult, low-
status work. The goddess of the letter demanded that instead of fishing, the Mallahs should devote themselves completely to becoming her *bhagat*s, or devotees.

During the following weeks, the letter from God circulated in several of the
colonial administrative districts surrounding Varanasi. Mallah community leaders
debated its relevance and authenticity. A meeting was organized in order to decide
what, if anything, to do about the letter and the rumors circulating. The meeting

was held on April 13, a Saturday, during a religious fair at a local pilgrimage site to the northeast of the city, near the village of Balua.

The particulars of the letter and the debate were recorded in the regional English press because of a subsequent set of events that occurred at the festival and that heightened the millenarian stakes of the goddess' demand. These events, which culminated in several violent deaths and the intervention of the police, are offered by the press as exemplary of the macabre religiosity of Indians, and particularly Hindus, in the absence of British intervention. The week of the Balua fair, marking the beginning of the Hindu solar year and coinciding with festivals throughout the country, was otherwise represented in English papers in terms of the lack of what was termed "incident." The memories of the failed rebellion known as the "Indian Mutiny" and of its aftermath were less than a decade old. Religious festivals were frequently read by colonial authorities as dangerous sites that could incite local passions. Most reports from correspondents to British Indian newspapers that week reported the success of pacification campaigns abolishing what were at the time seen as among the bloodiest and most rabble-rousing of Hindu rituals, the devotional piercings and other mortifications of the flesh that the British grouped under the heading of hook-swinging.[2]

Amid this litany of successes in curtailing religious license, the Varanasi correspondent to the *Pioneer*, in a letter appearing on April 19, reported on an unexpected failure: an incident of violence among the Mallahs gathered at Balua:

BENARES

April 15th.—A very singular occurrence took place, on the 13th instant, at Bulooa, in this district, which terminated in the violent death of two of the boatman caste of that place. It seems that the *mullas* [Mallahs] of Bulooa, whilst engaged in *sonee poojah* [propitiation of the inauspicious planet Saturn, or Sani, it being Saturday], got it into their heads that if blood were shed, some benefit would accrue to their community, and that the parties slain would rise again and live for ever! Two of the most enthusiastic in the cause accordingly consented to meet death at the hands of the brotherhood. The throats of the wretched men were immediately cut, while their parents stood by and exhorted them to bear the pain, as they would be sure to return and live for ever. The police now interfered, and met with some rough treatment at the hands of these strange creatures, who did not approve of their orgies being interrupted.[3]

One must wade through the brutal language of the colonial grotesque. No letter is mentioned initially; it appears two days later in a second report along with other new details. One such detail almost escapes notice, scarcely relevant to the correspondent save as a further sign of the irrationality of the Hindu lower orders: allusion is made to local interest in the behavior of an old woman, interest that somehow relates the debate over Kali's letter to the subsequent violence.

The second report begins with a reprisal of the two deaths, depicting the violence as characteristic of such religious assemblies, and goes on to describe the interventions of the police at considerable length. It then turns to the letter:

It appeared that two "seers," had been down to Calcutta in charge of some boats, and on their return had brought with them a letter addressed to the caste, calling on them to become *Buggutts*, and not to kill or eat fish any more. This letter seems to have been circulated in the Benares, Ghazeepore, and Azimghur districts; and *the belief in its truth seems to have been strengthened by the fact of an old woman giving up her food for five days and nights, during which period she sat shaking her head about.* On the occasion in question the people of the caste acted a regular play, three of the defendants in the case representing Ram, Mahabeer, and Mahadeo, Junior, and the two deceased, Uttril and Mahadeo, Senior: the latter were slain by the former, Ram having promised to bring them to life again. Among those captured are the three surviving gods, who have confessed their guilt [italics mine].[4]

The narrative link between the dangers of popular enthusiasm and the bloody orgies that inevitably follow is "the fact of an old woman." Not just an old woman, but a woman shaking her head about: the motion a classic sign of the *pagli*, the madwoman, for many in north India. And not just an old *pagli*, but one whose complete and sustained refusal of food takes her entirely out of the transactional frame of being a person, in particular of being an old and dependent person, and places her in that space of power and death from which her shaking silence speaks. In the decade following the failed hopes and repressive sequelae of rebellion, within a colonial text affirming the irrational nature of local violence, the mad old woman of the millennium makes an appearance within a text that does not know quite what to do with her.

I came across the old woman, and the events at Balua, while sitting in the India Office Library in London looking for probate cases in which children attempted to use a changing colonial legal system to prove an old parent was of unsound mind. The brevity of her appearance, despite its critical location in the narrative, sent me in search of further mention of a figure whose refusal to accept food and whose shaking head was offered as a source of valid knowledge. In several variants of Indian epistemology, any such source of valid knowledge would be termed a *pramāṇa*. How did the "fact of an old woman" serve as a *pramāṇa* for the resurrectional moment of the Mallahs?

Despite their "being uncommon and out of the way," the deaths in Balua were not widely reported. The *Bengal Hurkaru and India Gazette* of May 3 offered a description of the events with no mention of the old woman but with greater detail pertaining to the divine origin and contents of the letter and with a revised list of the five gods involved. However, other figures of old women and descriptions of their relation to religious practice were not foreign to the pages of the *Hurkaru* that month. On April 13, the date of the Balua affair, the paper reported on pilgrims who had journeyed to immerse themselves in the Ganges far upriver at the religious fair at Hardwar. The correspondent is preoccupied with the women as they emerge from the water, dripping:

A large proportion of the bathers were women who journeyed to this distance from the southern and eastern districts of Bengal, the central provinces and central India, and amongst these thousands, it does not say much for the beauty of the houris of the east, not a single really beautiful woman could be seen. Old and decrepit women seemed to counterbalance the young, and when these, after the immersion arose from the waters "like Venus of the sea" they did not strike the spectator as possessing in any remarkable degree the grace and beauty of the form divine.

Here, as a comic figure of the spiritual and physical decrepitude of the east, the British editors offer the vision of a national body composed of old women. Doddering and even mad old bodies appear in the press of the time as frequent signs of the strangeness of India, as frequently as do dangerous and enthusiastic young men like those of Balua. After casting his eye over the aged Venuses of Hardwar, the *Hurkaru* correspondent notes the pathetic folly of "one old Raja," who "to pave his way to the regions of bliss everlasting, gave 55,000 Rupees [to Brahman priests officiating], and would have given more but that the unfortunate and crazed creature kicked the bucket before he could finish his almsgivings."[5]

Against the colonial repetition of the decrepit or crazed old person as a sign of Indianness, the figure of the old woman who in her gestures and refusals proves that Kali's time is imminent remains apparitional. What she signifies, what she achieves—that which makes the letter from God readable—is not available to the English papers, for which she is but one sign of local irrationality among many. Who is she? I abandoned the archiving of probate cases to search unsuccessfully for her in the local Hindi and English press. Yet the question of the old madwoman, and of her movement and her silence, remains.

This book is about the representation of old people as mad or otherwise *different* in what they do or say, and about the relation of such difference to other sorts of realities, such as a millenarian moment in the history of Varanasi Mallahs. One of my goals in writing it is to suggest that age, as a way of representing and understanding other sorts of differences between individuals and classes of individuals, is critical to the articulation not only of individual bodies but of collective ones. The Balua affair suggests the importance of old age to the articulation of a specific moment of radical social possibility, to a new vision of culture and community. How and why might the old body serve as a critical site in the constitution of collective meaning and practice?

Current debates on old age in India and elsewhere engage other collective frames, particularly that of the nation. The "nation" has always been an important category in how the subset of social scientists known as gerontologists think about old age, but inevitably in a single and very specific way: there are, or will be, too many old people in our country, or in other people's countries, and so we—the guardians of the nation, or of the welfare of other nations—must do something about this problem. Thus the connection of old age, understood as a problem, to the category of the nation is central to many of the books on gerontology that have recently appeared in India, a number of which bear the identical title: *Aging in India*. In part I write as a contribution to the ongoing critique of such alarmist arguments and the effects they may have on real people, old and less old, particularly when the arguments extend across national boundaries. Thus, in part, the reason for my own title, *No Aging in India*.

But there are other, and perhaps more interesting, arguments to be made, and many other absences that the *No* of the title is meant to suggest. The old woman of Balua, whose refusal of the dependency normally constitutive of old age seems momentarily to signify a moment of radical transformation for the Mallahs, points to a different intersection of age, gender, and nation. Much recent work in the social sciences and humanities has examined the relationship between gendered and sexual representations and the politics of empire and the postcolonial nation,[6] but *age* has far less frequently been examined as a form of difference in its own right. How do collectivities and polities articulate themselves through or against such generational and age-specific representations? Can we learn something about the politics and histories of communities, nations, and empires through the study of where, how, and in which bodies age matters? How does the study of the body in time offer a way into the ongoing articulation of something called India?

THE AGE OF ALZHEIMER'S

I approach the body in time through the exploration of what has perhaps been its dominant medicalization during the years of my research, the set of bodily conditions and social practices organized and known as Alzheimer's disease.

When I was a kid we talked about senility as a vague sort of thing, losing your marbles, in old people who weren't getting enough blood to their brains. When I went to college, it was still possible for a professor in psychology to lecture that senility was a cognitive defense against the mindlessness of institutionalized old age. My friends and I knew—from films, journalistic exposés, and visits to old relatives—that nursing homes could make you senile. The etiological dilemma of *King Lear*—is it his old age or his daughters' actions that precipitate Lear's madness?—bespoke something real.

Well over a decade later, I was sitting in a cafeteria writing an early draft of this book and overheard, at the next table, "It must be my Alzheimer's, dear." I rarely hear senility discussed anymore. Friends ask me: "Isn't there a difference? Isn't Alzheimer's a disease but senility the normal process?" *Newsweek* articles I read in Varanasi when I was doing the research for this book proclaimed Alzheimer's "the fourth leading killer of adults," a "bomb," and an "epidemic" requiring "the equivalent of a Manhattan Project."[7] We are, it seems, ever on the verge of a cure; not a season went by during the writing of this book but some lab claimed to have definitively identified the Alzheimer's gene or to have recombinantly produced an animal model of the disease or to have developed an inexpensive test to identify and label future victims. Whatever the degree of market-driven hype, new knowledges have clearly emerged and further breakthroughs are likely. Something has happened: something learned; perhaps something forgotten.

No Aging in India is written about a different place, different friends, and different memories and lapses of memory, but its earliest roots lie in my coming of age in Canada and the United States, in my witnessing the emergence of the age of Alzheimer's in North America. Michael Agar writes that anthropologists interpret culture through Heideggerian "breakdowns"—through insight gained when events difficult to explain with one's own framework or "schema" for making sense of them force one into the realization of a different schema.[8] The juxtaposition, in my own life, of the age of senility with that of Alzheimer's constituted the earliest breakdown, the beginning of an insight that to talk about the behavior of old people was to invoke far more than blood flow, brain cells, nursing homes, or marbles.

The genre of contemporary writing about Alzheimer's dementia is often High Gothic, reflecting senility's newer and far more virulent identity as "the brain killer." Any alternative framework to the reductively pathophysiological to frame what's at stake in the lives of demented persons and their families is increasingly delegitimated. Karen Lyman has called this winnowing of what constitutes acceptable discourse the progressive "biomedicalization" of dementia.[9] I agree but resist the implication that the impetus for the shift lies primarily with a purportedly hegemonic abstraction called biomedicine. Hegemonies are not so easily reduced to institutions. Something far deeper, something more pervasive is at work. The ever more inescapable obviousness of dementia greatly exceeds the sites of its professional management. As at Balua, but in very different ways, there is far more to the representation of the old person than the specificity of the aging body.

I am neither interested in denying the relevance of the brain nor in making light of what families experience. This book will challenge us to think about what some of us understand as Alzheimer's in terms other than or in addition to those of a diagnosis or a disease: as a set of local and contingent practices rooted in culture and political economy. To do so it will draw on data across class, gender, caste, and regional and national boundaries and will focus on what is at stake in the representation, experience, and negotiation of old age in a place increasingly labeled postcolonial India. Yet its argument is as rooted in the materiality of contemporary clinical knowledge and the specifics of my own personal and clinical experience in the United States as it is in the Varanasi, Delhi, Calcutta, and Bombay ethnographies and Indian and European archival work that form the bulk of the research.

Before undertaking the Indian research, I examined geriatric and gerontological practice in the United States at multiple sites: at a school of public health, studying community-based geriatric health care; at governmental and nongovernmental social welfare agencies, designing older worker employment and training programs; at a medical school, being trained as a medical student in evaluating neurobiological research and conducting geriatric assessments and dementia workups; at a minimally funded nursing home in a Boston slum, working as a nursing aide and tying patients to their chairs each day and to their beds each night to protect them from falling; at well-funded nursing homes, working as a medical student and learning about milieu therapy and behavioral management; at local chapters of the Alzheimer's Disease and Related Disorders Association, joining support groups for the families of Alzheimer's patients; and at home and in the world, watching as not only relatives but two mentors, whose advice and example were integral to different stages of this project, grew increasingly forgetful and faced the diagnosis of Alzheimer's and the stigma of its label.

Yet exhaustive appeals to experience like these I have just made, frequent in the gerontological literature, may disguise as much as they disclose. Jaber Gubrium has drawn attention to the emergence of an Alzheimer's disease movement among family members and gerontological professionals, and to the nature of its practice: the continual reenactment, through meetings and a prolific literature of articles, books, and videos, of the status of Alzheimer's as a real and a biological disease. He suggests that repetition allows those involved with the movement to deny the inherent ambiguity in maintaining a distinction between normal aging and pathological dementia.[10] In the early chapters of this book, I will suggest that the iterative quality of Alzheimer's discourse further allows its victim to be reconstituted as a nonperson, and I will argue that it is not the biological processes of dementia as much as the social processes of its construction that deprives the demented elder of selfhood. Roland Barthes, in *Sade, Fourier, Loyola*, frames the problem of repetition more generally, looking through what he terms such "enumerative obsessions" in language and narrative to a set of vacancies that they expose.[11] Barthes is a presence throughout this book; central to its method is my interest in cultural representation not only as a structural field but as a set of obsessions and absences. For before one sees through representational surfaces to some notion of underlying architecture, the anthropologist's abstraction of culture, one needs to think about the repetitions of signs and narratives on those surfaces: culture as a kind of semiotic frottage.

At stake both in the voices of the old persons discussed below and in the institutions and narratives through which these voices are heard is a multitude of repetitions. Many enumerative obsessions, not only the elaboration of Alzheimer's, anchor my arguments here. These will become apparent in the first few chapters, as the narrative shifts from Boston to Varanasi via an interlude in Zagreb. Against Alzheimer's, I examine the "decline of the joint family"—the central narrative in Indian gerontology—and its relation to the language and practices defining the behavior of old people. In juxtaposing these two obsessions—rather than, for example, two cultural systems or structures—I try to move beyond an overly essentializing anthropology, mindful of Ronald Inden's and T. N. Madan's critiques of attempts particularly by Europeans and Americans to uncover the essential India.[12] Against the anthropological reification of ethnographic difference as *necessarily* privileged and essential, I struggle to bring together the competing and crosscutting totalizations of the modern body, of local and global economies and practices, and of culture as structure organizing at every turn one's orientation to self and the world.

These latter sorts of questions are of great interest to me as an anthropologist, but they may seem less compelling to readers more interested in Alzheimer's and old age; the relations of mind, body, and memory over time; or the sociology and politics of urban north India. I have tried throughout to strike a balance between the different sorts of interests and degrees of familiarity with medicine, gerontology, anthropology, and South Asia with which different readers may approach this text. Two other balancing acts inform my writing: writing for readers from India and elsewhere; and writing for imagined specialists and imagined general readers.

Balance is of course not a neutral term, as anthropologist Laura Nader would remind us[13] and as the language of balance framing the old person in middle-class neighborhoods in Varanasi will reveal. Other metaphors of how one can bridge the multiplicity of theories, persons, and politics informing one's writing—Donna Haraway's cat's cradle, the play of approaches held in interlacing and productive tension, and Wendy Doniger's home cooking and tool kit, the celebration of usefully messy bricolage[14] —may evoke a sense of the approach used here. Like some of the people about whom I write, I will at points elect a rather unbalanced aesthetic in pushing the reader to make certain connections, a juxtapositional ethnography of sorts. In the chapters that follow, discussions of seventeenth- and nineteenth-century European cultural history will come perilously close to readings of American supermarket tabloids and ethnographic descriptions of American support groups for Alzheimer's disease caregivers; these in turn are inserted into a text that focuses on several neighborhoods in one north Indian city but that includes discussions of an Italian pharmaceutical house in Bombay, a government ministry in New Delhi, an old age home in Calcutta, and geriatric clinics in Madras and Dehradun. Contemporary journalism rubs shoulders with Sanskrit epics and folklore, Hindi films and magazine ads, sociological anthologies, and religious calendar art. The author's two grandmothers make their appearance.

There is method to all this, and some constructive models in social theory. I will not belabor these here—each juxtaposition must stand on its own—save to make a few points relevant to this particular project. Field sites—to use the term anthropologists give to the places about which they write—are plural. Each of the people I will invoke and remember below is located in terms of multiple sites: brain, body, psyche, family, household, neighborhood, religion, caste, ethnicity, class, sex, language, episteme, city, nation, world system, and so forth. These sites articulate with one another in various ways—stable and shifting—in time and space. I juxtapose variant classes of disparate material in different portions of this text to highlight one or another of these articulations and some of the political and interpretative issues at stake in each case. This method leads to a book that is far from Aristotelian in the sorts of unities it offers. Unlike the conventional sociology and anthropology of India, it is not quite "about India." Nor is it really a comparison, for in at least one strong sense there is no place called "the West" out there with which "India" can be compared. A genealogy of contemporary gerontological practice in India, for example, must draw upon the specifics of a European history of medical practice as opposed to reifying the latter yet again as a sort of black box called "Western medicine." It must ask what is at stake in the construction of a postcolonial social science around the figure of an old body, and in so doing turn to the governmental, nongovernmental, and commercial sites where such a science takes shape. It must take seriously the multiple and interlocking worlds of meaning and institutions of social regulation within which a body becomes a series of subjects over time. Such a project requires an examination of many sites of cultural production, from changing readings of Brahmanic and anti-Brahmanic Hindu texts to different sorts of emerging urban spaces and the social dramas they frame to images and understandings incited by advertising. It must be a response to a world ever more global and yet trenchantly and often tragically ever more local in the ways poverty, violence, disease, and other viscerally real effects of marginal subjectivity are imported, isolated, and maintained within ever *less* porous borders.

So, the book is about senility, dementia, hot brain, sixtyishness, Alzheimer's disease, dotage, weakness, enchantment, and other states not named but which might strike one who is familiar with one or another of these formerly used terms as being recognizable. That is, it is about the language of behavioral inappropriateness and the practices of exclusion that come to encompass the lived experience of many old people. It is about the structures—bodies, generations, households, neighborhoods, neurons, classes, and cultures—that mediate and sustain the relationship between experience, significance, and practice. It is ultimately about the differences between bodies that explode efforts to ground an analysis in any of these frames—biological, political, or cultural—without rethinking the relationships between them.

THE VIEW FROM THE RIVER

The river, again. We are in a boat: myself, two other passengers—railway workers from the nearby town of Mughalsarai—and the boatman, who is pulling hard against the current and ferrying us upstream. We are on the Ganges, in Varanasi, and on our left the ghats glide by, flights of stone steps leading up to the lanes of the city. A few men and women, some quite old and stooped, are bathing. The scene—river, ghats, lanes, boats, and bathers—is clichéd. It has come to stand in for the city as a whole in a variety of registers: religious, touristic, sanitary, scholarly. Its meanings—what we four on the boat can make, respectively, of what we see—are overdetermined.

Other boats glide by. I don't remember their passengers, but they might have held parties of religious pilgrims come to see and bathe in the river at this sacred site, or tourists from larger cities or from abroad doing the prescribed early morning boat ride—cameras poised to catch the houris in dripping saris, the smoldering cremation pyres, the fisherman drawing in their nets glinting against the sunrise, or the suspicious-looking objects floating in the water. Or they might have been parties of men crossing the river to the wide and empty other bank for an outing, one of the lazy pleasures of *banārsipan*, the much-elaborated essence of being a Varanasi resident.[15] Or of development workers engaged in an often-publicized multinational effort to fight pollution and "save the Ganges."

It is 1989. The boatman's name is Shankar, and I know him because his wife cleans house for Marwari Mataji, the old lady who lives upstairs from me. Mataji and I share a building overlooking the river, owned by a temple trust; the principal trustees are the Peshwas, descendants of the former rulers of much of western India. Mataji was once a wealthy widow who came to Varanasi to live out her days in the religiously meritorious act of being a *kāśīvāsī*, a dweller in Kashi. (Kashi is another, venerable name for this city in the easternmost part of Uttar Pradesh.) Marwari Mataji became a disciple of Karpatri, an ascetic leader of the Hindu political right, who himself used to stay in this house by the river. Karpatriji had long since died (though his ghost would later come to haunt me in the person of Tambe the madman), and Marwari Mataji kept his memory alive.

Shankar is grizzled, wiry, and white-haired. When I first met him I thought he was in his sixties. But he is considerably younger. "Shankar works hard," I remember Marwari Mataji saying. "He just looks old." I would rent Shankar's boat for exercise on occasion, but even without passengers found it difficult to propel its lengthy wooden oars. Amid the traffic of other people's boats, I would spin in circles while Shankar watched from Mataji's window.

The two men from Mughalsarai are looking at me and I at them. They ask me if I'm a tourist. I get a little defensive. I tell them I'm a medical student and an anthropologist learning about what some people call the *kamzorī* (weakness) of *dimāg* (brain) in old age, what others joke about as "going sixtyish," *saṭhiyānā*. One of the two men leans forward and asks me to explain, as an expert, why the brains of Muslim old people stay *sahī*, right or correct, and why Muslim elders usually don't get angry, confused, or obstinate. Why that is, they do not go sixtyish.

The two men are Hindu and working class. It is a time in which political writers—in Varanasi and around the world—are worrying about rising communal tensions between Hindus and Muslims, and I am therefore struck that a poor Hindu man is framing the old brain of the Muslim as somehow more "right." But I lack a good answer to the railway worker's question, and I tell him so. I play it safe. I admit that I have never noticed any differences between Hindu and Muslim brains and ask him why he posed the question. He pauses. He says he wonders whether the fact that "we Hindus fight far more with our old parents and are less disciplined in family affairs than Muslims" might have an effect on the behavior of old people. These are not his exact words; as a social anthropologist, my practice was to write down the details of remembered conversations such as this one each evening before retiring.

Rereading what I had written in my notes of this conversation over subsequent weeks, I came to doubt whether I had interpreted the meaning of the man from Mughalsarai correctly. Differences ascribed to Muslim brains were neither a feature of Indian popular discourse on old age nor were they apparent within the language or practice of most persons I interviewed. Yet over the course of two years in Varanasi studying when and why old people were understood to be behaving differently and with what sorts of social and bodily consequences, I was a dozen or so times asked the same question, about the *sahī* brains of Muslims, and always by working or middle class Hindus.[16] The question came to haunt me. I would ask friends, acquaintances, or interview respondents in the four neighborhoods where I spent most of my time whether there were any differences between Hindus and Muslims in old age, and they would inevitably answer in the negative. Despite the putative advantage the railway worker's question seemed to offer to Muslims, the Varanasi Muslims with whom I spoke were unanimous in rejecting the idea that there could be any difference between Hindu and Muslim bodies and brains, seeing in the observation primarily a threat to their ultimately more strategic assertion that all persons were the same.

Yet each time I was ready to abandon the question, someone else in a different neighborhood and different context would pose some variant of it. I would press each new person for his or her own ideas, and I usually was told something like what the railman had first said: Muslim *families* are different; they are *sahī*, unlike our own, which in contrast are somehow spoiled or excessive or undisciplined or simply bad. And bad families produce weak-brained old people. Yet none of these interlocutors were happy with the sufficiency of this answer: thus their initial posing of Muslim difference as a question for an academic "expert." And so I begin by posing their question here, yet again. For me, it is a variant of the question raised by the old madwoman of the Balua affair. What might be at stake in the act of speaking about old brains and the behavior of old people, such that their being invoked moves us so seamlessly from the old body to the status of families and entire communities, religions, or nations?

✍ *Dulari* ☙

She would crouch at the edge of a crossing of muddy lanes or against the wall of a house. She had on an old grayish sari, and her thin arms reached around her squatting legs to grasp one another; then, with a motion of hand and head, she rocked slowly back and forth. She was small and dusty, easy to miss; I probably had passed the crossing several times without noticing her. It was her voice, rising and falling as she rocked, muttering quietly and incessantly, that I finally heard. Syllables thrust together—gurgling, "my daughter," "nothing, nothing"—in a monotone. A kid passed by, saw me listening, and grinned: "It's *bakbak*." Muttering, nonsense. Another kid: "She's crazy, a *pagli*."

She wasn't always at the crossing, but I heard her there a fair amount before I knew who she was and where she lived. Always the rocking back and forth, with her head bent down and to the side, and the rhythmic *bakbak*. Then one day, as I was hurrying by one of her habitual spots, she looked up with a steady gaze and spoke: "I have no one." And then, "I'm hungry." I hesitated, embarrassed, and she began to talk. *Bakbak* of a different kind, cogent stories and cogent demands, but repeated again and again, a new cadence set against the absence of a good old age and the presence of the hope that I might be one of the Christian Fathers come to redeem her suffering with money.

She talked and talked: of the death of a daughter under mysterious circumstances, of her own subsequent abandonment by her family, of her renting from distant relations a room in Nagwa slum, along with a male cousin, an old childless widower, who pulled a rickshaw in the city to support them. I began spending time with the two of them, helping out some, quid pro quo for listening to the story of Dulari—that was her name—the repetition of her missing daughter. But it is the *bakbak* of the old madwoman of the crossing I most remember, its vagueness, its rare and almost impossible coherence.

She was in a way expected in Varanasi. Almost everyone's Banaras had an abstracted old woman as an icon of the place, from Brahmanical panegyrics and the colonial picturesque down to Allen Ginsberg and Raja Rao.[1] Writ more broadly, she was India as the site of cheap solicitude under the sign of Mother Teresa, a metonym for the land of starving ancients awaiting the administration of that last loving cup. And not just cheap solicitude: the poor widow has become one of the focal points of a new critical analysis of Indian political economy, in the work of Martha Chen, Jean Drèze, and more indirectly, Bina Agarwal and Amartya Sen.[2]

I returned to Nagwa in the autumn of 1989, after some months' absence. Dulari was no longer at any of her crossroad spots. The cousin had died, and with him her source of food and rent. The relatives from whom she had rented a room told me her health had worsened from the sadness, and that they had no choice but to ask her to leave. They said they had asked one of the Christian Fathers to find her a space somewhere. Some kilometers north, Mother Teresa's Varanasi house stood set back from the river. It was a small version of her Calcutta operation; the sisters and staff told of periodic sweeps of the train station in search of abandoned or destitute elders needing shelter and a place to die. I found Dulari there, lying on a bed with her hair closely cropped.

Her look struck me: first, a bit mad and then, as two of the sisters walked by, conspiratorial. She pulled out a piece of paper from under her sheets and quickly thrust it into my hands: "They can't have this!" It was a picture of the goddess Durga. The nuns walked by, waiting.

ONE

Orientations

in which anthropologists construe, and neurons and nations conjoin

THE ZAGREB TAMASHA

Who is it that can tell me who I am?
KING LEAR I.IV.230

Tamasha in Hindi is a commotion, a performance—song and dance, tragedy, burlesque, and romance strung together with lots of noise—as in its heir, the modern Hindi film. In 1988 anthropologists from around the world convened in Zagreb for a global conference.[1] Several sessions were devoted to old age. At one, an anthropologist from India presented a paper speculating on the long lives of elders in a hill tribe in northeastern India. Afterward, the floor was opened for questions.

An American anthropologist asked the speaker about the prevalence of dementia among the elders. Dementia is a clinical term, which in 1988 signified progressive and long-term cognitive losses. Most of the anthropologists in the room were from North America, and they knew that dementia was more prevalent among the oldest old, persons in their eighties and nineties, like those of the superannuated hill tribe just described. The question seemed reasonable.

But the speaker did not follow it. There was a pause, and the American repeated the question, varying the key word: *senile dementia? Alzheimer's disease?* The speaker did not seem familiar with the terms. The room became still. The speaker's scholarship was not in question—he had presented a careful ethnography and had addressed questions of deep concern to Indian anthropology and to the emerging field of Indian gerontology—but Alzheimer's disease was not central to his frame of reference. Yet what had been a lackluster session on a hot afternoon suddenly grew focused and then animated as the audience, mostly from the United States, Canada, and western Europe, struggled to explain what to many of them seemed utterly obvious. Terms flew across the dais.

I was sitting in the back row, en route to India to begin the fieldwork for this book. I sensed in the sudden impasse between audience and speaker a soupçon of tamasha, of what the anthropologist Victor Turner might have called a "social drama."[2] Turner counseled paying attention to such moments of disruption, chaos, and conflict, as much as to more everyday things, in the study of social processes and structures. I had been trained as an anthropologist, to do *fieldwork*, and had romantic visions of writing field notes, of that moment when my life would cease to be just a more or less enjoyable middle-class existence and would become an instrument of knowledge. At that moment in Zagreb I had my own little "breakdown," my own collapse of expectation into a sense of possibility and confusion. I remember deciding that fieldwork had officially begun; I started to write. That the scholars I was writing about might not be so easily reducible to separate "American" and "Indian" camps, and that they were far more subtle and sophisticated in their work than the momentary tamasha I was able to exploit might indicate, did not occur to me at that moment. I was learning one of my first lessons about anthropological desire: it offered Archimedean possibilities, totalities out there for the taking. Everything, everywhere, all the time, was grist for one's interpretive mill: one had only to pretend a stance of complete innocence—life as Holden Caulfield, Harriet the Spy, Candide.[3]

The various words offered by the audience to the speaker did not clarify the original question for him. People kept trying to explain the obvious, until one exuberant participant shouted out "Crazy old people!" The audience's attention shifted quickly to the newcomer. That was not what was meant, they assured the speaker, not at all. They were gerontologists; they were not ageist. They were referring only to specific biological diseases. The efforts to explain Alzheimer's resumed.

I began to wonder, Candide in the back with notebook cocked, whether the anxiety around this challenge to gerontological aesthetics might carry greater significance. In calling into question the translatability of the medical language of dementia, the speaker seemed to have pushed his interlocutors down a slippery slope culminating in an admission (instantly resisted) that these medical terms pointed to the aberrant behavior of elderly persons, to old crazies. And not only was a link between disease and difficult old people being both offered and resisted, but it was being framed as a moral imperative, that *to ask about the minds of old people is essential and expected.*

The obviousness of Alzheimer's for the majority of the Zagreb participants mirrored its social and clinical construction in much of North America and Europe as a discrete, virulent, and unambiguous form of pathology. In rethinking the events of the Zagreb conference some years later, I was reminded of the format of family support groups sponsored by the Alzheimer's Association in the United States.[4] I attended several meetings of such groups in the Boston area from 1990 to 1992. In most sessions, family members were encouraged by a facilitator to acknowledge—openly, to other group members—that their relative had a brain disease. The repeated exhortations to *acknowledge* Alzheimer's were performative; that is, they conveyed meaning as much in the act as in the content of speech. Obviously, group members already knew their relatives were demented: this knowledge had brought them to the group in the first place. But the communal acknowledgment of Alzheimer's, through this adaptation of the confessional rhetoric of the American self-help movement, was framed as a critical first step toward "gaining control of our lives." There is much at stake, whether in self-help sessions or at international conferences, in the confessional naming and renaming of Alzheimer's. The aggressive and iterative obviousness of dementia discloses its structure as a *moral* discourse.

Against this particular normative content, the Zagreb session offered a contrasting and equally normative construction, that of the speaker. "What we mean," another participant told him, "is senility." "Ah, senility . . . ," the Indian anthropologist noted, and the audience relaxed, the hermeneutic circle finally having collapsed. "But you see," the speaker explained patiently, "there is no senility in this tribe." To him this truth was redundant. The point of his lecture had been to describe an isolated society in which the traditional Indian joint family was not yet threatened. Old people in such a society were well-cared for and did not become senile.

The speaker's invocation of the joint family as the sole criterion for assessing the well-being of old people is an important feature of post-Independence Indian literature on old age. Indian gerontology is built around a narrative of the inevitable decline of the universal joint family secondary to the four horsemen of contemporary apocalypse: modernization, industrialization, urbanization, and Westernization. The status and health of old people is consequently declining; solutions must be looked for in the highly developed technologies of Western gerontology and geriatrics. The West occupies a split role in this narrative, as the source of both the problem and the solution. For the speaker, "senility" was counterposed to the "joint family," the latter an index of Indianness and the former, in consequence, of Westernization. He seemed to suggest that it is only meaningful to speak of senile old bodies in the context of fragmented or nonexistent—and thus "Western"—families.

Those audience members not from India did not appear convinced of either the lack of "senility" among this tribe or of the speaker's explanation for it as an index of Westernization. The American who had asked the original question regarding the prevalence of dementia remarked to me later over dinner at a Croatian castle that, assuming that the proportion of tribal elders over the age of seventy was as high as the speaker had suggested, dementia was in all likelihood a more significant problem. Most of the audience, given the zest with which they took up the effort to translate the term, would probably have agreed. Two distinct and seamless narratives emerged: for many of the Americans and Europeans, senile pathology was located in specific and isolatable disease processes; for many of the Indians, senile pathology was located in family dynamics and cultural crisis.

Each narrative—repetitive, necessary, obvious—articulated the particular commitments of what after Arthur Kleinman I will call a local moral world.[5] Against the global vision of the Zagreb conference, worlds collided.

WHAT'S WRONG WITH THIS PICTURE?

No one else, of course, seemed to notice the detritus of collision. The following morning I left the conference, took a bus to the Dalmatian coast, bringing along *King Lear* as reading (my passage to India, reading materials and all, choreographed long before I left Boston), and boarded a ferry to the island of Rab. On the boat I met two South Asian medical students taking a vacation from studying for their exams, and we got to talking. They were being trained in Zagreb, and were from Pakistan. Their families, before Partition, were from villages now in India. We got on well: they saw me as an accomplice in their plan to meet German babes, I saw them as fodder for my new life-as-fieldwork. I steered the topic around to my project, hoping for a repetition of Zagreb, a little bit of potted tamasha. Not surprisingly, the two were fluent in the minutiae of senile dementia. Did they think there was much of it in India and Pakistan? One did, one didn't. The one who didn't brought up some of the points made by the Indian anthropologist in Zagreb. The other student recapitulated the point made by the American anthropologist at the castle. But no clear disjuncture of moral worlds emerged as the boat pushed along the Adriatic coast. Sensing my irrelevance, the two students lost interest, returning to a discussion between themselves about their chances of getting laid on the island. I drifted back to my seat and buried myself in Shakespeare. Real life, unlike the best-laid plans of anthropologists, seldom follow the logic of the excluded middle.

Lear: "The art of our necessities is strange."

THE BETTER BRAIN

I am happy to know that you are conducting your 10th Anniversary Conference of Alzheimer's Disease International. . . . God loves you.

MOTHER TERESA

In 1985 an article in the biweekly news magazine *India Today* reported on a search for the characteristic neuropathological signs of Alzheimer's disease, its "plaques" and "tangles," in Indian brains. A team of neurologists and neuropathologists in the city of Madras studied the brains of a sampling of local corpses and found that the tissues they examined appeared to lack these stigmata. They concluded that some sort of protective factor might be preventing the occurrence of Alzheimer's disease in India. Genetic, environmental, and behavioral hypotheses were raised.

As described in *India Today*, the finding was singularly unimpressive. Neurofibrillary tangles are ubiquitous, not limited to the brains of demented persons, and the scientists' reported claim not to have found even one suggests a significant misunderstanding on the part of either the research team or the journalist detailing the study. The data seemed to have come from work with too few brains to generate much certainty, and the brains studied were from persons who had died in their sixties and not their seventies and eighties. There was little to no clinical data on the persons whose brains were used. And the sampling was haphazard.

Yet in some sense the article was not just about—or even primarily about—the prevalence of senile dementia in India. The terms "Alzheimer's disease" and "senile dementia" do not appear. The term used to link the search for plaques and tangles to everyday life is the less technical "senile persons." As in Zagreb, senile persons are not being made sense of in terms of their own bodies as much as within a relational context, here one explicitly comparative: the article is entitled "The Better Brain," and it begins by noting that "the little grey cells in Indian brains have a lot going for them. Recent medical research by some neuropathologists and neurologists has produced the interesting revelation that in Indians, brains grow senile and degenerate much slower than westerners and the number of senile persons in India is far less than that abroad. In other words, the researchers claim, the Indian brain retains its agility and sharpness much longer."

These are resonant and densely referential sentences. Writing about the brain here demands a comparative language; more than Hercule Poirot is invoked in the mention of little gray cells as the site of national difference. The rate of degeneration of Indian as opposed to European brain tissue was a subject frequently addressed in British colonial debate on both tropical medicine and imperial pedagogy. The article reverses the classic assertion of such literatures, that Indian brain tissue ripens quickly but rots still more quickly. Indians and not Englishmen get to play the great detective.

Ultimately, as in Zagreb, the dominant referent of the comparison is to a moral world in which senility is a benchmark of the tragedy of modernity through the mediation of the Bad Family. Thus, again and again, in modern life old people are less respected and they become senile. India's relationship to such a debilitating modernity is ambiguous. In comparison to its own remembered past (or to that of a Northeast hill tribe, which can stand in for this past), modern India engenders senility. But set against something termed the West, ever reimaginable as constituted by infinitely worse families, the inalienable difference of Indianness is retrievable as the better brain.

The centerpiece of the article is a photograph of Professor R. Sarasa Bharati, head of the department of neuropathology at Madras Medical College, sitting next to a large electron microscope. Near the photograph, the text notes:

> Medical studies have revealed that nearly 15 per cent of westerners over 60 have such tangles in their brains. Says Bharati emphatically: "Such tangles have not been spotted in Indian brains at all. In all the brains which came for autopsy and which I examined, I haven't seen a single neurofibrillary tangle." And her observations have

been done under a powerful electron microscope—the first of its kind in India—which magnifies the minutest brain segments an incredible 1.2 million times.[6]

The microscope dwarfs the professor. Not only is the size of the machine impressive, reminiscent of the grandeur of Nehruvian big science,[7] but it is offered within a set of other extremes. The machine is "the first of its kind." It operates through the deployment of numeric extremes: infinities and zero. Indian flesh can be magnified almost infinitely, revealing its position in a global hierarchy of tissues. The existence of pathology—here neurofibrillary tangles—is reduced to an absolute nothingness.

In the subsequent decade, increasingly sophisticated clinical and laboratory researchers would begin to discover the existence of plaques and tangles throughout India. An Alzheimer's movement, primarily composed of physicians from South India, began to take shape. The globalization of gerontological practice, which I will describe in detail in chapter 3, grew more diverse and international groups advocating increased knowledge of and commitment to Alzheimer's disease appeared, such as Alzheimer's Disease International (ADI). This group in turn encouraged the growth of associations such as the Alzheimer's and Related Disorders Society of India (ARDSI). While I sat in the India Office library transfixed by the old woman of Balua, ADI held a tenth anniversary conference in Scotland in September 1994 on the occasion of "World Alzheimer's Day," bringing together representatives from around the world. ADI and ARDSI, like the American Alzheimer's Association, were organized to spread the message: the necessity of acknowledging Alzheimer's as disease, despite the absence of effective treatment to date. But against the spreading moral imperative of the senile confessional—*we too have Alzheimer's in our country*—the first entry of Alzheimer's into popular middle-class discourse is as an absolute negation: the better brain of 1985, free of even a single stigmatizing tangle. Against the ephemerality of the Western brain, there is no senility in India. The powerful gaze of a West "which magnifies the minutest brain segments an incredible 1.2 million times" is purchased and redeployed to materialize national difference on the cellular level: "Indian brains show fewer physical symptoms of senility than their western counterparts."[8]

TROPICAL SOFTENING

All the institutions and habits of the Bengalis tend materially to abbreviate the term of existence—their premature decay being in perfect accordance with their early and forced development.
JAMES MARTIN, *THE INFLUENCE OF TROPICAL CLIMATES ON EUROPEAN CONSTITUTIONS*

The interpenetration of discussions of neuropathology and the moral implications of senile bodies long precedes the emergence of Alzheimer's and its stigmata. The dominant literature of mid-nineteenth- through early-twentieth-century neuropathology, centered in western and central Europe, was sensitive to the texture of the brains of the apoplectic and demented. "Cerebral softening" was associated with atherosclerosis and described in a rich and almost gothic language of liquefaction as a powerful sign uniting physiological, psychological, and moral decay.[9] Softened brains could be cut like overripe fruit into slices to reveal dank pockets of mush within. This softness of brain tissues at times dovetailed with a very different but roughly contemporary framework for marking the progression of bodily decay, that of the various climacterics, or critical periods of late life. Nineteenth- and early-twentieth-century climacteric theory, reading the life course as a series of nodal moments that, if unsuccessfully negotiated, would lead to the acceleration of mental and physical disorder, framed the life history of the demented as the failed negotiation of an age-specific grand or senile climacteric.[10] Climacteric failure, which I take up in the next chapter, was rooted in an often explicit moral softness, particularly in the failure to adopt an appropriate stance of disengagement befitting the dignity of old age.

Softening and the dementia and associated moral weakness it invoked took on additional meaning in the emergence of British tropical medicine in the colonies and particularly India, linking the softening character of the tropics to the aging brains of its inhabitants. The disease of "tropical softening" was a dual concern for British authors in the second half of the nineteenth century and the beginning of the twentieth, both a climactic and physiological threat, given the shifting European experience of tropical humidity, and a moral threat, given what was perceived as the unsettling fluidity of Indian manners and reasoning. The tropics had the same effect as old age upon the physically and morally unprepared body. Both softened the tissues: colonial life was fundamentally climacterical.

The tropics aged one: the theme long precedes the stabilizing and controlling processes of colonial medicine. Montesquieu's eighteenth-century *Spirit of the Laws* notes that in their political life, persons in the hot South of the world are like timid old men, unlike the more youthful peoples of the cold North. The senescence of southern populations is one source of their acquiescence to despotic rule. In a different argument, Montesquieu explains despotic rule by the need to control southern women, whose premature physical aging makes randy young women a threat to public order. The early ripening and rot of tropical bodies is here split: the physical body ages early, but not the reasoning faculties. Young women threaten in part because they lack the intellectual maturity to moderate their quickened physical desire. Beauty and Reason, as Montesquieu puts it, are disjunct. Beauty comes and goes, before Reason, apparently more impervious to climate, can ripen.[11]

The emergence of a science of tropical effects upon globalizing European bodies is predicated upon the logic of a world like that which Montesquieu offers. The intellectual and the corporeal are peculiarly disjunct in the South and East of this world. The body of Desire is infantile, the body of Reason old and wizened. The moral quality of the body of Reason is often gendered in its representation. Unworldly but benevolent and wise old men (Kipling's old monk in *Kim*, Forster's Professor Godbole in *A Passage to India*) and virulent and dangerously smart old hags

(Haggard's several murderous old witches) dot colonial literature.[12] The relation of this old body and its brand of Reason to the corporeal, to the body of Beauty and the world of power and desire, is a problem. For Hegel, in India the Idea is cut adrift from the external, from its dialectic with and within the World. Reason, culture, and aesthetic form drift within a symbolic realm coincident with pure imagination and dream. The relations of Indian culture to the material world are arbitrary.[13] A sociology of India, within the logic of tropical decrepitude, can frame all considerations of power and corporeality as residual. Medically, the physical decay of the southern body, internally split with Reason preserved, does not present a systemic crisis. European bodies are at a different kind of risk. Reason must be policed, and the minds of arriving colonials watched for liquifactious behavior.

The softening effects upon European bodies become increasingly pronounced in the later nineteenth century. The difference between southern and northern bodies is rearticulated in the emergent languages of tropical and sanitary medicine. A 1907 health manual for the British family in India links tropical liquefaction to cerebral softening through the medium of blood and a collapse of one's "system": "There is little doubt that the exposure of Europeans to the effects of continued tropical heat during a series of years produces a debilitated condition of the system, consequent on blood-degeneration, favorable to brain-softening." Treatment is futile; softening is inherent in the unremitting heat of tropical life and the only long-term solution is "removal to a temperate climate."[14] The text is concerned primarily with European bodies; Indian bodies and particularly Indian blood have already acclimatized, existing in the split degeneration of a *longue durée* that preserves its queer Reason from the extremes of climate.

Throughout the nineteenth century, attention to corporeal decay and its management intensifies as a European mode of understanding Indian difference, and the biopolitics of empire increasingly encompass Reason, no longer invulnerable to precocious decline. Indian minds are naturally soft and, though not in danger of sudden softening, are in a sense congenitally senile. Such softness is predominantly a figure of moral difference. Sir Henry Maine, jurist, educator, and early anthropologist, phrased British concern pithily in an 1866 address on the future of Indian education: "The fact is, *that the educated Native mind requires hardening.*"[15] Maine's comments are part of his defense of memory as a tool of empire, and I will return to them in a discussion of memory, capital, and exchange in the fourth chapter. Like the neuropathological varieties of softening in the medical manuals, the moral versions were similarly rooted in physiological difference. In challenging the view of English alarmists that the imperial pedagogy of memorization favors the superficial mind of the Indian (thought to be more adept at rote learning), Maine suggests in contrast that the difference between Indian and English minds is an epiphenomenon of their occupying different climactic frames. Native minds flower early and luxuriantly but putrefy and rot as quickly, posing no threat to English control in the context of an all-too-ephemeral precocity. Senility, the tendency of all things tropical to evolve into imbecility, is the dominant trope of imperial appraisal.

In a 1921 psychiatric text, the everyday fluidity of Indian tissue leads to the different clinical presentation of local versus European lunatics. A. W. Overbeck-Wright's *Lunacy in India* incorporates toxemic along with racial and climatological levels of explanation to locate the character of Indian lunatics within a broader explanatory triad of the tropical, the hereditary, and the unclean. The triad helps specify the differences between Indians and Europeans and their respective susceptibilities to lunacy. Europeans hold in their bowel movements, and the accumulation of fecal toxins not only slowly poisons their system but builds up alarming levels of bodily heat. However adaptive in temperate climates, the warming effect of anal retention in the tropics leads to serious toxemia and fever. Europeans in India build up heat and become weak. This fact allows Overbeck-Wright to explain their often explosive and violent behavior in the tropics. The object of this symptomatic violence is left unstated.

Indians, more constitutionally soft and placid, suffer from the contrary disposition: they let everything out. They survive the heat, but at the cost of any attention to boundaries or to physical hygiene. Indians are filthy and fluid; Indian lunatics are particularly prone to besmear themselves or others with excrement.[16] In describing Indian mental derangement, Overbeck-Wright draws not on the language of constipation but of diarrhea, of a national identity not like the British filled with shit but rather one covered in it. Softening and diarrhea here supplement one another as figures of liquefaction and the abject nature of the Indian's lack of boundaries.

Softening—as a figuratively powerful and clinically vague term—retains some of its currency in contemporary Indian English. A 1992 article in *India Today* on leftist politics in Kerala noted that "younger cadres . . . are opposed to the septuagenarian Seetharanaiah because they feel the softening of the brain which can afflict the elderly is seeping into his policies."[17] Here the softness of senile policy seeps, an image again of the incontinent brain. And in lay terms, one can still invoke tropical difference to collapse an inferiorized self and debilitated body. "Perhaps it is the water," Marwari Mataji's son-in-law in Varanasi used to remind me from time to time, "because in this country, at sixty-five to seventy people's brains often get weak."

Yet though a few European academics throughout the colonial period continued to lament the paucity of data on the "peculiarities of tropical neurology,"[18] colonial medical engagements on the civic and national levels were dominated by the dangers of external infection rather than internal constitution.[19] Clinical details of the particular effects of cerebral softening on the natives are scant: softening is more powerful as an ideological figure glossing the tropical body than as a medical technology of intervention or control. There is a similar dearth of references to senility and senile dementia in late colonial medical and psychiatric literature.

EMBODYING PROBATE

Such terms abound, however, in colonial legal texts of the early twentieth century, as part of discussions of probate law and of testamentary capacity: who is of sound enough mind to prepare his or her will? Both "senile dementia" and "senility" are mentioned in debates on testamentary capacity in texts detailing the Indian Lunacy Act of 1912 and its amendments and replacements. The terms are necessary, Beotra notes in his 1965 introduction to the Act, because "in all civilised countries the law has thrown the mantle of protection over infants, idiots, and lunatics." The two terms thus constitute not only a mantle of protection but a guarantee of India's claims to civilization.

According to the Lunacy Act, senile dementia is defined as insanity secondary to a "degeneration of mental faculties" in which "judgement, memory, interest, and control over emotions are impaired."[20] The Act includes dementia as a central component of its delineation of testamentary capacity, based on a requirement reinstated in the Indian Succession Act of 1925 and corollary Hindu and Muslim personal law that testators be "of sound mind."[21] Beotra notes that such laws are designed to protect both old persons falsely accused of lunacy and potential beneficiaries wrongly cut out of a will.[22] He notes further that, under the secular code of the Indian Succession Act, dementia certified by a medical practitioner is a sufficient challenge to testamentary capacity, but concludes that in general the Lunacy and Succession Acts have been framed in subsequent case law to discourage magistrates from basing judgments solely on medical opinion.

Medical opinion, Beotra points out, is too ambiguous. Part of the problem lies in the effort to determine the relationship between pathology and normality in old age. The Lunacy and Succession Acts differentiate between losses of capacity due to "mere" old age versus those due to "extreme" old age: "Mere old age does not deprive a man of the capacity of making a will. Yet if a man in his old age becomes a very child again in his understanding or by reason of extreme old age or other infirmity he becomes so forgetful that he does not know his own name, he is not fit to make a will."[23] To complicate matters, in the literature on these Acts mere old age is often referred to as senility. In Beotra's discussion of the Lunacy Act, senile dementia is clearly a ground for challenging testamentary capacity, but memory impairment and "senility following old age" are not.[24] Other digests and commentaries refer to senility as a form of simple degeneration, dementia as a form of lunacy, and both as legitimate challenges to testamentary capacity.[25]

Yet the legal possibilities of such ambiguities were seldom exploited by those Varanasi and Calcutta lawyers handling probate cases whom I interviewed. Wills were often contested, but challenges to testamentary capacity drew more on other bodily changes than on unsound mind. I spent the most time following the case load of Mr. Tiwari, a lawyer with an old and busy practice in the heart of Varanasi. He was the brother of Mrs. Sharma, my landlady in the Varanasi neighborhood of Nandanagar, where I lived for a year in 1988. Tiwari-sahib's office was off Vishwanath *gaī*, the famous lane leading to the city's most important temples. During business hours, which often stretched late into the evening, it was full of clients and their families, assistants, and friends all seated together in Tiwari-sahib's small inner chamber. Tea flowed, legal books and documents littered the mattresses on which everyone sat. Tiwari was a voluble man who would describe various cases of his for me in which testamentary capacity had been at issue. During rare pauses, the friends, clients, and assistants would make supplementary observations.

Much of Mr. Tiwari's practice involved intrafamilial litigation concerning testamentary matters, but in his experience the various definitions of senility and dementia in case law and commentary were peripheral to the construction of useful argument. Testamentary capacity in practice was more narrowly embodied than in the law, far less often a matter of the soundness of mind and far more often a matter of the weakness of the senses. Children were far more likely to stress the impaired vision or hearing of an elderly parent than draw upon "unsound mind," far more likely to stress misrecognition than misunderstanding.

Matters of inheritance in India are subject to one of several parallel legal codes: the Hindu, Muslim, and secular personal laws. Textbooks of contemporary Muslim and Hindu law often refer to the secular Indian Succession Act in matters of defining soundness of mind. The Hindu Succession Act of 1956 throws its mantle of protection only on "persons who are deaf and dumb and blind."[26] Even where discussions of "mind" appear in the English-language codes of contemporary Hindu and Muslim law, commentaries do not elaborate categories of lunacy.

The differential embodiment of family crisis extends to the Bombay cinema. In the 1989 Hindi film hit *Ram Lakhan*, the story begins with an old landowner with failing eyesight being tricked by a corrupt lawyer into signing a sham will. As opposed to the 1865 story in the *Hurkaru*, wherein the mental capacities of testate old rajas are continually being exploited by an army of temple priests, *Ram Lakhan* offers a different embodiment of the weakness of old people and of the crises it may engender. The weak eyes of the old man, and not his weak mind, become a metonym for the generalized weakness of old age. The old body *means* differently. Despite the colonial embodiment of testamentary capacity as mind—as in the mentalist language of the Lunacy and Succession Acts and of those that replace them—within the everyday practice of probate law in Varanasi in the 1980s and within the representation of probate in Hindi film, the unsound mind of an elder is framed as a problem of recognition, not judgment. The relevance of globalizing systems of classification—of colonial medicine, and law, and their heirs—is neither unitary nor obvious.

A MEDICAL EXPLANATION

What would happen if he were to become senile as President? he was asked.
Mr. Reagan said he would resign.

How would he know that he had become senile?
Mr. Reagan said he expected his doctors to check him. Then he interrupted the interview to ask
for a medical explanation of senility.
NEW YORK TIMES, NOVEMBER 8, 1984

The ambiguities surrounding the relationship of "senility" and "senile dementia" in the Indian probate literature reflect a process of their continually shifting professional and lay definition. Even in the last decade, the two primary international classifications of dementia have shifted in significant ways. I want to introduce some of these recent shifts before turning to a redefinition of senility as an ideal type enabling certain kinds of analysis.

Dementia is a clinical as opposed to a diagnostic term, one that conveys a particular behavioral picture but in itself implies no particular causal model. Clinically, it is defined primarily as a set of multiple and relatively stable cognitive deficits, and in particular a deficit of memory. I must be careful when I say "*it* is defined," for the ontological status of dementia—its claims to being a *thing* at all—eroded in the early 1990s in the United States. The primary American manual defining and classifying psychiatric and some neurological disorders is the *Diagnostic and Statistical Manual of the American Psychiatric Association* (DSM). When I began my fieldwork for this book, DSM-III-R (the then-current revised third edition of the American Psychiatric Association's *Diagnostic and Statistical Manual*) defined *dementia* like other entities in DSM by a list of signs and symptoms, of which the person so diagnosed must exhibit a designated number. The section of DSM-III-R on dementia began with such a list, by which a clinician could make a diagnosis "of dementia." DSM-III-R went on to define a set of subtypes, the two principal ones being dementias of the "Alzheimer's type" and "multi-infarct dementias." The subtypes, unlike the general category, implied not only a clinical syndrome but a causal model: the primary degeneration of brain tissue in the case of dementias of the Alzheimer's type; and the secondary degeneration of brain tissue in the case of multi-infarct dementias, the primary process being the constriction and eventual blockage of small blood vessels supplying the brain leading to numerous tiny strokes.

By DSM-IV's appearance in 1994, the initial description of dementia in the manual had been shortened and no longer included any diagnostic criteria. That is, one could no longer be formally diagnosed "with dementia" but *only* with its former subtypes, which now took on the status of independent entities grouped together because of clinical resemblance. In the context of DSM, dementia *tout court* in the United States ceases to exist in 1994.[27]

The former subtypes change dramatically as well. "Multi-infarct" disappears, to be replaced with "vascular dementia," a term that had only a decade earlier been banished to nosological purgatory. The previous century had seen a continuous set of reversals of the primacy of vascular versus brain models of dementia. Atherosclerotic dementia—and the consequent reduction of blood flow to the brain—dominated until the 1960s and 1970s, when Alzheimer's disease was in sense rediscovered. Vascular flow models did not disappear, but were replaced by multi-infarct models in which the effects of vascular disease were secondary as a result of the multiple small strokes. The career of vascular dementia, the dominant medical model for senility for much of the twentieth century, all but erased in the wake of the reemergence of Alzheimer's disease and now making a pronounced reappearance, raises critical questions and will be taken up in the next chapter.

A second change in the delineation of the former subtypes in DSM-IV is the continued deemphasis of a once-critical distinction between the presenile and senile dementias. Alois Alzheimer's first "Alzheimer's" patients were middle-aged people; their premature senility generated the social concern and clinical interest that led the German pathologist to identify a set of neuropathological signs—the many "plaques and tangles" of Alzheimer's disease—with a "presenile" disease process. Within a few years of Alzheimer's published findings, other neuropathological investigators reported similar findings in the case of senile dementias and suggested that the presenile-senile distinction might be abandoned, but it persisted for decades. In DSM-IV, it lingers as a pair of subclasses of Alzheimer's Type, "early onset" versus "late onset." With the emergence of more sophisticated genetic modeling exploding the unitary category of Alzheimer's, it may regain its once coherent ontological status.

Two other broad subtypes of dementia complete the DSM-IV picture, dementia due to other "general medical conditions" such as Parkinson's disease or AIDS, and the various "mixed" and other less easily classifiable dementias, which often suggest a combination of primary and secondary dementing processes. The number of categories of mixed or "other" dementias has expanded in DSM-IV, even as the former subtypes of Alzheimer's and multi-infarct dementia take on a new ontological primacy as distinct classes not reducible to an overarching category. Thus by the early 1990s the ontology of dementing illness comes to focus primarily on causal models and not clinical syndromes, yet against conceptual clarity the vague and mixed classes proliferate.

Despite the disappearance of dementia-in-itself as a diagnosis in DSM-IV, the different subtypes share a set of core criteria. These shared criteria have continued to shift toward the emphasis of cognitive and the deemphasis of noncognitive symptoms and signs. They are worth examining closely. DSM-III-R is written in a more cookbooklike style, with a focus specifically on "memory" as opposed to cognition more generally, and stresses the clinical elicitation and enumeration of symptoms:

> A. Demonstrable evidence of impairment in short- and long-term memory.
> Impairment in short-term memory (inability to learn new information) may be indicated by inability to remember three objects after five minutes. Long-term memory impairment (inability to remember information that was known in the past) may be indicated by inability to remember past personal information (e.g., what happened yesterday, birthplace, occupation) or facts of common knowledge (e.g., past Presidents, well-known dates).

B. At least one of the following:
  1. impairment in abstract thinking, as indicated by inability to find similarities and differences between related words, difficulties in defining words and concepts, and other similar tasks
  2. impaired judgement, as indicated by inability to make reasonable plans to deal with interpersonal, family, and job-related problems and issues
  3. other disturbances of higher cortical function, such as aphasia (disorder of language), apraxia (inability to carry out motor activities despite intact comprehension and motor function), agnosia (failure to recognize or identify objects despite intact sensory function), and "constructional difficulty" (e.g., inability to copy three-dimensional figures, assemble blocks, or arrange sticks in specific designs)
  4. personality change, i.e., alteration or accentuation of premorbid traits.
C. The disturbance in A and B significantly interferes with work or usual social activities or relationships with others.[28]

The noncognitive, barely present in the DSM-III-R inclusion of personality change, is expunged entirely in DSM-IV.

A. The development of multiple cognitive deficits manifest by both
  1. memory impairment (impaired ability to learn new information or to recall previously learned information)
  2. one (or more) of the following cognitive disturbances:
    a. aphasia (language disturbance)
    b. apraxia (impaired ability to carry out motor activities despite intact motor function)
    c. agnosia (failure to recognize or identify objects despite intact sensory function)
    d. disturbance in executive functioning (i.e., planning, organizing, sequencing, abstracting)
B. The cognitive deficits in Criteria A1 and A2 each cause significant impairment in social or occupational functioning and represent a significant decline from a previous level of functioning.[29]

Even social function is expressed in explicitly cognitive terms. The word "cognitive" appears again and again throughout the DSM-IV lists of criteria for the various dementias, far exceeding the simple act of its signification: an excess of language. Helena Chang Chui, in a 1989 review, noted that "although dementia focuses on cognitive deficits, emotional and personality changes usually occur concomitantly."[30] The cognitive formulation of symptomatic relevance is offered despite the repeated suggestion, in the dementia literature, that more than cognitive change is involved.

The other internationally recognized classificatory scheme, the International Statistical Classification of Diseases of the World Health Organization, was reissued in 1992 as the ICD-10. The ICD series parallels the DSM both in its nosological structure and general direction of change, though the ICD changes often lag by a few years. ICD-10 still includes a more developed noncognitive component. Dementia—which retains its ontological priority as a general category in ICD—has four criteria, the third of which is "emotional":

> There is a decline in emotional control or motivation, or a change in social behavior manifest as at least one of the following:
>
> (1) emotional lability;
> (2) irritability;
> (3) apathy;
> (4) coarsening of social behavior.

Despite the difference between the two manuals, they share a fundamental opposition between the cognitive and the affective as an evaluative structure and the emphasis upon the former as the primary sign of pathology.[31]

Many of the changes in DSM-IV are a response to terminological confusion. In American geriatric training in the 1980s, students were taught to differentiate *acute* causes of cognitive change and confusion ("delerium") from *chronic* conditions ("dementia"), and in the case of chronic dementia, to differentiate *reversible* (potentially treatable) and *pseudo-* dementias (in which apparent cognitive losses reflect an underlying depression) from the *irreversible* and progressive causes of deterioration, the major dementia subtypes of DSM-III-R. The so-called reversible dementias include various metabolic, toxic, and systemic changes, often secondary to medication, alcohol, or other drugs or to chronic undernutrition; normal pressure hydrocephalus, treatable with surgery; intracranial infections; and other potentially treatable causes including sensory deprivation, cancer, immunologic disorders, hematomas, and fecal impaction. The strongest argument for the medicalization and internationalization of dementia, the agenda of groups like ADI, is that some of the dementias are ameliorable. However, many reversible dementias are not necessarily reversible, and few blinded studies of their treatment exist.[32] Nor are the irreversible dementias necessarily irreversible, though the literature on their successful treatment reflects in significant measure the often dubious claims of various pharmaceutical houses to have developed an effective magic bullet. Some studies suggest the progression of some vascular dementias may be halted with tight blood-pressure control.[33] DSM-IV has excised the language of "progressive" and "reversible."

The distinction between Alzheimer's Type and Vascular Dementia and their terminological predecessors has been used to generate comparative epidemiological data on dementia worldwide. The most frequent "cross-cultural" issue in dementia research has been a well-known finding that whereas in western Europe and North America well over half of all dementias in persons over sixty-five are diagnosed as probable Alzheimer's disease and less than a fifth as vascular dementia,[34] in Japan Alzheimer's is diagnosed only half as often as vascular dementia.[35] Some studies in Russia have suggested a picture similar to that of Japan.[36] Attempts to explain such national differences have focused on efforts to suggest these are artifacts of different study designs or of how different communities of physicians are trained to diagnosis dementia, *or* to try to make sense of it in terms of real epidemiological difference, whether rooted in genetic, environmental, or social factors or some combination. Examples of the first sort of argument have suggested that vascular dementia is underdiagnosed in North America and Europe and overdiagnosed in Japan, that prevalence measures are in general poor data for research on the causes of dementia, and that most measurements of the prevalence of either Alzheimer's or vascular dementia have widely differing criteria as to the inclusion of the so-called mixed dementias and are difficult to consider comparatively.[37] Examples of the second sort of argument have pointed out the high rate of stroke in Japan, consistent with the observed higher prevalence of vascular dementia there, as Graves and her colleagues note.[38]

The opposition of the prevalence of vascular and Alzheimer's dementias is epidemiologically and semiotically dense. Alzheimer's type dementias are found on average at a later age than vascular dementias and more often in women than men—in part in consequence of the fact that more women than men survive into extreme old age.[39] Differential prevalence rates of the two types of dementia in different historical and material settings may suggest many things: that slightly younger persons are more likely to be brought to medical attention and be counted than older ones, as are men rather than women; that persons in general do not live long enough to be diagnosed with Alzheimer's as opposed to vascular dementia; and that the extent to which old women's versus old men's bodies were and are institutionally available for enumeration and study might determine what sorts of figures predominate in an emerging science of the senile body. Furthermore, given that epidemiological difference seems to place Japan and Russia together in opposition to the United States and Western Europe—superimposing a West versus the rest opposition onto the distinction between Alzheimer's and vascular dementia—not only the gendered but also the nationalist implications of these categories may be relevant to how they come to matter as they travel ever more globally.

Thus, the recent findings that vascular dementias are far more prevalent than Alzheimer's type dementias in India and Africa must be approached carefully: such findings reflect complex demographic differences in who survives, gender- and class-specific patterns of which bodies are likely to be presented to a medical gaze, and the postcolonial prospects of the better brain.[40] A 1991 review of the epidemiology of dementia in the Third World from B. O. Osuntokun and colleagues at the University of Ibadan in Nigeria offers a case in point of the extension of the Japan model globally. The authors begin with a startling finding, but one reminiscent of R. Sarasa Bharati's Madras research reported in *India Today*: "No authentic case of AD [Alzheimer's disease] has been reported in an indigenous Black African. In one community-based study to assess the magnitude of neurological disorders, reported in 1987 from Nigeria, involving a door-to-door survey of nearly 19,000 subjects, 4% of whom were over 65 years of age, no patients with dementia were seen."

The authors go on to note that one of them has had thirty-three years experience in a practice in a premier teaching hospital, "during which *over 14 million patients* had been seen including 4% aged 65 years or more: the diagnosis of AD had not been substantiated in *any* patient" [my emphasis]. They then offer another pair of figures, first 37 patients seen between 1984 and 1989, of which "none had AD, but 18 clearly suffered from multi-infarct dementia," and second, autopsies "on 198 brains of Nigerians aged 40 years and above (including 45 older than 65 years)," of which none showed the "senile plaques, neurofibrillary tangles, beta amyloid deposit, pathognomonic [uniquely characteristic] of AD."

Against this data, they note that the prevalence of Alzheimer's among African Americans is at least as high as that of white Americans, and thus reject a genetic hypothesis to explain their data. They suggest in contrast that their data indicates grounds "for the hypothesis that AD is the consequence of some exposure to some environmental factors in which *homo sapiens* is not adapted and which are not present in non-industrialized countries."[41] Alzheimer's is again framed as the disease of modernity, but not the result of a bad family, as perceived in Zagreb, but rather the result of the implied effects of changes in diet or of pollution or other toxic exposures.

The hypothesis in itself is interesting, though it hints at the false assumption that life in Ibadan or elsewhere in the "nonindustrialized world" is more rather than less free from pollutants and toxins as a result of its relative marginality within the global economy. I recall a discussion over tea at a roadside stall near the university hospital in Varanasi with a professor who suggested that India might have less Alzheimer's because of less exposure to aluminum in its "traditional diet," the effects of exposure to the metal periodically being a hot topic in Alzheimer's research. While we talked, large trucks and buses inched their way through traffic, spewing noxious fumes that swirled around us. And our tea was being boiled in a large aluminum pot and served to us from a long aluminum dipper.

Like India's better brain, the Nigerian study deals in infinitudes and absences rather than in the realm of the statistically significant. Nineteen thousand persons are examined in the community, or an incredible 14 million in the clinic of the senior investigator, and not a single case of Alzheimer's is found. The discussion of multi-infarct dementia is striking for the return to more cautious enumeration: 18 persons with this dementia out of 37 examined. "Dementia," in summary, appears split here into a realm of Alzheimer's characterized by fantastic reportage and absolute knowledge, and a realm of vascular dementia characterized by more negotiable possibilities. Africa is simultaneously a place located out of time, space, and contingency, in which no case of Alzheimer's and no plaque or tangle has ever been found (no aging in Africa, in effect), and in which a physician can effectively screen 14 million patients; and a place within the world, in which epidemiology is a shifting terrain, demographics change, and diet, pollutants, and toxins may or may not play different roles in the causation of dementia over time.

Alzheimer's as the site of the fantastic is not limited to the narratives of the scientific periphery. The underdiagnosis of other dementias relative to Alzheimer's in the United States correlates with the latter's symbolic importance as the dominant sign of senility. The anthropologists in Zagreb first tried to gloss dementia by referring to "Alzheimer's." In American popular discourse, "Alzheimer's" has all but replaced "senility" as a word with multiple contextual uses—in joking about, insulting, despairing of, and analyzing the behavior of oneself and others. The Alzheimer's Disease and Related Disorders Association, informally the Alzheimer's Association, eventually had the confusing "and Related Disorders" officially excised. At meetings sponsored by the association, expert speakers alternate between attention to the multiple types of dementia in the content of their presentations and the continual evocation of "Alzheimer's" to sum up what they mean. Alzheimer's—not vascular dementia, not the questionably reversible dementias nor the many other possible diagnoses—receives the most lingering gaze, remains the brain killer, the "time bomb" that (citing *Newsweek*'s phrase book again) is "ticking away."[42] The force of the explosion is anticipated in the endlessly repeated fact of its terrifying ubiquity: "[I]t may be ticking, in fact, for all of us." Alzheimer's is about "all of us." It is as much a sign of identity for American readers of *Newsweek* as debate over the better brain has become a sign of difference for the readers of *India Today*. When brains become powerful indices of "us" and "them," how do we approach the globalization of plaques and tangles?

THE SENILE BODY

Senility, senile dementia, and Alzheimer's are not stable and invariant terms within several of the contexts we have begun to discuss. The putative lingua franca of the world of electron microscopes and white-coated researchers pictured in *India Today* quickly disaggregates into the different ways of engaging old age and different projects of materializing the senile body evidenced in Zagreb. The easiest response to these differences—indeed, the classic anthropological strategy—is to read them as variations in something called *culture*. In making sense of Zagreb, for example, one could draw upon the frequently cited insight of ethnographers that within a comparative context many Americans and Europeans act and experience themselves as autonomous and bounded entities, highly individuated selves within quite separate bodies, while many Indians act and experience themselves primarily in terms of their relations with others, as linked and interdependent selves continually sharing and exchanging substance with other bodies.[43] Along such lines, the more embodied and individuated senility of Americans versus the more social and comparative senility of the Indians at Zagreb makes a bit more sense. At times I will draw upon such "culturalist" logics, if in somewhat less grand formulations, when they seem particularly compelling.

But the immediate move to culture as the ground sufficient for situating difference obscures many other and more immediate forms of understanding and collapses more nuanced analyses into a necessarily misread totality, reinstating the anthropological predicament James Clifford and others have been addressing for some time.[44] Against both camps in Zagreb, each convinced the other was missing the point, and against their easy reification *only* into two discrete moral worlds, I draw upon some additional tools. I begin by constructing an ideal type from the one word that momentarily appeared to link the Zagreb conferees: *senility*.

I use *senility* precisely because of the contested and shifting meanings of the term. I refer by it to *the attribution of difference or discontinuity to an old person or to old people as a group, when this difference is embodied as behavior—as actions or utterances—and when it is to some degree stigmatized.* For the moment I will use "old" loosely, begging for now the specifics of how it translates, taking it as a generalized way of marking and signifying someone whose body, demeanor, behavior, social position, or history is suggestive of the later decades of the life course in a given place or time.

This definition of senility puts aside the question of causation, or in medical terms *etiology*, by suggesting that it may be useful to look at senility as a process, something that is articulated in time.[45] In part, the processual nature of senility is comprehensible within the frame of the various physiological models that we will examine below, whether we are speaking in terms of progressive disorders like Alzheimer's disease, of bad families, of nineteenth-century European theories of the male climacteric or tropical softening, or of Indian Ayurvedic discussions on the excess of wind. But a processual analysis of senility is not exhausted by any of these models. Colleen and Frank Johnson have shown how the timing of the diagnosis of Alzheimer's among the American families they studied in the 1980s was correlated more closely with levels of family stress than levels of dementing illness as measured by a mental status examination.[46] Caregivers appeared to defer diagnoses for family members until such time as they felt they could no longer care for them. One of the implications of the Johnsons' study is that the practice of diagnosing dementing illness functions as a critical legitimation for institutionalization. Bodily events—diagnosis, institutionalization, and their beneficial or traumatic outcomes—cannot be reduced solely to a body's internal workings. Senility is acutely attributional: it almost always requires two bodies, a senile body and a second body that recognizes a change in the first. As with the politics of madness, discussions of medical ontology are inseparable from the culture and politics of attribution. Without dismissing the material nature of senility, we need to recognize that "going sixtyish" in Varanasi or "being a victim of Alzheimer's" in the United States are fundamentally dialogic processes, involving both an old person and some other.

Thus the types of knowledge and practice that structure the experience of senility and make it comprehensible emerge within a particular relation of desire between the senile and the attributing body. Is the senile body the speaker's own? Knowledge of and engagement with and within one's own body I term *first-person*. Is the body in question that of some known other, whether parent, spouse, relative, or friend, or of someone differentiated from the speaker along axes of class or caste or gender? Knowledge of and engagement with another's body I term *second-*

person. Or is the senile body generalized, a body we can imagine as universal? Here the lines of desire between speaking and senile bodies get blurred, encompassed by some form of universalizing reason. The senile body emerges as a collective representation, as a fact in the world. Knowledge of and engagement with such a body I term *third-person.* Like my use of *senility*, these types of knowledge and practice are at best heuristic tools. Like any tools, they will come in handy at some times and not others, when it may be more useful to collapse them or ask different sorts of questions.

AN ANTHROPOLOGICAL PICARESQUE

Do not trouble to test me
I am always in the forefront
When it comes to bearing
The burden of grief.

FROM POEM BY "AKBAR PEHLWAN," WRESTLER AND HIRED MUSCLE, AS RECITED TO PSYCHOANALYST
SUDHIR KAKAR AFTER THE LATTER HAD ATTEMPTED TO ADMINISTER A PSYCHOLOGICAL TEST

Heuristic tools became necessary as a way of confronting a traumatic first year of research. I arrived in Varanasi in September of 1988 to begin what became a futile search for something remotely resembling what I was medically trained to recognize as senile dementia. Like Professor Sarasa Bharati, I could not find it.

In theory, I wasn't supposed to be looking for an "it" at all. I was trained to avoid what Arthur Kleinman has called a "category fallacy," the too-hasty reification of a historically and culturally specific concept like "dementia" as a necessarily universal tool for cross-cultural analysis.[47] I did not wish to presume the existence of a cultural equivalent of dementia in Varanasi, merely to "change the labels" as Catherine Lutz has put it.[48] I knew from previous years in Varanasi that few old persons were brought to hospitals or doctors' offices with anything like dementia and that few families ever spoke of such a thing. I organized my initial fieldwork in recognition of these insights, not in terms of clinics but rather households across class. On a previous trip to Varanasi in 1987 I had begun to speak with community leaders in two neighborhoods about the possibility of going from house to house and interviewing older persons and, when possible, others in their households. My interviews would be open-ended and not limited to glossing some dementia-equivalent.

But inherent to my imagined project was my belief that lurking somewhere in the prelinguistic realm of bodily stuff was something enough like dementia that I could use a "culturally appropriate" mental status examination (MSE) to create a sample of old persons who elsewhere might be termed demented.[49] If I went to enough households and talked with enough old people, I would be sure to find a few who were enough "like" demented persons that I could then ask their families if I could interview the elders and others in the household more extensively over the subsequent year. In this way I could learn what *would* be the relevant questions to ask of such families and such persons, so as not to presume the language and logic of biomedicine and so as to avoid the category fallacy. Armed with a set of better categories, I could then return and construct a larger sample of persons to interview and generate some better quantitative data. I could not see that the search for the better category was not a way out of category fallacy. Nor did I have a sense of why any categories, fallacious or not, should *matter* in these neighborhoods.

Despite such best-laid plans, none of the older persons I initially met—even the very aged and frail ones—appeared to be clinically demented. Or if, like Dulari, an old woman or man did at first seem demented, subsequent acquaintance suggested otherwise. I returned home each night to my room at the Sharmas to construct elaborate maps of my neighborhoods and to devise ever more intensive sampling techniques. Nothing appeared to work. Each night I would stare at my brightly colored Neelgagan-brand notebooks, unable to write. Something was wrong. I grew ever more desperate. I found myself, two months into fieldwork, stalking an old woman who was muttering to herself, following her through the lanes of the city at what I thought was a discreet distance, hoping she would lead me to her home where I could then interview her neighbors—until I saw the strangeness of my endeavor mirrored in the harsh stare of a woman passing by the two of us, the anthropological field-worker and the old woman his quarry.

There were obvious initial problems. I had spent a month rebuilding the links I had begun to make in 1987 with community leaders, and then with neighborhood supervision I had begun house-to-house interviews, first in Nagwa slum. Within a week, I realized that any MSE was an inadequate sampling tool for working in economically and politically marginal neighborhoods. Changing questions from something like "name the president" to "name the prime minister" was not adequate. Most tests presumed literacy, numeracy, knowledge of current events, and knowledge of words, figures, and narrative forms learned in school and developed through class-specific practice. But access to viable schooling and to the media differed across class and gender. Not only were existing MSEs inordinately biased,[50] but the use of examination techniques of knowledge gathering replicated other forms of state and police interrogation. Even with provisional corrections for formal biases, therefore, their use in places like Nagwa reasserted certain dynamics of power in such a way as to produce a response of learned helplessness—and low scores—from persons being interviewed. According to any of a bevy of such tests, almost the entire population of Nagwa, young and old, was severely demented.

But even less formal assessments didn't generate my hoped-for sample. Was I confirming the better brain? I began to consider demographics more carefully. The state of Uttar Pradesh had not undergone the "demographic transition" of several south Indian states and various regions and communities around the country: lower infant mortality, greater longevity, and a shift from a predominantly youthful population to one with a greater proportion of middle-aged and elderly persons. The demographics of Nagwa slum were further tilted toward the young, with a handful of persons, among several thousand residents, who thought they were over seventy. Like Shankar the boatman, people became "old" in Nagwa in their forties and fifties, old not only in name but in body. Sick old people seldom had independent access to medical resources, and died more quickly than chronically ill persons in other neighborhoods of the city.

The proportion of persons sixty-five and over in India overall was measured at 3 to 4 percent of the country's total population in 1980,[51] a figure far lower than the proportion of persons at or over sixty-five in most of Europe and North America. Few of the Indian group survived their seventies; according to United Nations estimates, .3 percent of the population of India was aged eighty years or older in 1980 and .4 percent will be eighty or older in 2000.[52] Poor old people fail to survive, as we will see in later chapters, less because of a lack of secondary and tertiary medical resources than because a dearth of affordable primary health care in the context of endemic poverty and the related feeling of many adult children that limited health resources—what we may term the severely circumscribed "health capital" of many families—are wasted on the old.

Framing my dilemma in terms of demography initially seemed to solve another dilemma: the social geography of the emerging Alzheimer's movement in India. The ARDSI began in Kerala, in South India. Though it has spread to middle-class enclaves in large metropolitan centers, it remains particularly widespread in cities and towns in South India. Other significant interest in dementia research in India has occurred in Madurai and Madras, in the neighboring southern state of Tamil Nadu, and among middle-class or wealthy urban communities elsewhere, such as among Parsis in Bombay.[53] In the former cases these are areas, particularly in Kerala, where a significant demographic transition has occurred;[54] the demographics of the relatively affluent Parsi community are similarly posttransition. Despite the claims of Bharati and of Osuntokun, a growing number of neuropathological and community studies suggest that the neuropathological stigmata and associated behavioral changes of Alzheimer's disease do exist in India.[55] In the absence of compelling data for "preindustrial" populations where the very old are uniformly spared such changes, it seems reasonable to expect that there may well be more old people with more plaques and tangles in Kerala, people who are probably more forgetful and more confused than they would otherwise be.

But my initial dilemma in Nagwa pushed me in a direction I could never have anticipated had I contented myself with work among persons labeled *demented* in a metropolitan middle-class or "posttransition" area. For though I did come to meet many older persons in Varanasi (slowly, over the course of months) who would have been labeled demented by most physicians, other questions had come to the fore, questions that became more central than the debate between the enthusiastic, nascent Alzheimer's movement and the proponents of the better brain theory advanced by nationalist science. I slowly learned to practice what was obvious to me in theory: to listen to the ways in which old age *mattered* to people in Nagwa and elsewhere, to ask the question Kleinman taught me to foreground: *what is at stake* is asking about old age?

As I stared despairingly at my notebooks night after night in Nandanagar, Mrs. Sharma began to worry. "Ask Munni to help you," she offered, referring to the eldest of her five daughters. Munni and her sister Sapna suggested I talk to the old lady next door: "She's quite mad." Increasingly, as my project became known to friends and acquaintances in each of the four neighborhoods, they began to offer me the names of old persons who they thought would be appropriate for my work; but almost inevitably these were old people in *other* people's homes, not their own. In Varanasi, it was only when I abandoned *looking* for what I understood as dementia that I began to find it, throughout the city. Why the existence of difficult and "weak-brained" old people raised questions of self and other—our household versus that of our neighbors, our devotion to parents as opposed to that of other kin, Hindu versus Muslim mental weakness—emerged as a critical problem, as well as raised new issues of interpretation. This led to what I will discuss below as familial bodies, dying spaces, and phenomenologies of the voice.

In the remainder of the two years that followed my fruitless first few months of house-to-house MSEs, as these new lenses became central to my learning and writing, I did end up meeting many more persons who would be considered demented in allopathic, biomedical terms. I could not suspend making such clinical assessments, when they seemed germane, nor would I wish to; such a practice of selective bracketing only reproduces a vulgar Orientalism and replaces critical engagement with anthropological romance. But a division of Varanasi elders into demented and not demented persons often obscured as much as it revealed: such a distinction was not the most critical determinant of the physical survival of old people, of their or their families' well-being, or of how the old body was experienced and contested and cared for.

"Dementia" is not at the center of this book *not* because it is a social construction with no bearing on the lives and bodies of persons in Varanasi, and *not* because to use the term enacts Western biomedical hegemony. To read critical tools such as hegemony as being located seamlessly with "the West" and "biomedicine" is to replace a coherent theory of language and class with a set of easy oppositions—East/West, traditional medicine/biomedicine. The relation of terms like clinically demented and practices like dementia exams and prevalence studies to local and global asymmetries is far more complex and requires a theory of how such language and practice engage the body. To speak of dementia is to engage the body in at least two critical ways.

Like all human efforts to act in the world, the speaking of dementia is of necessity social; its analysis in social terms must include both a pragmatic engagement with and debate over its usefulness and relevance as a tool and a theorization of how the languages and practices constituting it enact a certain sort of embodied subject. To reduce this analysis only to the tamasha of competing cultures is to fail on both counts. Dementia may or may not be useful in clinical terms, but the question of its usefulness may have far more to do with why most old people in Varanasi fail to survive very long than with a disembodied field of cultural difference. On the one hand, speaking of and measuring dementia may invoke a powerful tool—which though a historically and culturally located representation can engage the fate of bodies and lives in a manner not reducible to the obviousness of its being a social construction. However meaningless the language and practices instantiating Alzheimer's in much of Varanasi in the 1980s, their use could in theory lead, for example, to the diagnosis and treatment of normal pressure hydrocephalus in a confused and forgetful older person who might otherwise not recover what in the different neighborhoods of the city would be termed balance or strength. I say *in theory* because this diagnosis and treatment require far more than an assemblage of ideas and practices but presume a local economy and world system in which the human and technical resources necessary for such a diagnosis and treatment are widely available and not far more pressingly required for primary health care.

On the other hand, speaking of dementia not only creates a set of more or less useful and appropriate tools but invokes a moral world like that represented by the Americans at Zagreb and, as we shall see, made to matter by a plethora of foreign agencies from the United Nations to international Alzheimer's groups to multinational pharmaceutical corporations. Following Judith Butler, one could say that to speak of dementia is to call upon an aging body in a certain way and not in another and in a sense to materialize the body—literally and figuratively to make it *matter*—in a necessarily contingent manner. Butler reworks the analysis by the French Marxist philosopher Althusser of how persons are hailed or "interpellated" as subjects into a discussion of how persons are hailed as bodies.[56] Her own argument centers on the politics of sexual difference, but one can apply it to the materialization of dementia in India in terms both of a local politics of generation, gender, caste, and class and of a larger politics of global capital and postcoloniality. Speaking of dementia pushes bodies to matter as old, as poor, and as global in new ways.

Each of these processes involves both material things and the political terrains through which these are articulated over time. At stake in speaking of dementia is not the often banal narrative of an earlier medical anthropology: Is an embodied state biological or cultural? Rather, what is critical may be to find a way to engage language and practice *both* as tools the usefulness of which we can test and debate and rethink—whether that means researching the genetic basis of amyloid deposition or struggling for primary health care in a community—*and* as the always already politicized grounds of how we can know and engage our bodies at all.

Senility, dementia, and senile dementia continually resurface in ambiguous ways in Indian medical literature, always in terms of both their prevalence in "the West" and their absence in any of a number of senses in India. Readings of this absence vary, from Bharati's, who argues from laboratory research that Indian brains lack plaques and tangles, to that of the founders of the ARDSI in South

India, who argue from clinical experience that Indian doctors must stop denying the prevalence of Alzheimer's disease. What unites these very different assessments is the way they express Indian difference as a lack: of tangles, of commitments. Psychiatrists I interviewed in 1989 at the National Institute of Mental Health and Neurological Science (NIMHANS) in Bangalore who were then involved in a study of Alzheimer's disease reported to me a predicament opposite to the findings of Bharati, a third variety of absence. They found that autopsy studies utilizing dead brains were relatively easy to structure and clearly demonstrated the existence of plaques and tangles similar to those found in age-matched studies abroad. However, clinical studies using both outpatient and institutionalized patients at NIMHANS were far more difficult to set up; few very old patients were brought for treatment; fewer still were demented. The psychiatrists with whom I spoke were shifting their emphasis from clinical to neuropathological work; dead persons were more amenable than live ones to the elicitation of senile pathology.

OF VARANASI

I worked primarily in the city of Varanasi; I had lived there on several previous occasions as a student of comparative religion and was familiar with its neighborhoods. Varanasi is among other things a sacred city, built along the archetypically sacred Ganges, Ganga in India. From the river, Kashi is Shiva's city—that is, a unity, the oft-described and continually researched "sacred city of the Hindus." The river anchors the pilgrim's construction of Kashi as the most famous of *tīrthas*: "crossing over" places, junctures with the transcendent experiential order of moksha, or release. It has anchored as well the colonial construction of Varanasi as the essence of the imagined Hindu. Our understanding of its sacredness is filtered through its importance as a sign of the essential India in colonial representations of the touristic, Cohn's observational/travel modality: "a repertoire of images and typifactions that determined what was significant to the European eye."[57] Cohn points to depictions of the Varanasi riverfront as a central image within the commodified portraiture of the essential Hindu, alternately exotic, docile, threatening, superstitious, bestial, and otherworldly.

The riverfront offers an overdetermined reading within the Indological construction of India as "the one and the many," "unity in diversity," and so forth. Its imaging out of time and beyond commerce and politics allows its continued representation as the confrontation of a teeming plurality with a negative oneness. Thus its primary icon, the line of stepped quays, or ghats, which stretch along the river's broad curve studded with mandirs (temples), maths (monastic communities), palaces, and the two cremation ghats, and flanked by the empty sands and distant tree line of the opposite bank of the river, *us pār*. On the one side, majestic, hierarchical, labyrinthine, and ultimately redundant dharma, or righteous action, divisible into myriad identical units (the ghats), each of which stands for and replicates the whole. On the other, the emptiness of *us pār*, the sandy and desolate expanses of the uninhabited other bank. Foreign constructions of Varanasi in particular have tended to read the city through the perceived logic of its riverfront and its unambiguous religious meaning. Apologists see the glories of the inhabited bank and the solemn realities of the other; critics see the crowd (and sense communal frenzy), hear the clamor (and sense spiritual infantilism), and smell the filth (and sense bestial humanity) of the inhabited bank, and espy the fatalistic "life-negation" of Hinduism on the empty other.[58] It is the great Orientalist scene.

Within such a context, Nita Kumar's reinterpretation in *The Artisans of Banaras*[59] of the riverfront, the "other side," and their significance through a localized culture of pleasure—the language and practice of "Banaras-ness"—is radical. She reveals a different self-consciousness of the city, one alive to sensuality, to craft and commerce, and to Indo-Muslim culture, located within networks of trade and artisanship and the interpellation of its citizens within local and national discourses of their being *bhaiyās* and Banarsi thugs: North Indian rednecks, cheats, and ruffians. Following her lead, I will examine one of the stock characters of Varanasi, the devout and often destitute old person on the ghats, but only by placing this body within the context of the myriad other old bodies of the city, rereading the touristic.

Varanasi is a particularly interesting place to study old age. One of the key signs in the iconic representation of Varanasi is the old person and particularly the old widow, who has come to Varanasi and the Ganga to live out her last days or to die or at least be cremated here. The motives of these "dwellers in Kashi," or *kāśīvāsīs*, are ambivalently structured by many Varanasi natives with whom I spoke: on the one hand, they are said to have come out of great devotion (bhakti) to God to die in this sacred place; on the other, they have been cast out by unloving families or have lost their kin through untold tragedies. Might some of the *kāśīvāsīs*, I initially wondered, be demented as well?

Varanasi as sacred center is also home to hundreds, at times thousands, of sannyasis, renunciates, and other sadhus, or holy men. *Sannyāsa* is the last stage of *āśramadharma*—the idealized four-stage life cycle in the ethical and legal tradition of classical *dharmaśāstra*—and is conceptualized as a time of complete renunciation of secular life and pleasures, with one's mind focused on God and on the numenal world beyond appearances.[60] The goal of this fourth stage is the fourth of the classical goals of human existence—righteous action, pleasure, profit, and liberation from suffering. Moksha, or liberation, is often conceptualized as radical cognitive transformation in which one *learns to forget* the illusions of the phenomenal world. Old age as a radical cognitive transformation involving a practice of forgetting? Is *sannyāsa*, I initially wondered, ever a radical rethinking of senility?

Finally, Varanasi is an important center for medical and textual research and practice, with several colleges and universities. Scholars of biomedical (or "allopathic," as it is known in India, having no exclusive claim to being either biological or medical) and Ayurvedic medicine abound, and there are several notable practitioners of homeopathic and Islamic Unani medicine. Pandits who could lead one through medical, legal, philosophical, and narrative texts are many. The presence of other forms of expertise not as localized to Varanasi—particularly in social work and law—also drew me.

I organized my fieldwork in Varanasi into three overlapping spheres: (1) a study of old people and their families over two years in several neighborhoods, roughly stratified by class; (2) a study of formal and informal institutions—ashrams, monasteries, widow houses, government homes for the aged, charitable homes for the dying, local support networks—for *kāśivāsīs* and sannyasis, and extensive work with individuals; and (3) a study of local institutions and practitioners, including allopathy (neurology, psychiatry, general practice), Ayurveda, exorcists, the civil courts, and political and religious associations.

I spent several months outside of Varanasi doing research in other types of institutions. In Delhi I worked with volunteer-supported old-age advocacy and fundraising groups, with the Ministry of Welfare, with police missing-persons bureaus, and with several additional families of friends and acquaintances who told me their parents or grandparents were or had been senile. In Bombay I worked with a multinational pharmaceutical company marketing a drug to ameliorate dementia. In Calcutta I worked in two old-age homes founded by a women's volunteer association, at the missing-persons desk of the local news department at the national television network of Doordarshan, and, as in Delhi, with the families of friends and others. In Madras, Bangalore, and Madurai, I met with several physicians and researchers working on old age. In Dehradun, I visited two very different institutions, a wealthy retirement ashram and a geriatric clinic. I spent several days each at ashrams in the religious centers of Brindavin and Hardwar, sacred sites with somewhat different institutional relationships to older persons than found in Varanasi. Finally, in Allahabad, I visited the camp of Devraha Baba during the great convocation of ascetics, the Kumbh Mela; Baba, who has passed away since that time, was a famous superannuated saint then said to be at least 140 years old.

Despite the breadth of this ethnography, it centers in four neighborhoods of Varanasi. The city is spread along the west bank of the Ganga as it briefly courses northward. The older neighborhoods of the city, the *pakkā mahal*, lie closest to the river. The *pakkā mahal* consists of a narrow strip of neighborhoods, primarily Hindu, stretching for many kilometers along the river; another strip alongside the first one, which is mostly Muslim; and beyond these a patchwork of neighborhoods. Farther out from the lanes of the *pakkā mahal* is the *kaccā mahal* with its hodgepodge of slums, or bastis, middle- and upper-class "colonies," urbanized villages, large estates, the former British cantonment, and to the north the village of Sarnath, sacred site of the Buddha's first teaching.

Ravindrapuri colony is in the south of the city, just south and west of *pakkā mahal* Muslim and Hindu neighborhoods, north of a low-caste Chamar slum, and east of other similar colonies. Its inhabitants are the families of higher level government bureaucrats, professors, doctors, engineers and other professionals, business executives, and families with other sources of income. Nandanagar colony, where I lived with the Sharmas from 1988–89, is on the southern outskirts of the city, on the western rim of the vast semicircular campus of Banaras Hindu University, bordering a low-caste area of the village of Karaundi. It is smaller and less wealthy than Ravindrapuri, but its residents are similarly primarily the families of bureaucrats and other government officials, professors, and professionals. I treat these two communities together in the fifth chapter.

Nagwa Harijan Basti is a low-caste slum near the river just south of the southernmost of the major ghats, Assi. On its north is the stream of the Assi and beyond that another poor, though more mixed-caste, neighborhood on the east fields and the river, and on the west and south wealthier colonies. Unlike the colonies, which are primarily inhabited by upper- and middle-caste Hindus, the slum is almost exclusively Chamar, an untouchable jati, or caste group, whose low status is "explained" by its traditional and polluting occupation of working with leather. Some residents of Nagwa do work with leather, running the shoe- and sandal-checking stands outside some of the city's many large temples; most are involved in numerous other jobs. Women work as domestics, running small shops, selling vegetables in the Lanka market nearby, in construction, as midwives, as possession healers, and as beggars; men may do these, midwifery and usually beggary excepted, and also work as teachers, rickshaw pullers, petty bureaucrats, students, and migrant laborers. Some residents work seasonally on their family's land or on land to which they have obligations, in villages to the south and west of the city. The sixth chapter focuses on Nagwa slum.

Bengali Tola—the Bengali quarter—lies deep in the *pakkā mahal* along the river, between the major bathing ghats of Kedar to the south and Dasashwamedh to the north. Many Bengalis live here, as well as local Hindi- and Bhojpuri-speaking Banarsis and a significant community of Telegu- and Tamil-speaking south Indians. The area is cosmopolitan, crowded, and complex, with large homes known as *haveli*s and small hovels, remnants of erstwhile palaces and water buffalo pastures tucked away around a corner, and dotted with numerous religious institutions. Many *kāśīvāsī* widows, *kāśīvāsī* old men, and superannuated sannyasis live along the lanes of the quarter, and it was here, during the year 1989–90 when I lived in the quarter below Marwari Mataji, that I did most of my *kāśīvāsī* interviews.

The interdisciplinary site known as South Asian studies has changed considerably since I was a college freshman. Nowadays I pause before admitting that I have chosen to work in Varanasi, and not in other, less conventional and less touristic places. Whenever I return to the city and board at one of the several guest houses catering to visiting scholars, the variegated combination of expatriates I always run into presents an unpleasant reflection, perhaps one too close for comfort: religious seekers complaining about the locals, would-be sitar masters doing the George Harrison thing, students seeking the real India in the city's narrow and seemingly timeless lanes, and budget travelers counting the days until they can escape for the "hassle-free" vistas of Kathmandu.

For all the international attention and the prodigious literature it has generated, "Banaras" continues to be framed as a cultural domain unto itself, paradigmatic yet exquisitely local. In part, this localism originates in the Orientalist imagination, in part in parallel maneuvers to render the city timeless and unique, undertaken by Brahmanical pangyrists, national and international tour operators, and increasingly the so-called Hindu right. Bombay film has circulated depictions of "Banaras-ness" widely through films like *Banarsi Thug* and *Banarsi Babu.* Anthropologists like Jonathan Parry, Nita Kumar, and Joseph Alter have produced careful, complexly theorized, and richly textured ethnographies of the city, all of which have chosen to highlight practices understood as unambiguously traditional and particularly local.[61]

I began this book trained to do something similar, but in confronting the limits of my initial endeavor and in being forced to ask in different ways what was at stake in studying old age in a given place and time, I came to redefine the boundaries of my "field" in its dual sense: where and who I study, and how and for whom I write.[62] Varanasi has receded from its position as the center of this book, figuratively and literally, and has become a site in a different way, as a set of linkages from the intimate to the global, but particularly in between.

✧ *World Wide Web* ✧

Flexible ethnography for a fallen age: use Netscape to get on the Web, get into the database of the Alzheimer's Association, and wait for a prompt.

Enter keyword(s):   [   ]   [Search] [Reset]

Type "**India**," to be disappointed with a polite no. "Sorry, I didn't find any documents that matched your search for **India**"! Play around a bit; collect bits of the words and pictures filling the screen. An ad for *A Long Good-bye: Reflections on Dealing with Alzheimer's*, accompanied by photographs of its author, Dr. Linda Morrison Combs, as a little girl, a photograph of Linda's mother before she developed Alzheimer's, a "Personal message from Linda," and a Secure Online Ordering form. A collection of media releases: "Ronald and Nancy Reagan join forces with Alzheimer's Association," followed by "Government Abandoning Alzheimer Families through Medicaid Cuts." The ICD-10 description of Primary Degenerative Dementia of the Alzheimer Type. And the Alzheimer Page from the Alzheimer's Disease Research Center in St. Louis, which offers another prompt.[1] Again, try "**India**." This time, success, even after weeding out the majority of references to the other (Native American) Indians.

Two threads—"thread" being the term for a set of related postings on an Internet newsgroup—appear most promising. Both are culled from a newsgroup devoted to online discussions about Alzheimer's. The first is a debate on the relationship of Alzheimer's to a core New Age term, "oxidation," and subsequently on the antioxidant effects of a vegetarian diet. The debate leads one contributor to ask: "What is the incidence of AD . . . say in India . . . where 900,000,000 people are vegetarian?" The thread concludes, "A medical web site in India would be the one to check, I suppose?"[2] Oh yes.

The second is an appeal from one Austin Lobo at rpi.edu in the United States, whose mother-in-law is in Bombay, diagnosed since 1993 with Alzheimer's ("later confirmed by a thorough exam at Columbia-Presbyterian Hospital in NYC"). Back in Bombay, with her husband "as sole care-giver," the mother-in-law "paces about her house, hiding things and accusing everyone around her of stealing from her." Mr. Lobo laments the impossibility of institutionalization and the lack of support groups: "In India, the social conditions are such that putting a parent in a nursing home is almost unthinkable. And AD or any other mental condition is treated as 'madness in the family [*sic*],' with as much of a stigma as leprosy in biblical times."[3]

In response, a sympathetic poster notes that "with the awareness of Alzheimer's disease and dementia expanding globally, even in traditional societies such as India there is some recognition developing of the enormous strain placed on the family unit and the additional burden of social ostracism";[4] she goes on to recommend a contact person in Bombay. In India: site of the biblical, hundreds of millions of vegetarians, medical Web sites for the curious, the "unthinkable."

TWO

Alzheimer's Hell

in which Alzheimer's is revealed as a metaphor for old age, senility has a history, and the relation between witches and kings offers a subaltern physiology

NO AGING IN AMERICA! LEADING SCIENTISTS REVEAL

Well, at least you have a grandmother. Mine has Alzheimer's disease. It's like she's not even there. Enjoy your stay in Hollywood!
VALUE RENT-A-CAR SALESWOMAN HANDING ME THE KEYS AT FORT LAUDERDALE AIRPORT
AND NODDING TOWARD MY GRANDMOTHER, AFTER I HAD COMPLAINED ABOUT THE WEATHER

"Dapper Dana Andrews' Alzheimer's Hell" screamed a 1992 headline in the *Globe*, an American supermarket tabloid.[1] I read the tabloids a lot when writing the first incarnation of this book, their lurid headlines scanned while I waited in line to purchase more caffeine and carbohydrates to fuel my scholarship. Old age was a frequent theme, particularly astonishing tales of age incongruities: centenarian men marrying young women, old women or young girls giving birth, grandmothers (inevitably described as "grannies") doing daredevil acts. Amid this cavalcade, the Hollywood celebrity with Alzheimer's was a frequent figure. The "Alzheimer's hell" article chronicles the transformation of the "dashing matinee idol" Andrews into a "pathetic victim of Alzheimer's disease"; the disease is described through a sequence of violent metaphors: mangling, ravaging. Below the headline, two cameo-style photographs of the former actor are placed side by side, with the caption "From this to this in 4 years." In both, Andrews is smiling and well-dressed. In the first, taken we are told when he was seventy-nine, Andrews has jet black hair and stares out at the camera, about to say something. In the second, labeled "his mind and body fail him," Andrews has a head of gray hair and stares off at an angle, looking as if he has just finished speaking. The only apparent signs of mind and body mangling are the hair color and the hint of speech, imminent or completed. Old old Andrews stares past us; we are offered no connection to him. He has already spoken; the wisdom of experience, the possibility on the opening lips of young old Andrews, has flown with the hair color. We are left with a "pathetic, mindless shell," a truth rooted less in the devastations of brain disease than of a particular vision of old age

Why the turn here to American supermarkets and to Hollywood? The simplest answer is that the tabloids form part of a disparate collection of texts and events that have helped me both unthink and rethink what is at stake in talking about Alzheimer's, senility, and attempts to improve the welfare of old people. For readers more in sympathy with the North American position at Zagreb than with the others (the Indian position or my own back row pretense of Archimedean distance), this unthinking may be necessary to grasp why the medical practices by which the behavior of certain old people has been comprehended and sometimes altered are locally and historically particular, their analysis exhausted neither by the very real biology of the brain nor the very real political economy of age, the family, professional knowledge and the state. The tabloids help me express why something like culture remains critical, and yet their silliness—a particular kind of irony—renders the whole project of stabilizing and systematizing culture slightly parodic, a necessary stance.

The following two chapters are partial efforts at such rethinking. This chapter isolates several particulars of an American sociology and a European history of senility, particulars that help me tell a specific story about conjunctures and debates in India. It is neither a comprehensive historiography nor a focused sociology of science. Such broader approaches are critical and, at the time of this writing, unrealized, but they are not central to the particular history of the present I am writing, a history in some senses *about* but never simply located *in* India. This is an anthropologist's book, and though it eschews the particular unities of either the monocultural or the world systems anthropological text, it nonetheless is rooted in an attempt to provide materials for a genealogy of the particular.[2]

The particular social facts most relevant to how I have chosen *not* to write about senility and Alzheimer's are the following:

1. During the decade of this project and into the short-term foreseeable future, there has been and remains no effective treatment for most degenerative dementias. Nor does a radical technical or conceptual shift in the treatment of the major dementias appear imminent.
2. As noted in the last chapter, the practices which materialize Alzheimer's and the dementias more generally tend to be attributional, involving two classes of bodies, those in which the disease is located and those (the "caregivers") in which the disease is publicly experienced, through which it is made to matter.

Each of these points will lead me to certain emphases and deferrals. In terms of emphases, I note the second point. Writing about Alzheimer's pushes me to examine the difference between these two classes of bodies and to think about other modes or axes of difference through or against which this difference between the diseased (and usually older) and the care-giving (and usually younger) may be framed. The axis of difference that I will foreground here as most useful to a history of senility is that of gender. Mutually constitutive relations between age and other axes of difference have already been suggested in the preface and introduction: the colonial, caste, and class difference rearticulated in the moment of the old woman of Balua, the religious difference deployed in the self-construction of working class Hindus on the boat, and the colonial and racial difference materialized in the figures of tropical ripening and softening.

Given the first point, I have chosen not to focus on the Alzheimer's gene, Alzheimer's mouse, or other sites of biological research.[3] As the science of senility changes conceptually and technically, these sites will become more relevant to the kind of project undertaken here. Paul Rabinow draws on Baudelaire and Foucault in cautioning students of science against the easy nostalgia and *ressentiment* of "despising the present."[4] Though what constitutes nostalgia and *ressentiment* may not be obvious, depending a fair amount upon where one is sitting, the point is critical. I have no a priori interest in deconstructing Alzheimer's or in offering a nativist "Indian" category or conjuncture in its place. But both the stories of Alzheimer's in this chapter and of the Bad Family in the next are uniquely *negative* stories, about absence and difference, perhaps because they are so critically narratives of loss (of self, of material resources, of culture) and death. Similarly, J. P. S. Uberoi once offered a critique of an earlier version of this material, saying that it was so unrelentingly about negation, a sociology not of reason but its absence.[5] Yet to the extent medical practice, and in particular the medicine of old age, is a social engagement less with recuperation than with loss and death, it may engage a peculiar type of negative reason and demand a peculiar sort of critical response.

Given these two points, we might say that practical knowledge of Alzheimer's is organized around two maneuvers. First, it involves an *iteration* of its pathology as opposed to its normality, despite the lack of a cure. Second, it involves a *circulation*: of legitimate suffering, between diseased and care-giving bodies. These maneuvers, of iteration and circulation, will be important to keep in mind as the story I tell tacks back and forth between India and other places.

The tabloids I have been referring to are a particular subgenre of American journalism that appears weekly next to supermarket checkout lines and in convenience stores and combines celebrity gossip with miracle diets, psychic predictions, and a steady reportage of the shocking and weird. Their language of extremity and excess has characterized presentations of senility in the United States that were far more highbrow during the decade (1985–95) in which I was actively engaged in learning about senility. Below I will move from tabloid sensationalism through mainstream journalism and into the language of dementia professionals, stressing the thematic continuities: how a culturally and historically distinct obsession with what the *Globe* called "Alzheimer's hell" informs more reasonable discourse.

Additionally, I will use the tabloids as a shorthand for raising questions about American class consciousness and any attempt to articulate a cultural study in the

United States, even of the potted comparative sort that expatriate anthropologists implicitly engage in. Put simply, through their carnivalesque scenarios American tabloids offer ironic readings of the "leading experts" or "leading scientists" whose ubiquitous revelations suffuse the text but are never quite taken at face value, unlike the expert sound bites of more mainstream media. This irony is not simply the highbrow irony of kitsch, and it will help to trouble the certitudes of mainstream public culture and its partially manufactured consensus on how Americans think.

Finally, I will use tabloids themselves metaphorically, as a sign of the effects of a style of anthropological and social reasoning still prevalent in South Asian studies. The anthropologist's India has its tabloid quality, and its truths are often framed in terms of a similar straight-faced extremity. Graduate students who elect to study India are exposed to a discursive morass with its own hermetic logic, which generates carnivalesque truths that could appear, if there were but a market for them, on the covers of the *Globe* and its fellow tabloids: "Indians prefer hierarchy to equality, unlike modern French"; "Indians not individuals, leading scientists reveal"; "Indian men ruined by devastating childhood practices: their mothers split in two!"; "Bizarre Hindu village discovered where bodies are fluid," or "Secret pact between British and Brahmans discovered—it's all a colonial plot!" Still, this anthropological India is seldom just the sum of its colonial and postcolonial rhetoric. It *can* offer the basis for a "good enough" engagement with the world out there, to borrow again Scheper-Hughes's phrasing of a response to anthropology's obsession with its own reflexivity. Like the tabloids as I read them here, the anthropologist's India signifies powerful truths through the very excess that renders it parodic.

Protesting too much, I return to the senility of the rich and famous. Andrews "can't remember a thing," "has like a five-second attention span and then he's gone," "doesn't know you've even been there," and "started getting lost." Deficits in memory and attention are the key symptoms of the mangling of minds. A 1990 article in the *Star* tells the same horror story about comedian Harvey Korman, who "mixes up his wife and kids," "began showing up uninvited at his former houses," and has "been knocking on neighbor [and ex-Charlie's Angel] Jaclyn Smith's front door and saying 'I'm home.'" The extreme forgetfulness elaborated in these articles is hell because it implies a loss of self. Not only are the "mindless" victims of Alzheimer's no longer the persons they once were, they are in a sense no longer persons at all. Mind and self come to stand for one another.

Again, the victim is not the one who suffers in this hell: "[T]he only blessing is that the horrible disease destroyed the actor's mind before he could realize what was happening." The disease was "harder on his wife and three grown children." The article suggests that Korman, confusing his wife with sex symbol Smith, could be doing far worse. The relatives are the victims, as in the case of Andrews's wife:

> Just as painful was the effect Dana's disease had on his wife. . . . She was forced to sell their luxurious $600,000 home in Studio City to help pay for her husband's care.

"It was a big life change for Mom when he had to go in," says Stephen. "It's a shock to the system to suddenly be on your own after all that time together with someone you love."

She had a big house to run without Dad around. . . . "

Illness, Arthur Kleinman suggests in *The Illness Narratives*, may act like a sponge, soaking up meaning from the life world of the sufferer and recasting it in terms of itself.[6] Alzheimer's soaks up meaning less from the life of the initial "victim" than from those around him or her, casting all effort and experience of relatives—the "other victims"—in terms of the embodied signs of this mangling process. This exchange of symptoms—the body of the caretaker for the body of the Alzheimer's patient—dominates the middlebrow literature on senility.

Yet the irony of Alzheimer's—the suffering of the stricken brain being experienced primarily by those with brains intact—is in its tabloid version underscored by a deeper irony absent in middlebrow and expert versions, a hermeneutic of suspicion regarding the victimhood of rich relatives of famous people. Andrew's wife, forced to give up her then expensive home, becomes in a mocking gesture the poor little rich girl. Suspicion as to family motives mirrors another age-related tabloid genre: the violent contest between generations. Intergenerational squabbles, often involving a negotiation over the prerogatives of an older generation refusing to hand over its authority, erupt in the tabloids in grotesque fashion. In a delightfully hideous *Sun* piece from 1988, a struggle over institutionalizing a seventy-two-year-old parent suggests that a family's putative suffering in the mode of the other victim may point to a desire for the old person's disappearance.[7] Tabloid irony forces open the question of *King Lear*—incoherent within middlebrow and expert variants of Alzheimer's—the question of the relation between a family's gerontocidal desire and the insanity of old age. Whence the loss of self?

The piece begins with an image of the old person as excessive wanderer, "lost 5 years," yet immediately this ubiquitous figure within gerontological literature is grotesquely transformed, the truth of her wandering revealed as lethal immobility.

GRANNY, LOST 5 YRS, FOUND IN MURPHY BED!
—SHE WAS MUMMIFIED

A woman's final trip to her old family home turned into a horrifying nightmare when she discovered her grandmother's mummified corpse stuffed into a folding bed—still wearing her favorite nightgown.

Police in suburban Liverpool, England, say Abigail Larson, 72, died when her fold-away bed—commonly known as a Murphy bed—lurched backward into its cabinet as she slept, pinning the gray-haired granny between the mattress and the wall.

As the granddaughter, the voice of both innocence and irony here, discovers that her wandering grandmother has never left home, she offers us a different trajectory for the old woman's movement, one in which wandering and fixity continually shift referents:

Abigail's granddaughter, Janet Biggers, told officials she hadn't seen her grand-mother for more than five years, and the family assumed the spunky senior citizen had run away after a bitter fight regarding their plans to put her in a nursing home.

"Grandma was starting to fail, and my mother and uncle both felt it was unsafe for her to live in that big house all by herself," Janet explains. "Mother was especially fearful Grandma would fall down the stairs and hurt herself.

"However, Grandma couldn't stand the idea of selling the family home and liv-ing in a nursing home, and she told my mother so in no uncertain terms. She threat-ened to run away before she'd let them take her away."

According to Janet, the discussion ended on a bitter note, and several days passed before her mother decided to visit the stubborn old woman. But when she ar-rived, the house was empty and Abigail was nowhere to be found.

"We searched all over, certain she had fallen or hurt herself, but we couldn't find Grandma anywhere," Janet notes.

Mindless wandering may or may not be desperate running away; being stuck in a nursing home becomes being mummified in a Murphy bed. The desire by Lar-son's children to sell that big house and rid themselves of its burden affirms the disposable figure of the granny. The article evokes the image of Mrs. Fletcher, roughly contemporary with it, a figure from an American advertisement for a communication device designed for old people. In the ad, an old woman has fallen down and pathetically intones, "I've fallen and I can't get up." Repeating Mrs. Fletcher's monotonous cry for help briefly became an American national craze.

"We notified authorities she was missing, but they gave up looking after a couple of weeks. All we could do was hope she would call and say she was all right."

Five years passed, and Janet's family decided there was no use in hanging on to Abigail's three-bedroom home. "My mother cried when she called the real estate agent," she says. "It was one of the hardest things she's ever done. She knew Grandma would be furious, but after five years she felt she had no choice. The up-keep on the house was breaking us financially."

Here is tabloid irony, the crocodile tears of the other victim: Janet's mother, all too eager to sell the family home in the first place, now can afford to wait five expen-sive years with Larson gone. Then, the final revelation:

Janet stopped by later to clean up and walk through the house one last time. On im-pulse she opened the folding bed in her grandmother's bedroom, and it was then that she made her grisly discovery. . . .

"There was Grandma laid out flat, still wearing her favorite purple and pink nightgown. Her skin was withered and tough like leather, but other than that she looked as if she were still asleep. I guess the Murphy bed just flipped backward and took her with it. . . . "

With this inverted fall and the image of the dead granny, pathetically lost in her own home, among her own family, the embodiment of conflict shifts once again, from the fallen back to the lost and confused senile body:

Janet notes the family is saddened by her grandmother's passing, but relieved to know she isn't out in the street lost and confused.

"I'm just glad to know Grandma died in familiar surroundings," she declares. "I'm going to miss her a lot."[8]

The absurdity of this piece—suffocation in a Murphy bed transformed into a wholesome death in familiar surroundings—underscores the irony of intergenerational conflict. Care is interchangeable with control; the rhetoric of falling justifies institutionalization, but once Larson is lost and her children are free five years seem blithely to go by. Confusion and wandering are presented as far less dangerous than the lonely and deadly embrace of the family home, where Grandma can be missed because she is fixed, all too literally, in the plans of her children.

ALZHEIMER'S, SUBJECTIVITY, AND THE OLD WEST

I now begin the journey that will lead me into the sunset of my life. I know that for America there will always be a bright dawn ahead.

RONALD REAGAN, LETTER TO THE AMERICAN PEOPLE ANNOUNCING HIS ALZHEIMER'S

The multiple ironies that help sell tabloids were absent from writing on senility in the mainstream American press during the 1985–95 decade, but the same themes—the devastation of Alzheimer's and the transposing of the identity of its suffering onto family members—continued to be elaborated. Missing was a tabloid sensibility that the elaboration of the devastation and the suffering of family members were language games with potential winners and losers. The 1989 set of articles in *Newsweek* that I referred to earlier, collectively entitled "All about Alzheimer's," framed the disease through similarly violent imagery leading to an erasure of self: stripped of "every vestige of mind and identity," the primary victim simply "ceases to exist."[9]

The threat to selfhood posed by Alzheimer's within the middlebrow text remains dual, both the loss of self of the old individual and the loss of self of the other victim. *Newsweek* focuses on a seventy-one-year-old Boston woman, Ina, who from the start is represented through a series of losses: she forgets things, is "apathetic," "the logic is gone," "she has lost her sense of temperature," and so forth. These losses challenge our conception of a just world, placing the faux horror of the tabloid article within a far more impressive theodicy:

> Her name is Ina Connolly. She is 71 years old and she is a victim of Alzheimer's disease. But that is not all she is. She is also the mother of six grown children and the grandmother of seven. When her children describe their mother, they invariably mention her strength and her kindness. "She was the Rock of Gibraltar," says her son Frank, 34. "She was always doing things for people," says her daughter Kathy, 39.
>
> But the disease that is slowly destroying Ina Connolly's mind is not a respecter of past deeds. It does not matter that, as a young girl growing up in Boston, Massachusetts, she helped to raise her seven brothers and sisters and that she took care of her

elderly mother. It does not matter that she was once able to fix plumbing, hang wall-paper and prepare a full dinner every night, while keeping six kids out of major trou-ble. It does not matter that she could once swim faster than anyone in her family, that she secretly yearned to be a basketball star, that her late husband considered her the most beautiful woman he'd ever seen.

Alzheimer's is *unfair*. Within the late twentieth-century comparative aesthetics of the plague (until the advent of AIDS Alzheimer's was proclaimed the disease of the century),[10] Alzheimer's is framed as the disease that happens to good people. The contrast with AIDS in this moral sense is often explicit. Our sense of the tragic escalates through the portrayal of a kind of victim very different from the social portrayal of the AIDS sufferer: Ina is a mother, a grandmother, a sister, a daughter, a cook, a homemaker, a woman with secret yearnings, the most beauti-ful woman ever to her late husband.

The moral outrage the article invokes in its construction of Ina is immediately displaced onto the body of her family. Through the ever-present violent imagery, Ina shifts from being victim to victimizer. For her family, beyond the layered and tragic absences is an ever-present fear should "she ever became violent . . . espe-cially toward the baby [her granddaughter]." Ina is a physical threat to the body of little Amanda, as well as a psychological threat to the ability of her son Frank and daughter-in-law Mary Ellen to lead sane and normal lives.

The excess of Alzheimer's is structured not only as an explosion of violence but of time. *Newsweek* describes Alzheimer's as "a marathon," an "exhausting vigil" given bodies "who need to be constantly watched or restrained," an "ordeal," "round-the-clock," and most tellingly, an "endless funeral."[11] Such terms echo the title of the most well known American how-to book for families of persons with Alzheimer's disease and other dementias, *The 36-Hour Day*.[12] The suffering con-veyed by such temporal language is not that of the old person, who is here the agent but not the subject of disease. What is lacking from the repetitive language of Alzheimer's is much of a sense of the subjectivity of the old person, his or her *presence*. The *Newsweek* articles center on "the other victims"; Ina's past self is dis-played as an icon of family virtue, but the moral indignation around the unfair-ness of the disease glides quickly into the family's lament. The continually reiter-ated discovery of Alzheimer's journalism is that it is the caretaker who is the *real* victim. The endlessness and virulence of Alzheimer's is her experience.

What of the absent agent of disease? His or her incoherent voice as a person with dementing illness is offered in lieu of an attempt to acknowledge a subjectiv-ity and distinct selfhood. All we know of Ina now is that she can't speak coherently into a tape recorder and claims to be the president of Harvard. The logic of the text denies any possibility of continuity and any meaningfulness in taking Ina—with all her confusion—as still fundamentally a person. All we are allowed to hear is a set of aphasic, confused, and angry sounds presented to us as the sum of Ina and thus confirmation of the death of selfhood.

Within much of the specialized literature, such as *The 36-Hour Day*, prepared for families of persons diagnosed with Alzheimer's and other dementias, this era-sure generates some reflexive concern. *The 36-Hour Day* begins with the story of Mary, a woman struggling to cope with memory loss and an increasingly confus-ing and terrifying world. Her story is prefaced by an admission of the different agendas of families and "sufferers":

> Although this book was written for the families of people with dementing illnesses, we recognize that other people, including those suffering from these conditions, may read this book. We welcome this. We hope that the use of such words as patient and brain-injured person will not discourage those who have these illnesses. These words were chosen because we want to emphasize that the people who suffer from these conditions are ill, not "just old." We hope the tone of the book conveys that we think of you as individuals and people and never as objects.[13]

Unlike Ina, Mary as a person is not placed entirely within an idealized past. Alzheimer's is less of a totalizing construct—it neither stands for all dementias nor is it framed in as violent a language. The authors' goal, which they share with sup-port groups like those of the Alzheimer's Association, is to help families through a reconstruction, rather than an outright denial, of the subjectivity of the person with the dementing illness. Perhaps the most compelling narrative of such a re-construction is a 1994 film by Deborah Hoffmann, *Complaints of a Dutiful Daughter*, in which Hoffmann shows both the progression of her mother's dementia and of her own efforts to take care of the older woman and to cope. Like the tabloids, Hoffmann uses humor as a critical tool. Her story has an epiphany: before it, she is split between Sisyphean efforts to keep her mother, Doris, the same and a grow-ing frustration at Doris's refusal to remain who she was. But she comes to realize that her mother is changing and to make sense of Doris's actions by learning to re-construct continually who she is. Humor allows Hoffmann to read the absurdity of her mother's actions as the experience of a self in escalating flux, and not as the extinction of self.

In practice, the reconstruction of subjectivity is a more contested process, and the best of intentions often produce troubling results. In one family support group meeting I went to, held at the offices of ADRDA of eastern Massachusetts in 1992, there were seven persons besides myself in attendance: a male neuropsychologist who was leading the group; a female nursing home administrator, setting up an "Alzheimer's unit"; four sisters in their twenties through forties, daughters of a woman diagnosed with Alzheimer's the previous year; and a woman in her fifties, married three years ago, who was taking care of a demented mother-in-law.

The meeting lasted over two hours. We each introduced ourselves, starting with the psychologist. Two of the daughters were married, the other two lived together, and their mother was shuttled between their three households. The four women had differences among themselves as to how their mother should be helped and responded to but seemed content to share the task of caring for and watching her. The fiftyish daughter-in-law was less comfortable with caretaking, feeling trapped by her mother-in-law's illness ("It's disgusting, yes, that is just what it is, disgusting!"), her husband's inability to appreciate what she was going through, and the resistance of his family to putting the old woman into an institution. She told us that she had begun taking tranquilizers to cope. The nursing home representative and I introduced ourselves, and then the psychologist reintroduced himself, this time as a fellow family member of a person with dementia, and described several years of caring for a parent.

As in other support groups for secondarily victimized families, such as those set up for the family members of alcoholics, the process of each of us establishing our credentials as suffering caretakers—through a ritual of going around the room and revealing something personal—created what Victor Turner calls *communitas*, a temporary sense of community and shared purpose, allowing us to share intimate details and to reach new insights.[14] What differentiates the Alzheimer's Association from other such groups—which name themselves "Parents of," "Children of," or "Spouses of"—is the naming of this familial suffering not as adjunct to but constitutive of the experience of Alzheimer's itself. The organization is not Children or Other Relatives of People with Alzheimer's—it is, simply, the Alzheimer's Association. It is the absent victims, as in the introduction to *The 36-hour Day*, who are adjunct.

Following introductions, the psychologist introduced the agenda. The discussion was organized around a paired denial and reclamation of the absent victim's subjectivity. Our first goal was to regain control of our own lives, by recognizing dementia for what it is: the loss of self in the old person. Our second goal was to learn to communicate with the person with dementia, in effect by reconstituting a self. The first goal was achieved through an fairly exhaustive discussion by the psychologist of the pathophysiology of Alzheimer's and other dementias. Few questions were asked during this segment. Family members were interested, but did not engage this knowledge, nor did they try to apply it directly to their own situations. Its content as a statement was performative: the discussion did not seem to provide group members with much specific information, but its utterance reinforced their sense that Alzheimer's was something powerful, complex, and wholly other. It did this through the speaker's language, itself powerful, complex, and different from the language we were using as a group.

Given this performative structure, the psychologist's blurring of the nosology of dementia in his presentation was not surprising. He began by contrasting "Alzheimer's" with "pseudodementia," using the latter term to encompass all the potentially reversible dementias and not only those felt to be related to depression. Dementia was transformed from a clinical category into a specific disease through this equation of real dementia with endless suffering, and thus with the existential situation of these families. Multi-infarct and other less reversible dementias were briefly discussed, but despite their epidemiological importance did not carry the same semantic weight of virulence and chronicity as the plaques and tangles of

Alzheimer's disease and so were not elaborated upon. The performative usage of neuropathology was heightened near the end of this segment during a discussion of amyloid deposits. The daughter-in-law, whose open bitterness toward her mother-in-law made the synthesis between control and understanding the psychologist was striving for less appealing, broke in. "You talk about how this protein affects their brains. How about how it affects my brain!" For this woman, discussions of pathology did not engage her own victimization, but rather challenged its authenticity through impersonal medical language. Her goal, placing the origins of her victimization in the old woman's "disgusting" behavior and not in her body and brain, differed from that of the others at the meeting.

The presentation of neuropathology gave way to a discussion of how group members were making decisions and whether these were informed by an honest acknowledgment of Alzheimer's and its progression. Group members united in trying to convince the daughter-in-law that her husband needed to acknowledge the disease; she persisted that he was incapable of doing so. The group's sense that the common reality that "family members often refuse to acknowledge dementia" was at the root of the trouble was of limited success here; in a session "all about Alzheimer's," the relationship between husband and wife as the source of much of the problem could not be addressed.

The conflict between the received wisdom of the Alzheimer's movement and the complex needs of families was more acutely brought out in a debate between the psychologist and one of the unmarried daughters. The psychologist began by invoking clinical knowledge: persons with dementia are often disoriented and are further destabilized with a change of environment. He suggested that to keep shuttling the mother between her daughters was continually to disrupt her environment and do her no good. "For her sake," he suggested, "you need to make some difficult decisions."

Two of the daughters nodded assent. A third objected: "If we don't split the task of caring for my mother, one of us will ending up bearing all the burden; all of us have very busy lives. What you're suggesting means we'll end up putting her in a nursing home, which I don't think would be good for her. She knows each of us, and knows she's with her family. This is her life. That's what's important."

Debate continued along these lines. The dissenting daughter challenged the importance of tending primarily to her mother's cognitive state, viewing her within a network of relationships and through a life history. The psychologist continued to deny the legitimacy of the errant daughter's concerns, repeatedly restating the cognitive facts of the case and suggesting that the daughter needed to separate her needs from those of her mother by unselfishly institutionalizing the old woman.

He then continued with the second objective of the session. To understand and communicate with a demented person, he said, don't look to them but to yourself. Imagine yourself with the disease. "You have Alzheimer's disease. How would you feel? How would you cope?" The empathetic technique of *The 36-Hour Day* is invoked, but within a two-part scheme. Only when family members have "acknowledged Alzheimer's," have denied meaningful agency and subjectivity to the person with dementia, can these be reintroduced through the superimposition of their own subjectivity onto the experience of the other: *You have Alzheimer's disease.*

Against the emphasis on "the other victim" I have been tracing, the seldom heard voice of the person with dementing illness surfaces at critical junctures. I mention two of the most prominently featured voices. When Janet Adkins, diagnosed with Alzheimer's disease, succeeded in committing suicide as the first known beneficiary of Dr. Jack Kevorkian's "suicide machine" in the back of a van in a Michigan campground in 1990, her last utterance, thanking the maverick pathologist profusely, was widely reported.[15] In the media, Adkins's voice—her gratitude to the physician for terminating her endless funeral at its onset—was meaningful, and her actions could be placed within the context of her life as continuity:

> Mrs. Adkins, who had greeted middle age by climbing to the top of Mount Hood and trekking in the Himalayas, had approached her death with the same zest and independence that she had shown during her life.[16]

Only at the moment when the "Alzheimer's patient" removes herself from being a burden to family and society is her subjectivity acknowledged. In freeing us, she is granted personhood.

When Ronald and Nancy Reagan and their publicists reported the former president's Alzheimer's through a letter purportedly written by Reagan himself, the incident received enormous coverage and was repeatedly lauded as a selfless act of the couple (and especially Mrs. Reagan) in its popularization and destigmatizing of the Alzheimer's confessional.[17] Like Adkins, Reagan is presented in continuity with his pre-Alzheimer's self, and also like Adkins, the images used are those of the rugged American West and the gritty leather-skinned selfhood it is supposed to produce. In the brilliantly crafted letter, Reagan writes of himself riding off into "the sunset of my life."[18] The phrase, read by the news media as quintessential Reagan, collapsed the former president's future decline into a timeless image of the heroic cowboy. The future Reagan is narratively exhausted of any meaning but, rather than being read like Ina as an absence, is continually returned to this iconic moment of the ride into the sunset. In addition to erasing the future, and in a less visceral way than Adkins, Reagan ends the letter by elaborating the only real victim of the illness, his wife, and by extension, the American people, acknowledging his sorrow at any suffering they may have to bear on his account but affirming their ability, as tough stock, to ride it out.

In the weeks and months prior to his admission of illness, Reagan's utterances had been read by the media as confused or as politically ironic: "Asked [around the time of Nixon's funeral, when Reagan's confusion was publicly noted] what Reagan had finally thought about Watergate, the epic scandal of this age, Reagan fell silent. 'Forgive me,' he said, 'but at my age, my memory is just not as good as it used to be.' "[19]

But as soon as the whispers and allegations of senility, building on years of criticism by his opponents that as president Reagan was confused and forgetful, were recast as Alzheimer's, the possibility of irony vanished. Though his primary authorship of the letter is contestable, it was cast—in its clarity, its collapse of time and erasure of a future, and its elaboration of the trials of his caretakers—as the one authentic voice.[20] Despite occasional later and poorly publicized rumors (like that of Reagan urinating in the middle of a hotel lobby, surrounded by Secret Service agents keeping photographers at bay), the media respected and retained this voice as Reagan's last and truly presidential word. His back to us, Reagan retreats in silence. His heroism is epic, and in an age of identity through victimization his sacrifice inverts the classic Christian narrative: Reagan demands none of his own victimhood, and offers it all up to us, the nation as other victim. In granting us his suffering, we are redeemed: he rides off into the sunset, Nancy and we struggle through the endless funeral, and yet through the gift of his ennobling victimization he frees us: "I know that for America there will always be a bright dawn ahead."

In contrast to the redemptive aesthetics of the Alzheimer's victim removing herself, the daily experience of the demented person's family is read as Grand Guignol. When in *Newsweek* Frank and his sister redecorated Ina's bedroom, we learn that "it was an exhausting effort. They were often up late at night, cleaning out the closet and drawers full of the junk that had accumulated." And Frank laments the days when he could just up and leave his job for a month, hitchhiking around America and sleeping on the ground.

The suffering of families is intensely real. The difficulty of approaching the subjectivity of persons with dementing illnesses is enormous. But the intensity of this suffering and the enormity of this difficulty are culturally constructed and elaborated realities. Frank suffers in large measure because of how he and his society experience the dependency of a parent: on its own terms, cleaning up Mom's bedroom should not be construable as the worst torture the twentieth century has had to offer, and yet here it is. *Newsweek* cannot reach Ina as subject because its writers share certain assumptions about what constitutes selfhood. The power of Alzheimer's as popular category lies in its expression of a structuring of social relations in which dependency is equivalent to the loss of identity. Ina's non-sense suggests a nonself. Selves, to remain selves, must account for themselves. Ina *does not tell us who she is*: she cannot be represented, save as an absence.

The second threat to selfhood that Alzheimer's has come to represent is the threat to one's autonomy when one's parents become dependent. Frank has a wife, a steady job, his own children, and other responsibilities, but it is his mother Ina who represents the image of his lost selfhood—figured as a solitary and quintessentially American journey away from home and into the West, sleeping on the ground—and not these others. If one's parents signify the point of departure for a selfhood experienced as a journey, parents who become seriously dependent challenge the very essence of their children's selfhood, Frank's abandoned back-woods odyssey. The endless funeral is his, not Ina's.[21] Reagan remains heroic; Frank, unable to join him, must watch from Ina's bedroom.

THE GERIATRIC PARADOX

In calling such a theory a dogma we do not mean at all to disparage it, but rather to stress its scope and repercussions.

GEORGES CANGUILHEM, *THE NORMAL AND THE PATHOLOGICAL* (1943)

Despite the insistence of a few geriatric experts that Janet Adkins's future was not as unremittingly bleak as she, her family, and Dr. Kevorkian feared, the popular and professional construction of dementia has framed the case otherwise. Alzheimer's, though cleanly separated from old age by the force of the geronto-logical ideology that old age is normal, is continually and iteratively identified with the inevitable consequences of old age: decline and death. *Alzheimer's comes to replace old age in the structural understanding of the life course.* Old age is rendered "normal," freed from its inherent associations with decline and death, but in a paradoxical move that locates decline and death within a disease construct standing vigil at the borders of old age and negotiable only through the language of medical expertise and clinical enumeration: plaques, tangles, functional assessment, and mental sta-tus scores. The paradox of Alzheimer's reflects a larger paradox within the mod-ernist understanding of old age, of growing concern in the 1990s, leading in turn for calls for a "postmodern" perspective on old age and even a "postmodern life course."[22] But *plus ça change,* as we shall see.

The *Newsweek* articles stress the need to "face the facts": Alzheimer's is the *fourth leading killer,* there are few options for families, there are as yet no effective treat-ments, it ruins the brain. The articles again and again affirm the radical split of the pre- and postdiagnosis self, through the elaboration of the claim that Alzheimer's is not a normal part of aging. The third of the three *Newsweek* pieces opens with a picture of a neuropathologist holding a diseased brain up to the camera lens, sum-ming up the essence of the disease. Alzheimer's is a brain disease; that it occurs primarily in old people is registered nonchalantly, as almost incidental.

The pathology of Alzheimer's versus the normalcy of old age is a foundational principle of the Alzheimer's Association and other advocacy groups. Yet in elabo-rating the enormity and ubiquity of Alzheimer's as plague, these groups uninten-tionally reaffirm its identity with old age. *Newsweek* differentiates Alzheimer's from old age by virtue of the former being fatal and incurable, as if death did not linger on the horizons of old age and as if aging, like pseudodementia, were reversible. In playing the numbers game—Alzheimer's as the nation's fourth leading killer, cutting down one out of ten Americans over sixty-five, nearly half of those over eight-five, and the majority of the superannuated—this literature affirms a com-monsense view that Alzheimer's is obviously a matter of old age. The older you get, the more likely you are to have Alzheimer's: a fact the Alzheimer's advocates will not let you forget. From this to this.

Plaques and tangles form in all aging brains; memory loss occurs routinely in aging. "Benign senescent forgetfulness" (or BSF) emerged in the 1980s as the heir to senility's mantle of normal forgetfulness. Though benign and by definition normal, it remains a medical term. The line between the ambiguous normality of BSF and the unremitting pathology of dementia is itself not clear. How much forgetting is disease? How many plaques does it take?

In the face of this uncertainty, we might wish to locate the persistent and perhaps scientifically dubious search for *the* Alzheimer's gene and for other indelible and unitary markers to determine definitively who has or will someday have Alzheimer's and who does and will not: at once the hope for an eventual cure and an attempt to resolve the troublesome resistance of the normal and the pathological to remaining distinct from one another. On the day in 1990 when Janet Adkins's suicide was reported in the *New York Times*, another article appeared in the same paper on a "puzzling protein" that "shows up only in those with Alzheimer's." Researchers were attempting to locate the protein, at that point detected only in autopsy-derived tissues, in the cerebrospinal fluid of living persons to create a diagnostic test for the disease.[23] Other, less invasive tests have since been developed.[24] Presumably, such a test might have surprised Janet Adkins, revealing to her that she did not have Alzheimer's and sparing her and her family her decision to commit suicide; more likely, the test would have confirmed the diagnosis, and could spur many others at even younger ages to seek out Dr. Kevorkian or to buy and use Derek Humphry's best-selling how-to suicide manual *Final Exit*.[25]

Jaber Gubrium musters both neurological and fieldwork evidence to suggest that "it is not yet possible to clearly differentiate dementing illness from normal aging, and that the attempt to do so is a social construction to create order from the disorderly aspects of living with dementia."[26] Lyman has presented a comprehensive review of how the "biomedicalization of dementia" reifies as objective and necessary a way of looking at individuals grounded in particular relations of authority and control while it denies the relevance of these relations in the emergence and response to cognitive and behavioral change. In brief, she argues that "the myth of 'senility'" has been replaced by the "myth of 'Alzheimer's disease.'" That is, the acceptance of the inevitability and normalcy of cognitive decline in old age has been replaced by a disease model that, even as it challenges ageist presumptions, pigeonholes individuals as Alzheimer's victims through the "ready acceptance by clinicians, service providers, and families of an oversimplified diagnosis and prognosis."[27] Like Gubrium, she questions the ease with which the Alzheimer's movement differentiates the normal from the pathological, and cites studies of institutionalized people considered troublesome wanderers to make the observation that individuals who continue to act as they did before being institutionalized, that is, by the "normal" rules of life outside the nursing home, pose a challenge to institutional routine and are far more likely to be labeled as demented.[28] Medicalization, Lyman notes, "through medical labels, disease typifications, and medical authority, justifies control as appropriate treatment for the good of the patient."[29]

The maintenance of a sharp distinction between the normal and the pathological in the demarcation of and care for the senile body draws on a tension central to the discourse and practice of geriatric medicine. Like Alzheimer's disease, the explicit idea of geriatrics—of a branch of medicine and its allied professions devoted to the care of the old body—emerged early in this century. I. L. Nascher, a New York physician who during his medical training in the 1880s had been struck by the frequency with which more senior physicians used "It's just old age" to avoid disentangling the complex medical problems of elderly patients, coined the term in 1909 to parallel the nascent field of pediatrics. Nascher's goal was to demonstrate that old age was not equivalent to illness, and that the normal and the pathological were as distinguishable in old age as in younger adulthood.

Nascher later would retell the birth of geriatrics as the narrative of an epiphany, generated by an encounter with an old woman patient he had as a medical student. Visiting a slum workhouse with mostly elderly inmates, young Nascher and his medical preceptor are accosted by a woman complaining of her pain. The preceptor ignores the woman, and finally Nascher gets up the courage to ask why they are not trying to help her. "It's just old age," his preceptor explains. It is at this point that Nascher recounts the realization that founded (and continues to dominate) the field: *it's not just old age*. In the declaration of old age's normality, Nascher has the vision of geriatrics.[30]

This separation of the normal from the pathological structures Nascher's founding text, *Geriatrics*. He separates the text into two sections: Physiological Old Age and Pathological Old Age.[31] His division draws upon a century of medical debate theorizing the relationship between the normal and the pathological;[32] in particular, Nascher draws upon some of the early work of the preeminent French physician J. M. Charcot. Charcot's 1866–67 *Leçons Cliniques sur les Maladies des Vieillards et les Maladies Chroniques* remained the preeminent text in the field and had been translated and made widely available in English.[33] Like Nascher, Charcot placed the origins of his interest in the old body in an institutional encounter with old women. Take away the employees, the lunatics, the idiots, and the epileptics, he reports noting to his students, most of the remaining residents at the Salpêtrière hospital (formally the *Hospice de la Vieillesse-Femmes*) are old women of the socially least favored classes, presenting an ideal population for study.[34]

Charcot built upon the work of C. R. Prus, who had been the head of the medical service at the both the Salpêtrière and the Bicêtre (*Hospice de la Vieillesse-Hommes*) in the 1830s and 1840s and who utilized the growing population of the institutionalized old poor in Paris to articulate a natural history of the old body in decline.[35] Prus wrote of the medicine of the elderly in the future tense: as modern, yet unattainable; his declaration that "*la médecine des vieillards est encore à faire*" became an aphorism of the mid-nineteenth-century clinic.[36] Charcot's method of clinico-pathological correlation offered a realization of Prus's hope for the Salpêtrière and its human material. Old age provided a particular vantage onto the relationship between norms and pathology: "changes which old age sometimes induces in the organism sometimes attain such a point that the physiological and the pathological states seem to mingle by an imperceptible transition, and to be no longer sharply distinguishable."[37]

Charcot attempts to distinguish between the two; his focus, summarized in his title, is on pathology, and he interpolates from his delineation of the pathological to the possibility of a senile physiology. Yet the distinction is tempered by what for Charcot is the differand of the diseases of old age: normal and pathological are not easily separable: they implode. Charcot's moral stance is not that different from Nascher's: against their neglect, the diseases of old persons need to be studied, understood, and whenever possible treated. But the system he creates is strikingly different, based as it is on his sense that a rigorous shepherding of bodily processes into the normal and the pathological is not useful in the study of old age.[38]

Charcot places old age at the limits of the project of contemporary Parisian medicine, as depicted by the historian and philosopher Georges Canguilhem. Canguilhem suggested that the mid-nineteenth-century European articulation of the normal and the pathological as "quantitatively identical" (the pathological being a state of excess or deficiency of the normal but not something substantively different) was of a piece with an era in which disease was denied its own separate reality: "The denial of an ontological conception of disease, a negative corollary of the assertion of a quantitative identity between the normal and the pathological, is first, perhaps, the deeper refusal to confirm evil."[39] In Charcot's framing of old age, the ontological conception of disease is not only denied but the quantitative identity of the normal and the pathological collapses altogether: at the margins of life, normality *is* excess or deficiency.

The historian Thomas Cole, in his discussion of early to mid-nineteenth-century hygienic perfectionism, offers a somewhat different reading than Canguilhem of a related denial in the American construction of the natural death, the "broader cultural effort to eliminate death as a force in life and to remove both the pain and preparation previously considered essential to dying well." Cole charts the ascendancy of a national ethic of self-reliance and the transformation it necessitated: "But how could the ideology and psychology of self-reliance be squared with decay of the body? Only by denying its inevitability and labeling it as failure."[40] The denial of inevitable decay takes a different form in the later nineteenth century as old age becomes the site of scientific management. A language of perfectionism gives way to one of normalization.[41]

Canguilhem suggests the partial reemergence, in late-nineteenth- and early-twentieth-century Europe and America, of an ontological conception of disease, linked both to shifts in the understanding of infectious disease and neurology and to the violent laboratory of the First World War. Geriatrics emerges not only, as Cole suggests, within the context of the denial of decay, but additionally as disease comes again to take on a qualitative distinctiveness. The difference between the nineteenth-century Charcot, who saw himself as able to collapse the normal and the pathological in old age, and Nascher, who in 1909 attempted unsuccessfully to separate them and to offer disease in old age an independent ontological status, is in this latter context striking.

Nascher begins with the assumption that old age itself is normal. In the section of *Geriatrics* devoted to physiology, he attempts to quantify the bounds of the normal in old age, system by physiological system. He then moves on to pathology, where he catalogues the diseases of old age. But though the book is divided neatly into two parts, the same symptoms, syndromes, and processes are frequently described under both headings. The division between the normal and the pathological, though carefully nurtured, seeps, leaks, and eventually collapses. Unlike Charcot's *Leçons*, where the collapse is taken as the point of departure in studying the old body, in the foundational text of American geriatrics the central figure of normal aging runs counter to the demands of its content.

The difficulty of maintaining the separation and Nascher's efforts to do so characterize his writing on dementia as well. Like Charcot, Nascher associates clinical dementia with the pathological finding of cerebral softening, but he is careful to differentiate softening as pathology from softening as "normal senile degeneration." Clinically, however, the distinction between the two states in *Geriatrics* is unclear, and neither is described in a normalizing language. Ultimately, Nascher must collapse the two, as distinct causes of a single clinical entity, "primary senile dementia."[42]

To maintain a pathological reading of senility, Nascher draws upon a plethora of competing and complexly interlocking concepts coming out of the late nineteenth and early twentieth century. His resulting typology—softening, arteriosclerosis, psychosis, and atrophy—is an attempt to unite these dominant theories of the diseased old mind against some notion of the mind's normal aging.

Softening we have encountered already, in relation to its penchant for the tropics. Descriptions of the "very soft and liquefied" brains of persons who had died with diagnoses of apoplexy or palsy frequent early-nineteenth-century discussions of neuropathology and continue to be used into the twentieth.[43] Léon Rostan wrote *Recherches sur le Ramollissement du Cerveau* in 1823, analyzing the relationship between apoplectic events, mental symptomatology, and *le ramollissement*, or softening, through examinations of Salpêtrière women and autopsies of their brains. Unlike the later Salpêtrière physicians Prus and Charcot, Rostan does not center his researches on the old age of the female cadavers he examines. "Senile dementia" for Rostan, like "mental alienation" more generally, is one of several signs of latent softening in the absence of apoplexy.[44] Dora Weiner has discussed the Revolutionary shift in the formal status of Salpêtrière inmates from indigents to citizen-patients under the liberal welfare regime of Philippe Pinel, noting the famous physician's attention to the age-specific illnesses of the primarily elderly inmates of the hospital. That the old age of the citizen-patient could be noted and treated was an effective sign of the scope of Pinel's humanism, but the old body and cadaver for Pinel and Rostan were not the sites of the limits of normalization as they would become for Charcot.[45]

Rostan noted that softening was a problem of climactic extremes, most prevalent in very hot or cold climates, but British approaches to the gross pathology imported from France differed. Softening of the brain as a general figure of lay and medical speech did accord well with mounting concerns over the effects of the tropics on European constitutions. Yet as the formal collection of medical statistics became a critical component of colonial administration,[46] London-based physicians like Richard Rowland could reread the tropics against the rhetoric of softening: "Cerebral softening does not appear to be a prevalent affection in warm climates. The Army Medical Reports rather lead to the conclusion that it is less frequent in those latitudes than with us." Rowland's understanding of the temperate and arctic spaces of softening is not simply his reading of available quantitative data, however; it accords with his sense that palsy and apoplexy, the two clinical states correlated with softening, are nervous affections more likely to occur in modern urban settings and among professions involved in mental labor.[47]

J. Hughlings Jackson in 1875 criticized the nonspecific use of softening and the tendency to equate it with general atrophy of the brain. Softening is local necrosis of brain tissue and its causes are arterial. Attempts like Rowland's to see primary nervous symptomatology as the cause of softening reverse the causal equation. The key to the study of softening is the careful study of the arterial system and its pathology.[48]

Arteriosclerosis, leading to diminished blood flow and increased pressure with effects independent of strokes and hemorrhages, was the second of Nascher's categories; by the early twentieth century, it had become a ubiquitous concept for explaining the changes of aging, so often invoked that its use had become the subject of conscious irony.[49] Like softening, arteriosclerosis had particular resonance for tropical bodies. Both Emil Kraepelin's modernist psychiatric nosology and Eugen Bleuler's later revision examined the relationship between arteriosclerosis, insanity, and heat. Hot climates, hot baths, and the like make blood rush to the head, exacerbating the diminished elasticity and self-regulation of arterial vessels in old age and potentiating not only the likelihood of softening, but more diffuse tissue damage leading to "arteriosclerotic insanity."[50]

Psychosis: Nascher drew on a third set of ideas, engaging the language of madness as primary, independent of softening, arteriosclerosis, or atrophy in framing senility as *senile insanity* or *senile psychosis*. Preventing or at least forestalling senility was one of the preoccupations of the nineteenth-century concern with moral hygiene, manifest as two contradictory strategies, a conservation model stressing rest and the prudent expenditure of nervous energy and an activity model stressing continual exercise of the mental faculties.[51] Both strategies drew on a set of ideas about involutional psychosis and the senile climacteric that structured the onset of old age as a dangerous passage that must be negotiated with forbearance and moral strength to avoid a decline into senile pathology.[52] Both strategies stressed the need for order, and both extended a tradition that looked to Roger Bacon's thirteenth-century exposition on the prevention of old age through an ordered life, translated by the seventeenth-century English physician Richard Browne and frequently reprinted.[53]

Against the moral hygienic discussion of madness as the failure of order and appropriate behavior in old age drawing on traditions of prolongevity is an equally venerable argument that senility is inevitable. Against Browne, another seventeenth-century text frequently cited over the subsequent two centuries is the English physician John Smith's exegesis of the twelfth and final chapter of Ecclesiastes. Smith's reading is lengthy, and complex; its gist is an interpretation of the Biblical chapter as a fairly exhaustive and anatomically detailed description of the physical changes of old age: the decrepit body as memento mori. Moral order can not forestall the process; rather, the process signifies the need for a moral order outside and beyond the body.[54] This other moral economy of old age is deemphasized during the nineteenth century, as Cole suggests, but it does not disappear. The different gerontologies of Browne and Smith are both drawn into later formulations.

In the mid-nineteenth century, the Scottish physician Maclachlan juxtaposed both approaches in noting that, despite inevitable bodily decay, old people are often the wisest in a society. From this observation he suggested that the brain and the rest of the body decay at different rates. For Maclachlan, the brain's staying power lay in its close relationship to the mind and the soul. He combined a moral hygienic with an arteriosclerotic model: mental distress in most older people, he argued, is *either* a derangement of character brought on by poor moral hygiene *or* a disease process, such as softening. However, Maclachlan had also to confront the eventual decay of all flesh, and he posited a two-stage model. Whatever the status of its moral economy, ultimately the brain in extremis must decay: "All flesh is grass, but thus the immortal portion of our nature asserts its independence, and long outlives the decay that surrounds it. A period generally arrives, however, in the progress of years, when, like the frame itself, the intellectual faculties betoken the destructive effects of time."[55] Moral decay, pathological disease, and normal degeneration are all accommodated. The maneuver, to resolve a debate around the pathology of behavior in old age by splitting the life stage into two halves, younger and older, became a frequent structural response to the difficulty of constituting norms.

The opposition between the moral and the degenerative was recast with the emergence of a biological psychiatry. The relation between senile insanity and senile dementia concerned Kraepelin in the formation of his classification of mental illness, ancestor of both the DSM and ICD series. For Kraepelin in 1904, what was translated as *involutional melancholia* was a psychosis setting in "at the beginning of old age in men, and in women from the period of the menopause onwards. . . . About a third of patients make a complete recovery. In severe and protracted cases, emotional dullness may remain, with faint traces of the apprehensive tendency. Judgement and memory may also undergo considerable deterioration."[56]

This psychosis retained traces of its climacteric origin. It is a state passed through, not necessarily an endpoint, and it can be treated and cured. Against the generally good course of involutional insanity, the state of senile dementia or senile imbecility has a poor outcome. Both involutional psychosis and senile dementia were for Kraepelin secondary to "the general failure of strength and vitality in old age . . . a time when the power of resistance is reduced."[57] Dementia differed from involutional psychosis clinically in its more variable and labile affect, increased hypochondriasis, and the significant loss of short-term memory. Kraepelin, structuring his nosology through behavioral rather than other clinical or pathological criteria, had far less difficulty than Charcot or Nascher in separating the normal and the pathological. The critical and difficult boundary for him was between varieties of the pathological, between acute psychiatric illness (insanity or melancholia) and chronic neurological illness (imbecility or dementia).

Insanity, rooted in the reversible and morally weighted effects of a weakened person's melancholic response to the irreversible involution of old age, remains part of Nascher's typology.

The language of the climacteric and of senile involution will be discussed below in terms of the relation between the "senile" and the "female" climacteric; here I would note the late-nineteenth-century emergence of involution as a critical site for the incorporation of Darwinian ideas into discussions of old age. The gross anatomical term *involution*, a structure turning in upon itself, comes to take on a teleological cast in the mid-nineteenth century primarily in discussions of the involuting uterus as a metonym of the aging woman whose purpose has been fulfilled.[58] The site of involution in succeeding decades both expands to define the old body more generally and diffuses to describe the cellular and subcellular atoms of decline.[59] Involution as a figure comes to embody the late-nineteenth-century reading of moral hygiene, no longer a perfectionist vision of prolongevity but a process of evolutionary triage in which the old must pass over social and reproductive privilege to the young for the sake of the species.

Nascher's own prewar writings on involution and the climacteric engage a cavalcade of social types, stereotypic depictions of classes, genders, and professions, and their moral ability to negotiate the onset of old age.[60] The old person who has failed to accept old age and act accordingly is framed as hypersexual and pathetic, in the tradition of Renaissance and Restoration pantaloons and bawds, but representing a greater and increasingly eugenic threat. Physicians, not the least of whom was Alois Alzheimer, were being drawn into debates over the dangers of particular classes of persons to the species (and in some settings, to the race) and over the evolutionary meaning of bodily weakness.[61] Following the First World

War, most American discussions of involution centered on the presumed peri- and postmenopausal insanity of older women, but eugenic concerns remained. The pathologist Aldred Warthin, in his 1929 book *Old Age: The Major Involution,* argued that human development represented an energic balance between growth and involution and cautioned against efforts to disturb this balance by extending the afflicted lives of the oldest old. Warthin differentiated the minor involutions of pre- and postnatal growth, necessary for the survival of the individual, from the major involution of old age, necessary for the survival of what he alternately called the species or the race. Warthin's energics were based upon an understanding of the body as a machine for the propagation of germ plasm through time. In old age, "the individual human machine has fulfilled its function, and, now useless, stands in the way of the progressive evolution of the species. . . . The Universe, by its very nature, demands mortality for the individual if the life of the species is to attain immortality."[62]

Warthin's explicit concerns were the energy depletion resulting from an aging population and the lowered adaptability of a senescent and backward-looking race, not the explicit degeneration of the germ plasm resulting from aged semen. Yet his book was particularly concerned with a sexualized vision of the old and mortal versus young and immortal bodies. Scientific photographs of naked men, primarily black-and-white full frontal shots, are interspersed through the book. The accompanying descriptions focus on the face and posture, but the photographs themselves additionally present a progression of visible penises. The "lad of eighteen years" stares optimistically upward into the distance, his body thrust forward in anticipation of the future; the "youth of twenty-two years" stares more noncommittally ahead, his body erect. Further stages follow, until one reaches the "father of eighty years and son of thirty-seven years." Both men are standing side by side, naked, with the son's pulled-down pants visible at his ankles. The text notes: "[T]he weary, worn-out machine of the old man contrasted with the insolent aggressiveness of the son at the height of maturity tells the story of the meaning of involution and old age more effectively than any detailed scientific description can do."[63] The unspoken juxtaposition of father's and son's nakedness tells a slightly different story that presumes an interested observer. The hygiene of involution has shifted into a new moral vision of immortal and insolent male bodies.

Atrophy is the fourth of Nascher's considerations. Like Maclachlan and Kraepelin, Nascher positioned irreversible atrophy in late life, against other causes of behavioral change in those less superannuated. Atrophy provided the greatest challenge to the distinctiveness of the normal and the pathological. Even with normal aging, things eventually fell apart. A more clearly pathological understanding of atrophy developed through the work of Alois Alzheimer, a German neuropathologist. Although Alzheimer first located his plaques and tangles in the "presenile" brains of individuals in their fifties and was far more interested in the problem of presenile dementia, within a decade of his initial 1906 report many

European and American pathologists had gone on to note similar findings in senile brains and to suggest a single pathological process across the life course.[64]

Though described as both presenile and senile, Alzheimer's disease did not supplant arteriosclerosis, psychosis, softening, and normal aging as a critical concept in the study of senility. The diagnosis remained "nearly medically dormant until the 1960s";[65] arteriosclerotic models dominated, along with the emergence of a pharmacotherapy based on a class of drugs marketed as vasodilators, which, given the dominant paradigm, were intended to open up arteries to get more blood to the brain. Despite the many studies following immediately upon Alzheimer's own work suggesting that his findings also might explain senile dementia, the model was left largely alone for half a century. Patrick Fox has traced the role of a "handful of neuroscientists" and of the infrastructure of the National Institutes of Health in mobilizing resources for the creation of a popular "Alzheimer's movement" in the United States in the 1960s and 1970s.[66] By the 1980s, with the exception of multi-infarct dementia, vascular models were all but passé,[67] Vladimir Hachinski being all but the only North American who advocated retaining some concept of limited blood flow in the study of senility; in the 1990s, a variant of vascular dementia had returned to acceptability.

Nascher's book was retitled *The Care of the Aged* by his successor, Malford Thewlis. "Geriatrics" remained a seldom used neologism in the country where it was coined until after the Second World War, and large-scale subspecialization did not emerge until the 1960s and 1970s. The term began to return to vogue when the same images that dominate Nascher's retelling of the origins of the term—institutionalized old bodies and an unhearing medical profession—began recurring with great frequency in the American press and in many books "exposing" the situation of old people.[68] Against the ageism of physicians and institutions in an antipsychiatric era, geriatrics' offer of "normal aging" against "It's just old age" emerged as a powerful tool to demedicalize old age. The Alzheimer's era represented a shift in the negotiation of the divide: old age was declared to be entirely normal; benign senescent forgetfulness was offered to neutralize the ambiguity of normality and then allowed to drop out of sight. Those relegated to the victimhood of Alzheimer's now had to bear the dehumanizing brunt of a total and unquestionable pathology. Far from demedicalizing old age, geriatrics' insistence on normality instantiated a far more totalizing medical regime.

From its inception, geriatrics presented a paradox—a field insisting on the normality of old people but constructed through their differentiation and isolation, defining them as distinct from adults and requiring a separate and ancillary profession modeled on the care of children. The paradox is evident in both the politics of geriatric practice within the tertiary hospital setting and in the internal contradictions that define the geriatric body as a locus of knowledge.

The language of "normal aging" is critical in gerontological and geriatric training; my field experience here is based on my own training from 1982 to 1986 in geriatric medicine, social work, and nursing home work, and on formal field-work with geriatric professionals in hospitals and nursing homes in Boston. In a session I attended as a student, a geriatrician at a community hospital was trying to teach medical students about "normal aging." Most of the students resisted her. If old age is normal, why are old people so frequently hospitalized? Why is so much of internal medical practice geriatric?

The physician persisted; she was used to the objections. Old people often have more health problems, but these are diagnosable and mandate therapy; too often, a physician focuses on a limited differential for the chief complaint when a pa-tient's multiple problems, social situation, and often multiple medications may have direct bearing on etiology, diagnosis, choice of therapy, and outcome. The class was unimpressed. Yes, these are all to the good, but what is the point of all this talk of normal aging if geriatrics is invoked precisely to treat complex pathol-ogy? Most students left the meeting without a sense of what defining old age as normal offered. The physician's invocation of the geriatric paradox had deflected her message about the need to rethink the goals of internal medical practice.

Internists and other specialists in Harvard hospitals throughout my own train-ing often remarked with both humor and scorn, "There's no need for geriatrics; internal medicine [or neurology, etc.] is geriatric medicine." House staff and med-ical students were usually discouraged from seeking geriatric consults; when these were sought, the recommendations of the geriatric team were usually criticized as impractical and having little bearing on what were seen as the critical medical is-sues: "So they take off a drug or two, big deal." Despite the increasing routiniza-tion of geriatrics as a certifiable specialization within American medicine, its le-gitimacy among tertiary care physicians remains marginal.

Such marginal status is a pity, for the hospital practice of internal medicine re-mains profoundly ageist, characterized by the rich and well-documented language of "little old ladies," "gomers," "flogs," "slugs" and so forth (institutional elabora-tions of Mrs. Fletcher, the "I've fallen and can't get up" lady), by the Sisyphus-like determination of many house staff to get patients off the service and their conse-quent resentment of the immobility of sick elderly, and by the almost reflex ob-session with obtaining DNR (do not resuscitate) statuses on old patients from them or their relatives. Amid such a milieu, where old bodies often challenge the smooth functioning of house staff practice, the geriatric aesthetic of normal aging does not engage the agenda of house staff nor does it offer a coherent challenge. Geri-atric ideology subverts its own goals.

OUBLIER POSTMODERN AGING

When I first wrote a draft of this section, in 1991, there did not seem to be many critical voices raising similar concerns. Within American medical anthropology, gerontologists took on the project of geriatric normality with little apparent reflexivity, discovering in other cultures oases where the words of Nascher's preceptor, "It's just old age," could never be uttered meaningfully.[69] But the 1990s has seen an efflorescence of a self-consciously critical gerontology.[70] Much of what I am arguing here has been already (and often far more elegantly) put forward. One variant of this turn has been a move away from the normalizing language of the Nascherian epiphany to a recognition of geriatrics' silencing of the existential and embodied *abnormality* of the last years of the longest human lives. Several scholars have called this a "postmodern" recognition: Cole has charted the move from the modern construction of old age—in terms of liberal capitalism, ideologies of self-reliance, retirement, and the scientific management of aging and both its perfectibility and normalization—to the postmodern, through the failure of liberalism, renewed alarmism about an aging population, the rejection of Nascherian dualism, and the return to a dialogue with death and an *ars moriendi*.[71]

But there is reason to pause. The rise of critical gerontology in the United States—and of its recognition of the medicalizing and dehumanizing dualism of the geriatric paradox—comes precisely when the political economic apparatus that funds most gerontological research is looking for ways to demedicalize, to deinstitutionalize, and more generally to defund the care of older persons, the majority of whom are not wealthy and face not the withdrawal of futile but of needed health resources. In the United States, the policy debate of the 1990s brings together ethicists like Daniel Callahan who question how much futile medical care a society should be providing the oldest old[72] and political initiatives to cut Medicare and Medicaid without serious attention to the intersection of age, class, race, and gender.

The response of American gerontology to the paradoxes of its normalization has traditionally been and continues to be the splitting of old age into ever finer categories: the "young old" versus the "old old," "successful aging" versus "the frail elderly," and so forth. Nascher's failed effort to separate out the normal from the pathological is realized by splitting the objects of inquiry and policy into those defined by their normality (and not coincidentally by their constitution as a market segment) and those defined by their pathology (and not coincidentally by their constitution as an economic liability). Within the logic of such a split and its ever more trenchant rematerialization of failed efforts at normal aging as the dehumanized domain of Alzheimer's disease, the "recognition" of the profound ambiguity of old age seems less postmodern revelation than the latest turn of the screw by the professional compradors of gerontology, what I have elsewhere criticized as the "trope of ambiguity" running through much gerontological anthropology.[73]

To find a language to write about old age that fetishizes neither essentialized normality nor essentialized ambiguity, I want to move back a step and examine age itself, as a particular kind of difference made to matter in terms of narratives and practices constituted in terms of other culturally available kinds of difference. To make my meaning clearer, I begin by articulating a provisional European genealogy of senility. Why should it be interesting that the emergence of things like dotage, the senile climacteric, and Alzheimer's disease as *medical* problems is rooted in discourses of and debates on the bodies of women?

A WITCH'S CURSE

That it was an old woman who inspired Nascher's epiphany recalls Charcot's rationale for his own interest in old age, the ready material of the many old women of the Salpêtrière. The institutional availability of certain types of bodies differs as an origin story from Nascher's rite of discovery but informs a reading of the latter: concern for the old person in Nascher's case is similarly predicated on her institutionalized immobility. What is the relationship between this recurrent figure of the old woman—the much abused "granny" of popular myth—and the universal old person who is the object of geriatrics?

The relationship might at first seem a result of demography and of the effects of patrilineal household structure: if women live longer and there are more old women than old men, and if old men are more likely to retain property, to remarry and to be able to depend on children and others—and thus less likely to be institutionalized—the recurring old woman of the geriatric text reflects little more than the demographics of old age and the political economy of the household. Women's bodies, however, are notoriously good for men to think with, and I want here to examine briefly three moments in the history of the senile body in western Europe and the United States: the medicalization of the dotard, the rise and fall of senile climacteric, and the question of Alzheimer's women.

Dotage and senility enter medical discourse in Europe as juridical entities— things about which the physician can claim not only knowledge but authority from the state—through an appropriation of the body of the middle-aged and older woman from the gaze of the Inquisitor. Sixteenth-century physicians like Johannes Weyer and Reginald Scot argued that most of those burnt as witches under ecclesiastical authority never did the evil deeds to which they had confessed but were, whether they were possessed or not, melancholic, decrepit, and doting old women. Demonic possession was not ruled out, but was replaced by doting melancholy as the subject of medical—and state—concern.

Weyer, in a letter to his patron Duke William of Cleve accompanying publication of his *De praestigiis daemonum*, makes the juridical content of this new dotage explicit:

> To you, Prince, I dedicate the fruit of my thought. For thirteen years your physician, I have heard expressed in your court the most varied opinions concerning witches; but none so agree with my own as do yours, that witches can harm no one through the most malicious will or the ugliest exorcism, that rather their imagination— inflamed by the demons in a way not understandable to us—and the torture of melancholy makes them only fancy that they have caused all sorts of evil. . . . You do not, like others, impose heavy penalty on perplexed, poor old women. You demand evidence.[74]

Weyer returns to these women throughout *De praestigiis daemonum*. George Mora has catalogued his descriptive terms: "raving, poor, simple, useless, ignorant, gullible, stupid, vile, uneducated, infatuated, toothless, silly, unsteady, decrepit old women."[75]

Weyer details innumerable case histories of alleged witches. They are unpleasant tales. An eighty-year-old woman is accused of practicing enchantments. Suspicion is confirmed when her son gives her a packet of earth so that she might free herself of her chains. Weyer goes to meet her. Though she frequently "seemed to fall into a state of unconsciousness," she managed to explain that the packet was in fact linen, to tend to her ulcerated legs, injured when earlier inquisitors had poured boiling oil on them to generate a confession.[76] Other women are far less lucid, a state that, though indicating a state of sin, implies no threat to any save themselves: "Certain deluded old women . . . their brains—the organs of their thoughts and imaginings—so firmly ensnared by rare and deceptive phantasms and forms because of their unbelief . . . that they know of nothing else."[77] Weyer invokes the authority of medicine not to deny the relation of sin to behavior, but to transform its valence from threat to pathos.

In England, Reginald Scot invoked melancholy more explicitly in his 1584 work, *The Discoverie of Witchcraft*. Scot places accusation in the context not of the evil Inquisitor but of daily life in the community: these women are not witches, but melancholics, and their lack of control over their voice raises the suspicion of others when misfortune strikes.

> See also what persons complaine upon them . . . waie what accusations and crimes they laie to their charge, namelie: She was at my house of late, she would have had a pot of milke, she departed in a chase bicause she had it not, she railed, she curssed, she mumbled and whispered, and finallie she said she would be even with me: and soone after my child, my cow, my sow, or my pullet died, or was strangelie taken.[78]

Scot's attentiveness, like Weyer's, is to the *voice* of the supposed witch. The identity of witches and women, in the Inquisitorial handbook *Malleus Maleficarum* of 1486, the embodiment of a woman's carnality and weakness, is in her "slippery tongue."[79] Scot resists explaining the tongue in terms of womanly nature. He invokes a catalog of decrepitude similar to Weyer's:

> women which be commonly old, lame, bleare-eied, pale, fowle, and full of wrinkles; poore, sullen, superstitious, and papists; or such as knowe no religion: in whose drousie minds the divell hath goten a fine seat. . . . They are leane and deformed, shewing melancholie in their faces, to the horror of all that see them. They are doting, scolds, mad, divelish. . . .
>
> These miserable wretches are so odious unto all their neighbors, and so feared, as few dare offend them, or denie them anie thing they aske.[80]

The impossibility of hearing the old woman's request as just that—a request—is central to Scot's analysis, as in the example of the indigent woman coming over to borrow milk. Women accused of witchcraft in England and the English colonies in America were often solitary, indigent, and dependent on the charity of neighbors for survival. Alan Macfarlane's 1970 study of witchcraft accusations in the English county of Essex in the sixteenth and seventeenth centuries suggested that the rise of accusations should be understand in the context of shifting definitions of community and the delegitimation of the old woman's claims on her neighbors' resources. The powerful and increasingly angry voice of the indigent older woman demanding what was less and less her due became increasingly unhearable and incoherent.[81]

I do not wish to argue that most, or even some, of the accused witches were demented. The "old women" of these catalogues were not necessarily over sixty; the qualities ascribed to them are numerous. Diverse persons were vulnerable to being named witches. And "melancholy" has many associations. The point is simpler: medical authority, in conjunction with the prince, is invoked to define the signifiably old body when that body is female. Doting, melancholy, and demanding voices of old people are otherwise no strangers to Renaissance texts—Lear has come down to us with all his rage intact—but these voices are heard differently across gender. Lear may rail, but his is an abject voice. The old woman's curse, however, is powerful and must be contained. In the efforts of Weyer and Scot, medicine is invoked to defuse the threat and appropriate the voice. Before Scot's *Discoverie* and since, English physicians writing as natural theologians or philosophers would detail the signs of dotage and decrepitude as memento mori or social commentary; but in the doting voice of the old witch, medicine claims a different kind of knowledge and hails a different sort of old body.

THE SENILE CLIMACTERIC

The rediscovery and elaboration by Renaissance authors of "the dangerous graduall yeares, called climactericke," seldom referred to the bodies of women.[82] Climacterics were periodic points along the life course—at ages that were usually multiples of seven or nine—when the body was particularly susceptible to humoral excess and its accompanying emotion and morbidity. The ungendered (and thus inevitably male) climacteric continued to be cited well into the nineteenth century, the Irish physician Kennedy remarking in 1844 that

> from the time of Galen to the present period it has been nearly universally believed, that certain epochs of human life are very liable to be accompanied by disease of a certain character. A good deal of trouble has been taken to ascertain at what exact periods of life such a disease shows itself, and particular years, such as the forty-second and sixty-third, have been determined on: the latter of these periods has indeed been called the grand climacteric, as being the time above all others when the disease is apt to declare itself.[83]

Increasingly for nineteenth-century analysts, the existence of this grand climacteric and in particular the usefulness of its particular multiplication of sevens and nines was questionable. Kennedy himself concludes the above description by not-

ing that "in the cases of climacteric disease which have come under my own notice, I have not been able to confirm any of these points. . . . " Well before
Kennedy's time, the ungendered grand climacteric was becoming less tied to the
chronological precision of a magical multiplication of sevens and nines and more
to the emerging and gendered obviousness of what grew increasingly medicalized
as "the menopause."[84] On the one hand, the life course is disenchanted through a
process of its rational feminization. On the other, the shift reflects the larger transformation Thomas Laqueur has suggested in European medical constructions of
the sexual body, from a unitary anatomy in which the female body is a partial or
degenerate but not qualitatively different variant of the male to a binary anatomy
in which male and female bodies are mirroring opposites, qualitatively different
things.[85] The increasing taken-for-grantedness of the menopause replaces the invocation of Galenic tradition as proof of an ever more elusive and paradoxically
ever more male climacteric. Whereas eighteenth-century arguments for the existence of the menopause invoked the Galenic climacteric, by 1865 the climacteric
has been unambiguously speciated into male and female varieties and the gendering of what is obvious in the decline of old age has been inverted and split. C. M.
Durrant can derive the male climacteric solely through the female: "We are so
much accustomed to regard with interest and anxiety the peculiar changes which
take place in the constitution of the female at mid-age, that we are apt to forget
and overlook the phenomena which, in a more or less marked manner, attend the
turning point towards a downhill course in the opposite sex."[86]

The gendered shift in what was obvious and what derivative begins in Britain
early in the nineteenth century. In 1813, Henry Halford wrote what became a classic text on the climacteric, splitting the crisis along gendered lines and placing the
two newly distinct phenomena side to side. Halford contrasted the different embodiments of each: the male climacteric being a "deficiency in the energy of the
brain itself," leading, if not negotiated with care, to chronic mental deficiency. The
female transition was not of the brain but of the body, and it was of a sufficiently
marked character as to "render subsequent alterations less perceptible"; that is, female energy was so closely tied to the womb as to render the question of mental
crisis irrelevant.[87]

Nineteenth-century discussions of the dual climactera continued to cite Halford as the author of the split.[88] The characterization of the male climacteric as
cerebral and progressive and the female as visceral and acute lingered for over a
century: in 1933, Edward Podolsky could still write that "there is a definite male
climacterium in the same sense that there is a female climacterium, with the notable exception of course that in a man there does not occur those physical
changes which serve as a visible means of indicating the change of life. In the male
real and definite changes take place, but the physical element is negligible; the
mental upheaval is quite considerable."[89]

As the obviousness of this male climacteric begins to unravel in turn, in the first
decades of the twentieth century, numerous explanatory models are floated by its

proponents to explain the reasons for the dual climactera. Heredity, arteriosclerosis, toxemia, and neurasthenia were invoked.[90] Endocrine explanations dominated, reflecting both the emergence of the gland as a key concept in medical research and more generally the incorporation of evolutionary (climacteric as involution) and ecological (climacteric as reorientation of relations between body and environment) narratives. Gonadal endocrine models exploited the radical differences in the signification of ovaries and testes. Galloway in 1933 argued that involution is a paired process: "the homologous organs which show the changes of involution first in one sex should be those which degenerate first in the other." This principle of equivalence must break down, however, because "in the human female there is no need to follow the subject, the symptoms being so distinctive, culminating in the only objective sign we possess, the cessation of menstruation. It is some centuries since the great Belgian physician, Jean Baptiste Helmont, said 'woman is made what she is by her ovaries.' Thus attention is at once concentrated on them and the ductless glands under whose dominance they act."[91] Men were complex and not uniglandular; Galloway describes a network of testicular, adrenal, and pancreatic secretions. Hormonal logic separated the simpler pelvic and ductless female embodiment of the transition to old age from its more layered and polysemically ducted male embodiment. As male hormones were interacting within a rationally ordered system rather than simply drying up, the male climacteric occurred later than the female.[92]

Nascher turned to the climacteric to help resolve the tension between the normal and the pathological, particularly in regards to the senile mind. In his discussion of normal aging, Nascher offered images of old people as weak, willful, dependent, and decaying. In simultaneously moving to free old age from pathology, he constructed what one might term a subaltern physiology, legitimating the study of the old body as both normal and different by framing its normality in terms of other classes of subordinate bodies. To construct a senile physiology, Nascher drew upon other alternative physiologies, those of the child and of the woman. Old people were normal in the same way women and children could be normal.

In the case of the child, discipline as metaphor was supplanted by disciplinary object as metaphor. Less relevant for the new geriatrics were the formal congruencies between the child and the old person, and more relevant were substantive similarities between their behavior, their demeanor, and the degree of autonomy of which they were or should be capable. Nascher opened *Geriatrics* by declaring: "Senility is often called Second Childhood."[93] He used the term loosely, as a synonym for old age; elsewhere in *Geriatrics* he defined it more narrowly as the domain of those oldest old who have passed through the "senile climacteric." In equating very old age with second childhood, Nascher did not so much demonstrate the common structural concerns of pediatrics and geriatrics, as play on a powerful sign of the mentally impaired elder as legitimation for a new field of knowledge. In appropriating the child, *Geriatrics* positioned childish behavior at the center of the new physiology.

Nascher explored the climacteric at length in a 1915 article, "Evidences of Senile Mental Impairment." The piece is a discussion of both normal and pathological old minds through the presentation of eight cases, a progression of stock characters: "The oldest in this series of eight is a retired minister; of the others, one is a retired merchant, one is a manufacturer still in active business, one is a physician, one is a lawyer, and one is a humble shopworker. There are two women (widows), one living alone, the other living with her daughter."

The eight exhibit "various phases of senile mental impairment": the physician's mind is "extremely clear and alert"; both the minister and manufacturer are egotistical and forgetful; the lawyer is similarly so, and additionally "becomes confused or rambles"; the shop worker has "moments where the mind seems like a mental blank"; and the merchant is in the terminal stages of senile dementia. Nascher finds it difficult to place the two women along this progression; their vignettes stress less cognitive status than demeanor and the type of relationships the women have created.[94]

In delineating a "senile" as opposed to a "male" climacteric, Nascher attempted to routinize the senile body within a rational and ungendered discourse of geriatrics. Yet the possibilities of the normality he articulated remain rooted in a gendered logic. Unlike Galloway, he did not contrast the simple gonadal decline of women with the higher glandular embodiment of men. Rather than both sexes declining—albeit in different sites and at different rates—old men and old women, in *Geriatrics*, approached one another: "In childhood the growth force is exerted in two directions, or rather with two distinct purposes, accumulation of tissue and differentiation of the sexes. In old age . . . this growth force is now mainly exerted toward the approximation of the sexes and in old age they approach a neutral type."[95]

Not quite neutral, for the process "is more pronounced in the virilescence of the female." In noting the heightened masculinity of old women, Nascher may have been responding to more than their mustaches (to which, however, he had a tendency to return throughout *Geriatrics*). Whether the enhanced power of old women has been a universal archetype[96] or a culturally and politically located strategy of resistance,[97] it presented for Nascher a concern that challenges the central meaning of old age and its physiology of decline. He responded by interpreting the strong female old body as performative health, the failure of women to look as senile as they really are: "The obvious manifestations of senility appear later in the female, for the reason that she makes an effort to remain attractive, the psychic factor involved in the production of the senile slouch in the male being overcome by her vanity."

Beyond strategic vanity, the performance of the wrong normality was an indication of a woman's cognitive limitation: "Women being more impressionable than men, they are more amenable to religious teachings, they become more readily resigned to the inevitable through their faith and hope of eternal life hereafter, and being more cheerful they do not present the disagreeable, gloomy appearance of aged men." The performance of health masked the process of decline, depriving women of what limited brain power the terms of discourse granted them in the first place. Thus "the mental changes in the female generally include all of the intellectual faculties and proceed to the extent of complete dementia far more often than in the male."[98] One could not so easily, therefore, measure and rank women's cognitive status, it being a matter of all or nothing, performative health shifting quickly to complete dementia.

Dementia more generally is the result of the poorly negotiated climacteric. Negotiation is dependent on one's moral sense: "Occasionally there is a recrudescence of sexual desire, to gratify which he may attempt rape upon little girls. Such crimes do not arise from depravity, but through weakened mentality involving a weakened moral sense, inability to realize the nature of the act or its consequences, loss of control over conduct, and an irrepressible sexual fury."[99] If the climacteric represents a sexual gauntlet conditioned by a moral sense, dementia is the end stage of having failed to control one's sexuality. Unlike Warthin, Nascher retains the legacy of Victorian perfectibility. Mental control is an explicitly economic process of the prudent management of limited resources. The physician—not surprisingly, the hero of the "Evidences" article—whose thinking is clear and alert, has negotiated the climacteric successfully. His old age is characterized as conservative: "more serious, less aggressive, less energetic."

The merchant and the shop worker pass through the climacteric inefficiently and at great cost. Unproductive emotional excess at their retirements depletes their vital resources and sets the stage for their poor negotiation of the climacteric. The lawyer, the minister, and the manufacturer are all still negotiating their respective climacterics. They are all emotionally excessive and somewhat egotistical. The women resist climacteric readings. The eldest

> has been living alone since the death of her husband nearly twenty years ago. Before his death, she was hospitable, sociable and charitable, but soon after his demise she became irritable and suspicious. . . . For the past ten years there has been coming on a slow mental impairment. Her interests in life have become restricted, until today she cares about nothing except her life and her little home, including a cat—her sole companion. . . . Aside from [buying food], she does not leave her house, admits no one to her rooms, and in fact leads a hermit life.

The woman's struggle at the time of her becoming a widow is analogous to the preclimacteric dilemmas of the merchant and shop worker. But no eruptive climacteric follows, just steady decline. Has the meaning of the climacteric been exhausted in her undergoing the menopause? The one hint we have here is the archetype through which Nascher presents her, that of the crone: willfully alone, her irritable voice, the hermit hut, the telltale cat. In Nascher's offering us—through the solitary and demented old woman—a figure of the witch, we come full circle to Weyer's substitution of the witch for the doting old woman. Female physiology is relevant primarily to anchor construction of a (male) body subaltern in its old age; its climacteric language of gonadal weakness and absent cognition is exhausted in the signification of old men. There is an unsignifiable gap between this senile physiology, predicated upon a naturalized rhetoric of gender difference, and the bodies of women Nascher encounters. If old men are normal but weak, and to be normal and weak is to be like a woman, what are old women like? They seem to be like men: independent, mustachioed. But this must be performance, a magical physiology. Nascher falls back upon the archetype of the witch.

Similarly, the second widow, "82 years of age, is fond of society, especially of the young, and tries to appear young by resorting to facial artists, hair-dressers, beautifiers, and dressing in youthful garments and conducting herself like a young woman. She takes seriously the joking propositions of marriage made by young men who know her weakness."

Now "her memory is weak, she loses her way," and yet "on the whole her conversation is rational and coherent, though inappropriate for a woman of her age."[100] Her cognitive state is difficult to assess; she is presented as alternately rational and confused. Her state in some ways seems analogous to that of the mid-climacteric "egotistical" lawyer and minister. But Nascher does not use a language of pathological selfhood—he does not call her "egotistical," as he called the three men—so much as he stresses her social pathology, her inappropriateness. She is the old bawd, and her role encompasses her pathology more seamlessly than its mirror, the old pantaloon, can represent the experience of climacteric men. Bawd and witch: the two women are offered not as a series, not as a moral economy of aging as for the men, but as totalizing caricatures that obviate a processual physiology negotiating the normal and the pathological through moral choice. The male body is made to contain the distinction through the invocation of the taken-for-granted logic of the female climacteric. The female body is made to contain the distinction through a set of archetypes preventing counterhegemonic readings of its sexuality. Throughout, the fusion of physiology and pathology is not threatening to geriatric ideology, for it is read as difference in gender and not difference in age.

ALZHEIMER'S FAMILY

A compelling historiography of Alzheimer's disease has been emerging, one that centers on Kraepelin's motives in naming an "*eigenartige*" 1906 finding of his student and colleague Alzheimer as a distinct disease.[101] *Eigenartige* has been translated as characteristic or peculiar. The standard narrative of Alzheimer's assumes the former gloss, that Alzheimer was conscious of identifying a pattern of neural degeneration and plaque formation suggestive of a pathological syndrome distinct from the "normal" anatomical findings of senile dementia, and that Kraepelin was merely honoring his achievement in eponymously naming the syndrome Alzheimer's disease. G. E. Berrios has convincingly and rather elegantly suggested the latter gloss, that Alzheimer was struck by the peculiar characteristics of the symptomatology of the middle-aged housewife brought into his clinic by her husband and of the neuropathology of her sliced and silver-stained brain.

For Berrios, the critical and still-opaque moment is the decision of Kraepelin and his colleagues to in effect rewrite Alzheimer's case materials, stressing only cognitive symptoms rather than cognitive, affective, and delusional symptoms, only a degenerative etiology and not arteriosclerotic and degenerative etiologies, and only onset in middle age rather than a span encompassing middle and old age. Through this set of exclusions Kraepelin could construct a distinct disease category, whereas for Alzheimer and most of his contemporaries the case of the middle-aged housewife was peculiar precisely in its early onset and extreme presentation of an existing disease category. Berrios notes: "The most common interpretation by those living and writing during Alzheimer's period was that the 'new' disease simply named cases with early onset, marked severity and focal symptoms. As the cognitive paradigm consolidated, a clear move toward narrowing down the syndrome by, for example, dismissing the presence of delusions and hallucinations can be detected. Likewise, arteriosclerosis was quietly dropped, and became an exclusion criterion."[102]

Kraepelin's motives remain a puzzle for Berrios, perhaps given his tendency to split Kraepelin's practice into distinct and fairly seamless "scientific" and "nonscientific" realms.[103] His analysis, however, still helps clarify the central puzzle of the historiography of the disease, its disappearance and rebirth. As Berrios notes, the correlation of plaques and tangles with the symptoms of dementia preceded Alzheimer's 1907 report,[104] and subsequent work demonstrated the same constellation of symptoms and pathology with clinical onset in old age.[105] The classic narrative of the modern Alzheimer's movement—that the great pathologist was limited by the ageism of the time and could only see presenile dementia as pathological, awaiting the late 1960s for medicine to recognize that Alzheimer's was also an apt characterization for senile dementia and thus to inaugurate the separation of normal aging from pathological dementia—presumes Kraepelin's exclusions. Yet the disappearance of Alzheimer's disease, its failure to capture the language of senility treatment and research for half a century, suggests two alternative processes not adequately framed by "ageism," the first of which Berrios illuminates: Kraepelin's exclusionary construction of a presenile nosology ran against an emerging consensus and failed to provide a fruitful site for the laboratory or clinic.[106]

The other critical process, of course, was the development of arteriosclerotic dementia, which far from being relegated to the sidelines by Kraepelin's exclusion, became the dominant concept in senile dementia research and clinical practice for much of the twentieth century. Unlike the degenerative changes of Alzheimer's, the vascular changes of arteriosclerosis were central sites of pharmaceutical research and intervention, and new classes of vasodilatory drugs emerged as senility treatments. Conceptual and commercial practices sustained one another well into the 1970s, in the United States, and later in much of Europe, Asia, and elsewhere.

There are multiple ways to think about the events of the 1960s through 1980s, chronicled at length by Fox, Gubrium, and Lyman: the emergence of a profes-

sional and later a popular Alzheimer's movement in the United States, its powerful and in some senses ironic medicalization of old age, and the various routes of
its attempted globalization. The 1970s and 1980s movement chronicled by Fox and
Gubrium emerges explicitly in terms of the anti-ageist critique—stressing the
normalcy of old age—of geriatrics. But the ideology of geriatrics and Fox's careful micropolitical analysis beg the question of why Alzheimer's was rediscovered
as senile pathology precisely when it was and why the popular culture of Alzheimer's hell spread so quickly.

In part, Alzheimer's reemerges in the United States at an interesting time: the
middle- and upper-class "young old" were appropriating the mantle of the elderly
in the creation of a social movement, and popular and official concern in wealthier industrialized countries was increasingly taking up the imminent burdensomeness of a growing gray wave. On the one hand, groups like the American Association of Retired Persons (AARP) formed powerful and well-heeled lobbies,
promoters of pedophobic Sun Cities created planned gerontopoli where children
and not the elderly were marginal, and resistance to ageist economic practice such
as forced retirement spawned an "aging and work" subfield of social work and
fairly class-specific senior employment agencies like the American group Operation ABLE. The normalcy of decline—central to Nascher's physiology despite
the ideology of the new field—was increasingly resisted, and normal aging came
to signify the wealthy retirees having fun pictured on the pages of *Modern Maturity*,
the AARP's magazine. Normal aging signified an extension of the ideology of the
American Dream and of its dominant mood of fun.[107]

On the other hand, rejecting the burdensomeness of the dependent elderly and
preserving society's collective ability to leave home and roam America's byways—
like Frank in his fantasy of authentic pre-Alzheimer's personhood—was legitimated through a redefinition of the most needy elderly as encompassed by the
nonpersonhood of their disease. The thematic of Macfarlane's analysis of village
communities in Tudor and Stuart Essex is repeated: as the legitimacy of the gift—
no longer the giving of food to widows by individual householders but the guar-
anteed provision of income to all elders by the state—becomes contestable, so the
mind of old people—no longer marginalized older women but the so-called frail
elderly—becomes the object of unambiguous pathology, here not the subterranean associations of witchcraft but the earthly hell of Alzheimer's disease.

Given their rough class logic, the two turns—gerontocratic and gerontophobic—are not usually in opposition to one another. When an old American named
John Kingery was abandoned, apparently by his daughter to avoid the costs of
maintaining him at a nursing home, at a dog track in Idaho hundreds of miles
from his family, a spokesperson for the AARP lamented that such an action had to
happen but sympathized with the daughter:

> "granny dumping, as it's called, was unheard of 15 years ago but now the anecdotal
> evidence tells us it has become somewhat of a trend," said John Meyers, a

spokesman for the American Association of Retired Persons, which has 33 million members. "Not a day goes by when a hospital emergency room somewhere in America doesn't have a case where some elderly person has been abandoned, usually by the children". . . . "The fact that children abandon their parents, as horrible as it is, is indicative of the terrible balancing act that care-givers are stuck with."[108]

Meyers advocates federal support to families for adult day care centers, giving beleaguered children a break. AARP members are at least as likely to be givers as recipients of care; one can join and begin receiving various senior citizen discounts at age fifty. Meyers' response, like the *Newsweek* articles, reminds us that being a caregiver is experienced as the hell of the tabloids by older as well as younger children, that the desire behind the hegemony of Alzheimer's pathology and its denial of subjectivity to certain old bodies is located less in the politics of age per se than of generation. His response again underlines the critical role of gender in the structuring of pathology. *Mr.* Kingery is granny-dumped; his expendability is reinforced through the figure of the pathetic old woman. The Murphy bed reappears as a generational collective fantasy.

The language of legitimate pathology reflects not only the view under the microscope but the social construction of the person identified with the slice of tissue. The vascular damage and necrosis of multi-infarct dementia and the plaques and tangles of Alzheimer's continue to share the etiologic limelight, but it is plaques and tangles that become the key signs of the demented brain, and "Alzheimer's" that becomes a medical idiom for dementia and lay idiom for senility. The power of Alzheimer's over other medicalizations lies in part, as Gubrium and Lyman have pointed out, in its clear drawing of the line between normality and pathology and its legitimation of control as therapy. Beyond this, Alzheimer's is structured as an embodiment of excess. Its "gold standard" remains the plaques and tangles that appear in most aging brains but in excess in Alzheimer's.[109] Plaques are real, demonstrable, and countable. Given the emphasis within the Alzheimer's movement on the continual reiteration of the disease's pathology— one of the two "enumerative obsessions" present at Zagreb—plaques and tangles become the enumerable source of proof. Old parents place demands on their children; these demands do not make Frank's dream of freedom any more realizable. The behavior that has come to be called dementia makes particularly enormous demands on children; these are far from the only demands, but contribute critically to a moral economy in which the oldest old demand too much. Daughter Regan says to Lear, "I pray you, father, being weak, seem so."[110] The legitimacy of the claims of old persons on their children is inevitably contested. Excess plaques and tangles are demonstrable signs of a condition of this existential excess of the old. They come to stand for the person with dementia not because of their universality—vascular or multi-infarct and other types of dementia do not necessarily present with the pathology of Alzheimer's—but because of their semantic potential, as conveyers of what the patient means to others. The neuropathology of Alzheimer's—an unambiguous disease that can be counted, excess that can be revealed for all to see—proves the logic of senility. The interpersonal and existential crises of aging—its excessive demands—can be reduced to the disturbance of excessive mind. As the contest to define a person's old age is increasingly appropriated by children, Alzheimer's becomes the quantification of excess.

Unlike the language of climacteric excess, the modern concept of Alzheimer's resists the deployment of gendered pathology in naturalizing its claims to speak of age. Whereas Charcot and Nascher locate the conditions of possibility for a science of the old body with the institutionalized body of the old woman, Alzheimer's first patients are defined by him not as a priori institutional material for a science but persons from the outside whose reason for entry into the institution is in itself the critical fact anchoring a reading of their cellular pathology. The patient of the 1906 report had been "a woman, 51 years of age," who

> presented as the first most striking mental symptom, ideas of jealousy concerning her husband. Soon after, a rapidly developing mental weakening was noticed; she would lose her way about in her own home, throw things around and hide herself for fear of being killed. . . . In hospital she seemed perplexed, was disoriented for time and place, occasionally complained that she understood nothing. . . . The patient finally was completely demented; confined to bed with contractures of the lower extremities; and passed urine and feces involuntarily. In spite of greatest care decubitus developed. Death after a duration of 4 1/2 years.

Subsequently, "after the Bielschowsky silver impregnation method" Alzheimer noticed two features on slides of her cortical brain tissue: "tangled bundle[s] of fibrils" and "a deposition of peculiar stuffs."[111]

The second case of what had already become known as Alzheimer's disease, published in 1911, was of Johann F., a fifty-six-year-old day laborer and "moderate drinker" sent in 1907 to the Munich psychiatric clinic "by the overseers of the poor." For the previous six months he had "been forgetful; lost his way easily; could either not perform simple tasks or executed them awkwardly; stood about in an aimless manner . . . and no longer bathed." Over the course of the next three years Alzheimer documented Johann F.'s "manifest deterioration," efforts to pack his clothing and leave the institution, increased incontinence, continual weight loss, and eventual death "from symptoms of pneumonia."[112]

The fact that pathology is first searched for and discovered in a jealous and initially hysterical woman and then in an unproductive day laborer does not allow one to reduce either the materiality of dementia or Alzheimer's reasoning as a scientist to the equally material subalterity of these first "Alzheimer's patients." Yet behind the inquiry of the scientist wait the concerns of the husband and the overseer; Alzheimer's at its moment of origination is rooted in a specific need to explain the progressively more demented minds of the already dependent. Its indelible pathology—its incontrovertible plaques and tangles—demonstrates a pathology that is rooted in far more than the very real changes Alzheimer recognizes and reconstructs as clinical signs. The possibility of the neuropathological sign as stigmata draws on the social dependency of the person being redefined through it as unambiguously pathological. From its very first two cases, Alzheimer's has been situated at the moment of institutionalization and the conditions of its possibility.

This moment and these conditions are overdetermined. Social artifacts of shifting categories of dependency and technobiological artifacts of new drugs, new mice, and new clinical tests will affect and transform each other. Alzheimer's may take hold as clinical reality in India even in the absence of a so-called health transition. The impact of these new technobiological artifacts upon the local construction and negotiation of dependency across age, gender and class might well be studied as an ongoing process. At the moment and site of this research, such technobiological artifacts were of limited relevance to questions of local biology or local politics, and the following chapter turns to a narrative and set of practices of greater immediacy, those of the Bad Family.

Yet at this moment of enchantment, in which globalizing agents like the missionary physicians of Alzheimer's Disease International and multinational marketers of senility drugs proffer Alzheimer's as the answer to India's inevitably backward treatment of old people, the body of Alzheimer himself takes on unexpected and perhaps local forms. The Bangalore-based journal of the Indian Academy of Sciences, *Current Science*, devoted a 1992 issue to Alzheimer's disease, billing it as "an emerging issue for the developing countries."[113] The articles included were a mix of review articles, clinical overviews, and recent research and in their relative comprehensiveness suggested that a different kind of Alzheimer's practice had replaced the "better brain" project. On the cover of the special issue was a photograph of Alzheimer, but not the usual head shot accompanying books and articles on the topic in the United States and Europe.[114] The usual narrative of Alzheimer's life is one of tragedy, the template generated by Kraepelin's own essay on his junior colleague's various family losses and his premature death. But the Alzheimer who may be coming to matter in Indian science and whose invocation promises to restore aging in India is envisioned differently here. In his inaugural appearance in India, the great pathologist is pictured *en famille*, holding his son on his lap, seated next to his wife and daughter, and gazing through his ubiquitous monocle at their newborn baby.

A history of dotage wrested through the substance of old women's cries, gestures, bodies, and brains: the captive material of the Salpêtrière, for Charcot's theater of clinico-anatomical correlation, the old women who offer us knowledge, and through their inexhaustible numbers the possibility of a science of old age and of the boundaries of the pathological. But for a twentieth-century science of vivisection and recombination, the surplus material of old women was not enough; their live bodies could not circulate into the laboratory, and the search was on for the animal model, culminating in the arrival of several subspeciated brands of Alzheimer's mouse on the business pages of the *Wall Street Journal* and *New York Times* in 1995.

It is no longer a question of relative ethics, mice versus doting old women. Old women could not serve as the materialization of Alzheimer's as Alzheimer's was increasingly less a metonym of old age than a metaphor for it, its structural replacement. No one ever dies of old age anymore, but of the nation's fourth leading yet most insidious killer, and the material for a science can no longer be limited to the old. One looks for clues, rather, among the young: skin tests or other quick and painless assessments of future hell.

But the history of dotage still exacts its occasional pull: its reliance on the subaltern physiology of woman did not disappear with Alzheimer's plaques or with the celebrated arrival of genetically engineered mice. Like Scot with his witches and Charcot with his *vieille femmes*, a group of researchers at the University of Kentucky discovered the disciplinary possibilities of old nuns. One-third of the elderly School Sisters of Notre Dame were diagnosed with Alzheimer's, but all had kept written traces of their youth—autobiographical essays they had been instructed to write as novices, under the confessional authority of the church.

The Kentucky doctors found that the demented of the old nuns had, as young women, been more likely to have written simple sentences devoid of grammatical complexities; the old "mentally sharp" nuns when novices had in contrast written complex sentences. "Study Suggests Alzheimer's May Begin Early," ran the headline in the *San Francisco Chronicle*.[1] The possibilities for Alzheimer's swelled as the ever more contested distribution of intelligence—heretofore limited to the revived *Bell Curve* nature-nurture debates of the 1990s academy—could be framed as the harbinger of worse hard-wired horrors.[2] Once again, the institutionalized bodies of old women are the substrate for geriatric knowledge, but these bodies are now extended back in time to a plumbing of a youthful confession for new stigmata. Other explanations for the distribution of novitiate intelligence and for its correlation with the mental status of aged nuns were unimaginable.

From the wordplay of Mary Daly, ex-Catholic and self-proclaimed Witch: "academentia."[3] But real.

THREE

Knowledge, Practice, and the Bad Family

in which the old body is constituted as a site of national welfare,
as an embodiment of the bad family of middle class modernity

ON GERONTOLOGICAL OBJECTS

It is high time for the basis of discussion in these questions to be broadened and thickened up.
WILLIAM JAMES, *A PLURALISTIC UNIVERSE*

Against the taken-for-granted necessity of senile dementia, the anthropologist of northeast India in Zagreb offered the equally taken-for-granted declining status of the joint family as an index of senility. When families fall apart, children no longer respect and take care of their elderly parents. When old people are ignored or abandoned, their bodies, including and encompassing their minds, decline. About a dozen social scientists from India had come to Zagreb to give lectures on old age, and they shared the concerns of the ethnographer of the northeast hill tribe. The strength of the Indian contingent was indicative of the growth of social gerontology in India. To approach the construction of the senile body in Varanasi, I begin with an examination of Indian gerontological practice and some of its discursive and political milieus, to place the relation between the senile body and the structure of the family within the ongoing production of the taken-for-granted.

I start with the words of N. L. Kumar,[1] a Delhi-based activist for the elderly, spoken to me in an interview in 1989 at his home. I use Mr. Kumar's words to explore a different sort of gerontological paradox. I was struck by what, from my perspective, appeared as a set of ironies in Kumar's practice; I therefore want to note, at the outset, my respect for what Kumar has almost single-handedly accomplished, setting up what is by now a well-known nongovernmental organization (NGO) with unceasing passion and determination. This respect extends to Dr. S. K. Nayer, Mr. J. P. Sharma, and Mrs. Aloka Mitra, whose work for the welfare of the elderly I discuss below. I have tried to keep respect for their individual accomplishments, character, and visions distinct from a critical analysis of discourse and practice.

"You see, first, people did not know what a senior citizen is."

We were sitting in Kumar's living room having tea, and I was taping the interview. Kumar was noting the difficulty that he had initially in arousing interest in old age as a social issue. Searching after his own retirement for a cause to advocate, Kumar had chosen work in gerontology. He put the matter succinctly: "When I retired, I had the whole time. So I said I should do something. So, all of a sudden, this idea struck me. Because at that time, there was no aging in India."

Kumar's lament, which eventually led to his founding of the organization Age-Care India and of the journal *The Elderly*, is for the lack of "aging" as a field of knowledge. But it is expressed as a lament for a lack of categories. India lacks senior citizens and India lacks aging. Kumar thus formulated his cause: India needs senior citizens and India needs aging. The primary task of an Indian gerontology is here not to study aging but, notably, to create it.

This act of creation merits reflection. Since the early 1980s there has been an efflorescence of research projects, articles, books, projected welfare schemes, and commissions concerned with the experience of old people in India. Much of this emergent discipline of gerontology has shared the irony of Kumar's words. That is, it is a field that has erased its ostensible object, allowing for the paradox of no aging in India.

By *object*, I mean here not only an object of analysis but also the implicit beneficiary of an applied social science. The ostensible object of the new gerontology is the typical old Indian. Many recent gerontological reports offered this figure and his or her needs as their raison d'être. The face of a wizened old peasant or of an urban slum dweller has graced book covers.[2] Gerontological activists have invoked urban poor or rural elderly. HelpAge India, the country's premier gerontological social service organization, christened this object "the less privileged elderly" on the back of its 1989 Christmas cards.

This object is erased when, despite a plethora of state-sponsored studies suggesting that many old people fall between the cracks of self, family, and government assistance, the only significant form of state support remains a pension for a minority of relatively privileged elderly. It is erased when private gerontological institutions that constitute themselves as serving the needs of a lower-class majority in fact distribute most of their resources to an urban and often middle-class clientele. It is erased most profoundly when the structure of the scientific discourse of aging limits social analysis to the needs of urban elite elders and their families. The pensioner, the "senior citizen" whom Kumar searches for but will only find when he abandons the slums of Delhi for its wealthier colonies, remains the primary object of academic and applied gerontology in India.

How does the science of aging in India erase its object? Gerontological writing and practice is dominated by a powerful and seldom challenged narrative of the decline of the Indian joint family and the consequent emergence of old age as a time of difficulty. The narrative runs somewhat as follows: (1) Indian families were all once multigenerational "joint" households; (2) in such households, old people had all their needs taken care of, were listened to and respected, and had few complaints—old age was a pleasure; (3) with the advent of Westernization, modernization, industrialization, and urbanization, families began to break up, and the social support and respect for the elderly declined, along with their quality of life.

Far from a universalizable object of analysis, the old person who inhabits such a narrative maps primarily onto the experience of elite and urban middle-class elderly men. The object of gerontology is split between the "disadvantaged elder," who is the disciplinary icon, and the pensioner, who is the ultimate index of analysis. Analyses of the sociology of aging or proposals for government spending, usually constructed out of the experience of the pensioner, inevitably invoke the figure of the disadvantaged elder to legitimate their universality and claims for patronage. The pensioner and the disadvantaged old person come to stand for one another—through the denial of local disjunctions of class and power—in the constitution of a seamless gerontological object.

Most of the literature in English or Hindi on old age in contemporary India is organized around an imminent "problem of aging": more old people and less desire and ability—given the taken-for-granted decline of the joint family—to take care of them. This problem is deemed not only relevant but critical for immediate address in India: the language of gerontology is alarmist, almost apocalyptic. In both the studies on old age and the formal and informal charters of the institutions considered here, the problem of aging is taken as an originating point. It is assumed, not demonstrated.

THE "AGING IN INDIA" SERIES

The issue that brings him to a halt is nothing more or less than repetition.
KIERKEGAARD, *REPETITION*

I focus here on two texts. *Aging in India*, K. S. Soodan's sociological survey of urban Lucknow elderly, was published in 1975. *The Aging in India*, edited by A. B. Bose and K. D. Gangrade, appeared in 1988. The fact the two works share a title is not surprising: other recent English-language books on gerontology include the 1982 *Aging in India* and the 1987 *Aging in India*, as well as variants on the theme—the 1982 *Aging in South Asia*, the 1987 *Aging in Contemporary India*, and the 1989 *Aged in India*.[3] Even if we concur with Kumar that prior to the 1970s there was no aging in India, there seems to be naught but *Aging in India* since.[4]

The repetition merits analysis. "Aging" implies a universal, the idealized object of international gerontology, a thing that can be *in* India. Yet "India" is not a universal. "Aging in India" is oxymoronic. India is an Other that must be encompassed; the phrase sustains a relation between totalizing and subordinate universes. There are few gerontological works in India titled simply *Aging*: by itself, "aging" cannot articulate the relationship to an Other central to these works. "India" or "in India" is thus the requisite coda for gerontological formulations. The three most prominent organizations devoted to the elderly and based in New

Delhi are named HelpAge *India*, Age-Care *India*, and Age Aid *India*. Kumar, the founder of the second of these, described the genesis of its name:

> See, the name always matters. . . . I said, "Look here; this sort of organization, we don't have a proper name for it. Let's go, let's go out somewhere. We went to a restaurant, we went to a park, and we were relaxing. We walked over the grass. It was cool, you see, evening. And he suggested some names, I suggested some names. Then later, I suggested this name. Why not make it Age-Care? And we added *India*, to give it a specific.

Like Adam and Eve's naming of the animals, this garden idyll generated a universal category, with the "specific" of India an essential afterthought.

HelpAge India, the most prominent of these social service agencies, is more explicitly predicated on the legitimacy of internationalist universals. It began as a subsidiary of a British organization, HelpAge, which was spreading the message of caring for the aged worldwide. In a replaying of colonial experience, the Indian organization began with a Company phase, a few adventurous British social workers out to understand the problems of the aged in India. It moved into an imperial phase, the emergence of an organization modeled on British lines and run by an Englishman. And it matured into a neocolonial phase, an Indian-run organization, but still dependent for much of its funding and thus inspiration on several European HelpAges.[5] In moving from being a branch of HelpAge to independence as HelpAge India, the agency's one-way ties to British knowledge are not abandoned. By appending "India," HelpAge, Age-Care, Age Aid, and gerontological authors all claim local autonomy from internationalist discourse, but do so through a reassertion of epistemological subordination.

The *Aging in India* books share not just a title but the narrative of the Fall. To demonstrate an imminent crisis, their authors rely exclusively on numbers. There are no detailed case studies demonstrating the crisis, nor any historical analyses documenting change. Any documentation of experience is lacking. Like a geyser, the crisis lies beneath the surface of things; its explosive power cannot be seen before the fact and must be inferred. Projective demography thus lies at the center of this gerontology. The earliest of the series, Soodan's 1975 study of urban Lucknow elders, opens with a demographic demonstration of old age being a problem: "any person completing 55 years at the time of the survey was considered an aged person for the purpose of this survey. The number of such persons in India is now increasing at the rate of . . . 9.07 per cent for the decade. This rate of growth is likely to further increase as a result of longer survival ages enjoyed by elderly persons. The resulting problems posed by the increasing number of the aged now and in future [*sic*] will have to be faced by us sooner or later."[6]

The book begins by assuming "problems," but what they are remains unspecified and their timing is vague: "sooner or later." The numbers themselves are the principal signifiers here. Throughout the *Aging in India* series, demographics are used not to supplement but to represent the meaning of old age and the condition of old people. Despite this impressive rise in the number of old people, only near the end of the chapter does Soodan reveal that for the same decade (1951–61) the proportion of old people actually "fell slightly from 8.3 per cent of the population to 7.45."[7] The use of demography as legitimation of the a priori problematicity of old people is selective. Soodan goes on to cite figures reflecting a proportional increase of those over fifty-five in coming decades, but these again are offered as an affirmation of what is already assumed.

Most of the *Aging in India* books include chapters on demography; these tend to repeat one another. Implications are seldom assessed. As an example: the effect of a "gray wave" is examined through parameters such as dependency ratios. These assume that most young people are working and that most old people are not, neither of which is a tenable assumption in many Indian contexts. Further, the idea of "dependency" as a parameter of a problem rests on a set of culturally and historically located rules in which autonomy defines selfhood and individuals are responsible for the maintenance of their autonomy. Dependent old people break these rules, and lots of them challenge the playing of the game. Different rules mandate careful consideration to different challenges. Gerontology, by taking its problem for granted in structuring analyses, rarely asks which demographic information is useful or how it should be interpreted.

Soodan randomly samples households throughout the city of Lucknow, using an elaborate schedule that solicits residential, occupational, medical, familial, and emotional data from informants. He utilizes these data to suggest that old people have multiple problems: residential, occupational, medical, familial, and emotional. That Indian narrative and medical texts have made a similar point for millennia is no bar to Soodan tying these problems to a new problem of aging. A new problem mandates a new solution, and Soodan advocates financial assistance and professional attention for each of his classes of problematicity. His suggestions include a universal pension, increased funding for gerontological research, and the provision of health services, old age homes, clubs, day care centers, homemaker services, meals-on-wheels, and "friendly visits" by the state.

The complaint and the suffering Soodan documents are real. But the catalogue of needs he generates in his zeal to document multiple sources of distress, complaint, and suffering as The Problem is so broad as to approach the tautological. Soodan's "solution" ignores the economic limitations of state spending, the politics of state assistance, and the setting of welfare priorities. In proposing interventions like meals-on-wheels in the context of endemic undernutrition and limited access to potable water across generations, *Aging in India* approaches the absurd. Like the books that follow it, Soodan's detailed and well-intentioned study reinforces the bureaucratic equation of gerontology with a utopia beyond practical consideration. The generation of gerontological utopia legitimates the silence of the state.

The 1988 avatar of *Aging in India* develops the same set of themes. Its jacket alerts the reader to the fact that "the aging of populations is taking place in both developed and developing countries due to the lowering of birth rates and death rates and increased life expectancy. In India, too, the numbers as well as the proportion of the population 60+ are showing a rising trend. This gives an indication of the tasks that lie ahead, specially since about half of this population belongs to vulnerable socio-economic groups." Again: the demographic proof of an unspecified problem, the requisite positional coda "in India, too," and the legitimation of the field in terms of "vulnerable socio-economic groups." The protagonist is the disadvantaged elder, incarnate as the village peasant on the book's cover.

Yet gerontology's split object is evident. The volume is based on the proceedings of a seminar held jointly by the Citizenship Development Society and the Bombay-based Association for Senior Citizens (the latter group does not append "in India" to its name, but describes itself as "acting as the Indian chapter of the International Association of Senior Citizens based in Los Angeles"). Funding for the seminar was provided by the Friedrich Naumann Foundation of West Germany, dedicated to Naumann's faith in the "self-reliant individual." Articles in the volume—as they move from general exhortations nominally sensitive to both of gerontology's objects to specific proposals—presume individuals and families with economic resources sufficient to afford subsidized elderly housing and attend geriatric clinics and with a desire to identify themselves or their parents as senior citizens and initiate political action as an interest group. They presume, in other words, the pensioner or senior citizen, not the disadvantaged elder in whose name the volume is legitimated.

Thus C. Subrahmanium notes in his introductory remarks to this volume: "Among the aged there are two categories. The first category consists of men retired from active life—from Government service and other organised sectors. . . . Organizations to utilise the services of these senior citizens will have to be established." The pensioner is presented as active and as male, and his presence mandates the establishment of gerontological organizations. In contrast, "a different approach will have to be made for those who have become weak and disabled." For them, "family as an institution will have to play a crucial role in taking care of the aged."[8] The figure of the disadvantaged elder glides into that of the frail and weak body, and this latter, gender-neutral figure does not generate the promise of new institutional development but of recourse to the family—whose terminal decline is suddenly and mysteriously forgotten—with no mention of state patronage.

A third component of the *Aging in India* series, along with routinized demographics and the utopian response to the apocalyptic Problem, is an elaboration of tradition, contained within the obligatory narrative of the Fall. The 1988 *Aging in India* begins with appeals to demographic crisis and goes on: "By tradition, religious and cultural, the elders are given a high status in Indian society. . . . In the past, joint family was the common pattern that existed with the head of the family enjoying rights and responsibilities and commanding obedience and respect." However: "Under the impact of the Industrial Revolution the joint family system is fast breaking down."

The use of the image of a devastated joint family remains selective. But as the primary object of most of the *Aging in India* series is the pensioner, the references to the decline of the joint family are ubiquitous. Another article in the volume, a sociological analysis of intergenerational conflict, assumes that the premodern family was "a self-sufficient unit, socially and economically, the centre of the universe for the whole family, the arbiter of life's important decisions," and so forth.[9] The article proceeds with an analysis of "change" in family structure, with no data whatsoever on the presumed "before" of the picture.

Throughout the genre, the "traditional" family is conceived in idealized terms as an indivisible unit free from conflict and existing outside of the contingencies of time and space. A Golden Age is uncritically assumed. Normative exhortations to honor one's parents and the filial piety of moral cynosures such as Lord Ram or the devoted son Shravan Kumar are taken as evidence for an unambiguously gerontocratic society stretching from ancient Vedic days to the fondly remembered childhood of the author in question. Other traces of "tradition"—the elaborate descriptions of the decrepitude and humiliations of the old body in the texts known as Puranas, the stress in Ayurvedic medicine on the avoidance of old age altogether through longevity (*rasāyana*) therapy, the extensive soteriological use of the figure of the old person within Buddhist and Epic texts as sign of the materialist fallacy at its most pathetic—all are ignored in these readings.[10] Or, as we will see below in the case of Ayurveda, the location and meaning of decrepitude are extensively reworked. In closing inquiry to the richness and complexity of ritual and text as responses to, rather than merely injunctions about, aging and to the history of the family as more than a process of decline, gerontology denies itself the use of this history in its own creation. With the sealing off of the past, the discipline defines itself as having recourse only to "the West" for models to interpret a Fallen present.

INTERNATIONALIST SCIENCE

I have to thank you of America for the great attempt you are making to break down the barriers of this little world of ours . . . it has been given to thee to march at the vanguard of civilisation with the flag of harmony.

SWAMI VIVEKANANDA, *CHICAGO ADDRESSES*

The United Nations declared 1982 the International Year of the Aged. Representatives from around the world met that year in Vienna for a World Assembly on Aging. This meeting has come to assume near mythic status in Indian texts on gerontology. Its continual invocation[11] is reminiscent of the symbolic power of the 1893 World Parliament of Religions in Chicago where the Bengali religious leader Swami Vivekananda is said to have put Hinduism on an equal footing with the world's other great religions. But no such explicit counterhegemonic move came out of the Vienna conference. The structure of the World Assembly was less interactive than didactic, and its message—aging as a global problem—permitted no variant interpretations.

American gerontology texts of the same period as the Indian texts cited above seldom mentioned the World Assembly, unless they were by authors in the business of writing authoritatively about aging in non-American societies. "International gerontology" (as opposed to the specific citation of European and particularly Scandinavian experience) has had relatively little impact on American gerontology, yet American and European authors continue to dominate the field and set its agenda.

The unidirectional flow of information was illustrated by the appendix to the Assembly's report. Letters from four representative world leaders were included. Ronald Reagan was there for the developed West, Henryk Jablonski of Poland stood for the Eastern Bloc, Indira Gandhi spoke for the developing world, and the Pope held forth for Christendom. While Jablonski and Reagan extolled the virtues of the gerontological experience their respective systems of knowledge and power have produced, Mrs. Gandhi was more modest: "The pooling of experience and ideas from different countries will be useful in helping us to tackle our own problem."[12] Knowledge was neither produced nor transformed at the conference but transferred along well-rutted paths.

In preparation for the 1982 conference, both India and the United States produced status papers on the condition of old people. The American paper was implicitly constructed as a vehicle of *foreign* policy: it was produced by the Department of State.[13] The Indian paper was structured as a vehicle of *social* policy and was produced by the Ministry of Welfare.[14] The theme of the American document was success in meeting the challenges of the problem of aging, a theme reflected in the narrative structure of its system of classification in which old age is held aloft on pillars of "Health," "Income Security," "Social Services," and "Personal Fulfillment." The Indian document reflected two contradictory orientations: an openness to the importation of foreign gerontological technology, yet an adjoined critique of age-specific policy efforts. The paper suggested that gerontological concerns in India are being and should be met not through gerontology but through integrated planning for the welfare of the entire population. Kumar's "no aging in India," the acknowledged lack of state involvement in old age, was perceived simultaneously as a vacuum to be filled by the West and as a sign of a generationally indivisible familial self and polity in contrast to those of the West.

Yet the Indian document, with its ambivalence toward the relevance of a specifically gerontological epistemology, made no impact on the Vienna Assembly or its sequelae. The primary document to emerge from Vienna, and one to which the Indian Ministry of Welfare has had to devote considerable attention, was an "International Plan of Action," a set of recommendations (each beginning "Governments should . . . ") with the provision for follow-up questionnaires to examine individual governments' compliance with them. These questionnaires are composed of questions in the form "Does the Government have policies . . . ?" "Has the Government adopted a policy . . . ?" and so forth: they demand adherence to a single ideology of gerontological practice.[15]

The form of the Ministry's response to the questionnaire has been that of the confessional. Despite the partial critique contained within their own status paper, ministry officials I interviewed in 1989 interpreted their inability to answer many of the responses mandated by the International Plan as gerontological failure or, at best, as due to a lack of resources. Again and again, the questionnaire demanded "Does the Government . . . ," to which the ministry officials could only respond in the questionnaire they returned to Vienna: No, No, No.[16]

The American status paper stood in sharp contrast. A record of continuing successes, it pointed out the congruence of "international" and "American" gerontology. It offered a history of gerontology as a deepening recognition of the problematicity of "aging" and as a movement toward the standardization of a response. This movement was figured as a series of symposia, councils, and conferences. One reads that an emerging "awareness of aging as a national challenge . . . at the end of the nineteenth century" was formalized in 1938 through a symposium and companion volume, *Problems of Ageing*.[17] American institutions were offered as templates for international interventions, including those proposed by the World Assembly and its Plan of Action.

The knowledge to be gathered under this new movement, according to the status paper, assumed a division between the informed and the ignorant. From the outset, gerontology in the United States was framed as a missionary specialty. Thus, in the 1950s an "Inter-University Council on Social Gerontology [met to] further professional training" through "two month-long *indoctrination* programs for 75 college and university faculty members who had developed an interest in aging."[18] Conversion was followed by routinization; gerontology formalized its identity as an increasingly bureaucratized aging enterprise, and the direction of assumed rationalization was toward a merger with the state.

The 1982 World Assembly on Aging shared the two primary goals of the archetypal gerontological conference of which it is structured as an extension: naming old age as problem and inculcating the need for a uniform response among the ignorant. "International gerontology" was thus the effort to universalize through one-way communication a culturally specific epistemology: the invocation of a global community of knowledge to advance the claims of truth of a particular worldview we might term *internationalist*.

The epistemology underlying the World Assembly and its "collective" expertise is internationalist rather than international. It can be represented as a set of assumptions:

Universality: The old person and the old body are legitimate foundational points for a science whose assertions are universalizable. There is a universal old person, a universal old body, and a universal way of talking about them, and a gerontology is—and should be—about such universals. These universal objects of gerontology are not located within culturally and historically specific discourses.

> *Problematicity*: The old person and the old body—rather than old age—are conceptualized and signified a priori as problems. This problematicity can not be deflected onto other frames such as the family.
>
> *Moral Imperative*: To talk about old people and old bodies as problems is a moral and necessary act.
>
> *Threat*: The old person or old body as problem is not only essential and analyzable but inherently threatening. This threat is met by a metanarrative of "normalcy" or "functionality" that is superimposed upon the root problematicity of the old person or body, partially rendering that problematicity invisible.

That this epistemology and its claims are in point of fact not universal is read by international gerontology along evolutionary lines as legitimation of its civilizing mission.

Precisely what is at stake for international gerontology becomes clear in a charter of its goals created by one of its premier exponents, Donald Cowgill. In a 1979 article, "The International Development of Academic Gerontology," Cowgill and Rosemary Orgren noted that gerontology as a scientific discipline emerges only in certain social and historical contexts and its development is conditioned by further social and historical changes. More concretely we may posit that societies which have small proportions of their populations in advanced ages . . . will not develop a self-conscious analysis of old age and will not be concerned with the problems and conditions of aging."

Cowgill posited five stages of gerontological thought:

1. The absence of gerontology within "developing societies," for example, Brazil or Iran.
2. A "beginning interest," often a "transplanted interest stimulated by contact with gerontology elsewhere," for example, Thailand (where, as luck would have it, "a former student of mine is planning to study the inmates of their old folks residential homes") or Taiwan.
3. An intermediate stage of "research under way" where "few if any faculty describe themselves as gerontologists," for example, Australia or Japan.
4. "A full range of academic programs in gerontology," for example, most of western Europe.
5. Formal state-sponsored gerontological research, the transition to which the United States is undergoing.[19]

The gerontologist must not only study the old person at home, but should encourage gerontological transformation abroad. Cowgill's scheme of the evolution of gerontological knowledge paralleled his more well known evolutionary schema, presented in the 1972 volume he edited with Lowell Holmes, *Aging and Modernization*. In the 1960s and 1970s, Cowgill and others applied modernization theory—a powerful body of Cold War scholarship cutting across social scientific disciplines, which charted the progression of formerly colonized societies from "traditional" to "modern" guided by the controlled infusion, through market penetration, of foreign capital and expertise—to the study of old people. The theories of Parsons, Redfield, Rostow and others correlating the increased penetration of the United States into "developing economies" and the predicted rise of the socioeconomic conditions of the formerly colonized, were used to predict a corresponding decline in the status of old persons even as their societies advance, the fly in the modernization ointment.[20]

The sources of decline within this theory are multiple and overlapping. Industrialization and consequent urbanization lead to the migration of a younger generation away from villages; joint families are split and children, the traditional supports of their old parents, are displaced. Traditional knowledge and thus the legitimation of gerontocratic authority is rendered increasingly obsolete; intergenerational conflict rises and children come increasingly to identify themselves against their parents. Parental support is increasingly perceived as a burden. The lengthening of the life span and a decline in birth and mortality rates lead to more old people, numerically and proportionally; the burden is not only subjective but objective. Women move into less ascriptive roles and are less able to be home to care for an older generation. Aging and modernization theory reads these changes as iatrogenic side effects of an otherwise beneficent process: international gerontology becomes the prescribed treatment for the prognosticated ills of modernization.

Talcott Parsons himself articulated the transformations of old age with modernization:

> By comparison with other societies the United States assumes an extreme position in the isolation of old age from participation in the most important social structures and interests. . . . Two primary bases of the situation . . . [are first] the isolation of the individual conjugal family[:] . . . the parental couple is left without attachment to any continuous kinship group; [second] the occupational structure. As an individual's occupational status centers in a specific "job," he either holds the job or does not, and the tendency is to maintain the full level of functions up to a given point and then abruptly to retire.[21]

In *Aging in Western Societies*, Ernest Burgess developed these ideas at length, arguing that urbanization and mass production undermined the economic basis of the extended family, resulting in less family support and greater isolation for longer lived elderly.[22] That modernity was responsible for the "scandalous" position of the elderly achieved widespread intellectual and popular support through works like Simone de Beauvoir's *La Vieillesse*. Beauvoir argued that the dehumanization of the elderly could occur because modern society had no use for them. Old people are increasingly "defined by an exis, not by a praxis"; that is, they are seen as being objects and not actors, as being nonselves, persons without subjectivity.[23]

Aging and modernization theorists were more optimistic. A potential crisis of legitimacy for the foreign expert—the deleterious effects of development for old people—was transformed into a further rationale for their practice. International gerontology offered the West as both problem and solution, Hope in a Pandora's box of gerontophobic demons. The underdeveloped naif was falling and required the experience of the fallen to learn to cushion the blow. The decline in elder status with modernization was offset by the growth of formal gerontological knowledge.

Thus Erdman Palmore and Kenneth Manton could write: "When societies 'mature' the rates of change level off and the discrepancies between aged and non-aged decrease. There may be other factors such as the growth of new institutions to replace the farm and family in maintaining the status of the aged such as retirement benefits, more adult education and job retraining, policies against age discrimination in employment, etc." Modernization is redeemed. "The aged need not fear the advanced stages of modernization, because their average occupation and education status should no longer fall as in the early stages, and it may even begin to rise."[24]

Palmore and Manton attempted to quantify status and modernization in an effort to demonstrate both this rise and fall. Defining status as the "relative socio-economic position of the aged" (measuring the employment status, occupation, and education of those over sixty-five and comparing it to those twenty-five to sixty-four) and modernization in terms of increased productivity (measuring the per capita gross national product), the shift away from agriculture, and education (measuring literacy, the proportion of youth in school, and the proportion of the population receiving higher education), they presented data to suggest status does not simply decline with modernization but begins to improve. In defining aging and modernization not as a linear decline but as a "J-shaped relationship," Palmore and Manton argued that with the emergence of what Cowgill and Orgren would have termed a stage five level of sophistication (with its corollary of total state involvement), gerontology would eventually raise the status of old people to potentially unlimited horizons.

Palmore and Manton's and Cowgill and Orgren's constructions of the evolution of gerontology had to remain vague on origins. Gerontology was represented both as a natural function of the proportion of elderly within a society and, paradoxically, as a sophisticated technology requiring foreign insemination. Ultimately, the field is structured as an enterprise whose interests are tied to the state and whose members should advocate the continual expansion of its boundaries. Gerontology comes down from above, here in the person of the fifth- (and highest) stage American scholar sending his students around the world to spread the true gospel.

What makes this manifesto frightening is the absolute sincerity with which it was presented. That stage one and stage two societies might have elaborate, functional, reflexive, modernizing but *different* theories of aging and the life course (against the gerontological assumption of universality), that isolating and professionalizing these processes of thinking about aging—let alone allying them to the state—might have untoward effects on the lives of old people (against the gerontological assumption of the moral imperative), and that the process of knowledge production Cowgill offered is rooted in political inequities were not considered.

The center-periphery structure of international gerontology was evident in the "Plan of Action Questionnaire," which assumed the universality of aging as a problem and of the state as definer of problems and agent of solutions. The schedule of needs implicit in its questions maintained the hierarchy of gerontological development by defining the success or failure of local responses in terms of the acquisition of Euro-American gerontological technology. The Vienna office's demands included the following:

2.9   If the country has no research centre dealing with the aging of populations, does the Government contemplate establishing one or more such centres?

4.1   Has the Government adopted a policy concerning the protection of elderly consumers?

7.2a . . . please indicate which of the following social welfare services have been developed for the elderly?

> Financial assistance
> —— Senior centres and day-care centres (with health services)
> —— Distribution of basic foods to needy elderly
> —— Meals in group setting (soup kitchens, etc.)
> —— Home delivery of meals (i.e., "Meals on Wheels")
> —— Distribution of clothing and other basic items to needy elderly
> —— Clubs
> —— Home help (i.e., to assist in housekeeping, cleaning, shopping, personal hygiene, etc.)
> —— Laundry services
> —— Volunteer services for the aged
> —— Friendly visitors (for promoting social contact)
> —— Telephone contact systems

The document presumed a state that ensures the provision of basic resources to its citizens but may neglect to pay attention to the specific needs of the aged. Like the *Aging in India* series, it presented a utopian gerontological universe that in its incommensurability with Indian political economy marks the internationalist imperative as both a superordinate asymptote for gerontological striving (guaranteeing the need for an infinite production of discourse) and an avoidable impossibility for the state.

Other possibilities do exist. Against the utopian gerontology that emerges in the meeting of a local sociology of old age with a globalizing mission practice, the vigorous debate on social security begun by Amartya Sen and continued by Bina Agarwal, Marty Chen, and Jean Drèze, among others,[25] addresses the specific needs of the elderly generally and old widows in particular without isolating them from broader questions of entitlement, scarcity, the state, and public action.

Against the construction of the Indian elder as a unitary object within the narrative of the Fall, the efforts begun by Alfred De Souza and others at the Indian Social Institute in Delhi to address the class-specific needs of urban elderly and in particular the elderly poor offer the beginnings of a different sociology of old age.[26] But such possibilities will remain incoherent as long as state and global interest in utopian rhetoric and inexpensive inaction collude with the disciplinary structures of international gerontology.

THE "GOLDEN ISLES"

It is reported, that upon the Hills by Casmere *there are men that live some hundreds of years, and can hold their breaths, and lye in Trances for several years together, if they be but kept warm.*
JOHN MARSHAL, "A LETTER FROM THE EAST INDIES," *PHILOSOPHICAL TRANSACTIONS*

Peter Laslett, offering a historical critique of aging and modernization assumptions in Britain, noted that these theories posit a typology of before and after: the elderly before modernization were treated well; the elderly since modernization are treated poorly.[27] A second typology of there and here is superimposed on that of before and after. Corinne Nydegger termed the before and there stories gerontological myths: the "Golden Age" and the "Golden Isles"; they are united by the theme of the "Rosy Family" providing strength, love, and sustenance to all its members."[28]

Critiques of Aging and Modernization approaches have tackled either the before/after or the there/here versions. Dependency and world-systems critiques of modernization theory—which examine how neocolonial and core-periphery economic relations continue colonial processes of surplus extraction and collective impoverishment and intensify the marginal existence of the nonmetropolitan majority rather than "boost" underdeveloped economies—have been applied in a gerontological context by Peter Townsend and others. Townsend does not reject the central tenet of classical Aging and Modernization theory, that old age has become a bad age, but rather shifts the emphasis from status decline as an unfortunate epiphenomenon of an otherwise beneficent and natural process to decline as socially engineered:

> I am arguing, then, that society creates the framework of institutions and rules within which the general problems of the elderly emerge and, indeed, are manufactured. Decisions are being taken every day, in the management of the economy and in the maintenance and development of social institutions, which govern the position which the elderly occupy in national life, and these also contribute powerfully to the public consciousness of different meanings of ageing and old age.[29]

The decline in the quality of life of older people does not just "happen" with modernization; societies actively and continually produce dependency.

Sheila Neysmith and Joey Edwardth place Townsend's idea of the social dependency of the elderly into the context of Third World economic dependency.

They suggest that "the manner in which Third World nations respond to the human needs of their old is subject to the relationship that entwines Third World and capitalist industrialised nations," such that "social policy and human service models are nurtured by the ideology underlying these economic relations." The resulting institutions "at best support an elite. . . . This social structure, however, means that most people will never benefit from such programmes." Neysmith and Edwardth conclude:

> Third world countries must develop indigenous responses that reflect the needs of old people in their countries. Retirement and family policies as conceptualized in countries with developed market economies may be totally irrelevant; other programmes may not be. At a minimum, the assumptions behind service models must be critically examined. Our critique goes beyond the question of transferability of services. Service models merely reflect theories of aging, all of which are ideologically based.[30]

Most criticisms of Aging and Modernization challenge its universal typology of social change. Cowgill and Holmes culled material from a variety of decontextualized sources and ignored or explained away inconvenient data in their pursuit of universal patterns.[31] Palmore and Manton's work has been criticized for a similar tendency to use data selectively.[32] David Fischer has argued that their correlation of modernization and status decline is tautological, given that variables like educational status are used as an index both of status and of modernization.[33]

Sociologists and historians of aging writing primarily about the United States, Britain, and France have challenged the uniformity of the premodern before, the unambiguous valence of social change, and the correlation of the status of the elderly with industrialization. Georges Minois, in his comprehensive *Histoire de la Vieillesse en Occident*, traced the gerontophobic representation of the elder in Europe from Mediterranean classical antiquity through the Renaissance.[34] Fischer and Andrew Achenbaum, writing on the United States, did not challenge the existence of a Golden Age in itself but argued that declines in status were not necessarily a product of urbanization and industrialization.[35] For Fischer, the decline of a gerontocratic "cult of age" occurred early in the history of the republic and was tied to social and ideological changes associated with the American and French Revolutions. For Achenbaum, significant change came later, after the Civil War and on into the twentieth century, with "the impact of science and technology, of industrial innovations and bureaucratization, and of heightened age-consciousness and age-grading." Peter Stearns argued against the existence of a Golden Age in France.[36] Quadagno summarizes many similar studies: "The extended family household of traditional society is not universal but varies significantly over time and space. Retirement is not solely a phenomenon of modern society. Increased reliance on large-scale organizations is not necessarily a symbol of the breakdown of the family network. Further, some of the changes that did occur may have been operating in different directions at different times."[37]

Quadagno suggests that the empirical indicators used in this literature to assess status make multiple ethnocentric and historically located assumptions about what constitutes the physical and emotional security of old people, and she calls for a redefinition of what sociologists mean by "status" sensitive to local political and moral worlds.

Aging and Modernization theory projected the Golden Age onto Golden Isles even as it ironically forecast their destruction. Critiques of Golden Isles approaches have come from gerontological anthropologists. In writing of her fieldwork in Samoa, Ellen Rhoads did not question Samoa's status as a Golden Isle but suggested that different constructions of family, work, and intergenerational support seem "to have inhibited development of some of the more negative effects of modernization cited by Cowgill and Holmes."[38]

Janice Reid challenged both before and after in her work with members of the Australian Yolngu community. Cultural ideals, she argued, have far less to do with the fortunes of individual elders than do "their personalities and their differential location in the economic, political, and social structures." She stressed the variable effects of social change: "Some old Yolngu today have been able to take advantage of the direction of social change to enhance their status and material security; others have been bypassed or marginalised by the forces of modernisation and seen their forces dwindle with age."[39] Nydegger pointed out that the majority of studies on "the status of old people in . . . " have confounded "professed attitudes" with "actual treatment" and respect for parents within families with the provision of physical and emotional security for old persons as a group by society as a whole.[40]

Sociological and social anthropological studies of old age in India reflect both the initial enthusiasm for Aging and Modernization and the later emergence of a critique. Three of the early advocates of the decline of the joint family were Aileen Ross, F. G. Bailey, and Scarlett Epstein. In *The Hindu Family in Its Urban Setting*, Ross documented the opposed forces of "Break Down" and "Unity" within rural families. She was unable show a simple movement from one pole to the other, yet still concluded that with further modernization the forces of dissolution would prevail. In constructing a story of there-before, she conflated Sanskrit prescriptive traditions with social reality: "In the village they will have been largely brought up on the idealized conceptions of adult roles found in the *Mahābhārata* and *Rāmāyaṇa*." Her conclusions, like those of the *Aging in India* series, were entirely anticipatory: "These changes will bring older people many frustrations and anxieties. They will experience a loss of self-esteem, and may even feel intense social isolation. They may find it difficult to understand the revolt of their children and grandchildren against them."[41]

Bailey and Epstein both noted a significant decline in the joint family, despite the paucity of historical data they drew upon. Bailey, working in Orissa, attributed fission to economic diversification, secondary to the differential income of brothers.[42] Epstein found that only 8 to 10 percent of the families in the two Karnataka villages of her study fit her definition of "joint" as opposed to "elementary" families. She admitted that for poorer families without significant landholdings, a subsistence economy would have always mandated small family size. For landholding peasants in her initial study, however, family size had declined, probably secondary to the transformation from a subsistence to a cash economy.[43]

When Epstein returned to these villages a decade later, she further qualified her hypothesis. The families of wealthy farmers did not appear to be dissociating, and she concluded dissociation was a phenomenon of "middle-farmers."[44] Part of the problem may have lain in her definitions, which she adopted from I. P. Desai:[45] "I treated as joint families only those where all the following conditions in a unit larger than the elementary family were observed: 'common property and income, co-residence, commensality, co-worship and the performance of certain rights and obligations.' "[46] The definition, which makes unwarranted historical assumptions and which does not take into account local and regional variations in household structure and the definition of "family,"[47] may have contributed to Epstein's initial finding. Her 1973 data led her to complicate the picture with the description of an intermediate "share family" of multiple dwellings but shared income pooling and expenditure. Behind the share family lay her later finding that despite economic diversification, no villagers were ready to part with their land, "however unproductive it may be."[48] Her data eventually pushed Epstein beyond the predictions and models of Modernization Theory.

Multiple studies exist that suggest the joint family has not declined in any simple sense.[49] Studies of the Indian household have shifted away from the debate over before and after.[50] Yet, within the field of *Aging in India*, study after study repeats the same uncritical and unsubstantiated conclusions. The Golden Age and the Golden Isles thrive as the dominant figures of discourse. Neysmith and Edwardth called for an "indigenous" gerontology as a response to what they saw as knowledge and institutions produced by and through the core metropolitan location of international gerontology. But *Aging in India*, and the story of the Fall into the Bad Family it relates, is complexly local and reflects more than the global interest of the core and the class interest of the local metropolis.

GERONTOLOGY AS CULTURAL CRITIQUE

I hear that in America the old people are all abandoned.

MAN SITTING ACROSS FROM ME IN DELHI-VARANASI RAILWAY CARRIAGE,
OR ONE OF SEVERAL HUNDRED OTHER CHANCE INTERLOCUTORS.

Aging in India demands more than a hermeneutic of suspicion. The constant iteration of the decline of the joint family as the master trope of Indian gerontology against the evidence of historical and contemporary diversity is more than the domination of neocolonial modernization theory and its institutional correlates. It is more than the hegemony of the pensioner as the ultimate object of analysis and patronage. The endless repetition of the narrative of the Fall suggests that its telling is a powerful act; gerontology may convey at least as much performative as mimetic truth.

To locate the power of the narration I turn from the narrative's overt catalogue of signifiers to its metonymic structure, to examine the narrative after Barthes for the vacancies it exposes. Vladímir Propp's structural analysis of the folktale, despite the anthropological naïveté of its claims to universal employment, is helpful in viewing narrative as the elaboration of an abduction. Propp delineates a morphology, which I simplify here: (1) A victim is abducted from home; (2) a hero is (a) tested and passes the test, (b) receives the magical gifts of a donor, and (c) locates the victim; (3) the hero and the villainous abductor struggle until the villain is defeated; (4) the hero is rewarded and married.[51] In the gerontological narrative of the Fall the abducted victim is sometimes the old person, but more generally is a vague narrational presence we may call the imagined Indian self. The authors of articles in the *Aging in India* series, and the hundreds of middle-class persons who have related the decline of the joint family story to me in interviews, combine the old person with their own first person voice: "*We* no longer have the support of children; *our* families are breaking apart." One does not have to be old to experience the sense of loss. What is at stake may not be only the abduction of a good old age but that of the known self.

This abduction is from a state of wholeness marked as the joint family. The telling of the narrative presumes that the victim-narrator experiences his or her distance from this state of wholeness as an episode of violence in both space and in time. The villain who abducts is, in the oral narratives I collected, often modernity but more often "the West"; in the *Aging in India* series, the villain is unambiguously the latter. The originating point of the narrative as a temporal sequence, then, is located with the violent action of a villainous West.

To read the repetitious quality of Indian gerontology's insistence upon the Fall against "the facts" as but collusion with or mimicry of internationalist gerontology's Aging and Modernization paradigm is to ignore this centrality of the West as villain in the narrative. Gerontology in India is predicated upon a sense of Kulturkampf and of a consequent threat of the loss of self. Its movement both tracks this loss and challenges it through the reification of a morally superior Indianness, represented as the inclusive and embracing family.

Against both an imagined West and an experienced Here and Now, the family's internal relations are constituted not as shifting in time and potentially fractious but as anchored in a stable tradition and characterized by equipoise, love, and respect. The social memory of the joint family signifies a powerful alternative to the inferiorized self Ashis Nandy has posited as the enduring legacy of colonialism.[52] In *The Intimate Enemy*, Nandy, like Frantz Fanon, is concerned with the internalization of colonial difference by both colonizer and colonized and with the possibility of psychic decolonization, of a "recovery of self." Nandy's focus is upon the individual, and he uses the genre of biography to examine both the possibility and the pathos of individual efforts of decolonization. Many of his biographical subjects are critical figures in projects of religious and national construction, and the site of both loss and recovery of self in *The Intimate Enemy* tacks between the body and the nation.

For many individuals—for most of the adult residents of the two wealthier colonies of Varanasi and many in the Bengali quarter, and for many hundred middle-class interlocutors I have happened to meet in living rooms, clinics, coffeehouses and train compartments—the *family* rather than the autobiography or the vision of the nation was the site of loss and recovery in Nandy's sense. And if that which was lost and recovered is the "self," then it was very much a self *en famille*, the relational or "dividual" self psychological anthropologists and cultural psychologists continue to offer.[53] Yet unlike the telling of this anthropological story of India and its essentially familial self, I find the repetition of the decline of the joint family suggestive of familism (or relationality, fluidity, dividuality, and so forth), not as a static quality of "Indian culture" or "the Indian self" but rather as a site of anxiety and conflict, of the simultaneous maneuvers of loss and recovery in the construction of personhood and community within the space of an urban India modernity. Against history, against the particular experience of postcolonial modernity of an urban middle class, this repetition sustained the maintenance of an oppositional space of affect, memory, and wholeness called the Indian family.

That the self identified with this idealized joint family is "lost" within the temporal sequence of the narrative, abducted by Western modernity, is not a challenge to its authenticity. Even as the narrative charts this loss it affirms through its continual reiteration the ultimate equation of the Indian self with the joint family. The decline becomes less a loss than a superimposition of inauthentic Otherness.

By positing a decline from an idealized joint family, Indian gerontology maintains its critical difference from the West by keeping the "essential" India, where old people are never problems, apart from the actions of history, conceptualized as a progressive alienation from this essence. Through this exteriorized history, the move from a Golden Age in which old people never experience old age traumatically into the present—where families do undergo fission, generations do compete for control of authority and family resources, bodies do experience debility, and psyches do have difficulty negotiating these changes—never challenges the essentiality of the ideal family and of the enriched selfhood it sustains.

Thus, to read the repetitious and antimimetic quality of Indian gerontology's insistence upon the Fall as but collusion with or mimicry of internationalist gerontology's Aging and Modernization paradigm is to ignore the centrality of the West as villain in the narrative. As Susie Tharu in a different context has noted: "To suggest that . . . collusion is a total or adequate characterization of what takes place is to let the contestatory nature of . . . subaltern discourses slip through a theoretical sieve too gross for such fine gold." One must therefore be sensitive to "the subversions, elaborations, hybridizations, transformations, realignments or reappropriations that do take place within oppositional discourse."[54]

Obviously, the framing of the postcolonial Indian middle class as "subaltern" can be a troubling maneuver, and it has garnered its share of critics.[55] The ubiquity of the joint family narrative did not extend to lower-class families in the Bengali quarter and Nagwa slum, for whom it was virtually absent from discussions about old age. Still, in some strong sense I find it valuable to read *Aging in India* as "oppositional discourse." Gerontology in India is predicated upon a sense of difference that is mapped onto a polarity of India versus the West. Its originating point asserts the moral superiority of Indianness through its representation as the inclusive and embracing family. The continual invocation of the ideal joint family subverts both external and internal discourses of the inferiorized Indian self.

Even among the middle classes for whom the critique offered by Indian gerontology has relevance, its subversion of the unidirectionality of internationalist discourse can only be a partial one. On the one hand, the narrative implicit in Cowgill's vision of gerontology (the villain as native ignorance, the hero as the international gerontologist) is inverted. The West assumes the role of villain. On the other hand, the hero in the *Aging in India* narrative relies on a magical gift to defeat the villain: the gift is gerontological technology and its donor the international gerontologist. What is unique about gerontology as fairy tale is that the villain and the magical preceptor are one and the same. Despite the origins of narrative in a sense of the radical inappropriateness of Western experience, this very difference generates a preceptorship that assumes the universal applicability of a Western gerontological epistemology. As the narrative proceeds the role of the villain consequently shifts, from the West to the Indian government who will not fund these wonderful programs. The *Aging in India* series leaves us midnarrative: the hero now has the magical means to return the abducted victim home, but faces further trials as the victim's royal father (the state) has yet to relent and to allow a marriage between our hero and the victim. We are left with the hope that the king will relent and the victim will live happily ever after—but note—no longer defined by and for him or herself, but rather bound forever to a gerontological husbandry leavened with Western magic.

In two of the four institutions whose emergence I trace below, the founders soon discover that American gerontology doesn't work. But they do not turn to local models or epistemologies, for their narrative of the Fall erases these. Against the logic of the joint family narrative, they come to conclude that what is wrong with their practice is neither the technology nor its implementation but the errant nature of the Indian disciplinary object—the old Indian. Their response, interestingly, is to abandon her, to construct a gerontology without the contradictory presence of the old.

BP CHECKS: THE VOLUNTEER AGENCY

HelpAge India and its less prominent fellow agencies Age-Care India and Age Aid India have been among the most vocal advocates of the need for a response to the Fall. I focus here on Age-Care India and its founder N. L. Kumar. Kumar was a social worker by training, but his specific interest in gerontology was sparked by years spent living near the hill station resort of Mussourie, with its large expatriate community.

> I was in touch with some of the foreigners—mostly Americans, I would say—because Mussourie is, uh, their headquarters. So then what happened: I used to get literatures through them, about the old age homes and the old age social security measures abroad. I used to contact the embassies also to get some literature from the countries, and got interested. . . . I said, "This is a new field and a very pertinent area, to do the work for the aged, which is not looked after in our country."

Kumar, in the interview from which I am quoting, went on to offer a dismal picture of the condition of most elderly in India. The narrative flow here is not from the perception of a problem to the examination of the solutions others have found; rather, the admiration for the Other leads to the perception of not measuring up at home.

Kumar's first project was originally to be an old-age home. Though he and his colleagues could not acquire the land they wanted for the home and abandoned their plans, their choice of the old-age home, which they understood to be the exemplary site of gerontological practice in the United States and Europe, was noteworthy. The home, to have been built in the city of Dehradun, was not intended for impoverished old widows or other elderly destitutes but for wealthier retirees who were not wanted at home or who found living with their children difficult. The gap between Kumar's rhetoric of radical action and the intended beneficiaries of his early projects reflects the same duality as the *Aging in India* series.

Whereas Kumar's rhetoric was heartfelt, the founder of Age Aid India A. S. Bawa recognized that his organization is not structured to aid the poor and destitute. "The destitute receive assistance from the government and other quarters. But old people who are settled, who are middle class, may be entitled to a pension or other funds but lack the physical means or ability to get them. These old people are invisible. No one gives them much attention." Of these three Delhi-based organizations with the coda "India," Age Aid has been the least concerned with rural, poor, informal sector, and destitute elderly, and yet of the three its rhetoric most closely matches its practice. Age Aid's downplaying of the needs of the destitute suggests a denial rather than an erasure. Interestingly, of the three groups Age Aid is the least self-consciously modeled on a Western institution. Its literature has used the organization's Panjabi name "Birdh Sahaara" as often as the English title, and, not surprisingly, in the vernacular there has been no need for the "specific" of "Birdh Sahaara India." A Sikh-run organization at a time when Sikh identity does not suffer from a dearth of signifiers, Age Aid has incorporated both Western and Indian referents into its charter and practice, its origin narrative linking the exemplary actions of both the *Petits Frères des Pauvres* of Paris and the Sikh Gurus Nanak and Amar Das.

Kumar and Age-Care's next effort was designed specifically for lower-class elderly: a "mobile health checkup" aimed at those persons most deprived of health services. But the class specificity of the effort was signified more by Kumar and colleague's self-representation than by their actual intervention: "We went by the Delhi Transport Bus Service, because we didn't have any other means of communication. We were actually like Chinese barefoot doctors. And we adhered to that. We did everything on our two legs." The invocation of the imagery of rural-based populist health care was offered for an intervention planned around neighborhoods accessible to major urban bus lines; the aesthetics of mobility obscured questions of need.

The checkup was limited to a blood pressure test. Blood pressure, frequently referred to as *BP*, was central to middle- and upper-class narratives of aging and health for many of the people I interviewed. Men tended to "have BP" (whereas women tended to "have low BP"), and this having was frequently linked to the tensions associated with success. BP, when it appeared at all, was peripheral to lower-class narratives of illness in old age, and not the least because cardiovascular complaints were not as significant as the various manifestations of "weakness" in understanding the poor aging body. Debilitative complaints—what Djurfeldt and Lindberg have described as a coherent "poverty panorama"[56]—anchored the experience of the aging body in Nagwa slum and parts of the Bengali quarter. Such complaints suggest that the language of BP—the risks of accumulation, of the need for balance, of the hidden threats lurking within mandating a constant vigilance, thus "checkups"—may reflect a misplaced preventive effort. In contrast, the language of weakness brings out themes of hard labor by aged persons, of undernutrition, and of other forms of deprivation that might have informed a different understanding of aging. But to quote Kumar: "We sat down, decided that we should do [it] this way to reach the public and have our sort of educative awareness among the masses. . . . The people were ignorant. They did not know." The goal became convincing Delhi's poor elderly that they should be concerned about their blood pressure.

Once the mobile checkups began, along busy Delhi thoroughfares, two surprises confronted the Age-Care volunteers. First, few of those passersby who stopped for the checkup had high blood pressure. As Kumar indicated, "You'd be surprised—many cases were fine! Moneyed people or traders or businessmen would not come to us; they are more prone to these things. These—those that did come—are the people that are never checked by anyone. So when they came, we found generally these people didn't have much problem. Because they are physical workers, and they can stand any stress and strain."

Second, the few detected cases were not elderly persons but those in their thirties and forties. "We did not discriminate at that time because you could not find an old person on the roadside," said Kumar. This was not, in retrospect, such a tragedy. After all, Kumar concluded, "You can't do much to the old. Because they are having multiple problems. If you take care of the younger generation at that stage, you are doing a very useful work for the society.

The project was caught between conflicting interpretations of its object: an intervention designed for wealthier bodies indicated unexpected good health among the poor and confirmed the morality of their erasure; more salient criteria are ignored. An intervention located in a space traversed by younger bodies affirms the irrelevance of the old as gerontological object. Kumar realized that blood pressure checkups, roadside interventions, and age-segregated campaigns were inappropriate measures in Delhi. But rather than redefine the gerontological armamentarium, he blamed his failure upon the inappropriateness of lower-class elderly in and of themselves. As workers, "they can stand any stress and strain," and Kumar legitimated the narrowing of aid to that segment of Delhi for whom blood pressure was a critical sign of debility and control. And if "you can't do much to the old," old age itself is at fault, the impediment to successful gerontology. Thus the paradox for volunteer agencies searching for the signifiably deserving: barefoot doctoring for the middle class, Age-Care for the young.

FREE RADICAL EXCHANGE: THE GERIATRIC CLINIC

Geriatric clinics and research centers have begun to appear in several cities across India, most notably in the South, in Madurai, Madras, and Bangalore. In the history of the north Indian clinic I discuss below, the founder had a similar experience to that of N. L. Kumar and reached similar conclusions about the prospects for geriatrics in India. S. K. Nayer returned to India after more than twenty years practicing medicine in the United States, hoping "to make a difference" in India given his experience abroad. In his years among the old-age enclaves of southern Florida, he had become proficient in geriatric medicine. A geriatrics clinic seemed to make sense for Dehradun, the city where he settled, with its military and other enclaves with many retirees. Nayer had a large and well-appointed clinic built; a sign announced its specialty prominently: "Disha Geriatric Clinic."

As Nayer began to build a reputation as a highly competent physician, Disha's clientele slowly grew. They were not an exclusively or even primarily elderly group, however. "Geriatrics" was no more relevant to most patients' choice of a clinic than was "Disha." "People don't know what it means," laughed the clinic receptionist, referring to geriatrics. Yet the name is not meaningless, and even in Dehradun it has a local context. In nearby Mussourie, a physician's billboard that announced a bevy of degrees from Ayurveda to acupuncture to several spurious allopathic ("Western medical") certificates (but not the M.B.B.S. or M.D., the basic allopathic qualifications) had at the bottom of the list "geriatrician." Geriatrics has come to assume a particular authority in the signifying of medical competence. Throughout India, there are physicians who display the distinction *M.A.G.S.* on their billboards, acquired by joining the American Geriatrics Society. For most, it is a dubious qualification, but the frequency of appearance of *M.A.G.S.* suggests that even in legitimate contexts, the power of *geriatrics* may lie as much in the authority of the esoteric as in the discipline's specific content.

Treating a significantly younger population than he expected pushed Nayer to rethink his goals. In offering care to terminal cancer patients whom other medical institutions view as hopeless, he has maintained a commitment to defining medical care not in terms of cure but function, a central tenet of geriatrics. For the elderly and their families, however, he has realized that the medicalization of functionality is not marketable. Nayer has come to interpret this question of marketability in terms of the "practicality" of Indians, which he contrasted to the "always intervene" strategy of Americans. Indian practicality, he reflected in one of our conversations in 1989, masks the stinginess of an "agrarian personality." Yet the money spent by the families of terminal cancer patients in his clinic is at least as "impractical"; Nayer's analytic of medical realism is restricted to the elderly. Furthermore, though not all of the Disha patients were wealthy, most had means. "Making a difference" notwithstanding, this was an elite medical institution. Practicality as an explanation for the lack of old patients in a wealthy retirement community seemed insufficient. Like Kumar, Nayer discovered the resistance to a therapeutic practice exclusively for old people but did not question the relevance of his goals. Here again, the realization of the lack of aging as category led to self-blame and its displacement. For Kumar, the displacement was onto the mechanical invulnerability of the worker or the troublesome intractability of the old person; in Dehradun, Nayer invoked the shortsightedness of the agrarian personality.

Nayer's own interests suggest a different conception of the aim of geriatrics than that which he learned in the United States and was attempting to transpose to India. His office shelves were lined with a half-dozen geriatric medical textbooks, but with over twice as many American books on prolonged life extension: *The 120-Year Diet, Maximum Life Span, The Secrets of Long Life, Life Extension Reports, Prolongevity II, How to Live to Be 100, Anti-Aging News,* and the like. The authors of these books have sometimes represented their subject as geriatrics, but the self-help longevity genre runs counter to a central tenet of geriatric ideology, that the quality more than the quantity of life should be the physician's aim. Nayer was a good geriatrician in the strict sense of the term, but his heart lay with this alternative tradition of radical life extension and in particular with the theories of caloric undernourishment and free radicals of the American biologist Roy Walford.

Nayer's interest in Walford brought the imagined Other as possessor of the ideal technology of aging full circle, for Walford himself looks to India for inspiration. In brief, Walford has advocated a severely reduced caloric intake as essential for reducing free-radical damage to tissues on the molecular level.[57] He developed his thesis through laboratory research, but has offered as potential proofs of the preservative effects of undernutrition the superannuated yogis of India. Walford journeyed around India, and his travels culminated in a mountaintop rendezvous with an ancient guru. For the California scientist, the secret of successful aging was present in India's timeless customs.

Extremely well-read, Walford has cited *Suśruta* and *Caraka*—the classic Sanskrit medical texts—on *rasāyana* therapy as further evidence for his claim. *Rasāyana*, classical alchemy, is one of the eight traditional branches of Ayurvedic medicine and is concerned with therapies for extraordinary longevity. Given moves over the past century to legitimate Ayurveda by mapping each of its terms and concepts onto Western biomedical and folk categories, *rasāyana* has been labeled the "Indian geriatrics."[58] Because of the frequent appearance of Ayurveda and of *rasāyana* in texts and institutional settings that engage old age, I have devoted considerable attention to it in this book. But Walford's mention is brief, and the purging central to *rasāyana* and its associated *pancakarma* therapy differs significantly from the long-term caloric undernutrition he advocates.[59] Walford uses Indian terms rather like some Indian physicians profess membership in the community of geriatricians—as signifiers of legitimation by and through the unknown Other. Western "alternative science" in the 1970s and 1980s, most notably the writing of Fritjof Capra[60], frequently has used simplified and decontextualized images taken from Indian philosophy and religion to signify the universality and hermetic truth of its assertions. The signifier here is the superannuated Eastern Master, ubiquitously imagined with an undisclosed and powerful secret. From the Grand Abbot of Shangri-La to the Ancient One in *Doctor Strange* comic books to transplanted gurus like Muktananda, Maharishi, and Swami Bhaktivedanta of the Hare Krishna movement, the Eastern Master is a minor archetype in American popular culture. His secret stands for the true meaning of Eastern esoterica, inevitably lost to the Easterners themselves and only rediscovered through Western rationality. Thus the Grand Abbot, himself a European, waits until an Englishman lands in Shangri-La before handing over his reign; the Ancient One passes on his lore to Dr. Strange in Greenwich Village; and the late Bhaktivedanta's disciples founded a popular and beautiful temple in the holy town of Brindavin, where some gave lectures on the Bhagavad Gita when I visited there in 1983, proclaiming that only through its marriage with Western practicality can the esoteric truths of Hinduism be reclaimed. Similarly, through the power of physics and biochemistry, Capra and Walford offer their own disclosures of The Secret. Walford applies years of work with laboratory rats to offer his reader the philosopher's stone.

The lore of the Eastern Masters is more ambivalently perceived at home, and not because of a mythic lost essence. Though Walford cites *rasāyana* as a core element of Indian tradition, the creation of superannuation through medical therapy is "traditionally" viewed with considerable suspicion. Though they are prescribed for a long life span or extraordinary mental or physical powers, *rasāyana* tonics and other regenerative therapies in Ayurveda are frequently declared unsuitable for the elderly due to their extreme purgative or emetic effects. Many popular *rasāyana* medications, even one called "Geri-forte" and initially marketed for an older clientele, are primarily used by younger individuals for memory, virility, and strength, a point I will come back to in the next chapter. R. H. Singh of Banaras Hindu University, a prominent *rasāyana* scholar, noted both the difficulty in calling *rasāyana* geriatrics and the psychoactive properties of many *rasāyana* drugs in declaring, during an interview with me, that "*rasāyana* is not geriatrics; it is psychiatry."

Singh's contention builds on the ambiguity of the old body as legitimate medical object in classical medical and narrative traditions. As often as the fantastic restorations of *rasāyana* cures are described—the classic case is the restoration of the ancient sage, or rishi, Chyawan through a *rasāyana* preparation, the ubiquitous Chyawanprash subsequently named after him—so too are these cures portrayed as worthless panaceas.[61]

What is at stake in the "tradition" so insouciantly cited is well illustrated in Somadeva's eleventh-century compilation of tales, the *Kathāsaritsāgara*, in the story of the king Vinayashila. The king wants to remain forever young; he knows that as long as he remains youthful, the life of his kingdom will be happy and prosperous. When gray hairs appear, he summons his ministers to provide him with a longevity medicine. They demur, suggesting that in this fallen age such tonics can no longer be found, that any doctor who promises an end to old age is a quack, and that the physical changes of old age need not be viewed as decline but self-transformation and a path towards liberation. The king will not listen; he summons a duplicitous physician who promises a cure. Dr. Tarunachandra, or New Moon, places the king in a dark cave and feeds him strong purgatives that cause him to waste away from accelerated old age, *jarā;* eventually, the doctor kills the old king and replaces him with a young man who resembles him, and the story continues.[62]

The morality of geriatric intervention remains contested. At the session on *rasāyana* during the 1990 meetings of the International Association for the Study of Traditional Asian Medicine (IASTAM) in Bombay, the possibility of rejuvenating the elderly (as opposed to the middle aged) was a central and unresolved issue for delegates. Both in Somadeva's text and in Bombay, doctors with vested interests in the expensive transformations of *rasāyana* were certain of their geriatric applicability while others were more worried.[63]

The challenge in the *Kathāsaritsāgara* is not to the possibility of rejuvenation, but to its moral implications. Tarunachandra the doctor can kill the king not because the fruits of *rasāyana* are always iatrogenic but rather because seeing the primary task of aging as the denial of decline and death is unwise and unhealthy. In bringing geriatric knowledge to India, Nayer unintentionally assumes the role of Tarunachandra, who in claiming the old body as medical object denies the soteriologic power of old age. His interest in the latter-day *rasāyana* of Walford suggests that, like Kumar's, Nayer's heart lies with a preventive geriatrics aimed at the young; the old, like King Vinayashila, are ambivalent clinical subjects. The contours of Nayer's practice are split, between a desire to maximize function, treat those thought untreatable, and add life to years—the ideology of mainstream geriatrics—and the hope of adding years to life, of extending youthfulness by decades. Both the challenges of his clinical experience and his circuitous return to *rasāyana*, via California, offer Nayer the materials for a transformed geriatrics. In moving toward an intergenerational practice, Nayer takes up the challenge; but in his sense of failure and search for blame we confront again the split and unreconciled object, here the agrarian-minded peasant reluctant to medicalize old age, set against the hypergeriatric yogi, dedicated to the care of the aging body with superhuman results.

INTO THE WOODS: THE RETIREMENT ASHRAM

Not far from the Disha Clinic, a sign points one down a back lane to a "Vanaprastha Ashram" cum "human development centre." The sign, unlike that of the clinic, is in Hindi, and suggests an institution less immediately dependent on an imported universe of discourse. Ashrams, here connoting forest settlements of male and female sages who have renounced urban life, call to mind the isolated communities of elders visited by Ram and by the Pandava brothers during their years of exile in the Hindu Epics. *Ashram* here has a second meaning, a stage of life; the *vānaprastha āśrama* is one of the four stages of life (the order of *āśramadharma*) elaborated in the legal *dharmaśāstra* texts, the penultimate stage when individuals or couples leave their homes, having fulfilled their household obligations, and take up lives of renunciation in the forest.

The Manav Kalyan Kendra envisions itself as a refuge, a forest removed not only in space from the family and the life of the city or town, but in time, from the compulsions of modernity. In defining itself explicitly as a *vānaprastha* ashram, it draws on other "*vānaprastha* ashrams" founded in the colonial and post-Independence period, such as the large Arya Samaj ashram in Hardwar not far from Dehradun. The ideology and practice of the founders of the Manav Kalyan Kendra are in large measure rooted in Arya Samaj. This Hindu reform movement founded by Dayananda Sarasvati in 1875 quickly became popular among an emerging merchant-caste elite in Punjab and western Uttar Pradesh. In a series of handbooks, Dayananda had earlier offered his vision of renascent Hinduism to the urban middle classes of western India through a focus on the family and its ritual construction in space and time;[64] one important part of Arya Samaj practice was a close attention to the life course sacraments, or *saṃskāras*, and another, paralleling other contemporary reform movements, was attention to the plight of widows. The movement began building schools and other institutions in the 1880s; the building of widow houses, the forerunners to the *vānaprastha* ashrams, began in the early twentieth century.[65] The Hardwar ashram occupies a large physical plant, with both permanent residents and visitors, elderly women and men. Like the Manav Kalyan Kendra, it is a retirement ashram, a place of retreat and relaxation for urban middle-class pensioners and other elderly apart from their children, framed in terms of an ideology of a strong traditional family.

Retirement ashram: the phenomenon of fixed retirement for government servants and other formal sector workers is central here. The Manav Kalyan Kendra is a place to visit after retirement. The architecture of the human development proposed by the religious guide of its founders rests on the possibilities and expectations available within the formal sector. The ashram is an elite space, a resort in some ways similar to the Sun Cities of the United States but differing in its organization as a didactic, rather than recreational, community and as a place of retreat rather than neolocality. These *vanaprasthis* have not irrevocably disengaged from their families in Delhi and Bombay; their life in the forest is a sojourn rather than a departure. The ashram implies a mobile old body.

The charter behind the ashram frames it as a response to the decline of the joint family and the dangerous ascendancy of the West. The ashram was principally founded by Dr. J. P. Sharma, who runs a small homeopathic drug company. Sharma set up the Kendra as the embodiment of the ideals of his lifelong guru, Panditji; Panditji lives in the ashram and is supported by Sharma. In describing his vision for the ashram in an interview with me, Panditji enumerated the six principles that structure the practice of those who visit and stay there: devotion, contemplation, humanity, all are one, serve all, love all. The discipline he teaches, and its mode of enumeration, shares much with Arya Samaj practice.

When I spoke with Dr. Sharma, he was as much concerned with what Panditji represented as with the explicit content of the six principles: "You know, along with our country's improvements in industry and technology, etc., there is a dark side: the loss of values, of our religious heritage. India used to be a beacon to all. We are trying to preserve that tradition." For Sharma the central lost value is respect for the aged, the inverse benchmark of Westernization. Sharma and Panditji tried to approach the loss in two ways. First, they created the Vanaprastha ashram, a refuge from valueless modernity, for pensioners. Next, they created a second and parallel ashram, which was then being built next door: a Vriddhashram, or old age home, for the pensioners' parents. Old people will not come to this second home, they will be placed there. Side by side, the two ashrams call to mind two different images of the old body and two different responses to the "problem of aging." Sharma envisioned them, together, as a response to the lost family. Old people who have the option would leave their families and come to the Vanaprastha Ashram to study and develop. Other old people with different options would be taken care of in the Vriddhashram. Families, attracted by the Kendra's message, would settle nearby. Traditional values would radiate outward from Panditji and his aging disciples to infect the community—imagined as a large joint family— and the seed of a new Hindu renaissance would be planted. The disparate generational elements Sharma saw as characteristic of contemporary urban middle-class life—estranged old parents, nuclear households, and unwanted elders—are gathered in distinct spaces (development center, old age home, periphery) and placed in close proximity. Each of the spaces is justified as a metonym for the new family.

Thus, though a distinct alternative to family care and coresidence, the old age home can remain as a signifier for the strong Indian family. Against the experience of its residents, the ideology of the old age home offers them the inviolable and desirable family as the only legitimate gloss on identity. The family achieves a new hegemony at the moment it is perceived as being in decline; its inherent limitations, central to earlier constructions of old age, are no longer represented. The stage of *vānaprastha* is no longer an abandonment of the family, a moving beyond it to more essential truths appropriate to later life, but a return to "the family" as the very content of soteriology.

The neoorthodox Vriddhashram is distinct from the familiar institution of the widow house usually located in pilgrim towns like Brindavin and Varanasi. Such institutions still exist and will be discussed in chapter 8, but they differ from the Dehradun home in drawing meaning against—and not through—the family. The widows, beggars, and other poor elderly who live in or receive rations from charitable homes live the ethos of *sannyāsa*, the renunciate fourth stage, and not *gṛhasthya*, the familial second stage of the householder, or *vānaprastha*, the liminal third stage. In the stories they tell of their own lives and in the stories neighbors tell about them, their lives are made sense of in terms of a simultaneity of abandonment—the Bad Family, the travails of this world, the cruelty of God—and disengagement—the deeper truths of pilgrimage and prayer, the fruits of death at a *tīrtha*, a sacred place of crossing-over. The ambivalences of the widow house are brought out in Pankaj Butalia's film on widows in Brindavin.[66] Whether the stories of inmates are heard as tales of rejection by the family of the widow, or by the widow of the family, they suggest that old age is a time essentially in conflict with the values of younger family members, that the disengagement of the old body is predicated upon a rupture of familial continuity. The widow houses and charitable institutions of Varanasi are not reconstituted families: they are explicitly constructed as alternatives, whether understood as places of grace or wretchedness.

Sevā, or service to and respect for aged parents, is a domestic duty. Renunciation, the move away from the household through *vānaprastha* and *sannyāsa*, is in the Epic and Puranic texts framed as a move away from loving family members and from the comfort of receiving *sevā*. In setting up an old age home as the locus of *sevā*, the Manav Kalyan Kendra legitimates the dissociation of the dependent old body from the family. In claiming this old age home as an equivalent space to the family, the kendra denies the old person the alternative moral frame of disengagement through which to make sense of the alienation that it paradoxically demands. The only legitimate renunciates at the kendra are the mobile elderly, the pensioners who come on vacation. The object of gerontological solicitude is again dual: the aging self, the pensioner who leaves his or her family temporarily yet who is framed through the semantics of *vānaprastha;* and the aging other, the aged and dependent relative who becomes the embodiment of a revived ethic of *sevā* and is framed through the semantics of *gṛhasthya*, of the household. The order of the four *āśrama*s is inverted and collapsed as the totality of the family becomes the only legitimate narrative of the life cycle and its denouement.

MOTHERS VERSUS AUNTIES: THE OLD AGE HOME

Actually, she had no identifying mark on her. In fact, she was just an aunt. One of innumerable aunts. Not anyone's mother or father, just an aunt.

BANI BASU, "AUNTY"

Aloka Mitra has been instrumental in the creation of institutional environments for old people that are exemplars of the ideal old age home in American and European gerontological writing. At the two institutions—both called Nava Nir, or new nest—founded by the Women's Coordinating Council (WCC) of Calcutta in the early 1980s, the residents plan their own meals, discuss allotment of the budget, balance the books, control their own medication-taking whenever possible, and sometimes teach in neighborhood schools. The Nava Nir homes are highly permeable and decentered and do not resemble the total institutions described by Erving Goffman.[67] The decisions by staff and WCC members to allow residents to run many of the day-to-day affairs of Nava Nir are not an effort to create the "illusion of control" advocated in American old age home literature and social psychological research.[68] The old *māsimās*, the aunties, of Nava Nir must administer both the institution and their own lives; there is no one else to do it.

There is an irony in the juxtaposition of Nava Nir and the ideal geriatric institution in American professional literature. The latter suffers from the variant of the geriatric paradox discussed by Carroll Estes in *The Aging Enterprise*: interventions and institutions for old-age welfare offer a vision of normal and independent aging. These interventions are predicated upon the growth of an old-age welfare service sector. Such a sector of necessity demands dependent old bodies, and an "aging enterprise" emerges that maintains the very relations of dependency that its ideology challenges.[69] American gerontological efforts to produce old age homes that are less coercive and more open are often crude examples of the aging enterprise. A 1987 article in the *American Journal of Alzheimer's Care and Research*, "Design for Dementia: Re-creating the Loving Family," discussed how a "home-like environment" could be architecturally created that simultaneously offered patients "greater independence" and the staff "total control."[70] The design in question—multiple independent rooms ringing a central station from which staff could observe everything—is a literal translation of Jeremy Bentham's Panopticon prison design and is reminiscent of Foucault's discussion of permanent surveillance and disciplinary normalization in *Discipline and Punish*.[71]

In the Nava Nir homes, a different sort of economy of regulation and surveillance operates with the same surface effects as the panoptic institution. The disciplined order of Nava Nir is maintained not by a *planned* withdrawal of repressive institutional controls and their replacement by internalized and productive controls—the *māsimās* regulate their own movements, bodies, and lives and have no need of a staff to maintain their inmate status—but as a fiscal and social compromise by a welfare organization (the WCC) that could not afford to provide enough staff to take over many regulatory functions. One could read the almost complete absence of external regulation in the Nava Nir homes as the acme of either the "greater independence" the gerontological literature attempts to offer institutional inmates or the productive power of the welfare regime of Foucauldian modernity, but neither reading is sufficient.

What would be missing from such readings is an analysis of the sense of absence that permeates both the narratives of inmates and the interpretations of outsiders. For many persons of the Calcutta *bhadralok*, or middle class, who knew of the homes or who listened to my descriptions of them, the greater independence of residents was read as an abdication by a management that they felt could afford more staff and by children who had abandoned their parents. There was a strong contrast between my own initial perceptions of the Nava Nir homes and those of Calcuttan acquaintances: having long worked as a nursing aide in Boston in a home where inmates were routinely infantalized and in another where they were frequently physically restrained, and having worked to promote the concept of shared and interdependent living of groups of older persons, I was and remain enthralled by the independence of Nava Nir residents and by the openness of the institution. Mitra and her colleagues had created the fantasy home of mainstream gerontological literature, and had managed to do so without disciplinary training in gerontology. Social life within the home was not characterized by the redundancy and dehumanization found in more total institutions. Yet for the Calcutta residents whom I interviewed in 1989 and 1990, the Nava Nirs were pathetic places precisely because of the perceived lack of total dependence. The "independence" of residents pointed to the fact that they had no one to offer them proper *sevā*. Each of the multiple choices available to residents invoked their absent or uncaring children; their institutionally intensified individuality signified abject solitude.

This local critique assumed that the residents were put in Nava Nir, that they moved from a position of high to low dependency. The story Mitra told me of the homes' founding suggested a move in the opposite direction. During the United Nations Year of the Woman, Mitra related, she and several others within the WCC decided to create a refuge for poor old women "who had no one." Nava Nir would become a new family for homeless widows. Immediately, the institution was framed within an internationalist imperative and legitimated in terms of a triple-layered subordination: old, poor, and female.

The Nava Nir residents were almost all in their sixties or above, and from 1988–1990 all but one of the residents were women. But they were not the destitute widows Mitra's origin story envisioned. Two-thirds of the thirty I interviewed lacked sons to depend on. Only one resident out of the thirty came from a background of agricultural or urban labor; the others were all from middle- or upper-class families. Despite Nava Nir's subsidized costs, it remained out of reach for lower-class Calcuttans and rural Bengalis. The one exception, the only man at Nava Nir at the time, was sponsored by a kind employer. Yet this man was anything but sanguine about his good fortune when I met him: "Old age is a cursed life," he complained. "Go and talk to the man on the street. Why am I here? Very high accommodation here! Men like me are dying in the street!" He then glared at the superintendent. "Ask her!" She responded, "No, no, Dadu, that's not so."

The superintendent prided herself on establishing close kinlike ties with the old residents. They are not just addressed as her aunts and mothers, she noted, but think of her as their daughter. The old man rejected the institution as family: "If my friend didn't send money, do you think she would take care of me? Others live, they die, and their bodies are dumped into a handcart!" The old man's denial of Nava Nir as family differed from that of the middle-class Calcuttans whom I interviewed. For him, the rhetoric of the family was criticized not for disguising a lack of care for the old person and thus the decline of the joint family, but for disguising its rootedness in inequality and in the garbage bodies of the poor. He is lonely, the superintendent later confided to me. Yet in the old man's personal loneliness, the irony of his class position and the limits of any rhetoric of concern were manifest.

In another interview, Mitra offered a different charter of the institution, in which the initial impetus for Nava Nir preceded the International Year of the Woman. A WCC colleague of Mitra's was looking for an institution in which to place an elderly aunt but discovered that all available decent institutions were run by Christian orders like the Little Sisters of the Poor. She and others in the WCC began to consider the establishment of a nonsectarian home. Thus the second and underlying reason for the Nava Nirs: the need for an institution to house those elderly relatives of WCC members who lacked close family to support them.

These elderly relatives were all women. Nava Nir was founded primarily as a home for women; there were no undomicilable old uncles to generate a less gender-segregated institution. Old age presented different challenges to men and women, as the emergence of Nava Nir indicates; yet the *Aging in India* series and the agendas of most of the new Indian gerontological institutions have paid but passing reference to gender as critical to their field. In maintaining the polarity of the ideal and essential gerontocratic Indian past versus the fallen and inauthentic gerontophobic Indian present, the decline of the joint family narrative generates all difference from a single historical movement. Encompassing forms of difference such as class and gender that might suggest alternative readings of history are erased within the grand narrative of modernization and Westernization.

Who are the *māsimās*, poised between an external narrative viewing them as the cast-off mothers of the fallen joint family and an institutional history representing them as old aunts with less of a domiciliary claim upon their nephews and nephews' wives? Are they mothers or aunts, and what is the significance of this dichotomy? Both mothers and "aunts" are represented in Nava Nir, but the majority of residents had no sons: of my sample, one-third had living sons and two-thirds lacked them. Despite the narrative of the Decline, most of the "unwanted" residents are thus aunts, old women without sons who must depend on daughters who may be constrained by their husbands' families or upon more distant kin, and the rise of homes like Nava Nir suggest less a sloughing off of parents than the emergence of a different response to old people with weak claims upon family support.

Widows with and without sons are important markers in popular discourse, represented as mothers and as aunts. The needy old aunt is a prominent figure in Bengali and North Indian literature, classically in Banerji's *Pather Panchali* and Premchand's "*Būṛhī Kākī.*"[72] In each of these texts, the complex pathos of the family with an unproductive old woman is heightened by the absence of the figure of a selfish daughter-in-law. The nephew's wife, though she shares much of her persona with the daughter-in-law, is a more empathetic figure, struggling to support a family on threadbare wages with the added insult of an endlessly hungry old person who lacks a clear moral claim to a share of the food. Old-mother narratives, in contrast, are unforgiving in stressing the meanness of the daughter-in-law who abuses the old mother and the weakness of the son who lets her. In nineteenth-century Calcutta, this far less ambiguous narrative was visually represented in the art of the *patua* school of painters and woodcut printers as Ghar Kali, the End of the World: a wife riding on her husband's shoulders while his mendicant mother is dragged along on a leash held by her son (see frontispiece).[73]

These two figures embodying pathos—the old mother and the old aunt—are not only models of but models for making sense of aging within the family. The women of Nava Nir come from both groups; but the external critique envisions them all as mothers while the internal charter claims them all as aunts. Naming the old woman as aunt recognizes that old age is inherently a time of family stress, stress heightened when the moral claims of the old person upon the next generation are attenuated by distant kinship; the blame of imperfect *sevā* is deferred. Naming the old woman as mother, conversely, roots the difficulties of old age in the inadequacies of children.

The primary narrative of Indian gerontology, as I have stressed, elaborates the latter figure in a male or ungendered form: the neglected old parent. The errancy of children is displaced onto the West and its corruption, and is universalized. But the figure of the old mother has a more complex pedigree. Ghar Kali, the End of the World, bespeaks an apocalyptic consciousness. The young couple in the image neglecting their mother are not universal but located: the babu—the parvenu Indian government servant under the British—and his wife. The neglect of the old mother, the foppishness of the son, and the selfish disrespect of the modern wife together constitute a central image satirizing the emerging urban elite as emblematic of Kali Yuga, of the most corrupt last moments of the most corrupt age of humanity. Sumanta Banerjee has linked the *patua* folk art of mid- to late-nineteenth-century Calcutta to a broader critique of the babu in lower-class urban popular culture.[74] Following his argument, the figure of the old mother enters public narratives in the nineteenth century as a subaltern or proletarian symbol of elite excess.

Sumit Sarkar cautions against identifying the work of the *patua*s and associated genres with an exclusively or even primarily lower class level of culture. He suggests that "their patrons and consumers could include many of the bhadralok [the emerging urban bourgeoisie]. . . . In so far as a specific strata can be distinguished at all—always a problematical venture in matters of culture—it would be rather the world of genteel poverty, depressed upper-caste literati within a kind of pre-industrial lower middle class."[75] Ashis Nandy, in arguing that the upwardly mobile *bhadralok*—"made psychologically marginal by their exposure to Western impact"—turned to a reactionary defense of traditional prerogatives and in particular to an elaboration of "the fantasy of feminine aggression towards the husband," similarly suggests a Kulturkampf in which the satire of the Ghar Kali appealed to the parvenu *bhadralok* as well as to lumpen and marginalized groups.[76]

The appeal of the ironic trope in which the narrative of the abject old mother is popularized thus extends across class within the growing urban space of nineteenth-century Calcutta. The old mother is a complex sign upon which several distinct stories are superimposed: at the same time a mocking of upper-class morality, a lament for the decline of precolonial constellations of power, and a framing of the elite self against the corruptions demanded by a new politics of culture. However, within the uniformity assumed by the modern gerontological logic of a single universal problem of aging, the polysemy of the old mother is reduced to a monoglot narrative. The Ghar Kali image, sensitive to the cultural transformations of colonialism but rooted in a sense of internal difference and disequilibrium (of gender and social class), comes to signify the uniform aging of the theoretically classless and ungendered old person. The lower-class readings Ghar Kali that Banerjee documents are echoed in the old man's frustration at being in Nava Nir—the rejection of the rhetoric of universal care for the aged as upper-class self-interest—but find no place within the contemporary images constituting internationalist gerontology or *Aging in India*.

The modern discipline of *Aging in India* does not create the suffering old person; as the old mother and aunt, the figure was and is ubiquitous. What is created is an effort at hegemony, a universalization of a particular set of interpretations of the figure, rooted in the responses of urban elites and petty bourgeoisie to questions of identity within the colonial milieu. What is erased is the old woman as a signifier of social difference. In the social milieu enveloping Nava Nir, the old resident signifies the universal old mother, pointing to the callousness of children. In the informal charter of the institution discussed by Mitra, the threatening old mother is replaced by the more ambivalent old aunt, pointing to the existential dilemmas of aging. In the science of aging as constituted by *Aging in India*, the old woman is replaced by the putatively ungendered old man, pointing beyond the particular needs of real old persons to the search by elites and rising middle classes for a stable Indian identity, embodying crisis and absence and yet, in the sensibility of familism and *sevā* he invokes, offering the possibility of totality.

Aitaśa Pralāpa

The Athārva Veda, the fourth of the ancient Vedas whose authority grounds Brahmanical practice, has a section of its twentieth book termed the *Aitaśa pralāpa.* Ralph Griffith, at one time principal of the Sanskrit College in Varanasi, published an Athārva Veda translation in 1895 and 1896. Of the *Aitaśa pralāpa*, Griffith noted: "Regarded as uninspired productions, these hymns are hardly susceptible of intelligible translation or explanation."[1]

A later Vedic text, the Aitareya Brāhmana, offers a story explaining the origins of these verses' inexplicability. Aitaśa was a sage, of an important lineage. When he began to speak the words that would become the Athārva Veda hymns, one of his sons heard only incoherent sounds, prattle, *pralāpa.* In the terms of Nagwa slum, *bakbak.* The son tried to stop the father from talking, believing him mad. Aitaśa cursed his son for murdering his speech. Aitaśa's words were then spoken, and have been spoken by generation after generation ever since, in the monumental act of remembering, that is, learning to repeat the Veda.

Aitaśa, if he lived at all, lived long ago, and neither his words nor his story are necessarily paths toward thinking about parents, children, voice, silence, and madness today. And yet the story sticks. A father's speech, a son's inability to hear it as carrying meaning. An intergenerational conflict over the authority of interpreting the word. Accusations of madness versus the possibility of a sacred speaking. Anger giving coherence in the form of the curse versus *pralāpa* giving only a contested and feeble voice. The father defeating the son's efforts at reinterpretation and silencing, and generation after generation remembering and repeating the contested speech of the father. Until, for a far later generation, a Britisher teaching Sanskrit in Varanasi rereads the contest as a problem of philological science against obscurantism, erases the predicament of the Indian father amid his nation's own paternalist claims, and discovers the sad truth of *pralāpa*: "uninspired productions."

FOUR

Memory Banks

in which the conflicts of old age are differentially embodied,
memory is capital in a lottery-ticket world,
and philosophers debate what's left after everything is forgotten

THE EMBODIMENT OF ANXIETY

In *King Lear*, the origins of the old king's madness are disputed. "O sir, you are old," declare Lear's eldest daughters, but the king charges that it is "filial ingratitude" that has led him toward dotage, lunacy, and ruin. The etiologic debate is repeated in *Apne Begāne*, a 1989 Hindi film that draws on *Lear* in its tale of a father neglected by his two eldest sons and their wives and respected by his youngest son. The older sons and daughter-in-laws enfeeble the old man, and yet like Lear's the father's own inappropriate decisions allow his children to gain the initial advantage. In both narratives, old age and generational conflict reinforce each other as debilitating causes in a spiral of increasing senility, and in both, a similar question is posed: Is it the bodily logic of old age or the ingratitude and cruelty of the Bad Family that lead to the decline of the patriarch?

Lear has become a global site where the contested phenomenology of old age has been continually reinterpreted and reworked; in the United States, the play has been invoked to capture questions of Alzheimer's and identity.[1] *Apne Begāne* is a different sort of reworking. The film and the play differ on many points. Sons and their wives, not daughters, are envisioned as the primary caretakers of old persons in *Apne Begāne*. The old man in the film regains his prerogatives and his health at the end, and the selfish children are chastised and readmitted to the fold of the joint family. In *Lear*, to the end we are left not knowing if Cordelia's return and death have restored the king's mind or shattered it completely; his bitter closing lines vacillate between the howl of recognition and blithe confusion.

The narratives differ as well in how the signs of decline and suffering are represented. *King Lear* is a tale of escalating madness, an inversion of the conjoint wisdom and bodily debility of old age—

When the mind's free,
The body's delicate

into dotage and insensibility to physical degradation:

> the tempest in my mind
> Doth from my senses take all feeling else
> Save what beats there.[2]

Both old age and the Bad Family are experienced as a turbulence, located in the overlapping frames of mind and heart. The torment of mind is both set against the lesser malady of bodily aging and, as in the following quotation, united to it in a loss of self:

> we are not ourselves
> When nature, being oppressed, commands the mind
> To suffer with the body.[3]

Against the concern in Shakespeare's play with the mind and heart of old age and their complex relationship with the body and the family, the father in the Hindi film grows physically weaker and emotionally more depressed. His debility is never expressed as madness: the exterior wasteland of the play becomes the empty interiors of the unloving home or of the old man's weak body; the tempest becomes the silence of the marginalized or foolish voice. The debate over the origins of suffering in old age are mapped onto the old body in a different way, as a physical weakness encompassing strength and affect and not as a madness that troubles the hierarchy of mind and body.

In her ongoing study of an urbanized Hindi-speaking village near New Delhi, Sylvia Vatuk has examined the anxieties expressed by individuals confronting their own aging. The women and men she interviewed expressed frequent concern over the possibility of losing the support of their children in old age. Vatuk calls this concern "dependency anxiety"; we will turn to a fuller consideration of it in the next chapter. The persons she interviewed see physical debility as the most likely cause of the loss of support. By physical debility, Vatuk refers to the multiple embodiments of lost function described by those interviewed: the weakness (in Hindi, *kamzorī*) of ears, eyes, hands, feet, voice, and mind. Of these, hands and feet as a conjoint pair were the sine qua non of the projected losses of old age: "A phrase repeated [countless times] refers to the importance of having 'working hands and feet' (*hāth pair calte hue*) if one expects to receive respect and care from the younger generation." *Hāth pair* as the embodiment of anxiety is a frequent theme in the voices she cites:

> Old age is like a second childhood. In the first childhood, oh how lovable one seems to others! But do you think it is like that in old age? One can't walk properly, hands and feet don't do their work, eyes and ears become weak.

> As for old age, as long as one's hands and feet are working, everyone gives one food.

> It is good to die when one's hands and feet are still working: that is a good death.[4]

Second childhood—a frequent theme in European constructions of the aging self and senile body, including the text of *King Lear*—is expressed through multiple weaknesses and anchored by *hāth pair* rather than by mental weakness or madness.

The weakness of old age in these voices is not limited to work-related debility. In two of the three passages Vatuk cites that I include above, the informant goes on to move from *hāth pair* to the quality of the voice itself in old age:

> An old person says something and others just say, "Oh, let him babble! That's just the way he is!" . . .
>
> If you complain, they say, "Even in old age he wants to be satiated! He just lies there in bed all day and keeps giving orders! No work to do, no occupation, just lying there babbling about one thing or another all day long!"

Babbling here is read polysemically—as the refusal of children to listen to the meaningful requests of old people they no longer wish to support and as part of the primary weakness of old age itself. On the surface, the babble of Vatuk's informants translates into the doting prattle of Lear as heard by his elder daughters—always demanding, childish, and without meaning. But for the Delhi villagers of Vatuk's study, the troublesome voice is located within a very different embodiment. Whether its source be the biology or pathology of old age, or the social psychology and intergenerational politics of the family—the unresolved problèmatique of *Apne Begāne* and *King Lear*—the babble of the old voice is heard as emanating from very different constructions of the senile body.

That the personal and social distress of old age is *embodied*, and embodied in different ways at different times and for different communities, suggests a way into the unreflexive obviousness of Alzheimer's disease as American brain and body killer. In its specific construction as "the nation's fourth leading killer," Alzheimer's draws upon a culturally and historically located embodiment of the anxiety of getting old. This piece of epidemiological casuistry reflects the association between a clinical diagnosis of dementia and death, often secondary to pneumonia. On the surface, the relation between the progressive loss of brain function with Alzheimer's and a set of neurally mediated bodily processes that may precipitate pneumonia and other disease appears a matter of physiology *tout court*. But the move to understand this relationship as the primary cause of a person's illness and death suggests a different kind of language game. Institutionalized, chronically bedridden, and disoriented persons are likely candidates for pneumonia, but many of the precipitating causes of disease are not physiological and universal but social and contingent consequences of their diagnosis of Alzheimer's: being institutionalized and thus subject to a range of often virulent "nosocomial" pathogens, being physically restrained or being quickly and often forcibly fed by underpaid and disinterested staff and thus likely to get food into one's bronchial passages, being infantilized and left bereft of meaningful decisions and mindful activity and thus having one's disorientation and cognitive decline exacerbated. These pathogenic processes all stem from "Alzheimer's," but as physiological consequences of social responses to the old and demented body: its immobilization and infantilization, under the rationale of care and protection, within a discursive conjuncture in which Alzheimer's is a sign of the loss of selfhood. The language of "the nation's fourth leading killer" and the epidemiological practices that sustain such numbers erase this web of social and physiological pathogenesis, encompassing a complex set of practices—and possible sites of social intervention—within the seamless link between brain tissues and lung disease. The social production of the pathetic, institutionalized, and increasingly vulnerable senile body is reduced to the plaques and tangles of Alzheimer's. The death of weak and socially constrained old people is embodied through their brains. In old age, Alzheimer's becomes a critical metaphor for death.[5]

The centrality of Alzheimer's in America—the legitimacy of its consummate embodiment, such that one can simply and meaningfully say that someone died "of Alzheimer's"—is marked by its key symptom, forgetfulness. Memory loss, and "cognitive loss" more generally, becomes metonymically identified with the wide range of behavioral and neuropsychological changes consequent with dementia. As discussed in the last chapter, Berrios has convincingly suggested that the origins of this metonymy lie with Kraepelin's rewriting of Alzheimer's first cases to create a new and far less inclusive category of "Alzheimer's disease."[6] But the cognitive focus of Alzheimer's—as opposed, for example, to a focus on affective or other behavior change or on delusional symptomatology—suggests a broader cultural and historical consensus, that memory is the key to the self.

The forgotten word for many Americans immediately signals the devastations of "what's-his-name's disease." *Alzism* is a term used informally by some physicians to describe a syndrome of middle-aged and older Americans with complaints of memory loss and fears of Alzheimer's but no abnormal findings on neurological or mental status examinations. Other sources of memory loss—stress, the various paraphraxes traced by Freud,[7] the border category of benign senescent forgetfulness, the possibility of a cognitive style of "absentmindedness"—are increasingly forgotten. Reports of finding the traces of future Alzheimer's in the communicative patterns of young nuns, whatever the status of its science, intensify the anxiety around each unremembered name. A senior physician in Boston noted to me in 1990:

> My wife and I help each other out—she says, "What was his name . . . " and I finish the sentence. Together, we remember for each other. We joke about Alzheimer's—"what's his name's disease." We joke a lot, but our joking disguises a fair amount of concern. . . . My mother became disoriented last week, in her apartment building. My sister came for her and brought her back to her apartment, but my mother refused to believe that this was her apartment. My sister had to ask her again and again, "If this isn't your apartment, then whose pictures are on the wall?" . . . Each time we forget a word, we worry about ending up like that.

Memory, in both professional and popular literature and representations of Alzheimer's, becomes the necessary and sufficient index of the embodiment of aging, how one worries, in the words of this physician, about ending up.

Just as minds and brains are not the only possible embodiments of the etiologic and existential crises of old age, so weak memory is not the only way of perceiving the multiple losses of dementia. The following chapters suggest that in the Varanasi neighborhoods of my study, markers of affective change were often experienced as far more salient indices of pathological aging than memory loss per se. That old people forget, and that some forget far more than others, was common knowledge and common sense. But memory loss did not usually anchor the first-person narratives of persons exploring their own present or past aging or the second-person descriptions of others. When it was present, it tended to be as a loss experienced by middle-class families, particularly in their concern about old men. More generally, memory became a critical sign of the self primarily within third-person discourse, in the abstract discussion of the body and its relation to the community, the state, and the cosmos. Before I move beyond memory to the anger, silence, and babbling central to the narratives of my own fieldwork, I want to consider these third-person constructions. What does it mean to speak of memory and forgetting? What is the relationship between memory and bodily, social, and economic power? Are there other processes of embodiment—more critical than the anxiety of old age and the experience of senility—that soak up the act of forgetting?

THE PROMISE OF *RASĀYANA*

Ayurveda literally suggests the authoritative knowledge of longevity; as such, not only *rasāyana* but all *aṣṭānga*, all eight branches of medicine, are seen as critical to a clinical practice preserving and extending one's years. Contemporary Ayurveda draws on a multitude of clinical, commercial, regulatory, research, and pedagogic institutions; ongoing oral traditions of practice; and a series of primary and commentarial texts in defining its approach to the body and to therapy.[8]

Professional Ayurveda organizes itself through institutional forms parallel in most cases to allopathic biomedicine: Ayurvedic hospitals organized like colonial allopathic institutions; Ayurvedic medical schools that include a substantial international biological curriculum; Ayurvedic governing, accrediting, and regulating bodies; Ayurvedic pharmaceutical houses and "detail men" doing direct marketing to physicians; and Ayurvedic laboratories, research institutes, and journals. Charles Leslie and Paul Brass have described the diverging pulls of integrationist and purist schools of Ayurvedic practice. Integrationists have argued that medical care should go beyond the historical limitations of "systems" by introducing biomedicine into Ayurvedic physiology and methodology and Ayurveda's diagnostics, pharmacopaea, and allegedly holistic epistemology into other medical cultures. Purists have seen such compromise as a denial of the efficacy of Ayurveda as a totalizing and sufficient system of care.[9]

The integrationist-purist divide began to get recast in the late 1980s and 1990s in terms of the changed meanings of the global and the local, with particular relevance to the study of *rasāyana*. Two processes have been particularly critical: first, the intensified mass-marketing of "Ayurvedic" products to the middle class through the growth of television and print media, leading to changes in popular conceptions of Ayurveda as a set of indigenous commodities, and new debates over the boundaries of what can be termed "Ayurvedic"; second, the emergence of diasporic Indian ("nonresident Indian," or NRI) centers of Ayurveda, reconceptualizing and recommodifying it to both non-Indian and NRI consumers. The key figure in this latter process has been the allopathic physician turned New Age guru Deepak Chopra. Chopra is a fascinating figure in many respects: the nineties version of the Eastern Master in American popular culture, he has transformed the archetype. Out with the long beard and love beads, the appeal to timeless transcendence set to *khayal* music à la Ravi Shankar; Chopra is the guru in a business suit or semi-ethnic casual wear, whose infomercials appear gratis on public television, propelling the enormous American sales of his books offering an ageless body. Among Indian *vaidya*s, Ayurvedic doctors, sentiment toward these changes has been mixed. On the one hand, Ayurveda has become an internationally known and increasingly respected and remunerative field; on the other, Indian *vaidya*s, whether purist or not, have had ever less autonomy in defining the legitimate parameters of their field given rapid shifts in national and global markets.

Most Banarsis whom I interviewed through the better part of a decade conceptualized their alternatives in medical care not as a choice of system or epistemology but of the type of drug likely to be prescribed or of the physician's persona. Ayurveda was frequently identified with the charisma of a class of physicians, manifest in the quality of the *jaṛībūṭī*, the herbal preparations, selected and compounded under their supervision. *Jaṛībūṭī* was not only a matter for physicians; many householders, women and men but particularly women, learned to be proficient in the selection of herbs and other materials from the bazaar shops of herbalists and in their compounding and prescription. Professional Ayurveda differed not only in the physician's greater skill in diagnosis and therapy but in the quality of his herbs and of their preparation. With intensive advertising of standardized products by Ayurvedic pharmaceutical houses, the charisma inherent in the expert physician's *jaṛībūṭī* was being challenged by new forms of charisma, the familiarity of the clinical encounter and the authority of the local expert challenged by the familiarity and authority of the trademark.

Ayurveda is organized and popularly understood not only through these institutional and market structures but as indexical sets of practices and as iconic sets of texts. Pulse therapy, though peripheral to many textual constructions of the field, remains the sine qua non of the astute clinician who is said to be able to diagnose complex and previously untreatable disorders with a single reading of the afflicted person's pulse. The act of compounding—the assumed preparation of each composite drug with the specific patient in mind—similarly is a cardinal sign differentiating Ayurvedic practice from other kinds of healing. The manipulation of surfaces, entrances, and exits—the various and often violent purgations, eme-

ses, sweatings, oilings, and enemas of a set of practices often grouped together as
pancakarma—is a third critical component of the constitution of the discipline.[10]

Contemporary textual readings of Ayurveda are based on five classes of texts,
frequently cited by *vaidyas*—what are often called the greater triad and the lesser
triad, subsequent digests and commentaries, contemporary research monographs,
and internationalist apologia. The most authoritative are the two major texts of
the greater triad, the *Suśruta Saṃhitā* and the *Caraka Saṃhitā*, both dated by Jean
Filliozat in their redacted forms to the second or first century B.C.E. with little certainty.[11] These are the texts referred to by the biologist Roy Walford in his description of the journey to the mountaintop yogi.

Contemporary monographs draw on classical sources and modern research
protocols, and often are structured through a common narrative placing the re-
searcher's project within the twin legitimating frames of humoral holism and a
hodgepodge of scientific references drawing on theoretical physics, artificial intelligence, and various forms of systems theory.[12] Apologia by Western scientists
turning East—like Fritjof Capra's *The Tao of Physics*,[13] legitimating "Eastern
thought" because of its apparent congruencies with post-Newtonian physics—become powerful signs ratifying an oppositional construction of Ayurveda. At the
1983 annual Dhanvantari Puja function held by the Institute of Medical Sciences
of Banaras Hindu University (which had parallel biomedical and Ayurvedic faculties), paeans to Dhanvantari, a patron deity of medicine, and to Sushruta, the
redactor of the eponymous text who was by tradition a local Banarsi, were surpassed in number by equally routinized lauds to Capra.

Memory, *smṛti*, is explicitly fortified by many *rasāyana* remedies. The *vidanga
kalpa*, detailed in *Suśruta*, is typical of the extreme iatrogenic effects of *rasāyana*
therapy; against the aesthetics of oppositional holism, *rasāyana* offers a different vision of therapy:

> One Drona measure of Vidanga (seeds) should be boiled in the way of preparing
> cakes in an Indian cake-pan. When the watery portion (of the cakes) have been re-
> moved (evaporated) and the Vidanga-grains well boiled, they should be taken down
> and well pasted on a stone-slab. They should then be kept in a strong iron pitcher
> after having been mixed with a copious quantity of the decoction of Yashti-madhu.
> The pitcher should be buried in a heap of ashes inside a closed room during the
> rainy season and preserved there during the four months of rain; after that period
> the pitcher should be taken out (of the ashes). Its contents should then be conse-
> crated with (appropriate) Mantras by uttering them a thousand times and should be
> taken every morning in suitable quantities after the system has been thoroughly
> cleansed (by appropriate emetics and purgatives, etc.). The diet should consist of
> cooked rice and clarified butter mixed with a copious quantity of the soup of Mudga
> pulse and Amalaka cooked with a small quantity of Sneha and salt; and should be
> taken after the digestion of the medicine. The patient should lie on the ground (and
> not on a bedding). Worms would be found to have been issuing out of the body after
> the regular and continuous use of the medicine for a month, which should be ex-
> tracted with the aid of a pair of bamboo tongs or forceps after the body had been

anointed with the Anu-taila (described before). Ants would be coming out of the body during the second, and vermins [*sic*] (Yuka) in the third month of the use of the medicine which should also be removed as in the preceding manner. The hair, nails, and teeth begin to fall off and become dilapidated in the fourth month of its use.

The medicine destroys the old body through the sequential expulsion of its festering insides to build a new and transformed one, characterized by the guna (quality) of *sattva*, lightness and truth. The process of destruction both mirrors the decay of old age and through it offers a radical form of purification, ridding the body of its insectile temporality.

In the fifth month the body beams with a divine glow, becomes resplendent as the midday sun, and exhibits features which specifically belong to the etherial [*sic*] being. The ears become capable of hearing the faintest and remotest sound (under its use), and the vision extends far into space and beholds objects at a great range (which is not usually given to mortal eyes to descry). The mind, shorn of the qualities of Rajas (action) and Tamas (nescience), becomes possessed of Sattva (illuminating principles or true knowledge). Things are permanently and indelibly impressed upon his (user's) memory at a single hearing and the faculty of invention wonderfully expands. Old age and decay permanently vanish and youth returns to stay in him for good, bringing with it an elephantine strength and a horse-like speed, and he is enabled to live for eight hundred springs.[14]

This *sattvic* body is superhuman, with an incredible life span. Its powers include a mind, or *mānas*, capable of forming strong impressions and thus endowed with an indelible memory. Forgetting cannot occur because of the strength of the process of impression-formation.

Memory loss is here linked with the weaknesses of aging, and the idealized youthful body offered is a powerful rememberer. Memory is not distinct from bodily weakness, not compartmentalized because of its association with *mānas;* like vision and hearing, it is a bodily process linked to the actions of mind. "Mind" in *Suśruta* is understood through the categories of the Nyaya-Vaisheshika philosophical systems as an organ, atomic (that is, without significant mass or volume) and not restricted to the boundaries of the body with which it is associated. Mind is that organ that instantaneously travels through space, linking a perceived object with the sensory organ in the body through which it is seen and linking the self with sensory organs through the registering of impressions, or *saṃskāra*s. *Rasāyana*, through the fortification of *mānas*, generates ageless *saṃskāra*s.

Caraka summarizes the cumulative effects of *rasāyana*: "One attains longevity, memory [*smṛti*], intelligence [*medhā*], freedom from disorders, youthful age, excellence of lustre, complexion and voice, optimum strength of physique and sense organs, successful words, respectability and brilliance."[15]

These multiple qualities are not simply lumped together as the qualities of youth. *Rasāyana* is based on a physiology of decline in which the body suffers successive and periodized losses over the life course. A well-known line from a lesser triad text, the fourteenth-century *Śārṅgadhara saṃhitā*,[16] chronicles the progression of losses decade by decade: "Childhood, growth, colour and complexion, intelligence [*medhā*], skin health, vision, semen, valour, intelligence [*buddhi*], physical capacity, spirituality and life—these get lost in successive decades of life."[17] *Smṛti* is not explicitly mentioned in the *Śārṅgadhara* passage, raising the question of its association with either or both of the two losses translated as "intelligence," *medhā* and *buddhi*. For Ayurvedic physicians I interviewed in Varanasi, *medhā* differs from *buddhi* because of the former's explicit association with *smṛti*. The *Śārṅgadhara* passage is often cited, and it suggests that memory loss is located in the aging of younger bodies. *Medhā* in Hindi means "*bāt ko smaran rakhne kī mānsik śakti*," the mental power of retaining-remembering something.[18] The onset of diminished *medhā* is framed as a problem of a younger body.

Rasāyana's relevance to older bodies has been and remains contested. The destructive recreation of the body is too strenuous for certain classes of persons, according to most texts, including old persons. Tales of rejuvenated old persons, such as Rishi Chyavana, are exemplary but draw as much on the power of the ascetic as on that of the medicine. On the cover of J. K. Ojha's *Chyavanaprasha: A Scientific Study*, the sage serenely sits amid a group of scantily clothed young women bringing him platters full of *āmvlā* fruit and the other ingredients of Chyawanprash. The presence of the women both draws attention to the sage's indifference to their allure and yet offers the reader the object of *rasāyana* as a body steeped in sensuality.

Chyavana was a powerful and angry aged rishi who cursed a king whose daughter accidentally poked the rishi's eyes with a thorn. To win back the saint's affections and avoid the curse, the king married his daughter to Chyavana. The woman's body quickly wore down the old sage's vitality. When the divine twins and physicians the Asvins gave him the secret of Chyawanprash, he was rejuvenated: "This very saint regained youth and vitality by the use of this composition. The word youth means manhood and sex power, because saint Chyawan had become dear to innumerable virgin youths."

Though the promise of the drug is here the total rejuvenation of the old, Ojha's text is less a paean to its efficacy than a caveat to young men. Chyavana lost his vitality, Ojha warns us, because of semen loss consequent upon sex with his wife, "leaving him convalescent."

> In reality semen is not only the means of producing children but is also needed to regulate the glandular function of the body for its nourishment and development. Thus it regulates the life. Too much discharge of semen adversely affects the physical organs and reduces the human life by profusely weakening the body. Thus it is said "celibacy is life."[19]

The text details some early signs of semen loss—feeble voice, changes in the complexion—and roots senescence in sex and masturbation. Two "cures" are simultaneously offered, the supernatural transformation of Chyavana through the tonic and the injunction against ejaculation. Against the fantastic medicine possible for the exemplary body of the old sage, a therapy of seminal conservation is advocated. The meaning of *rasāyana* is translated from fortifying drugs for exemplary old bodies to fortified boundaries for normal young ones.

Chyawanprash, the gift of Chyavana to posterity, like the *vidanga* preparation described earlier in the classical texts, specifically preserves and improves memory among a host of other qualities. Associated with Chyavana's body, the drug offers memory to "even the old." *Caraka* offers the recipe for the drug and then notes:

> This is the famous "cyavanaprasa," an excellent rasayan. Particularly it alleviates cough and dyspnoea, is useful for the wasted, injured and old people and promotes development of children. It alleviates hoarseness of voice, chest diseases, heart disease, vatarakta, thirst and disorders of urine and semen. It should be taken in the dose which does not interfere with the food (intake and digestion). By using this (rasayan) the extremely old Cyavana regained youthful age. If this rasayan is used by the indoor method, even the old attains intellect, memory lustre, freedom from diseases, longevity, strength of senses, sexual vigour, increased agni (digestion and metabolism), fairness of complexion and carmination of wind. One, shedding the form of the old age, puts on that of the fresh youth. (Thus is said cyavanaprasa).[20]

Kuṭīpraveśikā, the "indoor method," refers to the importance of place in *rasāyana* therapy. *Rasāyana* is not just a compendium of drugs, but a series of orienting and purifying procedures at the center of which is the ingestion of the drug. The patient must be oriented both to time and to place. During the IASTAM session in Bombay discussed in the last chapter at which the applicability of *rasāyana* to the old was debated, a second debate was over the heightened commodification of the tonic. Over-the-counter, mass-produced *rasāyana* tonics, mostly variations on Chyawanprash, have been increasingly marketed as rejuvenators and energizers without the therapeutic context of *pancakarma* purification or the specification of the patient's environment. A vocal minority of those present in Bombay felt the sale of such tonics, without attention to therapeutic context, was dangerous or at best of no value to the patient.

The indoor method involves a hut for the patient to receive therapy, apart from the household space and the family. The separation of the body from family space suggests the third and fourth ascetic stages of life, *vānaprastha* and *sannyāsa*. Like *sannyāsa*, the entry into which involves a ritual death of the body and the creation of a "deathless" body separate from domestic space, the indoor treatment separates the body undergoing the more corporeal death and rebirth of *rasāyana*. The hut is both space of seclusion and womb of rebirth. As a space of seclusion, it can only be entered by certain types of persons:

> [A] cottage should be built in an auspicious ground, facing eastward or northward and in a locality which is inhabited by king, physician and brāhmaṇas, holy saints, is free from dangers, auspicious and with easy availability of necessary accessories. It should have sufficient space area and height, three interior chambers one after the other, a small opening, thick walls and should be comfortable for the seasons, well-

clean and favourable. It should be impermeable for undesirable sound etc. (sense objects), free from women, equipped with necessary accessories and attended by physician with medicaments and brāhmaṇas.[21]

Not only are women to be excluded, but for the practical reasons of the cost and time of the indoor method, all but the wealthy: "The indoor method of rasayana treatment is advised for those who are capable, disease-free, wise, self-controlled, leisurely and rich otherwise the outdoor method is advisable."[22] *Rasāyana* offers memory preservation to the young and, in some few cases, to the old. Old bodies can handle the milder remedy of Chyawanprash, but even then only through the technologically intensive "indoor method" restricted to wealthy men. The old person seems more to serve as exemplary than clinical body and points to the need to protect young bodies from being spent. Semen, money, memory: all are somehow linked. The primary currency of therapeutic protection, semen, glides easily into other forms of symbolic capital.

THE MARKETING OF MEMORY

The semantic network[23] linking memory, youth, masculinity, and money in textual sources of *rasāyana* characterizes the commodification and therapeutic use of the contemporary *rasāyana* tonic and of other drugs. To continue to explore the mapping of memory loss onto the cultural construction of the life span, I focus on two newly commodified "neo-*rasāyana*" tonics, Geri-forte and Kesari Jivan, and a tonic whose status as *rasāyana* is contested, ginseng.

To ask the question in a different way: Why do young men buy health tonics formulated explicitly for old people? Geri-forte is a pill marketed by the Ayurvedic drug company Himalayan as an "adaptogenic," a drug that enhances the strength and mental power of debilitated persons and fights stress. Himalayan has specialized in reformulating Ayurvedic herbal preparations, repackaging them in the symbolic forms of biomedical, "English" medicine—brightly colored capsules, plastic bottles, English labels—and distributing it by prescription primarily through biomedical physicians.[24]

Besides those in practice at the medical school of Banaras Hindu University and the lunatic asylum to the north of the city, there were two psychiatrists in private practice in Varanasi during the years of my fieldwork. Dr. Singh, the younger of the two, was not yet well-established. Often when I came by he was alone in the office, a sharp contrast to the psychiatric consulting rooms of the other private doctor and of the university clinic, in which a dozen or more persons besides clinician and patient occupied the room, most family members of patients waiting to be seen.[25] One afternoon when I came to call, Singh was seeing two persons who looked like and turned out to be farmers, father and son, and he motioned to me to take a seat. The young man was being treated for depression; his father brought him into town for the occasional visit. After several minutes of the father describing his son's limited improvement and the psychiatrist adjusting the medication, a short spell of silence followed. The young man looked expectantly and shyly down towards the floor. His father coughed, and excused himself to go urinate. Still shyly, the young man described being impotent and requested appropriate medicine. The psychiatrist wrote him a prescription for Geri-forte.

Geri-forte is explicitly named and classified as a drug for the elderly. Yet my interviews with several Varanasi physicians suggest that much of Geri-forte's market share comes from young to middle-aged men with the chief complaint of impotence. Mental weakness and impotence are marked by the same term, *kamzori*, literally weakness. More than a semantic glide is at stake. Himalayan-sponsored clinical research has suggested that Geri-forte may work as an anxiolytic, reducing a patient's anxiety and some associated symptoms.[26] But there may be more to the drug's efficacy across the life span than its possible anxiolytic effects.

The problem of Geri-forte is echoed in the marketing by the Zandu pharmaceutical company of Kesari Jivan, a mass-market preparation of the ubiquitous Chyawanprash with saffron. In one of the more memorable of the Kesari Jivan ads, shown on television and in vernacular and English newspapers and magazines, a young man is shown trying to catch a departing Bombay bus. He can't make it up until an older man reaches down and pulls him aboard; a young woman smirks in the background from her vantage point by a window. The legend, referring through the body of the old man to that of the young, reads, "Sixty years old or sixty years young?" Kesari Jivan, the ad suggests, has given the old man his vigor; but the ad is of course pitched to young men. Other Kesari Jivan ads show a gray-haired older man in a comfortable safari suit standing straight and tall and climbing a long flight of stairs with apparent ease, while lagging behind is a mustachioed and dark-haired young man dressed for success in a fashionable shirt and tie, puffing and bent over like his compatriot on the bus. A drug framed as an index of the strength of the old male body is addressed to the weakness of youth. The older body at sixty is paradoxically stronger than the younger body at thirty. The father leaves the room so the son can confess his impotence. Geri-forte.

In the wealthier colonies of my Varanasi fieldwork, Korean ginseng was a more popular tonic among young men than the various Chyawanprashes. Chyawanprash was something your mother spoon-fed you as a child. Ginseng carried with it both the appeal of Ayurveda and the exotic strength of East Asia. Over-the-counter preparations like Jensheng were packaged as potent red capsules with Chinese-style lettering and were often labeled "Ayurvedic." The young men in the colonies who used them—none of the young women in the colonies reported using ginseng or other vitality tonics—often referred to ginseng as Ayurvedic. Ayurveda here connoted the raw natural power of unadulterated herbs and the long-term transformative effects of *jaṛībūṭī* against the fly-by-night effects of *angrezī davā*, English (allopathic) medicine. Ayurveda was Indian and was something to take pride in. The Chinese lettering and the use of "Korean" paradoxically identified this medicine as something new and foreign: not Chyawanprash. East

Asian medicine offered an intriguing mediation of self and other: a powerful counterhegemony beating the West at its own game, a more inviolable self, the desired object of the tonic.

The Jensheng red capsule was not the only tonic to play on its phallic signification. Frequent newspaper ads for sexual vitality tonics continue to foreground the significance of the capsule shape: the image of a hand holding a massive capsule in ads for the sexual tonic 303 links together medicine, rifles (303 refers to a type of gun), and masturbation. Ginseng and the other tonics marketed for young men drew not only on *rasāyana* but on another of the eight branches of Ayurveda, the science of aphrodisiacs, or *vājīkaraṇa*. *Vājīkaraṇa* recipes are grouped with *rasāyana* therapies in most classical Ayurvedic texts, and their benefits overlap. *Rasāyana* recreates the body; *vājīkaraṇa* brings it the wealth of progeny and the pleasures of good sex.

In their therapeutic structure, the two specialties differ considerably: *vājīkaraṇa* lacks the elaborate locating and contextualizing of the body. *Vājīkaraṇa* remedies are usually not herbal and often involve eating the flesh or specific organs of animals. In *rasāyana*, the dismembered body is the patient's own, degraded through strong purgation within an enclosure reminiscent of the spatial construction of the sacrificial body: the patient is the dismembered and recreated Purusha, the sacrificial body of Vedic ritual.[27] In *vājīkaraṇa*, the sacrificed and dismembered body is that of the animal, and through its ingestion (as buffalo meat, cock's meat fried in crocodile's semen, the eggs of swan, goat's testicles, or pounded pork) the body becomes as powerful and the penis as large as that of a horse, bull, or elephant. For the young men of the colonies, ginseng differed from the classic *rasāyana* of Chyawanprash in its gendering: Chyawanprash implied the ingestion of mother's milk, something one had long since been weaned off of; ginseng suggested the ingestion of male body parts, not goat's testicles but a powerful red capsule.

Classical descriptions of *vājīkaraṇa*, like *rasāyana*, note its limited usefulness across the life course. Recipes that may be taken by old men are noted separately and are usually vegetarian.[28] The ingestion of the dismembered other, like the destruction of the self, assumes a young body.

Sanjay was a man in his early twenties who, at the time of the interviews with him that I draw on here, had finished with university and was preparing for his forestry civil service exams. He was the son of a professor at Banaras Hindu University, and at that time lived in his family compound in a village on the northern outskirts of the city fairly well known as the birthplace of the Hindi writer Premchand. Sanjay had recently been sick with intestinal cramping pain and diarrhea, and was worried about the effects of sickness on his studying for exams and specifically his ability to memorize. He decided to stop drinking unboiled water and began taking Jensheng.

Sanjay spoke of his illness both in localized terms—a "stomach" [*peṭ*] problem—and more generally, as *kamzorī*, weakness. Ginseng, he said, was a powerful

Ayurvedic tonic that his uncle, an allopathic government doctor, had recommended to him. Though ginseng was obviously Ayurvedic, Sanjay noted, it was a new product, probably the result of current Ayurvedic research transforming old formulae through recombination into powerful new drugs.

Ginseng is expensive, as Sanjay and most other men who chose to take it reminded me. In 1989, a packet of ten 250 milligram capsules in Varanasi ranged in cost from thirty to thirty-five rupees (then about two U.S. dollars, expensive for a tonic). Its price both limited its market and contributed to its appeal as a status item. Ginseng was in. One of the more heavily marketed ginseng preparations at the time was Thirty Plus, with ads featuring the Hindi film actor Jeetendra, then still known for his eternal youth and ability to garner young men's roles in middle age. Offering "stamina and performance," Thirty Plus combined ginseng ("revered by oriental scientists for centuries" and used by celebrities "including Indira Gandhi, Henry Kissinger and Marlon Brando") with the *rasāyana* drug Asvagandha ("a native root, mentioned in Vedic literature"). The drug tackled the debility of old age, here lowered to only thirty. The meaning of thirty in these ads as an index of progressive loss differs from that of sixty in the Kesari Jivan ad, a sign of exemplary power that younger men desire.

Ginseng grew phenomenally in popularity between 1988 and 1990. As the selling of the herb became increasingly bigger business, its questionable identity as Ayurvedic became of greater concern to ginseng distributors and their competitors. Neither quite Ayurvedic nor allopathic, ginseng drew on both systems of signification. Another ginseng preparation, Revital, inverted the recombinant aesthetics of Thirty Plus in joining the Korean herb to allopathic additives ("Minerals * Vitamins * Lipotropic Factors"). Revital, like Thirty Plus, offered an "alert mind" and "active body"; its slogan, "Better experienced than explained," acknowledges the drug's heteroglot resistance to rational description or systemic location.

Ginseng's upmarket position was echoed by a class of *rasāyana* Chyawanprash derivatives that explicitly marketed themselves to the then-newly named "puppies" (Punjabi), "guppies" (Gujurati), and other young urban professionals of the major cosmopolitan centers of the country. Chyawanshakti (*shakti* means power or energy) was a tough-sounding version of Chyawanprash, marketed to resist the mother's milk image of the latter. Ads for Chyawanshakti showed a successful thirty-something man in business clothes and appealed to the drug's power to alleviate the mental and physical weakness caused by the tensions of middle-class modernity. Baidyanath's Chyawanprash Special avoided children, mothers, and old people in its advertisements, showing before and after pictures of a young executive type who has gained "physical ability plus mental agility." Like many of the ginseng preparations, Chyawanprash Special drew on the physical potency of *rasāyana* and the sexual potency of *vājīkaraṇa* to offer a selective focus on mental fitness and memory power.

In the next chapter, I will turn to the generational politics and psychodynamics of the relationships between young and old bodies underlying these ads and a variety of other practices and discourses. Here I want to focus on distributional aspects of the losses and therapies detailed. For whom is mental weakness and memory loss medicalized? For whom is therapy created, and to whom is it marketed?

MEMORY AND CAPITAL

In Nagwa Harijan Basti, a pun played on the uselessness of tonics, whether Ayurvedic or allopathic. *Jhaṇḍū* is a particularly Banarsi term meaning "without further use," usually translated by slum residents as "what a lottery ticket is after the lottery." *Jhaṇḍū* was an exquisitely framed naming of abjection: like a lottery ticket after the lottery, someone who is *jhaṇḍū* probably had an infinitesimally small chance of making something of themselves in the first place, and now even that chance was over. Old people in Nagwa were often—jokingly or insultingly—called *jhaṇḍū*. "Zandu"—in Hindi the brand is indeed called *Jhaṇḍū*—was the name of the prominent Ayurvedic drug manufacturing house, makers of Kesari Jivan and other Chyawanprash derivatives and sponsor of the 1990 IASTAM meetings in Bombay. Thus the pun: "*jhaṇḍū* Chyawanprash"—useless Chyawanprash.

Jhaṇḍū played on more than the uselessness of tonics. Like the lottery, the neo-*rasāyana* tonic promises not only a stronger but a more successful and translocated body, the wealthy young professional of Chyawanshakti, the strong and erect sixty-year-old of Kesari Jivan. *Jhaṇḍū* implies not that Chyawanprash could never work or that it is a sham, but that whatever chances of translocation it offers are limited and inevitably past tense. The joke "*jhaṇḍū* Chyawanprash" points past the tonic to the slum body. Here in the slum we have *jhaṇḍū* old people, not strong men of sixty. Here even the young are *jhaṇḍū* and lack Sanjay's examinable body.

Tonic transactions in Nagwa differed from those in the colonies. In the family of Siranji, a woman in her late seventies or eighties who was one of the two oldest residents of the slum, tonics were given by her son Babu Lal to two of his more than one dozen family members living at home: to Siranji and to his young son Raju, still in grammar school. Raju's sisters had all been married, and several had left the household; those who remained were rarely offered tonics. Raju's older brothers had by then all left school and worked with Babu Lal, running the family vegetable shop, helping farm the family's small plot in their village to the south of the city, playing the drums at various religious ceremonies (a job expected of the low-status Chamar community, the dominant caste of the slum), and working at various day laboring jobs. They no longer take tonics. Like Sanjay, they were concerned about protecting their youthful strength, and they wore various amulets, rings, and strings around their necks, upper arms, wrists, and fingers, bindings given in empowering transactions by gurus, local exorcists, and other experts in spells and magic, mantra-tantra. Sanjay too wore several protective rings with stones appropriate to his astrological chart and personal history; the difference here was a matter of degree. The multiply girt body of Raju's brother, and to a lesser extent, of middle-class guys like Sanjay, was tightly bound up against leakage and loss, protected against the various depletions of women and upper castes and the desiring all-too-fluid self. But the family—through its purse controlled by Babu Lal and Parbati, his wife—invested little in these transactions. Raju's remained the potentially translocatable body; he received a vitamin tonic daily from a small and expensive bottle. He was not *jhaṇḍū;* he needed a strong body to study, to memorize, and to succeed. The chances of his radical translocation were slim, but they were not past tense.

Raju's *dādī* (grandmother) Siranji, whose multiple complaints and aggravated voice will be taken up in a later chapter, received a far less expensive mineral and "lipotropic" (fattening up) tonic from a bigger bottle, which sat on a shelf in the small courtyard that for most of the year doubled as bedroom for Siranji and the grandchildren and storage area for the vegetable shop. Siranji wanted treatment for her multiple ills and often saw the tonic as a substitute for proper care; family members either felt that her old age could not be treated or that any effective treatment was well beyond their means and not an appropriate use of the moral economy of the household.

The possibility of her tonic not being entirely *jhaṇḍū,* and by extension Siranji herself, lay in the affection behind the transaction. Siranji rejected her tonic, and said that it burned her; but she also rejected it because she saw it as a way of shutting her up, as a worthless panacea. For her family, the tonic was in one way an attempt to silence her unending complaints, but it was also an effort to respond, through the tonic as a gift that articulated a relationship between them, to a weakness that they understood to be beyond their means. From this perspective, the fact that the tonic might well be pharmacologically *jhaṇḍū* becomes immaterial; as a sign of the bonds that would transcend weakness, it retains a certain power.

For all in the family but Raju, weakness was seldom embodied as memory. One of Raju's older brothers, Munna, had a teach-yourself English text then popular in the city, which he studied in his spare time hoping for a better position or a college admission. But English was an avocation, and not memory power but time itself was the crucial missing commodity for him. Nor did Munna frame what was lacking in terms of a powerful paternal presence. Babu Lal, unlike Sanjay's father the university professor, had not achieved his status as one of the relatively more successful men of the slum through the kind of memory power that tonics like Chyawanshakti and ginseng augment. The figure of the successful older man in the safari suit climbing the stairs or standing erect on the bus—sixty years old or sixty years young—did not figure as a representation of the paternal-filial psychodynamics of Siranji's family.

Along one of the roads of Ravindrapuri Colony, a large sign advertised a tutorial coaching center for secondary and intercollege level students: "Memory Banks." Memory, here explicitly structured as capital in the pun of the organization's name, was offered for sale on the streets of the colonies, not the bastis. Tutorial programs, offering supplementary education to ensure success in school and state and national level competitive examinations, were all but required for academic success in the often fiercely competitive examinations for university entrance or civil service positions. Much was at stake in memory. When the multinational toy company Hasbro came to India, one of their first products marketed was "Memory," a card matching game, advertised in upmarket publications and offered as a didactic tool "designed to help your children develop their memory skills . . . [and] build visual recall."

The symbolic importance of memory in the structure of the Indian state and in the possibilities for the translocation of bodies characterized colonial British debate over the nature of native minds and the necessary safeguards thereof. Sir Henry Maine, in his lecture delivered at Calcutta in 1866 and briefly discussed earlier, addressed British concerns that the nature of competitive exams in Britain and India designed to routinize the staffing of a burgeoning empire were reducing education to "cramming" and the superficial knowledge gained by rapid memorization, and that the superficial mental faculties of native Indians, adept at such rote thinking and cramming but not at the sustained reflection of classical European thought, would overwhelm this emerging meritocracy by exam, to Britain's disadvantage. Maine disagreed, suggesting that knowledge gained by rapid memory was by no means any more superficial than what for him were increasingly antiquated methods.

> I wish, however, to say something of the whole class of objections implied in that one word, "cramming." If there is anything in them, you know, I suppose, that they have a far wider application to this University. They are constantly urged against the numerous competitive systems which are growing up in England, and in particular against the system under which the Civil Service of India, probably the most powerful official body in the world, is recruited, and will be recruited. . . .
>
> As far as I understand the word, it means nothing more than the rapid communication of knowledge,—communication, that is to say, at a rate unknown till recently.

In offering intensive memorization as a more rational didactic technique, Maine linked its strength of method with the powerful body of bureaucracy and empire. Memory-based learning, he suggested, works better than lengthier tutorial- or lecture-oriented approaches. A new regime of imperial power had opened up hitherto unexplored vistas of mental power.

As to the supposed and threatening superiority of Indians within the new regime, Maine demurred. "What appears to be meant is, that the Natives of India learn with singular rapidity. The fact may be so, though for my part, I doubt whether they learn with greater rapidity than English lads who once put their hearts into their work; and it may be also true, as some allege so positively, that their precocity is compensated by a greater bluntness of the faculties later in life." Here again is evidence of the polysemy of "softening," by which Maine characterized native minds, as an overlapping racial and generational pathology. For

Maine, the concern was not the greater cramming ability of Indians, negated even if it were true by the simultaneous softening and blunting of their minds, but the use to which they put memory and the new forms of knowledge Empire has crammed—literally—into them.

> I should rather venture to express disappointment at the use to which they some-times put it. It seems to me that not seldom they employ it for what I can best de-scribe as irrationally reactionary purposes. It is not to be concealed, and I see plainly that educated Natives do not conceal from themselves, that they have, by the fact of their education, broken for ever with much in their history, much in their customs, much in their creed. Yet I constantly read, and sometimes hear, elaborate attempts on their part to persuade themselves and others, that there is a sense in which these rejected portions of Native history, and usage and belief, are perfectly in harmony with the modern knowledge which the educated class has acquired. . . . They seem to believe, or they try to believe, that it was better to be a Brahmin or a scribe at-tached to the Court of some half mythical Hindu king, than to follow one of the pro-saic learned professions which the English have created. . . . The only India, in fact, to which he could hope to return—and that retrogression is not beyond the range of conceivable possibilities—is the India of Mahratta robbery and Mahomedan rule.[29]

Maine worried that memory as imperial pedagogy had rather paradoxically en-couraged a forgetting of the savage and corrupt Indian past. He argued that the new rationally crammed cosmos of the educated Indian—derived solely, he felt, from British education—was superimposed on the Indian past to reclaim the lat-ter as something it never was. Indian "softening" was ultimately less a matter of generalized forgetfulness, unlike European cerebral softening. Indian minds were soft as a result of their tendency to remember ever more falsely. The better trained in memory Indians became, the more they engaged in soft remembering.

"Memory" here suggests a two-edged commodity. Offered to India as a system of learning and advancement organized around the rapid cramming of European culture, it provided a tool for the colonized to re-member a dismembered social body. Within local postcolonial economies of examinations, bureaucracy, and translocation, the culturally elaborated domain of memory becomes a currency critical to the preservation and augmentation of certain classes of bodies—young, male, better off—and unavailable or irrelevant to others. "Memory loss" is experi-enced as, and signifies, something radically different for variously located bodies.

The embodiment of anxiety and weakness—Vatuk's informants' concern about their old age, Sanjay's concern about getting a job and succeeding his fa-ther, Raju's family's concern about his success in school, Siranji's concern about the illness raging inside her—is not just a function of universally meaningful symptoms that emerge out of an ideal and decontextualized suffering body. Old people often forget things, and some forget almost everything; everyone in the colonies and in the slum knows this. But despite such commonsense knowledge, memory loss and disordered mind did not go on to anchor the construction of the senile body or its infrequent medicalization. Siranji often forgot things, her family acknowledged, and other slum elders were similarly described as forgetful if you put the question to their family or neighbors. Among middle-class families, the situation differed somewhat.

Here I will briefly mention two old people whose families I knew in Calcutta; I will return to their stories in greater depth in chapters 6 and 9.[30] Somita Ray grew up in a Bengali village and was married in her early teens to a much older man who had become a lecturer in Calcutta; when I met her he had long since died, and she lived with her son and daughter-in-law in a small flat. The younger couple were at their wit's end as a result of Somita's behavior: they told me about false accusations, angry screaming, her hiding household objects to spite the daughter-in-law, and similar occurrences. They described the progression of her "maladjusted" behavior in terms of an exacerbation of previous personality traits, her inability over many years to adjust to her educated daughter-in-law intensified by her inability to adjust to old age. Memory loss was one piece of the lengthy descriptions of the previous several years they offered me in a course of interviews over six months, but it was not an organizing feature of how they understood Somita's difference over time.

Sudipta Basu was a very high ranking civil servant in West Bengal who was pushed into the civil service by his father despite his desire to become a historian, a fact he often retold to his children and grandchildren. He would have been a good historian, he used to say, because he had an especially good memory. His interest in memory and classification suffused his home life; his grandson, a friend of mine, recalls that even as a small child he found his grandfather's strict adherence to elaborate schedules and routines—to his *niyam*, a word difficult to translate but roughly his custom, practice, routine duty, or system[31] —remarkable: "I would play a game with him, lick his nose, and say, 'Is that your *niyam*?'"; "He used to have a lot of servants, and every morning each would have to do his precise task at just the right place and time. The fellow who shined his shoes had to place them by the chair where he ate breakfast, another would stand ready to carry his briefcase."

The grandfather had long since retired when his wife began to notice him forgetting words more and more frequently. She became upset: "You have bought all these books and yet you still can't remember this word!" "A man who was once chief engineer of Bengal is now reduced to this!" From losing memory, his grandson told me, he moved to progressively losing his *niyam*, which upset his family far more since it seemed so central to who he was. His wife became particularly concerned when he ceased to remember to offer his daily prayers to Krishna, a practice he had taken up after his retirement with her encouragement.

A friend of the family, a foreign-trained nephrologist, advised them that the old man probably had Alzheimer's and that he would progress from these losses to angry, violent, and suspicious behavior and finally to passivity, bodily failure, and death. As Sudipta progressed according to this prognosis and became increasingly difficult to relate to, the family looked continually for evidence of relational continuity. The grandson noted, "He continued to be warm to my father, which was important because they had been particularly close"; "a cousin-brother had recently been married and came with his wife to pay their respects—when they bent down to touch his feet, he leaned over to acknowledge them in turn, just as he always had done."

Unlike Somita's children, who focused on their mother's actions in terms of previous histories of family relationships, Sudipta's family additionally marked his last years in terms of the loss of memory and *niyam*, repeatedly framing these losses against the critical role of memory and routine in his earlier life as a student, examination taker, high-ranking civil servant, book collector, employer of many servants, and postretirement Vaishnavite devotee. Memory plays a powerful narrative role, along with family relations, in his grandson's retelling of Sudipta's decline, less because it was an index of being a person than as it suggested being a certain kind of person, someone cultivated, someone who was a master of order.

Such frames of gender and of socioeconomic difference mute the universal significance of the forgetful old person. Before turning more closely to the significance of relation, anger, and emotion as markers of difference, I want to highlight the one significant exception, the archetype of the universal elder as the site of a different sort of forgetting in a broad strand of normative Hindu thought: the last of the four life stages of *āśramadharma*, the sannyasi, or renouncer.

FORGETTING AS A PATH TO TRUTH

Smṛti, memory, is the subject of significant debate within most of the classical schools of Indian philosophy, or *darśanśāstra*. A central debate centers on the status of *smṛti* as a *pramāṇa*, or instrument of valid knowledge. Most schools of philosophy do not allow that memory can be a *pramāṇa*: first, it does not present but rather re-presents objects to consciousness; second, it may represent its object differently from the initial presentation; and third, it may involve secondary cognition and not be an immediate source of knowledge.[32] *Pramāṇa*, as B. K. Matilal suggested, conveys authority; memory, as but a copy of prior authoritative experience, in itself lacks authority and cannot be a *pramāṇa*.[33] And as copies need not be exact reproductions even though they may claim to be, memory can easily deceive.

Memory's status as a copy whose relationship to primary experience is uncertain undergirds its importance in the more soteriologically oriented philosophical systems of Vedanta and Yoga and in the great narrative and normative traditions of the Sanskrit Epics, Puranas, and *dharmaśāstra*, or legal compendia. These latter are collectively known as *smṛti*, that which is remembered, what Gerald Larson has referred to as the "important corporate memory of the community."[34] *Smṛti* is in this context contrast with *śruti*, the authoritative and always precedent knowledge revealed in the Vedas. Unlike *smṛti*, which is reflexively and explicitly told and thus accessible as a remembered narrative, *śruti* is always heard anew. *Smṛti* is the trace of authority, a derivative and potentially deceptive text. The Vedas, structured as prosodic oral recitative rather than prosaic narrative, are memorized to resist becoming text and thus a nonauthoritative copy. Thus a paradox: the "remembered" is narrativized, and loses its authority; the authoritative is memorized, to avoid degenerating into narrative.

Memory, in this contrast between *śruti* and *smṛti* literatures, signifies both the potentially deceptive nature of corporate memory—and all memory more generally—and the practical means by which authoritative knowledge avoids slipping into the inherent misreading of narrative. The polysemy of "*smṛti*," in other words, points both to the possibility of authority and illusion, both to things as they really are and things as we desire them to have been and thus be. This contradiction underscores the metaphorical language of memory and forgetting in the path-based philosophical soteriologies of Hinduism. Memory points us beyond the illusory confines of this life to the cyclical unfolding of multiple lives. Yet memory prevents us from forgetting the phenomenal, nonessential names and forms that seduce our understanding and thus prevents us from realizing that which is essential behind the veil of samsara, this cyclical and inherently unsatisfying cosmos. To discover the Real, we must "forget" the phenomenal world of names and forms; in forgetting, we "remember" our true identity beyond samsara.

In the fourfold scheme of stages of life, *āśramadharma*, the final stages of the forest dweller and of the renunciate are associated with both physical and cognitive withdrawal from attachment to the world of names and forms. This disengagement is in a sense a forgetting of domestic and political attachments and a remembering of an underlying transcendent self. Such transformative uses of memory are explored in depth in the monistic tradition of Vedanta. The philosopher Shankara, in his well-known fifth-century introduction to the *Brahmasutrabhasya*,[35] examines the nature of the error that prevents us from experiencing things as they really are. He does this through a concept of *adhyāsa*, superimposition. *Adhyāsa* is "the appearance, in the form of a memory, of something previously experienced in some other place." We recognize and remember our experience incorrectly by superimposing ourselves as the seat of consciousness on ourselves as autonomous bodies or distinct "selves."[36] Our memory of having been, in other words, conditions our self-perception as "selves," as something other than the pure consciousness of immediate being.

The power of memory to reify an erroneous conception of self lies in its constitution as multiple *saṃskāras*, as the impressions of perceived events and objects on the stuff of mind. These impressions are not only of the events of an individual's life witnessed by a single body, but subtle traces, or *vasanas*, of events of multiple past lives and, occasionally, of other coexistent bodies. *Saṃskāras* delineate a historical self that we mistake for the transcendent experiencer of that which is impressed. The subtler *vasanas* extend this historical self before our birth to other births; this subtle memory of past lives conditions our sense of having a jiva, a transmigrating soul. For great sages, memory may extend not only across lives but synchronically across bodies; rishis and other enlightened beings may remember the experience of other bodies.

Again the paradox of memory. Memory traps us within the illusion of the bounded and contingent self, yet memory explodes this self when, in remembering past lives or the lives of others, we discover the limitations of this world of samsara. As error is manifest as memory, so the path away from error involves forgetting; as memory on occasion points us to something beyond the self, so the path towards realization and moksha, release, involves remembering.

Wendy Doniger cites several stories from the ninth- to twelfth-century Kashmiri text *Yogavasiṣṭha* that play with the illusory yet transformative nature of memory. A young man assuages his brother's grief over their parents' death by reminding him of their multiple births and thus the relativity of death as an ending: "Punya added that he himself could clearly recall his own births as a parrot, a frog, a sparrow, a Pulinda [tribal hunter], a tree, a camel, a lovebird, a king, a tiger, a vulture, a crocodile, a lion, a quail, a king, and the son of a teacher named Saila." The remembering of karmic traces of past lives is usually framed less as revelatory than deluding: "Alas, the delusion that results from the karmic traces causes such misery among creatures." We experience subtle memory as desire for things we once enjoyed: a breast, possessions, the beloved. People are reborn, summarizes Doniger, "in a particular form because they want something. There is a hunger unsated in their present lives, that propels them across the barrier of death into a new birth, where this still unfulfilled longing leads them to do what they do."

She compares the karmic transfer across death and rebirth with the transfer of coded substance that McKim Marriott has suggested marks the construction of the person in South Asia.[37] "If people become a part of strangers in daily intercourse and give parts of themselves in return, the emotional reality of the karmic transfer across the barrier of death and rebirth could be very vivid indeed. The bonds with members of one's own family, one's own 'flesh and blood,' in the past and the future, are even stronger; one's family, and one's caste, are one's self in India."[38] If the ego is embedded in the transactional self of the family, the caste, and other local polities, then memory and forgetfulness point not just to the multiplicity of lives but of bodies that constitute the self. The fact that memory extends back to encompass all those whom one has been makes sense given its simultaneous encompassment of all those whom one is.

Forgetting and remembering as a dual path to truth are elaborated in several contemporary Hindu movements. In Lawrence Babb's discussion of the Brahma Kumari sect, belief in the apocalyptic vision of Dada Lekhraj, a "perfectly ordinary 'old man,'" translocates women and men to a position outside of history and beyond the cycle of time.

> A practitioner of raja yoga is characterized as one who "remembers." The Brahma Kumaris constantly employ the idiom of remembrance in discussing these matters. Raja yoga is "remembering father." The soul has "forgotten" its real nature and has identified with bodies. In yogic practice one should turn this upside down by "for-

getting the body" . . . and "remembering Shiv Baba." . . . In this most fundamental act of recollection—that is, in cultivating awareness of the Supreme Soul—one becomes aware of one's own soul and forgetful of the body and the world.[39]

Once again, the body of the exemplary old man—here explicitly the father— offers the promise of memory to a new generation. Despite the importance of the old man to the yogi's cultivated forgetfulness, the commonplace that old people often seem to forget things does not explicitly inform Brahmakumari practice. Though the normative model of the life course associates the renouncer's forgetting of the phenomenal world with the proper dharma, or moral practice, of old age, forgetful old bodies are seldom signifiers of the philosophical discourse of remembrance and forgetting.

In the *Kathāsaritsāgara* story of King Vinayashila and Dr. Tarunachandra discussed in the last chapter, the king is upset by his first shock of gray hair but cannot forget the pleasures of his life, particularly his wife. The king is a foolish old man not because he is beginning to forget himself but precisely because he cannot do so. The story continues after the physician and the young man have killed the king and thrown his body down a dry well and the young man has reemerged as the rejuvenated king, renamed by his loving populace Ajara, one free from old age. The doctor one day complained to Ajara that he was not receiving his due share of the kingdom's riches. The new king laughed at the physician's limited memory: "Ha! You are a fool. What man does anything for anyone, or gives anything to anyone? My friend, it is our deeds in a former state of existence that give and do." To demonstrate the karmic necessity of his ascension as against the doctor's agency, Ajara has the latter trace the source of five golden lotuses that they had seen floating downstream. The physician travels for several days, until "on the shore of a holy bathing-place in that stream, he beheld a great banyan tree, and a man's skeleton suspended on it. . . . [A] cloud came there and rained. And from that human skeleton . . . there fell drops of water. . . . [G]olden lotuses were immediately produced from them." Tarunachandra throws the skeleton into the river and returns to the palace, where Ajara informs him the skeleton was "my former body. I hung there in old time by my feet; and in that way performed asceticism, until I dried up my body and abandoned it."[40]

Two old bodies are contrasted in the story, the foolish old king who cannot forget and yet is fed *rasāyana* tonics, and the wise old sage who forgets all attachment and through his accumulated karma is reborn as a man who becomes a king and who remembers his past life. Foolish old people have a surfeit of static memory and delusional desire; exemplary old people forget but develop fluid and expansive memories extending over lifetimes. The senile body is represented through desire rather than memory. Desire closes off the possibility of movement: the body of the old king ends up in the dead end of a dry well, that of the old sage in the fluid space of the river.

Desire, emotion, and memory, more than forgetfulness in itself, are the stigmata of the foolish old body. In stories of foolish and weak elders or of the horrors of old age, an exemplary old person, like the old sage here, offers a way out. Despite the offer, desire blinds the deluded soul. The king rejects the advice of his ministers and opts for the false promises of medicine. Even when the promise of *rasāyana* is authentic, desire deflects its application. In a tale from the *Vikramacarita* of the thirteenth century or later,[41] a *rasāyana*-like magic fruit, is given to a poor Brahman, who decides to transfer the gift to the king, since eternal life without the strength to use it for the betterment of others is but delusion.

> In this city there was a certain brahman, who knew all the books of science, and had an exceptional acquaintance with charm-textbooks; yet he was a pauper. [The Brahman propitiates the goddess Parvati, who appears and grants him a wish; he chooses immortality.] The goddess gave him a divine fruit, and said: "My son, eat this fruit, and you shall be immune to old age and death."
>
> Then the brahman took that fruit, and went back to his own house; and when he had bathed and performed divine service, before he ate this thought occurred to his mind: "How now! After all I am a pauper; if I become immortal who will be helpt by me? . . . Real life is that which is lived by glorious and righteous men. A crow may live for a long time, by gulping morsels of rotten food.

The pathos of the long-lived weak and poor is represented through bestial images; only the wealthy and powerful merit the gift of the youthful body. But when the exemplary Brahman offers the fruit to the king, the unexpected happens. The king, after some reflection, realized that he could never endure the infinite separation that immortality would bring between him and his beloved queen, Anangasena. He gives the magic fruit to her. "But this Anangasena had a groom as lover, and she in turn, upon meditation, gave this fruit to him." Down through the body politic rushes the magic fruit towards its anticlimactic excretion.

> And there was a certain slave-girl, who was best-beloved of this groom; and he gave it to her. But the slave-girl was in love with a certain cowherd, and gave it to him. But he in turn had a great passion for a girl who carried cow-dung, and gave it to her.
>
> Now this girl was carrying cow-dung outside of the city, and had placed the basket of it on her head and thrown that fruit on the top.[42]

The king chances to see the fruit of immortality on its mountain of shit; disgusted with the inconstancy of desire—expressed as the shallow nature of women—he himself abandons the kingdom for the forest. The Brahman's exemplary gesture, offering his own immortal potential to the king, leads the king through the superficially enhanced memory of the *rasāyana* recipient to the remembering of the real nature of things, and thus to the final stage of life, *sannyāsa*. The delusion of *rasāyana*, here as in the story of the king and the physician, is not in its false promises but in the desire underlying its possibility.

Memory loss, in elite philosophical and narrative traditions of the path to truth and the fear of old age, is bound to emotion and desire. The impressions of *smṛti* link individuals to other bodies in time and in space. The valence of these linkages depends on whether they trap one within a world of desire or hint at alternative imaginings of the self. As a commodity, as something whose loss is explicitly resisted and culturally elaborated, memory in itself is a quality properly desired by "glorious and righteous men." As a sign of wisdom and of ignorance, and as a state rooted in desire, memory and its loss point to the centrality of the emotions and their relation to desire in old age. "He [or she] is old," I was told in many neighborhoods. "His brain is weak. So he is angry and irritable. His brain gets hot."

⨐ *Merī Latā Mahān* ⨑

To me and, I believe, to every Indian, Lata Mangeshkar is not so much a person as a voice—a voice that soars high and casts a magic spell over the hearts of millions of Indians from the Himalayas to Kanyakumari. It is a voice that is ageless.
GANGADHAR GADGIL, "MEET LATA MANGESHKAR," *ILLUSTRATED WEEKLY OF INDIA*, 1967

In the last years of Rajiv Gandhi's ministry, before India's only prime minister ever described as young lost a bitterly contested 1989 election to V. P. Singh's Janata Dal, a music video to promote both national integration and the Congress Party's projected image as the only force holding the country together was repeatedly broadcast on national television. *"Merā Bhārat Mahān"* featured music, film, and sports stars, each shown in his or her regional setting but each singing of and to the people of India as a whole. Region followed region, building toward a crescendo of unity in diversity.

Perhaps the most powerful sequence appeared near the end of the piece. A series of well-known film actresses was shown—Sharmila Tagore, Waheeda Rehman, and other former stars widely acknowledged to be beautiful but past their years of glory—and each actress sang against a scenic backdrop indicating her particular geographic or ethnic origins. Each sang the song's lyrics, expertly lip-synching in the style of the Bombay film. The series of film stars and backdrops then dissolved into the scene of a far older woman in the studio, in the act of recording the actual song you were hearing. The voice behind each actress, the unity behind the diversity of the tableaux was revealed: the great diva of "playback" singers Lata Mangeshkar, the Voice more than any other of independent India. And the song was memorable, echoing another sung for Nehru after a terrible war. In this video moment of time regained, grandson Rajiv became grandfather Jawaharlal and the nation was returned to itself.

The moment caught the viewer. Even jaded media watchers were known to shed a tear.[1] It was not the famous old song of famous old Lata that made the video remarkable, but rather that one got to *see* Lata in the very act of voicing the nation, the bodies of actresses, and oneself. It was the reflexivity in the final cut to Lata in the studio: the movement from actress to singer, region to nation, scenery to machinery, exterior to interior, body to voice, and young to old.

Lata is far older than the young actresses her voice usually animates on the screen. Her voice is unmistakable and has entered the realm of the signifiably timeless. Unlike the voice of the everyday old person, Lata's voice made no claims upon the listener and was seldom heard as simply old. Like the old woman of Balua, "giving up her food for five days and nights, during which period she sat shaking her head about," Lata's voice floated free of transactional ambivalence and could promise the millennium. The nation as what anthropologists might call, after Claude Levi-Strauss, a syntagmatic chain of beautiful women is a familiar theme, but unlike, for example, the Beach Boys' "California Girls," the chain here was not held together through a desiring male gaze alone. Lata's voice stringing together Sharmila, Waheeda, and Hema was the unity that materialized a desire for the nation as a whole.

Usually, Lata's voice is inextricable from the bodies of the actresses she sings through, whether in film or live performance. For audiences, the young body and the often far older voice are indivisible. If "Mother India" is part of the semantic network of the Voice of Lata, she is so while dancing as a far younger body. As with Geri-forte, the qualities of old and young circulate in interesting ways. In *Merā Bhārat Mahān*, this circulation became explicit. *Rasāyana*-like, old Lata's voice rejuvenated the middle-aged actresses, allowing them to reprise their moment of youthful cynosure when their bodies could stand for all India. The relation between actress and singer was made explicit: one did not experience the conjoint young body/old voice as seamless and obvious, but as anticipatory, as youthful body awaiting completion through the Voice. But under what conditions, in this age of Ghar Kali, may the young and old be reunited in time? In the moment of hoped-for national integration, under the political sign of the Son whose body spoke—still awkwardly but ever less hesitantly—with the voice of the Mother and Grandfather, Lata was called upon to reveal herself in flagrante delicto, amid the impressive but contingent modernity of the studio in which the Voice cum Nation is revealed as artifact. Beloved and unimaginably necessary, but requiring the *sevā* of those capable of mastering the ever more technical politics of keeping bodies and voices lip-synching to the future.

Lata on the stereo as I write. It is not to provoke accusations of postmodern superficiality that the chanteuse finds her way into this book, just as it is not to provoke accusations of old-fashioned Orientalism that I refer to debates on memory in Samkhya and Nyaya, and in the next chapter, to angry old rishis from the Sanskrit epics. Having watched *Merā Bhārat Mahān* work its magic in Varanasi during an election, when full-page Congress Party ads featuring pictures of baby dolls smashed into pieces as ominous signs of the future appeared daily and killings of Muslims in my neighborhood (apparently by Congress-aligned local "vested interests" in an effort to generate a soupçon of communal riot and bring home the need for a centrist party) were going on, I find it hard not to find the then-ruling party's deployment of age—old voices, younger bodies, smashed babies, fresh corpses—of critical importance. But this is the sort of appeal to experience that one should not have to rely upon. Lata is juxtaposed with Geri-forte, Kesari Jivan, "the voice," and other bits that lie ahead both to tell a story and to resist a telling, much as the angry rishis that lie ahead are not meant either to suggest a seamless link with the micropolitics of twentieth-century senility or to deny the possibility. A different sort of reading seems necessary: much as the voice of old age demands more than a sympathetic ear to be heard in a *jhaṇḍū* world. Much as Lata at her best demands something else besides your passive enjoyment of her voice on the stereo if you are really to be transformed from an aging body into the timeless beauty of Waheeda Rehman on the silver screen.

Shravan Kumar carrying his parents.

FIVE

The Anger of the Rishis

in which the voice of old age is given reason, body, and space

HOT BRAINS

What is left of this body now? Only my voice remains.
KRISHNA SOBTI, *AI LARKĪ*

In her twentieth-century retelling of the *Mahābhārata* epic, Kamala Subramaniam puzzles over the frequent anger of Parashurama, an ancient sage, or rishi: "The rishis, they say, have all their senses under control. But it is evident that anger is the one thing they have never been able to control. To think that such a great man as [Parashurama], a man who had practiced austerities for years and years, should have lost his temper so easily, is strange."[1]

The puzzle is this: the rishi is a paradigmatic type of realized individual, of an ascetic relation to the world exemplified by the final "stages" of *āśramadharma*: *vānaprastha* and *sannyāsa*. One moves, in the scheme of *āśramas*, from discipleship to the household to forest retirement to complete renunciation. The move is away from the connotations of *javānī*, of youth—hot and interactive—toward the colder and less interactive body. The scheme parallels the physiology of aging in the classical medical texts of Ayurveda, in which young adulthood is characterized by a surfeit of *pittā*, hot bile, with an increase of *vāyu*, cool wind, as one ages. Old bodies, socially and physiologically, are colder and more controlled.

The body of the rishi, narratively placed high on mountaintops or deep in forests, is the acme of the cold and noninteractive body. Rishi-like figures become legitimating icons for widely disparate projects. The cardiologist and American popular author Herbert Benson drew on the calm and collected rishi in discussing the cardiovascular benefits of the relaxation response.[2] Roy Walford offered the rishi's cooled down metabolism and dearth of free radicals as a sign of caloric undernutrition. Former Indian Prime Minister Narasimha Rao was often represented at the height of his power as a cool and withdrawn but exceedingly power-ful figure, with the connotation either of Brahman or rishi, in political cartoons.[3] Yet rishis are exquisitely prone to anger, which in the Varanasi neighborhoods was often experienced and described as a type of heat—hot brain.

Not only latter-day rishis and sannyasis but old people in general were often characterized to me in Varanasi as classically irritable and hot-brained; these typifications extend to local proverb and narrative. *Uskā dimāg garm ho gayā* (his or her brain has become hot), conveying a chronic state of anger, was frequently said of the old. Old people tended to dry up, and their decreased fluidity could be manifest as frictional heat and irritability. The dry and unyielding irritability of old people was often described in terms of the production of wind, the problema-tized voice.

The sort of categories and language games I highlight here—hot, cold, wet, dry, fluid, unyielding, interactive, not interactive—simultaneously open up and curtail forms of critical inquiry. To an anthropologist, they suggest the approach to language and myth developed by Lévi-Strauss, the analysis of paired opposi-tions like hot and cold as a means to imagine an abstract edifice called structure. Structuralist approaches of various sorts have been immensely fruitful in the analysis of society and of knowledge and practice in South Asia, but their mis-placed concreteness, frequent awkwardness in engaging questions of historical process and of difference and hegemony, and uncanny tendency to reprise various colonial nuggets of misinformation lead one to tread cautiously.

Structuralisms tend to be foreign affairs; the two most trenchant structuralist engagements in Indian sociology have been first, the work of Louis Dumont, his critics, and those who have taken his program in different directions, and second, what one might call the Chicago School and in particular the work of McKim Marriott, the early Ronald Inden, and many of their students and colleagues. Marriott's later work, and in particular a set of writings and interpretations grouped about an interpretive device sometimes termed "the cube," is exemplary both as an impressive heuristic, structuralist analytics of a certain sort taken to their logical extreme and offering powerful and unexpected insights, and as an un-comfortably reductionist Rosetta stone promising the final cracking of the hith-erto opaque code that is social behavior in India.[4]

Among the many trained in this sort of approach to India, the response to a radically changed sense of the necessary and obvious in anthropological practice has ranged: from total disavowal to the turn to "ethnohistory" to ever more local and nuanced structuralisms to the shift from questions of continuity to the more productive ground of diasporas, modernities, conflicts, ruptures, and "public cul-ture." My own approach has been to retain some of the crude but useful insights of a necessarily cosmopolitan reduction of continuity and difference to code, but here decentering rather than destructuring its claims to totality, in part through a perspectival language of first-, second-, and third-person accounts and in part by recognizing, as Margaret Trawick has suggested in an interesting synthesis of

Bourdieu and Lacan, that structuralist accounts offer not so much models of social life as models for (and against) it.[5]

The positioning of the old person in the third-person terms of hot/cold and other oppositions points not only to the physiological but the social body of the abstracted elder. As Marriott and others have suggested, the polarities of hot/ cold, wet/dry, and windy/still reflect a deeper framework for structuring experience. The windy and dry person, blowing both hot and cold, illuminates a wealth of positioned information. Heat, particularly in the context of the life cycle, may be read as the externalization of power. These oppositional rhetorics of thermodynamic sociality were more useful glosses in some interviews than in others, among some households more than others, in ways that did not cut neatly across class, caste, gender, or family history.

The ascetic path classically advocated in the latter stages of life centers on practices in which one cultivates tapas, ascetic heat or power, through physical stasis and disengagement. Tapas is sometimes demonstrable as siddhis—as superhuman feats—the most significant of which in contemporary India is longevity. Devraha Baba, an ascetic who died in 1990, was said to be 140 years old. He seldom spoke, but when he did his words were raptly listened to by thousands of pilgrims. The words of ascetics and particularly of contemporary babas are powerful, and demand the listener's attention. The internalized power of the ascetic, evident in his or her impersonal and "cold" seclusion and detachment, is manifest as the externalized power of a hot voice. The paradox of the aging voice, noted by Subramanian when she wonders about the anger of rishis, is on one level the intrinsic thermodynamics of tapas: accumulated power of the cold person who does not expend it through social abstinence builds to explosive pressures. Such explosions are described textually in classical Sanskrit and local narratives both as the prodigious sexual potential of the ascetic, most notably the god Shiva, and as the ascetic's fierce anger.[6]

Unlike the rarely emitted but destructive flame of Shiva's third eye, the hot ascetic voice can and should be heard, and, again in third-person humoral terms, is framed as relational, as part of exchanges between bodies. Relationality, in the recent analyses of Marriott and Daniel in other South Asian contexts, is often structured through the semantics of fluidity.[7] Babas and rishis have communicative and wet voices that melt the boundaries between them and their listeners. These voices are by definition meaningful, however opaque their overt signification; the ascetic voice, though turbulent, is not characterized by the "windy" attributes of incoherence and meaninglessness. Ascetics, even when like the Tantric Aghoris of Varanasi who often violently curse passersby, produce meaningful sounds.

Against the hot but meaningful exemplary voice that can transform the listener through its wisdom, most hot old voices in the real time of second-person referentiality are heard as irritability, as inappropriate anger. In humoral terms, the angry voice of the exemplary elder dries up in the everyday context of family life. The interpretation of the hot voice—the extent to which it can avoid desiccation, the sources of its hearing as inappropriate, humorous, threatening, or pathological— varies across class and gender and household structure and is changing with the globalization of Alzheimer's; I will take it up at length in the final four chapters. Here I want to locate the voice of hot brain in several more general ways: as emblematic of intergenerational conflict, as part of a set of old voices, as a particular embodiment of the family itself, and as a sign of what we might call a dying space.

SIXTYISHNESS AND SEVENTY-TWONESS

To be on this side
of the chasm,
with you
on the other,
son,
is a lie.

SUKRITA P. KUMAR,
"FATHERS AND SONS"

I begin with the third- and second-person frame of *saṭhiyānā*, which might be literally translated as "sixtyishness."

Dictionary definitions of *saṭhiyānā*, a Hindi word, stress its cognitive and performative implications. The 1987 edition of the *Samksipt Hindī Sabdsāgar* dictionary defines it as follows: "1. To be sixty years old. 2. To be old [*buṛṛha*]. Due to old age, to have a diminished intellect [*buddhi*]." *Sāṭh* is the word for sixty; *saṭhiyā jānā* is, literally, to go sixtyish. Other textual definitions mention a loss of *vivek*, discrimination, or of judgment. None explicitly mention forgetfulness or memory loss; though arguably encompassed in *buddhi*, they are not stressed.[8]

Despite its abstract definition as a loss of intellect, *saṭhiyānā* was seldom used as a descriptive term in third-person terms in any of the neighborhoods of this study. It was used more commonly about specific old people, humorously or derisively marking them as willful or stubborn. In this second-person spoken context, *saṭhiyānā* suggested less an abstract cognitive status and more the irritable and often hot-brained behavior of a known elder. Younger women and men might call friends of their own age *saṭhiyā*: you're acting like a stubborn old person. When I would attempt to describe someone who had been described to me as weak-brained or hot-brained as having gone sixtyish, the person to whom I was speaking might laugh or frown: I had changed the trope of the discussion.

In its semantic fluidity, its potential for insult or humor, and its link to chronological old age, *saṭhiyānā* shares features with the Indian English term "senility," into which it was on occasion translated by English speakers. But *saṭhiyānā*, unlike senility, was seldom used as an abstract signifier. It linked the thermodynamics of hot brain to the age of sixty and to a relational context: stubbornness, willfulness, and hot brain all suggested a struggle over authority within a household or, less frequently, a public or exterior space. Unlike other frames for describing the behavior of old persons, such as weakness and madness, sixtyishness was embedded within the contested forum of intergenerational relations.

The linkage of chronological age to the hot brain through *saṭhiyānā* is noteworthy. Other Indian languages similarly link the senile body to age-specific language. Among Panjabis, Haryanvis, and Himachalis in the city, to go *sattar bahattar* (seventy–seventy-two) was described through affectively loaded language similar to going sixtyish in Hindi. In the Bengali quarter, the language of sixtyishness was again displaced a decade; in Bengali, people got "caught by seventy-two"— *bāhāttūre*—connoting foolishness, willfulness, and inappropriate behavior. The Bengali term *bhīmrati* has a similar slant; in its etymology there is the suggestion of the oversexed and inappropriately youthful elder. *Bhīmrati* is not age-linked in itself, but a proverb told to me on a few occasions placed it at "seventy-seven years, seven months, and seven nights." Unlike *saṭhiyānā* but perhaps like *sattar bahattar jānā*, these phrases are endpoints, indices of willfulness and foolishness against which one can be measured. Thus a conversation, overheard by a friend in Calcutta:

> *She:* I have got *bhīmrati*.
>
> *He:* Well! Are you seventy-seven years old?
>
> *She:* Yes. Seventy-seven years, seven months, seven days, seven minutes, seven seconds . . .

And Sushil Kumar De's *Bangla Prabad*[9] quotes Dijendra Ray: "Has the old man reached *bhīmrati* or not?"

Sixty is a far more ambiguous marker. Though Banarsi friends joked that the difference between *saṭhiyānā* and *bāhāttūre* was that Bengalis preserved their brains by eating fish, sixty connoted far more than mental weakness and angry willfulness. An oft-quoted proverb in many local languages and dialects is some variant of "*Saṭṭhā ta paṭṭhā* (Sixty, thus strong)."[10]

The proverb evokes an important figure, the powerful patriarch; his structural forms are legion—the *tau* (father's elder brother), the zamindar (the feudal lord), and the *dādā* (literally grandfather or elder brother, but here connoting political boss or gang leader). The power of age was critical to political image–making during the years of this study. The septuagenarian Haryanvi politician Devi Lal styled himself the nation's *tau*, "uncle" here denoting not gentle advice so much as firm control. During this time, while Devi Lal foisted himself and his family—implicated in a variety of murders and at least one massacre—upon the nation through the Janata Dal party's dependence on his kulak vote bank, I could not help reflecting on the overdetermined sets of *taus* with which several friends were contending. One friend was forced into a marriage against his and his parents' will by his *tau;* another friend's family was evicted from their home after his father and his *tau* were estranged over the sharing of household resources and space. In styling him-self the nation's *tau*, Lal drew on a semantic network associating age and firm con-trol.

Unlike the former prime minister Morarji Desai, whose rejuvenative *rasāyana* experiments with urine did not put the semantics of old age to the most effective political use,[11] Lal used his age carefully. His seventy-fifth birthday party in Delhi was an elaborately scripted and staged event. Ritually elaborated rites of passage for the elderly were not common in north India, unlike the south. Lal's birthday party was a masterful piece of invented ritual, reminiscent, for an anthropologist, of Barbara Myerhoff's discussion of old people fashioning ritual in a southern California senior citizen's center.[12] But the stakes in Devi Lal's birthday party were massive. Drawing on traditions of the experienced world-conquering monarch, it presented Devi Lal to the nation as its cosmic center, the master of all he surveyed.

The ambiguity of sixty centers on issues of control. In ideal typic terms, the sixty-year-old is at the height of his or her control of kin, household, hearth, and other resources. The pressure from the next generation to transfer control is at its most intense as well. *Saṭhiyānā*—typifying the stubbornness and willfulness of the older adult—is not only an assessment and criticism of certain kinds of behavior by useless old people but it also expresses resentment against the perceived mind-set of those who hold power. At sixty, the figures of the powerful parent (*saṭṭhā ta paṭṭhā*) and the weak and useless parent (*wah saṭhiyā gayā*) coincide. More than the weakness of old brains, sixtyishness reflects the contested space between genera-tions. In the figure of the angry old person, these frameworks come together.

OEDIPUS IN INDIA

Nothing there is to lose,
Madam, if self there is none.
SUKRITA P. KUMAR, "MASSEY'S TALES"

We thus return to the Kesari Jivan ad: the young man, bent over, huffing and puffing, has just made it up onto the Bombay bus. The old man stands erect, to the side and slightly behind the younger man, his hand holding the younger man firmly in position, touching his lower back. A young woman laughs from a win-dow. The text reads:

60 years old or 60 years young?
Have you ever wondered why the old man who lives down the road is still full
of pep and vigour at 60, while you feel tired and run down at just 30?

Again, the paradox of sixty: is the old man the sixty-year-old senile *saṭhiyānevālā* or the sixty-year-young powerful uncle? The mystery deepens: old men of sixty seem to have the strength of young men of twenty or thirty, whereas younger men are as weak as one would expect old men to be.

From the vantage of a century of Freudian interpretive thought, I find it hard not to read the Kesari Jivan ad in the first instance through the figure of an erotic triangle,[13] with the young man who can't stand up straight (and the potential consumer who may identify with him) at its point of articulation and the figures suggesting his father and wife at the other corners. This kind of reading makes several demands upon me: how does the Kesari Jivan triangle relate to other erotic triangles in the contemporary public culture of which it is a part? And, how does any acknowledgment of the usefulness of such an analysis draw one into debates on the appropriateness of crude psychoanalytic approaches to Indian material, and to the history of such approaches?

My approach here will be to begin by reading the erotic triangle as a structural figure irreducible to any particular narrative or stage of human development. In his classic essay "The Indian Oedipus," A. K. Ramanujan counseled reading erotic triangles about conflicts between parents and children as abstractions of adult experience as much as of childhood.[14] The Kesari Jivan triangle can be contrasted with other triangular images framing the old body in relational terms in order to evaluate the limits of a universe of discourse in which the old body comes to matter in certain ways. The exercise must be seen as a playful one, its usefulness contingent upon the interpretive frames it may generate.

The tonic ad triangle differs from an earlier dilemma, that of the Ghar Kali painting of nineteenth-century Calcutta and of the twentieth-century literature on old mothers and aunts that succeeds it. Unlike either the classic oedipal son-mother-father or the Ghar Kali son-mother-wife groupings, the Zandu ad answers the question of "sixty years old or sixty years young," contrasting the weakness of father and son, in terms of the laughter of a young woman. In Ghar Kali the son and his wife represent a modern order against which the mother suffers; in the Kesari Jivan ad the son—weakened like the figures of young men in many *rasāyana* advertisements by the synergistic depletions of youthful excess and modern life—confronts a traditional order that separates him from his wife and that, through the tonic, he can aspire to embody.

In both cases, the predicament is the son's. In Ghar Kali, the babu-son is twice the size of his mother or wife, dominating the narrative frame; in the ad, the expected weakness of the old father is found to have afflicted the son instead. Within these frames, modernity is a pathology of an aging body in two different ways: as an order that functions by overturning generational hierarchy, generating a strong son and weak old mother, and as an order that functions by seducing the young and depleting their strength, generating a weak son and a strong old father. Within the limits of a structural comparison between a Bengali nineteenth-century image and a Bombay-based late twentieth-century advertisement, one might note that the old man here signifies strength and thus his son's abjection, the old woman weakness and thus her son's rejection.

Within these triangles, the young woman bears the blame for the breach between parent and child. The desire of daughters-in-law, many men and women advised me in Varanasi, can split families: brother against brother, parent against child. Everyday narratives of daughters-in-law that acknowledged their political marginality within families were rare. However politically peripheral, young women were symbolically central to intergenerational relations. In the Kesari Jivan ad, male intergenerational struggle is not represented save as implied competition for the respect of the woman. The possibility of contested relationships between fathers and sons over prerogatives, property, and other household resources is elided, or rather is embodied as the weakness of the son. Sons "lack pep."

When the figure of the *bahū* (daughter-in-law) is framed against that of her *sās* (mother-in-law), most commonly in the parlor dramas of Hindi film, the conflict is overt and not framed as embodied difference. Whether the older *sās* is the victimizer of a guileless *bahū* or the evil *bahū* terrorizes her helpless *sās*, the son, unlike the laughing woman of the ad, is passive. Though sons were politically central to the structure of female intergenerational relations within the patrilocal households I surveyed across class in Varanasi, in film narrative they were usually hapless observers. In the 1989 hit film *Chandni*, a son is turned against his fiancée by the complicity of his mother; in the same year's *Bivi Hai To Aisi*, the son remains blithely unaware of his mother's frequent attempts to murder his wife. Contrary to the position of the daughter-in-law in son/father and son/mother conflicts, sons in *sās/bahū* narratives are politically germane but symbolically elided within the family narrative.

Mothers and daughters-in-law are interchangeable in these narratives. Intergenerational politics are not represented as a continually deferred engagement with the older generation but as an ever-shifting struggle. The contest by older women for the preservation of their control over the household is chronic and overt. In the polarization of *sās* and *bahū*, the ambiguity of sixty—old men as inviolable bodies versus old men as weak and powerless bodies, with no narrative mediation possible between the two states—is given explicit narrative form across the life course. The opposition of powerful/powerless works differently in differently gendered narratives:[15] sixty points to the ambiguities of the old man's age and to the continuities of the old woman's.

Between mother and daughter a different sort of narrative emerges. Daughters, within the standard tableau of the patrilocal family, are married out and they become supplemental to the scene. Mother-daughter engagements, particularly between an elderly mother and a grown daughter, are more frequent in more highbrow literature than in popular texts or film. Perhaps the most arresting story of the old body in Hindi that appeared at the time of this research is Krishna Sobti's *Ai Laṛkī*, a dialogue primarily between an old woman bedridden with a fracture who senses her imminent death and her unmarried daughter, an artist, with whom she lives.[16] The daughter is available to the narrative and to the embodiment of her mother, in part because she has not married and had her own children. The daughter's very availability to her, the younger woman's not having gone on to love, to create life and in so doing to provide for her own old age, troubles the mother. Her son, reminiscent of Ghar Kali, is absent entirely; her hope that at the least he would appear to discharge his ritual obligations to her dying body remains unfulfilled at her death.

The territory between mother and daughter here is open, not anchored by a stable third and its ensuing triangular logic. Provisional triangles appear and dissolve as the mother, in articulating both her difference from and similarity to her independent and unmarried daughter, remembers her life anew. There are memories of a husband, and worries about a husband her daughter never had. There is a doctor who briefly stands in for the missing son but who can provide only life, not the proper closure the son never brings. There is a servant, Susan, who offers a different triangulation, a necessary and benign presence against which mother and daughter *together* create the possibility of memory rooted in death.[17]

In *Ai Laṛkī*, neither mother or daughter need embody weakness and death in the exclusive manner in which either the father or the son but not both must be the weak body negotiated at the site of sixtyishness. The Kesari Jivan image articulates one of the two generational possibilities: the father strong, the son weak. The choreography of the advertisement—its image of filial weakness with a soupçon of paternal penetration—is reminiscent of the psychoanalytic arguments for Indian adult male deferral to authority advanced by G. M. Carstairs and Sudhir Kakar and of the tales of paternal aggression collected and discussed by Ramanujan in "The Indian Oedipus."[18] Carstairs and Kakar offer narratives of Indian male psychosexual development that make sense of ethnographic and clinical findings by construing the self in question as more hierarchical and more desirous of its subordination to powerful male others: "more," that is, in relation to an implicit Western self that is presumed to resist subordination and to engage authority. The difficulty with this Indian Oedipus is in its all-too-convenient validation of the colonial construction of the Indian as desiring colonization, as sexually dependent on colonial difference.[19]

Carstairs's *The Twice-Born* illustrates the enormity of unrecognized countertransference in the putative psychoanalysis of culture. Carstairs wrote within the mid-twentieth-century idiom of Culture and Personality; his effort was to study the "genesis of national character" in India through "events which occur in the earliest stages of psychological maturation."[20] As in most studies of the "Indian self," the definition of "Indian" was limited to men of high status. Carstairs's argument engaged as scientific types figures with a lengthy pedigree: the split mother and the despotic father. He used careful ethnographic observation in a Rajasthani town to show that children, by which he meant boys, were pampered in early childhood in a maternal environment and then moved rather abruptly into a far more hierarchical world of paternal duty and demand, estranged from the mother. Thus:

> I suggest that this relatively late reversal of a previously dominating (although emotionally inconsistent) relationship with his mother has a profound effect upon the child's later development. The underlying mistrust which seems to cloud so many of my informants' adult personal relationships may well be derived from the phantasy

of a fickle mother who mysteriously withholds her caresses and attentions from time to time.

By inconstant, Carstairs referred to his observation that neither parent, in the presence of their elders, could show strong affection toward his or her child. The child, he suggested, would therefore experience the temporary and unpredictable loss of the mother's love. The result of both the inconstancy of the mother and the ultimate shift from the female to the male world was the fantasy and ubiquitous symbol, in Hindu devotional practice, of the bad mother, "someone terrible, revengeful, bloodthirsty and demanding in the same limitless way ... a horrific figure, decapitating men and drinking their blood." A child's mother, in short, was the goddess Kali, read as grotesque by Carstairs in a fashion more sympathetic to lurid missionary accounts of Thuggee practice than to the details of his own reported fieldwork. Her relationship to her son had to be contrasted "with the Western child whose familiarity with intermittent experiences of frustration and delayed satisfaction has enabled him to indulge his aggressive phantasies in moderation, only to be reassured by his mother's renewed affectionate attentions." Once the boy was deprived of maternal attention, his father became "intensely significant":

> From this time on his father's voice will be associated with commands which must be obeyed. The pain of defeat by the father in the oedipal situation is greatly intensified by the frequency with which the child is an involuntary witness of parental intercourse. It is not lightened, as in the West by the creation of a warm relationship between father and son. This has been prevented by the taboo upon the father's giving expression to affectionate feelings for his child. Instead, it appears to the boy that he has no choice other than that of unconditional surrender before this strong intruding stranger, his father. He must not only submit before this rival, but must deny any wish to compete with him. This is clearly reflected in the Hindu's later attitude towards his fellow men. To his father, and to figures of authority in general he owes unquestioning obedience.

Fathers sapped their sons' bodies, demanding not only obedience but hot youth:

> In effect all those who occupy the status of sons or younger brothers are required to enact a symbolic self-castration, denying themselves the right to lead an emotional or sexual life of their own so long as the father-figures still live and dominate them. This is implicit in the Hindus' willing subservience to autocratic Rajahs, to the rich, and to important officials.[21]

Sons not only castrated themselves in the presence of powerful others, they longed to be penetrated. Under the heading of "paranoia," Carstairs observed that Hindus were not only obsequious and passive, but that they could not be trusted and trusted no one in turn. This finding, too, could be laid at the door of the father:

> According to Freudian theory, paranoid reactions can be traced to one type of outcome of the Oedipus situation, namely that in which the boy assumes a passive role

and in phantasy has a homosexual love-relationship with his father. But while he longs to be possessed in this way, the child also fears and repudiates his desire; hence the transition from "I love him", through "I hate him", to "He hates me", on which delusions of persecution are based. . . . In my informants' phantasies . . . there is also a powerfully-repressed homosexual fixation on the father. This is shown not only in the ever-recurring paranoid reactions, but also, in indirect and sublimated form, in a man's feelings toward his Guru—the one context in which a warm affectionate relationship (although a passive and dependent one) is given free expression. Since this occurs at the stage of development when anal functions are the focus of keenest emotional interest, the conflict is usually expressed in anal terms.

Carstairs's vivid portrayal of upper-caste Rajasthani male Hindus as dominated by a singularly dysfunctional "covert pattern of irrational complexes"—stressing the "infantile" desire for authority and the "emasculate" desire for penetration—attempted to naturalize through a powerful and selectively applied rhetoric of child development a particular narrative of the Indian male self. The most well known formulation of this narrative is Dumont's *Homo Hierarchicus;* one of its most provocative critiques is that of Nandy in *The Intimate Enemy.*

Nandy examined both "the homology between childhood and the state of being colonized which a modern colonial system almost invariably uses" and "the homology between sexual and political dominance . . . the idea of colonial rule as a manly or husbandly or lordly prerogative." Using the same psychoanalytic terminology of the defensive identification with an aggressor that Carstairs drew on in describing male generational relations, Nandy suggested that many Indians internalized their colonial construction as less mature and less "male" (Nandy's analysis, like Carstairs's, founders on the possibility of female subjects). Against the naturalized passive "homosexuality" and childlike dependence on authority Carstairs roots in local child-rearing practice, Nandy argued that the psychodynamics of the gendered and generational ego must be evaluated in terms of the macropolitics of the colonial and postcolonial engagement.[22]

Juxtaposing Carstairs with Nandy, we are confronted with a peculiar absence in Carstairs's text. *The Twice-Born* presumes aggressive fathers who in the context of the bad mother transform their sons into virtual *hijras*, anal-receptive eunuchs,[23] but we actually learn very little about the phenomenology or psychodynamics of being a father over time. Carstairs's constant identification of his male informants with their filial position echoes the way British colonial officers articulated their relation to their native soldiers as being their *mai-bāp*, their mother and father. His effort to read experience through childhood precluded an attempt to make sense of the structure of adult male affection and aggression over time. The model he offers leaves little room for a coherent unfolding of male power, aggression, strategy, and heterosexuality; we do not learn how his informants get their genitals back and how, in the interim, they manage the appearance of masculinity in innumerable contexts.

For Nandy, the absent father is replaced by the colonial father, a position invisible in Carstairs's text as it constitutes the source of narrative, the position of anthropology.[24] A colonial gaze constituted the Indian as a split subjectivity: the infantile, narcissistic, and effeminate son (the subject of colonial rule) and the senescent, softened, and despotic father (the essence of Indian culture). Depersonalized and dispersed as "culture," the position of the father vanishes as a coherent site in a psychological anthropology; we are left with the son as the overdetermined site of selfhood.

Kakar's treatment of the Indian family in *The Inner World* is far more carefully constructed; Indian selfhood, again gendered male, is not presented as maladaptive psychopathology but successful adaptation to lived experience. The fractured oedipal triangle—the son with an ambivalent relationship to the bad mother and a passive anal eroticism towards the father—still predominates. The connection to the sociology of India is more explicit; in a section entitled the "Ontogeny of homo hierarchicus," Kakar explores "this resolution of the oedipal conflict by means of a submissive, apprentice-like stance toward elder men in the family," a stance that leaves

> a psycho-sexual residue in the unconscious that influences the rest of a boy's life; in the identity development of Indian men, this has generated a passive-receptive attitude towards authority figures of all kinds. The psycho-dynamic contours of this traditional and nearly ubiquitous stance towards authority become markedly plain in situations that reactivate the childhood conflict. Thus, for example, whereas in the West the unconscious passive homosexual temptations of patients that emerge at certain stages of psycho-analytic therapy invariably provoke intense anxiety, analogous fantasies and dreams among Indian patients have a relatively easier, less anxious access to consciousness.

Paralleling this observed difference between Western and Indian analysands in the degree of anxiety that "passive homosexual temptations" generate, Carstairs and Kakar differ in the concern they manifest about the *meaning* of such dreams and fantasies. For Carstairs, the Indian male psyche is envisioned as passively homosexual and coprophiliac to boot; no such "intense anxiety" or "analogous fantasies" attend Kakar's treatment of similar material. Men may dream, in the West and in India, about similar things; Indian men seem to interpret and experience one set of similar things with far less anxiety. "Homosexual" expression of male hierarchy is universal, Kakar suggests, extending to other primates. India is restored to the order of the normal; "the West" becomes an aberration:

> The erect penis and the offer of the anus among human males, as among many other primates, are symbolic of an attempt to establish a hierarchical order in their relationships. The fantasy among Indian patients of anal assault by an authority figure reflects not so much the occult pleasure and guilt of anal eroticism as it does the (relatively unconflicted) acceptance of the dominance of "those in authority" and the wish to incorporate some of their power into oneself. The high frequency

among adolescent boys and young men in India of swear-words with the general tenor, "fuck you in the anus", is another index of the common masculine preoccupation with hierarchical status.[25]

Kakar shifts the meaning of overt and fantasied references to anal sex away from discussions of sex and the body to a universal phenomenology of hierarchy. The move is far from satisfying—India is still identified *tout court* with hierarchy; the possibility of a psychology of women, identity and hierarchy remains at best murky; and critical questions of violence and of a multiplicity of desiring positions behind the language of "anal eroticism" remain[26]—and yet Kakar's move from pathology to politics offers a powerful rereading of Carstairs. The invocation of the primate order and the reflex naturalness of anal display—though dependent upon the circular reasoning involved in using models of primate behavior rooted in assumptions about human behavior to explain human behavior, and though reducing the possibility of homoerotic intentionality to neural reflex—shifts the tenor of social analysis away from hierarchy as an *essentially* Indian phenomenon, something that must be explained by recourse to the primacy of structure (Dumont) or familial pathology (Carstairs).

Finally, Kakar, unlike Carstairs, takes somewhat more seriously the study of Indian adulthood: "culture" lacks the narrative presence it has for the foreign anthropologist, and the father correspondingly rematerializes as a distinct subject. Still, in his contribution to his edited volume *Identity and Adulthood*, the adulthood discussed is the ideal model of *āśramadharma*: the father's disengagement is framed as a reflective and soteriologic individual process rather than a contested and ambivalent interpersonal one.[27] I will return to Kakar's model of normative Hindu adulthood; but to make sense of sixtyishness, we need yet to linger on the question of the exchanges between sons and fathers, between sons and mothers, and on the gifts entailed in these relationships.

Despite his significant interventions in reshaping the debate on Indian character, Kakar retains the young man's passive acceptance of older male authority as fundamental to the Indian male psyche. The logic of the tonic ad is consonant with such a retention. The young man feels weak, forgetful, and impotent at thirty and is attracted to the inviolable body of sixty. Through the purchase of the tonic, which alters young men's old age weakness through the transfer of old men's youthful strength, young men come to be as old men, *saṭṭhā ta paṭṭhā*, sixty therefore strong.

This narrative of trouble in male intergenerational relations as embodied in the son as opposed to in the political space between son and father assumes the son's infinite deferral of all conflict. The move from the construction of male self through the sixty-years-strong power of older men to the attribution of sixtyish behavior to older men happens only through a radical narrative break—the father's sudden development of serious physical, mental, and/or social debility—allowing the son to become the father unambiguously. Conflict between generations over whether the father is "sixty therefore strong" or "sixtyish" is not representable within these tales.

But one can shift the primary locus of repression, from sons to fathers, to suggest that what is repressed in such narratives is not the possibility of intergenerational conflict but rather its frequent enactment. Rather than simply deny the developmental story of boys that is told by these analysts—though I share Nandy's suspicion of such sorts of narrative, alternative modeling awaits far more and better studies of psychological development across gender, class, location, and family size[28] —I see it as but one part of a far more complex construction of the developing self. Conflict may well be deferred, such deferral may well be adaptive (after Kakar and against Carstairs), and such deferral may be more than the universal reflexes of homosocial relations (after Carstairs and against Kakar), but the importance of such deferrals does not legitimate the erasure of all contest. Such erasure may lie less in the psychodynamics of being a son and their basis in early childhood than in the political economy of patriarchal control in the propertied and landed households of the not-yet-gone-sixtyish.

Ramanujan observed that most Indian "oedipal" tales of same-sex intergenerational conflict are narrated from the intentional perspective of the father; that is, fathers hate sons and love daughters rather than sons hate fathers and love mothers.[29] More than Kakar, Ramanujan returned the father to the psychoanalytic family scene from which he had been deleted. Within the mythological literature Ramanujan cited, sons of course do defer engagement with fathers and willfully accept castration-like violence; the classic example is the origin story of the elephant-headed god Ganesha, who allows various older male figures (Shiva, Shani, Vishnu, Parashurama) to cut off his head and one of his tusks. Though this story has become a cynosure in the psychoanalytic study of Hindu myth,[30] its analysis usually reads the *repetition* of Ganesha's actions, his continually entering conflicts and then accepting mutilation, as but an intensification of the primary deferral. Yet the point that passes without comment is that Ganesha constantly returns to the fray: his frequent bearing of the "castrating" blow must be read in the context of his continued engagement in the field of conflict.

The acceptance of the burden of the father in such mythological narratives, as in Ganesha's allowing Shiva's ax to cut off his tusk, does not presume the necessarily strong body of the father. To reclaim the importance of ongoing intergenerational conflict in the psychic structure of the family, I examine two stories of the relations between sons and their parents well-known in Varanasi: from the *Mahābhārata*, the story of Yayati, and from the *Ramāyaṇa*, the story of Shravan (in folk tellings in Varanasi, Sharvan) Kumar.

COUNTING THE DAYS AND HOURS

The central family plot of the *Mahābhārata*—the horizontal and fraternal fission between the Pandava and Kaurava cousins—is preceded in genealogical time by the vertical fission between King Yayati and his sons. For breaking his marriage vow and taking his wife's servant and rival to bed, Yayati is cursed by his Brahman father-in-law Ushanas with premature decrepitude. Ushanas, in cursing Yayati, is portrayed as the archetypical angry rishi: "So it befell that Uśanas in anger cursed Yayāti Nāhuṣa. And he lost his previous youth and fell instantly to senility."

Senility is here the generalized decrepitude of the body. Ushanas curses out of the quick anger of the sage, and afterward attempts to mitigate his harsh words: "Such things I do not say idly. You have reached old age, king of the earth. But if you wish, you may pass on your old age to another. . . . The son who will give you his youth shall become the king, long-lived, famous, and rich in offspring." The play of generations is extended: Old Ushanas gives his son-in-law old age for disobeying him. But if Yayati's son will take on his father's old age in turn, Yayati can remain youthful, *saṭṭhā ta paṭṭhā*. The reward to Yayati's obedient son is the opposite of Yayati's punishment for disobedience: the son who takes on the father's old age will receive long life and the ultimate deferment of his own old age. The young who act young get old, the young who act old get young: again the logic of Geri-forte.

All but one of Yayati's sons, however, resist his request to exchange ages. They graphically cite the indignities and miseries of old age: their primary concern is the powerlessness of the old man. Only the youngest son, Puru, who stands farthest from the succession and therefore has the least to lose by deferring his youthful prerogative, is willing to take on Yayati's burden. Sons, the story suggests, do not willingly defer to the father, unless they have little to gain otherwise. Youngest sons, therefore, bear their father's old age more commonly than do their older brothers. Conflict, not deferral, is more likely to characterize the exchange of weakness between father and son.

Stricken with old age, Yayāti repaired to his castle and addressed his eldest and dearest son Yadu: "Son, old age and wrinkles and gray hairs have all laid hold of me, because of a curse of Uśanas Kāvya, and I am not yet sated of youth. You, Yadu, must take over my guilt with my old age, and with your own youth I shall slake my senses. When the millennium is full, I shall give your youth back to you, and take over the guilt and old age.

Yadu said:

Gray of head and beard, wretched, loosened by senility, the body wrinkled, ugly, weak, thin, incapable of achieving anything, and set upon by younger men and all the people that live off you? I do not crave old age.

Yayāti said:

You were born from my heart, but will not render your youth to me. Therefore, son, your offspring shall have no share in the kingdom!

Turvaśu, take over my guilt with my old age, and with your youth I shall slake my senses, my son. When the millennium is full, I shall give your youth back to you and take over my own guilt with my old age.

Turvaśu said:

I do not crave old age, father, which destroys all pleasure and joy, finishes strength and beauty, and puts an end to spirit and breath.

Yayāti said:

You were born from my heart but will not render your youth to me. Therefore, Turvaśu, your offspring will face distinction. Fool, you shall rule over people whose customs and laws are corrupt and whose walks of life run counter to decency, the lowest ones who feed on meat. They will lust after the wives of their gurus and couple with beasts; evil barbarians that follow the law of cattle are they whom you will rule!

Yayati's third son, Druhyu, rejects old age as well, drawing attention to the peculiar voice of the old person: "An old man enjoys neither elephant nor chariot nor horse nor woman, and speech fails him. I do not crave such old age." Anu, the fourth son, evokes the pathos of second childhood:

An old man eats his food like a baby, unclean, drooling, and at any time of the day. And he never offers to the fire in time. Such old age I do not crave.

Yayāti said:

You were born from my heart, but will not render your youth to me. You have spoken of the ills of old age, therefore you shall inherit them.

Only Puru, the youngest, accepts and is offered the inheritance of the kingdom. He trusts that his father will only hold on to power as long as is proper, and, the epic narrative relates, so Yayati does.

When he judged that the millennium was full, after having counted days and hours, being expert in Time, the mighty king spoke to his son Pūru: "I have sought pleasure, as I wished and could and had leisure, with your youth, my son, tamer of enemies. Pūru, I am pleased, I bless you. Now take back your own youth and likewise take the kingdom, for you are the son who did my pleasure." Whereupon the king Yayāti Nāhuṣa took on his old age and Pūru took on his youth.[31]

The text asserts that fathers are expert in Time and that their counting of days and hours is impartial. Yayati's sons demur; for them, his request is an overstepping of his hours and days and an appropriation of theirs. Old men, they suggest, claim mastery of Time but have lost the ability to know it: they eat at random hours, they cannot sacrifice in time. The narrative does not allow them to claim their prerogatives, but hints at a world of contest in which sons do not wait for but overthrow fathers.

Unlike to the unsuccessful filial rebellion against Yayati's demand, the story of Shravan Kumar in the *Ramāyaṇa* offers the idealized image of filial devotion and deferral. Shravan's devotion, however, presumes the powerless bodies of his parents and points us to a far more nuanced understanding of generational deferral. The story is popular in Varanasi. Baidyanath Sarasvati, in a book on emblematic practices of Varanasi culture, includes a photograph of Shravan being portrayed by a young man during the Ram Lila celebration.[32] In bazaars throughout the city, sellers of calendar art posters offer the image of the strong and youthful body of a young ascetic bearing his aged parents in baskets suspended from a yoke resting on his broad shoulders (see image on p. 152). The pair are calmly absorbed in religious devotion, counting their prayers on their *rudrākṣa*s, rosaries of the same type that becomes a leash in the Ghar Kali tableau. Around this image are pictorial vignettes of the story of Shravan's accidental death at the hands of Dasharath, the man who will be the father of the hero and divine incarnation Ram.

In Valmiki's *Ramāyaṇa*, the young ascetic is unnamed. Dasharath, when still "an intemperate youth," was eager to use his skills as an archer to go hunting at night. Like young Yayati, Dasharath seeks forbidden pleasures, here encompassed in his desire for his arrow to hit home in the darkness. But Dasharath, mistaking the young ascetic for an animal, mortally wounds him as he goes down to the river to fetch water. Not yet knowing his attacker, the ascetic speaks:

> It is not for the loss of my own life that I am grieving so. It is for two others I grieve that [I] am slain, my mother and father.
>
> For they are an aged couple and have long been dependent on me. When I am dead what sort of existence are they to lead?
>
> My aged mother and father and I all slain by a single arrow!

The son bids Dasharath to find his parents, and dies. Dasharath leads the pair, both blind, to their son's body.

> The wretched couple drew close, they touched their son and collapsed upon his body. And his father cried out:
>
> "My son, don't you love me any more? At least have regard for your mother then, righteous child. Why don't you embrace me, my son? Speak to me, my tender child.
>
> "Whom shall I hear late at night—how it used to touch my heart—so sweetly reciting the sacred texts or other works?
>
> "And after the twilight worship, the ritual bath, and offerings to the sacred fire, who will sit down beside me, my son, to allay the grief and fear that anguish me?
>
> "Who will bring me tubers and fruit and roots, and feed me like a welcome guest—me an invalid, without leader or guide?
>
> "And how, my son, shall I support your poor mother, blind and aged as she is, wretched and yearning for her son?"[33]

The desolate father curses Dasharath to die yearning for his own son; Dasharath recalls his deed when Ram has been exiled to the forest by his own unintended decree.

Shravan Kumar, as he is known to many who buy his calendar image, the son as perfect ascetic devoted to his parents, has become old not in bodily terms like Yayati's son Puru but in a deeper sense, of *āśramadharma*. He is called a forest dweller and ascetic; in his devotion to his parents, he has assumed the appropriate dharma, or duty of old age. But Shravan's enactment of old age—the ability to take on the burden that most of Yayati's sons refuse—presumes the powerful body of youth. Shravan is the source of solace that he is in his father's lament because he can carry both his parents. The image of the poster is far different than the generational embodiment of the Kesari Jivan ad. Shravan is upright and strong, and carries his parents easily. Their bodies, seated in the two baskets, are tiny in relation to his, almost doll-like. They are focused inward; the only sound the image suggests we can hear is the clicking of their rosaries.

Shravan is the epitome of *sevā*, devoted service, to one's parents. Far from a position of submission, the fantasied *sevā* of the Shravan Kumar image is represented as originating from a position of power that assumes the static, reduced, and silent bodies of the old parents. *Sevā*, as embodied in Shravan Kumar, his parents, and the king, is *the impossible gift by grown children of their body to aged parents while their superior position and the parents' passive and voiceless disengagement are maintained*. Impossible, as parents are not the reduced and almost weightless bodies of the narrative. Like Yayati, parents not only want and need *sevā*, they want to control the family, embodied as the youthful body contested by Yayati, his father-in-law, and his children. The transfer of such authority emerges through an extended process of conflict and negotiation. Children have powerful bodies, and parents have voices. Old age is seldom silent; as parents grow increasingly dependent upon their children, they are perceived by the latter more and more as a singular voice: the request. Yayati asks the same impossible question again and again and again: let *me* be *you*. Sylvia Vatuk has noted how the elderly with whom she worked near Delhi combined a sense of self as an ascetic with strong expectations of and worries over maintaining their comforts and prerogatives and over the substance of their children's *sevā*.[34] Siranji, in challenging her children's gift of the tonic, suggested that their *sevā* was but a performance. Her children, in protesting that they were doing all that they could for her, suggested that the performance may be generated not by callousness but love. The voice of parents, even those who perceive themselves as ascetics, grows ever louder as they age. Children can never be Shravan, whose success is framed by his parents' minimally transacting interiority. Like Ram and Dasharath, they are cursed never to be able to offer complete *sevā* nor to enjoy its fruits.

Old fathers cannot claim their sons' hot bodies for long. Their cooling and weak physiologies prevent them from exercising adequate control, and their demands for continued authority become empty and inappropriate, *bakbak*—so much nonsense or hot air. Sixtyishness points to the contested authority between generations, embodied as a disjunction between a cooling body and a will or brain that cannot recognize the process. From this perspective, the heat of old brains is a reaction to the reality of old and cold; it is the proverbial rope of Indian philosophy, mistaken for a snake along the road at dusk, the symptom of false consciousness.

Yet sons are no better counters of the hours than fathers. Parents resist handing over control of Time, knowing like the patriarch of the film *Apne Begāne* that most children, despite the assertions of Carstairs and Kakar, are not Shravan. Sixty, an age simultaneously old enough to convey the same inappropriate and hot-brained behavior as seventy-two and young enough to convey the powerful body of the paterfamilias, reflects neither only the reality of the Bombay bus man and Devi Lal nor that of Shravan's parents, but alludes to their superimposition and the contest, within families, involved in marking the body in time.

OLD WOMEN AT THE POLLS

Sau dafe dādī kahen, bād men daṇḍa māren.
[A hundred times they'll say "Grandmother"; afterward they'll beat you]
OLD WOMAN IN DELHI, ON WHY SHE NO LONGER VOTED
("THE ELECTION CERTAINLY HAS ITS LIGHTER MOMENTS . . . ," *TIMES OF INDIA*, 1989)

In Sobti's *Ai Laṛkī*, the old woman and her daughter together mark her dying body: the space between mother and daughter, unlike those between father and son or *sās* and *bahū*, suggests that the contest over the old body can be a productive site of meaning and exchange. A pair of poems by the Indian English poet Sukrita Kumar suggests a similar distinction: in "Fathers and Sons," cited in an epigraph above, a father frames his son as replacing him, a relation of *substitution* in which only one man at a time can occupy the position of virility; in "Mothers and Daughters," a mother frames an analogous realization of her daughter's maturing body as a relation of *identity*: mothers and daughters seeing themselves reflected in the aging of the other, and vice versa.[35] These ideal types of intergenerational dyads—mother/daughter, father/son, mother-in-law/daughter-in-law—structure a universe of discourse in which larger collectivities are continually materialized.

The relationship between an old mother and her son, as in the apocalyptic vision of modernity of Ghar Kali, may signify a larger frame than the intergenerational dynamics of substitution and identity. In this painting, later a popularly circulated lithograph, the old mother's abjection suggests the fallen present of the babu's Calcutta. The reality of the Kali Age, of the collapse of righteousness and dharma in the fallen present, is corporeally demonstrated in the figure of the old mother transformed into an alley dog, dragged along behind her son and *bahū* on a leash.

That the phenomenal universe ages, is destroyed and reabsorbed into the unmarked totality of God or Brahman, and after a period of cosmic night is created anew is a central theme of the medieval Puranic literature in Sanskrit. Kali Yuga, the Ghar Kali of the Bengali image, is the last of the four stages of devolution, in which dharma or righteousness, imagined as a cow, totters on its final leg in humanity and the universe's last gasp before their destruction. Marriott has offered the most compelling discussion of the relevance of this temporal order of the yugas to a contemporary sociology, reading the temporal axis as an index of "unmatching," the tendency of relations in the cosmos—between cause and effect, signifier and signified, totality and individual or group—to become unglued, increasingly less coherent.[36] Within the analytic frame of Kali Yuga, social and signifying relations will never be adequately encompassed by a structural logic of culture as totality, be it that of Dumont or Marriott himself.

The relation between the aging of the current universe, which takes place in four stages before its dissolution and rebirth, is not explicitly predicated on the aging of the person, in four stages before her dissolution and rebirth. *Sannyāsa* is not explicitly identified with Kali Yuga in textual discussions of either. The third and fourth positions of *āśramadharma* are after all steps or paths out of the illusory world of birth and rebirth, out of the cycle of decay: it is the old person caught by desire who fails to move on and leave the household, or the kingdom who decays and dries up, like the foolish king of the *Kathāsaritsāgara*, like the cosmos in Kali Yuga. Puranic descriptions of Kali Yuga and of the cosmic dissolution and reabsorption that follow often include descriptions of the aging of the body, in which old age is explicitly a sign of cosmic decay. Thus in the *Brahma Purana*, which the editors of the Motilal Banarsidass/UNESCO Puranic translation series assign to a period between the ninth and thirteenth centuries,[37] a section on the "natural reabsorption" of the cosmos is followed by a section on the "ultimate reabsorption" of the human body, a rather unpleasant meditation of the embodiment of ignorance. In old age,

> man undergoes many miseries as follows: His body is shattered by old age. His limbs are enfeebled and flaccid. His teeth are broken and loose. He is covered by wrinkles and protruding sinews and nerves and veins.
>
> His eyes are incapable of seeing anything far off. His pupils are fixed to the sky. Clusters of hair come out of his nostrils. The whole of his body shakes and shivers.
>
> His bones are laid bare. The bones at his back are bent. Since his gastric fire does not function, he takes but little food. He is capable of only a few movements.
>
> He experiences difficulties in rising up, in moving about, in lying down, in sitting and in his movements. His eyes and ears become less keen. Saliva exudes from his mouth and defiles his face.
>
> With his sense organs intractable, he looks up to his early death. He is not capable of remembering anything experienced at the very same moment.
>
> In uttering a sentence even once he has to put in great effort. He spends sleepless nights due to the strain of ailments such as asthma, bronchitis (cough) etc.
>
> The old man has to be lifted up or laid to rest with the help of another man. He is disdained and insulted by his servants, sons and wife.[38]

The description continues, and is followed by a discussion of the sufferings of the deathbed, the sufferings of hell, and the sufferings of the fetus in the womb and during childbirth: the cycle rolls on. The description is naturalistic, the normative order unless one acts to end one's ignorance, and the body in decline is gendered male. The sufferings of the old man under the sign of Kali Yuga, and in particular his treatment at the hands of his sons and wife, are inevitable and point not to Kali Yuga as metaphor for immediate cultural crisis but Kali Yuga as soteriologic frame. The slippage between the body of the father and the dharma of the Father is comprehended under the sign of Kali Yuga.

The decadence of Kali Yuga often includes reversals of gender: in a later text, the *Padma Purana*, in the last age "all men will be subjugated by women":[39] the figure of the babu's wife, astride her husband. But the image of the body of the

cosmos as an old woman is not a feature of the classic Puranic depiction. The abject mother, when she appears, points with immediacy to the neglectful son and an
inexplicable lack and not, unlike the abject father, to the inevitable substitution of
son for father.

Colonial rhetoric added additional dimensions to the decrepit old woman as
sign of a lack. The *Bengal Hurkaru* depiction of the aged "houris of the East," mentioned in the introduction, is predicated upon the colonial observer's hope of
glimpsing young native women in wet saris. All rots quickly in the tropics, and the
old woman stands at the juncture of colonial desire and the senescent logic of the
Other. Orientalist writing drew upon local figures of old women and repositioned
them. Sir William Jones, founder of the Asiatic Society and of many of the institutional and discursive forms of Indology, prefaced his translation of Kalidasa's
drama, *Śakuntalā*, with a "modern epigram" that had been "lately repeated to
me," concerning the great esteem in which the dramatist was held:

> Poetry was the sportful daughter of Vālmic, and, having been educated by Vyāsa,
> she chose Cālidās for her bridegroom after the manner of Viderbha: she was the
> mother of Amara, Sundar, Sanc'ha, Dhanic; but now, old and decrepit, her beauty
> faded, and her unadorned feet slipping as she walks, in whose cottage does she dis-
> dain to take shelter?[40]

The source of the quotation and its exact age are not mentioned by Jones; whatever its antiquity, it is of significance that Jones was told it as a *modern* epigram,
reflecting not just the decline of poetry under the general unmatching of Kali Yuga
but the particular decline of language in the world after Kalidasa and his successors. Jones's informant may have meant the final question and its accompanying
image as an unanswerable sign of contemporary cultural crisis, but in Jones's use of
it within his own project of translation and reclamation a different sort of answer
emerges: in the cottage of Sir William Jones, and the Asiatic Society he founds.

Such an answer has little direct relevance for the new urban world of Ghar
Kali; the presence of the British provides a new urgency to the question, but the
answer to the emerging dilemma of *bhadralok* culture took shape on different terrain. Partha Chatterjee has discussed the consequent development of a split between domestic and feminized interiority in which an authentic and uncompro-
mised selfhood could be maintained and a worldly and masculinized exteriority in
which the demands of colonial rule and cultural compromise could be sustained
with minimal loss of self.[41] The power of Ghar Kali may lie in its troubling of this
gendered splitting, through its reconfiguration of the interior world of woman as
a conflicted substitution of daughter-in-law for mother-in-law. Age challenges the
seamlessness of gender.

The predicament of Modern India as the predicament of the aged mother
awaiting the missing *sevā* of her inattentive son becomes instantiated as a central
narrative of post-Independence electoral politics. Politicians in election years frequently have their picture taken while bending down to touch the feet of an old

woman, her body framed by the doorway of a slum dwelling. The image is of the politician as the good son, healing the suffering of the citizen-as-mother by reestablishing the proper flow of *sevā* and thus undoing the wrongs of the Kali Age. On the front page of the *Times of India* on November 4, 1989, the powerful and by some accounts unscrupulous Congress politician Jagdish Tytler was pictured "seeking the blessings of an old woman by touching her feet during his campaign trail." As if to demonstrate its neutrality, the paper offered a candidate from the then-opposition Janata Dal party being "blessed by an elderly woman" the following week.[42] The *praṇām*, the respectful obeisance to one's seniors, becomes the populist gesture reminiscent of another society's kissing of babies.

Beyond their attempted appropriation by particular parties, old people and especially old women come to serve as symbols of the franchised citizen, of the electorate in itself. During the same national election, the Hindi daily *Dainak* offered a figure of a shrunken old widow in white sari and close-cropped hair walking steadfastly with the support of two young men toward a village polling place; her age was given as 120.[43] A *Times of India* article showed a grimacing old woman being carried to the polling place by a young man, while young women in line to vote look on. The article suggested, in discussing voting by the aged and infirm, that "democracy in India has come of age, has in fact really become mature." The image, with the old woman in the arms of the young man and the younger women displaced to the side, is the reverse of Ghar Kali. The son has come back to the old mother; the early uxorious flirtations of the babu have been replaced by a return to the family through the old body, and democracy has "come of age" from its unstated Indian infantilism.[44] Similar images and narratives circulated in the 1996 Lok Sabha elections.

One particular photograph of the old woman voting was frequently recycled in the *Times of India*: in 1989 she was the Muslim voter, in 1990 the archetypical Indian. Clad in the burka of a Muslim woman, she peers, bespectacled, over the ballot box and holds her ballot over the open slot (see photograph on p. 290).[45] A disembodied hand from the side of the picture points to the slot, directing her attention and activity. The pointing finger directs our gaze as well, but we do not know who points. The multiply subordinate figure—old, shortsighted, female, Muslim—may signify modern franchise in two ways: it suggests that even the weakest in society have the power of the vote, and conversely, that the voter is but an old woman, easily manipulated by interests dimly seen beyond the hand that directs one to the hole wherein one's future lies.

THE PHENOMENOLOGY OF THE VOICE

To locate the difference of old mothers and fathers more carefully, we move from vision to voice. When Banarsis in each of the four neighborhoods described what made a given old person different than before, it was often in terms of the quality or quantity of their voice. I began to learn to take *listening* seriously. Hot brain and sixtyishness were less seen than heard in their recounting, and this hearing emerged within a complex but bounded typology. In the neighborhoods, voices were described most often as angry, as repetitive, or as the nonvoice of silence, sadness, or loneliness. Each of these voices had a moral quality, heard either as positive and fluid (generative, wise, or transcendental) or negative and stagnant (selfish, meaningless, or pathetic). In Marriott's terminology, the stagnant voice was "unmatching." It was a signifier that was increasingly dissociated from what it purported to signify, registering, like *Aitaśa pralāpa*, only as incoherence. Its opposite, the fluid voice, was not the more neutral everyday language of the young in which the voice more or less signified as its expected content but something superordinately "matching." A fluid and powerful old voice was not only heard as its content but it made incontrovertible demands upon a listener, interpellating all within range as subjects of a generational economy.

Anger was not just the selfish demands of the hot-brained individual who could not adapt or who was too weak to contain him or herself. The angry voice of an old person could be transformative, and its heat carried the force of its powerful truth. In Nagwa slum, I was once sitting with a group of regulars at Secchan's tea stall. Harinath Prasad, the local schoolteacher or Masterji, an old man with whom I spoke frequently, came walking briskly by. He overheard the conversation we were having, one of those repeated discussions about how far away America was and how expensive it was to go there, and joined in, shifting the talk to a discussion of the earth and its spin. It was 1988, a leap year, and Harinath said that in this calendar year, "in 366 days" the earth completed a revolution around the sun. "You are mistaken, Masterji," said Secchan, that afternoon as most afternoons slightly drunk. "There are 365 days in a year." Harinath was delighted; someone had walked into his trap. But he looked furious. "Is that so? Are you contradicting me? Write down your claim. Write it down!" Which Secchan, illiterate, could not do. "You can't read or write! How can you know about these things?" A paper was produced, and Harinath asked everyone to remember how many days there had been in each month of that year. The tally totaled 366, and Harinath left in triumph.

"Why was he angry?" I asked, so used to hearing about angry old people. "He wasn't. He was *sahī*," correct, I was told by everyone, generating an opposition between being angry and being right. And Secchan himself, often an irreverent and mean-tempered drunk who had all but abandoned his own aged parents, said, "I am his son. He was teaching me. I know that a year has 365 days in it, but he somehow showed me that this time I was wrong." As an uncle with no claims on Secchan's earnings, Harinath could remain the counter of hours and days; the rectitude of the nonthreatening and the anger of the threatening speak with the same voice.

The voice was heard not only as hot but as *prolific*. Old people in several of the neighborhoods were said to speak uselessly or to *bakbak*. Vatuk's informants noted that when an old person could no longer contribute due to *hāth pair kī kamzorī*, the weakness of hand and foot, then they were heard only as babblers. Against babbling, the voice of old age was often framed as incredibly productive, a wise and inexhaustible source of experience and social memory. The classical figure of the endlessly productive wise voice, on television weekly that year, is that of the ancient warrior Grandfather Bhishma, one of the great heroes of the *Mahābhārata*. Bhishma brings up three generations of Kshatriya warriors and is in the end killed through the agency of one of them, his great-nephew and the hero of the epic, Arjuna. But Bhishma, his body immobilized by the innumerable arrows shot through him and forming a bed upon which he rests, does not die. Gifted with the boon of choosing the hour of his own death, Bhishma remains alive to narrate innumerable matters of statecraft and cosmology to his great-nephew, the future king Yuddhishtara. Effectively bodiless, Bhishma becomes pure voice and takes over the primary narration of the epic. He offers a lengthy discussion of dharma culled from his superannuated experience. Bhishma outlives most of the warriors on the battlefield and dies when the contest is over.

The line between productive wisdom and *bakbak*, as Vatuk's and my own informants often suggested, depends not only on the content of the productive voice but frequently on the politics of the hearing. Bhishma himself, in popular media discussions of the epic during its presentation as a two-year-long television serial, was on occasion presented as the epitome of *bakbak*. In describing the universality of Bhishma's character, the magazine *India Today* noted that "almost every home has an old, despondent man blabbering away, whose advice the younger lot may listen to, but rarely follow."[46]

The third voice of old age was that of *silence*. In third-person terms, old people in Varanasi were frequently described as lonely and depressed. The voice of the uncared-for elder could have been be sullen or tearful silence or a lament, but it was not heard by those for whom it was intended. Lonely voices were less heard than overheard, by others (relatives, neighbors, passersby) as neglected and pathetic markers of a lack of *sevā*. Yet the old person who was not heard might be spoken of by others as the old person who would not be heard, the latter-day forest-dweller. Silence, withdrawal, and a break in communication between young and old pointed as well to the transcendent voice of the *jīvanmukti*, the realized in life, or in more everyday language, to an old person heard as religious, as a serious bhakt, or devotee. The silent voice pointed toward a different politics of relationship and of knowledge, but one capable of making its own powerful demands upon the young. *Kāśīvāsīs* who came to die and be liberated in Kashi were alternately heard in the transfigured speech of the silently knowing and otherworldly or the pathetic speech of the abandoned. The hearing of silence, like that of anger and prolificacy, conveys a split moral understanding of the relation of an old person to his family and surroundings, and requires interpretation.

THE FAMILIAL BODY

. . . recalling his mother in the kitchen, pottering. "Jamun, the anger of parents is never anger."
UPAMANYU CHATTERJEE, *THE LAST BURDEN*

The old woman who lived across the road from a friend of mine in a middle-class Delhi colony frequently shouted and cursed at persons who were never there. Her voice was often heard by her neighbors as angry. I never saw the old woman in Delhi; my friend seemed reluctant to arrange a visit. I was told she was frail and that she lived alone, not with her family but with an attendant paid for by them. It seemed her late son had distanced himself from his parents and had brought up his own children with closer ties to their maternal relations. To the neighbors the old woman seemed clearly not well, *sahī nahīn* as Banarsi friends might have put it, but what was at stake in this not being quite right seemed to preclude a certain public articulation of the meaning of her voice for those wishing to maintain a cordial relationship with her children. She was named neither as mad or diseased nor as the victim of a bad family, though both frames were implied in the silence in which all that could be acknowledged was some sort of unmatching, things no longer being as they should.

To understand what suffering entails, Kleinman and Kleinman remind us, we must understand "what is at stake" for all those who define and are defined by particular moral worlds in which bodies are structurally fixed and intersubjectively lived.[47] Very often during this research, what was at stake when an old person was heard as an unmatched voice was the moral coherence of her or his family. To address the body of the old person is to address that body as embedded in a family and in the transactions that structure and maintain a family. Unlike other generational positions, the old body is not only embedded in its family but is, in a very real sense, appropriated by and *becomes* its family. The old woman's voice in Delhi in its incoherence is an unmatching: the breakdown of signification occurs simultaneously as a crisis in an individual body and in its family. The two are indivisible, the same thing. Her voice connotes a variety of possibilities for her middle-class neighbors—undifferentiated "mental weakness" or "senility," some kind of disease, her refusal to adjust to the inevitable and thus a state of "imbalance," the denouement of conflicts played out over decades, an exaggeration of already existing personality traits. But it denotes, in the immediacy of its hearing, an unmatching in the family, a breakdown of generations. To speak of her voice is to address the state of her family and of families more generally; one therefore may defer from speaking. Again and again during my work, I confronted what at first I took to be a matter of stigma, the reluctance of those with much at stake to share their hearing of a *sahī nahīn* voice, one not quite right. If it was stigma, it was not the stigmatized old body that was tainting its family by association. The old body was not stigmatized as "itself" but *as the body of the family*.

In writing of the familial body I reread the notion of the relational self in the psychological anthropology of the "non-West," particularly India. The "Indian self" has been constituted through the central thematic of the sociology and anthropology of India as being relational, primarily and reflexively structured through its relations to other "selves" and not in terms of an autonomous and interiorized individuality. In the work of Dumont and Carstairs and in much of Kakar, this relationality is read as hierarchy. In the responses to Dumont by Veena Das and Frédérique Marglin and in the work of Marriott and his students, hierarchy is but one dimension of the relationality of a "dividual" or "fluid" self.[48] In their discussions of Indian selfhood, Marriott, Valentine Daniel, and others extend this transactional framework to the body.

The consequences of this sort of rhetorical figures vary. Their limitations reside primarily in their oppositional and comparative origins. A "relational self" has little significance unless it is read from the position of a nonrelational self; the comparative anthropology of selfhood lumps together varieties of self-construction with little in common save their not being definitionally Western. In the case of India, despite the careful work of scholars like Richard Shweder,[49] the literature begins to lose its usefulness the more one weans oneself from crude comparison as the primary epistemological framework of anthropology.[50]

The "familial body" is in some senses a "relational" site, in which exchanges of material sustenance, medicine, and affection between generations constitute the lived body of the dependent elder. But I am neither interested in defining it *primarily* in contradistinction to the dynamics of age elsewhere, nor able to do so. If nothing else, there is an obvious comparative dimension to my use of the term, given the basic hermeneutic conditions of a suburban Jewish New Englander working in urban Varanasi. But I find the rhetoric I deploy here useful not because it helps me define aging in India against aging elsewhere; rather, the familial body, the old voice, and the dying space I write of below are offered as a shorthand that helped me understand and model relations between bodily experience, social dynamics, and particular universes of discourse in Varanasi and that may or may not be useful in other places. They are particularly useful in Varanasi and elsewhere in India given the centrality of the Bad Family as one of the key sites of a contested modernity, and indeed they may help explain the emergence of the Bad Family narrative. But they may provide tools by which to rethink the embodiment of old age in places where different narratives dominate, where rationalized terms like "caregiver" and even "disease" erase the centrality of the familial context of aging.

As a variant on the relational self, the familial body of the old and dependent person is not just constituted through "dividual" intergenerational exchanges. The welfare of the old body becomes a reflection of the welfare of family relations: it is less a relational body in itself than a signifier of relations elsewhere, between others. Old people become familial icons; their suffering, pleasures, and voice become increasingly exhausted in signifying the family and can point less and less to their distinct and separate needs, which become ever less signifiable and more and more identified with what I will term below a dying space.

Becoming one's family entails two linked processes: political marginalization and performative centralization. One must be unable or unwilling to assert a subjectivity that maintains a distinction between oneself and the family. Powerful old fathers and mothers-in-law are set against sons and daughters-in-law: Sons become fathers and daughters and mothers-in-law are opposed. Only when the old person can be politically encompassed by the family network, when there are no significant risks for grown children or gains in intergenerational opposition, does the old person become identified as not the superordinate but the symbolic center of the family.

These processes are complex. First, they are contested: thus the ambiguity of sixty, composed of, on the one hand, the resistance by the aging person to being identified as inappropriate and the effort to hold onto authority, on the other the effort by children to assume control of household resources and family prerogatives while maintaining the image of a stable generational hierarchy without disruption. Second, they are played out differently by various children, given what's at stake for each. Like Yayati's five sons or the three sons of *Apne Begāne*, older sons and daughters-in-law may seek to assume control and marginalize parental clout whereas younger children may ally with parents. In most of the neighborhoods of the study, old parents were more likely to live as part of their youngest son's household: older brothers successively fissioned off, taking whatever share of joint family property they could.

Though younger children may remain in positions of political alliance or subordination to parents, older children who have fissioned off—splitting entailing separate expenses and food and, rarely, shifts to new residences—may still request their parents' presence and support in circumscribed but symbolically dense areas in which the identity of family and household can be reasserted. These areas, in which old parents who have been left to younger siblings are reclaimed as familial bodies, center on the maintenance and commensal delineation of a *ghar*, a household: in rites of passage such as the Brahmanical *saṃskāras*, in other rituals of the household, in the training and surveillance of grandchildren, and in the greeting of (but not obtrusive involvement with) guests.

Old parents, within the logic of this ideal typology, are involved in two forms of *ghar*: the primary economic unit of the household, often with younger children, and the ritually reconstituted family. The division is a heuristic, a structural effort to delineate the substrate of political action. I use it to suggest that the familial body—and the social construction of old age debility—must be set within the context of the various strategies and overlapping structures of extended families and multiple households. The hearing of the voice, and the power of authoritative interpretation, are contingent on the community of listeners and their interrelationships.

For those on the periphery of a *ghar*, however defined, the *sahī nahīn* voice of an old person in Varanasi was often the sound of a morally "not right" family. Throughout the neighborhoods of this study, across class, outsiders—neighbors, daughters or sons critical of their siblings, passersby—often heard neglect in these voices. In interviews with me, they most often framed neglect as a transactional deficit: they do not give him or her enough food, enough clothing, or enough love: they do not offer enough *sevā*.

The perceived lack of *sevā* goes beyond the economics and attributional politics of households, families, and communities. If the self is relationally constituted, and if "family" becomes the monoglot index of relationality within the postcolonial context of the joint family story, then assaults on the inviolability of the family are particularly threatening. The assault, however, is unavoidable. Children, economically and politically and symbolically, eventually take on the position of their parents, but old parents do not necessarily disappear. No amount of *sevā* can reverse the process seamlessly.

"Respect" and "status" are ubiquitous and rarely examined constructs, either of social gerontology or of forms of local knowledge mandating filial piety. I suggest here that respect has two aspects: deferral to the powerful and performative deference to the no longer powerful. In the negotiated and contested forums of intergenerational life the distinction may not be so clear, but it is performative deference that the frequent and cross-cultural exhortations to honor one's parents imply. By performative I do not suggest "empty" practice, but rather that for the normative order of a family to be maintained, the emergent political hierarchy of children over parents must be reversed through symbolic action that generates a normative hierarchy of parents over children and yet does so without endangering the family's political order. By seeking parents' advice on decisions that they ultimately will not control, by placing their parents physically within shared family space or at the threshold as a sign defining *ghar*, domestic space, and the household, children identify their parents with the household and with authority over it. The elder is the household; his or her performative control over it signifies the moral integrity of the family.

Challenges to this integrity emerge through the familial body, heard as a voice of a neglected elder. Sources of the bad voice are multiple: they include the old-age weaknesses various actors in my story have called sixtyishness, hot brain, weak brain, senile dementia, senility, senile psychosis, and Alzheimer's disease. They also include more universal processes. Perfect *sevā*—the fantasy body of Shravan Kumar—is impossible. Shravan must die: in dying, he recognizes his failure: "I now see there is no reward for austerity."[51] The order of things—here framed as the body of the king, Dasharath, who cuts the perfect son down—prevents the realization of perfect filial service. Children cannot simultaneously be ascetics and householders. Few adult children I interviewed could do "enough" *sevā*, and its inevitable deficit was an anxiety central to many discussions of aged parents.

THE DYING SPACE

Isn't the classical codification of an individual life wise? Now and then I reflect on it—grihasthi
is the eye of the storm, I suppose—though that isn't entirely correct, because the eye connotes

stillness at the heart of tumult, doesn't it, and grihasthi is anything but. No, grihasthi is domes-
ticity, the family, and a mortal life'd be fragmentary without it; for sure, the three other rungs are
also significant to integrate a life, but the years before grihasthi seem to conduct you to it, and the
age after grihasthi winds away from it—it's the hub, the umbilicus, the skein of birth and death,
and one's so enmeshed in it, in the bonds and responsibilities of family, that one doesn't rumi-
nate on the central questions, not much, anyway—but there is isn't much spunk—oops, wrong
word—left in the years after grihasthi, and vanaprastha and sannyas are euphemisms, aren't
they, for rejection and dotage?

UPAMANYU CHATTERJEE, *THE LAST BURDEN*

The identity of family and body is mediated principally through the space of the home. Vatuk noted that "old people in India do most of their physical suffering, and ultimately their dying, at home."[52] In Rajan Khosa's short black-and-white film *Bodh Vṛkṣa* (*Wisdom Tree*), a young woman lives in a large house with her father and bedridden grandmother. The film is silent, save for a voice-over of the young woman's thoughts. The father is distant, wrapped up in his own unhappiness; the young woman is entirely responsible for the grandmother's care. As the old woman's illness progresses, the image of the grandmother and the house fuse through lingering shots of the house, the old body, and the young woman's desperation at being imprisoned by both. The house is empty, shadows and wind. The grandmother remains silent, immobile. The stillness is broken by the voice-over (translated from the Hindi by Khosa):

Why is it so still? What is it that inhabits the wind? Perhaps it is like me, watching it all, in silence, in stillness. . . .

Within this windy, silent body of *vāyu* and this windy, empty house, the grand-daughter senses heat:

Sometimes I can see it, a kind of grace, something pure and holy, which seems to grow in her as her body withers away. Every moment the disease eats further into her: her legs are rotten stumps, her bowels a mass of decay. Slowly, steadily, the whole house is bathed with her presence. There is a power—I have seen it.[53]

The grandmother continues to grow older and to decay, to die in a cold body and in a cold house, and yet, for her granddaughter, to wax more powerful: "[S]he burns in her pain with a flame of pure white heat."

By the end of the film, the granddaughter has left the house. The camera returns to empty rooms. Has the old woman died? Eventually, the camera approaches the deathbed. Grandmother is still there, silent. And then she stirs, slowly turns, and for the first time gets out of bed. Her immobility is somehow contingent upon the *sevā* of her granddaughter. Younger generations fix old bodies with their solicitude as much as they are fixed by the demands of care. The dying space, Grandmother's miraculous recovery suggests, is socially constructed and continually negotiated.

I was several times struck, in Varanasi, by children who spoke of taking care of their "dying" [*marnewāle*] parents, when to my eyes the old parents were not on their deathbed. But literally, of course, they often were: for the bed of old age is usually the deathbed, not the hospital bed, and without the intercession of the hospital or a machine, old age and death are structured as a continuity. These children defined a weak old age as a dying space, and to the extent that their parents could not or chose not to contest their reconstruction as old bodies, they defined it so as well.

The dying space may be an indoor bed, as in *Bodh Vṛkṣa*. In Ravindrapuri Colony in Varanasi, Amita Mukherjee and her mother, both elderly widows, lived in a large flat. Amita, in her sixties, taught at the Anandamai Ma Ashram girls' school; her mother stayed at home and rarely left her room. She could get about, and although she agreed with her daughter that she was quite weak and immobile, whenever I visited them and found Amita-di not at home, her old mother negotiated the entire house with relative ease. A north Indian physician who moved to Bangalore moved a television into his parents' bedroom so that they would never have to leave their bed to watch a program; like Amita's mother, they were less bedridden than bed-gifted, the immobilized object of solicitude. Significantly, these were years when the weekly *Mahābhārata* episode was televised each Sunday morning and was watched throughout the country by families and even entire communities crowded together; at the Bangalore doctor's house, the old parents sat on their own bed and watched apart.

The uncontested dying space is often spatially marginal to the household while remaining specularly central. The charpoy, the knotted rope and wood frame bed, is often placed near the threshold of the house or in a courtyard, and it suggests both the liminal and the exemplary position of its aged occupant. Not quite part of the household, the old person on the threshold was yet the first thing one would encounter in visiting. The "threshold function" of the family elder: for Sudipta Basu's family in Calcutta, the fact that despite his anger, confusion, and forgetting he could still greet visitors appropriately was very important. The charpoy was a ubiquitous and narratively elaborated site of the liminal old body: outside small dwellings in Nagwa slum, on the roofs and in the hallways of wealthy homes in Ravindrapuri, and in local representations of the village elder or elderly mother-in-law on his or her charpoy, the image is simultaneously that of confinement and repose, restriction and respect.

Another paradigmatic image conveying the spatial ambiguities of *sevā* is the *māliś*, the massage, classically by a dutiful daughter-in-law of her mother-in-law's *hāth pair*. A remembered image: I am sitting, up on the roof after a hot day in Varanasi, enjoying the urban delight of rooftop breezes. Around me flit the myriad kites of children; on surrounding rooftops, the hour of the *māliś* has arrived. The *sās* lolls on the charpoy, and her daughter-in-law squats next to her, massaging her leg. The older woman's arms and legs ache: *hāth pair*, the critical site of generational weakness. *Sevā* as *māliś* mandates an immobile body and tired limbs even as it marks the hierarchy of the superior older woman giving her feet to the younger and inferior.

TAKING VOICES SERIOUSLY

But dying spaces are contested, and we need to move from third-person frames of angry rishis and sixtyishness and second-person positioned accounts of the familial body to the first-person construction of experience, to the voices of old people, in and of themselves. Questions postponed must now take precedence: Do individuals experience their own aging as sixtyish or as powerful? As hot or as cold? Are these rhetorics of attribution relevant to the experience of old individuals? Do normative cultural frameworks like *āśramadharma* map onto personal experience? Ultimately, do individuals experience themselves as old in the first place? What does it mean to be "old"?

I have until this point evaded these questions, those of the phenomenology of the old body and the meaning of old in itself. They are important issues, sometimes neglected in the cross-cultural study of old age, but in posing them as distinct inquiries one may ascribe to the experience of old age a concreteness and distinctiveness it may lack. Sharon Kaufman has made the point, in her work with middle-class American elders, that

> when they talk about who they are and how their lives have been, they do not speak of being old as meaningful in itself; that is, they do not relate to aging or chronological age as a category of experience or meaning. To the contrary, when old people talk about themselves, they express a sense of self that is ageless—an identity that maintains continuity despite the physical and social changes that come with old age. . . . Being old per se is not a central feature of the self, nor is it a source of meaning.[54]

Kaufman's elegant assertion challenged the tenor of the phenomenology of old age, of projects like Cole and Gadow's edited collection *What Does It Mean to Grow Old?*, of solicitous tomes like de Beauvoir's *La Vieillesse*,[55] and more generally of efforts to track the aging subject as a set of distinct selves through the life course. In the next chapter, one of my informants will help me take issue with the universality of Kaufman's particular conception of the self; here I would note that in pointing out rather frequently that they do not feel old, Kaufman's informants seem to structure self *against* if not through old age: as the Other to selfhood here, old age remains critical to a phenomenology of the body and self in time, ever more the negative space as one ages, against which a continuity of lived experience asserts itself.

Kaufman's resistance to the meaningfulness of old age is suggestive of the ambiguity of the term within the American academy. Like the enumerative obsession of geriatrics with "normal aging," old age in American gerontology is organized as a paradox: the unmentionable object of discourse. Books often replace *old age* with *aging*, a term that rarely refers to the process of aging across the life span and far more often is a euphemism for old age. Thus Bernice Neugarten edited an early anthology in the field entitled *Middle Age and Aging*, in which the parallelism of "Middle Age and Old Age" is abandoned for a tropaic structure in which the whole must stand for the unspeakable part.[56] Gerontology as a field of knowledge presumes the importance of old age and old people as things to be studied, yet the professional language of social gerontology is structured around its erasure: thus the "World Assembly on Aging" and the "Aging in India" series.

For a generation of gerontological anthropologists, a corollary of the will to euphemize was the difficulty in articulating "old age" as anything other than a positive experience: against this difficulty, some of the current calls for a "postmodern life course." In her early work, Andrea Sankar contrasted what she found to be the "it's just old age" strategy of the Western medical tradition with traditional Chinese medicine, which she argued avoided using old age as an excuse not to take suffering seriously.[57] Sankar's discussion of old age, embodiment, and social networks among Buddhist nuns is among the more critically engaging work on old age in a Chinese community, but it was of necessity narrated through contemporary gerontological and medical anthropological critique of a "biomedical" straw man. Similar comparisons abounded in the medical anthropology of the 1970s and 1980s, as in Nancy Scheper-Hughes and Margaret Lock's classic article "The Mindful Body." The article elegantly demonstrates the ways in which the body as simultaneously experienced, social, and political should ground the social analysis of bodily phenomena, but then goes on to suggest that "Eastern" medicine does just that, easing in a sense the anthropologist's critical burden. A haiku and a tertiary-care hospital are offered to demonstrate the Kiplingesque division between aesthetic and holistic East and mechanistic and alienating West.[58] The apples and oranges comparison in the case of the Sankar article is similar, contrasting the tertiary care medicine of the West against the social milieus of Buddhist nuns of the East.

Beyond the comparison lies a central assumption: societies that label the experience of suffering, debility, or change within an old body as "old age" are *necessarily* distancing themselves from experience and healing rather than confronting the experience itself. In the Varanasi neighborhoods, "it's just old age" was a way frequently used by relatives and others to make sense of old people, as frequently used as the assertion that "in the West, you don't care for old people." Not only their relatives but old persons themselves throughout the neighborhoods of the study made use of statements of the "it's just old age" type. False consciousness awaiting gerontological pedagogy? Perhaps. Yet in denying the power of speaking "old age" as a personal and performative source against as well as for meaning, anthropologists may elide a dimension of the performative utterance (and nonutterance) of old age, its dialogic construction as both the expression and denial of experience and of suffering.

In rethinking the familial body and the dying space from first-person perspectives, we need to follow Kaufman and question the "obviousness" of being an old body, and to continually query the relation of the body in time to lived experience. Sylvia Vatuk shows in her discussion of the anxiety her informants expressed about becoming old, useless, and abandoned, that old age in the processual sense of *becoming* is critical to self-construction.[59] But becoming is not quite being. In the case of John Kingery, the old man who was "granny-dumped" at the Idaho dog track, the fact that the sympathies of the AARP spokesperson were more with the daughter who abandoned him than with the Alzheimer's victim suggests this. Like dependency anxiety, the social elaboration of Alzheimer's reflects the drawing of a boundary by younger adults to deflect the perceived transformations of their own old age.

It is difficult to address *being* old as a universal phenomenology or, pace Kaufman, as its absence. Kaufman's model presumes the possibility of role continuity, a possibility itself differentially available across class, gender, and other less predictable correlates of life experience. Widowhood may create dramatically different challenges for women than for men. A routinized form of retirement and the possibilities of pension are an option only for a minority of elderly; the effects of old age on those who must work as agricultural or construction laborers or who, like Dulari's cousin, pedal rickshaws until they literally drop dead may mitigate the possibilities of an ageless self. The various meanings of the charpoy for its occupant—repose, retirement, confinement, neglect, peripheralization—depend less on old age itself than on the varied conditions for the uninterrupted flow of *sevā* and the continued usefulness of the body.

Āśramadharma is similarly limited in anchoring a universal phenomenology of old age experience. Kakar offers its last two stages as an alternative to a psychoanalytic typology of maturity, with the accent on yogic desocialization as a rational response to mortality.[60] Few elderly informants, however, valorized disengagement from other persons as part of their sense of ideal self. Kakar's citing *āśramadharma* is reminiscent of a similar controversy in social gerontology in the 1970s over disengagement versus activity theories of first-person experience. The advocates of the former position suggested old people "naturally" disengage from social and other ties and turn inward; advocates of the latter held that old people when given the chance diversify and expand their sense of self once the limiting tasks of work and family have been passed on: ties and involvements should increase, not decrease.[61] The controversy prevented analysis from focusing on the ways individuals both disengage and broaden their ties and interests, on the importance but insufficiency of the forest as a model of old age. In *Non-renunciation,* T. N. Madan suggested that adulthood is characterized less by a movement from the dharma (duty), *kāma* (pleasure), and *artha* (profit) orientations of the householder to the moksha (liberation) orientation of the renunciate, than that the polarity of the *bhogī* (the hedonist) and yogi (the ascetic) frame the extremes between which individuals fashion life and self.[62] Repose, the position of a good old age, remains as much a celebration of *bhoga* as yoga.

In spatializing the adult life course as a move from the household to the forest to the peripatetic unmarked space of the sannyasi, *āśramadharma* legitimates the ambivalence of repose through its reconstruction as an ascetic state; like disengagement theory, it also provides a normative rationale for the enforced marginal-ization of the elder by others. Kakar suggests that the system offers the romantic possibility of the quest in old age against the more ironic constructions of old age in European thought, particularly psychoanalysis. Yet for old individuals, the dying space as the forest within the household is laden with irony, the same irony that follows the lengthier quest of the old person who travels the length of the country to die, transfigured but pathetically alone, in the holy necropolis of Kashi.

He was one of my idols; I had found his book *Lokayata* while a college freshman, wandering through the India stacks (*Ind* and *IndL*) in the subterranean recesses of Harvard's Widener Library, an imposing edifice gifted by the mother of a victim of the Titanic who had collected books. Thomas Wolfe, in *Of Time and the River*, had written of coming from the American South to Harvard and trying to read all the books in Widener, an attempt to master the place or at least to come to terms with it. But knowledge had continued to expand, and so did the numbers of books in the Widener stacks. Sir Henry Maine had observed that these were the conditions of empire. He advocated cramming. Too softened perhaps from television or suburban liberalism, I went instead for the particular and tried to come to terms with Ind and IndL, and did so not through cramming but by becoming a flaneur of the stacks.

I don't remember how I came to find the book. It was a very different sort of thing than either the Orientalia of my first year of college reading or the postcolonialism of my last, a dense amalgamation of Marxism, Hindu myth and philosophy, and nineteenth-century anthropology, a working through of Lewis Henry Morgan and Frederic Engels to reread Vedic and later philosophical texts for the remnants of an Indian materialism, a people's religion rooted in totemism and Mother-right. It was messy and anachronistic, but it brought together in a dizzying synthesis all the diverse knowledges necessary to being a Bengali Brahman and Marxist theoretician in the 1950s in Calcutta.

His name was Debiprasad Chattopadhyaya. He lived in Calcutta, in a large and drafty old house a few blocks south of the Victoria Memorial. His office was on the first floor, full of books and files, and he and his wife lived on the second. He was a scholar of the history of Ayurveda and of various schools of Hindu philosophy, and he had spent years learning about the botanical medicine of the Santal, "tribals" not too far from Calcutta and the object of both *bhadralok* and Marxist nostalgia. I went to see him to ask about *rasāyana* and its history, and as I mounted the stairs to his first floor office that first time, I saw her, an old woman in a white sari in a room next to the office, sitting on a bed and staring at the wall.

I wanted to ask about her, as the great historian and philosopher tried to answer my questions about *rasāyana* and senility, but felt a bit embarrassed. Each time I came calling, I would pass by the door of her room, hoping for something. What? Some days she was lying down. Some days like that first one she was sitting up. She never said anything, never seemed to do or notice anything, not me, anyway. It was very quiet in the big house. Her son the philosopher would be speaking, the sounds of the street muffled by all the books in the office. My mind would wander, listening for a sound from the next room.

He had written, in the book that I had come across in the library, about the relationship between voice and desire. He was analyzing a story from the *Chandogya Upaniṣad* in which dogs chanted for food like Brahmans chanting the Vedas. Against the usual interpretation, that the Upanisadic authors were mocking Vedic ritualism, he suggested the chanting dogs revealed the totemic origins of high religion, its rootedness in the desire for food and other material needs. Voice—the chanting as both language and song—was a magical means to fulfill desire, here for sustenance.

In Varanasi old people and dogs were seen to have a lot in common: abject dependence and a voice whose desire was no longer heard, so that it became more and more desperate and repetitive in its demand: ultimately, barking. The philosopher's particular critique of what he called idealism did not allow him to hear the chanting as an antinomian parody of this-worldly ritual. The dogs' chant was the innocent though desperate desire of the primitive collective, for survival.

In the next room, never a sound. The clock on the wall ticked, the philosopher spoke, from time to time the horns and yells from the street came through the curtains.

SIX

The Maladjustment of the Bourgeoisie

in which balance, pressure, and routine anchor the experience
of the old body and its degeneration, and multinational corporations take note

CIVILITY AND CONTEST

Meena lived in a middle-class residential colony in Pune, a city in western India. I visited her and her Maharashtrian Brahman family in 1988, before settling down in the Varanasi neighborhoods to begin my fieldwork. After offering tea to both me and a mutual friend, she began to speak of her mother-in-law.

> My *sās* was in her last years a subject for your study. The blood supply to one part of her brain was too little for just a minute. One cell died, and this dead cell grew and grew to cover much of the brain; she became more and more disoriented. . . .
>
> To others? We would say she's old, not doing well. Would you say to others she's crazy? We treated her well.
>
> Record this: an example of at least one Indian family. She went to both a physician and to a psychiatrist. And they conferred with each other. The physician took care of the medical side of things. At home, she was always respected. My children always knew she was the mother of their father. They never thought she was silly. When she began going down the stairs [to get out], they didn't watch and let her fall, but took her and said—this is not the way. She was never ridiculed, never "she is sick, she is old. . . . " We had to change her, as you would a baby's diapers.
>
> At that time, a German woman was staying with us [as a paying guest]. She asked me: "How can you put up with her? Why don't you send her to a home?" I explained that she had given much to my husband when he was young, and now we are doing the same when she needs it. But she did not understand. I asked her to leave. . . .
>
> You know, I think it comes down to this. We have the idea that as we treat our parents, so our children will learn to treat us. So I suppose it is selfish.

Meena offered me a story of the good daughter-in-law. The seriousness of her mother-in-law's condition, dramatized through a medicalized language invoking the wild cell growth of cancer as much as the cell death of an infarct dementia, underscored the depth of the intergenerational commitment of "one Indian family." The Decline of the Joint Family narrative was simultaneously brought forth and dismissed: against the presumption of the Fall, I was called to witness her family as perhaps the last outpost of Indian values. Against the hegemony of the West in the figure of the German woman, Indian families were then represented as caring for their parents. And yet, in describing her mother-in-law through the training of her children, Meena again doubted the possibility of true altruism. We care for old people as our social security. In describing the brain disease of her mother-in-law, Meena identified herself with the old woman. We are, we become the old. Brain disease did not render the *sās* radically "other": My children do not mock their grandmother. They do not say she is old. Old age, more than brain disease, is the final gloss on the *sās*, but her *bahū* is at pains to sustain her presence as within the continuity and connectedness of kinship: "the mother of their father."

Within the house, old age was not spoken; outside, it was used to defer the blunt reality of madness. Addressing the relational context of how to talk to the neighbors and to colleagues at work, Meena framed her *sās*—or rather, explicitly did not frame her—in terms of being mad. "We would say she's old, not doing well. Would you say to others she's crazy?" In representing her family, Meena played with two alternatives, old age and madness. Here the cellular model she began with lost its significance. Old age, which within the family was not spoken to preserve the unbroken continuity and identity of grandparents and grandchildren, became outside the deferral of more serious claims suggesting the Bad Family.

Madness—*pāgalpan* in Hindi, more commonly "mad" or "crazy" in English, and most commonly a language of mental imbalance or maladjustment in Hindi or English—was a frequent figure in the Varanasi middle-class colony interviews and in interviews in similar neighborhoods in Delhi and Dehradun. In this chapter I explore the particular salience of *balance* in these middle-class colonies, focusing at first on Ravindrapuri and Nandanagar in Varanasi, but including interviews in Delhi, Calcutta, Mussourie, and Dehradun in addition to Pune.

I was forced to cast my net widely. "You must find it difficult to research this subject; I do not think any one will talk with you about their old people," a young man from Delhi who worked for a multinational agribusiness concern had warned me. I assured him that given my experience in asking people about religious difference and about sexuality, two rather touchy topics, old age should not prove a challenge, but he was right. As I began to make acquaintances in the colonies and to be invited to people's homes to discuss my research, I found that most families remained interested in the project by redefining it: "There are many lonely and abandoned people, who have no one; this is an important work." But whenever I met the few families with old members who—according to whichever neighbor who had pointed them out—were weak-minded, senile, not right, or mad, younger family members were rarely willing to have me meet or even see the old relative. Unlike Meena, who knew me through a mutual friend and for whom I was a naive American guest rather than a professional interloper, few in the colonies were interested in being an "example." The connections that gave me legitimacy and eased my entry into the colonies' homes—my Banaras Hindu University connections, my several years of work with prominent local physicians—simultaneously structured me as an external and official presence, one apt not only to hear bad *sevā* in the familial body of the old person but through an imported medical gaze to see definitively and fix blame scientifically.

Against the challenges of most homes in the colonies, where most old people I was sent by neighbors to inquire about were asleep or too old or too sick to meet me, old friends in Varanasi, Delhi, Calcutta and elsewhere had no shortage of uncles, aunts, or grandparents for me to meet. In grouping these meetings and informal fieldwork together with my interviews from Varanasi colonies, I risk enlarging my "field" far too broadly and introducing a lot of regional and structural differences, confounding variables in the language of social science. I have tried to center my discussion on common political and rhetorical structures and processes, but I alert the reader in each case as to just where the vignette and the data are drawn from. I begin with the colonies, to locate the space between the home and the world in which the familial body signifies within a local Indian middle-class cosmology.

Ravindrapuri lay just west of the old *pakkā mahal*, half a kilometer to a kilometer's walk from the river. It consisted of large separate homes along a wide thoroughfare and numerous sequentially numbered side streets; at the southern end of the colony, then bordering two abandoned cinema halls and a slum, were several dry goods and tea shops and the carts of vegetable sellers. Vegetable sellers and other itinerant merchants went from home to home calling out their wares. The main street, two lanes with a divider, was one of the widest in the city, but neither end connected to a major traffic artery and the road, going nowhere and shadeless and unusable as common space, was usually deserted. For over a decade of my visits to Varanasi, it has been in a state of perpetual disrepair, with the politics of its forever-deferred or incompletely done paving shifting. The layout of Ravindrapuri was as much an iconic sign of its prestige and wealth and an index of its lack of community consensus and common purpose as a geography relating it to the rest of city. Residents of the adjoining slum, in contrast, used their franchise to construct a common "vote bank" in electoral appeals for basic resources.

Nandanagar hugged the great semicircular rim of Banaras Hindu University midway along its span, five kilometers south of the city proper. Less prepossessing than Ravindrapuri, its large individual homes were connected by several rutted dirt roads. It was smaller, more suburban, and more closely knit than Ravindrapuri. During the morning of the spring festival of Holi, groups of men, of women, of young men and boys, and of young women and girls from the colony gathered together, each traveling from house to house for Holi sweets and the spraying of colored water and lampblack on each other. Nandanagar's celebration was more controlled than the raucous color play and sexually explicit processions of gangs of young, intoxicated men in the city proper.[1] After the exchange of sweets and color, neighborhood residents made their way to an empty lot at one end of the colony. Filled with scrub and leftover building materials, the lot was transformed once a year into the neighborhood commons, the site of a bonfire for the holiday.

One colony resident, a university professor who had spent many years teaching about traditional Indian society and culture in the United States, tried to start a civic association and turn the plot into a park and playground. Jyoti Sharma, a housewife in the colony and for a time my landlady, expressed to me her contempt for the plan, which received no community support: "A stupid idea! He expected everyone to give him money and wanted to build a park! A waste. He got all these ideas—he thinks this is America. Well, we are not Americans."

Despite the peacefulness of the colonies, they were the site of frequent conflicts and occasional murders. Several well-planned deaths in Ravindrapuri during my fieldwork were rumored throughout the city to be the fruits of one resident's heavily criminal dealings with "black money." A local reporter took me on a rickshaw ride through the neighborhood, pointing out house after house where she alleged violent crimes had occurred. Residents feared theft and the murder of vulnerable family members. Articles on the violent deaths of old people sleeping alone in residential colonies appeared from time to time in local and national papers.

PUNJABI BAGH WOMAN STRANGLED

NEW DELHI, January 10: A 70-year old Leelawati of East Punjabi Bagh was found strangled with leggings in her house this morning. Her legs were bound and cloth stuffed in her mouth.

  Clothes were strewn all over the place and cupboards left open giving the impression that the house had been ransacked. The police suspect the motive to be robbery. . . . Her daughter-in-law, Mrs Sneh Gupta, wife of her only son, Mr Subhash Chand Gupta who is settled in the USA, was unable to provide much information. She . . . said that the previous night they had all retired at 11:30 p.m. The next morning her mother-in-law who normally slept in the "pooja" room was found strangled in the adjacent room. The police suspect that she was strangled in the "pooja" room and then dragged to the next room.[2]

Colonies at night were relatively empty and vulnerable places. The death of Leelawati in the puja room, site of the household prayers and one of the archetypical spaces of the old person within the household, challenges the integrity of the dying space. Readers of this article questioned whether the police, family servants or the choukidar (the night watchman) might not be in cahoots with the thieves, whether such deaths were inevitable when children abandoned parents for places like America, and whether the daughter-in-law herself, conveniently alone with her *sās* without her husband present, might not have had a hand in the murder. Thieves, servants, the corrupt state, or relatives: there were few sources of security.

Alliances, given the ability of community harmony to degenerate, were made warily and along family and regional lines. Mrs. Sharma told of the founding of Nandanagar. Her family had paid for several adjoining plots of land to plant a small field and garden next to the main house. Technically, such overbuying was against district regulations, but Mrs. Sharma dismissed such concerns with a brusque shake of her head: "Everyone does it . . . how else can a large family build a house? This is India." The colony resident in charge of land distribution, however, a professor whose plot adjoined the Sharmas, tried to force the family to sell back some of this land. This neighbor extended his own plot so as to prevent the Sharmas from having enough access to get a car onto their land.

Mr. Sharma, a government official whose posting was outside Varanasi in another city, was away. According to Jyoti Sharma's version of the tale, the neighbor threatened to bring some "student leaders," a euphemism on campus for *gundās* or mercenary toughs, to rough up her and her daughters.

> Late that night, my brother-in-law and I and my eldest daughter got tools and began building a wall giving us the agreed-upon access to the lane. Several student toughs appeared and began threatening us with curses. I had my daughter light the lamp. The boys realized I was holding a revolver. I said, first one to move gets shot. Then one of them recognized me. He said: "Auntie, I'm so and so's son, from Ghazipur." I had grown up with that family; his father was my brother. Okay, I said. You come in for tea; the rest of you, if you don't leave by the count of ten, you're dead.

Despite the civility of these new neighborhoods, there was often a violent edge to urban elite life in the colonies. Power was not primarily "local, continuous, productive, capillary, and exhaustive";[3] nor did it seem to be becoming so. There was far more at stake in the boundary of the household and the violently embodied moral economy of the community than the spontaneous *communitas* of events like Holi suggests.[4]

Ravindrapuri and Nandanagar were in some senses superficial communities, newly established and not yet "home" for their residents. Residents all had *ghar*s elsewhere, households of parents, siblings, or cousins with which they had extensive ties. Household size and generational composition were fluid, a core set of members continually supplemented with the arrival of rural or small-town relations taking advantage of the educational and bureaucratic opportunities of the city. Old parents, if they were not involved in the establishment of the new home, tended to spend more of their time in the extended family home with those children who could not establish a new urban or suburban household or who maintained more direct and interdependent economic ties with the parental household.

BALANCE AND ADJUSTMENT

Discussions of balance were always framed in second-person terms, those of the body of the known other. Once in Mussourie, a mountain resort in northwestern Uttar Pradesh, I met a group of middle-class women in their thirties and forties from Kanpur. They were on a sightseeing tour, and we sat in a lookout and discussed behavior and mind in old age. Their stories and reflections centered on *kamzorī*—on weakness as the reason for old people acting differently than they used to—and they rooted this weakness in "tension." In a Hindi conversation, they used this English word. Mental weakness was exacerbated by tension. When I substituted *cintā*, worry, for tension in rephrasing what one woman had told me, she corrected me: not worry, tension.

Tension points to a set of susceptible bodies. The Kanpur women noted that women have more tension then men. Men in the colonies claimed the opposite. Both groups noted that educated and respectable persons experienced more mental weakness, as they faced more tensions than the poor. The latter, noted the Kanpur women, do little more than work, eat, and sleep, and seldom have any more complex concerns. As the founder of Age-Care noted, "They can stand any stress and strain."

Middle-aged and old women and men in the colonies often spoke of their lives in terms of a polarity of tension versus shanti—peace, repose. Shanti was most often presented as an elusive goal. Sources of tension were constant, from the difficult responsibilities of marrying off one's daughters and settling one's sons and from the inadequate attention paid to one by busy sons and daughters-in-law. Shanti could come both from without and within, from a sense of the constant provision of *sevā* by children and from a balanced daily routine, or *niyam*. Within the colonies, old men spoke more of *niyam* than did old women; wealthier old men and women spoke more of *niyam* than did the less wealthy.

Adult children, in confronting my or another's query about the sixtyish or weak voice of their parents, inverted the language of tension: they themselves were tense, but their parents had a different problem, one of "balance." Again, one of several English words was frequently used: "He or she is fine; it's an 'adjustment' problem." From the perspective of balance, the anger of old people was at root an inability to adjust to changing times and shifting familial realities. Imbalance also connoted insanity, as it does in English elsewhere, but the central thrust of the term was positional: the old person was literally no longer able to balance on the increasingly thin line between high ascribed status and diminishing moral authority in the household. The avoidance of balance problems was for children rooted in a moral hygiene of adjustment.

Not surprisingly, in India the psychological literature on old age has centered on the operationalization of balance and adjustment.[5] Adjustment has similarly been a central theme of the sociology of aging literature, although overshadowed by the elaboration of the Fall in the *Aging in India* series. This emphasis reflects and is partially derivative of a similar concern of American social science in the 1950s and 1960s with the adjustment of old people,[6] but the American theme has been elaborated as the sine qua non of a social psychology of aging. In identifying adjustment as the key theme anchoring the lifeworlds of old people, this psychology of aging has reified a set of class-specific concerns as universal processes demanding critical attention.

The invocation of tension (in discussing oneself) or balance (in discussing older persons) exists within a semantic network that links the hydraulic physiology of tensions and pressures to the heart and high blood pressure. The polysemy of hypertension and blood pressure has of course not been limited to India, but the ways in which blood pressure was discussed in the Varanasi colonies are revealing. Concern over "BP" differed across class and gender, being far more prevalent in upper- and middle-class discussions of middle and old age than in discussions in the slum or the poorer dwellings of the Bengali quarter, and with men "having BP" while women had "low BP." Vijay Kumar, a lawyer from a well-to-do Bhumihar family in Tikri village outside of Varanasi, reflected on his seventyish grandfather becoming almost *pāgal*, mad, from time to time: it was due to his blood pressure. His neighbor felt differently, invoking mental against cardiovascular balance: "When a man gets old he can no longer do all the work; he has to retire; but he still wants to do the work—from this comes frustration, and mental problems." Others among the Bhumihars, the dominant caste in Tikri, identified these two models as versions of the same thing, different aspects of a single phenomenon.

BP is a prerogative of superordinate gender as well as class. The imbalance of old women was framed by family and neighbors more often in terms of a woman's need to be surrounded by others, her inability to adjust to solitude. Low BP, a common diagnosis for urban middle-class women, articulates a relation of body to pathology different from *having* BP. The more masculine BP was an outcome of possession: it is something one has.

The physiological systems of the body reflect status positions. Both as sites of pathology and as representations of the aging self, bodily systems were differentially distributed across the Varanasi neighborhoods. Cardiovascular disease signified the costs of power and wealth. The *Times of India* ran a feature in 1989, "Have a Heart," on the rise in cardiovascular disease among what was defined as India's emerging "yuppies." Cardiovascular diseases no longer signify old age, the article declared, but rather wealth and success: no longer are they the exclusive province of the old.

> Having a weak heart may be the in thing—a status symbol almost—amongst the Indian yuppies like neurasthenia and weak nerves were the fads of the Victorian age. However, the fact remains that AMI [acute myocardial infarction—note how acronyms crop up as markers of a disease's designer status] has ceased to be a problem exclusively of the elderly.[7]

When a new suburban housing complex outside Delhi (illegally built without adequate permits and pitched to future retirees and their families) advertised its attractions to potential buyers, prominent on the list was a projected "New Open-Heart Surgery Hospital." What was in hindsight a blatantly unrealizable claim underscores the rhetorical invocation of the heart and high tech in the construction of elite identity.

Balance shifts the locus of weak mind from children who give too little to parents who withhold too much; like BP, it is a position of possession in excess. In Ravindrapuri, B. K. Agrawal lived in an upstairs flat with his wife, their younger son, and three grandchildren. An older son used to live with them but at the time of my interviews with the family maintained a separate household. For B. K. Agrawal's grown children, he was a poorly adjusted and therefore difficult old man. If I were to have offered a biomedical assessment of Agrawal, I would by no means have diagnosed him as demented. He was known around the neighborhood as a bit weak-minded, and his frequent complaints—"Old age is a curse"—were a sort of *bakbak*. What was key for his family was that he refused to adjust to his elder son breaking economic ties from the extended household, a break the sons relate to the income disparity between them. For the senior Mr. Agrawal, what was key was that he faced enormous tensions daily, still having to work in his old age (as a legal clerk) to help pull his and his wife's weight and to contribute to the high school fees of his younger son's children. "If I did not work," he said in his anxious fashion, jerking his head toward the doorway through which his daughter-in-law occasionally glanced apprehensively at us, "how would they treat us?"

> *BKA:* In old age you are treated very poorly. Only if you have money and health are you treated well. If I did not work . . .
>
> *LC:* What of your wife?
>
> *BKA:* She has difficulty too. If we could hire someone to work in the kitchen. . . .
>
> *LC:* When does authority pass from *sās* to *bahū*?
>
> *BKA:* Well, when a *bahū* first comes, she doesn't know the household. But after five–six years, when she has adjusted, the fighting must begin. Then things stabilize. Then, when *sās* is tired, she lets the *bahū* take over.
>
> *LC:* What if your wife didn't work?
>
> *BKA:* Our daughter-in-law would say "You're not working!" And she would have to. Because she is still capable.

With the continued tensions of householdership and the impossibility of renunciation given today's children, "Where," Agrawal fretted, "can one find shanti?" "Are there no sources of shanti, then, for old people?" I asked. He paused. "Almighty God is the only source. But," he cautioned, "one would have to renounce material things and one's grandchildren, which I cannot do. There is a point to which we cannot aspire," Agrawal the clerk sadly noted: "the silence and repose of the sannyasi." For Agrawal, solace came only in the bhajan, the repeated hymn to God alone or in a community of other elderly singers, through which he temporarily experienced shanti. In bhajan his voice was again authoritative, its trope of repetition not *bakbak* but divinely meaningful. But transcendence—the *illud tempus* of bhajan and the *communitas* of the bhajan group—was fleeting. Between the never-ending tensions of *gṛhasthya* (householdership) and the always deferred peace of *sannyāsa*, Agrawal was unable to articulate the possibilities of *vānaprastha*, of a constructive rather than constrictive dying space. His children read this failure as imbalance and located it within the old father himself. Agrawal disagreed, locating balance in the spaces between family members and not in the old person. This relational interpretation characterized his definition of *saṭhiyānā*: "This means, after sixty, the conscious declines, the intelligence declines. Due to family environment, leading to a loss of mental balance and irritation."

Next door to the Agrawal family, Amita Mukherjee and her mother lived together, both elderly widows from Calcutta discussed briefly in the last chapter. The younger woman, in her early sixties, was not only a teacher in an Anandamai Ma girls' school but was an adept of Ma, a well-known religious teacher and for her devotees a divine incarnation who had spent much of her time in Varanasi. Mukherjee's mother at the time of our interviews was eighty-three. Mukherjee worked most of the day, and her mother remained at home in her own room, lying on her bed and getting up only to go to the bathroom. Other relations and a servant helped take care of the older woman.

Bhajan and a community of religiously minded old people were important in the lives of both mother and daughter. They had come to Varanasi in 1950, when the younger Mukherjee's husband was still alive, at the request of Ma herself. The younger woman has remained involved in various bhajan groups; she explained to me that the strength resulting from the deep meditation of bhajan singing has enabled her to both maintain her vigorous schedule and gain new insight on many things, including her mother's health.

Didima, the elder woman, the other Ma in Amita's life, complained of difficulty in breathing and of deafness. She had no other problems, she said. The visiting relatives concurred. "She can walk to the market, and she does; she doesn't obey us!" They laughed. They worried that she might fall en route and hurt herself, but felt no compulsion to restrain her. They offered their concern not as vexation with her poor adjustment—"She's completely fine"—but as signs of their desire to provide an environment of total dependency. I asked about *bhīmrati* and *bāhāttūre*, the seventyish Bengali variants of *saṭhiyānā*. The relatives and Didima laughed—"How did you come to know words like that?"—but made no link to Didima herself nor felt pressed to deny a connection. Didima herself explained *bhīmrati* as a matter of shock. "Due to a personal crisis," her relations added, and contrasted the usual effects of shock with Didima's strength in the face of adversity. "She has had a tragic life. Yet she is so happy. She has adjusted."

When the relations had left, Amita told me that she had noticed significant changes in her mother's memory. "She forgets things. Not names. Her memory for things past has improved; it is her memory of present things which has declined. Perhaps this selective loss, I have wondered through my meditation, is a person's refusal to deal with a present in which they feel neglected, if unconsciously." Mukherjee noticed memory loss and associated it with familial neglect, but as a subjective feeling in old age and not necessarily as an objective intergenerational deficit. This *feeling* of neglect by Didima seemed to suggest to Amita some maladjustment on her mother's part. Unlike the relational signs of overtly poor adjustment, however, Didima's memory loss did not provide an obvious narrative.

Months later, Didima's health began to decline. She didn't leave her bed; she refused things. A friend of Amita's, an old widower and fellow devotee, offered a "shock" model for Ma's health, drawing on the dangers of colony life and, indirectly, of the vulnerability of old people being left alone by their children: "About two or three years ago, she was alone in the house when some miscreants came by and tried to rob the house. They hit her several times on the face. She has not been the same, not in the same health."

Old people living alone may deny their pathetic construction, claiming to have adjusted. A few houses away from the Mukherjees, Arvind Rai and his wife lived in a flat by themselves. The neighbors who introduced me noted that the old man had a "nervous condition." Rai, a retired college professor, acknowledged no mental or other health problems. But he agreed that the failure to adjust was the primary impediment to achieving shanti.

> *AR:* People until sixty are very involved in material things. Then they become more involved in religion, in spiritual things. After seventy, one looks for a peaceful feeling.
>
> *LC:* What if they don't find peace, shanti?
>
> *AR:* Here people are attuned to religious things from a young age.
>
> *LC:* What about *saṭhiyānā?*
>
> *AR:* People become irritated; they get angry. This may be due to weakness.
>
> *LC:* Is there a cure for this?
>
> *AR:* No.
>
> *LC:* What about tonics? Like Chyawanprash?
>
> *AR:* No. [This process] is not weakness. But the mind stagnates.
>
> *LC:* Is *saṭhiyānā* real? Or just what young people say?
>
> *AR:* No it's real. For old people who may not adjust in old age they say "He's gone *saṭhiyā.*" Like the old man who yells at the kids going to the film because he doesn't approve. My son went to the Netherlands. He met a girl and he married her. He did not tell us. When we found out, he was married. So we adjusted. My neighbor's son married an American, and she did not adjust. I told her: "You have to adjust."

The adjustment of old age is seldom to physical change in itself but inevitably an accommodation to the desires of children. Unlike Agrawal, Rai neither needs nor feels pressured to work. Though he and his wife are "alone," with many visiting cousins but no sons in India, he has, unlike Agrawal, been able to adjust. For him, *āśramadharma* is a meaningful model of disengagement. Do the *āśrama*s exist these days? I ask him.

R: Certainly, they exist. Haven't you seen the many sannyasis in Varanasi?

LC: But for ordinary people?

R: They don't become sannyasis, but still they leave the material things. Some go to ashrams.

LC: And you?

R: Like a sannyasi. Not a pure sannyasi, as I am concerned about my granddaughter's admission and so forth, but I read *Mahābhārata*, *Gita*, and go to the Ma Anandamai Ashram. Bhakti is *sannyāsa*.

The life of bhakti, of devotion and love for God and guru, transforms the necessity of adjustment into a realizable form of *sannyāsa*.

When Sudipta Basu, the erstwhile chief engineer from Calcutta mentioned in earlier chapters, began to forget words and appointments, his wife would get angry, contrasting his memory loss with his vast library and former position, literal memory banks. But my friend their grandson related that his grandmother's concern really mounted when Sudipta forgot his daily puja, his devotional exercises. Sudipta had turned to religion after retirement, and it had become part of his successful and adjusted postretirement aging. "He has forgotten God," lamented his wife, the supreme act of amnesia bound up to the sudden imbalance of a latter-day sannyasi.

SENILITY AND MADNESS

The terms of metropolitan medicine—senility, dementia, and Alzheimer's—were invoked within the colonies, but as in Zagreb they pointed as much to a deficit in relationships as to the matter of the brain. The American preoccupation with senility as a disease had made few inroads in the late 1980s despite considerable efforts by multinational pharmaceutical corporations sensing a tremendous untapped market. Unlike balance, which shifted blame off the Bad Family, explicit disease models did not offer an alternative imaging of the familial body but begged the question of the family's role. They were not, at this juncture and for these families, useful to think with.

A letter to the editor of the *Times of India* in 1989 collapsed the language of vascular dementia with that of Alzheimer's, framing both within a moral economy of balance and adjustment. Mahinder Singh of Delhi wrote:

> In our country there is a misconception that senility sets in around the age of 70. . . . When an Indian had his 60th birthday . . . he is told by all and sundry to "rest" and "enjoy". These well-wishers little realize that rest at this age means degeneration and senility. An old person must be more active if he wants to remain happy and healthy.
>
> It is well known that the most significant factor in the ageing process is the blood flow to the brain which carries it[s] oxygen supply. With age, the diminishing oxygen supply leads to a deterioration of the neural function.

Research done by modern psychiatrists and geriatricians in countries like the United States shows that many of most fears about ageing are merely exaggerated. Senility, the most dreaded of all disabilities, is suffered by only 15 per cent of those above 65 years. Alzheimer's disease, considered the scourge of old age, accounts for more than half that number. . . .

Research done by a psychologist of the National Institute on Ageing's Gerontology Research Centre in Baltimore, U.S.A., proves that old age does not necessarily doom people to senility. . . .

After retirement from routine work, a new life of learning and activity must be started. New skills and knowledges must be sought and acquired. New habits and new routines keep the brain and the body young. In this way the elderly won't become a burden on youth.[8]

Senility's links to both sixty and seventy are acknowledged and then contested. Against the inevitability of mental weakness, Singh suggests a program of active adjustment through mental hygiene for the old, offered entirely in the imperative: they must shape up, initially to avoid senility and ultimately to avoid becoming "a burden on youth." Mental weakness is encompassed by Vatuk's dependency anxiety.

Internationalist science is repeatedly invoked as Singh offers the geriatric ideology of normal aging by denying the geriatric paradox. Alzheimer's and senility are deemphasized through the same numbers that highlight the ubiquity of Alzheimer's hell in the United States. Thus, senility is suffered "only by 15 per cent of those above 65 years," and to further downplay concern we are told that "Alzheimer's disease accounts for more than half that number." Alzheimer's here points to the need to shore up one's psychic defenses for the remainder of a life that will be increasingly spent adjusting to others.

In another Varanasi colony not far from Ravindrapuri, the extended family of the noted pathologist and litterateur Dr. B. S. Mehta shared a large home. Mehta continued to work part-time at the clinic he founded but which by then his son ran, and devoted much of his remaining time to his grandchildren, to voluntary public health efforts, and to the many cultural interests and commitments that came out of a life steeped in theater and literature. He joked with me about his own imminent senility; indeed, the phrase often came up in our conversations. Mehta has written humorous articles on old age, on the necessity and the difficulty of adjusting to the changes of old age without a retreat into self-pity or anger. Mehta's mother, he once noted to me, was "senile." He used the term to imply a pathological condition, senile dementia, drawing like Singh upon a combination of diminished oxygen, "brain softening" and "hardening of the arteries," language then out of favor in the United States but regnant in Indian allopathic practice.

She takes things and steals them—puts them up on high shelves. Sometimes she falls when she does this and then says, "It's nothing, it's nothing." She often sleeps in the day. At night she's up, and goes around the house. She gets angry, and accuses us, and goes off next door to my brother's house. She fights with my wife, who occasionally gets angry. She doesn't take interest—for example, when her brother died—she was not moved. She hides things—food—under her bed.

Mehta first mentioned his mother in the midst of a discussion we were having on social aspects of old age. "I am more interested in bodily change," I told him. "Ah, softening," he noted, and then described his eighty-eight-year-old mother having a "second childhood" due to softening.

Mehta never returned to the subject and resisted my efforts, over successive months, to do so. He would shrug his shoulders and make a dismissive gesture, suggesting that we both knew what was going on with her. I eventually stopped harassing him. A few months later, when I asked him, as I would routinely, how was his mother, he looked at me and said simply, "She is not eating." Curious about why her refusal of food had framed the first moment, Dr. Mehta allowed himself to return to speaking of her, I later asked his wife if I could meet her mother-in-law. "She is not eating," she repeated as she brought me into a large and spotless room whose only contents were a mattress and an old woman lying on it. The old woman, whom I called Dadiji, said that she was feeling weak and had no appetite. She was oriented to her surroundings and seemed to have a clear memory of the recent details of her illness. But for Dr. Mehta, his weakened mother was soft. Memory loss was irrelevant for the family of an old woman who, unlike Sudipta Basu, had never been crammed with imperial knowledge; but the litany of anger, accusation, apathy, and theft they described—all familiar to American "other victims" of Alzheimer's but peripheral to formal DSM diagnosis—presented an increasing challenge to the Mehtas' constitution of the familial. In refusing to accept food from her son and daughter-in-law, Dadiji undermined the authenticity of their care and awakened the anxiety of the Bad Family. Her son, daughter-in-law, and grandchildren never saw the fact of her not eating as fundamentally a relational gesture, and yet their concern seemed to exceed the issue of Dadiji's food intake, to become a metaphor for her inability to adjust: the refusal of the gift of well-intentioned *sevā*.

The position of extreme imbalance is madness. When the voice and body of the old person threaten not only to stigmatize the family but cause great physical, economic, and psychological stress to its members, insanity (*pāgalpan*) or some other rhetoric of bad mind (*dimāg kharāb*) is invoked and healers, including psychiatrists, may be sought out. Psychiatric care may consist of the prescription of neuroleptics, other sedating agents, or ergot alkaloids, the classic "senility drugs." Even then, madness is often but one contender within a semantic network centered on the family.

Mr. and Mrs. Kaul, their daughters, and Mr. Kaul's elderly father used to live in a government flat in Ahmedabad; Mr. Kaul was a senior cadre of the elite Indian Administrative Service. The old man had long since died, and I talked to the Kauls and their grown children at their current flat. Whenever we began to talk,

Mr. Kaul would say of his father: "Mad, just mad! Stark, raving mad!" Ignoring him, Mrs. Kaul would tell me that her father-in-law was just the way he had been in life, but in that exaggerated fashion characteristic of old age. The Kauls talked about the father's behavior as an oscillation between two voices, silence and anger. The anger also manifested itself as perverse behavior, such as his hiding excrement around the house, followed by a silence in which he would not admit to such surprises. It also emerged against his son in confused episodes when he would seem to mistake his daughter-in-law for his deceased wife and accuse his son of misbehavior, a substitution reminiscent of the Kesari Jivan triangle.

The grandfather would wander away from the house; these episodes were presented by the Kauls not as tales of the wanderer, as the moving body of American institutional narrative that resists benign confinement, but as a willful *voice* that resisted being stilled. "I'm going to jump in the Sabarmati River!" shouted the grandfather once as he stormed out of the house: his angry cry, more than his getting lost, defined the episode. Otherwise he would sit in his room and seldom respond to family members, least of all his son. "Mad!" interjected Mr. Kaul again.

For the Kauls, even Mr. Kaul, the old man's behavior was etiologically complex yet rooted in a resentment of his son's control of family resources. It suggested an effort by the old man to reach a position of minimal transaction with his son that occasionally collapsed when balance could not be maintained. This resentment was played out in his hiding his excrement and especially in his overtures to his daughter-in-law who, for her part, seemed to have maintained a close relationship of caring for the old man in part as an act of creating an autonomous space from her husband. Although this triangle was never explicitly articulated, the Kauls were quite open about both the old man's affection for Indira, his daughter-in-law, and about the exaggerated quality of her caring for him. The father's voice was bound up to his son's frustration and his daughter-in-law's efforts to achieve greater autonomy of a sort. Family dramas that emerged on lines of gender and generation structured perception of the relational old body. His madness reflected both the extremity of Grandfather's actions—hiding excrement, being unduly familiar with his daughter-in-law, threatening to kill himself—and the extremity of difference between father and son, the voice mad enough to fill the chasm of silence between them.

The categories of *āśramadharma*—particularly the disjunction between the behavior expected of householders versus that expected of renunciates—on at least one occasion offered a further gloss on madness. Ashok Tambe was the older of two brothers from Maharashtra, from a Brahman family with significant agricultural property. Both brothers when young had studied at Banaras Hindu University and had come into contact with the charismatic political and religious leader Swami Karpatri, the inhabitant of the house on the river that I later shared with his old disciple Marwari Mataji. Karpatri had been a tantric teacher and practitioner and a reactionary critic of pre- and post-Independence state policies that he felt challenged the autonomy and sacredness of Hindu principles. He had gathered around himself a coterie of Indian devotees and foreign students. Karpatri's mix of sexual and philosophical unorthodoxy and appeals to Hindu nationalism tinged with Aryan purity had a particular appeal for European intellectuals in the heady years before the Second World War when Varanasi was an international intellectual and cultural center; his particular conjunction of unorthodox erotics and a Hindu nationalist theory of history can be found, further transmuted, in the writings of his disciple, the French Indologist Alain Danielou.[9]

Into the mix came the young Tambe brothers. When they returned to Maharashtra to run their family dairy and other businesses, the promise of Varanasi and Karpatriji's particular vision of the Hindu nation lingered. As the brothers married, aged, raised daughters and sons and tried to get them well settled, tensions between them over the joint ownership of the dairy began to come to a head. The younger brother's sons saw Tambe senior as an unsympathetic *tau*, the classic powerful uncle working against one's interests, in this case trying various schemes to wrest control of the dairy for his sons alone.

The relationship between the aging brothers took a turn when the younger brother, widowed as a young man, decided to return to Kashi in his middle age to take up a life of study and eventually *sannyāsa*. In the scheme of *āśrama*s, the relationship between the two brothers was suddenly reversed: Tambe senior remained a householder while his brother "passed" him in going on to the final stage and taking on the legacy of their guru with greater fidelity. Tambe junior, now Swami to the group of widows in the holy city who took him as a guru and came to the talks he gave, maintained an interest in the worldly affairs of his sons, guiding their response to their *tau*'s efforts to gerrymander the inheritance. Tambe senior, for his part, presented himself when I met him as being as disinterested in worldly affairs as his sannyasi brother.

Their struggle over property had by the time I met the brothers shifted to a struggle over the definition of authority in old age. Tambe senior, still married, had come to Varanasi two years before I met him in 1989, to study the Vedas and their ritual with his brother. Their discussions often returned to the themes of the Karpatriji years, to the need for a particular marriage of modernity and Hindu tradition that did not, like Gandhian nonviolence or Nehruvian secularism, emasculate the nation. The discussion was sometimes framed as comparison between the contemporary relevance and moral ranking of the brothers' respective paths: asceticism and householdership. Tambe senior stayed in Varanasi for a year and a half, during which time no resolution emerged vis-à-vis the contested dairy. But he returned to Maharashtra with a new plan to demonstrate the supremacy and modernity of Hindu tradition, one that incidentally would require him to liquidate the disputed assets and use the cash in the name of Hindutva.

The plan for most who heard it was simply raving mad. Tambe wanted to create a center for Hindu learning on the site of the dairy that would be organized around the strength of the joint family and the rituals of married Brahmanical life. In describing the plan in his often perseverating and manic fashion, Tambe would allude to various persons he in particular wanted to impress, one of whom was a Christian missionary who ran his district's local mission school. Tambe spoke with well-founded concern over the continuing postcolonial expectation in India that quality primary education demanded "convent" or "mission" schools. He wanted to bring back the religious academy, or *pāṭhśālā*, and to train local boys in Hindu rather than Christian morality. The school would be centered not on the figures of celibate nuns or missionaries but on those of the Hindu family and its ritual. The guiding practice for students would be the Brahmanic ritual of the Agnihotra mantra, which Tambe planned to recite on a continuous twenty-four-hour basis. Admitting that he and his wife were unequal to the task of between them staying up all day and night, Tambe hoped to kill two birds with one stone: his wife had an orphaned cousin, the responsibility and considerable expense of whose marriage he had earlier taken on, as yet unsuccessfully. He proposed marrying the cousin as a second wife. His household would remain an auspicious and fertile site, and the three of them could split the task of supervising the boys in the recitation of the mantra. The intensive recitation of the mantra would bring rain. Tambe proposed using his engineering background to set up giant sprinklers around Australia to increase cloud formation; the mantra would then pour rain into the desert outback, converting it into an area as lush as the Gangetic plain. Tambe senior was crazy.

I speak less in a psychiatric than a personal voice. Given the DSM-III-R criteria of the time, Tambe senior might have been labeled with "297.10 Delusional Disorder, Grandiose Type," having a usual age of onset in "middle or late adult life."[10] He was not demented. Yet this rather irritating man resisted easy definition: he was no fool, and he was effective in taking pains to convince others that his ideas were not delusional. In 1989, he returned at the age of seventy-five to Varanasi at the request of his brother. Swamiji wished to dissuade him from the marriage, from the selling of their family resources, and from the foolishness of the project. Tambe resisted all efforts to deny the legitimacy of his plan. The taking of multiple wives was sanctioned by numerous divine and Epic examples. The efficacy of the Agnihotra mantra as a bringer of rain was outlined in *śruti* and *smṛti* texts. The desire to help Australia was a way of demonstrating the emptiness of any rhetoric of European superiority. According to Tambe: "The West tells us we are failures, that we have no science, that we are not developed. They give us fertilizers which destroy nature. If the Western science is correct, then why has it not worked there, in the West. Look at Australia. It's still a desert!"

Tambe drew on the Karpatri days, on Karpatri's belief that Brahmanic technology was the key to Indian development, and on Karpatri's great concern with the emasculation of the Hindu nation resulting from Gandhian-based mixing with untouchables: "To work the enormous areas of land [that] the mantra. with the aid of ocean sprinklers which will increase evaporation and cloud formation. will generate, we will solve India's population problem by sending all the harijans to Australia."

Swamiji for his part had no doubt as to the sanity of his brother: "I tell you, the man is crazy. I am going to have him locked up. He has these high ideas. He wrote to the minister in New Delhi about his plan. He writes letters to young women, wanting to marry them. He is crazy, and I may have him committed here for his own good. Whatever he tells you, I want you to tell me."

Tambe senior's sons and nephews differed on how they framed him, but all but the one son who seemed likely to benefit from the liquidation of the dairy agreed that he was old and weak-minded and could not adjust to turning the household over to others.

Despite his tough talk, Swamiji would not take matters to a head in attempting to commit him. The forum for determining Tambe senior's sanity, appropriately given the brothers' ideological commitment to Vedic science, was a local Varanasi *sabhā*, or council, of Maharashtrian Brahmans. And the question they agreed to debate was not whether Tambe senior was sane or insane, but whether he should remain a *grhasth*—a householder with the power to control his family's resources and to marry again—or whether as an old man he should be forced to hand over control of the family property to the next generation and take on *vānaprastha*, as Swamiji wished. The logic of the *āśramas* became the structure of confinement through which Swamiji hoped to control his mad brother. *Āśramadharma*, though elsewhere in my interviews not a central frame for confronting the extreme old voice of madness, here became a tool through which the old person, his family, and their community negotiated a contest over the nature of familial authority.

The unexpected intervention of foreigners, another echo of the Karpatri years, offered both parties new sources of legitimation. Eugene Thomas, an American psychologist studying old age and spiritual development in Varanasi on a Fulbright at the time, was introduced to Swamiji by his research assistant Om Prakash Sharma. Swami asked Thomas as an American expert to evaluate his older brother for senility, hoping to submit the evaluation to the Brahman *sabhā*. But Thomas was not a psychiatrist, and he responsibly deferred the diagnosis. Swamiji gave me a copy of the American's letter, wondering if I could advance his cause better. Thomas had concluded: "Finally, I have to say that I do not consider B. "crazy." Psychologically, to be declared incompetent a person must be shown to be disoriented. . . . B. clearly does not fall into this category. There may be some evidence of a senile brain syndrome, but that would take exhaustive clinical tests to determine." In sidestepping the psychiatric question of whether Tambe's ideas were delusional in favor of a cognitivist emphasis on disorientation and memory loss implying the necessity of "clinical tests," Thomas was able to minimize involvement with the Tambe affair.

Tambe senior, meanwhile, began to cultivate me extensively when he learned that I was living in one of Karpatri's former residences and knew of Danielou's Karpatri connection. Tambe hoped that I could be persuaded that Vedic science was firmly a matter of this world and "not just the stuff of lectures to old Nepali widows" (Swamiji had a big following among old Nepalis in the city). Tambe appealed to the ethos of the householder, making a strong case that the *grhasth* and not the sannyasi was the ultimate Hindu exemplar of dharma. "Reason in madness," to cite *Lear* again. He came by my house on the river nightly, presenting his vision of a societal analysis based on authentically Hindu categories rooted in the family.

His appeal won over the council, who decided in favor of Tambe senior remaining a householder but placed restrictions on which of his projects were in accordance with the shastras, the authoritative texts on dharma. In the case of Australia, the council was not able to deny the efficacy of the Vedas and dismiss the project entirely, but it made the suggestion that the application of Vedic technology to a foreign land, particularly given the presence of large unproductive tracts of land within India, was inappropriate. When last I saw Tambe senior, he had taken their decision to mean that the project was on and had jettisoned the outback for the great Indian wasteland, the Rann of Kutch. The family had triumphed over the confinement of *vānaprastha*.

LONELINESS AND MENOPAUSE

In 1989 after I gave a talk at the Vasant College for Girls on Raj Ghat in Varanasi, in which I cited the experience of old people in Nagwa to argue that gerontological agendas were usually based on the needs of urban elites, several audience members and college faculty approached me: "You haven't considered the loneliness of old people." They of course had a valid point: in my bluster, any careful attention to experience was missing. But what sort of experience did they expect in the specific demand that I address loneliness? Loneliness as a primary concern had not been expressed by most of the old people of either Nagwa or the colonies nor inferred by me. Over lunch following the seminar, students and faculty began offering examples of what they had meant: "On my lane, there are two old Bengali widows who live by themselves; their children never write them." None of the examples offered addressed the old age of the speaker's own parents or relations, nor of most old people in Varanasi who lived with or near their families. Rather the *kāśīvāsī*, and primarily the *kāśīvāsī* widow, came to stand for old age as a time of loneliness. She was further distanced from the family of most at the luncheon by being a Bengali widow; "in Bengal," non-Bengali Banarsis said to me on several occasions, "They talk much about their mothers; but then why do all these old Bengali mothers end up being abandoned here?" In the intimacy and immediacy with which these "interstitial" old women—inhabiting the interstices between domestic spaces, a point I will develop in the eighth chapter—were brought forward into our discussion, there was an exclusion of "domestic" elders, of the parents, aunts, and uncles of the Vasant College faculty or of other old people who might indexically represent them. These were absent from this discourse of the problem of aging perhaps because construed as problems they would have threatened to signify the Bad Family of the self.

The lonely old person in the Varanasi colonies was as inevitably the Other as the tense and overly burdened old person was associated with the self. Within the gendered terms of public iconography and reminiscent of the literary forms discussed in the third chapter, the old aunt rather than the old mother was the acceptable image of abjection. Koki (Auntie), a Bengali widow living in the stairwell of a wealthy family in Ravindrapuri, was quick to anger and was often spotted screaming at small children, dogs, or other passersby along her daily route. She was dressed in a ragged white sari and often had a wide-eyed glare, the image of the matted-lock *paglī*, or madwoman. But for Ravindrapuri residents, she was, in my hearing, never framed in terms of madness, imbalance, sixtyishness, or even weakness. "She has no one," I repeatedly heard. No one heard Koki as maladjusted, for there was no one to whom she had to adjust. She was not imbalanced, for there was no *bahū* against whom to balance. The interstice was her own.

The widowed old auntie without children seldom threatened the moral integrity of middle-class families or neighborhoods. Traditional behavioral restrictions on upper-caste Hindu widows and concerns over whether these were followed closely seldom formed an explicit part of local discussions of the morality of old widows. Younger and middle-aged widows offered a sexualized threat to the moral life of the colony; their behavior, particularly those women who were heads of households and those who worked outside the home, was inevitably if vaguely noted to be transgressive. One of the metaphoric registers through which the inappropriate behavior of such a woman might be marked was old age: by being prematurely marked as old, a widow could be seen to act in ways that were inappropriate for her age. The language of balance and adjustment could be invoked to frame what was wrong with such women in the contemporary absence of a shared public discourse on widowhood.

In Nandanagar, I was frequently told by young and middle-aged women to meet the old mad woman who rented a room from one of the colony families. This "old" woman was in her late forties, an educated Bihari woman widowed at eighteen with two children who managed to raise them without family support by obtaining a position working for the government on issues of rural health. She had married off both children; her son was posted in Rajasthan, she resented living alone but saw no alternative, and she was reluctant to discuss why she could not stay with the son and daughter-in-law. Unlike the many women in their forties in Nagwa basti who were frequently called old, in Nandanagar colony chronological age mattered and persons in their forties were simply not old. When I asked women in the colony who had called the widow old why they had done so, they did not answer directly but noted both her behavior and her bad family: her working in offices, her always coming and going, and her being abandoned by her children. There were hints of liaisons and infidelities, and even a soupçon of incest with the son offered by one neighborhood know-it-all.

Mrs. Seth, the widow herself, told me of great pressures and tensions. She had to struggle to marry off a daughter and get both her children postings, while working full time and bearing with neighborhood approbation. Her doctor had prescribed her minor tranquilizers, she told me soon after we began the interview; she had been told by the neighbor who had introduced us that I was becoming a *dimāgvāle dāktar,* a brain doctor or psychiatrist. She repeated throughout our conversation the difficulty of "tension," the impossibility of peace of mind, and the aid of medicine. This series was offered to deflect something, perhaps the sexual rumors or the complexities of the life behind them. Her taking tranquilizers was a fact several of the neighborhood women seemed to know and repeat. Though she worked a demanding job and had few interactions with anyone other than her landlords, she was offered by several in the colony as "mad." Descriptions of her pathology linked her nervous behavior, including "strange emotional outbursts," her femininity and indirectly her widowhood, and her obviously troubled relations with her children.

The menopause, during the 1980s, was emerging in settings like the Varanasi colonies as an increasingly powerful frame legitimating the pathology of difficult women like the Nandanagar widow.[11] Not (yet) a part of an everyday universe of discourse, the menopause was better known as a medical problem faced by middle-aged and middle-class women in particular, requiring psychotropic medication. Phenomenological descriptions of menopausal pathology in India have stressed its hysterical aspects, implying an opposition of cognitive male versus embodied female age reminiscent of earlier European climacteric literature. A 1981 study in a Varanasi colony adjoining Ravindrapuri began:

> The climacteric is a universal phenomenon which has received relatively little attention from psychiatrists, psychologists, sociologists, anthropologists and social workers all over the world, but almost no research on this subject has been carried out in the Third-World countries. This study, carried out in India, has been conducted for the purpose of unraveling the difficulties that Indian women have to face during the climacteric. 405 married women between 40 and 55 years of age from the general population were contacted and interviewed. The results, obtained with the menopausal symptom checklist prepared by the authors, indicate . . . that hot flushes, night sweats and insomnia seem to be clearly associated with the menopause. . . . Despite embarrassment or discomfort experienced from these symptoms by a majority of women, only 10% had apparently sought medical treatment.[12]

The study, which introduced considerable bias in (1) its preassessment of what could constitute relevant experience (respondents were read lists of discrete symptoms and asked which they had experienced), (2) its lack of attention to the breadth of experience that "hot flushes" and other symptoms may signify, and (3) the unrelenting programmatic goals of its investigators (who were seeking to show that India has as florid a menopause as anywhere else), found that far more Indian women reported symptomatology (for example, 59–61 percent of women across cohorts surveyed reported hot flushes) than most other populations worldwide.[13] Searching for India's missing menopause, the authors discovered the mother lode.

Another study of menopause and South Asian women, du Toit's on Indians in South Africa, similarly downplayed the neutral or positive "menopausal" experience of many of his informants, mentioned but not enumerated unlike sympto-matology more in keeping with contemporary metropolitan experience.[14] For most women in the colonies with whom I spoke, however, menopause was not pathologized in the florid way the authors of the Varanasi study describe. My own findings were far more consistent with George's study of immigrant Sikh women in Canada: relative to other Canadians, George found that "traditional psycho-logical and psychosomatic symptoms ascribed to menopause in the literature were notably absent in this group of women."[15]

The menopause was not a primary focus of my field research, and I do not want to offer a thin ethnography against the hundreds of detailed interviews the authors of the Varanasi study describe. Yet the excess of symptomatology they suggest was all but absent in my interviews with older women reflecting on their *own* aging and on the menopause. While my own sex, age, and foreignness almost certainly limited the sorts of discussions on the cessation of menses I was likely to engender (the male authors of the Varanasi study asked their wives to do the field-work), I stand by my sense that stories of anticipated or experienced bodily dis-comfort associated with the cessation of menses were neither public nor private markers of age for most persons in the Varanasi colonies. Medicalization, less of the menopause itself than of the postmenopausal body as a tremendous market for hormone therapy, may well change middle-class women's negotiation and ex-perience of the body in middle age, with the more far-reaching consequences Lock has outlined in the case of Japan.[16] Far more frequent in the late 1980s than the internalized medicalization of one's own body were attributions of pathologi-cal mood swings and more general bodily instability to *other* women, and particu-larly to those who, like the Nandanagar widow, presented a vague challenge to a local moral world.

The articulation of the senility of an old women may draw on other gendered life events. When I first met Mrs. Mishra in the Uttar Pradesh hill station of Mus-sourie, she was in her seventies and lived alone with her husband. Their eldest son was in government service in Orissa and the second had married and was living with his family nearby; their eldest daughter also lived nearby, a second was in Delhi, and the third abroad. Several cousins also lived nearby. I knew Mrs. Mishra's husband, and when he learned of my interest he invited me to visit him and his wife to help me with my book. As we walked down the steep hill to their home, which Mr. Mishra, in his seventies, negotiated several times a day, he told me that a visiting foreign doctor had diagnosed his wife with Alzheimer's disease and had told him that there was no cure. Mussourie was after all, as N. L. Kumar had noted to me in discussing its role in the founding of Age-Care India, the "headquarters" for many foreigners. Two of the Mishra children had married for-eigners, in one case leading to an estrangement between father and son that pre-vented Mr. Mishra from accepting his son's *sevā* and left him with sole responsibil-ity for his household and wife. As soon as we arrived at the house, he left to do his shopping.

I greeted Mrs. Mishra, who motioned to me to sit down. She stepped outside and began gathering twigs for a fire, placing them on top of the gas stove (which her husband kept disconnected when he was out) and looking around for matches to start a fire and make me some tea. When she went into the kitchen, I threw the twigs away, and she came out and began to process all over again. As I came to know Mrs. Mishra and the rest of her family, my clinical impression was that she was diagnosable with senile dementia, probably Alzheimer's disease. She had had steadily progressive loss of both short- and long-term memory and was seldom oriented to person (confusing her husband with her long-deceased father-in-law), place (wandering from the home each day and getting lost while her husband was at school), or time (she would frequently talk as if she were a young woman with small children). To frame what was wrong another way, Mrs. Mishra had grown mentally weak, with frequent bursts of anger and an often *bakbak* voice.

Mishra coped with the risks of his wife's affect, wandering, and disorientation through the help of many in the neighborhood. Neighbors and shopkeepers knew to keep an eye on her if she left the house, and to steer her in the right direction as she wandered about the market lanes. The nearby daughter came whenever her full-time job and household responsibilities allowed her time, and other relations helped with her care. For neighbors and for some of the relations, the cause of the old woman's *bakbak* and angry voice was more immediate than a foreign diagnosis and lay in what they saw as the improper *sevā* of the younger son who had married a foreigner. She had failed to adjust to his decision, they said; rather, it had caused a shock that weakened her mind and precipitated her current voice. In retelling the events of this marriage and her mother's decline, one of the daughters shifted the chronology of events to maintain the clear causality of her brother as the source of pathology.

Yet even within the world of these accusing sisters and cousins, bad *sevā* was an inadequate explanation. Mr. Mishra clearly *had* adjusted, though at the cost of a relationship with a loving son. He was neither sixtyish nor angry nor a *bakbak* type. In framing the difference between the two old people, relatives drew on a notion that I had heard a few times in the Varanasi colonies: women adjust more poorly than men. Men in Ravindrapuri framed this difference more in terms of innate differences; women in terms of the gendered events of the life course. The daughters of Mrs. Mishra recalled that their mother had become delirious during the birth of her last child years earlier: they defined this temporary period as *sannipat*, or derangement, a folk and classical Ayurvedic term denoting a literal derangement of all three bodily humors. Childbirth, they noted, carries its dangers: it weakens one and renders one vulnerable to shock. Women are less able to adjust because they have had to quite literally bear far more. In turning to the relational effects of childbirth to supplement the moral narrative of the bad son, the daughters echoed the typological difference discussed earlier, between fathers who negotiate all-or-nothing intergenerational relations of substitution and mothers who constitute and are constituted by their children's voices and effects.

BALANCE AND CARTESIAN POSSIBILITY

Balance and the power to adjust were differentially located across gender as well—as the following chapter will detail—as class. Briefly, in Nagwa slum, balance and adjustment were far less salient ways of making sense of an aging voice or forestalling the accusation of improper *sevā*. The possibility of balance is located within a particular embodiment of socially located experience.[17]

Dr. B. S. Mehta, in addition to his work as a pathologist and a student of theater, was a well-known raconteur. In 1989, he gave a talk on All India Radio Varanasi about growing old. In his talk, Mehta addressed a conflict in the aged construction of selfhood reminiscent of Sharon Kaufman's informants: feeling the same as one's youthful self but being socially and bodily marked as an old person. He explored several variations on the disjunction between what he framed as the ageless feeling of mind and age-bound experience of body. Ultimately for Mehta, unlike Kaufman's interviewees, both mind and body constitute authentic sources of selfhood. Rather than an alienation of identity from body, he describes a splitting of self.

In translating his address, I have included the original Hindi and Urdu terms for old age Mehta used, in part to show the subtleties of Banarsi Hindi's rich lexicon in the hands of a master and the ways Mehta can thus use local idiom to construct a thick phenomenology of old age.

> *Why get nervous at the coming of old age [piri]?*
> People tell you, you've gotten old [*būṛhe*]. It's for people who talk like that that it is said: They neither listen to God's praise, nor sing His songs, yet claim they can bring the heavens down. Only crookedness filters through: since they're washed up, so others must be destroyed. Well, let them be damned. What do you think? Perhaps you're humming: The heart remains young in love, and that, in the opinion of those who know, age [*umr*] is not measured in years but feeling. One sees them strong at sixty and aged [*būṛhā*] at twenty.

The paradox of sixtyishness is cited by Mehta to demonstrate the essential youthfulness of the self as heart and feeling. Yet sixtyishness is laden with irony, and Mehta goes on to suggest that the consciousness of oneself as youthful is sham, a denial of identity bound up with the prerogatives of *mast*, libertine pleasure. The first gray hair, a sign in Sanskrit literature of sexual decline, is an appropriately located index pointing to inward and essential change. And the hair is that of Dasharath, doomed to die of grief at the separation between generations for the sin of killing the perfect *sevā* of Shravan Kumar.

> Now on the other hand, after a time the mirror of King Dasharath seemed to say to him: Near the ear, white hair. The lesson: the mind is aging [*jaraṭhpan*]. And those who offer unsolicited advice say that when your hair is gray it is time to abandon wife and property and follow the path of Ramanath. All well and good—but might one not say: Old age [*buṛhāpā*] is mine, but being called old [*būṛhe*] has no support in my heart.

The split is not of mind and body. Heart—that is, desire—is young, and the body is old. Mind shuttles between, as mind is wont to do in Indian thought, reflecting Mehta's implicit insight that desire implies an absence, that the youthful heart of old age is predicated on an identity cognizant of its transformation. This transformed but authentic self is expressed in kinship terms, as a shift in one's relational identity from the lover to the "baba," the old man or uncle.

> To hell with white hairs and black mouths—neither are particularly affectionate. Of gray hair it is said that: White things all are fair, are fair save for hair, women won't bend nor enemies press, save in respect. Kesav Das used to moan: Kesav. . . . No enemy could do worse than these moon-bodied, doe-eyed ones. They call me baba and go. Now times have changed. Now a stretch-fabric beauty queen calls me "uncle" then disappears, leaving uncle scratching his head with his finger of wisdom.

A play upon embodiment: the mind as a contemplative "finger of wisdom," an impotent and useless appendage and a conflation of the weakness of *dimāg* with that of bodily *hāth pair* and of sexual potency. The very organ of reflection generating a sense of an ageless self is revealed as the phallus in decline, and the denial of the body as a source of selfhood becomes a pathetic effort to regain the seamless phallic hegemony of the body that does not signify its difference.[18] The multiple claims of heart, body, and mind are consolidated in a confrontation with one's mirror image: "And it is truly said, one wants to stand in front of this matter and to declare soundly: The world has come to witness a strange phase, continually changing in many ways, with surprise I look into the mirror, to see the oldness [*būṛhā sā*] of another one. The problem is that the perception of the mind [*man*] and body [*tan*] differ."[19]

Unlike Kaufman's informants, who in Mehta's terms take the interior claims of the mind and not the exterior ones of the body seriously in the constitution of the self, Mehta suggests that the self is simultaneously experienced as young and old and as hot and cold. Failure to manage this set of apparent paradoxes tips the equilibrium, and one becomes irritated and hot. Missing in Mehta's lexicon are terms for old age that stress experience and wisdom, as opposed to decline and abjection: the Sanskritic *vṛddha* against *jarā*, wise against decrepit old age,[20] or in this context the more neutral Urdu *buzurg*. Wisdom in this unmatching world is not a phenomenological given of old age, but a precarious state of balance between conflicting sources of the self.

Many people in the colonies framed the mental health of old people in terms of their *niyam*, their rule of conduct, and felt that through a balanced lifestyle they could maintain a state of shanti. For many in Nagwa and the poor of the Bengali quarter, the contrast Mehta evoked between a youthful heart or ageless mind and a weak body in old age neither paralleled experience nor was available as a rhetoric mapping intergenerational politics. Particularly in the lives of the Nagwa Chamar, dependency anxiety was rooted in a chronic sense of marginality, and old age was experienced less as a new Eriksonian challenge than as *plus ça change*.

Shanti was less a state of equilibrium than of asymptotic possibility, less the every-day coping with a dualism of self than the transcendence of extremity.

The last line of Mehta's radio address cited above, on the split between *man* and *tan*, mind and body, offers a play upon a verbal pair ubiquitous in Hindi poetics. Several variants of a couplet on *man* and *tan* in old age were told to me in Nagwa slum, ascribed to the late medieval poet-saint Kabir. I heard the first two versions over snacks at Secchan's tea stall, the initial one declaimed by the local *netā* (polit-ical leader) Seva Lal:

> *Nā tan mare nā man mare marmar jāt sarīr*
> *Āśā tṛṣṇā nā mare kaha gaye dās Kabīr.*

Neither body [*tan*] nor mind dies as the body [*sarīr*] keeps dying
Hope and thirst will not die, it's been said by Kabir Das.

When Seva Lal spoke the couplet, someone responded that there was no open-ing "*nā*" in the first line. But the tea stall audience was unanimous in hearing *man* and *tan* as a conjoint pair in both versions, linked to hope and thirst as things that lingered despite the decay of *sarīr* (or *śarīr*), the corporeal body not split into *tan* and *man*.

The two contradictory appearances of "body" in the couplet did not make sense to me, and I asked about them. A serious discussion of these terms followed, in which several people pointed out that *man* and *tan* were lasting ideational and material aspects, respectively, of human experience, whereas *sarīr* was the body *tout court*. One man called *tan* and *man* the soul (jiva), suggesting by the term that *tan* was the "subtle body" of Indian cosmology, that which transmigrated after death. Throughout, *man* and *tan* were not the ultimate and opposed alternatives they were in much of Mehta's text; rather, two different conceptualizations of body, one total (*sarīr*) and one discriminate (*man/tan*), constituted this framework of in-formal analysis. Against the transformations of age, mind and body were not op-posed but set together as a pair; the operant dualism was between a notion of body that decays and body that survives. *Man* and *tan* do *not* in themselves gener-ate a sense of irony; as the next chapter will suggest, the irony of aging in Nagwa lies in its meaninglessness, for all culturally elaborated frames for making sense of its transformations—weakness, renunciation, and the split self of Mehta's piece—have been exhausted in the comprehension of the marginality of low-caste youth.

Ambiguity is in the eye of the beholder. Viewed by younger others across the class spectrum, old people are split: experienced yet debilitated, peripheral yet icons of the family, hot-minded yet cold-bodied. In making sense of themselves, however, individuals experience the relationship of mind, body, and self relative to their own bodily histories, histories rooted in an individual's social position. The frequent but ethnographically crude invocation of Cartesian/non-Cartesian dis-tinctions in medical anthropology—viewing cultures as more or less dualistic in their construction of body and mind—must be sensitive to the dialogic constitution of the split self, to the dangers of equating mind (rather than body, or both) with identity, and, in particular, to the variable possibility of balance and dualistic thought across class.

THE DEMENTIA CLINIC

In 1989 I spent several weeks in an empty office adjoining the psychiatric outpatient clinic of the Banaras Hindu University Hospital. I had been advised by several hospital physicians that the psychiatry clinic, as opposed to the general medical or neurological clinics, would be the place to meet persons referred with diagnoses of senile dementia. Across the hall from where I would sit, several persons waiting for a consultation along with their family members crowded around the desk of the attending psychiatrist while he examined the patient whose turn it was and then prescribed something. More than a hundred patients were seen each day. Patients diagnosed with dementia by the attending psychiatrist were told about my study and asked if they would agree to a second clinical interview. At least, this was the plan, proposed by the attending psychiatrist and gratefully agreed to by me. During the month in which I scheduled these weekly sessions at the clinic, the attending psychiatrist with whom I was working diagnosed only six patients as potentially demented. They were all middle-aged adults, forty-five to sixty-five, each with a chief complaint of memory loss. None could be diagnosed as demented by DSM-III-R criteria.

1. KKB was a sixty-five-year-old male retired police superintendent with the chief complaint of memory loss. His past history was significant for a series of "nervous breakdowns": in 1962 when he was posted to Nepal and at the same time was involved in arranging for the marriages of his six sisters, in 1982 from the shock of having to cancel his daughter's wedding on the wedding day itself when he found out she was having an affair, and attacks of "nervousness" over the past year not associated by him with specific events. His father died several months ago and KKB became the head of the household; since then he had noticed a progressive memory loss.

2. TNR was a forty-five-year-old male stenographer living with his wife and two sons, with the chief complaint of memory loss. He reported that he had suffered from an "inferiority complex" and forgetfulness since childhood. He began "bad habits"—by which he meant masturbation though he hinted at occasional sex with female prostitutes or other men—in childhood, and accelerated them in the army. He was impotent with his wife, got little sleep, and felt fearful and hopeless.

3. UD was a forty-eight-year-old housewife brought to the clinic by her husband for refusing to eat; she was sent to me because of the attending physician's sense of her continually worsening disorientation and memory loss. Five months earlier, she began refusing food and became increasingly agitated. At that time she would refuse to look at anyone else and would close her eyes, lie immobile in bed, and refuse to move even to relieve herself elsewhere, would make vibrating noises but

no clear speech, and "forgot everyone and everything." She had had intermittent swelling of her face and extremities, intermittent abdominal pain and vomiting, and episodes of incontinence. A medical workup was negative; she was referred to the neurology clinic. One medical doctor suggested the symptoms were due to the menopause and would in time resolve. The first neurologist diagnosed her with "? schizophrenia"; the consulting neurologist noted on his report "? Alzheimer's Disease, Progressive deterioration of intellectual function. No objective neurological signs." She was referred to the psychiatric clinic and placed on Valium.

Simultaneously, her husband consulted with a pandit in the Sanskrit department of the university, an expert on astrology and mantra-tantra, spells and esoteric practices. He was concerned that his wife's behavior might be due to possession by a *bhūt*, a type of spirit that frequently attacked vulnerable and particularly female bodies. The pandit examined both the patient and her horoscope; he then prescribed an Ayurvedic medication and the reading of the *Durgā calisā*, a hymn to the goddess Durga, after which the patient's symptoms improved but did not resolve.

4. UsD was a forty-six-year-old female school principal with the chief complaint of memory loss and the continuation of headaches that she had had since a fatal scooter accident two years previously that killed her husband and during which she lost consciousness. She described finding out about his death, a week after regaining consciousness, as a great "shock." She developed headaches whenever she tried to do her work, could get little accomplished, and was afraid of losing her position. Her "memory kī kamzorī" (weakness), like her headaches, was associated with her job and her feeling of failure and inability to work. She received a provisional psychiatric diagnosis of "post-traumatic fear, psychosis" and was placed on Ativan, another anxiolytic medication.

5. SR was a fifty-year-old male file clerk with the chief complaint of memory loss. He had been seen at the clinic for a year with the primary diagnosis of depression and had been treated with antidepressant and anxiolytic medication. He felt the memory loss was a new problem and that his "mental depression" was cured. His past history was unremarkable, but he noted that he used to do too much "deep thinking" about his worries, particularly about getting all his daughters married.

6. H was a forty-seven-year-old male shopkeeper from a village in the district, whose chief complaints were memory loss and a hot brain (*dimāg*). He had a history of several decades of *ghabrāhaṭ* (nervousness, panic) to the point over the last few years of *pāgalpan* (madness). He had seen a series of medical doctors without relief until he had met the attending physician at the psychiatric clinic the previous year. Since then, he was receiving shanti from his medication, Halcion. He noted the medication helped to cool his *dimāg* but has not relieved his forgetfulness, a problem in keeping his accounts straight for his business.

In addition to developing a dementia workup including a mental status exam, I listened to whatever the patient and his or her family thought was most relevant to their situation. Only UD, the woman who wouldn't eat and who had been referred to psychiatry by the neurologists, had a score on the mental status examination that could be correlated with dementia; she had been the one patient whose file included the possibility of Alzheimer's. But her score, like that of many in Nagwa, seemed in itself little indication of much save her disinclination to be examined. The memory loss of the other five was not the demonstrable short or intermediate term memory loss in theory demonstrable on such an exam. Nor were UD's rapid course of decline, her sudden anorexia and aphasia, her history of swelling, and her family's sense that she got better with mantra-tantra treatment indicative of a clinical picture particularly suggestive of chronic dementia.

The clinical data of A. K. Venkoba Rao, the first psychiatrist in India to carry out extensive clinical and community-based surveys of mental health in the elderly, suggests that at least in the south Indian city of Madurai old persons less ambiguously diagnosable as demented form a majority of those over fifty-five referred and brought to the psychiatric clinic by their families.[21] In Varanasi, my own physician interviews, clinical interviews, and examinations of medical records with psychiatrists, neurologists, and internists suggested that although most old patients with cognitive deficits and behavioral or other "adjustment" problems were diagnosed as being demented or having Alzheimer's, few old people ever came to the clinic as patients for such things. More to the point, few old people were ever brought to the Varanasi clinic for anything. As I noted earlier, one answer to explain the difference between Madurai and Varanasi would be quantitative, the effect of the demographic and health transitions of south India: there are proportionally more old people and these live longer. Thus, there will be more senile pathology and more dementia, leading to more clinic visits.

But the Varanasi clinic as of 1989 was not characterized so much by fewer visits by persons over sixty-five as by their virtual absence. The behavioral difference of older people was seldom medicalized, independent of the proportion of persons over sixty-five within the population. If the difference between Varanasi and Madurai is related to the health transition of the south, it may be related more to the antecedents of the transition than to its effects. North-south differences within India in terms of family structure and their effects on life expectancy and mortality are a complex topic—as is evident in the data collected by scholars like Pauline Kolenda and Bina Agarwal[22] —and I do not think a satisfactory resolution of why Venkoba Rao's data so differs from clinical experience in Varanasi can easily emerge. What is missing from such a discussion is a sense of how the ideology of the Bad Family relates to the everyday negotiation of intergenerational relations and knowledge of the old body in different regions of India.

In Varanasi, dementia—as a medical site linked powerfully to memory—drew to it a host of life experiences that, unlike those of weak or hot brain, were embodied primarily through the idiom of amnesia. The memory loss of the patients I have described and of persons in the colonies with similar complaints was attributed to sorrow, shock, masturbation, attacks of nervousness and panic, depression and deep thinking, and a range of somatic experiences. Many of these persons' illness narratives were reminiscent of other idioms and frames of suffering—of *dhat*, or semen loss,[23] of *bhūt-pret*, or spirit possession—sometimes with explicit diagnostic and therapeutic links. The associations of masturbation and semen loss in particular evoked a semantic network of semen, capital, and memory, the space of the neo-*rasāyana* tonic. The psychiatric clinic, with the frames it tentatively offered, was but one of several sources of healing considered by sufferers and their families, most relevant for the families of middle-class and primarily male adults for whom memory loss as opposed to possession or depletion could be a primary idiom of experience.

The likelihood of physicians—and in particular psychiatrists and neurologists—to consider pushing a diagnosis of dementia was, in the two years of my primary fieldwork, most closely correlated with their interactions with pharmaceutical company representatives, or detail men. I followed the efforts of one multinational corporation to market an antidementia product to Indian physicians. In 1988, the Italian firm Farmitalia, under a dynamic new American manager of their Indian operations, began to promote nicergoline, a product sold in Europe as the antidementia drug Sermion, under the Indian brand name Dasovas. Company and product names differed in India, in part given then-current restrictions on multinational corporations prior to the economic liberalization of the 1990s. Farmitalia did business under a different name, as a company set up through the liquor baron and horse-racing enthusiast Vijay Mallaya.

The challenge for the firm was to sell a relatively expensive dementia drug in a market where, as Farmitalia's Indian medical director noted to me, senility was seldom medicalized. In the beginning of the campaign, he was unsure of strategy ("It's a mystery to us"). Six months later, in 1989, the company had formulated a strategy and was set to launch the new drug; I returned to Bombay to visit the medical director. He asked me what sorts of symptoms I was seeing in Varanasi. Somewhat warily, I answered that what I was seeing was that symptoms did not correlate with mental status exams in the ways I had been taught to expect in medical school. He responded "Frankly, we don't want doctors to do these tests. We're trying to push these drugs. How can we pressure—no, that's the wrong word—how can we convince doctors, GPs, that they should find out about memory?"

The medical director and his marketing team had sensed that marketing Dasovas as a memory tonic would reach a far wider market than marketing it as a specifically medicalized dementia drug. Curious, I asked him if he too had noted that adjustment problems and affective change were more salient criteria of old age weakness. He immediately noted: "Yes, but we want to stress memory. We want, when a fifty-year-old man comes in with other problems, the doctor to be alert to memory—how is his memory—and to be able to say 'You need this drug' and to treat the problem before dementia sets in."

Nicergoline was thus from the outset offered as preventive medicine through a radical pathologization of middle age. To legitimate the move, Farmitalia decided to begin with brain specialists but to advance the campaign quickly to include other practitioners: "We'll begin with the neurologists. Otherwise, no one else would prescribe the drug. But we want to move beyond them. We recognize that most, 80 percent, of people will only see a GP, so we have to target them. But how?"

The strategy was reasonable, and the question germane. Its answer came from a surprising quarter: "We want you to work with us. Perhaps you could publish an article—anonymously, if you wish—with us? Though I declined, Dasovas's medical, marketing, and management support team developed several successful strategies; the product's appeal did not suffer. When some months later I was in Madurai visiting the psychiatrist Venkoba Rao, several physicians connected with Madurai Medical College mentioned to me they had been visited by Dasovas representatives, and asked me what I thought of the drug.

By early 1990, when I again was in Bombay, Farmitalia had moved to new and far plusher offices, up from the basement to the fourteenth floor. Dasovas was doing well, though the pattern of its success surprised some in sales and marketing. Expecting the largest impact in urbanized areas of north India, particularly Delhi, they found their best sales to be in south and central India. Given feedback from detail men informing them that in central India Dasovas sold well to the middle-aged concerned about memory, they began to consider marketing the drug more explicitly as a brain tonic as a way to success in the north.

What did I think of the drug? I found the answer tough. Nicergoline is an ergot mesylate, a descendent of a class of drugs clinically labeled vasodilators and marketed extensively in the United States until the 1980s as treatments for senile and vascular dementia. In the days before Alzheimer's was a household word, when diminished cerebral blood supply secondary to arteriosclerosis explained senile behavior, vasodilators offered the prospects of increased blood flow. By the late 1970s, evidence had emerged to challenge the efficacy of these compounds against placebo;[24] simultaneously, the concept of Alzheimer's had shifted and was leading to a rapidly changing research climate in which vascular models were being eclipsed. By the mid-1980s, American vasodilator use was declining and behavioral interventions targeting the lingering "inappropriate prescribing" of the substances were being undertaken.[25]

Despite the American shift, European companies like Farmitalia continued to market and develop newer generations of ergot mesylates and to promote extensive clinical and experimental research. Cross-nationally, it is possible that the degree of decline in vasodilator use was correlated with the centrality of Alzheimer's in professional and popular conceptualizations of senility. The new generation of ergot drugs was rechristened, their function fortuitously rediscovered: no longer vasodilators, the drugs were now metabolic enhancers. A new rationale was advanced for their efficacy. Research findings favorable to the efficacy of nicergoline were extensively promoted by Farmitalia. Articles distributed by the firm were seldom paragons of impartial research design and reporting: sources of funding were seldom revealed,[26] placebo controls were not always included in study designs,[27] and the effects of the drug on long-term prognosis and on severe dementia were downplayed or ignored.

To explain the significance of metabolic enhancement, Dasovas literature relied on a somewhat tautological category of "chronic cerebral insufficiency," presented through the use of an acronym (CCI) as an accepted and experimentally confirmed biomedical fait accompli. CCI—which was a grab bag of lumped-together symptoms with complex differentials, including dizziness, depression, anxiety, memory loss, and "decreased performance"—was posited to occupy the gray space between the poles of the normal and the pathological of geriatric ideology. It was described as "a complex age-related degenerative process that can be considered an exaggeration of normal ageing," and "its symptomatology could be considered (as a working formulation) as lying midway between that of normal ageing and the one of senile dementia."[28]

CCI, like its liminal DSM cousin "benign senescent forgetfulness," allowed for the maintenance of the sharp division between the normal and the pathological through the containment of the geriatric paradox within itself. Presented as normal—thus universal—aging meriting consideration by physicians for all their patients, and as a pathological syndrome with its own "symptoms" and "management," CCI could become a synonym for the ambiguities of old age. In Dasovas literature, its invocation was followed by a description of the various dementias, further establishing a metonymic link between CCI and dementia and implicitly suggesting that to treat one was to treat the other. CCI played on the weak but certainly plausible evidence that nicergoline may in fact increase alertness and concentration in old adults with mild dementias.

In its construction as a sophisticated medical object, Dasovas was offered as a gatekeeper, a cure for the climacteric period between aging and the fall into severe dementia. The assumption throughout its literature was that if one could, through nicergoline, make an impact at the limen of pathology, one could forestall dementia forever. Thus the medical director's attempt to get to all fifty-year-olds "before dementia sets in." Thus the picture, in an article reporting one of the European clinical trials, of Lucas Cranach's Fountain of Youth.[29]

What moral are we to draw from the ongoing saga of Dasovas? That the senile body is being rampantly medicalized by the false promises of the encroaching world system in the incarnation of Italian companies, German researchers, American managers, and Indian medical directors? To assume that the usual excesses of the medical marketplace are so powerful as to recreate the cultural construction of the senile body in India is to assign the Indian consumer—physician, patient, bureaucrat, or relative—the thoroughly passive role of unwitting dupe in the play of markets, practices, and representations. But Farmitalia has its echoes elsewhere. Recall King Vinayashila, and the lesson of the *Kathāsaritsāgara*: it is the nature of physicians to promote their wares and to respond to the desires of some patients to forestall old age indefinitely. Recall Siranji's family, and the gift of the tonic: a drug was bought not as an agent of transformation but as a sign of *sevā* and the love of children. In contesting her children's gift, Siranji argued that it was a worthless tonic, that they needed to try again and not just to point to the abandoned big bottle on the shelf every time she complained of weakness.

Dasovas was offered as the cure for the senile climacteric: the drug that if given early enough will prevent further decline. It used a neuronal language synchronous with Alzheimer's to legitimate its vague model of efficacy. But its success may draw on other needs and other languages: the desire for the powerful gift, the quest for the neo-*rasāyana* tonic. Few physicians or families with whom I spoke were particularly convinced of Dasovas's promise. "We can," noted a Calcutta psychiatrist, "only keep trying." The children, he said, need to give something.

Dasovas was not cheap; if metabolic enhancement was but old wine in a new bottle, its being prescribed to those with marginal incomes would suggest pharmaceutical industry exploitation. But like the equally upmarket ginseng preparation Thirty Plus, Dasovas's price is a marker of its transactional value within the economy of the familial body. Whatever the ethics of Dasovas's availability or the sources of its popularity, Farmitalia is not suffering; on my last visit to Bombay before leaving India in 1990, the concern had just added a fifth car to its fleet of luxury vehicles. But to focus on the sale of upmarket tonics as sources of inequality in the construction of the senile body is to miss the point. Treating the senile body is itself a conceptual possibility only within a narrow window of the class spectrum. Medicalizing senility presumes a senescent geometry of balance, not weakness.

There were several roads into that part of Nagwa. One way to get in was to cross the new bridge over the Assi River, against whose banks the slum was poised, then to turn right at the lane between the Catholic Fathers' ashram and the house where the red-haired American evangelist rented a room. The ashram Fathers, unlike the evangelist and unlike the activist priest Paul, who lived farther in, didn't interact with Nagwa residents too often but gave gifts on occasion, which angered Paul as he felt it made people dependent and less likely to resist the ways in which they perpetuated their own marginality. John the evangelist had little success in spreading the Good News, in part a result of his lack of an ear for foreign language. The missionary girls up in Mussourie—the American headquarters with its mission language school where Mr. Mishra and his children had taught—would titter and call him Ji Han for the one Hindi word he had then been able to master and which he would in consequence interject incessantly, *jī han, jī han*, Yes. Repeated excitedly it sounded like braying. John's modest room overlooked the bridge, which had been built when the government moved the course of the Assi as a flood prevention measure. The river, little more than a trickle most of the year, had changed its course at least twice in the chronicles of the slum, the most recent being the result of the government effort and the first, according to a story I was once told in Nagwa, being the work of an angry rishi who cursed the once broad Assi after it had refused to speed up at his behest, the power of his voice reducing it to the diminutive stream that it remains.

A second approach was from the wealthier sections of Nagwa, off a road that brought one from the university. A colony of European expatriates, many of whom were students of Indian classical music, was nearby, prompting the Cardinal of Milan along with other curia officials to visit Nagwa and to conduct an inquiry into what attracted so many Catholic youth to the wellsprings of Ganga and

Kashi. His Eminence, accompanied by some of the ashram Fathers, passed through the slum en route, pausing briefly at the water pump across from the Ravi Das temple. Other luminaries have taken this way in, including erstwhile California governor and American presidential candidate Jerry Brown.

The approach into the slum most used by its residents led one through a series of lanes that began by the police station, or thana, at Lanka crossing. The police were also frequent visitors to the slum, but whereas the cardinal had limited his inquiries to the young the police had an interest in the old as well. A lot of young women in Nagwa worked in domestic service and were the prime suspects in local robberies of jewelry and gold, a few of which they may have abetted but most of which they clearly had not. Still, one often made oneself scarce after a robbery in an establishment where one worked, to avoid the trial-by-ordeal beatings of police custody. Thus the police interest in the parents of the absconders as sources of information about their children's whereabouts, and consequently the not-too-infrequent beatings of Nagwa elderly.

The "elderly": many in their late forties through early sixties, yet very much *būṛh*, old, in the terms of local knowledge. There were not too many persons in their seventies or older in Nagwa. Some people went back to relatives in their villages when they were too old to work; more died, failing to survive bouts of illness in the absence of sustained nutrition and health care by their children or others. It was a neighborhood of the young, a Shangri-La of the plains. A funny place to study old age, standing in queue behind the missionaries and politicians and police, each with their questions and each their good news: Yes.

SEVEN

Chapati Bodies

in which weakness, not maladjustment, anchors the body in time

NAGWA BY ITS RESIDENTS

Hori folded his tattered jacket carefully and placed it on the cot. "So you consider me an old man, do you? I'm not even forty yet. And men are still lusty as bulls at sixty."

"Not ones like you. Go look at your face in the mirror. Just how are you going to be lusty when you can't even get enough milk and butter to make a few drops of ointment for your eyes? It scares me to see the condition you're in—makes me wonder how we'll manage in our old age? Whose door will we beg at?"

Hori's momentary mellowness vanished as though consumed in the flames of reality. "I'll never reach sixty, Dhaniya," he said, picking up his stick. "I'll be gone long before that."
PREMCHAND, *GODAN*[1]

If the meaning of a bad old voice is deferred in cosmopolitan discourse and in the residential colonies through the invocation of the West as the origin of the Fall and the parabolic geometry of balance as the mapping of the life course, in Nagwa Harijan basti processes of deferral invoke the imposition of caste order as the origin of the Fall and the linear movement of weakness as its geometry. Weakness, *kamzorī*, is central to local experience and ideology in Nagwa. I again begin by locating a neighborhood within a particular cosmos through the narratives of its residents.

Varanasi got its name, according to a popular if dubious etymology, from the two tributaries of the Ganga—the Varuna River to the north and the Assi stream to the south—which form one version of its sacred borders. In between lies the city of Lord Shiva, held aloft on his trident and safe from cosmic dissolution, with its promise of liberation for those who bathe, live, die, and who are cremated there. Just south of the Assi the ground rises; on it sits the slum. Even when the course of the Assi was shifted, splitting the neighborhood in two, the part of the slum officially known as Nagwa Harijan basti remained outside the land between the rivers. Nagwa overlooks the field of liberation from the wrong side.

Most of the low-caste residents of the slum are Chamar, nominally a leather-working caste; fronting the slum on the Panchakosi Road are the homes of the relatively higher status Dhobis and the Catholic Kristapanthi ashram. On the opposite side of the road are a few homes, a small mosque, and fields that run along the Ganga. Further south and to the west lies an area of middle-class homes and a few wealthy estates.

The Panchakosi Road rings Varanasi and marks the route of pilgrims on a five-day seasonal circumambulation of the city. It is an alternative and more inclusive framing of the boundary of the sacred city.[2] Most city dwellers living beyond the greater circle of the Panchakosi Road were not particularly troubled by their location beyond redemptive space. For several slum residents, however, the question of boundary was more of an active challenge. They stressed their location within the Panchakosi Road—as opposed to beyond the Assi—as part of a move of inclusion and totality consonant with the political language of the slum, its ubiquitous plaint that "all people are the same."

Caste more than geography distanced Nagwa Chamar from the religious resources of their city. Residents did not feel comfortable at most temples, festivals, or processions, despite the successful struggle several decades earlier to open the city's important shrines to them. Through the cult of the fifteenth- or sixteenth-century poet saint Ravi Das, a Chamar who lived in and around Varanasi, Nagwa slum dwellers recreated the city as an accessible yet oppositional sacred center. His purity and virtue challenged by Brahmans, Ravi Das demonstrated his inner worth to the common people and to the king through a series of well-known miracles. In the most famous of these, when asked by his high-caste interlocutors where he kept his sacred thread (which as a Chamar he had never been invested with and could not wear) Ravi Das cut open his chest and produced not one but four threads, internalizing the fourfold caste order within the body as a sign of sameness.

Ravi Das's birthplace and the river ghat where he spent his days (and cut open his chest) are the sites of new temples. These were linked to low-caste bastis throughout the city on Ravi Das's birthday by a parade that wound its way through city streets to the site of the birthplace, just beyond the BHU campus. Nagwa, as one of the southernmost of the city's Chamar slums near the end of the parade route, would greet the floats, trucks, elephants, and tractors from throughout Varanasi district as they approached the final stretch. One of several competing "Ravi Das Committees" from the slum would raise funds for a floral arch, draped with a broad banner welcoming participants on behalf of the Nagwa committee. The subscription of funds and erection of the arch linked Nagwa slum with other Dalit communities[3] and appropriated the elaborate and Brahmanic sacred geography of Varanasi as authentically Chamar through the figure of Ravi Das.

Ravi Das was represented on posters in homes in Nagwa, along with images of a mother and child, the goddess Durga, and Dr. Ambedkar, the untouchable architect of the Indian constitution. There were two poster representations of Ravi Das: a vigorous black-bearded man and an old and emaciated white-bearded rishi type. The younger man tears open his chest to reveal his visceral caste and lots of blood; the older man sits in a meditative posture, a world-weary expression on his face.

A small shrine of the younger Ravi Das sat in an open area in the center of the slum, across from a government-erected pump and latrine. To the east of this clearing, the slum rose toward the Panchakosi Road. On the other three sides, the ground sharply descended: to the Assi on the north; to a water-filled gully and a field to the south, which until 1989 served as the slum's dish-washing pond or "tank" and its recreational space; and to the other half of the slum, spilling over into low-lying and periodically inundated land, on the west.

Between the summer of 1988, when I first began to interview residents, and the spring of 1990, when I left Varanasi for the United States, the physical environment of Nagwa changed significantly. A developer won the contested rights to the slum's common land—its tank and field—and the high brick and plaster walls of a new middle-class colony began to rise several meters from the Nagwa slum dwellings. The dense basti lost its commons; all that was left of the tank water were several small and stagnant pools. Overnight, the geography of Nagwa Harijan basti was transformed, from a poor urban village into something more closely resembling a Bombay or Calcutta slum.

Other physical transformations occurred in the basti during those two years. The urban administration of Varanasi freed up funds for subsidizing the building of household latrines, although the drainage system necessary for them to become operative was not repaired. Still, unusable latrines began to appear in most of the wealthier homes of the slum. Change came from other sources as well. The European priest and scholar known as Father Paul had lived in the slum since 1980, forsaking the comfort of the Kristapanthi ashram. Paul raised European funds to buy a plot of land a kilometer to the south of Nagwa basti, build a pump house for irrigation, and set up a vegetable growers' cooperative of slum residents. His efforts stressed self-reliance and communal control of the gardens. Residents who joined had to commit to a periodic membership payment and communal labor, but received the perpetual use of an irrigated garden plot.

Many residents were distrustful of his motives; several questioned where the cooperative dues went. Despite his years of service in the community, Paul was an ambiguous figure, seen by some to enjoy elite prerogatives—travel, university study, connections in high places—without giving any gifts. Unlike the periodic gift-giving of the ashram Fathers, his projects were not based on explicit gifting but rather on the creation of autonomy and a different kind of local reason. Yet as he was a foreigner, Paul's visa was continually subject to reexamination and to the

potential refusal of another extension. He could not guarantee that he would remain in the community to ensure residents' invulnerability from the claims of the
powerful and to protect the security of their investment.

The fear that the community garden would go the way of the commons drew
upon the experience of time and social structure in Nagwa. The history of
Nagwa, for its residents, was that of a Fall from greatness into a state of dependency characterized by unstable sources of patronage. The destruction of the
commons, the latest incursion into the Nagwa slum by persons locally identified as
Thakurs, members of several land-owning and latter-day baronial castes, was but
the repetition of a historical pattern. The Fall of Nagwa took shape within a local
ideology of Chamar and other Dalits as the autochthonous bearers of authentic
religion and polity, of an Adi Dharm. Several residents claimed that Nagwa's
sanctity antecedes that of Varanasi itself. Adi Dharm is literally the original
dharma. It was described as the true Indian religion and polity, before the foreign
invasion of the Vedic Aryans and the imposition of caste and its naturalization.
The lowest "scheduled" castes and tribal groups were thus the true heirs of a pre-
Aryan and pre-Brahmanical Indian religion.

Local versions of Nagwa's sacred geography demonstrated the area's claim to
precedence over the superimposed sanctity of Kashi. Several hundred meters
south of the basti along the Panchakosi road was a stone worshipped as a protective demigod, Baru Baba. Ram Lakhan, one of the most articulate ideologues of
the slum, suggested that Baru Baba was a naga, a snake deity. He suggested that
naga worship was central to Adi Dharm, and furthermore that the name for
Nagwa itself came from naga. Ram Lakhan envisioned Nagwa as a forgotten center for naga worship. The woman who ran the tea stall across from Baru Baba
concurred. One day, she noted, a *motevālā* (a fat man, here a pejorative term connoting power and position) came by to look at Baru Baba. The Fatman pointed to
the local mosque, located next to where her tea shop now stands. He told her that
Baba originally came from the top of a former temple, the site of which is cur-
rently occupied by the mosque. Muslims, the *motevālā* was suggesting, were responsible for the destruction of Nagwa's heritage.

The indexicality of the Fatman's finger was resisted. Muslims were seldom invoked as the agents of decline in the history of Nagwa; they were viewed ambivalently. On the one hand, they were competitors for limited state and private patronage for the poor, not as truly deserving as the Nagwa residents. On the other,
they were seen as living *sahī*, correctly, as having good families and not getting
weak minded in old age, and as bearers of an egalitarian ideology. Efforts by characters like tea-shop Fatmen to pin the decline of Adi Dharm on Muslims begged
what for most residents was the primary source of their debility, the upper-caste
triad of Brahman, Kshatriya, and Vaishya, who destroyed Adi Dharm and en-
slaved and dehumanized its adherents. This original Aryan colonization was continually relived in local narrative: people spoke of the collusion of "Brahman,

Thakur, Bania" (priest, landowner, merchant) in the ongoing appropriation of their rights and resources.

The relationship of Nagwa residents to powerful others that emerged from collective memory was not just a simple opposition of us versus them. The antiquity of Baru Baba notwithstanding, few in Nagwa were certain that their grandparents or great-grandparents lived there; most had family ties in villages south of Varanasi across the Ganga or northwest toward Jaunpur district. Several families who rented in the colony were migrants from Bihar or Bangladesh. An alternative origin story stressed not the antiquity of the area but its historical founding by Bula Babu, a Bengali who built a grand house on what had formerly been only fields. Jhalli Ram, an "old man" (*būṛh*) in his early sixties who continually shuttled between the households of two of his sons, told me that many of the large mansions near the Ganga had been built by Bula Babu and sold to various princes, including the King of Nepal. These rajas gave great gifts to the poor, who clustered nearby. Jhalli Ram thought that the emergence of Nagwa basti occurred in 1931.

Jhalli told of Bula Babu willing one of his mansions to his gardener, a story suggesting the extent of Bula's largesse. But opportunists—again, rich Thakurs—wrested the house from the gardener. Jhalli Ram tied the founding of the community to the gifts of outsiders, here Bengalis and Nepalis, and its decline to local elites. The theme was repeated in other sets of narratives. Jawahar, a vegetable seller in his sixties, noted that Nagwa's land was originally owned by the Maharaja of Varanasi, but that the new Indian state took the land from him and sold it to rich Thakurs. The Maharaja had given the land where the slum and its tank and common field were to the Harijans. But just as the Thakurs secured the other royal lands, they have managed to appropriate the commons.

Narayan, a laborer and poet in his seventies, recalled that he used to work a plot of land near the Assi River that was owned by the Maharaja. When the government took over the land, he said, "the Congress Party workers urged me to press my claims to the land. But I wanted [the land] to go over to the Rani [the queen]. When my father came here, this was all jungle. They came from M.P. or Haryana to Banaras on pilgrimage, and felt that they should stay here. They built these homes. Others came from elsewhere. The Maharaja gave them the land." Narayan suggested that through his fealty to the family of the Maharaja, his family's initial benefactor, he lost control of his former plot. Now, in his old age, he could not depend on owning land and was far more vulnerable. He summed up his state in one of his ballads, which he would sing to fellow patrons at a tea stall in Lanka crossing. In the ballad a bull butts the narrator from behind when he is not looking, knocking him down. Oh, Bull, went Narayan's refrain, why did you hit me? The bull in Narayan's ballad reflected the two "bulls" in his experience, old age and his declining resources, both of which caught him unawares. He paralleled the physical *kamzorī* of old age with the economic weakness of being both old and Chamar.

Others of Narayan's songs were less ironic. He sang heroic ballads about Dr. Ambedkar and Indira Gandhi, the latter whom he, like most other older people in Nagwa, considered a hero in contrast with her son, then prime minister. With Mrs. Gandhi's policies, he would sing, the proud Thakur became a rickshaw puller and the lowly Chamar a moneylender. Like the Maharaja and Bula Babu, Indira Gandhi was the paradigmatic giver, but like these others her gifts were appropriated when different rulers came to power.

Given the instability of gifts and the self-interest of the powerful, political and religious ideology in Nagwa stressed self-reliance and strategies of minimization. Political machines were distrusted and local party affiliations would continually shift. As in R. H. Khare's study of "worldly asceticism" among Lucknow Chamar,[4] politics in Nagwa were often framed in terms of a self-reliant asceticism. Many men and a few women in Nagwa had a guru, a teacher who trains and counsels one in both political and religious matters. Gurus were usually older men from outside the slum, often from other Dalit communities. Gurus were also teachers from the past. Religious life in Nagwa centered on a quartet of four historical and saintly gurus: Kabir, Isa Masi [Jesus], Guru Nanak, and, most of all, Ravi Das.

As related by Nagwa disciples, the message of gurus—contemporary and historical, ethical and exemplary—challenged not the fact of low-caste weakness but its meaning, suggesting that weakness demonstrated not the necessity of hierarchy but the identity and, consequently, equality of all people. The gods of Vaisnavite and Saivite Hinduism and the pretensions to authority and purity of Brahmans, Thakurs, and Banias were but the legitimation of exploitative practice. Local celebrations of the historical gurus included the lampooning of caste Hindu piety. On the day before Ravi Das's birthday in 1989, the local leader Seva Lal and several friends acting as a Ravi Das Committee organized a performance in another Dalit neighborhood, that of Seva Lal's guru. Secchan, the ever-inebriated tea shop proprietor, was transformed into Lord Shiva; in leopard skin and colored deep blue from head to toe, he held court over a celestial audience of prostitutes and dancing boys.

As leather-workers, Chamar were called upon to drum in the celebrations of many other groups in the city, events of varying sanctimoniousness. Part of Chamar performance often included satiric skits, in which reversals of age, gender, and sexual desire along with those of caste and class offered social satire ranging from barbed to highly muted, depending on the audience and occasion.[5] In another skit, the weaver and part-time musician and comic Ramji played an old and deaf village man, newly married to a young girl, who undertakes a pilgrimage to the holy city of Varanasi with his bride. They meet an unscrupulous Brahman *paṇḍā*, or religious guide, on the road, who offers to take them around the city with hopes of bilking and even cuckolding the old man. The deaf old man misunderstands each of the Brahman's instructions, praying "*Jai Murgā Mai*" (Hail Mother Goddess Chicken) instead of "*Jai Durgā Mai*" (Hail Mother Goddess Durga) at the

Durgā temple, and so forth. The temples that the mismatched couple visit are those that many of the Chamar audience work outside of, guarding the polluting shoes of worshippers.

WEAKNESS AS STRUCTURE

The figure of the decrepit old man played by Ramji is as central to Nagwa ideology as it is to Brahmanical and Buddhist thought. In Ramji's depiction, the old man's weakness symbolizes both the perversion and ultimate failure of elite desire, its object here the young woman. Elders, no matter how powerful, cannot hold onto youth forever, and eventually confuse goddesses with chickens. Chicken, *murgā*, is a dense signifier in Nagwa, suggestive among many other things of the humiliating and painful position the local thana policemen may have one assume as a milder weapon from their armamentarium of torture. In the end, the skit insists, it all comes down to chicken. The weakness of the aged is a double sign in Nagwa ideology, both part of the overall weakness of Adi Dharm people generated by an exploitative society (the overdetermination of suffering in Narayan's lament, the allusions to the police in Ramji's potted panegyrics) and proof of the equality of all beings (the decline of generational power in Ramji's portrayal). In the poetry of Ravi Das, both figures (the old person as tragic victim and as humbled victor) are brought together:

> As high as you can build, as low as you can dig,
>> your size will never swell the dimensions of a grave;
> Those lovely curls, that turban tied so rakishly—
>> they'll soon be turned to ash.
> If you've counted on the beauty of your wife and home
>> without the name of Ram, you've already lost the game.
> And me: even though my birth is mean,
>> my ancestry by everyone despised,
> I have always trusted in you, King Ram,
>> says Ravidas, a tanner of hides.
> The house is large, its kitchen vast,
>> but only after a moment's passed, it's vacant.
> This body is like a scaffold made of grass:
>> the flames will consume it and render it dust.
> Even your family—your brothers and friends—
>> clamor to have you removed at dawn.
> The lady of the house, who once clung to your chest,
>> shouts "Ghost! Ghost!" now and runs away,
> The world, says Ravidas, loots and plunders all—
>> except me, for I have slipped away
>> by saying the name of God.[6]

Old age and death, framed as a unity, give the lie to the pretense of social difference claimed by the powerful, the signs of an ephemeral world that "loots and plunders all." The old body is presented simultaneously as sign of exploiter and exploited, of the strong and the weak.

Weakness, *kamzorī*, was as central to descriptions of aging and of particular old persons in Nagwa as it was in the Bengali quarter and the residential colonies. However, weakness attributions in Nagwa conveyed something additional and quite different, for statements like "Look, he's old, so he's weak; his hands and feet (i.e., his ability to work) are weak, his mind, too, so what?" were enclosed within family weakness narratives: "We are poor folks, not rich; we are weak; we cannot give (our children, our parents) decent food." Transactional deficits central to narratives of the family and the familial body elsewhere in the city were here linked more forcefully to *kamzorī* and quantified. The quantification was usually in terms of pieces of bread, roti or chapati: we can only give him so many chapatis. Bodies were approached through chapati counts. A never-adequate rhetoric of self-justification soaked up all other difference. The experience of old age, the narratives of family members implied, is encompassed by the experience of being poor and Chamar.[7] She is weak because we are weak. Far less often families looked to failed processes of adjustment, adaptation, or balance to explain bad voices. And to explain them away: weakness, like balance, worked as much against meaning as for it, against the moral threat of certain kinds of old voices. Weakness encompassed difference and diverted the need for intrafamilial accountability.

Old age weakness was linked to caste weakness both causally and essentially. Causally, old people were understood to be weak because they had not eaten enough good food in life, because they did not have access to real medication as opposed to tonics, and because they had to work until they dropped, like Dulari's cousin the rickshaw-puller. Essentially, old people were said to be weak because of their inherent social weakness as Chamar. Again and again in my interviews and discussions in Nagwa basti, mention of hot *dimāg* and other voices would glide into old age weakness, which in turn would glide into social weakness. Lost in this seamless glide was the familial body and the role of intergenerational politics in the emergence of the aberrant voices of weak old people.

Before we can turn to individual families, to examine the relationships between generations and individuals and the negotiation of the weakened body and its meanings for different actors, we might explore further the ideology of weakness in Nagwa, to see what is at stake in this glide. I suggest that "weakness" is the structural principle that both generates the order of castes for the residents of Nagwa and provides the structural basis for its critique. In so doing I respond to a central debate in the sociology of India since the 1960s regarding the relationship of individuals to the social order, and respond in particular to a more specific debate about the relationship of "untouchables" to this order. These debates have a routinized and somewhat cathartic form: the ongoing and perhaps compulsive need to undo the work on India of the French sociologist Louis Dumont, principally his *Homo Hierarchicus*.[8] Thus the myriad critiques of his position that continue to emerge long after the beast was thought dead. My brief comments here are no exception.

The Dumontian analysis placed the pure/impure opposition at the center of the analysis of society in India and considered the discursive practices of Brahmans as the sole authoritative source for a reflexive Indian sociology. Earlier critical responses to Dumont emerged on at least two levels, either as criticisms of his privileging of the "ideological" against the material basis of caste ideology, or, for those accepting the role of cultural structures as determinants of history, as criticisms of the limits Dumont placed on what constituted the ideological. Discussions centering on low-caste groups often have tended to ignore or dismiss Dumont, the assumption being that his domain of Indian society is a crude reframing of the dominant ideology.[9] Discussions of middle and higher castes and particularly of dominant and baronial castes have argued that the "political" domain of the state is as central to the underlying ideological structure of Indian society as is the "religious" domain of purity and pollution, and that this structure has a history.[10] These post-Dumontian structuralist accounts of caste concern themselves with the relationship between elites, their competing ideologies, rationalities, and transactional styles, and their underlying epistemes. The central problèmatique is the relation between king and Brahman and between princely and priestly authority, with attention to the colonial delegitimation of non-Brahmanic ideologies.

Both sets of critiques are of limited appeal in approaching the body and society in Nagwa. Materialist objections to Dumont are powerful but frame the poor and marginal as speaking truth to power with little effort to grasp the texture of necessity by which dominant and dominated ideologies and practices are reproduced. Language and practice in Nagwa slum were layered and complex; their structural contours pointed to more than infrastructures all the way down. Here I focus on two opposed but ubiquitous themes explicit in local discourse and implicit in practice: *identity*, the frequent assertion that "all persons are the same," and *weakness*, the tendency for people in Nagwa to rank others in terms of their ability to weaken or be weakened by them.

In so doing, I attempt a strategy in some ways parallel to the alternative critical position on Dumont, focusing on the normalization of social difference through a set of competing or, to paraphrase Charles Malamoud,[11] "revolving" hierarchies rooted in complementary figures of totality and gift. This alternative critique has had widely differing formulations,[12] but few of them have been of particular use in exploring the possibilities of this expanded and post-Dumontian play of structure for the religion, politics, and embodied life of the socially marginal and outcaste. Following R. S. Khare,[13] I want to look at the Nagwa Chamar language of strength and weakness in structural terms, as an ideological generation of a hierarchical world from a moral opposition rooted in a particular class of transactions.

In noting the centrality of *kamzorī* in the perception and negotiation of social difference and political relations in Nagwa, I want to suggest how hegemonic constructions such as the naturalization of hierarchy as organic difference—pollution—simultaneously determine the position and experience of bodies and are fundamentally reworked by them. Weakness takes shape, like pollution, as organic and embodied difference, but as difference that preserves the moral integrity of the weakened against the weakener. Residents are weak, *kamzor*, in opposition not to the wealthy or powerful as individuals but as the triad of Brahman, Thakur, and Bania, who as corporate groups challenge the individual moral relationship of the gift between patron and poor. The Maharaja's sense of feudal obligation and the Bengali Babu's gift of his own home to his gardener narratively evoke an ideal transactional frame in which class and weakness are not synonymous. This frame is disrupted by Thakurs, by Brahmans, by petty bureaucrats and by the police in the stories residents tell of where they live and who they are. These disruptive actors reverse the moral order of society: they take rather than give, and they weaken the poor.

Through the imposition of new transactional orders creating weakness within a local version of the Fall, Chamar narratively come to have bodies different from others. To speak of weakness constituted the recognition by basti residents that their *bodies* were different from those of Brahmans, Thakurs, and Banias, more than their identities *tout court. Kamzorī* was not only weakness but thinness; all states of weakness were embodied as lack. *Kamzorī* is a depletion of bodily substance—semen and menstrual blood, but more particularly the coarser primary tissues: food juices, blood, flesh, and flesh. Weak bodies were thin, dry, and cold, in contrast to the *motevāle*, the Fat Ones, who came and made pronouncements on Nagwa and who stole its land and its water and offered in their place toilets. Weakening challenged the moral order of caste by substituting for it a different moral order, one equally rooted in the inevitability of organic difference. Difference was embodied as weakness, not pollution: caste was a medical condition.

Upper-caste differences were reconfigured within a field generated by the differential strategies of each caste group as weakeners, drawing on stereotyped local transactional strategies of Brahmans, Thakurs, and Banias. Banias demanded high interest and siphoned all one's earnings. Thakurs appropriated land and intimidated residents through thugs or the police, particularly the infamous Lanka thana. Brahmans controlled academic and service positions, maintained the image of Harijans as *gandā* (dirty, polluted), cloaked all action as moral imperative, and were more effective claimants of Thakur, Bania, and state patronage.

The ideology of weakness disguised as well as disclosed relationships. First, the language of *kamzorī* reflected the performative dynamics of fieldwork. Like the police, I came to take something: I was, and remain, another *motevāla*. "The old woman is weak because we are weak" was dialogic, referring not only to the old woman and the "we" of the formulation but to myself: "She is weak because we are weak—are you a weakener or a patron?" The language of weakness forced me to remain aware of what was differentially at stake in an interview, and pushed me to define myself transactionally. "We are weak—what do you intend to do about it?"

Thus I initially came, in the course of fieldwork, to discount the significance of *kamzorī*, reading it as a rhetorical strategy on the part of those I interviewed, an expression of need, dependency, anger, and at times suffering, but not as central to experience as its frequent mention seemed to suggest. But rhetorical strategies draw upon a limited universe of discourse. The more time I spent with families and the more exposure to both daily life and social dramas that I gained, the more I came to accept the language of weakness as indicative of the structure of lived experience in Nagwa and to recontextualize my initial interpretive anxieties within an unfolding social world.

Second, beyond these issues, the ideology of weakness blurs distinctions of class and gender within Nagwa basti. The experience of rural migrants who pedaled rickshaws versus established petty functionaries who worked for the municipal administration or the Banaras Hindu University differed vastly but drew upon the same language of weakness in framing the body in time. Ram Nath and his brother and cousin had each recently rebuilt their houses; the houses were larger and more frequently whitewashed than others in the area. Ram Nath addressed the question of *dimāg kī kamzorī*—brain weakness—through continual reference to "them," the illiterate others of Nagwa: "They cannot read or write—they are all *bevakuf* [stupid]—so their minds go quickly. I am older. I have survived severe injury [he detailed getting an electric shock and falling off a roof, and surviving], but my mind and my health are still correct." In speaking of the worries of old age, Ram Nath and others like him were more likely than others in the slum to frame a discussion of weakness in the supplementary moral terms of tension and balance. Literally, in Ram Nath's case: he lost his balance, falling off a roof and injuring his head, and yet through tenacity has survived both weakness and imbalance.

Third, *kamzorī* was differentially constituted as a threat to men and women, a distinction men tended to discuss in terms of the paired losses of semen and menstrual blood. This androcentric discourse in Nagwa took male fluid loss as a threat to oneself and female fluid loss as the necessary control of women's heat. The elaboration by men of these losses—in personal narratives, in restrictions against menstruating women, and in the experience of semen loss anxiety—was more muted than in middle-class and higher-caste neighborhoods.[14] Like the weakening of old age, the weakening of sexual fluid loss was framed within a broader context of diminished substance. For men, *kamzorī* as impotence was overshadowed by *kamzorī* as thinness. Both men and women downplayed gender differences in discussions of old age weakness, framing it primarily in terms of limited roti and bad families.

However, even in Nagwa differences between men's and women's care of their bodies bespoke a differential concern with the maintenance of the bounded male body—but not the female—from threats of diminution and weakness. As in the

Bengali quarter and more often than in the colonies, men bound themselves, and gurus and women bound men, with varieties of protective amulets, strings, vows, spells, and rings.[15] *Aslī Baṛā Indrajal* ("True Great Magic")—the primary text of Chaman Lal the *ojhā*, the charismatic exorcist who was the guru of several men in Nagwa—contained numerous spells to protect men from the diminution caused by their enemies and by women, but few protective charms for women.[16]

Menstruation, some men in Nagwa argued, was necessary to let out a woman's heat. Secchan, who played Shiva on Ravi Das' birthday, noted that the process was necessary for women's daily health and that amenorrhea, the absence of menses, led to an accumulation of heat and thus fever, jaundice, tuberculosis, or eye diseases. Other men at his tea stall disagreed, stressing that menstruation weakened women incrementally and that they aged more quickly as a conse-quence: "They are old by fifty. Have you noticed?" Women in Nagwa reversed the male gloss, from a loss of heat or strength to a process of removing fatigue. Sev-eral women in Narayan's family contrasted the *tākat* (strength) of women and men. His daughter-in-law told me, "Women get more tired. They give birth, raise chil-dren, and worry about them." I responded, "But men work . . . ?" to which she said, "But they eat more; they fill their stomachs. . . . Men are built stronger. Women thus have their monthly [period], when their fatigue comes out. With the blood. So they won't become too weak." Weakness does not come to women as some "natural" consequence of menstruation, these women suggest, but rather is a constituent feature of their social situation and its physical ramifications— chronic undernutrition and constant labor. And weakness for women unlike men is not just a lack, a diminution of substance, it is rather a quantity that can be ex-creted. Both the nature of a woman's life and the prerogatives of men maintain her as weak, but the body and its fluids are claimed as a (quite literally) empower-ing response.[17]

What of the cessation of menstruation in the slum? The menopause as either a pathologized or simply a marked category of experience did not seem to exist in Nagwa in 1988 and 1989, in dramatic contrast to Sharma and Saxena's data for the colonies. Despite the elaboration of menstruation as the excretion of weak-ness, the end of menstrual bleeding was described jokingly by most women as a time of relief. Men sometimes had a different perspective. Secchan, in suggesting that amenorrhea led to illness, was concerned with the premature cessation of bleeding and the buildup of heat. Old women, he noted, were inherently colder; they did not need periods. The men who felt that strength was lost during the menses viewed old age and the mental weakness of old women as a cumulative effect of earlier menstruation and not due to a climacteric period such as the menopause.

In my earliest discussions with men and women in Nagwa, including those about menstruation and weakness, I worked with a BHU student, Rajesh Pathak, who would come with me to Nagwa from time to time and would afterward edi-torialize. Rajesh felt that more was at stake for the women discussing the cessation of menses than they were letting on. "This is a difficult time," he said, "when a woman thinks, 'I am no longer a woman' and gets upset." Like Sharma and Saxena, Rajesh expected a gendered embodiment of the imbalance of old age. In Nagwa, however, older women were amused when I tried to press the question of a menopause against their assertion that if anything they experienced a relief at the cessation of much fuss and bother. If these women's experience as women changes, as Rajesh insisted, the change was not keyed to a bodily event like the menopause. For women and men in Nagwa, my discussions of gender difference obscured the centrality in old age weakness of being Chamar. *Būṛhe hain, kamzor hain, garīb hain*, they are old, thin/weak, poor. Flesh and fat, more than blood and semen, were at stake in *kamzorī* and in old age.

MUSLIMS AND OTHER SAINTS

"What things characterize old age?" I would ask during interviews in Nagwa as elsewhere. Sitting with Bageshera, Narayan the poet's elder sister, and her family, a volley of responses came from both the old woman and the younger people. Bageshera began by listing problems:

their eyes
their teeth
they can't work well
their minds don't sit quite right.

Her grandchildren joined in, their responses less embodied:

they get agitated
they are weak
their minds rot
they just babble, *paṭ paṭ paṭ paṭ.*

Bageshera looked vexed: "He writes all this down. Say some good things about old people!"

Like Bageshera's family, in focusing on imbalance, anger, and weak mind, I offer a skewed portraiture of old age in India. The problem is heightened in Nagwa, where old age is almost inevitably called *buṛhāpā* (the embodied and rather decrepit state connoting weakness) and seldom *vṛddhāvasthā* (experienced and more disembodied old age) and where weakness is the dominant metanarrative of social relations.[18] Yet *buṛhāpā*, in its privileging the hearing of old voices as *bakbak* or *paṭ paṭ*, does not exhaust the experience of being old or knowing or loving an older person. "Use *buzurg*," Masterji the tailor suggested when I called someone *vṛddh*, offering me the Urdu for the Sanskritized word, as "people will understand." I seldom heard *buzurg* used in informal conversation, but in my more abstract discussions with Masterji, Ram Lakhan, and other ideologues of the neighborhood, *buzurg* like *vṛddh* suggested an ideal and *sahī*, correct, old age.

A *sahī* old age was often linked to Islam, through the turn to a more Urduized or Persianized construction of utterance as well as in narrative. "You should talk to Muslims," I was repeatedly told in the poorer Hindu neighborhoods of the city, as during that boat ride early on. "Their *dimāg* remains *sahī*." Muslim friends, I should note, were either amused by or suspicious of this generalization but they rarely concurred with it, seeing in it the potential deployment of a Hindu strategy of the differentiation and ultimately dehumanization of the Muslim body. But the women and men in poorer neighborhoods who offered the Muslim *dimāg* as a gold standard in old age were not being disparaging. They did not know why the difference occurred ("You're the doctor, you tell us!") but it was somehow obvious. When I asked people to speculate, their answers varied. In Nagwa, a man named Lakhan had this to say: "Hindu minds tend to deteriorate in old age but Muslim minds tend to expand. Muslims are richer, more successful. They have less worries, thus less mental problems. They are more hard-working, and single-mindedly devote themselves to the task at hand. We are too gregarious, too outward-oriented." Another response to why Muslim old people don't get weak minds was that their family relations were better. Always implied was that Muslims did *sevā* to their elders, that they preserved their *izzat*, their honor. The Muslim self was more directed and less selfish, and the Muslim family tighter.

T. N. Madan has argued that Indian male householders position themselves dialectically between the poles of the renunciate yogi and the libertine *bhogī*. To the extent that his argument is relevant for poor men in Varanasi, the Muslim occupies the discursive position of the yogi. He is a paradigm of the "worldly ascetic" that Khare suggests is the exemplary actor in the ideology of Lucknow Chamar. To be ascetic in domestic relations, the invocation of the Muslim suggests, is to preserve oneself and one's parents from mental weakness. The Muslim as sign of the exemplary elder and family again suggests the anxiety surrounding the impossibility of true *sevā*. As other, the Muslim can occupy a position against the construction of the self. Why Muslims? In the question, I sensed an unspoken narrative of *sevā* anxiety: "I am a creature of desire and selfishness; I am the imperfect family. In perfect families, composed of ascetics, there is perfect *sevā*, there is no weakness in old age. Look at the other, look at the Muslim." The Muslim can be placed outside the opposition of weakening and weakened; his Otherness is in theory exchangeable with one's imperfect selfhood. Unlike Brahmans, Thakurs, and Banias, who achieve a reprieve from weakened mind through their weakening practice, which guarantees them access to good food and medical care and the absence of worries, Muslims escape the economy of weakness (and become rich) through a process of renunciation, not of taking but of not taking.

Muslims are ambiguous signifiers in Nagwa. Some persons would speak of the *sahī* mind of the Muslim, most had no opinion, and some, like Muslims, felt the whole question was ridiculous. Sannyasis, ubiquitous in Varanasi, are viewed less ambivalently. True renunciation in old age in Nagwa is seldom identified with the Brahmanic ideals of *vānaprastha* and *sannyāsa*. The classic renunciate is rejected as the idealized self for four reasons: (1) *sannyāsa* is an option by and large open only to upper-caste Hindus; (2) *sannyāsa* is morally ambiguous for all householders, of high and low caste, in its challenge of household morality;[19] (3) in Nagwa, upper-caste renunciates are held to be false claimants to local patronage who appropriate the gift from the deserving weak; and (4) all Banarsis have the jaded locals' experience of numerous "false sadhus," faux holy men seeking easy money or on the run from a criminal past. Against *sannyāsa*—neither available to nor desired by Chamar—the ideal self is described as a person of restraint and self-sufficiency. This worldly renunciate does not abandon—literally or symbolically—the household. Renunciation is not in opposition to householdership, but rather is the ethos characterizing the ideal householder.[20] The life stage model of *āśramadharma* folds into the constant asceticism of the weakened. Old age, as *buzurg*, is not a break with material pleasure but a distillation of a lifetime of restraint into a powerful voice. This voice is seldom heard—the silent voice of the ascetic—and when it is heard it is as the legitimate anger of the rishi. Angry rishis, along with the Maharaja and Baru Baba, populate the history of Nagwa and of other slums and villages around Varanasi. A rishi's curse, after all, had dried up the once mighty Assi separating Nagwa from Varanasi, turning the river into a small stream.

In examining the ideology of worldly asceticism of Lucknow Chamar, Khare helps us to place the transformations of age in political and ideological contexts. Appadurai has summarized Khare's argument:

> Instead of playing the impure foil to the Brahman, the Untouchable becomes his civilizational critic and his moral conscience. No longer a product of some sort of "karmic" Fall, the Untouchable becomes a brutalized representative of the ascetic ideal in ordinary life. His degradation and oppression are no more regarded as a just working out of the joint scheme of dharma (social law) and karma (cosmic causal law) but of the blindness of the Brahmanic social order to the axioms underlying its own existence. . . . In Dumont's own evocative usage, here is an Indic conception of equality and individuality that "encompasses" Brahmanic notions of hierarchy and social categories.[21]

Through the directed learning or hearing of the message of a guru, many men and some women in Nagwa spoke of themselves as this-worldly ascetics, both framing their lives and struggles within a meaningful and spiritually directed discourse while embodying a direct critique of "Hindu" ideology and practice similar to that which Khare outlines.

The position of ascetic engagement glided into the dying space. Vipat, the father of the two slightly higher-caste Dhobi men who lived in adjoining households on the edge of the slum facing wealthier homes, was said by many to be the oldest person in Nagwa. He was very weak, lying most of the day on his charpoy outside the house of his younger son, and he was seen to be so. But he was not *heard* to be so—that is, his mind was *sahī*. Vipat seldom spoke, and when he did, in measured and quiet tones, he rarely complained or asked for much from his family. He lay out on the bed all day and all night, his time punctuated only by meals and long, slow walks the half a kilometer or so to the banks of the Ganga to relieve himself.

Vipat's charpoy was an unambiguous dying space. He was a *marnevālā*, a "dying one." Neighbors and family said he was very old. "Over one hundred," claimed an adult grandson. Using the age he remembered himself to be during famous floods and Partition, my usual method, I had figured him to be in his late seventies or early eighties.

Vipat's two remaining sons were from his two sequential marriages, and he was again a widower. His sons had split, according to Vipat, some ten or twelve years ago. The elder, Hiralal, had had his own job at the time while the younger Lallu had none, and economic "tension" between the brothers had mounted. Hiralal had wanted Lallu and his other half-brother Motilal (now deceased) to obey him. They refused; and when Motilal got married he and his wife began eating separately. After Motilal's death, Hiralal separated completely from his brother. A wall was built dividing the house and the few square meters of land in front of it roughly into halves. Vipat remained with Lallu, as his youngest son had no work at the time; Vipat supported him and his family. Six years ago, Vipat gave over ownership of the house to his sons.

Vipat cried when he recalled to me the split between his sons. Their feuding and public split provided the context for the Bad Family that explains the weak mind and angry voice of other old people. But Vipat did not have a weak mind, and neighbors and relatives pointed to his sons' *sevā*—he was receiving food and drink, he was not wanting. Bodily weakness and the Bad Family were central to the construction of weak and hot mind, but they were not sufficient.

Vipat had achieved a state of shanti, of repose. He did not allow himself—nor was he impelled to by existential or neurophysiological crises—to be interpreted as empty heat or *bakbak*. He was weak, but he interpreted his weakness as consonant with his great age and the pain of his sons splitting—facts of life that must be accepted. He would sit on his charpoy, talk to the handful of other Nagwa residents who had reached their seventies and eighties, eat, and walk to the Ganga. He embodied, in his shanti, his household as a still-unified entity; he was an emblem—in front of the two halves of the split house, linking them on his charpoy—of the rightness of his family. Through Vipat, they were, against the inevitability of their history, also *sahī*.

Though family fission did not generate weak mind, weak mind pointed to family fission. In Nagwa, challenges to shanti were rooted in the economics of limited family resources and the often bitter family splits and debilitative and untreated chronic illnesses that emerged in the context of these economics. Out of the seventy-five households in Nagwa in which I did interviews, there were at most a dozen "old old" persons, those whom I then estimated were about or over seventy-five years of age. Assuming an age-related peaking of clinical dementia in the ninth decade of life, similar to that of Europe and the United States, there were fewer old people in Nagwa who were likely to become demented, unlike in the residential colonies. But the voices of old people whose minds were not *sahī*—the hearing of anger and *bakbak* and even outright madness—were integral to the phenomenology of old age in the slum. There were many threats to shanti.

Earlier I offered Harinath Prasad's besting of the tea shop owner Secchan as an example of the explicitly *sahī* anger of the experienced elder. Harinath was Narayan and Bageshera's younger brother. He was sixty-two when I first met him, a fact that he stated emphatically, daring me to challenge him. My age-estimation questions about marriages and floods had become well-known. Mr. Prasad had been a "Masterji," a school teacher. He continued to "give tuitions" full-time after retirement, to offer Memory Bank–style supplementary tutoring to petty bourgeois families somewhat wealthier than most of those in Nagwa. These were students trained in "Hindi-medium" institutions, not those schooled to remember in the more bankable English. Like Vipat, his mind was *sahī*, though he seemed the antithesis of the other man in terms of personal style. Forceful, direct, and proud, he did not back away from argument. He was an angry old man, but his hot voice was taken at its worth, as the mildly funny but deserved chastisement of one of the most educated older men in Nagwa. His mind was not weak.

Harinath controlled this resource, staging infrequent and impromptu displays of his mastery over time and space. Secchan, who when he got married told his own father that he could not afford to contribute his income to that of his parents—effectively denying them any significant support in their old age—heard the anger of Harinath Prasad as undemanding and useful. He could call himself Harinath's son; his own father's angry voice, however, structured as the demand and the lament, was too demanding and could only be heard as *jhandū*, all used up.

Harinath's wife died, and one of his two sons found a good job in a different part of the state. His other son, Chandan, was unmarried and an intercollege (preuniversity) student. Chandan had worked as a dancer in a troupe like Ranji's; he may have been a male prostitute as well, and sometimes dressed like a woman.[22] Chandan was devoted to his father. Harinath long ago had had a fight with Narayan, and the two brothers were not on speaking terms. With a distant son and daughter-in-law, with the need to work because Chandan brought in no income yet, with his anticipated difficulty in ever getting Chandan married, and with an alienated brother and his family, Harinath was not seen to have a peaceful old age. He was denied the repose of a charpoy.

But Harinath's learning, his having amassed some measure of symbolic capital and his effective management of it, was not suggestive of repose denied. For neighbors who did not know him so intimately, Harinath's continual activity demonstrated his continued mastery over his world. He illustrated the proverb *satthā ta patthā*, sixty therefore mighty, and not the sixtyish mind. He gave neighbors no cause to invoke the Bad Family.

Mangri, a widow in her sixties, lived with her daughter, who was separated from her husband, and grandson in a small, one-room house. Her daughter worked to support the family and her grandson was in school. Mangri managed the household, as well as much of the communal affairs of her part of the slum. Her voice, criticizing municipal workers who didn't do their job, neighbors who stole from other neighbors, or anthropologists who wasted people's time, was well-known. But she leavened her scolding with humor and self-deprecation. Her requests, the substance of her angry voice, were rarely phrased as threatening complaints or outright demands. She interrupted me one day as I was talking to someone else, about old age: "*This* old woman walks naked. You should give me some clothes." Young teenagers in the lane would joke with her, calling her *jhaṇḍū*. But her angry voice was often listened to; it meant something. Mangri lacked Harinath Prasad's learning and was poorer and less powerful than he. She had bouts of weakness, and her neighbor Father Paul brought her five "bottles of strength," vitamin tonics, which she said helped a bit. Though an old widow, like Harinath she was able to maintain a powerful and *sahī* persona through the manipulation of an angry voice. She was somewhat less successful than him in being heard as a useful and therefore meaningful voice; Harinath was never called *jhaṇḍū*. As in the colonies, the voice of the marginal widow was at greater risk for being heard as not *sahī*.

Most old people in Nagwa who could no longer work as laborers or who feared being considered *jhaṇḍū* in the household attempted to develop new sources of income. One of the more common routes, for those who could advance the necessary capital, was to open up a small shop, often in a doorway or window of the family house facing out onto the lane. There were several such shops in Nagwa Basti, stocking biscuits, matches, cheap bidi leaf-wrapped cigarettes, paper kites, and so forth. Raghu Ram ran one of them. He was, according to one of his sons, ninety-five years old; he himself was unsure, and extrapolating from the ages of his children I estimated that he was in his seventies. Like Vipat, he was a widower whose sons had split. Of Raghu Ram's nine surviving children, five daughters married and moved to their husbands' homes, and the families of the four sons lived separately in adjoining compounds. Raghu ate with his second-youngest son, Lallan. Like Vipat, Raghu Ram was represented as a superannuated icon of auspicious old age by his family. Still, Raghu felt compelled to work to avoid being a potential burden to Lallu's family. Vatuk has noted in her discussion of dependency anxiety that the elderly feared the consequences for themselves of their physical incapacity and resulting burdensomeness to their children. In Nagwa, old people with some savings forestalled the possibility of becoming a burden as long as possible through small enterprises or outside labor.

Shanti, here as for Mr. Agrawal in Ravindrapuri, was continually deferred. Raghu Ram's son Ram Lakhan, in speaking of his father and old people in general, located their *dimāg*, or brain, between cool shanti and hot anger: "There is neither a lot of peace, nor a lot of heat. It is like India. Sometimes the weather is hot, sometimes cold, and there are the monsoons." Raghu Ram avoided being considered *jhaṇḍū*, but at the same time he relinquished his claims to a charpoy to a position of repose. But his tiny shop, where he eked out a token income, was in a sense a dying space. He was identified with the shop, could always be found there, and was in a way restricted to it much as Vipat was restricted to life lived from the charpoy. His position, for his son, the elegantly philosophical Ram Lakhan, was one of ambiguity, neither the voice in repose nor that of anger. Still, as long as he could maintain his shop, Raghu Ram remained *sahī*.

GENERATION AND WEAKNESS REVISITED

When were old voices heard as mentally weak in Nagwa? When did angry voices become willful and selfish, and silences become lonely and pathetic? In the histories of the families with whom I spoke, two transitions marked shifts in the perception of the old person's voice and weakness: *the loss of authority* and *the loss of usefulness*. Both were gradual and contested processes, but each marked, fitfully, a shift in how an old parent was heard. The first, the loss of authority over household decisions and resources, was associated with the emergence of anger and a hot *dimāg*. The second, the loss of usefulness, that is, of any significant interpersonal role within the household, was associated with emerging criticisms of the old person babbling meaninglessly—*bakbak, paṭ paṭ, baṛbaṛ*.

"If you have property," many across the four neighborhoods informed me, "or if you have money, your children will do your *sevā*." Few in Nagwa had significant property or savings to guarantee filial obedience. As in the colonies but more quickly and not necessarily for the same incentives, brothers tended to fission off one by one starting with the eldest, ultimately leaving parents with the youngest son. Thus Ganga Jali lived in a single room, literally a hole in the wall, with her youngest, a repairer of bicycles and tires who some said was himself weak-brained and who could barely earn enough to feed himself. Across the lane lived Ganga Jali's two married sons and their wives and children. Their households would occasionally feed Ganga Jali but were not responsible for her daily support.

Residents in Nagwa, unlike those in the colonies, did not seem to think that such families were recent or unusual phenomena. Nor did they look to the modern or to the West to ground a rhetoric of why families collapse. The rural villages in neighboring districts to the south of the city from which many families had migrated were not remembered as places where the politics of intergenerational support were that different, and these memories are consistent with Bernard Cohn's data for Chamar family size thirty to forty years earlier in a village similar to those that Nagwa residents or their recent ancestors had left, where the majority of households were nuclear and several composed of a single aged individual.[23]

Vishwanath lived with his wife Juguli and three sons and their families in one of the larger houses on the main road. He told me he was about seventy. As usual I asked my series of questions about floods, marriage, kids, and Partition, and estimated he was in his mid-sixties. He no longer worked, but owned the family house and had some savings. His sons drove or pedaled rickshaws or worked as day laborers: none were financially secure, and all remained dependent upon their parents' property and savings. They had not separated into separate *ghars*; Vishwanath was proud of this fact. "I am the head of the household. They give me their earnings." His pride, unlike that of families in the colonies, did not rest on being a "joint family"; the concept, as such, was rarely articulated in Nagwa. Rather, the unified house was testimony to Vishwanath's strength, to his ability to fend off weakness.

Yet his sons fought among themselves. Why? "Because sons want to take over." Intergenerational stress, among the majority of families in Nagwa, was usually manifest as horizontal stress, particularly between brothers. The narrative of the consequent theodicy—of the effort by parents to comprehend the bitter fighting of their children—ran as follows: "If I had property, I could keep my sons together." Without such imagined property, fathers could not become the powerful bodies of the Kesari Jivan ad, sixty therefore strong. The ubiquity of the Carstairs-Kakar construction of oedipal deferral, generated within their theoretical formulations from a figure of the powerful Father, is delimited by class and inheritance. Vipat experienced his family's torment through the fighting between his sons, not in their construction of his marginalized dying space. Vishwanath repeatedly articulated the fact that if he did not have sufficient property, his sons would break apart, making him politically marginal. "They would take power forcefully. If one has property, he is obeyed out of fear; if not, he is not." Would he, like Vipat, have transferred his property to his sons? "No. If I had no more money, my sons might no longer take care of me."

In reality, Vishwanath was not as autonomous as he claimed. His sons were not giving him most of their wages, and they were making separate purchases for their families. "But they tell me whatever they buy." His authority had already shifted, from active control to performative validation. Vishwanath could still maintain himself as *ghar kā mālik*, as the boss of the household, but the meaning of boss had changed, giving his sons greater autonomy—from him and from each other—while preserving a sense of common purpose and coherence by maintaining the father's centrality through performative *sevā*. Given the limited resources of Vishwanath's sons, the lack of a significant differential between their incomes, their father's property, and the old man's unreadiness—unlike his neighbor Vipat—to lie down on his charpoy, there was more to be gained by staying together.

Juguli, his wife, was about a decade younger than Vishwanath. She had two daughters-in-law at home; her middle son's wife had died. Juguli no longer had control over all domestic purchases, but she still organized the labor of her *bahūs*, her daughters-in-law. Vishwanath said: "When she is too weak to work, the daughter-in-law will take over. When, for example, if she were to make roti and to do so would kill her." There was no single contender for Juguli's authority: she had two daughters-in-law, not one, and as long as the households remained together Juguli was not the primary rival to her daughter-in-laws' control. She and Vishwanath were both concerned about quarrels between the *bahūs*, for they felt that family fission was rooted in daughters-in-law fighting. Juguli's role as a grandmother was heightened by her two motherless grandchildren. Given her ability to work, but more important her central role in running the household and in acting as a surrogate mother, Juguli's voice, angry at times, was not heard as useless, hot, and weak.[24]

Next door, Tapeshwara's four sons had already split: each along with his family occupied a small room in the house. A widow, probably in her late sixties, Tapeshwara ate with her youngest son, Gulam, and his wife. There was little room in the small house, and Tapeshwara would say that she wished her sons would move away. But more, she wished they would stop fighting with one another. "We don't think she is a burden," her youngest daughter-in-law, with whom she eats, said to me. Tapeshwara looked upset, and remained silent, I thought a bit sullen. Her *bahū* looked at her, and then said: "Her sons have grown up and left their mother." Tapeshwara sighed, and spoke after some time. "In the old times, old people were respected. Not now. If you have money, they pay attention. If not, they don't." Tapeshwara was lamenting a decline not so much in an institution (the family) as in a more generalized set of relations. The reciprocity of the gift relationship had been replaced by self-interest. Tapeshwara's lament is the history of Nagwa, in which relations of weakening replace those of true *sevā*.

Tapeshwara experienced her sons' fighting with one another, their denial of her pleas for unity, as feelings of weakness and worry. Her *dimāg* "runs from here to there." She, and the daughter-in-law who had invested the most in feeding her, said that these feelings were directly attributable to the behavior of the other sons. Tapeshwara, more than her daughter-in-law, blamed the local version of a declining cosmos in which people came to act for their individual interest and others get weak, and not just her own sons per se. Her relatives deny bad-family explanations: She feels weak because she is old. She is weak because we are weak. Look at how many rooms we live in, look at how many chapatis we can give our children.

In Chittupur, another Harijan settlement not far from Nagwa but slightly wealthier, the old patriarch Mausaji lived on a charpoy in a little wooden shelter constructed in the middle of the family courtyard. His sons had long ago separated, and his wife was still receiving a steady income as a housekeeper. I learned of Mausaji through his wife's niece, Tara Devi, who sometimes cooked for me.[25] "What do you ask old people?" Tara once asked me. I told her. "Well," she said after a pause, "my uncle is like that."

> *TD:* Durga [his daughter-in-law] used to give him food. When she gave him a roti, he would always ask for more: *Aur do!* and at first she used to give it to him. But he would keep asking, and she saw that he was hiding them under his bed.
>
> *LC:* What does she do?
>
> *TD:* They don't want to give him food. It is expensive! The other sons don't give him any, it is only Durga who gives him. She says, he is my father. . . .
>
> *LC:* What about Mausiji [his wife]?

TD: She says, "I do not know this one."

LC: And if they don't give him [food], that is, anything more than is necessary?

TD: Then he will keep asking for more. And he will get angry. . . . And he swears a lot.

Tara began with food and its transaction. Food was given by some but not others, food was demanded when there was not enough, food was hidden under a mattress. The currency of measuring food transactions—for what she was addressing were moral challenges to a domestic economy—was the chapati. Hiding food was here less importantly a sign of cognitive loss or of maladjustment and imbalance, and more obviously a challenge to who wields authority over basic resources. On the one hand, Mausaji unfairly demanded more chapatis when others should have had them. He was the old fool of the Ravi Das poems who has not gotten beyond ego; he was weakening his family by demanding more than his share. Yet his sons had split and had in consequence forsaken Mausaji. His demands for roti could alternatively be read as the hot *dimāg* of the abandoned elder, weakened by the Bad Family, the poor old man of the Ravi Das poems whose wife screams "Ghost!"— or in this case, "I do not know this one."

Tara was enough of an insider in Mausaji's family to know what Durga and Mausiji might have said, but distant enough to broach the subject with me. What she had at stake was different from what was at stake for the other women, who heard Mausaji's demands as the weak mind of the Bad Family. "He is treated," she said at one point, "like a dog." Mausiji, however, put things differently: "This happens with age. Yes, I'm fine now, but in time . . . "—she bent over like a hunchback and felt her way along as one who could no longer walk or see. Invoking the general weakness of old age, Mausiji shifted the terms of the question I had put to her, which had been about *matha* (brain, mind), turning it through the figure of the blind and crippled hunchback to one on the nature of *kamzorī*. When I first visited Chittupur, after I had met Mausaji, Mausaji, his wife, was eager for me to meet another old woman, their neighbor Shanti. Despite her name, she was presented to me as a *bakbakvālī*. "She has no one," Mausiji said. Shanti was offered for the anthropologist's gaze as an example of true degradation and as a matter of voice and of *dimāg*, versus the understandable eccentricities of the frail old age of Mausaji.

Mausaji told me he was born in 1906; but given his children's ages and their recollections, I felt that he was probably born some ten to fifteen years later. Over a decade ago he could no longer work as a laborer and he opened up a small shop selling pan, or betel leaf. Six years ago he had to stop selling; he "got a wind" (*havā lagā*) and could no longer lift things with his left hand. "Getting a wind" might be expressed in American lay culture as "having a stroke," but conveyed more in its utilization of the semantics of *havā*, air or wind. For the old person in particular (for getting a wind was not restricted to the old), wind and breath were key markers structuring the experience of extremely weak old age. Mausaji's family framed his weakness as *hāth pair;* for Tara and for others who knew Mausaji from a greater distance, his *kamzorī* was embodied through an angry voice and a hot *dimāg.* But Mausaji himself experienced his weakness as a disability of breath and wind. He had difficulty breathing; he coughed; and *havā* had wasted his arm. The identification of wind with the experienced old body and its narrative elaboration is not surprising in the context of undernutrition, endemic tuberculosis, heavy tobacco smoking, urban air pollution, ineffectively regulated workplace hazards, and the increased cardiopulmonary complaints of later life. The experience of *havā* was rooted in the economic, environmental, and epidemiologic conditions of working-class Varanasi.

Wind, *vāyu* or *vata* in Ayurvedic and folk traditions, is the humor that predominates in old age. It is associated less with pulmonary complaints than with ailments often translated in allopathic terms as "nervous diseases." *Vāyu* is the agent of motion and direction. "It is so called," the god Dhanvantari reveals in *Suśruta,* "from the fact of its coursing throughout the universe."[26] Zimmermann has reexamined Āyurveda as a science of cooking, the therapeutic manipulation of the relations between classes of terrains, plants, animals, humans, and disorders in terms of the food chains that link them and transmit and transform certain essences or flavors, *rasa.* "What the Rishis, the seers of Vedic times, quite literally saw was that the universe is a kitchen, a kind of chemistry of rasa."[27] The function of *vāyu* was conceived of in *Suśruta* as moving food and its successive incarnations through the cooking vessels of the body.[28]

Excesses of *vāyu* are disorders of motion and are suffered as such: as convulsions, paralyses, and problems with the feet,[29] and as changes in mental state. Mind, *mānas,* in several of the *darśanas,* or classical systems of philosophy, is that which moves between sense organs, objects perceived, and the stuff of consciousness. Like *hāth pair kī kamzorī,* the weakness of breath and application of wind for Mausaji concern his inability to move about in several senses. Mausaji, however, did not root his weakness and wind problems merely in his old age. "*Khānā nahīn hai,*" he said bitterly, there is no food, referring both to his marginalized present and specifically to his getting wind six years earlier. His family immediately objected to this accusation of bad *sevā:* he lost his memory then, they told me, and thus he wrongly thinks that he did not eat. Memory loss was thus invoked long after I was successively reintroduced to Mausaji's weakness by Tara, Durga, Mausiji, his sons, and Mausaji himself. And it was invoked to explain a discrepancy between Mausaji's and his family's memory of a history of food transactions. Memory loss in Chittupur was a second-order problem, not central to weakness like angry voice, hand-foot loss, or wind and breath trouble, but an obvious symptom of weakness that need only be mentioned to deny the Bad Family, here indexed by chapati counts.

The relationship between the hearing of hot brain and the loss of authority in the family was clearest when there was a generational divide of the old parent or parents versus a single son, daughter, or daughter-in-law. With these cases the contest for control of the household was more vertical than with the successive splittings off of multiple siblings. Kapura, in her sixties, lived with her son, daughter-in-law, and grandchildren. She took care of the grandchildren and kept the house clean. Her daughter-in-law saw Kapura as a weak and meddlesome fool, harshly calling her such—"*Cūtiyā!*" [a term of abuse]—whenever Kapura ventured to interrupt. Kapura was terrified of this rather mean-tempered *bahū*, but the latter heard Kapura as a willful and meddlesome voice. In the case of Siranji, whose resistance to taking a tonic has been discussed, family relations were less of a caricature.

Siranji was "not less than one hundred," as she put it; her grandchildren's guesses ranged, but centered on about eighty. My own guess was that Siranji was in her mid-eighties. She was, in short, quite old, vying with Vipat for the distinction of the oldest person in Nagwa. She had lost three sons older than Babu Lal, the only one left alive and then in his fifties. Siranji lived with Babu Lal, his wife Parbati, their five sons and their unmarried daughters, the sons' families, and a young village man who worked for Babu Lal in exchange for room and board. She had a grandson from one of her older sons, but according to this man, Lakhan, Siranji and Babu Lal cast out his widowed mother after his father died. The two compounds, Babu Lal's and Lakhan's, were adjoining, but there was no *matlab*, literally meaning or significance and connoting relationship, between them. Both were among the larger households in Nagwa Basti, especially Babu Lal's with its two courtyards, animal pens, and vegetable shop. Babu Lal and his sons were involved in several small enterprises, had some land, ran the vegetable shop, and worked as drummers as did several Chamar families in Nagwa. The household was large and, as a result of Babu Lal's success, has remained joint. Parbati managed the household with the aid of three daughters-in-law and their children, as well as that of her remaining daughters.

With the emergence of Parbati's role as *sās*, as the mother-in-law of this joint family, her ongoing role as *bahū* to Siranji became increasingly redundant. Siranji still attempted to direct many of the household's affairs, but Parbati increasingly paid her no heed. She did not cross Siranji openly, and in some ways still maintained the deference of a *bahū*, but there were no domains of the household not under her firm control. Siranji knew this, and over the years, the forum of contestation shifted from the *ghar* and the *cūlhā* (the hearth) and increasingly to the body of Siranji itself. This shift was that of *Lear*, of the progressive compression of the king's domain from England to his court to a few retainers to his body and wits.

More and more, the primary item of contestation was *davā*, medicine. Siranji lived in pain, which she described as an intermittent fever or a hotness in her stomach and a chronic difficulty in breathing. She interpreted these experiences as sickness, *bimārī*, and felt that with proper medicine she would be cured. Proper medicine consisted, for Siranji, of powerful pills from a good private doctor. It did not consist of injections or of the big bottle on the shelf. She recalled with anger and some fright her visit "a long time ago" to the free clinic at the BHU Hospital, when the doctors gave her "saline IV," which she hated. Siranji's constant demand—to her family and of me—was for good medicine, and when I tried to take her to a doctor friend of mine who saw patients at the hospital, she got upset: "They will make me stay at the hospital. If I go, they will give me an injection and I'll die. So I will not go there."

The big bottle of vitamin tonic sat on a shelf in the small outer room that Siranji and her grandchildren slept in and where the drums were kept. Pointing to the tonic, she told me, "It burns me." In a stage whisper, Siranji added to me, about Parbati, "She wouldn't care if I die. She abuses me." As Siranji pointed to *davā* as an index of transactional inadequacy, her son and grandchildren (Parbati as the good *bahū* never openly criticized Siranji) pointed to the chapati count. Siranji, Babu Lal, his eldest son Amarnath and Amarnath's wife Gita, Rajesh Pathak, and I were in the outer courtyard where the animals were kept and where, in winter months, Siranji would sit outdoors. She was fixing a basket as we others were talking of types of food and of her illness. "I eat one chapati [daily], sometimes two," said Siranji. Gita laughed and turned to me. "She eats four!" Babu Lal, Gita, Amarnath, and Rajesh all found this image, of the old woman and her four chapatis, of the hypocritical abstinence of the hungry old, exceedingly funny. Siranji denied eating four, angrily, but her son kept giggling and telling me, "Ask her if she eats four! Ask her if she eats four!"

Gita's joke was of a common pattern, the frequent teasing of Siranji by her granddaughters-in-law and especially her granddaughters. Whereas Gita and her fellow *bahūs* were quiet in Parbati's presence, around Siranji more of a joking relationship prevailed, echoing the anthropologist Radcliffe-Brown's classic observation.[30] For the granddaughters, teasing Siranji was an art. Controlling her granddaughters' demeanor was one of the domains Siranji had no intention of relinquishing. When they would thus provoke her by acting "unseemly," Siranji would get upset and begin abusing them: "*Cūtiyā*s! I'll break their teeth!" and so forth. Getting Siranji to produce her hot and weak-minded voice was a favorite pastime in Babu Lal's house. Within the walls of their compound, the family joked with Siranji. She responded with her curses and mutterings, sometimes in anger and, sometimes, it seemed, in disguised good humor. Through her weak and hot persona, Siranji could take center stage and criticize her family for perceived neglect. Her complaints were ignored but her cursing was warmly received.

Outsiders differed on the causes of Siranji's hot brain—the ever-cursing voice that could be heard from the lane—beyond the definitionally obvious, that it was due to the weakness of old age. The central explanation, again, was the Bad Family, her family's not giving her medicine, "especially when they have so much money." Economic difference played a central role in neighbors' perceptions of Siranji, for Babu Lal was among the richest men in his part of the basti. Siranji, from this perspective, was not only a member of a rich family and therefore, given the logic of weakening, not really all that weak, but as a superannuated old woman she stood for her family and was an icon of its social and political position. Many, therefore, identified her with Babu Lal's various political and factional ties, and in general, with a perception that this family was not weakened. Despite its literal presence, day and night, in the lane, her voice was not really heard all that often, unlike the often less heated voices of other elders like Dulari and Ganga Jali who "had no one" and were thus unambiguously weak-brained. Siranji, for such outsiders, was weak to the extent that her weakness suggested the wrongness of Babu Lal's family.

For the family, their hearing of and love for Siranji shifted frames outside of household space. When my efforts to get her to go with me the BHU Hospital continued to fail, I took Siranji one morning to a private doctor in the city. Her granddaughter Hoshila, then unmarried and still Siranji's chief tormentor in the household, carefully dressed and wrapped a shawl around Siranji and led her outside toward the rickshaw I had hired. I was struck by the pair of women, within the household "madwoman" and "wretch" to each other, slowly and lovingly making their way through the lane out to the main road.

Unlike Mrs. Mishra in Mussourie, Siranji was only hot-brained at certain times and from certain perspectives. Her heat could be selectively produced by her family by joking with her, and Siranji was aware of this process. But both women were called weak and hot-brained. Both engendered certain threats and certain responses. Where Siranji's "weak brain" differed was in the fact that her family was able to keep it within the household. Siranji for her part knew when not to speak. Her battle was within; she did not challenge her children by shaming the household. Her voice usually did not present the same threat to meaning. Mrs. Mishra's weak brain, however, could not be contained. She wandered; she made accusations to strangers; she had hit strangers on occasion; and perhaps more important, her strained relations with her son and daughter-in-law were well-known. The weakness of her familial body could not be convincingly reframed. The challenge of old people like Mrs. Mishra, whom I would have identified as demented, did not demand a new set of categories, meanings, or models; she was encompassed within the same idioms of distress as Siranji. What differed was in how and when these categories were used, and in the implications for the quality of familial relations.

JHAṆḌŪ AND THE SOUND OF DYING

Siranji, for all her frequent displays of hot mind, was never *jhaṇḍū*. She took care of the family's goats and cow, repaired baskets and other housewares, and minded her grandchildren and great-grandchildren. Increasingly in the year before her death in 1990, she spent most of her time on her charpoy in the small outer room or in the outer courtyard, but despite her pain she tried her best to be productive, not to be a burden. Like Vatuk's informants expressing dependency anxiety, she worried about not doing enough.

Though Mangri, the old woman who lived with her daughter and grandson, kept house, took care of her grandson, and did minor repair work on the house, she was called *jhaṇḍū* by neighborhood kids. Unlike Siranji, whose charpoy was in an enclosed courtyard (though not the main family courtyard where Parbati held court), Mangri's everyday space was far more permeable to public communication. Though she was humorous and quick-tongued, in calling her a *bakbak* maker children superimposed the expected voice of weak old age. Mangri's exposure to public hearing as much as the content of her speech set her up for *bakbak*.

Bakbak could also be cultivated as a performative style, however, used by, as well as attributed to, the old. Several old widows in Nagwa *bakbak*'ed in public spaces, especially, like Dulari, at the intersections of lanes. Anupa lived with her only son Mir Chand, his wife, and their younger son and his family. Her oldest grandson lived next door; the grandchildren's households had separated eight years earlier. The family was poorer than most in Nagwa; Mir Chand as well as his younger son pedaled rickshaws. Anupa, like Siranji, wanted to receive legitimate *davā* for her illness, and like Siranji she resisted its definition as weakness alone. She was weak because she was ill and needed medicine.

Unlike Siranji, Anupa was conceived of as a *marnevālī*, one at death's door, by her family and neighbors alike. This judgment seemed to reflect less an interpretation of specific bodily signs than her location and voice. Anupa often sat by an intersection across from her house. She would squat on the ground, her cane in one hand, and rock back and forth muttering to herself. The content of her muttering, when I was close enough to hear, was a repetitive lament—an elaboration of her losses and deprivations—and an appeal for some help. "Help me, baba, help me, baba, baba . . . " At times the lament did not seem to make sense. Around her, children played in the lane, and men and women went about their business. Anupa's *bakbak* was seldom heard, or rather, it was heard as part of the dying space of the very old and frail. "How is her *dimāg?*" I asked one of her grandsons. "She is dying," he answered.

Anupa, despite her desire for *davā* and for a cure, knew she was useless and a *marnevālī*. Similarly, Ganga Jali complained of neglect through a routinized outdoor *bakbak* lament and discussed her own imminent death. "He is *pāgal*" [crazy], she would say of her youngest son, Bijay, and his inability to bring in much money. "I go for days without food." Unlike Siranji, what was often at stake for Ganga Jali was enough food for her to eat, and she would explain her considerable suffering and her reputation as a *bakbak* maker in terms less of sickness than of hunger. Her older sons and daughters-in-law would repeat that her mind was *sahī* and that her weakness was only the weakness of old age and of their mutual poverty. She is dying, very weak, and so sounds this way; who can afford medicine, who can give her adequate chapatis? For Ganga Jali herself, her ever-present death was proof of her older children's neglect and suffering and yet at the same time the only respite she had to look forward to.

Old people in Nagwa often discussed their deaths. The lament of *bakbak* may include repeated wishes to die: "I want the Ganga [implying cremation and immersion]; take me to the Ganga." Mangri, whose brothers' families had long ago abandoned her and her daughter, described her death with great relish. "Then they will all come," she once told me, referring to the family who never supported her in life, "and they can behold my body as it turns into ash and is dumped into the Ganga river." She contrasted death with old age ironically: only in death was the broken family reunited. The familial body of the old person is rendered whole, she suggested bitterly, at the moment of its final destruction.

THE POSITION OF REPOSE

North of Nagwa was the neighborhood of Assi. Here in numerous small ashrams and rented rooms lived several hundred elderly sannyasis and *kāśīvāsī* widows who came to live out their days in Kashi and die there. Most were Brahman. On Assi Ghat itself, however, by a pump next to the Sangameshwar Temple, one low-caste old woman from Nagwa appeared each morning. She would squat down next to the pump and soon go into trance, loudly chanting bhajans, religious hymns, sometimes violently shaking her body or getting up and dancing, and demanding money from passersby. Some of the ghat residents said she was a madwoman; a few children called "*paglī*" out to her. Several grown-ups said the spirit of God had descended upon her and caused her to sing like this. Economic incentive and divine inspiration often coexisted comfortably in such ad hoc explanation.

When she first began begging on Assi Ghat, the old woman used to shout her possession. Virendra Singh, a well-known Hindi teacher, research advisor to foreign scholars, and longtime champion of neighborhood quiet against the growing use of loudspeakers, lived next to the pump. Annoyed by her constant noise, he approached the shouting woman one day: "I said to her, why are you screaming? People will give you much more money if you sing. And the next day, she began to sing. And she received more money." The Sangameshwar old woman modulated her voice, moving from hoarse *bakbak* to the more upscale and marketable bhajan. For those who understood her voice and passion as possession, she was able to shift her presentation of self from that which was interpretable as *bhūt-pret* or *ḍāin*, as the voice of a ghost or witch, to that which suggested God speaking through her. The first voice drew dramatic attention to her abject state, but put her at some risk of harassment by police, local toughs, or children and challenged Singh's efforts to construct a local civil society of balanced voice. The second, if presented like that of most widows, might have failed to elicit much notice or patronage, but the pump lady's bhajans combined the voice and vigor of a younger woman possessed by malign forces with the lyrics and more upmarket claims to patronage of the upper-caste widow. She was able to draw upon both the pity of passersby for her abject condition and their devotion to a God whom she had learned to embody.

Few aged and resourceless producers of a voice in Nagwa Basti could transform their laments and *bakbak* into such a resource. Even families who felt that an old person was a burden and who gave her fewer chapatis resented the shame that would befall them were she to go out and beg elsewhere. For most, the Assi Ghat old woman remained a beggar even as she drew upon the social space of the re-nunciate and of the one possessed. First, Chamar men and women could not eas-ily be true sannyasis or *kāśīvāsī* widows. Second, possession remained a largely do-mestic space of affliction, and one particularly for the young. When old women and sometimes old men from the slum went to *ojhā* healers, it was invariably for the exorcism and healing of a daughter, daughter-in-law, granddaughter, or grandson.

Ideal *sannyāsa*, for those few men in Nagwa who spoke of their old age in terms of it, came through the subjugation of the self: not to the upper castes or their in-stitutions, but to the self-chosen guru or teacher. Munna Lal was about sixty, and he lived with his wife and two sons in a house next to one in which his two younger brothers and their families lived, not far from the house of Narayan the poet. He spoke of old age in third-person terms, not of *kamzorī* but of a polarity of sadness and anger, on the one hand, versus shanti, on the other.

> If people follow a guru, stay in good company, and try to know God, they will achieve happiness and thus repose [shanti]. If they do not, they will be sad. There will not be peace; they will fight with family members in their old age. The guru can be anyone. Ram and Krishna also had gurus. It is because Krishna did not listen to the rishi Durvasas, his guru, when he told Krishna to apply *khir* [rice and milk] to his entire body, and neglected to put some on his ankle that he died. In this body, every-thing can be found. But how does one know this? One needs information and thus knowledge; thus, the guru.

Krishna was killed, incidentally, by a hunter named Jara, old age, the arrow strik-ing his vulnerable ankle. Shanti is opposed to decrepit old age, and one gains it through submission to a guru. This submission was contrast by Mr. Lal with the Brahmanical ideal of *sannyāsa*:

> Ravi Das was a *sant śiromaṇi*, that is, he was always living for others. . . . Listen: I'm in the householder stage . . . its dharma is giving blessings to your children. . . . This is greater than *sannyāsa*. Ram, Ravi Das, Kabir, Nanak were all householders. Ravi Das, as *sant śiromaṇi*, said one should always look out for others. He was a shoemaker. He only took three *paise* [cents] out of the four he received for a pair of shoes, and returned the rest or gave it to the poor. I read a book on Isa Masi [Jesus], too. He said religion is to love others; this is not what some others say it is.

The ideal old age, for Munna Lal, was one of continuity with adulthood. One re-mained a householder and continued to be the giver to one's children, no longer of material substance but of *āśīrvād*, of blessings. The debt remained, on the part of one's children. *Sannyāsa* is rejected, as is the religion of "others," as a philoso-phy associated with the powerful and their taking, and weakening. True knowl-edge could only come from a true asceticism that consisted of the giving of one-self. *Sannyāsa* is identified here with a position of not giving, in this case not giving the *āśīrvād* of old age. Yet paradoxically it was Munna Lal's own relative success and comfort that placed him in the position of repose and pushed him to reconfigure the languages of balance and of weakness in terms of one another.

Sannyasis in Varanasi were described by basti residents either as cheats or privileged retirees. True ascetics were the weakened poor who have no choice. The relationship between the dialectics of weakening and the emergence of the ascetic ideal was taken up by Raghu Ram's son Ram Lakhan in his discussion of Adi Dharm. The Aryan invaders forced the peaceful original Indians to become their slaves and degraded them. The emergent caste society offered no possibilities for mental peace. No one could be a giver: one either took or had nothing left to give. An ideology of *sannyāsa* emerged, in which the original principles of Adi Dharm were appropriated and placed at the end of a lifetime. Old age, the last stage, came to stand for the entire personhood of the original Indian. But this new scheme of the life cycle was warped, rooted in cultural theft and in the false splitting of values between a time of exploitation and a time of renunciation. Old age for Ram Lakhan, the preeminent Nagwa ideologue of his generation, was for the elite a warped version of Adi Dharm and for Nagwa dwellers but the nadir of their weakened status.

Neither the ideology of Khare's articulate informants nor the philosophy of Ram Lakhan, however, map well onto the stories most Nagwa residents tell about old age and weak mind. Munna Lal's description of aging stressed the possibility of achieving shanti if one was true to the guru's word. But weakness and hot mind, most residents argued, were unavoidable. Though Ram Lakhan suggested that dualistic thinking was externally imposed through Hindu categories, few in Nagwa could place themselves outside the framework of weakener and weakened. The rootedness of the language of weakness extended beyond community identity. For weak brain suggested not only Chamar versus Brahman-Thakur-Bania, but parent versus son or daughter-in-law. Nagwa residents spoke of themselves as weakened in opposition to "Hindus," but they classified themselves as Hindu in speaking of each other as the weakeners of old parents, occasionally in opposition to *sahī*-minded Muslims.

In the colonies, the sannyasi and especially the *kāśīvāsī* widow stood as markers of abjection, the lonely old person who "had no one," the narrative foil to one's own parents. In Nagwa, sannyasis were at best irrelevant. There were, however, several stock characters in Nagwa, individuals who "had no one" in dramatic ways and who offered an extreme picture of old age and weak brain against which most families and individuals could positively frame their own *sevā* and their own old age.

Dukni lived in a small house with her two sons and their families. There was little room, and the sons often stayed with their in-laws. She was a widow in her fifties; yet she called herself and was called *būṛhī*, old. "She acts old," I was told, perhaps a reference to her constant griping. As her name suggested (*dukh* is sadness), Dukni seldom found much enjoyment in life. Unlike Mangri who lived across the lane and whose financial situation was far worse than hers, Dukni never laughed.

In addition to her sons, Dukni had two daughters who lived nearby and who often visited. The adjoining household was that of Panvasi, Dukni's stepson from her late husband's first marriage. Panvasi and his wife, Gita Devi, and their children lived separately. They were an extremely ambitious couple, but without any support from Panvasi's family they had virtually no capital upon which to draw. They resorted to many schemes. Panvasi started a new Ravi Das committee, competing with the group ran by Seva Lal and Secchan. For a while Gita Devi ran a little store on the main road, a wooden box from which she sold snacks, kites, and matches. She was at pains to befriend all the "Fathers," all the missionaries associated with the Kristapanthi Ashram and other foreigners who might be sources of patronage. In 1988, when John the evangelist moved to the outskirts of the basti, most of his hopes of winning converts were pinned on Gita Devi and her family. Gita Devi often asked me to steer any new "researchers" her way; I was able to oblige.

The couple spent, or at least claimed to have spent, large sums (more than a thousand rupees) each year on the worship of Ravi Das. They took a vow of worshipping the guru properly for several years to ensure the health of their three sons. They had lost several infants, all girls, to illness already, Gita told me, and wanted to ensure their sons' health. An earlier Ravi Das Committee had built an open shrine for an image of the saint in the center of the basti, overlooking what was then the neighborhood tank; the saint now overlooks a large Thakur house. Each February when Ravi Das' birthday rolled around, several groups within Nagwa competed for the gifts to the guru each household might give. Panvasi would organize a Ravi Das puja, the offering of fruit and other items to the saint, each year, and would be entitled to receive some of the money and gifts back as a *dān*, as a gift for his services. Whether or not he lost much money each year, few in Nagwa viewed him as disinterested.

One day Dukni appeared in the main alley of the slum with bruises on her head, inflicted by policemen from the Lanka thana searching for her daughter. The daughter had been working as domestic help in a home in Ravindrapuri from which several gold bars were stolen. The employer, "the Thakur," had accused Dukni's daughter, who then fled, deciding to resist the inevitable beating as she was over eight months pregnant. Dukni would not reveal her daughter's whereabouts. I had heard several stories of police beatings of old women while I was working in Nagwa. These stories were offered as proof of the moral illegitimacy of the police and the district administration and their control by "Brahman, Thakur, Bania." They were, in effect, the flip side of the newspaper images of old woman voting. The old woman's body, icon par excellence of the individual in relation to the state, was in Nagwa materialized as the battered victim of the police. In talking of Dukni's beating, however, her neighbors also looked to her family. The rumor was that Dukni's daughter had been seduced by her employer, and when her husband discovered this and went to the Ravindrapuri house to complain, the rich man accused the daughter of stealing his gold to deflect the charge of adultery. The loose morals of Dukni's daughter, neighbors suggested, were in part responsible for her mother's condition. Dukni's national body pointed to the police; her familial body pointed to her daughter.

This daughter was eventually found and arrested; her husband was not in Varanasi and so Dukni gave Panvasi 260 rupees to bail her out and bribe the policemen. The daughter returned to Shukulpur, another basti near the Sankat Mochan temple further west, and had the baby. Several evenings later, Rajesh and I were about to call it a day when we heard a commotion near Babu Lal's house. We joined a group, including Siranji, wondering what was happening. We saw Dukni's other daughter run into the lane and begin screaming at Panvasi: "How could you beat my mother? Why not beat me instead? Go ahead! I am young! She is old!" Dukni came up to our group, holding out her arms. "Look what he did to me. He beat me. I will call the police. I will go to the thana." She turned to Panvasi and began to abuse him and Gita Devi: "Your wife is a whore. She has turned you against me. You're a pair of sinners." Panvasi screamed at her in turn, and they began again accusing each other of eating the other's money until the stepson again began to throw blows down upon Dukni.

The crowd separated them. Much of Nagwa had gathered by this time. Next to me Siranji, with a ringside view, was taking it all in quietly. Small groups broke off. Some accused Panvasi of being a bad son. "He should have helped her out with her debts, and not demanded that she repay them." Others blamed Dukni. "She is a quarrelsome woman. Her mind is not correct. She is always abusing him." People turned to me, knowing the limited categories I tended to think in, and told me to note that the relationship between a stepson and a stepmother would never lead to shanti or *sevā*.

What had been at stake was a loan for one thousand rupees taken from a moneylender by the daughter whom Panvasi had bailed out of jail and the daughter's husband. The two still owed eight hundred rupees on the loan. Panvasi, raising money for his annual Ravi Das birthday puja, found that the moneylender had put the word out that the family owed a significant sum of money and had no business collecting and spending further sums. Furious, Panvasi confronted his stepmother and demanded that she and her daughter pay back the eight hundred rupees remaining. He would front four hundred rupees if they would match it, and the brother-in-law could pay him back in the future. Dukni denied she agreed to anything. "I make ten rupees a day by scrubbing people's pots; where would I get four hundred rupees?" She offered the counteraccusation that Panvasi spent much of the bail money she had given him on liquor.

The social drama of Dukni and her stepson framed a set of complex and difficult issues for the slum—financial disagreements, false accusations, drinking, the abuse of women, hot-brained elderly—within a coherent narrative of the false family. Mangri and her daughter, Babu Lal, and Siranji, Ram Lakhan, and Raghu Ram, all heard in Dukni's and Panvasi's accusations a family situation qualitatively different from their own. The fundamental distance between this mother and son not related by blood generated an ideal type for understanding old age in terms of a weakened familial body, and at the same time distanced one's own experience.

The most extreme of *bakbak* voices in Nagwa basti was that of Dulari, the madwoman of the crossing who ended up with Mother Teresa's nuns and a purloined Durga. She represented a picture of total deprivation and old age weakness, so much so that neighbors would consistently use the language of madness—*bhūt* possession, cracked mind, half mind, ruined mind—as well as that of *kamzorī* to speak of her. Like Dukni, she represented an extreme of the Bad Family—in her case, the absent family. The epitome of the weak voice of *bakbak*, Dulari moved beyond the opposition of weakener-weakened. She had no one to withhold *sevā* from her. Beyond the possibility of even the Bad Family, she was heard as pure voice, pointing beyond itself—in her case, to nothing.

A Child Is Being Lifted

July 1996. A woman drowned in the Varuna, the northern limit to the sacred city. One week later, in trying to piece together what had happened, I found that her age kept shifting. I was with the contractor Ratnesh Pathak, who had worked with foreign anthropologists before and was writing a book about their pretensions. In the early afternoon, we reached the lane in Orderly Bazaar where the woman had been accused of being a child-lifter, or *lakaṛsunghvā*, and had been apprehended by a group of young men, tied up, held overnight, and either pushed or forced to jump into the river. At the head of the lane, a woman was selling pan; she turned out to be the one who had raised the alarm against the *lakaṛsunghvā* woman. She eyed us in anger and fear as she said to Ratnesh that the child-lifter was *karer*, tough, a word suggestive of a powerful adulthood, less of youth or old age. "She got in the house from the roof. I found her covered in oil, holding my one-year-old granddaughter and leading my four-year-old grandson by the hand, stealing them." The oil: several other rumored gangs of thieves were said to cover themselves in oil so as to be too slippery to catch, including the fabled Underwear Gang (*kacchā-baniyān*). Fear of the latter had led to several accusations and vigilante killings in the past.

The *lakaṛsunghvā* thief was strong and the oil prevented the grandmother from grabbing hold of and restraining her, so she held on to the thief's hair and started to scream for help. She held on until relatives and other neighbors appeared. Several of the men surrounded the child-lifter and tied her up. That was the last, she told us pointedly, that she saw of the oil-covered woman. Some of the pan-seller's relatives had since been arrested and were in custody. She repeated how strong the woman had been, and how serious the threat to the family. Ratnesh, going over the details of the interview after we left Orderly Bazaar, did not doubt that the drowned woman had been a child-lifter but thought the pan-seller was lying about what happened after her capture: "She had to know what happened to her."

The local police in the neighborhood thana concurred with some of what the pan-seller said. They had been responsible for rounding up suspects once the corpse of the *lakaṛsunghvā* woman had been found in the Varuna. The thana police were less committed to the grandmother's claim that her grandchildren were being kidnapped, but they worked in a world where kids were routinely sold or exchanged by adults and took the possibility of child-lifting gangs at face value. They did not mention the recent explosion of popular rumors of mysterious child-lifting gangs that had spread throughout this part of the state. They noted the age of the *lakaṛsunghvā* woman in prosaic terms: "She was about forty-five."

In a busy office, the superintendent of police for the city was dealing with several recent deaths of suspected *lakaṛsunghvā*s in the context of an escalating number of child-lifting rumors. He knew of the case, one of three persons in the city killed over the past month after being accused of child-lifting. He wasn't sure of the woman's age, but presumed that she was old given the connection of such rumors to fears of witchcraft. To explain, he began to construct typologies. There are two kinds of cases in which persons are killed as child-lifters, he told me. Either an old enmity or land dispute is being settled under the cover of a child-lifting accusation, or people come to believe that their victim is a child-lifter independent of any such vested interests.

In either case, he continued, the killing is justified in one of three ways. First, the victim is said to be part of an organized gang who steal children for adoption, bonded labor, prostitution, professional beggary, or, increasingly, the theft of their kidneys. Over the past five years, more and more poor Banarsis I knew had mentioned the possibility of selling one of their kidneys in exchange for needed cash; though donation of kidneys by live unrelated donors had been declared illegal and though Varanasi was not a center for informal-sector black-market donation, the possibility of such an exchange was universally believed and rumors of clinics where these were carried out abounded. Second, the victim is said to be a *ḍāin* or a *cuṛail*, a witch or a demoness. Though the two terms are distinct for many who use them—*ḍāin*s being old women who curse people with their angry voices, eager for their misfortune, and *cuṛail*s being ghosts of dead women in the form of young and beautiful enchantresses who kill people, eager for their livers—the superintendent of police collapsed them together as *ḍāin-cuṛail* and associated them with old and poor women. Third, the victim is said to be a *lakaṛsunghvā*, a child's bedtime terror come to life. *Lakaṛsunghvā*s carry sticks with a smell that attracts children, whom they kill, whose organs they may eat, and whose bodies they may dump under bridges. *Lakaṛsunghvā*s are often thought of as babas, as wandering old men or sannyasis. In 1996, these several types of outsiders hungry for children—younger gang members, old *ḍāin*s, and *lakaṛsunghvā* babas—coalesced. For the superintendent of police for the city, the existence of such gangs was questionable, and those killed as *lakaṛsunghvā*s were usually old, poor, and therefore at risk. The drowned woman became old: old women were necessary figures in a tableau of India as a Hobbesian world of vested interests and vulnerable individuals.

This officer's superior, the senior superintendent of police, or SSP, for Varanasi district, was not in the city but in the spacious cantonment. For him, the woman was old and half-naked, and he noted—using the language of the old Indian Lunacy Act—that her mind was probably unsound. She was most likely a doddering beggar who wandered into a neighborhood where she did not belong. When youth surrounded her and demanded to know why she was there and where she was from, she could not, given her confused mind, articulate an adequate response and confirmed her interlocutors' convictions that she was a child-lifter. Unlike the other officers, the SSP saw the matter as one simply of superstition and baseless rumor. Children had been mauled by wolves or hyenas to the northwest of Varanasi, killings widely reported in the press, and the panic had spread to urban areas like this one. If the police had been given rein to be more aggressive in combating the initial spread of rumor, he suggested in ending our interview, the epidemic would never have happened. The drowned woman was now not only old but senile, her nonsense mirroring the nonsensical world of the superstitious masses. In invoking the victim as old madwoman, the SSP offered a world of mass ignorance in which the police are not merely one more vested interest but an entity that offers the redemptive deployment of force.

What had happened? On March 1996, four months earlier, as the hot summer approached and more persons began to sleep outside, reports of hyenas coming into villages at night and stealing sleeping children began to spread in Sultanpur, Jaunpur, and Pratapgarh, three eastern districts of the state. Some of the missing children's bodies were recovered, with flesh and internal organs gouged out. The word for hyena, *lakaṛbagghā*, is consonant with the word for child-lifter, *lakaṛsunghvā*, and reflects local knowledge that small children are at particular risk, especially when sleeping outdoors, for being caught by predatory animals. *Lakaṛbagghā* stories, like *lakaṛsunghvā* stories, are told to children to keep them from wandering off.

As the number of reports of missing children grew, hyena tales were supplemented by those of *lakaṛsunghvā*s, witches, and child-lifting gangs. The number of deaths of persons thought to be culpable soon surpassed the number of missing children. Such explosions of child-lifting, or of child-lifting rumors, had occurred periodically in eastern Uttar Pradesh, the last a little over a decade earlier. Like the 1996 events, previous occurrences of rumor have combined fears of wild animals, old babas and witches, gangs, vested interests, and the stealing of children by physicians. But whereas during earlier episodes the actions of gangs and of physicians centered on international adoption, beggary, and sex work markets—often, it was said, financed by the desire of Gulf states for cheap Indian matériel—the 1996 rumors stressed the new world market in children's kidneys. One nursing home in Varanasi, and the physician who ran it, were at the center of kidney-stealing rumors, to the extent that he was forced to take a leave of absence and effectively shut down the home.[1]

In the districts where most of these children had died, local leaders organized fearful and angry villagers against perceived inaction by district administrations. A Varanasi-Lucknow train was stopped and some of its coaches were burned. A senior police team investigating the matter was waylaid and its members humiliated, forced to admit publicly the existence of a conspiracy, that a *lakarsunghva* and not a mere *lakarbaggha* was behind the deaths. Medical teams doing health checkups and vaccinations of children were similarly waylaid, and the summer's child health campaign came to a standstill.[2] In Lucknow and Delhi, such local responses were said to be the work of vested interests; still, pressure on the local administrative services mounted, and in late June after an intensive search a den of "man-eating" wolves was finally found and dispatched. The event was carried in the national press as the truth behind the rumors from backward eastern Uttar Pradesh. Locally, wolves were offered as a less sinister alternative to the dangerously alliterative *lakarbaggha*s.

Yet within hours of the capture, new missing children were being reported throughout the region.[3] Stories of captured wolves now competed with those of a new category collapsing *lakarsunghva* and *lakarbaggha*: according to the *Patrika* of July 2, "The [Pratapgarh] District Hospital was thronged today by people who wanted to have a glimpse of the alleged human hyena who was caught and handed over to the police. . . . The alleged human hyena is under police custody in the paying ward of the District Hospital and nobody is permitted to meet him. He behaves like a lunatic, which people say is a coverup to escape police action."[4]

The human hyena was eventually released, but reports of "a black thing"—"an animal-like figure which could run on two hind legs"—spread.[5] Gangs were said to employ persons expert in mimicking animals. Other government teams began to systematically hunt down wolves and the mainstream Hindi press began including tips on how to differentiate dogs, hyenas, and wolves.[6] On the side of the animals, Maneka Gandhi—member of parliament, daughter-in-law of the late prime minister Indira Gandhi, and longtime animal-rights activist—argued that innocent wolves and hyenas were being killed so that the state could avoid taking the prevalence of organized gangs and their convivial relationship to political leaders seriously.

Meanwhile, the beatings and killings of suspected lifters escalated, the victims usually being some combination of old, female, homeless, and mad.[7] A ragpicker woman in Kanpur was, in the words of a local headline, "roasted alive"; following her death, beggars and ragpickers in the city went into hiding.[8] An old man was walking with his grandson and was taken for a *lakarsunghva* baba, beaten, and delivered to the police. Whether because of the man's shock, the fact that no one would listen to him, or his unsoundness of mind, the police were no more able to hear his protests as intelligible than was the crowd that first caught him, and they beat him too.[9] And in Varanasi, a woman drowned. Her estimated age varied, depending upon whether one saw and heard her as a criminal, an accused witch, or an old madwoman, depending upon whether the grandmother's panic, the superintendent of police's realpolitik, or the senior superintendent of police's rationalism was most compelling.[10] Something was badly amiss, and a cavalcade of shape-shifting outsiders threatened the only sure entitlement of even the poorest families, their children. Old witch women and babas, doctors promising health for all, and human hyenas stood in for one another—each the uncanny incarnate, the Other to the family.

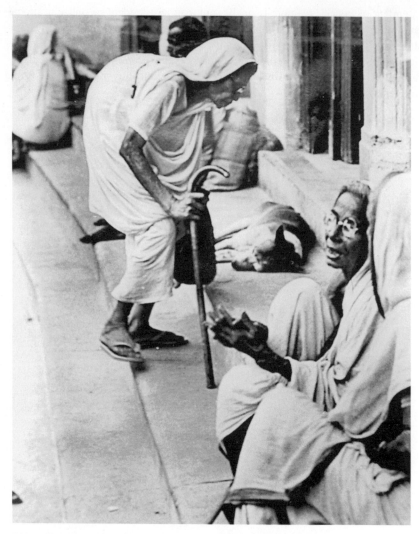

Elder's Day. Reproduced by arrangement with The Times of India Group.

EIGHT

Dog Ladies and the Beriya Baba

in which the gendered old body is heard differently at home and in the interstice

DOGS AND OLD WOMEN

Mashima, Auntie, lived in the Bengali quarter. Early each morning she left her small rented room with a bag of just-baked chapatis, made with flour bought from her monthly allowance. She stopped at the homes of several families in the quarter, Bengali Brahmans like herself, and collected a chapati or two from each. Thus armed, she would proceed slowly along the long lane running the length of the quarter. Her hungry companions would begin to follow, but Mashima was not yet ready for them and kept a steady pace. At Sonarpura crossing, she emerged from the network of lanes and crossed the main road to a well-known sweet shop, the Ocean of Milk. The owner was fond of Mashima and would give her sweet curds leftover from the previous day: "But they're not for humans, Mashima." Mashima reentered the lanes where her companions awaited her eagerly: they were all dogs. They followed behind her in a growing pack and growled furiously at any passerby who appeared in their dog's-eye view to threaten Mashima. When she reached her destination, a small clearing deep within the lanes where more dogs were waiting, Mashima sat down for a moment to catch her breath. Then she began her day's work, feeding the dogs of Varanasi.

Dogs were not beloved in the city. My friends the Banerjees, one of the Mashima's sources for chapatis, then had two pet dogs that they had trained; the family was considered eccentric. For Mr. Banerjee, a civil engineer who had insisted his wife attend graduate school against her initial wishes, and who then decided to raise his two daughters like sons so that they would always be self-sufficient, training purebred dogs was part of a consciously modernist fashioning of life and family. But for his neighbors, dogs were dirty—skulking in dank and odorous corners, barking incessantly at night, wandering over the cremation ghats, feeding on whatever they might find there—and not worth the effort. Children in the quarter played with dogs, learning from their siblings and friends in early childhood to elicit yelps by hitting, kicking, and stoning them. Dogs were interstitial creatures, essential inhabitants of the space between households, and as such had no strong claims to domestic support.

Dogs, Mashima told me, were her children. She would talk to, scold, and comfort them. She was always enlarging her route, waxing ever more powerful in old age by including more lanes and more dogs. "She has no one," noted her neighbors, framing her as the pathetic *kāśīvāsī* woman whom the professors at the Vasant College luncheon had once told me was the typical old person, the abject figure who comes to stand for the old age of others. She was a child widow, one who had lost her husband when she was fourteen and already the mother of a baby daughter. The daughter had been married for many years and lived in Calcutta. Mashima herself had lived in Calcutta until the early 1970s when she came to Kashi. She was now in her seventies. Her family was wealthy and, she told me, its members were cultured *bhadralok*: she had nephews in Canada and other foreign places and had met the filmmaker Satyajit Ray. Some of her brothers and her daughter sent her small monthly remittances, and she received a Central Government pension (minus five rupees to the postman to guarantee its delivery). Altogether, it was enough to live simply and pay the rent, with some funds left over for the dogs. Still, Mashima described herself as a religious mendicant oblivious to gain and surviving off the daily kindnesses of others.

"Why not feed . . . the cows?" a neighbor who objected to the daily parade of dogs once suggested. Other people fed cows, Mashima responded, but dogs too had claims upon us. Dogs, she used to say, were also mendicants, like the old people of the city. But most neighbors to whom I recounted the story of the Dog Lady resisted the explicit connection of old people and dogs that Mashima put forth. Dogs did not explicitly anchor the discourse of old age in the quarter or in the other three neighborhoods. Others besides old women and dogs shared the interstice; the neighbor's comment about cows suggested a more meaningful association. Like the old, cows were in theory objects of veneration found throughout the sacred city. But in practice both cows and widows were obstacles that blocked one's path. Banarsis frequently recited a couplet on the things visitors trip over when they reach the holy city:

Raṇḍ, sāṇṛ, sīṛhī, sannyāsī
Inse bache sevā to Kāśī.[1]

Widow, bull, steps, sannyasi,
Avoiding these one can enjoy Kashi.

Varanasi was the city of holy things in painful excess—liberated renunciates, steps descending to the Ganga, auspicious animals, and pious old widows—but it was also the city of a cultivated insouciance and joie de vivre. Widows, classically inauspicious in Hindu India, did, like cows, steps, and holy men, become part of the spiritual capital of Kashi as pilgrimage center. But for those who had to live in Varanasi everyday, the couplet suggested that life was more pleasurable to the extent that one avoided the claims of the pious and pure and their self-appointed protectors. The ambivalent image of widows in excess was perhaps more extreme in the temple town of Brindavin in western Uttar Pradesh, where a tout once accosted me and urged me to make a contribution to his family's temple where every night "ten thousand Bengali mothers" were fed. Fortified by my contribution, he promised, this gargantuan mass of widowed mothers would sing bhajans, hymns, to God, and garner me the resulting merit.

Mothers had to eat: thus the tout's claim upon me and the source of his not insignificant income. Mothers and cows were never of the interstice but belonged to someone and somewhere. Bhajan ashrams, homes for upper-caste Hindu widows where their voices could be collectivized and routinized as maternal blessing through the bhajan, transformed the threat of the individual widow's voice. Whatever limited resources such widow houses offered, old women who lacked even the slender protection of the domestication of their voice as bhajan were seldom heard as mothers. In the lanes of the old city, the voices of old *kāśīvāsī* women were heard less as mothers than as madwomen. Mashima did not mind the children who taunted her and cried *"paglī,"* she told me; she could talk back to them. The adults who made fun of her, who pulled at her clothes, or who accused her of being a witch and giving the dogs poison were less easily dismissible. She could talk back, but her Hindi was poor and in any case she tended to be misunderstood. As much as the conditions of mendicancy, this inability to make her voice heard as other than degraded or repetitive noise grounded Mashima's dog metaphor.

Like other elderly widows and old men of the quarter, Mashima spent the early mornings visiting friends and aiding those less mobile. The maintenance of these networks required considerable effort and mobility. The *kāśīvāsī* was constantly between households as she worked to domesticate the interstice. As the Dog Lady, Mashima was the most vivid example of an interstitial elder I knew, because in domesticating the interstice she attempted to transform its most pathetic signs—alley dogs—into a family. Her economic security, her Brahman and *bhadralok* status, and her personality all contributed to her fragile success. But most *kāśīvāsī* widows, and other widows whose caste did not privilege *kāśīvās* as a solution to the threat of destitution, were in danger of becoming Dog Ladies in a different sense, of being read through the interstice as embodiments of not only pathos but of a threatening bark and complete degradation. The genius in Mashima's eccentricity was in this: that she explicitly spoke of the condition of the *kāśīvāsī* elderly in refusing the lure of the bovine and claiming kinship with dogs.

Though not self-consciously invoked by most old people, dogs were powerful signs of the interstice and were frequently juxtaposed with figures of interstitial old women. The juxtaposition was sometimes iconic, that is, dogs and old women

were associated because they appeared to share certain qualities. Thus on the occasion of the United Nations–sponsored "Elders' Day," an internationalist holiday locally advocated by groups like HelpAge India, the *Times of India* in 1988
commemorated the occasion with a large photograph of three old women clad in
the white saris of widows and shown next to a sleeping dog, seemingly white in the
picture (see photograph on p. 262). One of the widows has her back to us, the second has her mouth open, and the third is severely hunchbacked and holds a small
cane. The sleeping dog was one more marginal white-clad figure in the gutter.[2]

The Elder's Day image also conveyed a symbolic juxtaposition, that is, a connection between dogs and old women based upon particular cultural associations.
In both classical Hindu and popular local narrative, dogs were one of several archetypical denizens of the ultimate dying spaces of the Hindu polis, the cremation
ghats. In Varanasi, necropolis par excellence, the fierce form of Lord Shiva known
as Bhairava was an important and powerfully transgressive deity and was closely
associated with dogs.[3] Each night, alongside the Ganga, dogs howled and barked
in menacingly lupine cadences: Bhairava was wandering the lanes and ghats, seeking expiation for his sin, the death of Brahma, the old man of the gods. David
White, in his essay "Dogs Die," examined the dog as hellhound in Vedic and other
Indo-European traditions.[4] In Varanasi, dogs signified degradation and putrescence as much as death: they not only frequented cremation grounds but ate what
they could find there. To be "treated like a dog" thus conveyed a complex set of associations suggesting both iconic dependency and noise and symbolic pollution
and threat.

OLD WOMEN AND MADWOMEN

*As the story goes, the king died and the queen lost her mind and the kingdom turned into
a wasteland.*

BHISHAM SAHNI, "*RĀNĪ MEHTO*"

Mashima recognized and could contain her dog-ness. She received family assistance and could afford to accept no cooked food for herself. She took chapatis—
and in doing so maintained a social network—only for the dogs. By refusing food
for herself and by transforming dogs into cows, she challenged what it meant to be
old and dependent on the interstice. If dogs could be cows, then Mashima
through her practice was not the abject aunt but the good mother, daily distributing the largesse of the Ocean of Milk.

Still, for most passersby she seemed pathetic. One neighbor was my friend
Bijay, through whom I had first met Mashima. He told me that he knew that I was
on the lookout for crazy old people. "She's been in the lane just outside my house
every morning for years," he told me one morning, "I wouldn't have noticed that
she was quite mad but for you." The powers of the imported gaze aside, however,
many local kids didn't need me to tell them the Dog Lady was a mad old *paglī*. The
frequency with which local children sought out and teased old women—calling

them madwomen—was one of the reasons the project of studying senility in Varanasi had evolved in the first place. In 1983 during an earlier stay in the Bengali quarter, I was sitting outside my rented room on Pandey Ghat while five or six children were playing nearby. A hunchbacked old woman wearing a dirty white sari appeared in the lane and quietly set about collecting some dung patties that were not her own from a wall on which they were drying. One of the children saw her, motioned to his friends, and the whole gang ran over, shouting *"Paglī! paglī!"* and pelting her with small stones. The woman began cursing the children. Strong and archaic curses from the frail old hunchback sounded funny to the kids, and they laughed and laughed. The *paglī* left off stealing dung patties and limped away.

Koki, the old Bengali widow who lived in the Ravindrapuri stairwell, was similarly an interstitial elder at high risk for becoming a *paglī*. Though she called her stairwell home, Koki spent her days going from house to house and from institution to institution—visiting friends, receiving foodstuffs, going from the Ganga to the Durga temple. Continually on the road at a vigorous gait, Koki brooked no interruptions. Whenever I tried to talk to her in motion, she would tell me that she was busy: "Get lost!" Dogs and children were her other bêtes noirs. If a dog followed at her heels, Koki would turn and begin scolding it. Children, both those in the colony and from the slum across the road next to the abandoned cinema hall, would come running to watch the mad widow talk to dogs. Children found Koki—with her busy gait and sharp voice—a delight to mock and call *paglī*. Koki, unlike genteel Mashima, would quickly let loose with a string of Bengali curses that few of the children could understand. The heteroglossia of the old voice—its incomprehensible and varying cadences of class, rural life, region, and level of education—added to the pleasures of its elicitation.

Years after the Bengali quarter stoning, I asked many of the younger brothers and sisters of the erstwhile Pandey Ghat gang what was the reason for stoning a *paglī*. The kids all said that you teased a *paglī* because of her voice. In particular, they hoped for the following sorts of things: *galīs*, or abuses, often quite obscene and usually in the form of a curse; errors, which widows—often from distant regions of India, Bangladesh, and Nepal—made when they spoke quickly in Hindi or Bengali; and *bakbak*, or utter nonsense.

Paglīs would curse, but their curses were empty and powerless. They were mad, but mad in the way usually only kids could see. Bijay and his neighbors saw Mashima as eccentric, but it took the transposed gaze of the ethnographic moment—"I wouldn't have noticed that she was quite mad but for you"—to transform pathos into pathology. Children, not yet mature enough to hear the familial body or its lack in the old voice, tended to hear its humor. Small children were sometimes frightened by such old women, and their older siblings and playmates might tease them with the threat that the old witch, like some *lakaṛsunghvā*, would get them. But for most kids, most of the time, old women's voices were not threatening in Varanasi. The madness heard by children in old voices was gendered; there were also *pāgal*, madmen, in the lanes of the quarter, but they were usually far younger men. The old men or babas who wandered the interstices of the city were heard differently. And yet the 1996 *lakaṛsunghvā* murders suggested that the hearing of interstitial voices in moments in which the familial and domestic appeared critically under attack could transform the usual scaffolding of gender and age in what rendered voices crazy, dangerous, and witchlike.

MADWOMEN AND WITCHES

The uncanny effect of epilepsy and of madness has the same origin. The layman sees in them the working of forces hitherto unsuspected in his fellowmen.

SIGMUND FREUD, "THE 'UNCANNY' "

Stolen dung, the voices of old women, and the movements of children mattered differently in Varanasi's rural hinterland. On the rare occasions when such things happened, suspected witches or *lakaṛsunghvā*s were attacked less as strangers whose voices could not be heard as meaningful other than indexing menace, and more as neighbors or relatives whose voices made demands that challenged shifting configurations of land, capital, and *sevā*.

Martha Chen and Jean Drèze's work on the survival and quality of life of Indian widows and Bina Agarwal's examination of the relation between land ownership and the survival and quality of life of women more generally have drawn attention to the correlation of witchcraft accusations and the contested ownership of land by unmarried, separated and widowed women.[5] Witchcraft has flourished in areas that have been rendered marginal through the intensification of a cash economy, the Sanskritization of practices of land tenure and patriarchal authority, and the delegitimation of women's rights in land. Earlier ethnographic work on rural witchcraft accusation and death in north India, such as Carstairs's *Death of a Witch*, has been reread by Chen in terms of the contested land ownership of the suspected witch.[6]

Such economic interpretations of witchcraft accusation have been lacking and are critical. Broader socioeconomic reasoning may also be useful to analyze why periodic intensifications of witchcraft and child-stealing accusation—as in 1996— occur when they do. Several social facts may lie some distance behind the *lakaṛsunghvā* rumors: the everyday violence, to use Nancy Scheper-Hughes's phrase,[7] when parents and other family members feel they are forced to bond or sell not only their children's labor but the rights to their bodies; the widespread knowledge, in eastern Uttar Pradesh, that there were brokers to whom one could sell one of one's kidneys for a relatively high price, thus the knowledge that the global market had an interest in separating one into salable parts; and the recent rise in the cost of numerous basic commodities with the decline in government controls and subsidies in the wake of neoliberal "structural adjustment," and its potential effect on people's sense of vulnerability within a growing space of marginality.

The question for us here is why and how certain old people become representative of the forces that seem to impinge upon households and communities, in both the normalized theodicy of everyday misfortune and violence and the extraordinary theodicy of social panics. How witchcraft may work as a way to confront misfortune has been one of the central themes in the anthropology of suffering.[8] My approach here will be to ask what is it that in extraordinary times makes the voice and appearance of certain persons not humorously or abjectly witchlike but frighteningly and uncannily so, and, moving in the other direction, to ask how the possibility or social memory of the uncanny may structure the everyday abjection of the interstitial dying space. How does the repetitive request of the elder for support become heard as a dangerous curse, and how do memories of the curse structure more everyday hearings?

In his essay on the experience of the *"unheimlich"* or "uncanny," Freud begins with two observations. First, after the philosopher Friedrich Schelling, he describes the class of things that tend to provoke an uncanny feeling in us as follows: "Everything is *unheimlich* that ought to have remained secret and hidden but has come to light." Second, he notes that the word's contrary, *heimlich* (and the same is true in different ways for "canny" and the more literal translation "homely"), can suggest not only the comfortable, trusted, and familiar but also the secretive and unpleasant, *"so that 'heimlich' comes to have the meaning usually ascribed to 'unheimlich.'"*[9] The familiar is suddenly strange: a rupture appears in the taken-for-grantedness of things. The old woman's everyday *bakbak* is suddenly weird and threatening.

This return of the repressed works on the usual two levels for Freud, suggesting both an earlier developmental stage of infantile narcissism and an earlier societal stage of primitive animism. Freud goes on to question why "the phenomenon of the 'double'"—the perceived repetition of events, likenesses, and experiences—often generates an uncanny feeling. For readers of Freud less committed to his specific narratives of child development and cultural evolution, the experience of the uncanny and particularly of the uncanny double has come to suggest a rupture in the symbolic order and a conflict between the meaning of a sign and its materiality.

The unexpected strangeness of the old body is rooted in the disruption of its familial significance. The familial body of the old person, whether literally displaced from its expected charpoy or hearth into the liminal space between households or discursively displaced from its familial context into a new administrative science of old age, regains a voice and is no longer the unhearable inhabitant of a dying space. For the urban middle class, over the past century, this displaced and suffering elder has periodically embodied a colonial and postcolonial predicament of culture in which the familiar and foreign form shifting hybrids.

For the rural and urban poor, we have seen how the politics and phenomenology of everyday weakness diminishes the unique significance of the old body. If the rupture of the familial itself is to an extent normalized, suffering old bodies may have less apocalyptic significance for the poor than for the *bhadralok* and structurally similar groups. Old bodies that bespeak millenarian promise—such as, perhaps, the old woman of the Balua affair who took no food for five days and nights—seem to do so by radically renouncing any familial dependency. Within the transactional networks sustaining persons and families in communities like Nagwa, the bodies of vulnerable children more than those of vulnerable elders may become metonyms of family and *ghar* and of their transactional health. For Siranji's family, the old woman was a far more ambivalent vehicle of the adequacy of their gifts than was her grandson Raju. Throughout Nagwa, old people were at risk for being perceived as useless mouths continually demanding chapatis destined for the equally vulnerable but far more promising young. When as in 1996 the relation between a marginalized community's health and the well-being and survival of its children appears radically threatened, particularly given the chapati counts that frame the young and old as contestants for survival, old persons may be at greater risk of becoming strange threats: witches, *lakarsunghvās*.

In gerontopolitan Varanasi, the ubiquity and ideological centrality of interstitial old bodies and voices renders them part of the normalized topography of the urban exterior: *rāṇḍ*, *sāṇḍ*, *sīṛhī*, sannyasi. Like cows and steps, widows and babas are familiar and only occasionally irksome features of the landscape. Interstitial old voices in the city do not threaten any but the youngest children. These are often teased by their older playmates—see the old woman, she's a witch, a *ḍāin*—and are shushed into bed by the admonitions of mothers and aunts: hush, or the *lakaṛsunghvā* will get you. Such scary tales might be seen to evoke and rehearse the crises of child development, after Freud, but in the context of everyday and extraordinary concerns surrounding child survival their ubiquity takes on a different cast.

The figure of the old baba or witch of play and bedtime fantasy, ready to devour or steal young children, recalls an uncanny circulation between the very old and very young, offering a grammar for a different sort of intimate enemy than the alienated familial bodies of Ghar Kali. In everyday play, the monstrous elderly are invoked to stabilize differences of age: the old but not very old tell of them to their children; the young but not very young tell of them to their younger siblings: young is to old as innocence and vulnerability are to knowledge and danger. But witches recall the fragility of the familial. At critical moments when the hegemonic obviousness and necessity of the social order threaten to collapse—when the strangeness of the order of things overwhelms its functional content—the order of generation itself is rendered unstable and opaque.

Michael Taussig in *The Devil and Commodity Fetishism in South America* described how Bolivian peasants in the context of the introduction of tin mining, the intensification of wage labor, and the commodification of body, time, land, relationships, and life, "captured" the transformations of commodity fetishization by "subjecting [them] to a paganism." The devil in peasant narrative is monstrous but not terrifying, an ambivalent figure reflecting the conflicted yet critical consciousness of peasants regarding the source of their growing affliction.[10] Witches and dangerous old babas are ambivalent in a different sense, humorous figures of everyday generational difference periodically transformed into monstrous figures of emergency. The oscillation between these may reflect an effort to capture a set of social processes by which both rural peasants and urban slum-dwellers are constituted as subjects through intensifying forms of commodification—of one's children, of one's body parts—that explode the borders of both the family and the body.

In the everyday play of children as well as in the literature of affliction of the region around Varanasi and more generally in north India, the relation between terror and abjection circles around the female witch.[11] Old men as babas, as I will discuss below, draw upon the dense field of the renunciate and the rishi. The ambiguity of the doubled figure of widow-witch specifically indexes the ambiguity of mother-aunt in the narrative of the Bad Family. Dogs, ghouls, and Bhairava are joined on their cremation ghat perambulations in urban folklore by the figures of *ḍāin*s and *curail*-like vampiresses; the old woman as dog and madwoman draws upon the stock figure of the *ḍāin*.

The psychoanalytic readings of Carstairs and Kakar identify the ubiquity of witches and demonesses in north Indian folklore and mythology in terms of the bad mother so central to their analyses: the demonic or witchlike bad mother is an oedipal archetype of the Indian child's perceived rejection by his inconstant mother when extended family pressure forces her to relinquish him to his father and uncles.[12] Such bad-mother explanations are impoverished, ignoring the experience of girls and women, the cross-societal frequency of witches and their historical transformations, the relation of witch accusations to land disputes, and the oscillation between the everyday and the monstrous. Even from within a psychodynamic framework—one attentive to the relation of sociocultural dimensions of child-rearing to the constitution of local worlds, to what Gananath Obeysekere has called deep structure[13] —the bad mother narrative avoids more interesting questions. Old witches are grandmothers or aunts far more than mothers. To exhaust their meaning within the framework of kinship in terms of the mother or her transformations is to elide the importance of other kin in family structure and particularly in the raising of children.[14]

In his discussion of the accused "witch" Dhapu in a Rajasthani village, Carstairs attempted to suggest that the old woman's aggressively angry voice—of which other villagers had long been resentful and sometimes afraid—laid the seeds for her eventual accusation as having caused various severe illnesses and misfortunes and her being hacked to death. Dhapu looked out for her own family's interests to an extreme; she was resented by all the other women and men of the village. Dhapu may have been at risk because she had "acted in such a manly fashion" throughout a series of land disputes. Chen has reinterpreted this material, showing the centrality of these land disputes to Dhapu's accusation and death.[15]

The relation between the exploitation of interstitial old women and the contested hearing of their voice emerges sharply in a 1911 short story by the Hindi writer Premchand, *Garīb kī hai*, "The Lament of the Poor." Premchand often wrote of life in the villages near Varanasi where he grew up. Manga, a Brahman widow like Mashima and Koki, entrusts her late husband's pension to the wealthy village advocate, Munshi Ramsevak, for safekeeping. She discovers only too late that he has spent much of it and has no intention of returning any. Manga goes to the village council for justice, "but a poor widow's anger is just the sound of a blank bullet that may scare a child but has no real effect at all." Manga stops working, stops keeping house, and devotes herself single-mindedly to her hatred of Munshi Ramsevak. Her progress from anger to *bakbak* to silence, culminating in her death, is narrated by Premchand as a chronicle of the metonymic voice.

This voice is at first barely present: there is no one, Premchand reminds us, who will listen to the voice of an old and poor widow. But her obsession transforms Manga dramatically, from a weak and unheard body into one increasingly identified entirely with her voice: "All day and all night, walking or sitting, she had only one idea: to inveigh against Munshi Ramsevak. Seated day and night at the door of her hut she fervently cursed him. For the most part in her pronouncements she employed poetic speech and metaphors so that people who heard her were astonished." Manga's voice moves from a direct language of complaint, which cannot be heard, to a rich and bloody use of metaphor, which is. As she shifts into a metalanguage in which she conveys her anger through the poetry of madness, Manga as voice finally gains an audience. There is, however, a price in becoming just a voice. Adults are astonished, children make fun of her, and "gradually her mind gave way. Bare-headed, bare-bodied, with a little hatchet in her hand, she would sit in desolate places. She abandoned her hut and was seen wandering around the ruins in a cremation ghat along the river—disheveled, red-eyed, grimacing crazily, her arms and legs emaciated."

The repetitive voice is located within the social marginality of the interstice, and precedes the fact of madness. As she becomes increasingly demonic, Manga moves from object of derision to one of fear: "When they saw her like this people were frightened. Now no one teased her even for fun." Manga becomes like a female ascetic, immersed in the signs of death; she is like a bitch, scrounging around the cremation ghat. And these transformations are expressed through her voice: "She had earned the title of the local mad woman [*pagli*]. She would sit alone, talking to herself for hours, expressing her intense desire to eat, smash, pinch and tear Ramsevak's flesh, bones, eyes, liver and the like, and when her hatred reached its climax she would turn her face toward Ramsevak's house and shriek the terrible words, 'I'll drink your blood!'"

Manga's voice is now that of the vampire witch. It is no longer the old person's lament for food: like the old woman of Balua, Manga refuses all transaction. "Manga ate nothing. . . . Even after a barrage of threats and abuse she refused to eat." All that remains is the primal voice—as witch, as beast, and as that epitome of inauspiciousness and danger, the owl: "More terrible than her words was her wild laughter. In the imagined pleasure of drinking Munshiji's blood she would burst into laughter that resounded with such demoniacal violence, such bestial ferocity that when people heard it in the night their blood was chilled. It seemed as though hundreds of owls were hooting together."

Manga lies on Munshi Ramsevak's threshold. Only one child—Ramsevak's own wayward son Ramgulam—continues to torment her. Eventually her cry subsides, she retreats into the last, silent voice of old age, and she dies on Ramsevak's doorstep. The advocate is ostracized for the murder of a Brahman, but for him and his wife a greater torment than the now-angry villagers is Manga herself, bodiless but still present as a voice. "Several times a low voice reached them from within the earth: 'I'll drink your blood. . . . '"[16] Ramsevak's wife dies of fright, Ramsevak ultimately immolates himself, taking on the classic fate of the abject widow, and Ramgulam, the mocker of old *paglīs*, winds up in the reformatory.

Premchand as social critic transforms the *paglī* from object of derision into agent of retributive justice. He does so through her voice, drawing on a heteroglot complex of interstitial voices contained in the lament of the *paglī*: dog, owl, fearsome ascetic witch. Yet Manga's victory requires her death: only the killing of a Brahman on his doorstep explodes the fiction of Munshi's reputation for *sevā*, the source of his moral standing. His family unravels. Manga's voice, previously discountable as that of the interstitial old woman and then bewildering as the curse of the madwoman, is ultimately located on the threshold of a bad family—which explains and redeems it. Again, Ghar Kālī.

The old woman of Ghar Kali is bare-breasted, a complex sign of her disengagement from material concerns and of her degraded treatment. The sexually explicit old widow also draws upon the erotic connotations of the widow as the unhusbanded woman and as the prostitute. A common word for "widow" also connotes whore. Saraswati, in his study of *kāśīvāsī* widows, noted the association frequently made by his Varanasi informants between widows and prostitutes. Young widows in particular were seen as having few other sources for meeting their economic needs and sensual cravings.[17]

The threat of both the young widow's body and the old widow's voice was mediated through its institutionalization in bhajan. Bhajan was central to middle-class piety in the colonies. Amita Mukherjee and many of her neighbors attended groups of older women and sometimes men who sang hymns together, daily or weekly. For indigent widows, bhajan was not only a site of community but a source of livelihood.

On Mir Ghat, not far from the cremation pyres of Manikarnika Ghat, a beautiful old red brick building that had seen finer days housed one such bhajan ashram. Here both young and old widows stayed in exchange for their voices. They sang bhajans throughout the day, financed by patrons who accumulated merit through both the gift itself and the praises of God sung. The threat of the widow's body was inverted: in the ashram, nonwidows threatened. The building was well-guarded by neighbors and the widows themselves. On an early visit, a widow who decided that I was up to no good chased me up the steps of the ghat with a stick. The separation of the bhajan ashram from the dangers of the interstice was aggressively maintained.

The production of bhajan transformed the repetitious voice from *bakbak* to divine rhythm, and offered a space to contain the simultaneously dangerous and endangered body. The voice *of* the body—the complaint of the destitute or uncared for or sexually ambiguous widow—is silenced; it becomes the voice *without* a body, or rather, is given a new body, the divine body of Krishna. But constant disembodiment was a burden for most of the ashram widows; they tended to grind through their bhajans soullessly. Their rather mournful noise, early in the morning on Mir Ghat, was occasionally punctuated by the voices of women on pilgrimage—as the boats of the latter drifted by the windows of the room—chanting bhajans joyously. For its hearers, there was irony in the institutionalized bhajan; it could not but point elsewhere. "How is their health?" I asked a young man who lives behind the Mir Ghat Bhajan Ashram, about the widows. He shrugged, "They are old." "And how are their minds?" I continued. He shrugged again, "They sing bhajans." Safe from being heard as doglike or witchlike, these voices of God still spoke to the absence of family and to the unhappy mind of the interstitial old woman.

DOGS AND OLD MEN

In his well-known story "*Būṛhī kākī*" ("Old Aunt"), Premchand tells of an unnamed elderly aunt, a childless widow, whose nephew Buddhiram ceases to care for her once she makes over her property to him. Like Manga, the old aunt suffers because she has "no one," but though she is treated like a *paglī* she does not become one. Her two grandnephews persecute her because "children have a natural antipathy to the old": "One would pinch her and flee; the other would douse her with water. Auntie would shriek and start to cry. But it was well known that she only cried for food, so no one would have paid attention to her grief and cries of distress."

The aunt is reduced to a voice identified solely with her demands upon her family for food; she is not heard otherwise. She is treated like a *paglī* but her voice, within domestic space, never threatens to become inhuman. The conflict between the *sās* and *bahū* is lifelong. Though the aunt is marginalized, she remains conceived by her relations as an active combatant in the chapati wars, in the contested economy of the hearth. The domestic old woman is here less a dog than a child. In the context of the old aunt, Premchand notes that "old age is often a return to childhood." Childhood is here a return to a less abject orality than that of the dog, to the mind's identification with the mouth and its paired functions of eating and lament: "The old aunt had no effort left for anything save the pleasures of the tongue, and to attract attention to her troubles she had no means but to cry."[18] The child suggests the inversion of power and of role, but it remains within the language of kinship, within the space of domestic logic.

Buddhiram organizes a feast to celebrate his son's engagement ceremony, or tilak. The old aunt is beside herself smelling all the food being prepared. But she is afraid she'll incur her nephew's wife's wrath if she should step near the hearth.

She cannot control herself, however, and twice comes out of her room at inappropriate times to ask for a *purī*, a piece of bread. Both times she is soundly scolded and sent back without anything, and in the end she is forgotten about. Her grandniece, the one family member sympathetic to her, leads her during the night to the soiled plates of the guests, where the old Brahman aunt stuffs the polluted leftovers into her mouth. She has at last become a beast. Her nephew's wife discovers her there, and at last recognizes the Bad Family in the unexpected image of the dog. The story ends not in the chaos of the voice and then death, but in the return from second childhood toward a reclaimed adulthood. The voice of the old aunt comes again to represent her reasonable needs and claims to status and is no longer an icon of an infinite desire. Once transactional flows are restored, once the nephew's wife allows the Bad Family to heal, the question of second childhood recedes.

As old *kāśīvāsī* women are more frequently the dogs of the interstice than are old babas; old men are more frequently the dogs of domestic space. Mausaji was frequently described as a dog by his family in Chittupur: eating, shitting, pissing, barking. The identification of the old man with the dog recurs in classical Puranic and Ayurvedic descriptions of old age. When the old man—who had symbolically maintained his youth, "sixty years young," against the weakness of the son—finally does fall into powerless decrepitude, the move from head of household to supplicant conveys a far more abject reality than the cyclical politics of *bahū* and *sās*. Old men who give up household power are described in the *Bhāgavata Purana*:

> Being unable to maintain his family, the unfortunate fellow, whose all attempts have ended in failure, becomes destitute of wealth and miserable. Being at a loss to know what to do; the wretch goes on brooding and sighing. Just as miserly farmers neglect old (and hence useless bulls), his wife and others do not treat him with respect as before, as he has become incapable of maintaining them. . . . He is now nourished by those whom he had brought up. He stays in the house like a dog eating what is contemptuously thrown to him.[19]

In the Bengali quarter, an old friend of mine had announced along with Bijay his interest in helping me find crazy old people. Bijay "realized" the appropriateness of the Dog Lady within several days, but my friend Bishwanath waited six months before suggesting one day that I visit his maternal grandfather, his *dādū*, who talked funny in a way he thought I would find interesting. When the invitation came, I had already developed my little symbolic interactionist tool kit and decided without too much reflection that Dadu's *sahī nahīn* voice had of course suggested the threat of bad *sevā* to his family, and my being introduced to him thus carried some risk. I was less interested in plumbing the violence and grace surrounding a friendship.

There was another issue. That I was introduced to Dadu at all may have had to do in part with the different connotations within domestic space of the weak old voice across gender. I was introduced by friends to far more "not right"–voiced old men than old women. A family was more often on the defensive about the nature of an old woman's voice. Much might explain such an "observation," but within the sorts of differently gendered semantic networks I was exploring I found the more naturalized state of domestic old men being-the-dog at least a partial way into thinking about their slightly diminished threat of bad *sevā*. To frame the difference another way: old men were less ambivalently placed within a dying space than were old women.

At a friend's anniversary party in New Delhi, a rather drunk businessman in his fifties from Chandigarh told me a story about aging and becoming a dog. He approached me and asked me what I studied, and I answered "senility." He said: "You know what we call this here. . . . "

"*Saṭhiyānā?*" I finished his sentence for him, eager to demonstrate some cultural legitimacy. "Yes," he said, although he was about to offer a different answer and tried the question again. "But in Punjab, do you know that we say . . . " "*Sattar-bahattar*," I jumped the gun again. "Yes." He paused. "And why do you think there is a twelve-year difference between the U.P.-walas and Biharis and the Punjabis . . . ?" A group had gathered by then, and we laughed at the joke, although we never did articulate just what that difference might be. The man went on to bring up the Bengali term "*bāhāttūre*" as well, and the group played with the ethnic distinctions the terms allowed. A Bengali man joined the group and began to explain the distinction between the Bengali and Hindi terms through elaborate references to astrology and the life cycle. His explanation went on for some time, and people began to drift away until the first man jumped in with a joke:

> When God was handing out life spans to all the creatures of the world, they all stood in line. Each animal was handed a packet of forty years. For this animal, for that one. All received the same amount. Last in line was man, and God handed him a packet with forty years in it, too. I'm sorry, said God, but that's all I have left. You're last in line. I'm all out of years to give.
>
> But the ox said to man, "I really don't want forty years of hard labor. I'll be glad to give you twenty of mine.
>
> And then the dog said, "And my life isn't worth forty years. I'll give you twenty, too."
>
> Finally, the monkey too decided that forty years of hopping about trees was more than enough and gave twenty of his years to man.
>
> So now man had a life span of one hundred years.
>
> For the first forty years of our life, therefore, we are truly men—the years God gave to us.
>
> Then, from forty to sixty, we are living the years of the ox, working for the wife, for our sons, supporting everyone else in the family, nothing for oneself.
>
> Then, from sixty to eighty, we are a dog! [He laughed.] The son asks us to mind the house, mind the children—"We're going out." And so we stay at home, guarding the house. And barking: Always asking for this or that, again and again and again. Like the dog.
>
> And then, from eighty to one hundred, we're living the monkey's years, without teeth, without speech, just making the motions of being human.

A man's aging is illustrated through a bestiary. Against the cosmic theories of *āśramadharma* the other man was offering, the first man offers a refiguring of the life course in terms of three distinct but each unpleasant forms of dehumanization. Adulthood here peaks at forty, envisioned as the burden of carrying along one's wife and weak sons. Sixty remains the time of political inversion, when the meaning of debility shifts from the burden of the powerful (the father as ox) to the subordinate duties of the grandfather (the father as dog). After sixty, the voice becomes central, the abject request of the man forced to beg from his own son. At eighty, a different meaning of senility is offered, not the political abjection of the dog, but the far more embodied decay of the voiceless old man, for whom the request has degenerated thoroughly into meaninglessness: the monkey.

Dogs, within the bestiary of human abjection, draw upon particular genealogies of the gift. In a lengthy enumeration of the duties of the mature householder, the *Bhāgavata Purāṇa* places the food-giver at the center of the cosmos. All creatures are his children: "One should look upon beasts, camels, donkeys, monkeys, rats, serpents, birds and flies like one's own sons." One should allow, the text suggests, these animals access to one's house and fields. Rats and snakes and monkeys, like sons, take. Beyond taking, the text goes to define a specific category of those who must be given to: "He should duly share his objects of enjoyment with all down to dogs, sinners and people belonging to the lowest strata of the society."[20] Dogs are the embodiments of those too degraded even to take, within a gendered mode of exchange between fathers and sons in which the gift does not rehumanize, as it does for Premchand's Old Aunt, but marks the end of manhood and thus one's humanity.

OLD MEN AND BABAS

Near my house in the Bengali quarter, an old East Bengali Brahman schoolteacher lived alone in a small room. "His family didn't want him," my neighbor told me, her story thoroughly unsubstantiated. The room was dark and only four feet in height, and the old man would crouch inside, making his food, his voice eerily projecting from his little cave. Unlike the old *kāśīvāsī* women in the area, the old saffron-clad man was seldom teased, though he seemed to have all the ingredients: no apparent family, an eccentric manner, frequent requests for raw foodstuffs, and a funny voice. Two doors down from this man lived another former Bengali schoolteacher, in his seventies, with his family. Unlike the saffron man they called Baba, the children of neighbors made fun of this man for his frequent and pathetic complaining. In hearing Baba, however, kids and passersby drew on a more complex hermeneutic of generosity: Baba seemed to be a sannyasi, and his voice was many things to different people—beneficent, guileful, hypocritical, transgressive, or enlightening—but seldom meaningless or strange.

The old man in the little room was not attached to any *sampradaya*, any particular ascetic order. In the late 1960s, Surajit Sinha and Baidyanath Saraswati studied the sannyasis of Varanasi and calculated that the number of ascetics residing more or less permanently in the city in monastic institutions called maths was 1,284. About 300 ascetics were not attached to a math, but maintained ties to a *sampradaya* while living on their own. Sinha and Saraswati suggested that of the total population of the city during their study in the 1970s, 1 in 240 persons was an ascetic.[21] This ratio did not include the considerable numbers of sadhus (holy men) of various sorts who arrived and stayed in the city seasonally; nor did it include individuals like this old Baba, who did not belong to any religious order but dressed the part, participated with friends in any of a number of the myriad devotional, educational, and recreational opportunities of Kashi, wandered the lanes of the city, and worked the foreign "hippies" for a living.

The last task was one of Baba's more challenging but remunerative. He spent time on Dasashwamedh Ghat, the busiest and the most central of the ghats, striking up conversations with the many young foreigners who arrived each day in the city. Varanasi remained one of the principal stops on another latter-day touristic, that of "Asia on a shoestring" budget travelers, for whom the city's yogis, musicians, and cremations—along with Goa's beaches, Mother Teresa's Calcutta homes for the dying, Dharamsala's Tibetans and treks, and Kathmandu's evergreen psychedelic scene—reworked the colonial grand tour Cohn has described. Within the narrative of the budget tour, Varanasi was a microcosm of India, particularly in being a "love it or hate it" kind of place, the mother lode of the negative currency of the young traveler, "the hassles." An inveterate teacher and relatively fluent English speaker, Baba delighted in introducing interested young tourists hassle-free into the mysteries of Hinduism. The challenge was to make the foreigners, who tended to take Baba along with the river, the cremation fires, and the cows as a found object, and who got nervous at the hint of a quid pro quo, lighten their own material burden a bit without losing their feeling of control.

Banarsis heard the voices of sannyasis with some ambivalence, either as the wheedling of charlatans or the blessing of the god-realized, or both. The former hearing dominated; Banarsis, who contend with sannyasis on a daily basis, were apt to be jaded. Like old widows, old babas were part of a topography. But the interstitial location of their voices redeemed them. Sannyasis and other sadhus and babas who lived throughout the Hindu neighborhoods of the *pakkā mahal* had voices that were hearable as benign and on occasion positively transformative: those of latter-day rishis. One could make fun of Baba on Dasashwamedh, with his hippies, but in the neighborhood he was neither a figure of derision or pity. And the hearing of his voice drew upon more famous, and archetypal, voices, of renowned old holy men in the city or the state whose voices were distinguished by their radically unusual tenor. Some of these men blessed through swears, sexual language, and curses; some spoke on rare occasions only; some never spoke.

On Assi Ghat, a few feet from where the woman from Nagwa would come to sing by the Sangameswar Temple, was a small Saivite math, a place for sannyasis headed by Ramu Baba. Like most strangely voiced babas, Ramu Baba was said to be superannuated by the men from the community who frequented the math's nightly *āratī*, the worship service, in the small shrine adjoining his room. He was eighty, ninety, one hundred, or more. Ramu Baba remained in his room all day in meditation. He came out publicly once a day, in the evening after the *āratī*, to give these men a darshan, a viewing of him. He would say nothing; he never spoke. His *nazar*, his gaze, seemed all the more powerful. His eyes burnt into you; they seemed to know all that needed to be known about you. They were joking, thoughtful, deadly serious. Ramu Baba was an archetype of the silent voice, of the *jīvanmukta*, the realized in life.

Samne Ghat was on the Ganga bank just south of Nagwa and east of the sprawling BHU campus. At that time, it was the staging point for the passenger ferries across the river to Ramnagar during the monsoons; the rest of the year, a pontoon bridge linked the city to Ramnagar via the ghat. Since the mid-1990s, a bridge has been built spanning the river; its pylons were, according to a persistent but usually humorous rumor, build on the bodies of children collected by the state through its *lakaṛsunghvā* agents. In the late 1980s, one took a ferry or hired a small boat. A Banarsi friend once cryptically told me that halfway between Ramnagar and Samne Ghat, on the water, I would meet someone "for your project." Later, after I had met the Beriya Baba, I returned and asked the friend why he thought to mention him to me. I got an answer similar to the one Bijay gave me about Mashima; contemplating my project, this man for the first time decided that the Baba might be mad.

I went down to Samne Ghat, that first day. Across the water I saw a small wooden houseboat. "Who lives there?" I asked the tea shop regulars presiding over the coming and going of boats.

"That's Beriya Baba."
"Who is he?"
"He's an old baba."
"How old?"
"I don't know . . . about eighty?"
"Can I visit him?"
"He doesn't ever want to be bothered. He'll just curse you."

But one of the boatmen agreed to take me across. On the way, he told me to be extremely respectful.

"Make sure you greet him very politely [*praṇām karnā*]. He's very old."
"How old?"
"Oh, at least a hundred."

"Where does his name come from?" I asked. "From a *ber* (plum or jujube) tree," said the boatman. "He uses it for his worship." Another friend later said that Beriya Baba used to live up a tree, and had vowed never set foot on the ground. That was why he now lived on a boat, neither on one shore nor the other. The image of King Ajara's former sannyasi body in the *Kathāsaritsāgara* story, hanging from a tree, came to mind. Several superannuated babas were famed for their never having touched the ground in recent memory. The most famous was Devraha Baba, at 140 the oldest of them all. Devraha Baba lived in small stilted huts, and when he was transported was lifted into the car or boat by which he was transported. Both babas structured their practice as radically disjunctive from the material world through their literal embodiment as luftmenschen.

The Plum-Tree Baba was sitting crouched in the small enclosed deck that doubled as bedroom and kitchen. He was naked except for a sweater. "*Praṇām*, Maharaj," I perhaps too obsequiously intoned, trained less by the boatman's admonition than by my frequent watching of the tv serial *Mahābhārata* in which all old rishis as well as kings were so addressed. "Sister-fucker," Baba immediately replied. He showered a variety of curses down upon me, and then began a discourse on proper dharma, punctuated by references to sex and illustrated by frequent obscene gestures: his continually simulating sex with his fingers and his panting out "thrust, withdraw, thrust, withdraw." For Beriya Baba, material reality without God was bestial, just eating and having sex.

> If people don't sing *bhajans*, if they don't keep their mind on God, they are no better than a dog or a bitch. Thrust withdraw thrust withdraw. The government—the police and the inspectors—are just hungry animals. Thrust withdraw thrust withdraw. They rape everyone's daughters. They like to fuck their own daughters. Thrust withdraw thrust withdraw. All the government wants is cunt, is ass. Sister fuckers. Ass fuckers. Split everyone's ass right open by the fucking inspectors. Thrust withdraw thrust withdraw. Just dogs. Bitches.

Somewhat taken aback by the force of Baba's discourse, I nervously changed the subject. "How old are you, Baba?" "120 years." I looked at him; he didn't seem a day over 80. Perhaps sensing my questioning gaze, he downplayed his age. "But that's nothing, Devraha Baba is 140!"

Young at 120, Baba resumed his lesson, describing citizens as policemen's daughters, seeking incestuous liaisons with power. I left some money as my gift, and Baba gave the boatman and me some sweets as prasad, the materialization of his grace, in return. We returned to shore. I asked the tea shop crowd why Baba swore so much. "Well, to keep people away," one man answered. But some had other ideas. Baba used insults to tell us: You are a *bhogī*, a seeker after pleasure. I am a yogi. So you should not come here. And you should give up acting like animals if you want to discover God.

But why, I persisted, if Baba is indeed a *jīvanmukta*, one liberated in this life, is he so obsessed with sex? The men in the shop concurred in their answer: "It's because you are the *bhogī* that Baba is goaded to challenge your right to be on his boat. He is a mirror of yourself." Baba combined one of the great ascetic archetypes of the city, the aghori baba, the transgressive ascetic who curses, drinks, lives and meditates in the inhuman and impure space of the cremation ghat and eats the ashes from cremations.[22] Like an aghori, Beriya Baba cursed to bless. His words were transformative, cutting through the fondness for pleasure that deafens one to reality. Like the anger of the rishis, the curses of the babas *give*.

I left Samne Ghat, and went home to Nandanagar colony where I was then still living. I mentioned meeting Beriya Baba to Mrs. Sharma; she doubted that he was 120 or that his words were of any spiritual import. He was a fake, "not the same thing as Devraha Baba," she concluded. Beriya Baba was not always heard as a spiritual cynosure. But though he was considered a charlatan by quite a few, his interstitial role cut off any connection to a familial body and its associated critical hearing. One did not say of any of the many babas, big or small time, in the city: "He has no one." Old men were heard differently in the interstice. And every local fake pointed to true ones. Beriya Baba might not be 120, but Devraha Baba's 140 years were seldom challenged.

BABAS AND THE STATE

Though Beriya Baba criticized the sarkar, the government, and its representatives the police, he proudly told us that the Prime Minister Indira Gandhi herself had sent him a letter. The tea shop men told me that another prime minister, Charan Singh, had visited Baba years back. "He swears at all of them," they assured me. Baba's curses are not only heard to be powerful, they are powerful. Politicians come to collect them.

Stanley Tambiah, in his study of the Thai Buddhist cult of amulets, broadened the Weberian notion of charisma to include its objectification and translocation through economies of force or exchange. In concluding, he notes that ascetic masters claiming supranormal powers "have been taken up and assiduously visited by the country's politicians, bureaucrats, and intelligentsia—especially from the metropolis." Like the amulets in which a saint's charisma is recognized to be embedded, the visit to a saint itself becomes a fetishized commodity, which ruling elites with increasingly questionable legitimacy collect. Tambiah indicates: "The political center is losing its self-confidence, but it has not lost its might; it searches for and latches onto the merit of the holy men who are the center of religion but peripheral to its established forms."[23]

The visit, in Uttar Pradesh in India, to a superannuated saint allows for the transfer of charisma through the several sensory pathways through which the baba and the political visitor mix their substance, and the various media record and disseminate the transaction. Intergenerational charismatic transfers increasingly depend upon the image of the transfer, suggesting that the process Tambiah records is dual: the politician's personal need for a renewable source of old age charisma, and the necessary production of simulacra of the transaction for its effectiveness.

Each of these sensorial modes can be thus approached both in terms of an anthropology and a political economy of the senses.[24] *Seeing* the baba, in the first instance, is a form of darshan. As Eck has noted, darshan can be a central act of

Hindu worship; seeing and being seen potentiates a transfer of substance between deity and devotee, and the act extends to holy persons:

> When Mahatma Gandhi traveled through India, . . . they would throng the train stations for a passing glimpse of the Mahatma in his compartment. Similarly, when Swami Karpatri, a well-known sannyasi who is also a writer and political leader, comes to Varanasi to spend the rainy season "retreat" period, people flock to his daily lectures not only to hear him, but to see him. However, even an ordinary sannyasi or sadhu is held in esteem in traditional Hindu culture. He is a living symbol.[25]

The examples of Gandhi and Karpatri are instructive in other, quite different, ways. Shahid Amin has explored the complexity of Gandhi darshan in eastern Uttar Pradesh, suggesting that peasants and landlords took away different and often opposed forms of charismatic empowerment from the phenomena of massive Gandhi darshan rallies in the early 1920s.[26] The darshan of the late Karpatri, whose house I chanced to rent and who haunted the memories of Marwari Mataji and of the Tambe brothers discussed above, differently helped to realize the various projects of his urban anti-Chamar supporters and his royal patrons. Similarly, the charisma of the politician's Devraha Baba darshan became an increasingly contested site in the 1980s, and the effectiveness of living symbols came to depend upon the effectiveness of media management.

Tasting as a mode of charismatic transfer establishes a symbolic hierarchy between the charismatic source and the recipient who is willing to accept the theoretically polluted but auspicious leftovers of the deity or saint. In the commensal transaction of a puja, the worshipper offers appropriate foodstuffs to God, who consumes the essence of the gift and allows the giver to partake of the seemingly intact but now "leftover" portion as the grace of prasad. Beriya Baba offered me his own food—literal leftovers, in his case—as prasad. The transaction was more complex because as a patron I had given him money. The hierarchy established through an exchange of coded substance, in the sense of Marriott and his students, which confirmed my willingness to accept his pollution, rhetorically extinguished the traces of a different hierarchy in which Baba was a client. When one gave to widows, the gift was unidirectional, save in the collective institution of the bhajan ashram through the mediation of a management who kept most of the gift, and here food was exchanged solely for voice.

Touching is similarly a mode of establishing the unambiguous direction of the flow of charismatic power. The tea stall men and the boatman reminded me to stay off of Baba's boat. To step aboard would have been to lift myself above him as well as to bring to earth, in a sense, his distanced position. Central to the embodied performance of hierarchy was the polarity of head and foot. For Devraha Baba, given his position on a platform on stilts, encounters with visitors were more easily managed. The main practice for the politician taking darshan of Devraha Baba was to have Baba place his feet directly on the politician's head. The image—simultaneously that of extreme obeisance and powerful legitimation—

appeared in newspapers throughout the country whenever an important politician came to Devraha Baba for darshan. More than any other sensory mode, the choreography of the touch translated into the national darshan of the aged saint with his feet on the prime minister, an image akin to the politician-son touching the feet of the old widow-mother but with one critical difference: no matter how opportunistic politicians might try to stage-manage their encounters with Baba, he remained a source of charisma whose presence was never exhausted by the hypocrisy of the filial scene.

Finally, charisma is transferred through its hearing. Beriya Baba cursed, and his supplicants took away blessings. Devraha Baba would sit silently in front of his little hut during those festivals when he was available for darshan, and would not speak. The tension for the listener would grow, until Baba would suddenly begin to offer a discourse, usually on Krishna devotion as a path opposed to the pleasures of this world. Like Beriya Baba's voice, Devraha's voice challenged in its unpredictability: he would withhold his presence and voice, sitting hidden inside his aerial hut and then would suddenly appear, sit silently in view, and then suddenly speak.

The importance of the voice draws more on generational than divine transaction. The old body becomes a source of powerful charisma when it no longer constitutes a threat to children seeking legitimation of the morality of their appropriation of the household. Like Buddhist amulets, old bodies enshrined in well-kept dying spaces become powerful icons and indices of the moral legitimacy of a family. The old body, in a sense, is fetishized, and as such becomes available as a critical marker within the legitimating discourse of the nation-state and its discontents.

But familiar old bodies degenerate, provoking the continual crises of *sevā* anxiety. The charisma of older male authority—among politicians, figures from Devi Lal and Laloo Prasad Yadav to the late N. T. Rama Rao and M. G. Ramachandran before their final decline come to mind—must eventually give way to the abjection of the weak old father forced to beg like a dog. The baba out there—as a sannyasi already ritually dead, as a latter-day rishi living apart from society—offers a voice that cannot devolve into lament. When babas threaten, as in the nursery stories of child-stealing babas with large sacks, told to children, or as in the collapse of the language of witchcraft, international conspiracy, and child-lifting babas into the 1996 *lakaṛsunghvā* panic, they threaten in an uncanny conjuncture of the domestic and interstitial old man, as a double to the father. As authority and charisma out there, they mirror the father as a site of male authority; as the domestic old man, they are a simulacrum of male authority, its pale shadow—"without speech, just making the motions of being human"—save for the sound of an infinite and ever more impossible desire, the bark.

The old "babas" beaten in 1996 were often with children, usually their grandchildren or other relations, when they were seen and heard to be uncanny and dangerous, and what was very hard to read was the nature of their desire. For most old men with access to the rhetorical possibilities of *sannyāsa*, even a partial relocation of their identity from home to interstice was insufficient to transform their relations with family and neighbors from the pathetic request of the old grandfather to the inviolate liminality of the luftmensch.

Every sixteen years, the great astrological festival the Kumbh Mela is held in Allahabad, the closest city of similar size to Varanasi and also a pilgrimage site of long standing. Sannyasis and other interstitial holy men and women from throughout the country gather along with millions of pilgrims in what has become perhaps the largest single assemblage of persons in human history. A city is erected for the sannyasis and others, a literal center out there in Victor Turner's sense.[27] In 1989 as in previous Kumbh Melas, Devraha Baba would not camp within the bounds of the interstitial city, this decentered center. A sannyasi's sannyasi, he maintained his separation even during the festival's collapse of the boundaries.

I attended the Allahabad Kumbh Mela that year along with my friend Pankaj Mishra and an estimated 15 million others. To visit Devraha Baba, we had to walk for several kilometers away from the tent city at the confluence of the Ganga and the Yamuna, along the sandy banks. Hundreds of pilgrims formed a line across the sand ahead of us, making the same trek. Baba's management had set up a corral of sorts, into which we pushed our away. Inside, I saw Baba's familiar hut on stilts; I had seen it at other pilgrimage centers, but had never had the chance for a Devraha darshan. Baba was inside the hut, not visible to us, when we drew as close as we could. Hundreds of villagers were waiting for darshan and a sermon. Closest to Baba's hut, several well-dressed people in suits and fashionable saris waited with photographers in attendance. Someone nearby told his companion: "Politicians." They too were part of the expected scene.

While we all waited, a man in a politician's pressed white pajama-kurta and paunch gave us a long talk on the message of Devraha Baba and Hindu dharma. The talk was uninspiring, save for the fact that already by 1989 any linkage of the importance for the nation of "Hindutva," or Hindu-ness, particularly in the presence of politicians, suggested the then-coalescing rhetoric of the recently revitalized populist Hindu right. Despite his offering his feet, with detached equanimity, to Congress, Janata Dal, and Bharitiya Janata Party [BJP] supplicants alike, Baba's superannuated charisma was coming to signify the meaning of tradition in very specific ways. The man exhorted the audience to go and buy a three-volume set on the life and worship of Krishna, available at the edge of the enclosure, which Baba would then bless with his feet. A line of peasants formed by the book counter.

Baba's head briefly stuck itself out the door of the hut and then disappeared back inside. He looked, I thought, far older than Beriya Baba. Many Banarsis with whom I talked about Devraha Baba told me the same routinized narrative of how old Baba must be:

When I was a boy, my grandfather took me to see Deoria Baba [another name for Devraha, who is said to come from the town of Deoria]. He looked the same then as

he does now. And my grandfather told me that when he was young, he was taken to
see Baba, and was old then, too!

Grandfathers take grandsons who become grandfathers themselves; Baba remains
the stable icon anchoring this narrative of skipped generations. The visit to the
baba suggests a framing of time—the infamous "cyclical time" of the non-West[28]
—distinct from the proximate temporality between father and son dependent on
the father's ageless—sixty but strong—body; A. R. Radcliffe-Brown long ago suggested that the social reproduction of culture and time worked through these two
modes, parents to children and grandparents to grandchildren.[29] Each mode presumes a certain sort of body in time: the relation between father and son presumes
the ageless body of the father, able to carry its hegemony agelessly without the
signs of decrepitude locating and delimiting its power; the relation between
grandfather and grandson presumes the body of the ageless—*but aged*—baba, not
that of the grandfather himself who may relationally framed as weak and in decline but of Old Age out there, transfigured. Devraha Baba's old age is the sign of
a different order of culture and power, and it is an order intensely appealing to
politicians constituted by a different order. I heard the grandfather story frequently, its details seldom varying from telling to telling. As an urban folk tale, it
reflected both the importance of Devraha's really being old—against the easy suspicion lavished on lesser figures like Beriya Baba—and the power of the interstitial old man as a sign of an alternate masculine order of age and power than the
dynamics of generational domesticity.

Devraha's authenticity was maintained by his firm colonization of the periphery. Not only Indira Gandhi but members of both Congress and the various opposition parties in the 1989 national elections sought out Baba's feet, photographers on hand. The home minister in Rajiv Gandhi's cabinet, the Sikh Buta
Singh, came to Devraha Baba in search of Hindu legitimacy. BJP politicians
brought bricks for the Ram temple to be built on the site of the disputed mosque
in Ayodhya; Baba placed his feet on these, too. In the year following the Kumbh
Mela, the last year of his long life, Baba became increasingly identified with a
"pro-Hindu" political stance, less and less of the antinomian center out there.
Brought down to earth perhaps, in the end, by the colonization of the forest as explicitly Hindu, as opposed to antinomian, space, Baba died in 1990.

Until the end, many besides the powerful continued to take Baba's darshan, his
voice, his books, and if fortunate, his feet. Baba's longevity, I was frequently told,
came from his mastery of yoga. Many yoga masters in Varanasi were known to
have lived for generations through both their accumulated siddhis or "mind-over-
matter" powers, and more specifically through breath control. As the number of
one's breaths in the course of a lifetime is fixed, a venerable yogic idea, a key to
longevity is learning to breathe less often. Even if one didn't attempt the practice
of yoga, the charismatic transaction with the master of his or her body was itself
an embodied encounter. Devraha, the master of the body, offered its gifts as so

many siddhis: health, fertility, potency, power, wealth. Unlike the hegemonic order of the politician and father, which worked time by denying its effects—like the agelessness of the "sixty years young" adult able to defer the claims of old age— the order of the charismatic baba insisted on its elaborated embodiment: the 140 year old visage, the matchstick limbs, the feet gingerly lowered, the careful location in a tree, or on a boat.

The Age of the Anthropologist

The problem, said the Friend, one of the closest I had made during the years of *No Aging in India*, is that we have grown up. It was over a decade since both project and friendship had been conceived, and I was back in Delhi writing another final draft. New timetables had intruded: a job, a relationship, changes in the economy, the imponderabilia of life. Things seemed different, and we waited for a sign from one another across the minor embarrassment that was our sense of ourselves in time.

Barbara Myerhoff wrote that to be an anthropologist in the country of the Old was to study the Other that is one's future self.[1] Myerhoff died of cancer before becoming the old lady of her imagined future, and the tragic irony of her effort to number her days—to see how the self and the world were unmade and remade in time and therefore to know oneself in it—gifted us with a sense of the gerontological sublime. A teacher of mine once said we become doctors because we are afraid of death, and something similar could be argued for gerontologists and more generally for moderns. Gerontology in this sense may be the quintessentially modern social science, marking off the shifting limits to interiority and to life. The failure of its sublime for me may lie in being part of a cohort of persons hard hit by AIDS, many of whom did not or will not live to be old—and thus the fears I seem to carry with me each day and which inflect and infect my sense of a horizon—though I distrust my sentiments here. This book has charted some of the many other places and reasons for the failure of such a sublime, the "No" of its title.

But it is not just as a body set against death that one does and writes, but as one set against time, and change, and decay. These are obviously related but distinct things, and the book has been centered on the last of them. The decay of the body, the social and material fact against which modern gerontology was organized and around which "postmodern" gerontology is being articulated, has presented a critical problem to anthropology since its origins. One of the discipline's charter narratives was that of the dying and regenerated god-king of James Frazer's *The Golden Bough*. Primitives and tropicals make tropaic errors, in Frazer, and confuse the well-being of the social body with that of the individual body of the king or priest totemically standing for it. At the first sign of physical decay, the individual body must be replaced by a younger one: the struggle in the sacred grove, the regeneration of the social body through the killing of the king and his replacement by a body once again ageless, like the substitution of Ajara for Vinayashila in the *Kathāsarītsāgara*.

Frazer can be read as more than an armchair anthropologist brandishing a theory of primitive error; his category of "magic," the nexus between the decay of the individual and the social body, becomes the realm of the symbolic for both later anthropologists and for psychoanalysts. The story of the Golden Bough, of the violent rupture at the heart of the sacred, offers a way to think about the relation of the body in time to the totalization of social relations as a seamless, purposeful, and atemporal hegemony, the anthropologist's Culture. The position of the king, priest, or god—in psychoanalytic terms the position of the father—is not only a position in and of language (as it was for Max Muller and would be for some Lacanians) but is, for Frazer, a fundamentally *embodied* stance: when the body reveals its temporality with the first recognizable signs of old age, the king/god/father must die. The body of language and culture is not simply the body of the powerful but of the powerful able to stand outside of time, a body hegemonic in not revealing its temporal contingency but appearing just so. The powerful individual body and the social body are metonymically linked as presences out of time, obviously and necessarily just so, totalities whose comportment and configuration are maps of the self-evident relations between their parts.

But the "ageless" individual body becomes *marked*: age comes to matter. The recognizable signs of decay—the white hairs that alert Vinayashila to the collapse of his world, framed as his ability to hold onto his subjects and to younger women—create a scene in which the hierarchical relations between king and subject, man and woman, and old and young become palpable and contestable. A younger body, one not recognizable as *aging*, must be substituted so that the seamless continuity of the social world can be maintained.

This need for the continuity of the world in time is formally a matter of primitive error for Frazer, but one that as cultural critique he implicitly extends to his own modern Christian world. Primitive error in *The Golden Bough*—the desire for the maintenance of a totalized world in space and time through signifying practices of metaphor and metonymy—suggests the potential for an analytics of culture that recognizes the problem of history—of change, death, and time. If culture is the possibility of the coherence of things in time, the story of the dying and regenerated king in Frazer locates the violence at its heart. The act of suture, which preserves the order of things through a substitution of bodies, is an act of destruction, the heart of darkness that for Frazer ultimately lies not in the nature of primitivism or civilization or the desire of the child but in the possibility of meaning, of the move from time to totality, hegemony to culture, body to sign. And if modernity and coloniality replace this possibility of the coherence of things in time with a normalizing reason and a frozen metanarrative of absence and loss, then the decaying body moves from its secret place in the sacred grove into the full light of day, and the body of the king and the father is replaced by the new corporeality of the citizen, of the old woman at the polls.

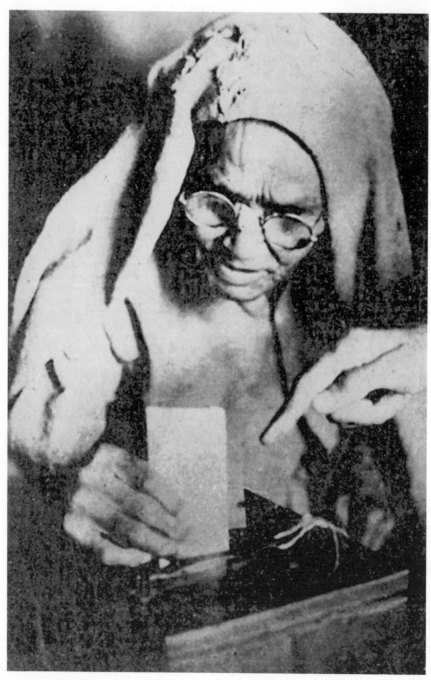

Old woman voting. Reproduced by arrangement with The Times of India Group.

NINE

The Body in Time

in which things disappear, or merely seem to

MY GRANDMOTHER'S LETTERS

"I notice," I said, "that most of your trips ended in disaster of some sort or another, and yet you went on making them, which strikes one as a little strange."
H. RIDER HAGGARD, "A TALE OF THREE LIONS"[1]

Three decades before me, my grandmother came to Varanasi. She and my Grandpa Bill, a carpet distributor and later a sales manager for a Bible Belt carpet manufacturer from Tennessee, traveled around the world combining business and pleasure. In their later years of globetrotting, they were joined by Mr. and Mrs. J., the carpet manufacturer and his wife, to form a quartet. The Tennessee couple were devoted to spreading Jesus's message, and a friend once suggested to me the source of my grandfather's unlikely friendship with Mr. J: "Your Grandpa sold carpets, he sold Jesus." While the men were selling, Grandma and Mrs. J. took long walks through the parks and museums of whichever city they were in, and wrote. Grandma kept a travel diary and Mrs. J. wrote poetry. This *vānaprastha* idyll did not last: my grandparents grew older, during their African safari a vulture made off with part of Mrs. J.'s hand, and then my grandfather died suddenly, in a hotel room in Tokyo on one of his trips alone. Some years later, still struck by the manner of his exit and desirous of some greater connection with that generation, I tried to enroll in a course on Japan at college. The professor was not captivated by the origins of my interest, and declined to admit me. At the suggestion of a friend I joined another seminar that had an opening, one on religion in India. The rest, as they say, is history, and though Akhil Gupta and James Ferguson appropriately dismiss such banal accounts of the anthropologist's "choice of a field"[2] (a concern of a piece with Philippe Bourgois's critique of the anthropology of suburbanized alienation), of such cloth are redemptive encounters fashioned for many.

My grandmother was less ruffled, either by vultures or her place in history. She fondly remembered her Benares and that early morning boat ride on the Ganges. When my grandfather was still alive, the two of them would give slide shows in the lobby of their co-op apartment in Florida: the round-the-world adventures of the footloose Cohens. Grandpa drew on Hollywood images in advertising the shows: "Call Me Bwana" and the Crosby-Hope *Road to . . .* pictures. I remember being all of eleven and fascinated, sitting in the lobby during Christmas vacation, by the adventure and the animals. Sensing this, Grandpa took me to Lion Country Safari the next day. But Grandma's advice for me, on the eve of my first departure for India, was more practical. "Don't give the beggars money, dear," she warned me, and then explained: "If you give something to one beggar, then they all come after you and follow you for hours, and won't go away until you give each one something." She paused: "It will break your heart."

Years later, uncomfortable with that heartbreaking vision of the sightseer, I tried to deflect the family legacy of beggars and beasts through the mediations of anthropology. Yet the field as it was often taught reenacted a more subtle touristic mode. The Grand Tour for the anthropologist of South Asia in the 1980s did not skim along the Ganga at sunrise, but dipped into the equally overdetermined waters of the relational self. Though I became critically engaged with the liquefactions and softenings of the embodiment of colonial difference, I somehow managed to replicate them through participation in the fluid dynamics (selves, signs, polities) of the Chicago School and its dispersed successors.[3] The traces linger. Indians, when push comes to shove in much of this book, are written of through a relational, fluid, and soft language of anger and affect, and Europeans and Americans through a monadic and hard-wired one of memory and cognition.

This tenacity of troublesome metaphor within the contemporary touristic mode of the anthropologist—the continual failure of the best of intentions—remains rooted in the attempt to capture difference within the language of "they're not like us." This linguistic awkwardness cannot be avoided; difference as the organizing principle of anthropological knowledge attracts normatively polarized statements like flypaper. My sense that in Varanasi memory was seldom as central as anger in anchoring discussions of behavioral change and of the self in old age was one such two-edged sword. The language of hot brain allowed me to question the "naturalness" of forgetfulness as a necessary figuration of the senile body. But in suggesting that affective, rather than cognitive, change was strongly marked in the social construction of senility in India, I managed to resuscitate an older and less liberating opposition: the Occident as the rational brain, the Orient as the emotional body. Like the nineteenth- and early-twentieth-century European climacteric theorists I have discussed who distinguished between male cerebral dementia and female genital menopause, I have perpetuated a reading of the Self as cerebral and its Other as quite literally subcortical: Reason versus Nature.

What is to be done? The irony is not simple; I remain committed to the project of interrogating naturalized categories like dementia, memory, and cognition.

Emotion and affect are complex domains of thought and are not the antithesis of reason; one could make strong neurobiological arguments for their importance to dementia research and treatment, despite the language of DSM-IV. A cultural politics of generation that hears old voices as hot and dry and unstable, and younger voices as colder and wetter and more stable, may indeed revisit simplified structuralisms that can only work through colonial erasures of much of social life. But to assume that the generational politics of the former is simply encompassed by the colonial politics of the latter is naive and risks yet a more powerful erasure of the subject. To work through these and several other frames of difference, conjoint but not congruent, I have sketched a perspectivist model whereby the anthropologist pays attention to first-, second-, and third-person "knowledges" as distinct windows onto local processes.

Generational difference, like colonial difference, is here not simply an object of social science; it forms a central question of method. The study of generational difference is fraught with its own colonialism; most gerontologists are simply not all that old. The tourism in gerontology is less overt. But like Cohn's description of the touristic mode for knowing India, the country of the old has its route, the passage to and through an exotic realm by those who wish to master it. The stops along the route—the appeals to ageism, the bittersweet oral history, the reproduction of the "aging enterprise" through the necessity of grant hustling and the reduction of anthropology to "qualitative methods" and cookbook methodology—are well marked.

At a first glance, the politics of this engagement differ from that other, overtly colonial encounter. The natives of the country of the old, for those of us who visit as tourists, are our own future selves. There are no hermeneutic impasses to be broached; we are all aging. Yet I always pause when I discuss my work with my grandmother. Why? The hesitancy—and the slight embarrassment that generates it—is in the first place my sense of the hubris in proclaiming myself to her as an old age expert. I may be aging, but I am not old. The aging enterprise reminds me of the Varanasi land surveyors standing outside Nagwa slum and its pond and measuring the commons: it would soon be a well-groomed colony, but not for its current users. Gerontology as colonialism offers a self-conscious theory of improving the natives—"to make old age a good age" is its frequent refrain, another hint that without the field there would be "no aging"—and for me to claim the status of future native is of necessity to imagine a world in which parents and grandparents have been erased, in which I will be the redeemed old body of this imagined horizon.

Time and generation, the markers of colonial difference, are imploded by gerontological theory in several ways, blurring the political context of its practice. Thus the ever imminent demographic explosion glides the anticipated future—too many old people, requiring new forms of generational regulation—into the present. The urgency of the apocalypse legitimates the delegation of gerontological authority to experts. Disaster scenarios offer the postapocalyptic old bodies of their authors as truer objects of gerontological practice, practice that is imposed on the present bodies of pre-apocalyptic elders: we will suffer from the explosion's fallout, so we study you. Like the "other victims" of Alzheimer's, apocalyptic gerontology hints at a truer victimhood than that which can be claimed by the proximate objects of practice, old people here and now.

The move is similar to the American deployment of other, nondemographic, forms of apocalypse: particularly, given market-driven anxiety over the costs of the increasingly mechanized and expensive but still low-yield intensive care of the elderly, the deployment of a rhetoric of "futility" and "rational death" by an interesting alliance of rational-choice theologians and policy elites under the sign of Ethics.[4] Not surprisingly, those most resistant to the rationality of withholding futile care are groups with disproportionately lower access to basic health.[5] The rational calculus of appropriateness and limits presumes a world of available care challenged by an aging population: the old become those who would take resources from the poor, an equation of particular significance in the American context of corporate medicine.

Throughout the two years I lived in Nandanagar and in the Bengali quarter, my grandmother's regular letters from Montreal or Florida reminded me of the complexity of what was at stake in being old back home. The letters never mentioned "old age," either in Grandma's questions about my work or in her discussions about herself. She wrote about my aunts, uncles, and cousins, about who had had a baby or a bat mitzvah, and about the annoying habits of her neighbors in the Florida co-op where she had lived for over two decades. Like Kaufman's interviewees, my grandmother did not write "as" an old woman. She wrote as herself.

My other—maternal—grandmother, who migrated from a violent corner of Europe between the world wars and who lost much of her extended family to the Holocaust, was neither comfortable in English nor with the particular civilities of middle-class Anglo-American life in which both myself and my paternal grandmother had been raised. She never wrote. But in phone conversations before, during, and after my period of fieldwork, she mentioned old age frequently. "What can I tell you, Lawrence? I'm an old lady. I have problems, problems, you shouldn't know what problems." (In a sense, I can only rewrite her voice as shtick: its *bakbak* insistence on idioms of the body became a nostalgic site for a generation of American Jews marking an affectionate difference from their parents, and is by now a national cliché.) Then, and since, old age has remained a central interpretive category for her. It is not a conspicuous silence, marked by the ominous changes noted in everything around her, as in the letters of my other grandmother. Old age is proclaimed from the rooftops. "I am old" appears to soak up all meaning.

I thought often, in the course of this work, of the disparity between my grandmothers' reflection on their embodied worlds. Their experience of their age and of their bodies has differed radically, though their clinical histories do not differ considerably and they are only a few months apart in age. But they are old quite differently. They both came into the world the daughters of eastern European Jews, but on different continents and in radically different social and economic circumstances. They both lived most of their adult lives in Montreal, but in different neighborhoods amid different institutions: home/factory/market/clinic/old age home versus home/college/synagogue/golf club/retirement co-op. The logic of geriatrics, embodied old age as unremitting normality, makes sense for the life-world of only one of them. The meaning behind the intensely embodied life world of my other grandmother was taught to me during my formal training in geriatrics: "hypochondriasis." Some old patients, I was once told by a caring preceptor as we strolled the regimented and kinless floors of the old age home where I was clerking, only speak of their ailments: they have a pathological need for attention. He spoke without irony.

The seeming universality of old age draws simultaneously on the hegemony of certain representations of the old and on the universals of the body. Around the world, for those who survive into old age, eventual debility and death are certainties. But the material effects of death are as variable and specific as are those of taxes: death for Anupa, who mutters, "I want the Ganga, take me to the Ganga," over and over in her corner of the slum, is not the same as death for the poet Narayan, who celebrates life in all its indignity. Debility in Nagwa means something quite different from debility in the colonies or debility, for that matter, in Montreal.

Though my paternal grandmother never mentioned being old in her letters, old age was addressed obliquely throughout. She favored a vigorous morning constitutional and swim. The letters frequently mentioned other residents of the co-op who would sit by the pool all day and talk, too complacent to consider an ocean swim or a walk along the shore. Immersed in accusations of Banarsi *bakbak*, I sensed congruencies. "Some old people," she would write, "do nothing but complain all day of all their troubles, or of how their children never visit them. They're bored, and boring. They have nothing to do because they do nothing. No one visits them because they just complain and complain."

Old age, throughout our correspondence, was represented by its absence. I avoided old age in avoiding discussing the content of my research. My grandmother projected old age onto other "old people." These old people were the others of the apartment complex. Over two years of these letters, the inertia and *bakbak* of the co-op crowd grew and grew. My grandmother chronicled the aging of her world, a change that touched her deeply and yet was kept at arm's length. "I have more things wrong with me than she does, but I just keep my mouth shut. What's the point of dwelling on such things?"

Behavioral difference and threats to autonomy in the lives of these others were particularly noted by my grandmother. More and more of the women who had been her friends for years were increasingly described by her as "changed." Few old friends escaped her disapprobation. Some of my relatives wondered if my grandmother herself was developing Alzheimer's, "forgetting" all her old friends. They asked me as a student of dementia what I thought. What I thought was that something particularly important was at stake, for all of us in the family, in this question of mental status. Alzheimer's was simultaneously something feared and denied and yet the ever-present idiom, in North America, of the old body in relation to others. In the middle of fieldwork, I returned to Montreal for a family wedding. I learned that a great aunt had been put in an old age home two blocks from where I was staying. I asked my paternal grandmother if she wanted to come visit her sister-in-law. She said no, but when I decided to go anyway she changed her mind. When we arrived on the floor, my great aunt was in the day room along with the other residents, awaiting her lunch. She didn't recognize me but did recognize my grandmother. But the residents were being wheeled in for lunch. After several months of being socialized to the imperatives of the total institution, my aunt became nervous at our potential violation of the routinized meal time. Afraid of missing her meal and more afraid of asking the nursing aide if she could delay eating or take the meal in her room, she urged my grandmother to wait outside the dining room for ten minutes. We waited, on a bench in the hallway by the nurse's station, near the physiological monitors. Across from us, an old man sat unattended in a wheelchair, staring fixedly out in space, a line of drool coming from his mouth. My grandmother grew increasingly uncomfortable, and after a minute and a half into the ten she told me she would wait downstairs.

My great aunt represented the sort of threat for my grandmother that I have rarely seen in India, a threat magnified but not encompassed by the old age institution. More than old age in itself, senility and dementia were the silence in my letters to Grandma, the things it seemed bad form to mention to the grandmother for whom bad form would matter. Despite her frequent discussions of the old complainers, my grandmother seldom brought up demented or institutionalized persons like her sister-in-law. My grandmother was herself old, equally subject to the paradoxes of geriatrics. She could not constitute herself as the primary, "other" victim: she was no tourist.

When my other grandmother decided she wanted to live in the Jewish *Centre d'Accueil*, another Montreal old age home, she was from the beginning openly concerned about "the crazies" she was now forced to endure. They were upsetting to her—one rather vicious old woman in particular—but they were not things from which one averted one's gaze or noted through silences or displacements. Though she was not as sharp as she used to be and after a year in the home was noted by my family to have lost some short-term memory, encounters with other demented people were for her from the outset not some grim foreshadowing of a future without personhood but one more set of embodied incidents, confirming a continuity of experience.

These are "Aunt Minnie" stories, invocations of one's own old relatives in gerontological argument analogous to the anthropological defense: "Not in *my* village." But not only does it seem fair play to invoke one's own grandmothers if one

is in the business of writing about everyone else's, but their quite different embodied histories and second-person experience of other people's old age are cautions
to a parceling out of styles of embodied old age along simplistic cultural lines. The
Varanasi stories I have told are similarly varied, though they share a world in
which biomedicine, as of the late 1980s, had failed to articulate significantly with
the practices of being old, being old and sick, or dying. The final vignette turns
back to Somita Ray in Calcutta, whose children's understanding of their mother's
strange behavior—hiding utensils, calling out to the neighbors that she was being
beaten—was that these actions were of a piece with a lifetime of distrusting her
daughter-in-law. But then the plaques and tangles of Alzheimer's—through the
mediation of the superintendent of the Nava Nir home, of the detail men from
Farmitalia, of the geriatrics collection of the British Library, and of a foreign anthropologist—came to matter, in an interesting way.

NO ONE HERE CARES ABOUT ALZHEIMER'S

Somita Ray and her husband the professor had had one son, Mithun; as a result of
the estrangement between the mismatched couple, Mithun became the primary
outlet for his unhappy mother's affections. The anthropologist Manisha Roy has
written of this particular triangulation as common among the Bengali middle class,
Sudhir Kakar has suggested it is common to the Indian family,[6] and others have
framed it as a more general figure of male narcissism and female dependency. But
for Mithun and particularly for his wife, Sharmila, Somita's dependence on her son
and her consequent dislike of her daughter-in-law were unique and extreme.

Mithun became a photographer; Sharmila, a librarian at the British Library.
Sharmila resented her mother-in-law's dependence on Mithun; Somita, she felt,
had never made any efforts to acknowledge her from the wedding day onward.
Mithun could not find steady work and grew increasingly depressed. Sharmila
continued to work full-time in the library. Her salary supported the family, and
after Mithun's father, the professor, died the three were forced to move to a downstairs flat in her parents' house.

In the house of her daughter-in-law's parents, Somita increasingly began to
wander. She would get lost in the neighborhood; Sharmila began to feel embarrassed. What kind of daughter-in-law was she, people must be asking, who allows
her mother-in-law to go about like a beggar? She began noticing more and more
utensils missing, finding them among her mother-in-law's possessions. Mithun
began spending most of his time at home to watch his mother; he stopped looking
for work. One day Somita called out the window, "Get the police, get the police,"
accusing her family of maltreating her. Sharmila interpreted all these episodes—
to her husband, to a few close family friends, and to myself—as an exacerbation of
Somita's hatred of her. She accused Somita of destroying Mithun's career to keep
him home with her. The strains between the three in the small, one-bedroom flat
were considerable.

Mithun had a wealthy cousin, Aloka Mitra, whom we have earlier met as one of the founders of the Nava Nir homes in Calcutta. At Sharmila's urging, he approached her to see if Somita might be admitted to one of the homes. Like the other "old aunties," the poor relations of the Nava Nir founders, Somita was eventually admitted. But the old age home is here the beginning, and not the end of the story. Three days later, the superintendent of the Nava Nir sent word to Sharmila and Mithun that they must take back their mother: she was unacceptable for the home.

The couple arrived at the institution to find Somita sitting outside. Sharmila's description of this moment, several months later, is vivid. A transformed Somita crouched on the stoop; her eyes were flashing, her hair was in wild disarray. The figure Sharmila paints is the classic *paglī*. In her retelling, the institution itself had transformed Somita, or at the least brought out a truth concealed until then. The superintendent, however, a short woman with the demeanor of a drill sergeant, refused to believe that anything had changed. "You lied to me," she angrily accused them. "She is crazy. She doesn't belong here; she is your responsibility."

Crazy old people do not belong in old age homes: they invoke the Bad Family, and challenge the institution's benevolent self-construction. Somita required considerable care, the one thing the Nava Nirs could not provide, despite their rhetoric of neolocal kinship. The superintendent took refuge in the Bad Family only at this juncture; earlier, Somita was defined as the poor old aunt of a board member.

The image of the *paglī* articulated and legitimated a next move for Sharmila, her seeking out psychiatric care with the hope of diagnosing her mother-in-law as mad, like the superintendent had said, and having her admitted to a psychiatric nursing home. Though madness in itself was stigmatizing, it was less of a threat than the dangers of the Bad Family that a screaming mother-in-law at the window or an accusing superintendent evoked. The couple took Somita to the clinic of one of Calcutta's best known psychiatric families. They were seen by the junior member of the family, Dr. S. Nandi. Recently trained, Nandi was familiar with the differential diagnosis of dementia; its limited clinical salience was less of a problem for him than its importance in the texts of international cosmopolitan medicine. He had been visited the previous month by detail men pushing Dasovas. They had stressed the increasing prevalence of Alzheimer's disease and the need for vigilance: Ask about memory. They gave Nandi a free sample.

For Nandi, Somita offered a rare opportunity to do a dementia workup and to evaluate the claims of the Farmitalia men. He told Sharmila that he felt her mother-in-law had a serious disease of the brain tissue known as Alzheimer's, about which there was much information in the West but little yet in India. He noted that few medicines appeared to have much effect. He admitted his uncertainty as to whether Dasovas would work, but Sharmila and he agreed to try it for Somita. He said that Sharmila should not feel guilty; Alzheimer's was a biological condition.

The psychiatrist told Somita that he could not be certain if Alzheimer's were the problem. He therefore recommended a computerized tomography (CT) scan of the brain to enable him to make a more definitive diagnosis. Following the scan, he told the family that the result confirmed his opinion: Somita had Alzheimer's. An unfamiliar diagnosis is affirmed through the largely symbolic use of high technology. CT scans are neither necessary nor sufficient tools for diagnosing dementia; the changes in cortical and ventricular size they measure are nonspecific. They may rule in a rare diagnosis, normal pressure hydrocephalus, but NPH can be suspected by a classic set of symptoms that did not characterize Somita's behavior. More than offer the psychiatrist new information, the CT placed Somita in a new framework of high technology. Like Dr. Bharati's electron microscope in the *India Today* article, "The Better Brain," the CT scanner can reveal the truth about brains, truths hitherto unavailable in India. The machine allows for the possibility of Alzheimer's.

Armed with a diagnosis of a complex biological disease, Sharmila was considerably relieved. To friends and acquaintances who knew of the family situation, she announced the fact that Somita had a brain disease. The medications did not seem to have much effect, but Somita was diseased and a legitimate candidate for a psychiatric nursing home. The couple began investigating homes with great expectations. Then came the surprise: Despite the old woman's diagnosis, none would consider Somita. Even armed with the elaborate medical diagnosis of Alzheimer's, Sharmila was made to feel that responsibility both for Somita's care and her condition lay with her. Her new lament: "No one here cares about Alzheimer's." The couple were advised to care for Somita at home, the same advice they had been receiving before the diagnosis of Alzheimer's. The only homes that would take her were very expensive facilities.

One home, in the far north of the city near the airport, eventually accepted Somita. It was a one- to two-hour commute in Calcutta traffic, and her family rarely could visit Somita. When I visited her there, her nurses reminded me—defensively, it seemed—that this old woman had a serious medical condition.

What was wrong with Somita? Diagnosis is contested, as is the future of her body. Sharmila believed Somita had always hated her and that she had just gotten worse in old age. The relation echoed classic *sās-bahū* narratives. Sharmila represented Somita as the cruel mother-in-law. Somita, although conversations with her had little evident give-and-take, suggested through gesture and the occasional accusation that the problem lay with the evil daughter-in-law who was trying to turn her son against her and even to kill her. Her accusations gained in coherence from the figure they drew upon, the selfish wife and weak husband of Ghar Kali. Sharmila's firm control over her husband and their unusual matrilocal residence reinforced the meaningfulness of Somita's words and the locus of pathology in the *sās-bahū* relationship and not merely her aged body.

Sharmila resisted the Bad Family, blaming Somita's lifelong inability to adjust to her for all that is wrong with her life, chiefly her husband's failure—and consequently hers—to amount to much. The episode at the old age home pathologized what had until then been a contested family matter. In hearing and labeling Somita a crazy woman, the superintendent meant by madness less an index pointing to the old woman than a sign of family neglect. When Sharmila arrived for Somita, she for the first time saw her mother-in-law as a madwoman, with the pathognomonic Medusa-like eyes and hair of a woman possessed. She reinterpreted the accusation of madness to point to the old woman and went to see Dr. Nandi.

With the diagnosis of Alzheimer's, mediated through the fortuitous appearance of the drug salesmen and the visualizing power of expensive machine technology, the family could shift the locus of pathology from themselves onto Somita's brain. The diagnosis also offered them an armamentarium, drugs like Dasovas. But these did not seem to work very well, nor did the diagnosis of Alzheimer's gain Somita admission into a psychiatric institution during an anxious year of application. Alzheimer's, as of 1990, could not displace the stigma of the Bad Family. It did not cure Somita and was an ineffectual response to the family drama delineated by her weak body and angry voice. Sharmila's considerable pain at the rigors of putting up with Somita and the added insult of being seen as the cause of her own suffering was healed by the understanding that she was not to blame, much as families in Varanasi used understandings of balance or weakness to deflect the Bad Family stigma.

But balance and weakness point simultaneously to the old person and her environment; not so Alzheimer's. Rather than responding to the critical issues of familial interdependence and the maintenance of a familial self, the disease isolates the body of the old person and denies her intersubjectivity. Sharmila has a diagnosis, a CT scan, and a drug, but her newfound explanation does not engage Somita's familial body or its location in postapocalyptic time and space as fully as its scientific and global origins initially promised.

Did Somita have Alzheimer's? Quite possibly. Alzheimer's disease makes rational sense of Somita's situation in the process of unmaking the sense of her family. It suggests to Sharmila that Somita does not hide household objects under her bed to spite her; it might suggest to neighbors, friends, and passersby that Somita is not necessarily the tortured and neglected old woman she is heard to be. It offers her family the hope of a cure and—even if Dasovas is not significantly better than placebo over the long run—it offers them at the very least the opportunity of the gift, a chance to maintain the flow of *sevā*.

Yet in locating the problem solely in the old person's brain, Alzheimer's denies these multiple frames of difference in the constitution of the senile body. Somita's family is unhappy, in a Ghar Kali sort of way. Sharmila all but silences Mithun while blaming all their troubles on his mother; he for his part has consistently refused to intervene to effect some kind of truce between the two women in his life that might have laid the grounds for a less traumatic negotiation of what the family now faces. To flip the *sās-bahū* narrative around: Somita has long been jealous of her daughter-in-law and has done little to make her life easy. The tensions and silences that riddle the history of these three frame their responses to each other's behavior. The family share a small, one-bedroom apartment in a crowded city. There is little room for any of the three to escape the others, even for a moment. The presence of Sharmila's parents upstairs adds to the intensity of a *sahī nahīn* situation.

The family's economic position structures both the possibility of Somita's survival and the inability of a way out. The old man in Nava Nir who angrily reflected on the old age of his class fellows, dumped in a handcart, reminds us that far more than even Nagwa slum, the majority of Calcuttan elderly simply aren't: that is, they are unlikely to survive as old for very long. *Kamzorī* is its own cure: weakness, thinness, and death are all bound together. Somita eats—there is barely enough money for rent, but there is no shortage on food in this family—and survives.

The invocation of Alzheimer's and other dementias pushes the complex sources of the hearing of a bad voice aside. The multiple valences of weakness and balance, the culture and politics of the family, the commodification of memory loss by Dasovas detail men, and the local moral world of this family and their community are silenced. Like balance, weakness, and the narrative of the Fall, Alzheimer's is as much knowledge against as for meaning, allowing families to move the locus of aging from transactions between family members onto the old person or onto larger social processes.

A classic debate in medical anthropology centers on the status of what Kleinman and Byron Good, along with several colleagues, defined as "explanatory models." In an early work, *Patients and Healers in the Context of Culture*,[7] Kleinman developed the explanatory model (or EM) as a heuristic to suggest that a similar narrative process constitutes professional, folk, and popular discourse on the body. In so doing he created a useful tool to challenge the marginalization of patient narrative and experience by physicians as being peripheral to well-being. "EM theory" advanced a model of clinical engagement as communicative action, the continual renegotiation of the meaning of an illness experience among and between patients and healers.

Allan Young in a 1981 article criticized EM theory for what he took as its cardinal assumption: that the practice and experience of people confronting illness are structured primarily as organized and rational models. People who fall sick do not so much construct models, Young suggested, as draw upon different types of what he termed prototypical knowledge.[8] Here I would focus less on the debate than on some shared assumptions that may have made it possible: that theodicy is the work of culture, that people make and live their worlds to "make sense" of suffering and loss, and that the business of the anthropologist is to come up with a framework to represent this process of making sense and its differential constitution.

But the important question of how people make sense of suffering may obscure a different anthropological question. The work of culture is not only or always to make sense of illness, particularly when what is at stake is the ontology of the non-sensical. The bad voice of old age threatens because its hearing already and powerfully *presumes* a sense, in this case that of the inadequate transactions that have failed to sustain a familial body. The meanings given to the senile body are not just a making sense of experience, but a response to the already meaningful world in which bodies in time mean far too much. I have suggested three sorts of knowledge that are drawn on to resist the excessive signification of the old voice.

First, bodies decay and die and are politically marginalized, so persons turn to other frames of self and change—indignation, *niyam*, *sannyāsa*, the joke, grandparenthood, retirement, and the construction of a new category of "senior citizen"—to forestall particular anxieties of loss and dependency. Second, children become their parents and yet old parents do not go away, so children turn to the experiences of balance and weakness and to the ideological assemblages that gloss these. And third, societies are confronted with new circulations of technology and capital and new hierarchies of embodiment as their forms of marginalization within a world system shift, so they struggle for coherent narratives of the national and the modern—the Bad Family, the Forgotten Elder—to locate the absences of postcolonial modernity through bodies and in history. A meaning-centered analysis of the body is inadequate without tracing the ways in which knowledge is appropriated both for and against meaning, resists as well as creates coherence, and deforms as well as demands the possibility of a *scientia senilis*.

LOST AT THE FAIR

During the Kumbh Mela, while Devraha Baba gave his darshan, local newspapers contained several reports of lost old people.[9] Distraught children were interviewed; their parents had wandered off and were nowhere to be found. Reporters described the plight of the children, wandering among the hundreds of thousands at the fair, looking for their mother or father. Many Banarsis were cynical about such stories of missing parents. The many *kāśīvāsī* old people of the city, they suggested, did not come there solely out of a desire to die in holy Kashi, far from their land and their family. Children abandon their parents, people knew, sometimes just dumping them at the station. Whether or not it was a Forest of Bliss, no old householder would willingly renounce his or her home for Varanasi.

The lost old person was a familiar figure on television news. Local stations in the 1980s were given airtime to show photos of missing persons of all ages and describe their last known whereabouts; frequently, such missing persons were elderly. Their stories were similar: a family from a village or small town visits a big city. The old person wanders and gets lost in unfamiliar surroundings. The children consult the police; a report is filed. The old person is seldom found. When pressed by reporters, families of such persons noted that the lost person was old and mentally weak. The police inspector in the old city of Delhi responsible for missing persons concurred, telling me that most of his missing elderly cases were people with a "mental defect." Yet he also noted that many lost old persons in Delhi were eventually found at or near train stations, reinforcing the Banarsi hermeneutic of suspicion. "But I don't know for certain," he concluded. "Although we record and report these cases, our work is with the children." The sisters from Mother Teresa's Varanasi ashram, where Dulari from Nagwa eventually moved, regularly combed the train stations of the city for destitute old and sick people. They, too, agreed with local accusation: a son brings his mother on pilgrimage to Kashi and "loses" her at the train station, leaving her to die, liberated.

"You didn't speak of the *loneliness* of old people," the Vasant College faculty had told me. The wanderer wanders because he has been abandoned; the *bakbak* dog lady barks because she has no one. The Bad Family soaks up all meaning. Neither the policeman nor the nuns, whatever their institutional concerns with the traffic in children or Christians, were wrong. Wandering and being lost point in several directions. The suffering old body is simultaneously an autonomous entity in physical decline and a socially constituted entity in political decline. Both illuminate why so many lost old people get on television news. Old people may get disoriented, and confused; old people may be at greater risk for being neglected or abandoned by their younger relations. And old people are good to think with: their abjection becomes a sign that fixes the blame for the decay in the order of things, assigns it to bad children, an exploitative society, the seductions of modernity, the cruelties of Western culture. And perhaps, if demographic transitions take hold in north India and if certain kinds of medical knowledge become more useful, the decay in the order of things can be laid at the door of the brain, the cell, and the gene.

Though a century from now a different paradigm may have replaced it, I am of my time and irrevocably committed to the usefulness of Alzheimer's as an explanation for a set of behaviors contingently demarcated and grouped as dementia. But invoking Alzheimer's within the globalizing discursive milieu of Alzheimer's hell asserts that the cognitively organized clinical syndrome it represents is in every case the most real and relevant representation of what might be at stake. Invoking Alzheimer's asserts far more, asserts enough to send Janet Adkins into that final embrace with Dr. Kevorkian in the Michigan trailer park. Plaques and tangles point to embodied processes, however overdetermined their figuration of indelibility and plenitude, but they are not the font of all suffering nor of the meaning of a mindful body facing its decline. Alzheimer's ideology posits normal aging against total and unremitting pathology; in so doing, it both denies the complex experience and the personhood of the old persons it would represent and shifts attention away from the social origins of much of the weakness of the old.

Like suspicions as to how one gets "lost" at the fair, debates on Kevorkian have been a way for the American media and its various experts to raise the issue of a social constitution of a dying space. Unlike the triumphalist narrative of Adkins's authorizing her death, the 1996 case of Gerard Klooster, a retired physician from the San Francisco area diagnosed with dementia whose wife had considered the services of Dr. Kevorkian, was reported with greater ambivalence. One of

Klooster's children, also a physician, spirited his father away from the rest of the family when he became convinced they were trying to kill him, and the case ended up in the courts. Unlike Janet Adkins, Gerard Klooster could not offer a voice in the moment of its own extinction, and the question of assisted suicide versus forced euthanasia could not be resolved. The irony of the tears of the other victim, usually restricted to tabloid reality, could here break through into the mainstream press.[10]

As sorts of places to be abandoned, gerontopoli like Varanasi or Allahabad are different from the embrace of Dr. Kevorkian, if only in the ideology of renunciation they seem to embody, the radical frame by which families can divest themselves of the expectations of *sevā*. But Kevorkian's relationship to the disenchantment of the dying space is anything but obvious. In the summer of 1996, he responded to his critics in an address to the National Press Club in Washington, D.C. Against concerns that he and his various instruments of assisted suicide—the "Thanatron" and later the "Mercitron"—promised a less dignified death than his advocates claimed, the Michigan doctor responded:

> Well let's just take what people think is a dignified death. *Christ.* Was that a dignified death? Do you think it's dignified to *hang from wood* with *nails through your hands and feet bleeding,* hang for three or four days *slowly dying,* with people *jabbing spears* into your side, and people *jeering* you? Do you think that's dignified? Not by a long shot. Had Christ died in my van, with people around Him who loved Him, the way it was, it would be far more dignified. *In my rusty van.*[11]

The space of Kevorkian-death is not that of a household, but neither is it the modern institution of the hospital or the institutions—the legislature, the judiciary, the media, the church—which Kevorkian sees as ranged against him, sustaining the hospital's algorithms[12] of alienated machine death. Neither home nor hospital work as dying spaces here, but a middling space in between, characterized by an accessible pioneer ethos of the trailer-park wild, the rusty-van West, and the trash technology of tubes and gas masks and crazy pathologists who get off designing ever simpler and less alienating death machines. Jesus is reclaimed for this new world, but not the Crucifixion, not the resistance of suffering and death to their rational management. Kevorkian's rusty van offers a bloodless *Pietà,* a seamless move from life to the arms of the Mercitron, Mother of Death. Old age vanishes.

Perhaps the exemplary figure of this new bloodless comfort at the American end of the millennium is not Doctor Death but the man I see as his counterpart, a Doctor Life fashioning not middling death but middling life, and not out of tubes and the pioneer West, but out of exotic Indian wisdom, the language of hormones and genes, and the imagined Arthurian and pagan past of whiteness. Deepak Chopra, the great purveyor of neo-*rasāyana* to the world, in book after best-selling book and in repeatedly broadcast television shows and videos and motivational seminars, offers *Unconditional Life* and an *Ageless Body, Timeless Mind.*[13] His 1990s writing has turned ever-more toward Arthurian and other European imagined pasts of enchantment, integrating these with the ancient truths of Ayurveda.[14] Life and death, within Chopra's world of the ambient, are a nondualist blur, and middle-aged adults make their quietus by both ignoring and embracing decay yet seemingly never having to suffer it. Kevorkian-death and Chopra-life refashion the ends of time and the body, emptying sickness and frailty and confusion of any presence.

That a migrant from India can brilliantly recommodify his heritage into such a gift of no aging seems telling, at the close of the century amid the World Bank and Government of India's efforts to achieve a far greater articulation of India into the global market. Rishis travel well, though in the process they seem, like sage Chyavana, to grow younger. Chopra began his New Age career by trying to help his guru Maharishi Mahesh Yogi to bring Ayurveda to America. But at some point he seems to have outgrown Maharishi, and the figure most Americans associate with Ayurveda is not a white-bearded old rishi but his former disciple, the middle-aged Chopra, in business suit or leisure wear. Chopra offers an India without guilt, and for those who would embrace the other India, there is always Mother Teresa, ready like the Mercitron to make Third World death a good death. The Indian anthropologist at Zagreb could offer the good family against the cold biologism of the available West, though back at home the Bad Family awaited, and the absence to which it tried to speak. To that absence and to several of its own, such a West could in turn offer Reason, and Mercy.

❦ *A Last Few Trips up the River* ❧

Bakbak. My last morning, I got up at five and went out on the river in Shankar's boat to immerse my image of Saraswati, goddess of Culture, and have a final look at the fabled city. Shankar pushed off from the bank; I held Saraswati in my lap. I had learned about the immersion of festival images in that first class on Indian religion. Four years later in Calcutta, my first day in the country, I asked the physiologist who had picked me up from the airport (the nephew of the mother of a former tenant of my mom's secretary) to stop the car his aunt had hired so that we could watch a crowd of young men immersing a large image. I had arrived in the city the day after a major Puja, and I had been taught that after the period of worship God's presence no longer inhabited festival images and they were supposed to be immersed, returned to the river and to the elements. We had been talking about cancer research; he looked at me strangely, and declined to join me in running after the young men to the river's edge.

I had bought this particular image before Saraswati's annual celebration in 1989, from a lane lined with hundreds of Saraswati statues. Having the embodiment of Culture in the house of an ethnographer seemed a good idea. I no longer ran after processions and was spending more of my time talking to scientists; still, old habits die hard. But I held off immersing my 1989 Saraswati in the Ganga on the day after the Puja. It was a lovely image, and it seemed wise to keep it intact. But fieldwork was over.

Marwari Mataji, as always, watched from her window as Shankar pushed off. Far to the south, I could see Nagwa slum beyond the line of ghats and temples. When I was working full time in Nagwa, I had stopped coming to the ghats. Their dense groupings of religious things seemed to reinforce the exclusion the Nagwa Chamars often talked about. But such truths were difficult to live by for one brought up on the glories of ageless Varanasi, and when I turned to middle-class fieldwork I allowed myself to move back into the old city, to the home by the river that turned out to be the former residence of Swami Karpatriji, he of anti-Chamar politics.

It was still quite early, that final morning. This was the boat we had used when the two men from Mughalsarai had asked me why Muslims didn't get sixtyish. I had not been able to give them the answer they wanted. When I turned the question back to them, the man who replied had said it was all about who had bad families, and who didn't. But he thought there was more to it.

The two men had eventually disembarked, and I had stayed put, sitting there on the boat working it all out. Shankar had grunted and with a long oar pushed us back out onto the river. He began rowing upstream again—past Brahman experts, tourist vendors, old women bathers, appropriate-technology-armed Ganges savers, practicing wrestlers, argumentative babas, strolling policemen, and fisherman putting away their nets—and I theorized. Then Shankar spoke: "Don't listen to them, brother. Everyone is the same." Meaning Hindus and Muslims. He paused. "Except for money. If we poor people had some, we would never get so old and weak."

Shankar rowed hard against the current. I sat there. Each of us, on his own side of the boat and in his own way, imagined something like no aging in India. And on the bank, the timeless vision of Varanasi and its ghats drifted by, propelled by Shankar's hands and feet. No shortage of metaphor, in anthropology.

On that last day, we again sat silent and midstream, watching Saraswati the goddess of Culture sink and dissolve under our mutual gaze. Something about tourism in my family: "It will break your heart."

Shankar spoke: "Where to now?"

NOTES

THE GROUND OF THE ARGUMENT

1. Sahlins 1976: 55.
2. Rabinow 1992, Haraway 1991, Latour 1993.
3. Kierkegaard 1988: 9–15; I am indebted to Veena Das for many discussions about Kierkegaard's relevance for a philosophy of age (see Das 1996).
4. Strathern 1981.

ACKNOWLEDGMENTS

1. Cohn 1996.
2. Scheper-Hughes 1990.
3. Scheper-Hughes 1992.

INTRODUCTION

1. Kali was a larger-than-life figure for British correspondents, the emblem of all that was uncanny about the conditions of colonial rule and its effects, and one need take the attribution of the letter to her—along with most other religious specifics of the Balua affair—as the sediment of the available descriptive language of the time. Thus the otherwise confusing concatenation of Kali, Shani, and Lord Ram in the telling of the deaths at Balua.
2. Dirks 1992, Oddie 1995.
3. "Benares, April 15" 1865.
4. "Benares, April 17" 1865.
5. "The Gathering at Hurdwar" 1865.
6. The list is by now endless; see Parker et al. 1992, Chatterjee 1993, Mani 1989, Mc-Clintock 1995.
7. Cowley 1989, Gelman, Hager, and Quade 1989, Kantrowitz 1989.
8. Agar 1986.

9. Lyman 1989.
10. Gubrium 1986.
11. Barthes 1976.
12. Inden 1990, Madan 1994: 85–107.
13. Nader 1990.
14. See discussion of Haraway's cat's cradle in Allucquere Rosanne Stone 1995:21–22; Wendy Doniger O'Flaherty 1976.
15. Kumar 1988.
16. In the context of contemporary India, these terms—working class, middle class— elide as much as they reveal. The ongoing genealogy of class formation differs from that of European, American, and other contexts, a matter obscured by any common terminology (Chakrabarty 1989, Oberoi 1994). I use the terms in part as a shorthand, acknowledging the problems with them, and in part in the way they are often used locally in Varanasi, in English and in Hindi.

DULARI

1. Ginsberg 1984, Raja Rao 1989.
2. Chen 1996, Chen and Drèze 1992, Drèze and Sen 1989, Agarwal 1990, 1994.

CHAPTER 1. ORIENTATIONS

1. The XII International Congress of Anthropological and Ethnological Science was held from July 24 to 31, 1988.
2. Turner 1974.
3. I am indebted to James Bono for a conversation on Candide.
4. At the time, the group was known as the Alzheimer's Disease and Related Disorders Association.
5. A. Kleinman and J. Kleinman 1991.
6. Venkatramani 1985.
7. The equation of science, development, and culture in the first decades of independent India under Nehru was repeatedly articulated through the *immensity* of artifacts: dams, planned cities, new universities (Inden 1995, Visvanathan 1995).
8. I use *materialize* here rather than, for example, *construct* to avoid the frequent misreading of social constructionist language as idealist and antimaterialist by both its critics and some of its adherents and to suggest that any theory of the social and the subjective must articulate itself in careful relation to body and environment. This entails not only taking the body as the *site* of the social in the sense of Mauss (1992) and Bourdieu (1990) but as a more robust presence in theory (Rabinow 1993, 1994, A. Kleinman 1989, 1995). I will suggest some of what I mean by *robust* below. My use of *materialize* is in part indebted to Butler's *Bodies That Matter* (1993).
9. Maclachlan 1863, Charcot *Clinical Lectures on the Diseases* 1881, Nascher 1914.
10. Durrant 1865, Nascher 1915, Podolsky 1933.
11. Montesquieu 1989.
12. Kipling 1901, Forster 1924, Haggard 1885, 1886.
13. Hegel 1956.

14. Moore 1989 [1907]:74.

15. 1876:275, my emphasis.

16. 1921:182.

17. Menon 1992.

18. Palthe 1933.

19. Naraindas 1996, Arnold 1993, Harrison 1994.

20. Beotra 1965: iii.

21. Chaudhari and Chaudhari 1963, Roy Chowdhury and Saharay 1988, Hidayatullah and Hidayatullah 1985 [1977], Ramamurti 1980.

22. All India Reporter (Madras) 1940: 73.

23. Roy Chowdhury and Saharay 1988: 118.

24. Beotra 1965.

25. Roy Chowdhury and Saharay 1988: 112.

26. Chaudhari and Chaudhari 1963: 256.

27. DSM-IV 1995.

28. DSM-III-R 1987.

29. DSM IV 1995.

30. 1989: 806.

31. ICD-10 1992, ICD-10 1993.

32. Clarfield 1988.

33. Meyer et al. 1986.

34. Chui 1989, Graves et al. 1994.

35. WHO Scientific Group on Senile Dementia 1986, Graves et al. 1994, Homma and Hasegawa 1989.

36. Jorm et al. 1987.

37. Graves et al. 1994, Katzman et al. 1988, Rocca et al. 1990, Sulkava et al. 1985.

38. Graves et al. 1994, Jorm et al. 1987.

39. Henderson 1988, Meyer et al. 1988.

40. Wadia 1992; Osuntokun et al. 1991.

41. Osuntokun et al. 1991.

42. Gelman, Hager, and Quade 1989.

43. Marriott 1976.

44. Clifford 1988.

45. Moore 1986.

46. Johnson and Johnson 1983.

47. A. Kleinman 1977.

48. Lutz 1985: 89.

49. I began the process of developing appropriate MSEs first through training to use the Folstein MMS in clinical settings (Folstein et al. 1975), then through observation of the community-based home follow-up MSE testing of the East Boston Senior Health Project (n.d.), then through intensive literature reviews (Venkoba Rao et al. 1972, Pershad and Wig 1979, Venkoba Rao and Madhavan 1982, Chandra et al. 1994) and interviews with neurologists in five cities in India.

50. Chandra et al. 1994.

51. Department of International Economic and Social Affairs 1982, Keyfitz and Flieger 1990.

52. Department of International Economic and Social Affairs 1982.

53. Venkoba Rao 1989; Bharucha et al. 1987.

54. Krishnan 1976.

55. Wadia 1992.

56. Butler 1993, Althusser 1971.

57. Cohen 1996.

58. Schweitzer 1936.

59. Kumar 1988.

60. Patrick Olivelle (1993) has convincingly argued that *āśramadharma* emerged in *dharmaśāstra*, Hindu writings on normative social order, more as an edifice to encompass different prescriptive models of the religious life by containing them within a single scheme of "stages of life," and less as an effort to theorize the life course. His work is consonant with Sylvia Vatuk's more contemporary finding in a village in the vicinity of Delhi that people did not frame their old age in correspondence with the typology of *āśramadharma* (1980). Still, as Vatuk notes, though the last two stages of *vānaprastha* and *sannyāsa* are not models for old age in any strict sense, they are critical in how many persons reflect on their old age or that of others. Whatever the origins of the four stages, they have become part of the explicit or implicit terms by which many persons may think about age.

61. Parry 1994, Kumar 1988, Alter 1992.

62. See Mani 1990, Gupta and Ferguson in press.

WORLD WIDE WEB

1. http://www.infi.net/~combsdm/ALG.htmlpostings, http://www.infi.net/~combsdm/Secure-Book-Order-Form.html, http://www.alz.org/assoc/media/institut.html, http://www.alz.org/assoc/media/25.html, http://www.mentalhealth.com//icd/p22-or04. html, http://www.biostat.wustl.edu/alzheimer/ (all last downloaded 10/22/96).

2. http://www.biostat.wustl.edu/hyperlists/alzheimer/9512/0218.html (last downloaded 10/22/96).

3. http://www.biostat.wustl.edu/hyperlists/alzheimer/9502/0002.html (last downloaded 10/22/96).

4. http://www.biostat.wustl.edu/hyperlists/alzheimer/9502/0052.html (last downloaded 10/22/96).

CHAPTER 2. ALZHEIMER'S HELL

1. Michals 1992.

2. See Lock 1993 for an excellent example, in medical anthropology, of the selective use of European history in the construction of a Japanese ethnography and history of the present.

3. New genetically engineered subspecies of mice marketed as viable animal models of Alzheimer's disease for laboratory research have been patented in the United States. Newspaper reports of this research have been as likely to appear on business as science pages of American newspapers. See King 1995, Kolata 1995, Riordan 1995, "Alzheimer's Work Aided by New Breed of Mouse" 1996.

4. Rabinow 1989:7.

5. Comment made at a seminar at the Centre for the Study of Developing Societies, Delhi, 1990.

6. A. Kleinman "Illness Narratives" 1988. See Good and Good 1981.

7. I am grateful to Linda Hunt for providing me with a supply of supermarket tabloids when I was in Varanasi.

8. Donaldson 1988.

9. Cowley 1989, Gelman, Hager, and Quade 1989.

10. Fox 1989.

11. Cowley 1989, Gelman, Hager, and Quade 1989, Kantrowitz 1989.

12. Mace and Rabins 1981.

13. Ibid.: 14.

14. Turner 1969.

15. Egan 1990.

16. One might compare the publicity over Adkins's case with that over Gerald Klooster, a California obstetrician apparently diagnosed with Alzheimer's whose wife, Ruth, allegedly tried to involve Kevorkian in a hotly contested "assisted suicide" for her husband. A custody battle erupted, one son winning custody of Klooster in a Michigan court, "saving his life" from Kevorkian and Ruth Klooster, and a daughter regaining custody in a California court. Legal and other representatives of both children framed the issue to the court and press in terms of Klooster's suffering, but descriptions of this suffering invariably invoked the "other victim" (Lewin 1996, see pp. 303–4).

17. Ramos 1995, Stone 1994.

18. Sidey 1994

19. Ibid.

20. Morris (1995) points out the additional importance of Reagan having written out the letter by hand.

21. There are other ways children of parents diagnosed with dementia have approached its twin victimizations, avoiding both the pious silencings of Alzheimer's professionalism and its gerontocidal tabloid parody. Deborah Hoffmann's 1994 film, *Complaints of a Dutiful Daughter*, acknowledges her ambivalent and at times difficult relationship with her mother before and during the latter's illness, without the story ever falling into either Grand Guignol or granny-dumping. The mother in the film never ceases to be a person, however difficult or impoverished her relationships with others become. The filmmaker reports realizing that her initial problem with her mother during the progressive course of the latter's dementia lay in expecting her to be someone she no longer was. The message is that of *The 36-Hour Day*, but unlike its realization in the ADRDA meeting, the message here never degenerates into the denial of selfhood. Alzheimer's is acknowledged, but the acknowledgment does not replace the old woman as the heart of the story.

22. Cole 1992.

23. Angier 1990.

24. "Researchers Say Skin Test May Identify People with Brain Disease" 1993.

25. Humphry 1991.

26. Cited in Lyman 1989:599; see Gubrium 1986.

27. Lyman 1989: 599.

28. Dawson and Reid 1987, Rader 1987.

29. Lyman 1989: 602.

30. Thewlis 1941.

31. Nascher 1914.

32. Canguilhem 1989.

33. Charcot 1866, considerably revised as Charcot 1867. Early English versions included Tuke's *Clinical Lectures on Senile and Chronic Diseases* (1881) and an American edition, *Clinical Lectures on the Diseases of Old Age*, trans. L. H. Hunt (1881). Alain Lellouch (1992) offers a far broader catalogue of Charcot's writings on "la pathologie sénile."

34. Charcot, *Clinical Lectures on the Diseases*: 17. See also Lellouch 1992: 86.

35. Prus 1840.

36. Lellouch, p. 94n. "The medicine of old people is still to be made."

37. Charcot, *Clinical Lectures on the Diseases*: 20.

38. Thomas Cole, attempting to insert Charcot into a narrative of the ever more routinized split of the normal and the pathological in the movement toward geriatrics, downplays Charcot's observation that the distinction collapses in old age (1992: 201–2). But Canguilhem's discussion, cited by Cole, troubles the seamless movement Cole suggests, as I will discuss below.

39. Canguilhem 1992: 104.

40. Cole 1992: 106.

41. Ibid.: 199–200.

42. Nascher 1914: 195.

43. Maclachlan 1863.

44. Rostan 1823: 217, 244.

45. Weiner 1993: 188–89.

46. Cohn 1996, Rabinow 1989.

47. Rowland 1851: 50–55.

48. Jackson 1875.

49. Dieulafoy 1918: 983.

50. Kraepelin 1968 [1904], Bleuler 1924.

51. Maclachlan 1863: 24, see also Sicherman 1981. Flint 1879: 669.

52. See Cole 1992.

53. Bacon 1683: 11.

54. Smith 1752.

55. Maclachlan 1863: 21.

56. Kraepelin 1968 [1904]: 9.

57. Ibid.: 221.

58. Tanner 1860, cited in the *Oxford English Dictionary* (OED) 1989 (8): 56.

59. Power and Sedgwick 1888, cited in OED 1989 (8):56.

60. Nascher 1915, discussed below.

61. On Alzheimer, see Kraepelin 1987.

62. Warthin 1929: 77–78.

63. Ibid.: 113, 115.

64. Barrett 1910, Simchowicz 1910, Fuller 1911, Tiffany 1913–14.

65. Gubrium 1987.

66. Fox 1989.

67. The lone voice in the wilderness was the Canadian neuropathologist Vladimir Hachinski (e.g., Hachinski 1990).

68. Curtin 1972, de Beauvoir 1972, Blau 1973, Butler 1975, Gubrium 1975.

69. Sankar 1984.

70. Luborsky and Sankar 1993; see also Cohen 1994.

71. Cole 1992.

72. Callahan 1987, 1993.

73. Cohen 1994.

74. Cited in Mora 1991: lviii.

75. Ibid.: lxii.

76. Weyer 1991 [1583]: 523–24.

77. Ibid.: 285.

78. Scot 1964 [1584]: 33.

79. Kramer and Sprenger, 1948: 44.

80. Scot 1964: 29.

81. Macfarlane 1970. See also Demos 1982 for attention to why the voices of certain women, particularly at midlife, presented a threat in seventeenth-century New England.

82. Pliny as translated by Philemon Holland (1601: vii: xlix: 182).

83. Kennedy 1844: 245–46.

84. Lock 1993: 303–29.

85. Laqueur 1990.

86. Durrant 1865: 233.

87. Halford 1833: 10–13.

88. Skae "Climacteric Insanity" 1865, Skae "Climacteric Insanity in the Male" 1865.

89. Podolsky 1933: 70.

90. De Fleury 1910, Gleason 1916.

91. Galloway 1933: 129.

92. Moinson 1934.

93. Nascher 1914: 1.

94. Nascher 1915: 541–43.

95. Nascher 1914: 6.

96. See, for example, Walker 1985.

97. See, for example, Martin 1987.

98. Nascher 1914: 16–17.

99. Ibid.: 18–19.

100. Nascher 1915: 541–44.

101. See Amaducci, Rocca, and Schoenberg 1986, Beach 1987, Berrios 1990, Berrios and Freeman (eds.) 1991.

102. Berrios 1990: 363.

103. Ibid.: 362.

104. Alzheimer 1907.

105. Berrios 1990: 359–63.

106. I am less certain than Berrios appears to be as to whether the Alzheimer of the 1907 paper is as much a part of this consensus as Berrios seems to suggest. Alzheimer repeatedly stresses, in that paper, the failure of existing classifications to capture the peculiarities of the case in question.

107. Wolfenstein 1955, FitzGerald 1986.

108. Egan 1992.

109. Chui 1989.

110. Shakespeare 1974: II: iv: 204.
111. Fuller 1912: 452–53, 453–54.
112. Ibid.: 541–43.
113. Ramaseshan and Martin (eds.) 1992.
114. See, for example, the cover of Berrios and Freeman (eds.) 1991.

NUNS AND DOCTORS

1. "Study Suggests . . . " 1996.
2. Herrnstein and Murray 1994.
3. Daly 1996.

CHAPTER 3. KNOWLEDGE, PRACTICE, AND THE BAD FAMILY

1. In an earlier draft of this chapter (Cohen 1992), I used pseudonyms for the four individuals I discuss at length here; in this version, I use the real names. With reflection, issues of honesty and accountability (mine) seemed of greater concern than an imagined and never requested need for confidentiality.

2. Bose and Gangrade 1988. Pati and Jena 1989.

3. Soodan 1975, Bose and Gangrade (eds.) 1988, Desai (ed.) 1982, Sharma and Dak (eds.) 1987, de Souza and Fernandes (eds.) 1982, Biswas (ed.) 1987, Pati and Jena (eds.) 1989.

4. Obviously, there have been books with other titles; the point here is to stress the degree of routinization and the epistemological consequences of social science that must be nominated as "in India." Other works with different titles but similar narratives include Bhatia 1983 and Vijaya Kumar 1991; works with different narratives are fewer, and include Marulasiddaiah's classic 1969 study.

5. See George Basalla's discussion of "the spread of Western science" in three similar but less ironically treated phases (1967), as well as Deepak Kumar's critique (1995).

6. Soodan 1975: 1.

7. Ibid.: 11.

8. Subrahmanium 1988: vi.

9. Gangrade 1988: 27.

10. See Cohen 1983.

11. Desai 1982, Desai 1987, Goyal 1989, Kohli 1987, Mishra 1989, Mohanty 1989, Ramnath 1989, Saxena 1988, Sinha 1989, Srivastava 1988, Subrahmanium 1988.

12. United Nations World Assembly on Aging 1982.

13. United States Department of State 1982.

14. India, Ministry of Welfare 1987.

15. United Nations Office at Vienna 1988.

16. India, Ministry of Welfare 1988.

17. United States Department of State 1982: 1.

18. Ibid.: 3, my italics.

19. Cowgill and Orgren 1979: 503–4

20. Cowgill and Holmes 1972. See Robertson 1984.

21. Parsons 1949: 230–31.

22. Burgess 1960.

23. De Beauvoir 1972: 321–22.
24. Palmore and Manton 1974: 210.
25. See Drèze and Sen 1989, Agarwal 1990, 1994, Chen and Drèze 1992.
26. De Souza 1981, De Souza and Fernandes (eds.) 1982.
27. Laslett 1985.
28. Nydegger 1983.
29. Townsend 1981: 9.
30. Neysmith and Edwardth 1984: 39.
31. Cowgill and Holmes 1972: 310–11.
32. Quadagno 1982: 5–6.
33. Fischer 1978. See also M. Johnson 1973.
34. Minois 1987, but see Cohen 1994 for a critique.
35. Fischer 1978; Achenbaum 1985.
36. Stearns 1977.
37. Quadagno 1982: 22–23.
38. Rhoads 1984: 249.
39. Reid 1985: 92.
40. Nydegger 1983.
41. Ross 1982: 286–90.
42. Bailey 1957.
43. Epstein 1962.
44. Epstein 1973: 210.
45. Desai 1956.
46. Epstein 1973: 201, citing Desai.
47. Kolenda 1967, Y. Singh 1973.
48. Epstein 1973: 206–10.
49. Cohn 1960, Madan 1965, Rao 1968, Gore 1968, Shah 1974, Van der Veen 1976.
50. Gray and Mearns (eds.) 1989.
51. Propp 1968.
52. Nandy 1983.
53. See Shweder and Miller 1985, Ramanujan 1989, Daniel 1984, Marriott 1976, 1989, Roland 1988.
54. Tharu 1989: 127.
55. Ahmad 1992.
56. Djurfeldt and Lindberg 1980. See de Souza 1981: 42 for the application of Djurfeldt and Lindberg to the study of the poor elderly.
57. Walford 1983.
58. Mahdihassan 1979.
59. Ojha and Kumar 1978.
60. Capra 1975.
61. Francis Zimmermann has recently offered a fairly lengthy critique of my work based upon the following few paragraphs on Chyawanprash (1995). Charging me with the faults of being on the one hand a "cultural relativist" and on the other a champion of bio-medical primacy in the tradition of the medical anthropologist George Foster, Zimmermann rightly suggests that any attention to the bodily politics of Chyawanprash is incomplete without an effort to analyze its efficacy and locate this efficacy within a genealogical narrative of herbal medicines ("*Si nous nous limitons à décrire les ressorts du succès de l'industrie*

ayurvédique qui satisfait à une demande artificiellement suscitée par la publicité et l'idéologie hindoue, comme le fait Cohen, sans poser la question de l'efficacité, nous sombrons dans le relativisme culturel et le cynicisme des observateurs comme George Foster . . . "). His effort to take my argument on the tonic in a different direction is welcome.

Unfortunately, Zimmermann seems less interested in engaging the arguments on the old body presented here than in reading them somewhat awkwardly within what seems to be a contemporary French anxiety over cultural relativism and the associated dangers of the American style. But the point in the paragraphs above is not that Chyawanprash is or is not reducible to the politics of its contemporary commercial or generational dynamics. Rather, it is that the old body is ambiguously framed as a legitimate medical object within a variety of textual and ethnographic materials, that this ambiguity can be heightened and exploited for a variety of clinical or other practical ends, and that efforts to think in third-person terms about the relation of "the old body" to particular old bodies in space and time need engage such uses of ambiguity. *This point is as relevant for the deployment of allopathy as for that of Ayurveda.*

62. Somadeva 1968 [1880].
63. See Cohen "The Epistemological Carnival" 1995.
64. Jordens 1978: 150–52.
65. Bakshi 1991: 88, 174.
66. Butalia 1993.
67. Goffman 1961, Gubrium 1975.
68. Langer 1989.
69. Estes 1980.
70. Stevens 1987.
71. Foucault 1977.
72. Banerji 1990 [1929]; Premchand 1978 [1921].
73. Paul 1983.
74. Banerjee 1989.
75. Sarkar 1989: 38.
76. Nandy 1980: 7–9.

AITAŚA PRALĀPA

1. *Atharva Veda* XX: 129–32. Griffith 1895–96: 437f.

CHAPTER 4. MEMORY BANKS

1. Denby 1994.
2. *King Lear* III: iv: 11–14.
3. *King Lear* II: iv: 108–10.
4. Vatuk 1990: 67.
5. Sontag 1978.
6. Berrios 1990. See also Amaducci, Rocca, and Schoenberg 1986.
7. Freud 1966.
8. Zimmermann l989.
9. Brass 1972, Leslie 1976.

10. D. Ojha and A. Kumar 1978, Zimmermann 1992.
11. Filliozat 1976.
12. Cohen "The Epistemological Carnival" 1995.
13. Capra 1975.
14. *Suśruta (Cikitsāsthānam* XXVII: 6) 1981 [1911]: vol. 2: 516–18.
15. *Caraka (Cikitsāsthānam* I: i: 7) 1983: vol. 2: 4.
16. Srikanta Murthy 1984: iii.
17. *Śārṅgadhara* (I: vii: 20) 1984: 30.
18. Varma 1987.
19. J. Ojha 1978: vii, 14–15.
20. *Caraka (Cikitsāsthānam* I: i: 68–74) 1983: vol. 2: 9–10.
21. Ibid. (I: i: 17–21) 1983: vol. 2: 4–5.
22. Ibid. (I: iv: 27) 1983: vol. 2: 31.
23. Good and Good 1981.
24. Nichter 1980.
25. See A. Kleinman "A Window on Mental Health" 1988.
26. Boral et al. 1989.
27. Hubert and Mauss 1981 [1898]: 21–28.
28. *Caraka (Cikitsāsthānam* II: 2: 14–17) 1983: vol. 2: 41–42.
29. Maine 1876: 283–90.
30. Both of these persons are described through pseudonyms: in one case the family requested not to be named and in the other I did not have the opportunity to meet all of the relatives I discuss in order to ask permission.
31. Biswas 1968: 892.
32. Potter 1977: 172–73, Larson 1992.
33. Matilal 1985: 208.
34. Larson 1992.
35. Potter 1981.
36. Ibid.: 69.
37. Marriott 1976.
38. O'Flaherty 1984: 209–10, 220, 224.
39. Babb 1987: 123.
40. Somadeva 1968: 374–75.
41. Edgerton 1926: lii–liv.
42. *Vikramacarita* 1926: 6–7.

MERĪ LATĀ MAHĀN

1. Discussion with the journalist and media critic Amita Malik, 17 June 1996.

CHAPTER 5. THE ANGER OF THE RISHIS

1. Subramaniam 1965: 49.
2. Benson 1975.
3. Ninan 1991.
4. Marriott 1989.

5. Trawick 1990.

6. O'Flaherty 1981.

7. Marriott 1976, 1989; Daniel 1984.

8. Varma 1987.

9. De 1986: 157.

10. B. Mishra and V. Mishra 1965.

11. The connections between contemporary *rasāyana* and urine therapy are minimal but do exist and are far from Desai's idiosyncrasy alone. See Mithal 1979, Patel 1978.

12. Myerhoff 1978.

13. The discussion of such triangles leads from Lévi-Strauss on the circulation of women to Rubin 1975 and Sedgwick 1985.

14. Ramanujan 1983.

15. See Das 1982.

16. Sobtī 1991.

17. See Das 1996.

18. Carstairs 1958; Kakar 1981.

19. Nandy 1983.

20. Carstairs 1958: 138, 153.

21. Ibid.: 158–60, my emphasis.

22. Nandy 1983: 4–18.

23. Such a description of Hijras, the "third gender" of India, is not mine but that of Carstairs, who saw Hijras as living metaphors for Rajasthani men. See Carstairs 1956, Cohen "The Pleasures of Castration" 1995.

24. Nandy 1983: 17–18.

25. Kakar 1982: 134–35.

26. See Cohen "Holi in Banaras" 1995.

27. Kakar 1979: 125–26.

28. Despite the emergence of several important works in psychological anthropology and sociology, such as Stanley Kurtz's critical rethinking of Oedipus in India literature (1992), as well as work on aspects of adult masculinity in Varanasi by Nita Kumar (1988), Joseph Alter (1992), and Steven Derne (1995), work on family relations and child development in north India paralleling Margaret Trawick's seminal work in Tamil Nadu (1990) has been limited.

29. Ramanujan 1983: 252.

30. Leach 1962, Courtright 1985, Obeysekere 1990, Cohen 1991.

31. *Mahābhārata* (1 [7.c]. 78: 30–80: 12) 1973: 191–94.

32. Saraswati 1975.

33. *Rāmāyana (Ayodhyakanda* 57, 58) 1986: 205–10.

34. Vatuk 1980: 147.

35. Poems read at the Indian Institute for Advanced Study, Simla, June 19, 1996.

36. Marriott 1989.

37. *Brahma Purāna,* Part 1, 1985: xix.

38. *Brahma Purāna* (126: 27–33), Part 3, 1986: 687. The editors' license in translating the text using contemporary medical terms (asthma, bronchitis) should be noted.

39. *Padma Purāna (Kriyāyogasārakhanda* 26: 26) Part 10, 1992: 3547.

40. Jones 1807: 368–69

41. Chatterjee 1993.

42. Chadha 1989, "The Janata Dal candidate" 1989.

43. "Paśchim Bangāl" 1989.
44. Bali 1989.
45. [Old woman voting] 1989. [Old woman voting] 1990.
46. Raza 1990.
47. A. Kleinman and J. Kleinman 1991.
48. Das 1982; Marglin 1977.
49. Shweder 1989, Shweder and Miller 1985.
50. See Das 1995.
51. *Ramāyana (Ayodhyakanda* 57: 32) 1986: 206.
52. Vatuk 1990: 82.
53. Khosa n.d.
54. Kaufman 1986: 7.
55. Cole and Gadow 1986; de Beauvoir 1972.
56. Neugarten 1968. See also Cohen 1994.
57. Sankar 1984.
58. Scheper-Hughes and Lock 1987.
59. Vatuk 1990.
60. Kakar 1979.
61. J. Levin and W. Levin 1980.
62. Madan 1987.

CHAPTER 6. THE MALADJUSTMENT OF THE BOURGEOISIE

1. Kumar 1988, Cohen "Holi in Banaras" 1995.
2. "Punjabi Bagh" 1990.
3. Fraser 1989: 22.
4. Turner 1969.
5. Anantharaman 1979, Ramamurthy 1979, Saraswathi and Dutta 1988: 120, S. Mishra 1989, Sinha 1989.
6. Burgess 1954, Havighurst 1954, Cumming and Henry 1961.
7. Dalvi and Gandhi 1989.
8. M. Singh 1989.
9. See for example Danielou 1964, 1982.
10. DSM-III-R 1987.
11. See Lock 1993 for a more extensive discussion of the issues raised here.
12. Sharma and Saxena 1981.
13. Lock 1993: 34–36.
14. Du Toit 1990.
15. George 1988.
16. Lock 1993.
17. See Laura Nader's critique of "harmony ideology" for a related discussion of the limits of balance as rhetoric (1990).
18. See Woodward 1991 for an exemplary effort to work through questions of subjectivity in old age in terms of a Lacanian concern with mirroring, identity, and difference.
19. Mehta 1989.
20. Cohen 1983.
21. Venkoba Rao 1989.

22. Kolenda 1967; Agarwal 1994.
23. Obeysekere 1985, Bottèro 1991.
24. Yesavage et al. 1979, Coffman 1979.
25. Avorn and Soumerai 1983, Soumerai and Avorn 1987.
26. Kugler and Agnoli 1988.
27. Kugler 1988.
28. "Therapeutic Effectiveness" n.d.
29. Kugler 1988.

CHAPTER 7. CHAPATI BODIES

1. Premchand 1968.
2. Eck 1982.
3. *Dalit* has become a term by which an increasing number of Varanasi Chamar identify their political commonality with other "untouchable" or "Harijan" communities; at the time of research in the late 1980s, however, it was seldom used by people in Nagwa to describe themselves and will not be used here. Chamar can be an offensive term in some contexts, but not it is hoped in the kind of writing offered here.
4. Khare 1984.
5. See Freeman (1979) for some discussion of untouchable caste performance.
6. Ravidas 1988. By permission of Oxford University Press, Inc.
7. For a structurally analogous situation, see Gaylene Becker's study of hearing-impaired old people, for whom lifelong identification as deaf transforms the everyday knowledge and experience of being old (1980).
8. Dumont 1980.
9. Berreman 1971, Mencher 1974.
10. Marglin 1977, Dirks 1987.
11. Malamoud 1988.
12. Appadurai 1986, Das 1982, Dirks 1987, Marglin 1977, Marriott 1989, Quigley 1993, Raheja 1989, Uberoi 1996.
13. Khare 1984.
14. See Searle-Chatterjee (1981) for a related finding.
15. The string amulet as differential signifier of the male body across class has been used in contemporary advertising campaigns, perhaps nowhere as explicitly in terms of its complex relation to *kamzorī* as in the television ad in which a wife enters the bedroom to find her husband, Bi-joy (a homoerotic play on the Bengali name Bijoy), in bed with a thinner, amulet-wearing *bhaiyā* (north Indian lumpen). The husband panics and scrambles to get dressed; the *bhaiyā* is thoroughly unconcerned. The ad, somewhat mysteriously designed to sell television sets (the wife drops their television in surprise), offers a doubled and inverted reading of *kamzorī*: both the rich Bijoy versus the lumpen *bhaiyā*, thin and protected by his amulet, and the unprotected and anal-receptive (notably Bengali) Bi-joy versus the amulet-protected and active *bhaiyā*. Televisions that do not break are being offered as protective wrapping to prevent middle-class weakness in the face of the receptivity of the new consumerism.
16. *Aslī Baṛā Indrajal* n.d.

17. One uses "empowering" with caution, given its overdetermined and class-laden context; yet menstrual blood in this context is literally empowering through its removal of embodied weakness.

18. See Cohen (1983), where I contrast the use of *jara* and *vṛddhatvā* in Epic and Puranic texts.

19. See Madan 1987.

20. See Khare 1984 for a lengthy discussion of similar themes.

21. Appadurai 1986: 752.

22. See Cohen "The Pleasures of Castration" 1995 for a discussion of Chandan.

23. Cohn 1955, 1960.

24. The eponymous grandmother of the internationally televised documentary film *Dadi and Her Family* (1982) is in many ways similar to Juguli in her concerns over the *bahū* as the cause of brothers separating and old parents being neglected.

25. Tara Devi's name is kept, at her request; the others have been changed.

26. *Suśruta* (*Nidānāsthānam* I: 3) 1981 [1911]: vol. 2: 2.

27. Zimmermann 1987: 8.

28. *Suśruta* (*Nidānāsthānam* I: 4–12) 1981 [1911]: vol. 2: 2–4.

29. Dash 1978: 24.

30. Radcliffe-Brown 1940.

A CHILD IS BEING LIFTED

1. See "Janpad men bheṛiye se zyādā aphvāhon kā jōr" 1996.

2. "Janpad men bheṛiye se zyādā aphvāhon kā jōr" 1996, "Lakaṛsunghvā ke aphvāh se svāsthy parīksaṇ nahīn ho sakā" 1996.

3. "Wolves Strike Again in Pratapgarh District" 1996, "Hyena Hunters Fail to Convince People" 1996.

4. "Human Hyena?" 1996.

5. "Hyena Strikes Again, Baby Saved" 1996, "Hyena Menace Still in Villages: Police Forced to Hand Over Killed Girl's Body" 1996, "Child-Killing: Police Still in Dark about Black Figure" 1996, "Three 'Wolf-Men' Lynched in U.P." 1996, "Mysterious Disappearances of Two-Year-Old Girl" 1996.

6. "Ādamkhor jānwar ne adhikāriyon va jantā kī nīnd uṛāī" 1996.

7. "Another Lynching by Mistake," *Northern Indian Patrika* 1996, "Another Burnt Alive in Kanpur" 1996.

8. "Kanpur Mob Roasts Woman Alive" 1996.

9. "Lakaṛsunghvā ke bhram men bābā ko pulis ke havāle kiyā" 1996.

10. See Scheper-Hughes (1990) for a discussion of the complex truths behind child-theft rumor.

CHAPTER 8. DOG LADIES AND THE BERIYA BABA

1. I have heard several versions of this couplet. I cite the variant printed in the 1909 *Benares Gazetteer* (Nevill 1909: 90–91), reading Nevill's "sewa" in the second line as the more grammatical *sevan*.

2. Chadha 1988.
3. Eck 1982.
4. White 1989.
5. Drèze and Chen 1992; Agarwal 1994.
6. Carstairs 1983; Chen n.d.
7. Scheper-Hughes 1992.
8. Evans-Pritchard 1937; Favret-Saada 1980.
9. Freud 1995: 126, 127.
10. Taussig 1980: 181, 230–31.
11. See the ethnographies of Saletore 1981 and Kapur 1983 and the writing of Premchand 1988, Bandyopadhyay 1990, and Devi 1990.
12. Carstairs 1958, Kakar 1981.
13. Obeysekere 1990.
14. See Kurtz 1992.
15. Carstairs 1983: 63; Chen n.d.
16. Premchand 1988: 35, 36.
17. Saraswati 1984.
18. Premchand 1978 [1921]: 144, 145 (my translation).
19. *Bhāgavata Purāṇa* (III. 30. 12–15), Part 1, 1976: 398.
20. *Bhāgavata Purāṇa* (VII. 14. 9, 11), Part 3, 1976: 980, 981.
21. S. Sinha and Saraswati 1978: 50.
22. Parry 1982, Svoboda 1986.
23. Tambiah 1984: 345.
24. For the former, see Howes (ed.) 1991.
25. Eck 1981: 4–5.
26. Amin 1988.
27. Turner 1974: 193–96.
28. Munn 1992., Östör 1993.
29. Radcliffe-Brown 1940.

THE AGE OF THE ANTHROPOLOGIST

1. Myerhoff 1978.

CHAPTER 9. THE BODY IN TIME

1. Haggard 1889.
2. Gupta and Ferguson n.d.
3. Daniel 1984, Marriott 1976, 1989.
4. See Callahan 1987, 1993.
5. Several white staff members at the American hospital on whose ethics committee I have been an observer noted with some exasperation, in a committee discussion of futility and appropriate care, that African American family members were far more likely to resist staff efforts to get them to agree to the withholding of intensive care when it was likely to be futile. The staff understood this resistance, for the most part, as suspiciousness—based upon a history of discrimination—that prevented rational decision-making.

6. Roy 1975; Kakar 1981.
7. Kleinman 1980.
8. Young 1981.
9. "Thousands Lost in Mela Yet to Be Reunited" 1989.
10. Lewin 1996.
11. Kevorkian 1996.
12. Farmer and Kleinman 1989.
13. Chopra 1992, 1993.
14. Chopra, *The Return of Merlin* 1995, *The Way of the Wizard* 1995.

GLOSSARY

āśrama	forest retreat; one of the four ideal stages of life
āśramadharma	the prescribed duties of the four ideal stages of life
baba	old man; grandfather; mendicant or holy man
bāhāttūre	seventy-two; Bengali expression for senility
bakbak	prattle; chatter
basti	slum
bhadralok	the urban Bengali elite
bhajan	devotional song
bhīmrati	Bengali expression for senility
bhūt	malevolent spirit that can possess people and make them ill
darshan	auspicious sighting (of a sacred image, person, or place)
davā	medicine
dharmaśāstra	classical Hindu legal codes; the authoritative literature on dharma
dimāg	brain; mind
ghar	home; household; in "*Ghar* Kali," cosmic age or *yuga*
hāth pair	hands and feet; used with *kamzorī* (weakness) to suggest general bodily fatigue or disability
jaṛībūṭī	herbal medicine; Ayurvedic remedies
kamzorī	weakness; fatigue; impotence
kaśīvāsī	one who moves to Kashi (Varanasi) to live out one's final years
ojhā	*bhūt* (malevolent spirit) exorcist

paglī	madwoman
pakkā mahal	the 'finished' or solidly built neighborhoods, the area of Varanasi closest to the Ganges
pancakarma	radical Ayurvedic purification treatment, the prerequisite for many al-chemical (*rasāyana*) longevity therapies
rasāyana	alchemy; the branch of Ayurvedic medine concerned with extending life and forestalling old age
rishi	literally, a seer; a semi-divine sage who imparts sacred knowledge
sahī	right, correct (*sahī nahīn*: incorrect)
saṃskāra	karmic memory trace from the past or a previous life; life cycle rite for caste Hindus
sannyāsa	renunciation; the fourth stage of life
saṭhiyānā	to go sixtyish; to become senile, stubborn, difficult, or confused
sevā	filial respect, caring, service
shanti	peace, repose
tamasha	spectacle; show
thana	local police post
vānaprastha	forest-dwelling; life apart from the family, the third stage of life

REFERENCES

POPULAR MEDIA

"Ādamkhor jānwar ne adhikāriyon va jantā kī nīnd uṛāī." *Dainak Jāgraṇ.* July 3, 1996.

Altman, Lawrence K. "Reagan and Alzheimer's: Following a Path His Mother Traveled." *New York Times* 144: B6 (N). November 8, 1994.

"Alzheimer's Work Aided by New Breed of Mouse." *New York Times* 145: A12 (N). October 4, 1996.

Angier, Natalie. "Scientists Link Protein Fragments to Alzheimer's." *New York Times* 139: B6. May 29, 1990.

"Another Burnt Alive in Kanpur." *Northern Indian Patrika.* July 7, 1996.

"Another Lynching by Mistake." *Northern Indian Patrika.* July 6, 1996.

Aslī Baṛā Indrajāl. Calcutta: *Sri Loknath Pustaklay,* n.d.

"Benares, April 15." *Pioneer* (Allahabad) 1 (47). April 19, 1865, p. 4.

"Benares, April 17." *Pioneer* (Allahabad) 1 (48). April 21, 1865, p. 5.

Benson, Herbert. *The Relaxation Response.* New York: Morrow, 1975.

Blau, Zena Smith. *Old Age in a Changing Society.* New York: New Viewpoints, 1973.

Butler, Robert N. *Why Survive? Being Old in America.* New York: Harper and Row, 1975.

Capra, Fritjof. *The Tao of Physics: An Exploration of the Parallels between Modern Physics and Eastern Mysticism.* Berkeley: Shambala, 1975.

"Child-Killing: Police Still in Dark about Black Figure." *Northern Indian Patrika.* July 13, 1996.

Chopra, Deepak. *Unconditional Life: Discovering the Power to Fulfill Your Dreams.* New York: Bantam Books, 1992.

———. *Ageless Body, Timeless Mind: The Quantum Alternative to Growing Old.* New York: Harmony Books, 1993.

———. *The Return of Merlin: A Novel.* New York: Harmony Books, 1995.

———. *The Way of the Wizard: Twenty Spiritual Lessons in Creating the Life You Want.* New York: Harmony Books, 1995.

Cowley, Geoffrey. "Medical Mystery Tour: What Causes Alzheimer's Disease, and How Does It Ruin the Brain?" *Newsweek.* December 18, 1989.

Curtin, Sharon R. *Nobody Ever Died of Old Age*. Boston: Little, Brown, 1972.

Dalvi, Bharat, and Naresh Gandhi. "Have a Heart." *Times of India*. April 22, 1989.

Daly, Mary. "Sin Big." *New Yorker*. February 26, 1996.

Denby, David. "Queen Lear." *New Yorker*. October 3, 1994.

Donaldson, Stanley. "Granny, Lost 5 Yrs, Found in Murphy Bed!—She Was Mummified." *Sun*. August 23, 1988.

Egan, Timothy. "Her Mind Was Everything, Dead Woman's Husband Says." *New York Times* 139: B6 (L). June 6, 1990.

———. "As Memory and Music Faded, Alzheimer Patient Met Death." *New York Times* 139: A1 (N). June 7, 1990.

———. "Robbed by Alzheimer's, a Man Is Cast Away." *New York Times* 141: A1 (N). March 26, 1992.

"The Election Certainly Has Its Lighter Moments. . . . " *Times of India*. November 13, 1989.

"Friends Fear Alzheimer's Is Taking Toll on Harvey Korman Who Can't Even Remember Where He Lives." *Star*. August 14, 1990.

Gadgil, Gangadhar. "Meet Lata Mangeshkar: An Interview." *Illustrated Weekly of India*. April 1967.

"The Gathering at Hurdwar." *Bengal Hurkaru and India Gazette* (Calcutta). April 13, 1865, p. 46.

Gelman, David, Mary Hager, and Vicky Quade. "The Brain Killer." *Newsweek*. December 18, 1989.

Gordon, Michael R. "In Poignant Public Letter, Reagan Reveals That He Has Alzheimer's." *New York Times* 144: 1 (L). November 6, 1994.

"Human Hyena?" *Northern Indian Patrika*. July 2, 1996.

Humphry, Derek. *Final Exit: The Practicalities of Self-Deliverance and Assisted Suicide for the Dying*. Eugene: Hemlock Society, 1991.

"Hyena Hunters Fail to Convince People." *Northern Indian Patrika*. July 2, 1996.

"Hyena Menace Still in Villages: Police Forced to Hand Over Killed Girl's Body." *Northern Indian Patrika*. July 13, 1996.

"Hyena Strikes Again, Baby Saved." *Northern Indian Patrika*. July 12, 1996.

"Janpad men bheriye se zyādā aphvāhon kā jōr." *Dainak Jāgraṇ*. July 26, 1996.

"Kanpur Mob Roasts Woman Alive." *Northern Indian Patrika*. July 6, 1996.

Kantrowitz, Barbara. "Trapped inside Her Own World." *Newsweek*. December 18, 1989.

Kevorkian, Jack. Talk given to the National Press Club, Washington, D.C., July 29, 1996.

King, Ralph T., Jr. "Scientists Make a Big Leap on Alzheimer's." *Wall Street Journal*: B6. February 9, 1995.

Kolata, Gina. "Alzheimer's Is Produced in Mice, Report Says." *New York Times* 144: A8 (N). February 9, 1995.

"Lakaṛsunghvā ke aphvāh se svāsthy parīksaṇ nahīn ho sakā." *Dainak Jāgraṇ*. July 24, 1996.

"Lakaṛsunghvā ke bhram men bābā ko pulis ke havāle kiyā." *Dainak Jāgraṇ*. July 1996.

Lewin, Tamar. "Life and Death Choice Splits a Family." *New York Times* 145: A8 (N). January 19, 1996.

Mace, Nancy L., and Peter V. Rabins. *The 36-Hour Day: A Family Guide to Caring for Persons with Alzheimer's Disease, Related Dementing Illnesses, and Memory Loss in Later Life*. Baltimore: Johns Hopkins University Press, 1981.

Mahdihassan, S. *Indian Alchemy or Rasayana in the Light of Asceticism and Geriatrics*. New Delhi: Vikas, 1979.

Mehta, Bhanusankar. "Amde pirin se ghabrātā hai kyūn?" *Āpka Svāsthy*, 1989.

Menon, A. K. "Newsnotes: Blunting the Sickle: Naxalites Cool Fire." *India Today*. April 15, 1992.

Michals, Bob. "Dapper Dana Andrews' Alzheimer's Hell." *Globe*. March 3, 1992.

Morris, Edmund. "This Living Hand." *New Yorker*. January 16, 1995.

"Mysterious Disappearances of Two-Year-Old Girl." *Northern Indian Patrika*. July 21, 1996.

"Punjabi Bagh Woman Strangled." *Times of India*. January 11, 1990.

Ramos, George. "East L.A. Has a Reason to Be Grateful to Reagan." *Los Angeles Times* 114: B3. January 9, 1995.

Raza, Rahi Masoom. Interview. *India Today*. January 31, 1990.

"Researchers Say Skin Test May Identify People with Brain Disease." *New York Times* 142: C18. September 1, 1993.

Riordan, Teresa. "A Mouse Engineered to Get Alzheimer's." *New York Times* 144: C2 (N). April 3, 1995.

Sidey, Hugh. "The Sunset of My Life." *Time*. November 14, 1994.

Singh, Mahinder. "Ageing Process." Letter to the editor. *Times of India*. September 21, 1989.

Stone, Jerome H. "Reagan's Help Spurred Alzheimer's Funding." *Wall Street Journal*: A11. December 29, 1994.

"Study Suggests Alzheimer's May Begin Early." *San Francisco Chronicle*: A3. February 21, 1996.

Svoboda, Robert E. *Aghora: At the Left Hand of God*. Albuquerque: Brotherhood of Life, 1986.

"Thousands Lost in Mela Yet to Be Reunited." *Northern Indian Patrika*. February 9, 1989.

"Three 'Wolf-Men' Lynched in U.P." *Northern Indian Patrika*. July 19, 1996.

Venkatramani, S. H. "Neurology: The Better Brain." *India Today*. September 15, 1985.

Walford, Roy L. *Maximum Life Span*. New York: Norton, 1983.

Walker, Barbara. *The Crone: Woman of Age, Wisdom, and Power*. San Francisco: Harper and Row, 1985.

"Wolves Strike Again in Pratapgarh District." *Northern Indian Patrika*. July 2, 1996.

CLASSICAL AND LITERARY WORKS

[Aitareya Brahmana.] *Rigveda Brahmanas: The Aitareya and Kausitaki Brahmanas of the Rigveda*. Arthur Berriedale Keith, trans. Cambridge: Harvard University Press, 1920.

Atharva Veda. Ralph T. H. Griffith, trans. Benares: E. J. Lazarus, 1895–96.

Bandyopadhyay, Tarashankar. "The Witch." Kalpana Bardhan, trans. *Of Women, Outcastes, Peasants, and Rebels: A Selection of Bengali Short Stories*. Kalpana Bardhan, ed. Berkeley and Los Angeles: University of California Press, 1990 [1940].

Banerji, Bibhutibhushan. *Pather Panchali*. T. W. Clark and Tarapada Mukherji, trans. Calcutta: Rupa, 1990 [1929].

Bhāgavata Purāṇa. Ganesh Vasudeo Tagare, ed. and trans. Parts 1 and 3. *Puranas*, vols. 7 and 9. Unesco Collection of Representative Works, Indian Series. Delhi: Motilal Banarsidass, 1976.

Brahma Purāṇa. "A Board of Scholars," ed. and trans. Parts 1 and 3. *Puranas*, vols. 33 and 35. Unesco Collection of Representative Works, Indian Series. Delhi: Motilal Banarsidass, 1985–86.

Chatterjee, Upamanyu. *The Last Burden*. New Delhi: Viking, 1993.

Devi, Mahasweta. "The Witch-Hunt." Kalpana Bardhan, trans. *Of Women, Outcastes, Peasants, and Rebels: A Selection of Bengali Short Stories.* Kalpana Bardhan, ed. Berkeley and Los Angeles: University of California Press, 1990 [1979].

Forster, E. M. *A Passage to India.* London: E. Arnold and Co., 1924.

Ginsberg, Allen. *Collected Poems, 1947–1980.* New York: Harper and Row, 1984.

Haggard, H. Rider. *King Solomon's Mines.* London: Cassell and Company, 1885.

———. *She.* New York: McKinlay, Stone and Mackenzie, 1886.

———. "A Tale of Three Lions." *Allan's Wife, and Other Tales.* London: S. Blackett, 1889.

Kipling, Rudyard. *Kim.* London: Macmillan and Co., 1901.

Kramer, Heinrich, and James Sprenger. *Malleus Maleficarum.* Montague Summers, ed. London: Pushkin Press, 1948.

The Mahābhārata. Van Buitenen, J. A. B., trans. and ed. Vol. 1. Chicago: University of Chicago Press, 1973.

Merrill, James Ingram. *Selected Poems, 1946–1985.* New York: Knopf, 1992.

Padma Purāṇa. N. A. Deshpande and "a Board of Scholars," eds. and trans. Part 10. *Puranas,* vol. 48. Unesco Collection of Representative Works, Indian Series. Delhi, Motilal Banarsidass, 1992.

Pliny, the Elder. *The historie of the world. Commonly called, the Natvrall historie of C. Plinivs Secvndvs.* Philemon Holland, trans. London: A. Islip, 1601.

Premchand. [Premacānda]. "Būṛhī Kākī." *Mānsarovar.* Ilāhābād: Hans Prakāśan, 1959 [1921].

———*The Gift of a Cow [Godān].* Gordon C. Roadarmel, trans. Bloomington: Indiana University Press, 1968.

———. "The Power of a Curse" ["Garib ki Hay," literally "Lament of the Poor"]. *Deliverance and Other Stories.* David Rubin, trans. New Delhi: Penguin, 1988 [1911].

Raja Rao. *On the Ganga Ghat.* New Delhi: Vision Books, 1989.

Ravidas. "Poems of Ravidas." *Songs of the Saints of India.* John Stratton Hawley, ed. John Stratton Hawley and Mark Juergensmeyer, trans. New York: Oxford University Press, 1988.

Shakespeare, William. *King Lear. The Riverside Shakespeare,* G. Blakemore Evans, ed. Boston: Houghton Mifflin, 1974.

Sobtī, Kṛṣṇā. *Ai Laṛkī.* Naī Dillī: Rājkamal Prakāśan, 1991.

Somadeva [Bhaṭṭa]. *Kathāsaritsāgara.* English translation by C. H. Tawney. Delhi: Munshiram Manoharlal, 1968 [1880]. Hindi translation by Kedarnath Sharma Sarasvat. Patna: Bihar Rashtrabhasha Parishad, 1971.

Subramaniam, Kamala. *Mahābhārata.* Bombay: Bharatiya Vidya Bhavan, 1965.

Valmiki. *Ramāyana.* Vol. 2 of *Ayodhyākāṇḍa.* Sheldon I. Pollock, trans. Robert P. Goldman, ed. Princeton: Princeton University Press, 1986.

[*Vikramacarita*] *Vikrama's Adventures or the Thirty-Two Tales of the Throne.* Franklin Edgerton, ed. and trans. Part 1: Translation, in Four Parallel Recensions. Harvard Oriental Series. Vol. 26. Cambridge: Harvard University Press, 1926.

ELECTRONIC SITES

http://www.alz.org/assoc/media/institut.html. Downloaded 10/22/96.
http://www.alz.org/assoc/media/25. html. Downloaded 10/22/96.

http://www.biostat.wustl.edu/alzheimer/. Downloaded 10/22/96.
http://www.biostat.wustl.edu/hyperlists/alzheimer/9502/0002.html. Downloaded 10/22/96.
http://www.biostat.wustl.edu/hyperlists/alzheimer/9502/0052.html. Downloaded 10/22/96.
http://www.biostat.wustl.edu/hyperlists/alzheimer/9512/0218.html. Downloaded 10/22/96.
http://www.infi.net/~combsdm/ALG.htmlpostings. Downloaded 10/22/96.
http://www.infi.net/~combsdm/Secure-Book- Order-Form.html. Downloaded 10/22/96.
http://www.mentalhealth.com//icd/p22-0r04.html. Downloaded 10/22/96.

FILMS AND VISUAL MATERIAL

Bali, Suryakant. "All Voting Generations." Photograph. *Times of India*. December 5, 1989.

Butalia, Pankaj, director. *Moksha* [Salvation]. Film. 1993.

Chadha, S. K. "Elder's day was observed on Friday." Photograph. *Times of India*. November 19, 1988.

———. "Mr Jagdish Tytler, Congress candidate from the Sadar parliamentary constituency, seeking the blessings of an old woman by touching her feet during his campaign trail in the Subzi Mandi area in Delhi." Photograph. *Times of India*. November 4, 1989.

Camerini, Michael, and Rina Gill, directors. *Dadi and her Family*. Film. Worldview Productions. 1980.

Hoffman, Deborah, producer and director. *Complaints of a Dutiful Daughter*. Film. New York: Women Make Movies. 1994.

"The Janata Dal candidate from the Outer Delhi seat, Mr Tarif Singh, is blessed by an elderly woman in one of the padyatras through his constituency." Photograph. *Times of India*. November 10, 1989.

Khosa, Rajan. *Bodh Vṛkṣa* (Wisdom Tree). Film. Voice-over translated by Rajan Khosa. Unreleased.

Ninan, Ajit. "P. V. Narasimha Rao: Gaining in Stature." Cartoon. *India Today*. December 31, 1991.

[Old woman voting]. Photograph. *Times of India*. November 16, 1989.

[Old woman voting]. Photograph. *Times of India*. March 23, 1990.

"Paśchim Bangāl ke barsāt kṣetr men 120 varṣiya jān bībī matdān karne jā rahī hain." Photograph. *Dainak Jāgraṇ*. November 29, 1989.

Paul, Ashit, ed. *Woodcut Prints of Nineteenth Century Calcutta*. Calcutta: Seagull, 1983.

Tejpal, Madhu, director. *Apne Begāne*. Film. 1989.

MEDICAL WRITINGS (COSMOPOLITAN)

Alzheimer, Alois. "Uber eine eigenartige Erkrankung der Hirnride." *Allgemeine Zeitschrift für Psychiatrie* 64: 146–48. 1907.

Avorn, Jerome, and Stephen B. Soumerai. "Improving Drug-Therapy Decisions through Educational Outreach: A Randomized Controlled Trial of Academically Based "Detailing." *New England Journal of Medicine* 308 (24): 1457–63. 1983.

Bacon, Roger. *The Care of Old Age and Preservation of Youth*. Richard Browne, ed. and trans. London: Thomas Flesber, Edward Evets, 1683.

Barrett, Albert M. "Degeneration of Intracellular Neurofibrils with Miliary Gliosis in Psychoses of the Senile Period." *Proceedings of the American Medico-Psychological Association* 17: 393. 1910.

Bharucha, N. E., E. P. Bharucha, H. D. Dastur, and B. S. Schoenberg. "Pilot Survey of the Prevalence of Neurologic Disorders in the Parsi Community of Bombay." *American Journal of Preventive Medicine* 3 (5): 293–99. 1987.

Bleuler, Eugen. *Textbook of Psychiatry*. A. A. Brill, ed. Authorized English edition. New York: Macmillan, 1924.

Chandra, V., M. Ganguli, G. Ratcliff, R. Pandav, S. Sharma, J. Gilby, S. Belle, C. Ryan, C. Baker, E. Seaberg et al. "Studies of the Epidemiology of Dementia: Comparisons between Developed and Developing Countries." *Aging* 6 (5): 307–21. 1994.

Charcot, Jean Martin. *Leçons Cliniques sur les Maladies des Vieillards et les Maladies Chroniques*. Paris: P. Asselin, 1866.

———. *Leçons Cliniques sur les Maladies des Vieillards et les Maladies Chroniques*. Paris: A. Delahaye, 1867.

———. *Clinical Lectures on the Diseases of Old Age*. Leigh H. Hunt, trans. New York: W. Wood and Co., 1881.

———. *Clinical Lectures on Senile and Chronic Diseases*. William S. Tuke, trans. London: New Sydenham Society, 1881.

Chui, H. C. "Dementia: A Review Emphasizing Clinicopathologic Correlation and Brain-Behavior Relationships." *Archives of Neurology* 46 (7): 806–14. 1989.

Clarfield, A. M. "The Reversible Dementias: Do They Reverse?" *Annals of Internal Medicine* 109 (6): 476–86. 1988.

Coffman, J. D. "Drug Therapy: Vasodilator Drugs in Peripheral Vascular Disease." *New England Journal of Medicine* 300: 713–17. 1979.

Dawson, P., and D. W. Reid. "Behavioral Dimensions of Patients at Risk of Wandering." *Gerontologist* 27 (1): 104–7. 1987.

De Fleury, Maurice. "French Clinical Lecture on the Change of Life in Man." *Medical Press* 89: 566–67. 1910.

Diagnostic and Statistical Manual of Mental Disorders: DSM-III-R. Washington: American Psychiatric Association, 1987.

Diagnostic and Statistical Manual of Mental Disorders: DSM-IV: International Version with ICD-10 Codes. Washington: American Psychiatric Association, 1995.

Dieulafoy, G. *Manuel de Pathologie Interne*. Sixteenth edition. Paris: Masson, 1918.

Durrant, C. M. "On the Commencing Climacteric Period in the Male." *British Medical Journal* 2: 233–35. 1865.

East Boston Senior Health Project. "Interview Seven—Home Follow-Up." Form SH15 OMB 0925–0248, n.d. [1988].

Flint, Austin. *Clinical Medicine*. Philadelphia: Henry C. Lea, 1879.

Folstein, Marshal F., S. E. Folstein, and P. R. McHugh. "'Mini-Mental State': A Practical Method for Grading the Cognitive State of Patients for the Clinician." *Journal of Psychiatric Research* 12: 189–98. 1975.

Fuller, Solomon C. "Alzheimer's Disease (Senium Præcox): The Report of a Case and Review of Published Cases." *Journal of Nervous and Mental Disorders* 39: 440–55, 536–57. 1912.

Galloway, D. "The Male Climacteric." *Malayan Medical Journal* 8: 129–33. 1933.

George, T. "Menopause: Some Interpretations of the Results of a Study among a Non-Western Group." *Maturitas* 10 (2): 109–16. 1988.

Gleason, W. Stanton. "The Crucial Age of Man." *Medical Record* 90 (21): 881–89. 1916.

Graves, Amy B., Eric B. Larson, Lon R. White, Evelyn L. Teng, and Akira Homma. "Opportunities and Challenges in International Collaborative Epidemiologic Research of Dementia and Its Subtypes: Studies between Japan and the U.S." *International Psychogeriatrics* 6 (2): 209–23. 1994.

Hachinski, Vladimir C. "The Decline and Resurgence of Vascular Dementia." *Canadian Medical Association Journal* 142 (2): 107–111. 1990.

Halford, Henry. *Essays and Orations.* London: John Murray, 1833.

Henderson A. S. "The Risk Factors for Alzheimer's Disease: A Review and a Hypothesis." *Acta Psychiatrica Scandinavica* 78 (3): 257–75. 1988.

Homma, A., and K. Hasegawa. "Recent Developments in Gerontopsychiatric Research on Age-Associated Dementia in Japan." *International Psychogeriatrics* 1 (1): 31–49. 1989.

The ICD-10 Classification of Mental and Behavioural Disorders: Clinical Descriptions and Diagnostic Guidelines. Geneva: World Health Organization, 1992.

The ICD-10 Classification of Mental and Behavioural Disorders: Diagnostic Criteria for Research. Geneva: World Health Organization, 1993.

Jackson, J. Hughlings. "A Lecture on Softening of the Brain." *Lancet* 2 (2714). 1875.

Jorm, A. F., A. E. Korten, and A. S. Henderson. "The Prevalence of Dementia: A Quantitative Integration of the Literature." *Acta Psychiatrica Scandinavica* 76 (5): 465–79. 1987.

Katzman, R., M. Y. Zhang, Ouang-Ya-Qu, Z. Y. Wang, W. T. Liu, E. Yu, S. C. Wong, D. P. Salmon, and I. Grant. "A Chinese Version of the Mini-Mental State Examination: Impact of Illiteracy in a Shanghai Dementia Survey." *Journal of Clinical Epidemiology* 41 (10): 971–78. 1988.

Kennedy, Henry. "Observations on Climacteric Disease, with Cases." *Dublin Journal of Medical Science* 25: 245–66. 1844.

Kraepelin, Emil. *Lectures on Clinical Psychiatry.* Revised English edition. London: Baillière, Tindall and Cox, 1968 [1904].

———. *Memoirs.* H. Hippius, G. Peters, and D. Ploog, eds. Cheryl Woodin-Deane, trans. Berlin: Springer-Verlag, 1987.

Kugler, J. "Electroencephalographic and Psychometric Measurements during Treatment of Cerebral Insufficiency with Nicergoline and Co-dergocrine Mesylate." *Ergot Alkaloids and Aging Brain: An Update on Nicergoline.* J. Kugler and A. Agnoli, eds. Amsterdam: Excerpta Medica, 1988.

Kugler, J., and A. Agnoli, eds. *Ergot Alkaloids and Aging Brain: An Update on Nicergoline.* Amsterdam: Excerpta Medica, 1988.

Maclachlan, Daniel. *A Practical Treatise on the Diseases and Infirmities of Advanced Life.* London: John Churchill, 1863.

Martin, James Ranald. *The Influence of Tropical Climates on European Constitutions, including Practical Observations on the Nature and Treatment of the Diseases of Europeans on Their Return from Tropical Climates.* New edition. London: John Churchill. 1856.

Meyer, J. S., B. W. Judd, T. Tawaklna, R. L. Rogers, and K. F. Mortel. *Improved Cognition after Control of Risk Factors for Multi-infarct Dementia.* Journal of the American Medical Association 256 (16): 2203–9. 1986.

Meyer, J. S., K. L. McClintic, R. L. Rogers, P. Sims, and K. F. Mortel. "Aetiological Considerations and Risk Factors for Multi-Infarct Dementia." *Journal of Neurology, Neurosurgery and Psychiatry* 51 (12): 1489–97. 1988.

Moinson, Louis. "Retour d'Age Chez la Femme et Chez l'Homme." *Journal de Médecine de Paris* 54: 345–46. 1934.

Moore, William. *A Manual of Family Medicine and Hygiene for India*. Seventh edition. Delhi: Sri Satguru, 1989 [1907].

Nascher, I. L. *Geriatrics: The Diseases of Old Age and Their Treatment*. Philadelphia: P. Blakiston's, 1914.

———. "Evidences of Senile Mental Impairment." *American Journal of Clinical Medicine* 22: 541–45. 1915.

Osuntokun, B. O., A. O. Ogunniyi, G. U. Lekwauwa, and A. B. Oyediran. "Epidemiology of Age-Related Dementias in the Third World and Aetiological Clues of Alzheimer's Disease." *Tropical and Geographical Medicine* 43 (4): 345–51. 1991.

Overbeck-Wright, A. W. *Lunacy in India*. London: Ballière, Tindall, and Cox, 1921.

Palthe, Van Wulfften. "Psychiatry and Neurology in the Tropics." *Malayan Medical Journal* 8: 133ff. 1933.

Pershad, Dwarka, and N. N. Wig. *P.G.I. Memory Scale: Abridged Manual with Additional Norms*. Chandigarh: Postgraduate Institute of Medical Education and Research, 1979.

Podolsky, Edward. "The Critical Period in a Man's Life." *Sind Medical Journal* 6: 70–73. 1933.

Power, Henry, and Leonard W. Sedgwick, eds. *The New Sydenham Society's Lexicon of Medicine and the Allied Sciences*. Vol. 3. London: New Sydenham Society, 1888.

Prus, Clovis René. "Recherches sur les Maladies de la Vieillesse." *Archives Generales de Medicine* 8: 1–27. 1840.

Rader J. "A Comprehensive Staff Approach to Problem Wandering." *Gerontologist* 27 (6): 756–60. 1987.

Ramaseshan, S., and G. M. Martin, eds. *Current Science* 63 (8). 1992.

Rocca, W. A., S. Bonaiuto, A. Lippi, P. Luciani, F. Turtu, F. Cavarzeran, and L. Amaducci. "Prevalence of Clinically Diagnosed Alzheimer's Disease and Other Dementing Disorders: A Door-to-door Survey in Appignano, Macerata Province, Italy." *Neurology* 40 (4): 626–31. 1990.

Rostan, Léon Louis. *Recherches sur le Ramollissement du Cerveau*. Paris: Chez Bechet Jeune, 1823.

Rowland, Richard. *On the Nature and Treatment of Softening of the Brain*. London: Highley and Son, 1851.

Scot, Reginald. *The Discoverie of Witchcraft*. Arundel: Centaur, 1964 [1584].

Sharma, V. K., and M. S. Saxena. "Climacteric Symptoms: A Study in the Indian Context." *Maturitas* 3 (1): 11–20. 1981.

Simchowicz, Teofil. "La Maladie d'Alzheimer et son Rapport avec la Démence Sénile." *L'Encéphale* 9 (1): 218–31. 1914.

Skae, Francis. "Climacteric Insanity." *Edinburgh Medical Journal* 10: 703–16. 1865.

———. "Climacteric Insanity in the Male." *Edinburgh Medical Journal* 11: 232–44. 1865.

Smith, John. *The Portrait of Old Age. Wherein Is Contained a Sacred Anatomy Both of Soul and Body, and a Perfect Account of the Infirmities of Age Incident to Them Both*. Third edition. London: E. Eithers, 1752.

Soumerai, Stephen B., and Jerry Avorn. "Predictors of Physician Prescribing Change in an Educational Experiment to Improve Medication Use." *Medical Care* 25 (3): 210–21. 1987.

Stevens, Preston S., Jr. "Design for Dementia: Re-creating the Loving Family." *American Journal of Alzheimer's Care and Research* 2 (1):16–22. 1987.

Sulkava, R., J. Wikstrom, A. Aromaa, R. Raitasalo, V. Lehtinen, K. Lahtela, and J. Palo. "Prevalence of Severe Dementia in Finland." *Neurology* 35 (7): 1025–29. 1985.

Tanner, Thomas Hawkes. *On the Signs of Diseases of Pregnancy.* London: Renshaw, 1860.

"Therapeutical Effectiveness in Ageing Disorders: Advances in Clinical and Experimental Nicergoline Research." Pamphlet. Bombay: Dominion Chemical Industries, n.d.

Thewlis, Malford Wilcox. *The Care of the Aged (Geriatrics).* St. Louis: C. V. Mosby, 1941.

Tiffany, William J. "The Occurrence of Miliary Plaques in Senile Brains." *American Journal of Insanity* 70: 207–51. 1913–14.

Venkoba Rao, A. K. *Psychiatry of Old Age in India.* Ahmedabad: Torrent Laboratories, 1989.

Venkoba Rao, A. K., and T. Madhavan. "Geropsychiatric Morbidity Survey in a Semi-Urban Area near Madurai." *Indian Journal of Psychiatry* 24: 258–67. 1982.

Venkoba Rao, A. K., B. S. Virudhagirinathan, and R. Malathi. "Mental Illness in Patients Aged Fifty and Over (A Psychiatric, Psychological and Sociological Study)." *Indian Journal of Psychiatry* 14: 319–32. 1972.

Wadia, Noshir H. "Experience with the Differential Diagnosis and Prevalence of Dementing Illness in India." *Current Science* 63 (8): 419–30. 1992.

Warthin, Aldred Scott. *Old Age, the Major Involution: The Physiology and Pathology of the Aging Process.* New York: P. B. Hoeber, 1929.

Weyer, Johannes. *Witches, Devils, and Doctors in the Renaissance* [*De praestigiis daemonum*]. Georges Mora, ed. John Shea, trans. Binghamton: Medieval and Renaissance Texts and Studies, 1991 [1583].

WHO Scientific Group on Senile Dementia. *Dementia in Later Life: Research and Action.* Technical Report Series 730: 1–74. 1986.

Yesavage, J. A., J. R. Tinklenberg, L. E. Hollister et al. "Vasodilators in Senile Dementias: A Review of the Literature." *Archives of General Psychiatry* 36: 220. 1979.

MEDICAL WRITINGS (AYURVEDIC)

Boral, G. C., Gautam Bandopadyaya, Anjan Boral, N. N. Das, and P. S. Nandi. "Geriforte in Anxiety Neurosis." *Indian Journal of Psychiatry* 31 (3): 237, 258–60. 1989.

Caraka saṃhitā. Priyavrat Sharma, ed., trans. Varanasi: Chaukhambha Orientalia, 1983.

Dash, Bhagwan. *Fundamentals of Ayurvedic Medicine.* Delhi: Bansal and Co., 1978.

Mithal, C. P. *Miracles of Urine Therapy.* Second revised edition. New Delhi: Pankaj Publications, 1979.

Ojha, Divakar, and Ashok Kumar. *Panchakarma-Therapy in Ayurveda.* Varanasi: Chaukhamba Amarabharati Prakashan, 1978.

Ojha, J. K. *Chyavanaprasha: A Scientific Study.* Varanasi: Tara Publications, 1978.

Patel, Raojibhai Manibhai. *Manav Mootra = Auto-Urine Therapy: A Treatise and Urine for Universal Health.* Santilal M. Desai, ed. Third revised edition. Ahmedabad: Bharat Sevak Samaj Publications, 1978.

Śārṅgadhara saṃhitā. K. R. Srikanta Murthy, trans. Varanasi: Chaukhamba Orientalia, 1984.

Srikanta Murthy, K. R. Introduction to *Śārṅgadhara saṃhitā*. K. R. Srikanta Murthy, trans. Varanasi: Chaukhamba Orientalia, 1984.

[*Suśruta saṃhitā*] Sushruta Samhitā. Kunja Lal Bhishagratna, trans. Third edition. Varanasi: Chowkhamba Sanskrit Series Office, 1981 [1911].

LEGAL TEXTS AND GOVERNMENT DOCUMENTS

All India Reporter [AIR]. *Madras Section.* Nagpur, 1940

Beotra, Rai Sahib B. R. *The Indian Lunacy Act (Act IV of 1912) (Central and States).* Allahabad: Law Book Co., 1965.

Chaudhari, D. H., and A. D. Chaudhari. *The Hindu Succession Act, 1956: Act No. 30 of 1956.* Third edition. Calcutta: Eastern Law House, 1963.

Department of International Economic and Social Affairs. *Demographic Indicators of Countries: Estimates and Projections as Assessed in 1980.* New York: United Nations, 1982.

Hidayatullah, M., and Arshad Hidayatullah. *[Mulla's] Principles of Mahomedan Law.* Eighteenth edition. Bombay: N. M. Tripathi, 1985 [1977].

India, Ministry of Welfare. "The Aged in India: Policies and Programmes. Status Paper for the World Assembly on Aging." *Aging in India: Challenge for the Society.* M. L. Sharma and T. N. Dak, eds. Delhi: Ajanta, 1987.

India, Ministry of Welfare. "Responses, Prepared for United Nations Office at Vienna, Centre for Social Development and Humanitarian Affairs in Response to 1988 Questionnaire: Second Review and Appraisal of Implementation of the Vienna International Plan of Action on Aging (United Nations Document Number V.88–20838)." New Delhi: Ministry of Welfare, 1988.

Nevill, H. R. *Benares: A Gazetteer.* Allahabad: Government Press, United Provinces, 1909.

Ramamurti, Mantha. *Law of Wills in India and Pakistan.* Third edition. Allahabad: Law Publishers, 1980.

Roy Chowdhury, Salil K. and H. K. Saharay. *[Paruck's] Indian Succession Act, 1925 (Act XXXIX of 1925).* Seventh edition. Bombay: N. M. Tripathi, 1988.

United Nations Office at Vienna, Centre for Social Development and Humanitarian Affairs. "Questionnaire: Second Review and Appraisal of Implementation of the Vienna International Plan of Action on Aging." United Nations Document Number V. 88–20838. 1988.

United Nations World Assembly on Aging. "Report." United Nations Document Number A/CONF. 113/31. 1982.

United States Department of State. "U.S. National Report on Aging for the United Nations World Assembly on Aging." Washington: Department of State, 1982.

SCHOLARLY WORKS

Achenbaum, W. Andrew. "Societal Perceptions of the Aging and the Aged." *Handbook of Aging and the Social Sciences.* Second edition. Robert H. Binstock and Ethel Shanas, eds. New York: Van Nostrand, 1985.

Agar, Michael. *Speaking of Ethnography.* Beverly Hills: Sage, 1986.

Agarwal, Bina. "Social Security and the Family: Coping with Seasonality and Calamity in Rural India." *Journal of Peasant Studies* 17 (3): 341–412. 1990.

————. *A Field of One's Own: Gender and Land Rights in South Asia*. Cambridge: Cambridge University Press, 1994.

Ahmad, Aijaz. *In Theory: Classes, Nations, Literatures*. London: Verso, 1992.

Alter, Joseph S. *The Wrestler's Body: Identity and Ideology in North India*. Berkeley and Los Angeles: University of California Press, 1992.

Althusser, Louis. *Lenin and Philosophy, and Other Essays*. Ben Brewster, trans. London: New Left Books, 1971.

Amaducci, L. A., W. A. Rocca, and B. S. Schoenberg. "Origin of the Distinction between Alzheimer's Disease and Senile Dementia: How History Can Clarify Nosology." *Neurology* 36 (11): 1497–99. 1986.

Amin, Shahid. "Gandhi as Mahatma: Gorakhpur District, Eastern UP, 1921–2." *Selected Subaltern Studies*. Ranajit Guha and Gayatri Chakravorty Spivak, eds. New York: Oxford University Press, 1988.

Anantharaman, R. N. "Adjustment and Its Correlates in Old Age." *Indian Journal of Clinical Psychology* 6: 165–68. 1979.

Appadurai, Arjun. "Is Homo Hierarchicus?" *American Ethnologist* 13 (4): 745–61. 1986.

Arnold, David. *Colonizing the Body: State Medicine and Epidemic Disease in Nineteenth-Century India*. Berkeley and Los Angeles: University of California Press, 1993.

Babb, Lawrence A. *Redemptive Encounters: Three Modern Styles in the Hindu Tradition*. Delhi: Oxford University Press, 1987.

Bailey, F. G. *Caste and the Economic Frontier*. Manchester: Manchester University Press, 1957.

Bakshi, S. R. *Arya Samaj: Swami Dayananda and His Ideology*. Vol. 1. Delhi: Anmol, 1991.

Banerjee, Sumanta. *The Parlour and the Streets: Elite and Popular Culture in Nineteenth Century Calcutta*. Calcutta: Seagull, 1989.

Barthes, Roland. *Sade, Fourier, Loyola*. Richard Miller, trans. New York: Hill and Wang, 1976.

Basalla, George. "The Spread of Western Science." *Science* 156: 611–22. 1967.

Beach, Thomas G. "The History of Alzheimer's Disease: Three Debates." *Journal of the History of Medicine and Allied Sciences* 42: 327–49. 1987.

Becker, Gaylene. *Growing Old in Silence*. Berkeley and Los Angeles: University of California Press, 1980.

Berreman, Gerald. "The Brahmanical View of Caste." *Contributions to Indian Sociology* (N.S.) 5: 16–23. 1971.

Berrios, G. E. "Alzheimer's Disease: A Conceptual History." *International Journal of Geriatric Psychiatry* 5 (6): 355–65. 1990.

Berrios, G. E., and H. L. Freeman, eds. "Alzheimer and the Dementias." London: Royal Society of Medicine Services, 1991.

Bhatia, H. S. *Aging and Society: A Sociological Study of Retired Public Servants*. Udaipur: Arya's Book Centre, 1983.

Biswas, Sailendra, ed. *Samsad Bengali-English Dictionary*. Subodhchandra Sengupta, revision ed. Calcutta: Sahitya Samsad, 1968.

Biswas, Suhas K., ed. *Aging in Contemporary India*. Calcutta: Indian Anthropological Society, 1987.

Bose, A. B., and K. D. Gangrade, eds. *The Aging in India: Problems and Possibilities*. New Delhi: Abhinav, 1988.

Bottèro, Alain. "Consumption by Semen Loss in India and Elsewhere." *Culture, Medicine, and Psychiatry* 15 (3): 303–20. 1991.

Bourdieu, Pierre. *The Logic of Practice.* Richard Nice, trans. Stanford: Stanford University Press, 1990.

Bourgois, Philippe I. *In Search of Respect: Selling Crack in El Barrio.* Cambridge: Cambridge University Press, 1995.

Brass, Paul. "The Politics of Ayurvedic Education: A Case Study of Revivalism and Modernization in India." *Education and Politics in India: Studies in Organization, Society, and Policy.* Susanne Hoeber Rudolph and Lloyd I. Rudolph, eds. Cambridge: Harvard University Press, 1972.

Burgess, Ernest W. "Social Relations, Activities, and Personal Adjustment." *American Journal of Sociology* 59: 352–60. 1954.

———. *Aging in Western Societies.* Chicago: University of Chicago Press, 1960.

Butler, Judith P. *Bodies That Matter: On the Discursive Limits of "Sex."* New York: Routledge, 1993.

Callahan, Daniel. *Setting Limits: Medical Goals in an Aging Society.* New York: Simon and Schuster, 1987.

———. *The Troubled Dream of Life: Living with Mortality.* New York: Simon and Schuster, 1993.

Canguilhem, Georges. *The Normal and the Pathological.* Carolyn R. Fawcett, trans. New York: Zone Books, 1989.

Carstairs, G. Morris. "Hinjra and Jiryan: Two Derivatives of Hindu Attitude to Sexuality." *British Journal of Medical Psychiatry* 29: 128–38. 1956.

———. *The Twice-Born: A Study of a Community of High-Caste Hindus.* Bloomington: Indiana University Press, 1958.

———. *Death of a Witch: A Village in North India, 1950–81.* London: Hutchinson, 1983.

Chakrabarty, Dipesh. *Rethinking Working-Class History: Bengal, 1890–1940.* Princeton: Princeton University Press, 1989.

Chatterjee, Partha. *The Nation and Its Fragments: Colonial and Postcolonial Histories.* Princeton: Princeton University Press, 1993.

Chen, Martha Alter. "Responses to Widowhood: The Lives of Widows in Rural India." Manuscripts, September 1996.

Chen, Martha Alter, and Jean Drèze, "Widows and Health in Rural North India." *Economic and Political Weekly*: WS81-WS92, October 24–31. 1992.

Clifford, James. *The Predicament of Culture: Twentieth-Century Ethnography, Literature, and Art.* Cambridge: Harvard University Press, 1988.

Cohen, Lawrence. "Continuity and Change in the Fullness of Days: Traditional Hindu Attitudes toward Old Age." Thesis, Committee for the Study of Religion. Harvard University Archives HU 89. 208.0002. 1983.

———. "The Wives of Gaṇeśa." *Ganesh: Studies of an Asian God.* Robert L. Brown, ed. Albany: State University of New York Press, 1991.

———. "No Aging in India: The Uses of Gerontology." *Culture, Medicine, and Psychiatry* 16 (2): 123–61. 1992.

———. "Old Age: Cultural and Critical Perspectives." *Annual Review of Anthropology* 23: 137–58. 1994.

———. "The Epistemological Carnival: Meditations on Disciplinary Intentionality and Āyurveda." *Knowledge and the Scholarly Medical Traditions.* Don Bates, ed. Pp. 320–43. Cambridge: Cambridge University Press, 1995.

———. "Holi in Banaras and the *Mahaland* of Modernity." *GLQ—A Journal of Lesbian and Gay Studies* 2 (4): 399–424. 1995.

———. "The Pleasures of Castration: The Postoperative Status of Hijras, Jankhas, and Academics." *Sexual Nature, Sexual Culture*. Paul R. Abramson and Steven D. Pinkerton, eds. Pp. 276–304. Chicago: University of Chicago Press, 1995.

———. "Toward an Anthropology of Senility: Anger, Weakness, and Alzheimer's in Banaras, India." *Medical Anthropology Quarterly* 9 (3): 314–34. 1995.

Cohn, Bernard S. "The Changing Status of a Depressed Caste." *Village India*. McKim Marriott, ed. Chicago: University of Chicago Press, 1955.

———. "Chamar Family in a North Indian Village: A Structural Contingent." *Journal of Asian Studies* 19 (4). 1960.

———. *Colonialism and Its Forms of Knowledge: The British in India*. Princeton: Princeton University Press, 1996.

Cole, Thomas R. *The Journey of Life: A Cultural History of Aging in America*. Cambridge: Cambridge University Press, 1992.

Cole, Thomas R., and Sally A. Gadow, eds. *What Does It Mean to Grow Old? Reflections from the Humanities*. Durham: Duke University Press, 1986.

Courtright, Paul B. *Gaṇeśa: Lord of Obstacles, Lord of Beginnings*. New York: Oxford University Press, 1985.

Cowgill, Donald O., and Lowell Holmes, eds. *Aging and Modernization*. New York: Appleton-Century-Crofts, 1972.

Cowgill, Donald O., and Rosemary A. Orgren. "The International Development of Academic Gerontology." *Promoting the Growth of Gerontology in Higher Education*. Belmont: Wadsworth, 1979.

Cumming, Elaine, and William H. Henry. *Growing Old: The Process of Disengagement*. New York: Basic Books, 1961.

Daniel, E. Valentine. *Fluid Signs: Being a Person the Tamil Way*. Berkeley and Los Angeles: University of California Press, 1984.

Danielou, Alain. *Hindu Polytheism*. New York: Bollingen [Pantheon], 1964.

———. *Shiva and Dionysus*. K. F. Hurry, trans. London: East-West Publications, 1982.

Das, Veena. *Structure and Cognition: Aspects of Hindu Caste and Ritual*. Second edition. Delhi: Oxford University Press, 1982.

———. *Critical Events: An Anthropological Perspective on Contemporary India*. Delhi: Oxford University Press, 1995.

———. "The Aesthetics of Ageing." Talk given at the Townsend Center for the Humanities, University of California at Berkeley, 1996.

De, Sushil Kumar. *Bangla Prabād*. Third edition. Bhabatosha Datta and Tushara Cattopadhyaya, eds. Kalikata: E. Mukharji, 1986 [1392].

de Beauvoir, Simone. *The Coming of Age [La Vieillesse]*. Patrick O'Brian, trans. New York: G. P. Putnam's Sons. 1972 [1970].

Deliège, Robert. "Replication and Consensus: Untouchability, Caste, and Ideology in India." *Man* (N.S.) 27: 155–73. 1992.

Demos, John Putnam. *Entertaining Satan: Witchcraft and the Culture of Early New England*. Oxford: Oxford University Press, 1982.

Derne, Steve. *Cultures in Action: Family Life, Emotion, and Male Dominance in Banaras, India*. Albany: State University of New York Press, 1995.

Desai, I. P. "The Joint Family in India: An Analysis." *Sociological Bulletin* 5: 146–56. 1956.

Desai, K. G. Introduction to *Aging in India*. K. G. Desai, ed. Bombay: Tata Institute of Social Sciences, 1982.

———. "Situation of the Aged in India." *Aging in Contemporary India*. Suhas K. Biswas, ed. Calcutta: Indian Anthropological Society, 1987.

Desai, K. G., ed. *Aging in India*. Bombay: Tata Institute of Social Sciences, 1982.

De Souza, Alfred. *The Social Organisation of Aging among the Urban Poor*. New Delhi: Indian Social Institute, 1981.

De Souza, Alfred, and Walter Fernandes, eds. *Aging in South Asia*. New Delhi: Indian Social Institute, 1982.

Dirks, Nicolas. *The Hollow Crown: Ethnohistory of an Indian Kingdom*. Cambridge: Cambridge University Press, 1987.

———. "The Policing of Tradition: Colonialism and Anthropology in Southern India." Paper presented at Center for International Affairs, Harvard University, Cambridge, Mass., 1992.

Djurfeldt, Goran, and Staffan Lindberg. *Pills against Poverty: A Study of the Introduction of Western Medicine in a Tamil Village*. New Delhi: Macmillan, 1980.

Drèze, Jean, and Amartya K. Sen. *Hunger and Public Action*. Oxford: Clarendon Press, 1989.

Dumont, Louis. *Homo Hierarchicus: The Caste System and Its Implications*. Revised English edition. Marc Sainsbury, Louis Dumont, and Basia Gulati, trans. Chicago: University of Chicago Press, 1980.

du Toit, Brian M. *Aging and Menopause among Indian South African Women*. Albany: State University of New York Press, 1990.

Eck, Diana L. *Darsan: Seeing the Divine Image in India*. Chambersburg: Anima, 1981.

———. *Banaras: City of Light*. New York: Knopf, 1982.

Edgerton, Franklin. Introduction to *Vikrama's Adventures or the Thirty-Two Tales of the Throne*. Franklin Edgerton, ed. and trans. Part 1: Translation, in Four Parallel Recensions. Harvard Oriental Series. Vol. 26. Cambridge: Harvard University Press, 1926.

Epstein, T. Scarlett. *Economic Development and Social Change in South India*. Manchester: Manchester University Press, 1962.

———. *South India: Yesterday, Today, and Tomorrow*. London: Macmillan, 1973.

Estes, Carroll L. *The Aging Enterprise: A Critical Examination of Social Policies and Services for the Aged*. San Francisco: Jossey-Bass, 1980.

Evans-Pritchard, E. E. *Witchcraft, Oracles and Magic among the Azande*. Oxford: Clarendon Press, 1937.

Farmer, Paul, and Arthur Kleinman. "AIDS as Human Suffering." *Daedalus* 118 (2): 135–50. 1989.

Favret-Saada, Jeanne. *Deadly Words: Witchcraft in the Bocage*. Catherine Cullen, trans. Cambridge: Cambridge University Press, 1980.

Filliozat, Jean. *The Classical Doctrine of Indian Medicine*. Delhi: Munshiram Manoharlal, 1976.

Fischer, David Hackett. *Growing Old in America*. Oxford: Oxford University Press, 1978.

FitzGerald, Frances. *Cities on a Hill: A Journey through Contemporary American Cultures*. New York: Simon and Schuster, 1986.

Foucault, Michel. *Discipline and Punish: The Birth of the Prison*. Alan Sheridan, trans. New York: Pantheon, 1977.

Fox, Patrick. "From Senility to Alzheimer's Disease: The Rise of the Alzheimer's Disease Movement." *Milbank Quarterly* 67 (1): 58–102. 1989.

Fraser, Nancy. *Unruly Practices: Power, Discourse, and Gender in Contemporary Social Theory*. Minneapolis: University of Minnesota Press, 1989.

Freeman, James M. *Untouchable: An Indian Life History*. Stanford: Stanford University Press, 1979.

Freud, Sigmund. *The Psychopathology of Everyday Life*. Alan Tyson, trans. James Strachey, ed. New York: Norton, 1966 [1901].

——. "The 'Uncanny.'" Alix Strachey, trans. *Psychological Writings and Letters*. Sander L. Gilman, ed. New York: Continuum, 1995 [1919].

Gangrade, K. D. "Crisis of Values: A Sociological Study of the Old and the Young." *The Aging in India: Problems and Possibilities*. Bose, A. B. and K. D. Gangrade, eds. New Delhi: Abhinav, 1988.

Goffman, Erving. *Asylums*. Garden City, N.Y.: Doubleday, 1961.

Good, Byron. *Medicine, Rationality, and Experience: An Anthropological Perspective*. Cambridge: Cambridge University Press, 1994.

Good, Byron, and Mary-Jo DelVecchio Good. "The Semantics of Medical Discourse." *Sciences and Cultures*. Everett Mendelsohn and Yehuda Elkana, eds. Pp. 177–212. Sociology of the Sciences. Vol. 5. Dordrecht: D. Reidel, 1981.

Gore, M. S. *Urbanization and Family Change*. Bombay: Popular Prakashan, 1968.

Goyal, R. S. "Some Aspects of Ageing in India." *Aged in India (Socio-Demographic Dimensions)*. R. N. Pati and B. Jena, eds. New Delhi: Ashish, 1989.

Gray, John N., and David J. Mearns, eds. *Society from the Inside Out: Anthropological Perspectives on the South Asian Household*. New Delhi: Sage, 1989.

Gubrium, Jaber F. *Living and Dying at Murray Manor*. New York: St. Martin's Press, 1975.

——. *Oldtimers and Alzheimer's: The Descriptive Organization of Senility*. Greenwich: JAI Press, 1986.

——. "Structuring and Destructuring the Course of Illness: The Alzheimer's Disease Experience." *Sociology of Health and Illness* 9: 1–24. 1987.

Gupta, Akhil, and James Ferguson. "Discipline and Practice: 'The Field' as Site, Method, and Location in Anthropology." *Anthropology and "the Field": Boundaries, Areas, and Grounds in the Constitution of a Discipline*. Akhil Gupta and James Ferguson, eds. In press.

Haraway, Donna Jeanne. *Simians, Cyborgs, and Women: The Reinvention of Nature*. New York: Routledge, 1991.

Harrison, Mark. *Public Health in British India: Anglo-Indian Preventive Medicine, 1859–1914*. Cambridge: Cambridge University Press, 1994.

Havighurst, Robert J. "Flexibility and the Social Roles of the Retired." *American Journal of Sociology* 59: 309–11. 1954.

Hegel, Georg Wilhelm Friedrich. *The Philosophy of History*. J. Sibree, trans. New York: Dover, 1956.

Herrnstein, Richard J., and Charles Murray. *The Bell Curve: Intelligence and Class Structure in American Life*. New York: Free Press, 1994.

Howes, David, ed. *The Varieties of Sensory Experience: A Sourcebook in the Anthropology of the Senses*. Toronto: University of Toronto Press, 1991.

Hubert, Henri, and Marcel Mauss. *Sacrifice: Its Nature and Function*. Chicago: University of Chicago Press, 1981 [1898].

Inden, Ronald B. *Imagining India*. Oxford: Basil Blackwell, 1990.

——. "Embodying God: From Imperial Progresses to National Progress in India." *Economy and Society* 24 (2): 245–78. 1995.

James, William. *A Pluralistic Universe*. Cambridge: Harvard University Press, 1977.

Johnson, Colleen Leahy, and Frank A. Johnson. "A Micro-Analysis of 'Senility': The Responses of the Family and the Health Professionals." *Culture, Medicine and Psychiatry* 7: 77–96. 1983.

Johnson, M. "A Comment on Palmore and Whittington's Index of Similarity." *Social Forces* 51: 490–92. 1973.

Jones, William. "Introduction to 'Sacontala; or, the Fatal Ring: An Indian Drama by Calidas.'" *The Works of Sir William Jones*. Vol. 9. London: John Stockdale and John Walker, 1807.

Jordens, J. T. F. *Dayānanda Sarasvatī: His Life and Ideas*. Delhi: Oxford University Press, 1978.

Kakar, Sudhir. "Relative Realities: Images of Adulthood in Psychoanalysis and the Yogas." *Identity and Adulthood*. Sudhir Kakar, ed. Delhi: Oxford University Press, 1979.

———. *The Inner World: A Psycho-Analytic Study of Childhood and Society in India*. Delhi: Oxford University Press, 1981.

———. *The Colours of Violence*. New Delhi: Viking, 1995.

Kapur, Sohaila. *Witchcraft in Western India*. Hyderabad: Orient Longman, 1983.

Kaufman, Sharon R. *The Ageless Self: Sources of Meaning in Later Life*. New York: Meridian, 1986.

Keyfitz, Nathan, and Wilhelm Flieger. *World Population Growth and Aging: Demographic Trends in the Late Twentieth Century*. Chicago: University of Chicago Press, 1990.

Khare, R. S. *The Untouchable as Himself: Ideology, Identity, and Pragmatism among the Lucknow Chamars*. Cambridge: Cambridge University Press, 1984.

Kierkegaard, Soren. *Fear and Trembling; Repetition*. Howard V. Hong and Edna H. Hong, eds. and trans. Princeton: Princeton University Press, 1983.

———. *Stages on Life's Way: Studies by Various Persons*. Howard V. Hong and Edna H. Hong, eds. and trans. Princeton: Princeton University Press, 1988.

Kleinman, Arthur. "Depression, Somatization, and the New Cross-Cultural Psychiatry." *Social Science and Medicine* 11: 3–10. 1977.

———. *Patients and Healers in the Context of Culture: An Exploration of the Borderland between Anthropology, Medicine, and Psychiatry*. Berkeley and Los Angeles: University of California Press, 1980.

———. *The Illness Narratives: Suffering, Healing, and the Human Condition*. New York: Basic Books, 1988.

———. "A Window on Mental Health in China." *American Scientist* 76: 22–27. 1988.

———. "Social Sources of Pain, Distress, and Misery: A Medical Anthropological Perspective on the Symbolic Bridge between Social Structure and Physiology." *Kroeber Anthropological Society Papers* (Berkeley) 69–70: 14–22. 1989.

———. *Writing at the Margin: Discourse between Anthropology and Medicine*. Berkeley and Los Angeles: University of California Press, 1995.

Kleinman, Arthur, and Joan Kleinman. "Suffering and Its Professional Transformation: Toward an Ethnography of Interpersonal Experience." *Culture, Medicine, and Psychiatry* 15 (3): 275–301. 1991.

———. "The Appeal of Experience; The Dismay of Images: Cultural Appropriations of Suffering in Our Times." *Daedalus* 125 (1): 1–23. 1996.

Kohli, D. R. "Challenge of Aging." *Aging in India: Challenge for the Society*. M. L. Sharma and T. N. Dak, eds. Delhi: Ajanta, 1987.

Kolenda, Pauline. *Regional Differences in Family Structure in India*. Jaipur: Rawat, 1967.

Krishnan, T. N. "Demographic Transition in Kerala: Facts and Factors." *Economic and Political Weekly*, Special Number. 1976.

Kumar, Deepak. *Science and the Raj, 1857–1905*. Delhi: Oxford University Press, 1995.

Kumar, Nita. *The Artisans of Banaras: Popular Culture and Identity, 1880–1986*. Princeton: Princeton University Press, 1988.

Kurtz, Stanley N. *All the Mothers Are One: Hindu India and the Cultural Reshaping of Psychoanalysis*. New York: Columbia University Press, 1992.

Langer, Ellen J. *Mindfulness*. Reading: Addison-Wesley, 1989.

Laqueur, Thomas Walter. *Making Sex: Body and Gender from the Greeks to Freud*. Cambridge: Harvard University Press, 1990.

Larson, Gerald James. "The Trimurti of Smṛti in Classical Indian Thought." Paper presented at South Asia Symposium on Myth, Memory and History, University of Virginia, Charlottesville, 1992.

Laslett, Peter. "Societal Development and Aging." *Handbook of Aging and the Social Sciences*. Second edition. Robert H. Binstock and Ethel Shanas, eds. New York: Van Nostrand, 1985.

Latour, Bruno. *We Have Never Been Modern*. Catherine Porter, trans. Cambridge: Harvard University Press, 1993.

Leach, Edmund R. "Pulleyar and the Lord Buddha: Aspects of Religious Syncretism in Ceylon." *Psychoanalysis and the Psychoanalytic Review* 49: 80–102. 1962.

Lellouch, Alain. *Jean Martin Charcot et les Origines de la Geriatrie: Recherches Historiques sur le Fonds d'Archives de la Salpetriere*. Paris: Payot, 1992.

Leslie, Charles. "The Ambiguities of Medical Revalism in Modern India." *Asian Medical Systems: A Comparative Study*. Charles Leslie, ed. Pp. 356–67. Berkeley and Los Angeles: University of California Press, 1976.

Levin, Jack, and William C. Levin. *Ageism*. Belmont: Wadsworth, 1980.

Lock, Margaret M. *Encounters with Aging: Mythologies of Menopause in Japan and North America*. Berkeley and Los Angeles: University of California Press, 1993.

Luborsky, Mark R., and Andrea Sankar. "Extending the Critical Gerontology Perspective: Cultural Dimensions." *Gerontologist* 33 (4): 440. 1993.

Lutz, Catherine. "Depression and the Translation of Emotional Worlds." *Culture and Depression: Studies in the Anthropology and Cross-Cultural Psychiatry of Affect and Disorder*. Arthur Kleinman and Byron Good, eds. Berkeley and Los Angeles: University of California Press, 1985.

Lyman, Karen A. "Bringing the Social Back In: A Critique of the Biomedicalization of Dementia." *Gerontologist* 29 (5): 597–605. 1989.

Macfarlane, Alan. *Witchcraft in Tudor and Stuart England: A Regional and Comparative Study*. New York: Harper and Row, 1970.

Madan, T. N. *Family and Kinship: A Study of the Pandits of Rural Kashmir*. New York: Asia, 1965.

———. *Non-renunciation: Themes and Interpretations of Hindu Culture*. Delhi: Oxford University Press, 1987.

———. *Pathways: Approaches to the Study of Society in India*. Delhi: Oxford University Press, 1994.

Maine, Henry Sumner. *Village-Communities in the East and West with Other Lectures, Addresses, and Essays*. New York: Henry Holt, 1876.

Malamoud, Charles. "On the Rhetoric and Semantics of Purusartha." *Way of Life: King, Householder, Renouncer*. T. N. Madan, ed. Delhi: Motilal Banarsidass, 1988.

Mani, Lata. "Contentious Traditions." *Recasting Women: Essays in Colonial History*. Kumkum Sangari and Sudesh Vaid, eds. New Delhi: Kali for Women, 1989.

―――. "Multiple Mediations: Feminist Scholarship in the Age of Multinational Reception." *Feminist Review* 35 (summer): 24. 1990.

Marglin, Frédérique Apffel. "Power, Purity and Pollution: Aspects of the Caste System Reconsidered." *Contributions to Indian Sociology* (N.S.) 11 (2). 1977.

Marriott, McKim. "Hindu Transactions: Diversity without Dualism." *Transaction and Meaning: Directions in the Anthropology of Exchange and Symbolic Behavior*. Bruce Kapferer, ed. Philadelphia: Institute for the Study of Human Issues, 1976.

―――. "Constructing an Indian Ethnosociology." *Contributions to Indian Sociology* (N.S.) 23: 1. 1989.

Martin, Emily. *The Woman in the Body: A Cultural Analysis of Reproduction*. Boston: Beacon Press, 1987.

Marulasiddaiah, H. M. *Old People of Makunti*. Dharwar: Karnatak University, 1969.

Matilal, Bimal Krishna. *Logic, Language, and Reality: An Introduction to Indian Philosophical Studies*. Delhi: Motilal Banarsidass, 1985.

Mauss, Marcel. "Techniques of the Body." *Incorporations*. Jonathan Crary and Sanford Kwinter, eds. New York: Zone, 1992.

McClintock, Anne. *Imperial Leather: Race, Gender, and Sexuality in the Colonial Contest*. New York: Routledge, 1995.

Mencher, Joan. "The Caste System Upside Down, or the Not-So-Mysterious East." *Current Anthropology* 15: 469–93. 1974.

Minois, Georges. *Histoire de la Vieillesse en Occident de l'Antiquité à la Renaissance*. Paris: Fayard, 1987.

Mishra, Bhuvaneswarnath, and Vikramaditya Mishra, eds. *Kahavat Kos*. Patna: Bihar Rastrabhasa Parisad, 1965.

Mishra, Saraswati. *Problems and Social Adjustment in Old Age: A Sociological Analysis*. New Delhi: Gian, 1989.

Moffatt, Michael. *An Untouchable Community in South India: Structure and Consensus*. Princeton: Princeton University Press, 1979.

Mohanty, S. P. "Demographic and Socio-Cultural Aspects of Ageing in India—Some Emerging Issues." *Aged in India (Socio-Demographic Dimensions)*. R. N. Pati and B. Jena, eds. New Delhi: Ashish, 1989.

Montesquieu, Charles de Secondat. *The Spirit of the Laws*. Anne M. Cohler, Basia Carolyn Miller, and Harold Samuel Stone, trans. Cambridge: Cambridge University Press, 1989.

Moore, Sally Falk. *Social Facts and Fabrications: "Customary" Law on Kilimanjaro, 1880–1980*. Cambridge: Cambridge University Press, 1986.

Mora, George. Introduction to *Witches, Devils, and Doctors in the Renaissance* [Johannes Weyer, *De praestigiis daemonum*]. Georges Mora, ed. John Shea, trans. Binghamton, N.Y.: Medieval and Renaissance Texts and Studies, 1991.

Munn, Nancy D. "Cultural Anthropology of Time: A Critical Essay." *Annual Review of Anthropology* 21: 93–123. 1992.

Myerhoff, Barbara. *Number Our Days*. New York: Simon and Schuster, 1978.

Nader, Laura. *Harmony Ideology: Justice and Control in a Zapotec Mountain Village*. Stanford: Stanford University Press, 1990.

Nandy, Ashis. "Sati: A Nineteenth Century Tale of Women, Violence, and Protest." *At the Edge of Psychology*. Delhi: Oxford University Press, 1980.

————. *The Intimate Enemy: Loss and Recovery of Self under Colonialism*. Delhi: Oxford University Press, 1983.

Naraindas, Harish. "Poisons, Putrescence and the Weather: A Genealogy of the Advent of Tropical Medicine." *Contributions to Indian Sociology* 30 (1): 1–35. 1996.

Neugarten, Bernice, ed. *Middle Age and Aging*. Chicago: University of Chicago Press, 1968.

Neysmith, Sheila M., and Joey Edwardth. "Economic Dependency in the 1980s: Its Impact on Third World Elderly." *Aging and Society* 4 (1): 21–44. 1984.

Nichter, Mark. "The Layperson's Perception of Medicine as Perspective into the Utilization of Multiple Therapy Systems in the Indian Context." *Social Science and Medicine* 156: 225–33. 1980.

Nydegger, Corinne N. "Family Ties of the Aged in Cross-Cultural Perspective." *Gerontologist* 23: 26–32. 1983.

Oberoi, Harjot. *The Construction of Religious Boundaries: Culture, Identity, and Diversity in the Sikh Tradition*. Chicago: University of Chicago Press, 1994.

Obeysekere, Gananath. "Depression, Buddhism, and the Work of Culture in Sri Lanka." *Culture and Depression: Studies in the Anthropology and Cross-Cultural Psychiatry of Affect and Disorder*. Arthur Kleinman and Byron Good, eds. Berkeley and Los Angeles: University of California Press, 1985.

————. *The Work of Culture: Symbolic Transformation in Psychoanalysis and Anthropology*. Chicago: University of Chicago Press, 1990.

Oddie, Geoffrey A. *Popular Religion, Elites, and Reforms: Hook-Swinging and its Prohibition in Colonial India, 1800–1894*. New Delhi: Manohar, 1995.

O'Flaherty, Wendy Doniger. *The Origins of Evil in Hindu Mythology*. Berkeley and Los Angeles: University of California Press, 1976.

————. *Śiva, the Erotic Ascetic*. New York: Oxford University Press, 1981 [1973].

————. *Dreams, Illusion and Other Realities*. Chicago: University of Chicago Press, 1984.

Olivelle, Patrick. *The Āśrama System: The History and Hermeneutics of a Religious Institution*. New York: Oxford University Press, 1993.

Östör, Ákos. *Vessels of Time: An Essay on Temporal Change and Social Transformation*. Delhi: Oxford University Press, 1993.

Palmore, Erdman B., and Kenneth Manton. "Modernization and Status of the Aged: International Correlations." *Journal of Gerontology* 29: 205–10. 1974.

Parker, Andrew et al., eds. *Nationalisms and Sexualities*. New York: Routledge, 1992.

Parry, Jonathan P. "Sacrificial Death and the Necrophagous Ascetic." *Death and the Regeneration of Life*. Maurice Bloch and Jonathan Parry, eds. Cambridge: Cambridge University Press, 1982.

————. *Death in Banaras*. Cambridge: Cambridge University Press, 1994.

Parsons, Talcott. *Essays in Sociological Theory: Pure and Applied*. Glencoe: Free Press, 1949.

Pati, R. N. and B. Jena, eds. *Aged in India*. New Delhi: Ashish, 1989.

Peirce, Charles Sanders. *Selected Writings (Values in a Universe of Chance)*. Philip P. Wiener, ed. New York: Dover Publications, 1966 [1958].

Potter, Karl, ed. *The Tradition of Nyaya-Vaisesika up to Gangesa*. Vol. 2, *Encyclopedia of Indian Philosophies*. Delhi: Motilal Banarsidass, 1977.

————. *Advaita Vedanta up to Sankara and His Pupils*. Vol. 3, *Encyclopedia of Indian Philosophies*. Delhi: Motilal Banarsidass, 1981.

Propp, Vladimir. *Morphology of the Folktale*. Second edition. Louis A. Wagner, ed. Laurence Scott, trans. Austin: University of Texas Press, 1968.

Quadagno, Jill. *Aging in Early Industrial Society: Work, Family, and Social Policy in Nineteenth-Century England*. New York: Academic Press, 1982.

Quigley, Declan. *The Interpretation of Caste*. New York: Oxford University Press, 1993.

Rabinow, Paul. *French Modern: Norms and Forms of the Social Environment*. Cambridge: MIT Press, 1989.

———. "Artificiality and Enlightenment: From Sociobiology to Biosociality." *Incorporations*. Jonathan Crary and Sanford Kwinter, eds. New York: Zone, 1992.

———. "Galton's Regret and DNA Typing." *Culture, Medicine, and Psychiatry* 17 (1): 59–65. 1993.

Radcliffe-Brown, A. R. "On Joking Relationships." *Africa* 13 (3): 195–210. 1940.

Raheja, Gloria Goodwin. "Centrality, Mutuality and Hierarchy: Shifting Aspects of Inter-Caste Relationships in North India." *Contributions to Indian Sociology* (N S.) 23 (1): 79–101. 1989.

Ramamurthy, P. V. "Psychological Research of the Aged in India: Problems and Perspectives." *Developmental Psychology*. E. G. Parameshwaran and S. Bhogle, eds. New Delhi: Light and Life, 1979.

Ramanujan, A. K. "The Indian Oedipus." *Oedipus: A Folklore Casebook*. Lowell Edmunds and Alan Dundes, eds. New York: Garland, 1983.

———. "Is There An Indian Way of Thinking? An Informal Essay." *Contributions to Indian Sociology* 23 (1): 41–58. 1989.

Ramnath, Rajalakshmi. "Problems of the Aged." *Aged in India (Socio-Demographic Dimensions)*. R. N. Pati and B. Jena, eds. New Delhi: Ashish, 1989.

Rao, M. S. A. "Occupational Diversification and Joint Household Organization." *Contributions to Indian Sociology* (N.S.) 2: 98–111. 1968.

Reid, Janice. "'Going Up' or 'Going Down': The Status of Old People in an Australian Aboriginal Society." *Ageing and Society* 5: 69–95. 1985.

Rhoads, Ellen C. "Reevaluation of the Aging and Modernization Theory: The Samoan Evidence." *Gerontologist* 24: 243–50. 1984.

Robertson, A. F. *People and the State: An Anthropology of Planned Development*. Cambridge: Cambridge University Press, 1984.

Roland, Alan. *In Search of Self in India and Japan: Toward a Cross-Cultural Psychology*. Princeton: Princeton University Press, 1988.

Ross, Aileen D. *The Hindu Family in Its Urban Setting*. Toronto: University of Toronto Press, 1961.

Roy, Manisha. *Bengali Women*. Chicago: University of Chicago Press, 1975.

Rubin, Gayle, "The Traffic in Women: Notes on the 'Political Economy' of Sex." *Toward an Anthropology of Women*. Rayna Rapp Reiter, ed. New York: Monthly Review Press, 1975.

Sahlins, Marshall David. *Culture and Practical Reason*. Chicago: University of Chicago Press, 1976.

Saletore, R. N. *Indian Witchcraft*. New Delhi: Abhinav, 1981.

Sankar, Andrea. "'It's Just Old Age': Old Age as a Diagnosis in American and Chinese Medicine." *Age and Anthropological Theory*. David I. Kertzer and Jennie Keith, eds. Ithaca: Cornell University Press, 1984.

Saraswathi, T. S., and Ranjana Dutta. "Current Trends in Developmental Psychology: A Life Span Perspective." Vol. 1. of *Psychology in India: The State-of-the-Art*. Janak Pandey, ed. New Delhi: Sage, 1988.

Saraswati, Baidyanath. *Kashi: Myth and Reality of a Classical Cultural Tradition.* Simla: Indian Institute of Advanced Study, 1975.

———. "Cultures in Crisis: An Anthropological Exploration of the Hindu Widows of Kashi." Manuscript, 1984.

Sarkar, Sumit. "The Kalki-Avatar of Bikrampur: A Village Scandal in Early Twentieth Century Bengal." *Subaltern Studies VI.* Ranajit Guha, ed. Delhi: Oxford University Press, 1989.

Saxena, D. N. "Senior Citizens: Their Problems and Potentialities." *The Aging in India: Problems and Possibilities.* A. B. Bose and K. D. Gangrade, eds. New Delhi: Abhinav, 1988.

Scheper-Hughes, Nancy. "Theft of Life." *Society* 27 (6): 57–62. 1990.

———. "Three Propositions for a Critically Applied Medical Anthropology." *Social Science and Medicine* 30 (2): 189–97. 1990.

———. *Death without Weeping: The Violence of Everyday Life in Brazil.* Berkeley and Los Angeles: University of California Press, 1992.

Scheper-Hughes, Nancy, and Margaret M. Lock. "The Mindful Body: A Prolegomenon to Future Work in Medical Anthropology." *Medical Anthropology Quarterly* (N.S.) 1 (1): 6–41. 1987.

Schweitzer, Albert. *Indian Thought and Its Development.* Mrs. Charles E. B. Russell, trans. New York: H. Holt and Company, 1936.

Searle-Chatterjee, Mary. *Reversible Sex Roles: The Special Case of Benare Sweepers.* Oxford: Pergamon, 1981.

Sedgwick, Eve Kosofsky. *Between Men: English Literature and Male Homosexual Desire.* New York: Columbia University Press, 1985.

Shah, A. M. *The Household Dimension of the Family in India.* Berkeley and Los Angeles: University of California Press, 1974.

Sharma, M. L., and T. N. Dak, eds. *Aging in India: Challenge for the Society.* Delhi: Ajanta, 1987.

Shweder, Richard A. "Ghost Busters in Anthropology." *Kroeber Anthropological Society Papers* 69–70: 100–108. 1989.

Shweder, Richard A., and Joan G. Miller. "The Social Construction of the Person: How Is It Possible?" *The Social Construction of the Person.* Kenneth J. Gergen and Keith E. Davis, eds. Pp. 41–69. New York: Springer-Verlag, 1985.

Sicherman, Barbara. "The Paradox of Prudence: Mental Health in the Gilded Age." *Madhouses, Mad-Doctors, and Madmen.* Andrew Scull, ed. Philadelphia: University of Pennsylvania Press, 1981.

Singer, Milton B. *Man's Glassy Essence: Explorations in Semiotic Anthropology.* Bloomington: Indiana University Press, 1984.

Singh, Yogendra. *Modernization of Indian Tradition.* Delhi: Thomson, 1973.

Sinha, J. N. P. *Problems of Ageing.* New Delhi: Classical, 1989.

Sinha, Surajit, and Baidyanath Saraswati. *Ascetics of Kashi: An Anthropological Exploration.* Varanasi: N. K. Bose Memorial Foundation, 1978.

Sontag, Susan. *Illness as Metaphor.* New York: Farrar, Straus, and Giroux, 1978.

Soodan, Kirpal Singh. *Aging in India.* Calcutta: Minerva, 1975.

Srivastava, R. S. "Service Centres for the Aging." *The Aging in India: Problems and Possibilities.* A. B. Bose and K. D. Gangrade, eds. New Delhi: Abhinav, 1988.

Stearns, Peter N. *Old Age in European Society: The Case of France.* London: Croom Helm, 1977.

Stone, Allucquere Rosanne. *The War of Desire and Technology at the Close of the Mechanical Age.* Cambridge: MIT Press, 1995.

Strathern, Marilyn. "Culture in a Netbag: The Manufacture of a Subdiscipline in Anthropology." *Man* 16: 665–88. 1981.

Subrahmanium, C. Foreword to *The Aging in India: Problems and Possibilities*. A. B. Bose and K. D. Gangrade, eds. New Delhi: Abhinav, 1988.

Tambiah, Stanley Jeyaraja. *The Buddhist Saints of the Forest and the Cult of Amulets*. Cambridge: Cambridge University Press, 1984.

Taussig, Michael T. *The Devil and Commodity Fetishism in South America*. Chapel Hill: University of North Carolina Press, 1980.

Tharu, Susie. "Response to Julie Stephens." *Subaltern Studies VI*. Ranajit Guha, ed. Delhi: Oxford University Press, 1989.

Townsend, Peter. "The Structured Dependency of the Elderly: A Creation of Social Policy in the Twentieth Century." *Aging and Society* 1: 5–28. 1981.

Trawick, Margaret. *Notes on Love in a Tamil Family*. Berkeley and Los Angeles: University of California Press, 1990.

Turner, Victor. *The Ritual Process: Structure and Anti-structure*. Chicago: Aldine, 1969.

———. *Dramas, Fields, and Metaphors: Symbolic Action in Human Society*. Ithaca: Cornell University Press, 1974.

Uberoi, J. P. Singh. *Religion, Civil Society and the State: A Study of Sikhism*. Delhi: Oxford University Press, 1996.

Van der Veen, Klaas W. "The Joint Family: Persistence or Decay?" *Aspects of Changing India*. S. Devadas Pillai, ed. Bombay: Popular Prakashan, 1976.

Varma, Ramchandra, ed. *Samksipt Hindi Sabdsagar*. Ninth edition. Kashi [Varanasi]: Nagaripracarini Sabha, 1987.

Vatuk, Sylvia. "Withdrawal and Disengagement as a Cultural Response to Aging in India." *Aging in Culture and Society*. Christine L. Fry, ed. South Hadley: Bergin and Garvey, 1980.

———. "To Be a Burden on Others": Dependency Anxiety among the Elderly in India. *Divine Passions: The Social Construction of Emotion in India*. Owen M. Lynch, ed. Berkeley and Los Angeles: University of California Press, 1990.

Vijaya Kumar, S. *Family Life and Socio-Economic Problems of the Aged*. Delhi: Ashish Publishing House, 1991.

Visvanathan, Shiv. *Organizing for Science: The Making of an Industrial Research Laboratory*. Delhi: Oxford University Press, 1985.

Vivekananda, Swami. *Chicago Addresses*. Calcutta: Advaita Ashrama, 1968.

Weiner, Dora B. *The Citizen-Patient in Revolutionary and Imperial Paris*. Baltimore: Johns Hopkins University Press, 1993.

White, David. "Dogs Die." *History of Religions* 23 (4): 283–303. 1989.

Wolfenstein, Martha. *Childhood in Contemporary Cultures*. Margaret Mead and Martha Wolfenstein, eds. Chicago: University of Chicago Press, 1955.

Woodward, Kathleen M. *Aging and Its Discontents: Freud and Other Fictions*. Bloomington: Indiana University Press, 1991.

Young, Allan. "When Rational Men Fall Sick: An Inquiry into Some Assumptions Made by Medical Anthropologists." *Culture, Medicine and Psychiatry* 5: 317–35. 1981.

———. "Rational Men and the Explanatory Model Approach." *Culture, Medicine and Psychiatry* 6: 57–71. 1982.

Zimmermann, Francis. *The Jungle and the Aroma of Meats: An Ecological Theme in Hindu Medicine*. Janet Lloyd, trans. Berkeley and Los Angeles: University of California Press, 1987 [1982].

————. *Le Discours des Remèdes au Pays des Épices: Enquête sur la Médecine Hindoue.* Paris: Payot, 1989.

————. "Gentle Purge: The Flower Power of Āyurveda." *Paths to Asian Medical Knowledge.* Charles Leslie and Allan Young, eds. Pp. 209–23. Berkeley and Los Angeles: University of California Press, 1992.

————. *Généalogie des Médecines Douces: de l'Inde à l'Occident.* Paris: Presses Universitaires de France, 1995.

INDEX

abjection, 23, 74, 137, 159, 173, 207, 250, 266, 269, 271, 275, 277, 303
absence, 5, 20, 31, 38–39, 49, 56, 58–59, 120, 173, 274, 289, 295, 302, 305
accusation, 72–74
Achenbaum, Andrew, 101, 317
activity/disengagement, 21, 65, 115, 185
adaptation, 230
adaptogenic, 133
adhyāsa, 143
Adi Dharm, 226, 229, 252
adjustment/maladjustment, 141, 194, 196, 198–201, 205, 207, 210–211, 216–217, 230, 244, 299
Adkins, Janet, 58, 60–61, 303–304, 313
affect, 24, 28–29, 80, 126, 210, 217, 292–293
Africa, 30–31
Agar, Michael, 6, 309
Agarwal, Bina, 14, 99, 216, 268, 310, 317, 322, 324
Agarwal family, Nandanagar, 207–208
age: incongruities, 47; materialization of, 289. *See also* difference, age as
Age Aid India, 90, 106–107
Age-Care India, 88–90, 106–109, 194, 209
ageism, 16, 61, 69–70, 80–81
aghori, 155, 280
aging, 88; enterprise, 95, 98, 116, 293; as euphemism, 183; normal, 60, 69–70, 80–81, 183, 200, 219; premature, 20–22, 222
"Aging in India," 4, 88–93, 99, 102–104, 106–107, 118, 120, 184, 194

Agnoli, A., 322
Agrawal family, Ravindrapuri, 196–197, 240
Ahmad, Aijaz, 317
Ahmedabad, 201
AIDS, 54
Aitareya Brāhmana, 121
Aitaśa pralāpa, 121, 175
Ajara, 145, 179, 288
alienation, 64, 293
Allahabad, 41, 284, 304
allopathy, 40–41, 127, 136–137, 318. *See also* biomedicine
Alter, Joseph, 43, 312, 320
Althusser, Louis, 38, 312
aluminum, 31
Alzheimer, Alois, 27, 67–69, 79–80, 83–84, 127, 314–315
Alzheimer's and Related Disorders Society of India (ARDSI), 20, 36, 38
Alzheimer's Association, 7–8, 16–17, 20, 32, 45, 55–58, 60, 310, 313
Alzheimer's disease, 123, 141, 185, 199–201, 209–210, 215–216, 218, 220, 296, 298–301; American discourse of, 7, 16, 20, 32, 45, 55–58, 60, 81–86, 125–127, 303, 313; American movement of, 80–81; animal model of, 5, 49, 85, 312; definition of, xv, 5–6, 26–27; diagnosis of, 33, 125–126; epidemiology of, 29–32, 36, 38, 125; gene for, 5, 18, 31, 49, 61; globalization of, 81, 84, 156; history of, 26–27, 68–69, 79–84, 126, 315; Indian

Alzheimer's disease *(continued)*
  discourse of, 15, 18–19, 20; Indian movement
    of, 20, 36; irony and, 51–53, 59, 81; material-
    ization of, 85; metaphor for old age and
    death, 47, 60, 85, 126; as "nation's fourth
    leading killer," 60, 85, 125–126; ontology of,
    126; plaques and tangles of, 18–20, 27, 31–32,
    36, 38–39, 56–57, 61, 68, 79–80, 82–83, 85,
    126, 297, 303; pneumonia and, 125; as pro-
    cess, 33; test for, 5, 61, 85–86, 126. *See also* de-
    mentia; senility
Alzheimer's Disease International (ADI), 18, 20,
    29, 84
Alzism, 126
Amaducci, L. A., 315, 318
Ambedkar, Dr., 225, 228
ambiguity, 112, 183, 213, 241, 271
American Association of Retired Persons
    (AARP), 81–82, 185
Amin, Shahid, 282, 324
anality, 23, 163–165
Anantharaman, R. N., 321
Andrews, Dana, 47, 50–51
anger, 74, 154, 158, 175, 177, 194, 198, 201–202,
    207, 210, 233, 235, 238, 240–241, 244–247,
    251, 272, 292. *See also* rishi, angry
anthropology, 7, 257, 287–288, 292, 308; Indian,
    15; medical, 70, 213; multi-sited, 8; psycho-
    logical, 178
Anupa, and family, 249
anxiety, 123, 125–127, 140, 201, 216; dependency,
    124, 185, 200, 212, 240, 248, 302; *ghabrāhat,*
    215; *sevā,* 180, 236
anxiolytics, 215
Apne Begāne, 123, 125, 170, 179
apoplexy, 64–65
Appadurai, Arjun, 237, 322–323
Arnold, David, 311
ars moriendi, 71
arteriosclerosis, 64–66, 69, 76, 80, 218
artha, 185
Arya Samaj, 113–114
ashram, 41; bhajan/widow, 41, 113, 115, 265, 273;
    Vanaprastha, 41, 113–115; Vriddh, 115
āśīrvād, 251–252
Aslī Baṛā Indrajal, 322
āśramadharma, 40, 113–115, 142–143, 153, 165, 169,
    172, 183, 185, 198, 202–203, 205, 237, 277, 312
astrology, 137, 215
Athārva Veda, 121, 318

atherosclerosis, 21
atrophy, 65–68
attribution, 183
aunt, 116–120, 159, 193, 206–207, 266, 270–271,
    274–275, 277, 296, 298; "Aunt Minnie" story,
    296; mashima, 116, 118
authority, 121, 241–242, 283
autonomy, 91
Avorn, Jerry, 322
Ayurveda, 33, 40–41, 93, 109–112, 127–138, 153,
    187, 210, 215, 245, 275, 305, 317–318

baba, 155, 212, 258, 260–261, 268, 270–271,
    278–281, 283, 285–286, 308
Baba, Bengali Quarter, 277–278
Babb, Lawrence, 144, 319
babu, 119–120, 159, 171
Bacon, Roger, 66, 314
Bageshera, and family, 235, 239
bāhāttūre, 157, 197, 276
bahū. See daughter-in-law
Baidyanath, 136
Bailey, F. G., 102, 317
bakbak, xxii, 13–14, 125, 170, 175–176, 196, 210,
    235–236, 238–239, 241–244, 249–250, 255,
    267, 272, 274, 294–295, 303, 307
Bakshi, S. R., 318
balance/imbalance, 8, 190, 193–199, 201, 207,
    211–212, 220, 223, 230, 233, 235, 244, 250,
    252, 300–302, 321
Balua. *See* old woman of Balua
Banaras. *See* Varanasi
Banaras Hindu University (BHU), 42, 112, 129,
    133, 135, 191, 193, 202, 214–215, 221, 224,
    233–234, 247–248, 279
banārsipan, 10, 40, 43
Bandyopadhyay, Tarashankar, 324
Banerjee, Sumanta, 119–120, 318
Banerjee family, 263
Banerji, 119, 318
Bangalore, 39, 41, 84, 109, 182
Bania, 227–228, 232, 236, 252–253
Barrett, Albert M., 314
Barthes, Roland, 7, 104, 310
Baru Baba, 226–227, 237
Basalla, George, 316
Basu family, 141–142, 182, 199, 201
Bawa, A. S., 107
bawd, 67, 79
Beach, Thomas G., 315

Becker, Gaylene, 322

Bengal Hurkaru, 3–4, 25, 173

Bengali Quarter, 42, 105–106, 108, 157, 195, 230, 234–235, 263–264, 267, 275, 277, 294

Benign Senescent Forgetfulness (BSF), 61, 126, 219

Benson, Herbert, 153, 319

Bentham, Jeremy, 116

Beotra, Rai Sahib B. R., 24, 311

Beriya Baba, 279–285

Berreman, Gerald, 322

Berrios, G. E., 79–80, 126, 315–316, 318

"Better Brain," 18–20, 32, 35–36, 84, 299

bhadralok, 117, 120, 173, 264–265, 269

Bhāgavata Purāna, 275, 277, 324

Bhairava, 266, 271

bhajan, 196–197, 250, 265, 273–74, 280. *See also* ashram, bhajan

bhakti, 176, 199

Bharati, 299

Bharati, R. Sarasa, 19, 30, 34, 36, 38–39

Bharatiya Janata Party (BJP), 285

Bharucha, N. E., 312

Bhatia, H. S., 316

bhīmrati, 157, 197

Bhishma, 176

bhoga/bhogī, 185, 236, 280

Bhumihar, 195

bhūt-pret possession, 215–216, 250–251, 255, 300

Biggers, Janet, 52–53

Bijay, 266–267, 275, 279

biomedicine, 6, 37, 40, 70, 127, 133, 184, 297. *See also* allopathy

biopolitics, 22

birthday party, 158

Bishwanath, and family, 275

Biswas, Suhas K., 316

Blau, Zena Smith, 329

Bleuler, Eugen, 65, 314

blood, 22; menstrual, 233; pressure (BP), 65, 108–109, 195–196

body, xvii, 21, 37–38, 69, 75, 79, 84, 132, 140, 155, 161, 232, 270–271, 285, 288–289, 292, 294–295; ageless, 285, 288; dismembered, 135, 140; divine, 274; examinable, 137; familial, 177–183, 191, 199, 220, 230, 250, 254, 269–270, 281, 300, 302; Hindu/Muslim, 236; as machine, 68; "mindful," 184, 303; national, 4, 254; old, xvii, 3, 6, 9, 11, 22, 25, 62, 67, 74, 76, 83, 112, 114, 131, 138, 145, 159–160, 174, 212, 216, 230, 245, 269, 283,

293; senile, 32–34, 52, 62, 72, 77, 87, 125–126, 140, 145, 219, 292, 300, 302; subtle, 213; *tan* versus *sarīr*, 212–213; translocatable, 138–139; tropical, 23; young, 130–138, 146, 150–151, 169–170, 289

Bombay (Mumbai), 41, 46, 112, 114, 132, 134, 137, 158–159, 170, 217–218, 225

Boral, G. C., 319

Bose, A. B., 89, 316

Bottero, Alain, 322

Bourdieu, Pierre, 155, 310

Bourgois, Philippe, 291

Brahma, 266

Brahman, 146, 154, 166, 188–189, 202–204, 224, 226, 228–229, 231–232, 236–237, 250–253, 263, 265, 272–273, 275, 277

Brahma Purana, 172, 320

brain, 75, 77, 240, 292; gross pathology of, 21, 60, 64–65, 79, 82–83; Indian, 19; Western, 20. *See also* mind; weakness, of brain/mind

Brass, Paul, 126, 318

breakdown, Heideggerian, 6, 16

breath control, 285

Brindavin, 41, 111, 115, 265

Browne, Richard, 66

Buddhism, 93, 229, 281, 283

Bula Babu, 227–228, 232

Burgess, Ernest, 97, 316, 321

Butalia, Pankaj, 115, 318

Butler, Judith, 38, 310, 312

Butler, Robert, 314

Calcutta, 24, 41, 116–120, 139, 141, 159, 171, 182, 187–188, 190–191, 197, 199, 220, 225, 264, 278, 297–299, 301, 307

Callahan, Daniel, 71, 315, 324

cancer, 110, 189

Canguilhem, Georges, 60, 63–64, 314

capital, 22, 38, 138, 217, 268; health, 36; spiritual, 265; symbolic, 133

Capra, Fritjof, 129, 317, 319

Caraka Samhitā, 110, 129–130, 132

caregiver/caretaker, 33, 54–56

Carstairs, George Morris, 161–166, 170, 178, 242, 268, 271, 320, 324

Cartesian dualism, 124, 213–214

caste, 33, 49, 223. *See also* Chamar; hierarchy

category fallacy, 34–35

Chakrabarty, Dipesh, 310

Chaman Lal, and family, 234

Chamar, xxii, 41–42, 137, 212, 224, 226–232, 235–237, 241, 246, 251–252, 282, 307–308, 322. *See also* Dalit; Harijan; Untouchable
Chandogya Upanisad, 188
Chandra, V., 311
chapati, 230, 233, 243–245, 247, 249, 251, 263, 266, 269, 274
Charcot, J. M., 62–65, 67, 72, 83, 85, 310, 314
charisma, 128, 281–286
charpoy, 182, 185, 237–239, 241–243, 249, 269
Chatterjee, Partha, 173, 309, 320
Chattopadhyaya, Debiprasad, 187–188
Chaudhari, A. D., 311
Chaudhari, D. H., 311
Chen, Martha, 14, 99, 268, 271, 310, 317, 324
Chicago School, 154, 292
chicken, 228–229
childbirth, 210
China, 184
Chittupur, 243–244, 275
Chopra, Deepak, 128, 304–305
Christianity, 94, 118, 204, 221–222, 224–225, 253, 288, 303–305
"Chronic cerebral insufficiency" (CCI), 219
Chui, Helena Chang, 28, 311, 315
Chyavana, 112, 131–132, 305
Chyawanprash, 112, 131–137, 198, 317–318
Chyawanshakti, 136, 138
circulation, 150; of suffering, 49, 53–54, 58
citizen, 174, 289
civil society, 250
Clarfield, A. M., 311
class, 33, 41, 49–50, 195, 213–214, 233, 242, 267, 301, 310
classification, 25
Clifford, James, 33, 311
climacteric, 21, 33, 72, 74–79, 83, 208, 219–220, 234, 292
climate, 21–23
Coffman, J. D., 322
cognitive, 27–29, 57, 77–80, 126, 205, 208, 216, 244, 292
Cohen, Lawrence, 312, 315–321, 323
Cohn, Bernard, xxii, 39, 241, 278, 293, 309, 314, 317, 323
Cole, Thomas R., 183, 313–315, 321
commodity/commodification, 128, 133–138, 140, 147, 270–271, 301
commons, 192, 225, 226
communitas, 56, 193, 196

confessional, 17, 20, 57–58, 85–86
Congress Party, 149–150, 174, 227, 285
Connolly family, 53–55, 59–60, 81–82
consciousness, conflicted, 270
corporeality, 22, 289
Courtright, Paul, 320
cow, 264–266, 270
Cowgill, Donald, 96, 98, 101–102, 316–317
cramming, 139–140, 187, 201
Cranach, Lucas, 219
cremation ground, 266, 272, 280
culture, 7, 22, 32, 48, 105, 159, 288–289, 297, 301, 307–308
Culture and Personality, idiom of, 161
Cumming, Elaine, 321
curail, 258, 271
Current Science, 84
curse, 247, 267, 269, 279–281, 283
Curtin, Sharon R., 314

dādā, 157
daīn, 250, 258, 270–271
Dainik, 174
Dak, T. N., 316
Dalit, 224, 226, 228, 322. *See also* Chamar
Daly, Mary, 86
Daniel, E. Valentine, 155, 178, 317, 320, 324
Danielou, Alain, 203, 205, 321
darśana, 245
darshan, 279, 281–285
Das, Veena, 178, 309, 320–322
Dash, Bhagwan, 323
Dasharath, 169–170, 180, 211
Dasovas, 217–220, 298, 300–301
daughter, 84, 118, 123, 125, 131, 160–161, 166, 171, 173, 179, 182, 185, 193–194, 207, 209–210, 214–215, 239–240, 246, 251, 253–254, 263–264, 280
daughter-in-law (*bahū*), 119, 123, 141, 159–160, 171, 173, 179, 182, 189–190, 192, 194, 196, 201–202, 209, 239, 242–243, 246, 248, 251, 275, 297, 299–300, 323
De, Sushil Kumar, 157, 320
death, 63, 71, 115, 124, 161, 182, 192, 213, 229, 250, 273, 275, 283, 287–288, 301–302, 304
de Beauvoir, Simone, 97, 183, 317, 321
decay (decrepitude, degeneration), xvii, 19, 20–22, 24, 63–64, 66, 76, 130, 172, 275, 287, 288, 289, 302
deference, 180, 246

deferral, 161, 166, 168, 180, 190, 223, 240, 242, 286

De Fleury, Maurice, 315

Dehradun, 41, 107, 109, 115, 190

Delhi, 41, 87, 100, 107–109, 114, 124, 158, 177, 190–191, 195, 199, 205, 209, 260, 276, 287, 302–303

delirium, 29

dementia, 127, 199, 292–293, 303; Alzheimer's-type, 26, 29–30, 45; atherosclerotic, 26, 80; "biomedicalization" of, 6, 61; causes of, 21, 78; "cross-cultural" research on, 29; definition of, xv, 15, 24–26; diagnosis of, 30, 32, 36; epidemiology of, 15, 17, 19, 29–32; gender and, 30; globalization of, 46; irreversible, 29; mixed, 27; multi-infarct, 26–27, 31, 56, 69; ontological status of, 26–27, 29, 33; presenile, 27, 68–69, 80; pseudo, 29, 56, 60; reversible, 29, 56, 60; rhetoric of, 37–38, 56–57; senile, 15, 18, 23, 32, 34, 64, 67, 69, 87, 200, 210, 214–218; treatment of, 48; vascular, 26–27, 29–32, 69, 218. *See also* Alzheimer's disease; senility

demographic transition, 35–36, 216, 303

demography, 31, 36, 92; alarmist, 4–5, 60, 71, 89–91, 293–294

dependency, 3, 5, 59, 74, 81, 83–84, 91, 117, 170, 197, 233, 266, 270

dependency theory, 100–101

depression, 29, 56, 133, 215–216

Derne, Steven, 320

Desai, I. P., 103, 317

Desai, K. G., 316

Desai, Morarji, 158, 320

desire, 33, 78, 144–147, 172–173, 188, 198, 212, 220, 236, 275, 283

De Souza, Alfred, 100, 314, 317

detail men, 127, 217–218, 297–298, 300–301

Devi, Mahasweta, 324

Devraha Baba, 41, 280–285, 302

Dhanvantari, 129, 245

dharma, 39, 176, 185, 206, 237, 251, 280

dharmaśāstra, 40, 113, 142, 206, 312

dhat, 216. *See also* semen loss

Dhobi, 224, 237

Diagnostic and Statistical Manual (DSM), 26, 66, 201, 219; *III-R*, 26–29, 204, 214, 311, 321; *IV*, 26–29, 293, 311

dialectic, 22

diaspora, Indian, 128

diet, 31

Dieulafoy, G., 314

difference, 19, 22, 29, 30, 38, 48–49, 212, 232, 292–293; age as, xv, 4–5, 33, 49, 71, 79, 213; behavioral, 216, 295

Dirks, Nicolas, 309, 322

"disadvantaged elder," 89, 92

disease, ontological conception of, 63–64

Djurfeldt, Goran, 108, 317

dog, 171, 207, 244, 263–268, 271, 274–277, 283, 303

domestic, 251, 268, 274–276, 283, 285

Doniger, Wendy, 8, 144, 310, 319

Doordarshan, 41

dotage, 72–74, 78, 85, 124

doubling, 269, 271, 283

Dreze, Jean, 14, 99, 268, 310, 317, 324

dualism; anthropological, xvi, 38; Cartesian, 124, 213–214; Nascherian, 71

Dulari, 13–14, 35, 185, 230, 248–249, 255, 303

Dumont, Louis, 154, 163, 165, 171, 178, 230–231, 237

Durrant, C. M., 75, 310, 315

du Toit, 208, 321

Dutta, Ranjana, 321

dying space, 37, 52–53, 178, 180–183, 186, 197, 237–238, 241, 269, 276, 283, 303–304

East Boston Senior Health Project, 311

Eastern Master, 128

Ecclesiastes, 66

Eck, Diana, 281, 322, 324

Edgerton, Franklin, 319

Edwardth, Joey, 100–101, 103, 317

embodiment, 24–25, 32, 37, 51–52, 71, 75, 120, 123–127, 140, 161, 170, 184, 208, 211–212, 216, 232, 238, 250, 274, 277, 282, 286, 288, 292, 294–297, 302–304

enchantment, 84

endocrine, 76

Engels, Frederic, 187

English medicine (*angrezī davā*), 133–134

Epics, 93, 113, 142

epistemology, 90, 95–96, 106

Epstein, T. Scarlett, 102–103, 317

ergot mesylates, 201, 218

Erikson, Erik, 212

erotic triangle, 159. *See also* Kesari Jivan, triangle

Estes, Caroll, 116, 318

eugenics, 67–68, 76

Evans-Pritchard, E. E., 324
excess, 20, 28, 31, 45, 49–50, 54, 60, 63, 65, 83, 85, 119, 196, 310
excluded middle, 18
excrement, 23, 146, 202
exorcism, 41
explanatory model (EM), 75, 301

Fall, 90, 93, 103–106, 194, 223, 226, 232, 237
falling, 52–53
family, 114–115, 180, 206, 261, 270–271, 301; bad, 11, 19, 33, 49, 84, 87, 103, 115, 123–124, 190, 199, 201, 206, 238–239, 243–245, 247, 255, 270, 275, 298, 302–303, 305; Hindu/Muslim, 10–11, 204, 236; joint/extended, 93, 113, 203, 242, 271; joint/extended, decline of, 7, 17, 87, 92, 102–106, 115, 118–120, 180, 190; "Rosy," 100; Western, 17, 19
Fanon, Frantz, 104
Farmer, Paul, 325
Farmitalia, 217–220, 297–298
father, 68, 121, 123–124, 133–134, 138, 140, 142, 144–145, 157, 159–174, 179, 181, 189, 193, 197, 201–202, 209, 239, 242–243, 271, 277, 283, 285–286, 288, 302, 304; absent, 163–165
Favret-Saada, Jeanne, 324
Ferguson, James, 291, 312, 324
Fernandes, Walter, 314, 317
Filliozat, Jean, 129, 319
film, Hindi, 15, 25, 43, 123–124, 136
Fischer, David, 101, 317
FitzGerald, Frances, 315
Fletcher, Mrs., 52, 70
Flint, Austin, 314
flow models, 26, 65, 69, 199, 218
fluidity, 105, 154–156, 175, 178, 292
Folstein, Marshal F., 311
Folstein MMS, 311
forgetfulness. *See* memory loss
Forster, E. M., 21, 310
Foucault, Michel, 116–117, 318
Fox, Patrick, 69, 80–81, 313–314
frailty, 81
Fraser, Nancy, 321
Frazer, James, 288
Freeman, H. L., 315–316
Freeman, James M., 322
Freud, Sigmund, 126, 162, 158, 268–270, 318, 324
Fuller, Solomon C., 314–315
futility, 71, 294

Gadow, Sally A., 183, 321
Galenic medicine, 74–75
Galloway, D., 76–77, 315
Gandhi, Indira, 94, 136, 149, 150, 228, 260, 281, 285
Gandhi, Mohandas, 203–204, 282
Gandhi, Rajiv, 149–150, 228, 285
Ganesha, 166
Ganga (Ganges), 1, 3, 9–10, 39–42, 221, 223–224, 227, 238, 250, 264, 266–267, 279, 284, 295, 307–308
Ganga Jali, and family, 241, 248, 249
Gangrade, K. D., 89, 316
Geertz, Clifford, xvi
gender, 5, 33, 74, 77–79, 160, 195, 211, 233, 235, 267, 275–276
generation, 51, 53, 93, 121, 156–157, 160, 165–166, 216, 230, 241–242, 270, 281, 293
George, T., 209, 321
geriatrics, 29, 41, 62–63, 69, 86, 109–112; discourse of, 77; geriatric paradox, 60, 69–71, 200, 219, 296; ideology of, 77, 79, 295
Geriatrics, 62, 69, 76–77
Geri-forte, 111, 133–134, 150–151, 167
gerontological sublime, 287
gerontological utopia, 91, 97
gerontology, 4, 7, 15–17, 60, 70–71, 87–106, 119, 183–184, 287, 293–294; international, 94–100. *See also* object, gerontological
gerontopolis, 81, 270
ghar, 179–180, 193, 242
Ghar Kali, 119–120, 150, 159–161, 169, 171–174, 270, 273, 299–300
gift, 81, 138, 146, 165, 170, 220, 225, 227–228, 231–232, 243, 251, 253, 270, 277, 280–282, 285
Ginsberg, Allen, 14, 310
ginseng, 133–136, 138, 220
Gleason, W. Stanton, 315
global/local, 37, 43, 45–46
globalization, 25, 32
Goffman, Erving, 116, 318
Golden Age, 93, 100–103, 105
Golden Isles, 100, 102–103
Good, Byron, 301, 313, 319
Good, Mary-Jo Delvecchio, 313, 319
Gore, M. S., 317
gothic, 21
Goyal, R. S., 316
"granny," 47, 51–52, 72, 81–82, 185, 313
Graves, Amy B., 30, 311
Gray, John N., 317

Griffith, Ralph, 121, 318
Gubrium, Jaber, 7, 61, 80–81, 310, 313–314, 318
Gupta, Akhil, 291, 312, 324
guru, 110, 137, 163, 199, 203, 228, 234, 251

Hachinski, Vladimir, 69, 314
Haggard, H. Rider, 22, 291, 310, 324
Halford, Henry, 75, 315
Haraway, Donna, xvi, 8, 309–310
Hardwar, 3, 41, 113
Harijan, 227, 243. *See also* Chamar
Harinath Prasad (Masterji), and family, 175, 235, 239–240
Harrison, Mark, 311
Hasbro, 139
Hasegawa, K., 311
havā/wind, 154, 244–245
Havighurst, Robert J., 321
health transition, 84, 216
heart, 124, 195–196, 212
Hegel, Georg Wilhelm Friedrich, 22, 310
hegemony, 6, 37, 79, 93, 103, 114–115, 120, 135, 190, 212, 232, 270, 283, 286, 288–289, 295
Helmont, Jean Baptiste, 76
HelpAge India, 88, 90, 106, 266
Henderson, A. S., 311
Henry, William H., 321
heteroglossia, 267
Hidayatullah, Arshad, 311
Hidayatullah, M., 311
hierarchy, 20, 164–165, 178–179, 183, 228, 231–232, 237; revolving, 231
hijra, 163, 320
Himalayan, 133–134
Himalayas, 58
Hinduism, 1–4, 10, 39–40, 93, 143–144, 202–204, 206, 228, 237, 252, 264, 278, 282; Brahma Kumari, 144–145; nationalist, 203–204, 284–285; Vaishnavite, 142
Hindu Succession Act of 1956, 25
Hoffman, Deborah, 55, 313
Holmes, Lowell, 96, 101–102, 316–317
homeopathy, 40
Homma, A., 311
homosexuality, 68, 135, 161–166, 239, 322
hook-swinging, 2
hot/cold, 23, 153–155, 181, 213, 233–234, 238, 246, 293
hot brain/mind (*dimāg*), 147, 153–157, 170, 175, 215–216, 230, 238, 244–245, 247–248, 252, 254, 292

householdership/householder (*grhasthya/grhast*), 113–115, 196, 202–203, 205, 214, 237, 251, 275, 277
Howes, David, 324
Hubert, Henri, 319
Humphry, Derek, 61, 313
hybridity, 269
hypochondriasis, 67, 295
hysteria, 208

icon, 89, 128, 178, 191, 213, 253, 265
identity, 120, 123, 171, 214, 228, 231, 283, 286, 288–289, 295
illusion of control, 116
impotence/potency, 133–136, 165, 212, 214
Inden, Ronald, 7, 154, 310
index, 128
Indian Lunacy Act of 1912, 24, 259
"Indian Mutiny," 2
Indian Succession Act of 1925, 24
India Today, 18, 23, 30, 32, 176, 299
industrialization, 17, 31, 89, 92
infantalism, 21, 174
Inquisition, 72–73
institutionalization/deinstitutionalization, 33, 46, 56–57, 61–62, 71–72, 83–84, 86, 116–120, 125, 274, 298
internalization, 163
International Association for the Study of Traditional Asian Medicine (IASTAM), 112
internationalism, 91, 93–100, 104
International Statistical Classification of Diseases (ICD), 28–29, 45, 66
International Year of the Aged, 93
International Year of the Woman, 117–118
interpretive, 121, 159, 178, 233
interstice, 206–207, 265–275, 278, 281, 283–284
intersubjectivity, 300
involution, 67–68, 76
irony, 213, 250, 274, 295
Islam/Muslim, 150, 174, 226, 235, 252, 308
iteration. *See* repetition
"It's just old age," 62, 69, 71, 184

Jablonski, Henryk, 94
Jackson, J. Hughlings, 65, 314
Janata Dal, 149, 157, 174
Japan, 29–30, 209
jarībūtī, 128, 134
jāvanī, 153
Jawahar, and family, 227

Jena, B., 316
Jensheng, 134–135
Jesus, 228, 251, 291, 304
Jhalli Ram, and family, 227
jhaṇḍū, xxii, 137–138, 151, 240, 248–249
jiva, 143, 213
jīvanmukta, 176, 279–280
John the evangelist, 221, 253
Johnson, Colleen, 33, 311
Johnson, Frank, 33, 311
Johnson, M., 317
Jones, William, 173, 320
Jordens, J. T. F., 318
Jorm, A. F., 311
juxtaposition, xvi, 6–8

Kabir, 213, 228, 251
kaccā mahal, 41
Kakar, Sudhir, 161, 164–166, 170, 178, 186, 242, 271, 297, 320–321, 324–325
Kali, 1–2, 4, 162, 309. *See also* Ghar Kali
kāma, 185
kamzorī. See weakness
Kanpur, 194, 260
Kapur, Sohaila, 324
Kapura, and family, 246
karma, 144–145, 237, 284
Karpatriji, Swami, 10, 202–205, 282, 308
Kashi. *See* Varanasi
kāśīvāsī, 176, 206, 302. *See also* widow, *kāśīvāsī*
Kathasāritsāgara, 112, 145, 172, 219, 279, 288
Katzman, R., 311
Kaufman, Sharon, 183, 185, 211–212, 321
Kaul family, 201–202
Kennedy, Henry, 74–75, 315
Kerala, 23, 36
Kesari Jivan, 133–134, 136–137, 151, 198, 242; triangle, 134, 158–161, 202
Kevorkian, Jack, 58, 60–61, 303–305, 313, 325
Khare, R. H., 228, 231, 236–237, 252, 322–323
Khosa, Rajan, 181, 321
Kierkegaard, Soren, xvi, 89, 309
king, 145–146, 158, 162, 167–169, 172, 288–289
Kingery, John, 81–82, 185
King Lear, 5, 15, 18, 51, 74, 123–125, 206, 246, 316, 318
Kipling, Rudyard, 21, 310
Kleinman, Arthur, 177, 301, 310–311, 313, 319, 321, 325
Kleinman, Joan, 177, 310, 321
Klooster, Gerard, 303–304, 313

knowledge, 251, 270, 301–302; first/second/third person, 33–34, 127, 154–156, 176, 184–185, 193, 251, 293, 297; imperial, 139, 201
Kohli, D. R., 316
Koki, 207, 272
Kolenda, Pauline, 216, 317, 322
Kraepelin, Emil, 65–68, 79–80, 84, 126, 314–315
Kramer, Heinrich, 315
Krishna, 141, 251, 274
Krishnan, T. N., 312
Kugler, J., 322
Kumar, Deepak, 316
Kumar, Ashok, 317, 319
Kumar, N. L., 87–88, 90, 106–110, 112, 209
Kumar, Nita, 40, 43, 310, 312, 320–321
Kumar, Sukrita, 156, 158, 171
Kumar, Vijay, and family, 195
Kumbh Mela, 41, 284–285, 302
Kurtz, Stanley, 320, 324
kuṭīpraveśikā, 132–133

lakaṛbagghā (hyena), 259–261
lakaṛsunghvā, 257–260, 267–268, 270, 279, 283
Lal, Devi, 157–158, 171, 293
Langer, Ellen J., 318
Laqueur, Thomas, 75, 315
Larson, Abigail, 51–53
Larson, Gerald, 142, 319
Laslett, Peter, 100, 317
Latour, Bruno, xvi, 309
Leach, Edmund R., 320
Lekhraj, Dada, 144
Lellouch, Alain, 314
Leslie, Charles, 126, 318
Levin, Jack, 321
Levin, William C., 321
Lévi-Strauss, Claude, 150, 154, 320
life course, 223; disenchantment of, 75; postmodern life course, 60, 70, 184
life extension, 110
Lindberg, Staffan, 108, 317
liquefaction, 21–23
"little old lady," 70
Little Sisters of the Poor, 118
Lock, Margaret, 184, 209, 312, 315, 321
loneliness, 175–176, 190, 206, 241, 303
longevity, 66–67, 110, 127, 130, 155. See also *rasāyana;* superannuation
Luborsky, Mark R., 315
Lucknow, 90–91, 228, 236–237, 260

Lutz, Catherine, 34, 311
Lyman, Karen, 6, 61–62, 80, 310, 313

Mace, Nancy L., 313; *The 36-Hour Day*, 54–55, 58
Macfarlane, Alan, 74, 81, 315
Maclachlan, Daniel, 66, 68, 310, 314
Madan, T. N., 7, 185, 236, 310, 317, 321, 323
madness, 123–125, 190, 195, 201–202, 205, 207–208, 239, 255, 266, 279. See also *pāgalpan; paglī*
Madras (Chennai), 18, 36, 41, 109
Madurai, 36, 41, 109, 216, 218
M.A.G.S., 109
Mahābhārata, 102, 153, 166–168, 176, 182, 199, 280, 320
Maharaja of Varanasi, 227–228, 232, 237
Mahdihassan, S., 317
mai-bāp, 163
Maine, Henry, 22, 139–140, 187, 319
Malamoud, Charles, 231, 322
mālīś, 182
Mallah, 1–5
Mallaya, Vijay, 217
Manav Kalyan Kendra, 113–115
Manga the widow, 272–274
Mangeshkar, Lata, 149–151
Mangri, and family, 239–240, 249–250, 252, 255
Mani, Lata, 309
Manton, Kenneth, 98, 101, 317
mantra-tantra 137, 215–216, 234
marginality, 124, 179, 212–213, 220, 242, 268, 270, 274, 302
Marglin, Frédérique, 178, 321–322
marnevālā, 238, 249
Marriott, McKim, 144, 154–155, 171, 175, 178, 311, 317, 319–320, 322, 324. *See also* unmatching
Martin, Emily, 315
Martin, G. M., 316
Marwari Mataji, 10, 23, 202, 282, 307
Marxism, 187–188
Mashima (of Bengali Quarter), 263–267, 272, 279
mast, 211
masturbation, 135, 214, 216–217
materialization, 32, 38, 48, 71, 171, 280, 310
math (monastery), 278
Matilal, B. K., 142, 319
Mausaji, and family, 243–245, 275, 323
Mauss, Marcel, 310, 319
meaning, 183, 228, 246, 248, 269, 301–303
meaninglessness, 213, 277

Mearns, David J., 317
medicalization, 29, 62, 72, 80, 140, 209, 216, 219
Meena, and family, 189–190
Mehta, B. S., and family, 200–201, 211–213, 321
melancholy, 72–74
memento mori, 66, 74
memory, 22, 24, 27–28, 59, 61, 67, 121, 123, 126–127, 129–133, 136–147, 216–217, 292, 298; loss, 40, 50, 53, 59, 61, 79, 126, 130, 156, 197, 199, 201, 205, 210, 214–216, 245, 292, 296; social, 104; subtle, 144
"Memory" (game), 139
Memory Banks, 138, 239
Mencher, Joan, 322
menopause, 68, 75–79, 206, 208–209, 215, 234–235, 292
Mental Status Examination (MSE), 33–35, 37, 215, 311
Merā Bhārat Mahān, 149–150
Mercitron, 304–305
metabolic enhancer, 218–220
methodology, 6–8, 10
metonym, 104, 114
Meyer, J. S., 311
middle age, 27, 79–80, 126, 214, 217–218, 310
middle class, 8, 36, 89, 104–108, 120, 127–128, 136, 177, 189–191, 193–195, 207, 225, 269, 307
millennarian, 1–5, 269
Miller, Joan G., 317, 321
mind, 25, 124, 127, 212, 255; *buddhi*, 131, 156; *dimāg*, 240, 243, 249; *man*, 212–213; *mānas*, 130, 245; *matha*, 244; *medhā*, 130–131. *See also* brain; weakness, of brain/mind
Ministry of Welfare, Government of India, 41, 94–95, 316
Minois, Georges, 101, 317
mirror, 212, 280, 283
Mishra, Saraswati, 316, 321
Mishra family, 209–210, 221
misrecognition, 25
missing persons, 41
Mithal, C. P., 320
Mitra, Aloka, 87, 116–118, 298
modernity, 19, 31, 62, 104–106, 113, 117, 119–120, 136, 159, 173, 203, 241, 287–289, 302–303
modernization, 17, 89, 96–98, 100–105
Mohanty, S. P., 316
Moinson, Louis, 315
moksha, 39–40, 143–144, 185

monstrosity, 270–271
Montesquieu, Charles de Secondat, 21, 310
Moore, Sally Falk, 311
Moore, William, 311
Mora, George, 315
moral, 17, 20; decay, 21, 66; economy, 66, 79, 138, 244; hygiene, 65, 67; world, 19, 33, 177, 301
Morgan, Lewis Henry, 187
Morris, Edmund, 313
motevālā, 226, 232
mother, 116–120, 126, 142, 150, 159–166, 169, 171, 173–174, 182, 187, 189, 197–198, 200–201, 210, 243, 254–255, 265–266, 270–271, 297, 302–303; "bad," 162, 271
Mother India, 150
mother-in-law (*sās*), 160, 171, 173, 179, 182, 189–190, 196, 201, 246, 275, 297–300
Mother Teresa, 14, 18, 255, 278, 303, 305
Mughalsarai, 308
Muller, F. Max, 288
Munn, Nancy D., 324
Munna Lal, and family, 251–252
Mussourie, 107, 109, 190, 193, 209, 221, 248
Myerhoff, Barbara, 158, 287, 320, 324

Nader, Laura, 8, 310, 321
naga, 226
Nagwa, xxii, 13–14, 35–36, 42, 106, 108, 137, 175, 182, 206, 211–213, 216, 221–243, 246, 249–255, 270, 278–279, 293, 295, 301, 303, 307
Nanak, Guru, 228, 251
Nandanagar, 24, 37, 42, 190–195, 207–209, 281, 294
Nandi, S., 298, 300
Nandy, Ashis, 104–105, 120, 163–164, 166, 317–318, 320
Naraindas, Harish, 311
Narayan, and family, 227–229, 235, 239, 251
narrative, 17–18, 31, 71, 84, 103–106, 123, 159, 165–166, 168, 198, 202, 210, 232, 242, 300; illness, 216
Nascher, I. L., 62–65, 67–69, 71–72, 76–79, 81, 83, 310, 314–315
nation, 4, 11, 19, 59
National Institute of Mental Health and Neurological Science (India), 39
National Institutes of Health (U.S.), 69
Nava Nir, 116–120, 298, 301
Nayer, S. K., 109–110, 112–113
Nehru, Jawaharlal, 149–150, 203, 310
neo-*rasāyana*, 133–136, 217, 220, 304

Neugarten, Bernice, 183, 321
neurasthenia, 76
neuroleptics, 201
neurology, 41
New Age, 45, 305
Newsweek, 5, 32, 53–54, 59–60
New York Times, 61
Neysmith, Sheila, 100–101, 103, 317
nicergoline, 217–218
Nichter, Mark, 319
Nigeria, 30–31
niyam, 141–142, 194, 212, 302
"no aging," 5, 88–89, 95, 287, 293
nongovernmental organization (NGO), 87
normal/pathological, 24, 49, 61–64, 66–69, 71, 76–77, 79–80, 82, 219. See also aging, normal
Normal Pressure Hydrocephalus (NPH), 299
nursing home. See old age home
Nydegger, Corinne, 100, 102, 317

Oberoi, Harjot, 310
Obeyesekere, Gananath, 271, 320, 322, 324
object, gerontological, 87–89, 92, 106, 113, 115
Oddie, Geoffrey A., 309
Oedipus, 152, 242; Indian, 159, 161, 166, 320
O'Flaherty, Wendy Doniger. See Doniger, Wendy
ojhā, 137, 234, 251
Ojha, Divakar, 317, 319
Ojha, J. K., 319
old age, xvii, 4, 21, 33, 63, 123–124, 127, 130, 172, 183–184, 190, 195, 205, 212, 239, 250–251, 275, 285, 288, 294–296, 304; *burhāpā*, 235; *buzurg*, 212, 235, 237; definition of, 235; *jarā*, 112, 212, 251, 323; split, 24, 47, 60, 66, 71, 213; *vṛddhāvasthā*, 212, 235, 323
old age home, 41, 52, 55–57, 61, 81–82, 107, 113–120, 296, 298
old man, 167, 172, 212, 268, 271, 274–277, 281
old woman, 3–4, 62, 67, 70, 72–79, 82, 85–86, 116–120, 173, 206, 240, 253, 258, 263–276; of Balua, 1–6, 11, 20, 150, 269, 272, 309; voting, 173–174, 253, 283, 289
Olivelle, Patrick, 312
Orgren, Rosemary, 96, 98, 316
Orientalism, 37, 40, 42, 150
Ostor, Akos, 324
Osuntokun, B. O., 30, 36, 311
Overbeck-Wright, A. W., 23

Padma Purana, 172, 320
pāgalpan, 201, 215, 249. See also madness

paglī, 3, 13, 207, 250, 265–268, 271–274, 298, 300.
    See also madness
pakkā mahal, 41, 191, 278
Palmore, Erdman, 98, 101, 317
Palthe, Van Wulfften, 311
pancakarma, 129, 132
Panchkosi Road, 224–226
Panditji, 114
pantaloon, 67, 79
paraphraxis, 126
Parashurama, 153, 166
parody, 48, 50
Parry, Jonathan, 43, 312, 324
Parsi, 36
Parsons, Talcott, 97, 316
Patel, Raojibhai Manibhai, 320
Pathak, Rajesh, 234–235, 247, 254
Pathak, Ratnesh, 257
Pati, R. N., 316
patua, 119–120
Paul, Father, 221, 225, 240
pedagogy, 22
pensioner, 89, 92, 103, 113, 115
perfectionism, 63, 67, 78
performative, 17, 56–57, 77, 79, 104, 170, 179,
    184, 232, 242, 249, 282
Pershad, Dwarka, 311
personal law, 24–25
pharmaceutical industry, 29, 38, 41, 80, 84,
    127–128, 133, 199, 217, 220
phenomenology, 123, 163, 183, 185, 208, 211–212,
    239, 269; of voice, 37
Pinel, Philippe, 65
Pioneer, 1–3
pittā, 153
placebo, 218–219
pneumonia, 83
Podolsky, Edward, 75, 310, 315
police, 2, 22, 35, 41, 222, 232, 250, 253–254,
    258–261, 280–281, 302–303
poverty panorama, 108
Potter, Karl, 319
practice, xvii, 33, 37, 48, 84, 87, 94, 126, 297
pramāṇa, 3, 142
praṇām, 174
Premchand, 119, 135, 223, 271–274, 277, 318, 322,
    324
print media, 128
probate, 24
process, xvii, 33, 79
Propp, Vladimir, 104, 317

Prus, C. R., 62–64, 314
psychiatry, 41, 65–66, 112, 133–134, 189,
    200–201, 205, 208, 214–217, 298–300
psychoanalysis, 159, 161, 164, 166, 186, 271
psychosis, 64; involutional, 66–68; senile, 65
puja, 199, 253, 282, 307
Pune, 189–190
Puranas, 93, 142, 171–173, 275
pure/polluted, 231–232

Quadagno, Jill, 101–102, 317
Quigley, Declan, 322

Rabinow, Paul, xvi, 49, 309–310, 312, 314
Rabins, Peter, 313; *The 36-Hour Day*, 54–55, 58
race, 23
Radcliffe–Brown, A. R., 285, 323–324
Rader, J., 313
Raghu Ram, and family, 240–241, 252, 255
Raheja, Gloria Goodwin, 322
Rai family, 198–199
Ram, 3, 93, 113, 169–170, 251, 309
Ramachandran, M. G., 283
Ramamurti, Mantha, 311
Ramamurthy, P. V., 321
Ramanujan, A. K., 159, 161, 166, 317, 320
Ramaseshan, S., 316
Ramāyaṇa, 102, 166, 168–169, 320–321
Ramji, 228–229
Ram Lakhan, 226, 235, 240–241, 252, 255
Ram Lakhan (film), 25
Ram Lila, 168
Ram Nath, and family, 233
Ramnath, Rajalakshmi, 316
Ramu Baba, 278–279
Rao, M. S. A., 317
Rao, Narasimha, 153
Rao, N. T. Rama, 283
Rao, Raja, 14, 310
rasa, 245
rasāyana, 93, 111–112, 127–138, 145–146, 150,
    158–159, 320
Ravi Das, 222, 224–225, 228–229, 234, 244, 251,
    253–254, 322
Ravindrapuri, 41–42, 138, 182, 190–200,
    207–208, 210, 240, 253–254, 267
Ray, Dijendra, 157
Ray family, Calcutta, 141–142, 297–301
Reagan, Ronald, 25, 46, 53, 58–60, 94
reason, 21–22, 49, 225, 289, 292, 305
recognition, 123, 170, 288

recollection, xvi–xvii
recuperation, xvii
Reid, Janice, 102, 317
rejuvenation. See *rasāyana*
renunciation. See *sannyāsa*
request/demand, 73–74, 83, 170, 269, 284
repetition, 7, 17–18, 49, 54, 89, 103–105, 166, 175, 265, 272
retirement, 101, 113–115
Revital, 136
Rhoads, Ellen, 102, 317
rishi, 112, 143–145, 245, 271, 283, 280, 305; angry, 150–151, 153–155, 167, 221, 237, 281
ritual, 132, 203–204, 283
Robertson, A. F., 316
Rocca, W. A., 311, 315, 318
Roland, Alan, 317
Ross, Aileen, 102, 317
Rostan, Leon, 64–65, 314
Rowland, Richard, 65, 314
Roy, Manisha, 297, 325
Roy Chowdhury, Salil K., 311
Rubin, Gayle, 320
rupture, xvii, 288

sadhu, 237, 278, 282
Saharay, H. K.,311
sahī/sahī nahin, 10–11, 175, 177, 179, 190, 226, 235–241, 249, 252, 254, 275, 301
Sahlins, Marshall, xvi, 309
Saletore, R. N., 324
Salpêtrière, 62–65, 72, 85
sampling, xvi, 19, 35
samsara, 143–144
saṃskāra: impression, 130, 143–145; rite, 113, 179
San Francisco Chronicle, 86
sanitation, 22
Sanjay, 135–138, 140
Sankar, Andrea, 184, 315, 321
sannipat, 210
sannyāsa/sannyasi (renunciation/renouncer), 40–42, 115, 133, 142–143, 145–146, 153, 153–155, 169–170, 172, 185, 196–197, 199, 202–203, 213, 236–237, 250–252, 264, 270–271, 277–279, 283–284, 302, 304
Sarasvati, Dayananda, 113
Saraswathi, T. S., 321
Saraswati, 307–308
Saraswati, Baidyanath, 168, 273, 277–278, 320, 324

Sarkar, Sumit, 119–120, 318
Śārṅgadhara saṃhitā, 131, 319
saṭhiyana. See sixtyishness
sattar-bahattar, 157, 276
"*saṭṭhā ta paṭṭha*," 134, 138, 157–159, 165–167, 211, 239, 242, 275
sattva, 130
Saxena, D. N., 316
Saxena, M. S., 234–235, 321
schema, 6
Scheper-Hughes, Nancy, xxiii, 50, 184, 268, 309, 321, 323–324
schizophrenia, 215
Schoenberg, B. S., 315, 318
Schweitzer, Albert, 312
scientia senilis, 302
Scot, Reginald, 72–74, 85, 315
Searl-Chatterjee, 322
Secchan, and family, 213, 228, 234, 239, 253
second childhood, 24, 76, 124–125, 168, 201, 274–275
Sedgwick, Eve Kosofsky, 320
self, 212, 236, 251; ageless, 185, 212; aging, 211; Indian/Western, 32, 161, 163–164, 178; loss of, 7, 50–51, 53–60, 124, 126; and memory, 126–127; relational/transactional, 3, 105, 155, 177–178, 180, 292; subjugation of, 251
semantic network, 133, 201, 217, 276
semen, 133, 217, 233; loss, 131–132, 216–217, 233
semiotic frottage, 7
Sen, Amartya, 14, 99, 310, 317
senility, 17, 19–20, 27, 38, 41, 64, 87, 127, 167, 199–200, 207, 276–277, 292, 296; versus Alzheimer's, 5, 17, 32, 61; definition of, xv–xvii, 24–26, 32–34; history of, 47–48, 71–84; as trope of imperial appraisal, 22–23
senior citizen, 88, 92, 302
Sermion, 217
sevā, 115, 117, 120, 170, 173–174, 176, 180, 182, 185, 191, 194, 201, 209–211, 220, 236, 238, 241–243, 245, 252, 254–255, 268, 273, 275–276, 283, 300, 304. *See also* anxiety, *sevā*
Seva Lal, and family, 213, 228, 253
Shah, A. M., 317
Shangri-La, 222
Shani, 166, 309
Shankar the boatman, 9–10, 36, 307–308
Shankara, 143
Sharma, J. P., 87, 114
Sharma, M. L., 316

Sharma, Om Prakash, 205
Sharma, V. K., 234–235, 321
Sharma family, 24, 35, 37, 42, 192–193, 281
shanti, 194–198, 213, 215, 238–241, 251–252, 254
Shiva, 39, 155, 166, 223, 228, 234, 266
shock, 198, 209, 214–216
Shravan Kumar, 93, 166, 168–171, 180, 211
Shweder, Richard A., 178, 317, 321
Sicherman, Barbara, 314
siddhi, 155, 285–286
sign, 288–289
silence, 124, 170, 175–176, 181, 202, 237, 241, 272, 279, 283, 296
Simchowicz, Teofil, 314
Singh, Dr. (Varanasi psychiatrist), 133–134
Singh, Mahinder, 199–200, 321
Singh, R. H., 111–112
Singh, Virendra, 250
Singh, Yogendra, 317
Sinha, J. N. P., 316, 321
Sinha, Surajit, 277–278, 324
Siranji Devi, and family, 137–138, 140, 170, 213, 220, 246–249, 254–255, 270
sixtyishness (*saṭhiyāna*), 10, 33, 156–158, 165–166, 170, 175, 194, 197–198, 207, 211, 239, 276, 308
Smith, John, 66, 314
smṛti: literature, 142–143, 146, 204; memory, 129–131
Sobti, Krishna, 153, 160–161, 171, 320
social drama, 233
sociology of India, 22
softening, 139–140, 164, 187, 200–201, 292; cerebral, 20–23, 64–66, 69, 140; tropical, 21–23, 33, 49, 64–65
Somadeva, 112, 318, 319
son, 68, 117–119, 121, 123, 133–135, 137, 141, 144, 150, 159–175, 177, 179, 188, 192, 194, 196, 198, 201–203, 205, 207, 209–210, 214, 228, 237–249, 251–255, 263, 275–277, 285, 297, 303
Sontag, Susan, 318
Soodan, K. S., 89–91, 316
Soumerai, Stephen B., 322
South Asian Studies, 42
South India, 216
Sprenger, James, 315
Srikanta Murthy, K. R., 319
Srivastava, R. S., 316
śruti, 142–143, 146, 204
state, 81, 88, 91–92, 98–99, 106, 253, 281

status, 102
stigma, 20, 33, 46, 58, 83, 86, 177, 300
Stearns, Peter, 101, 317
Stevens, Preston S., 318
Strathern, Marilyn, xvii, 309
structuralism, 154–155, 171, 230–231
subaltern, 105–106, 119; physiology, 76, 83
subjectivity, 37, 53–60, 97, 164, 179
sublime, genrontological, 287
Subrahmanium, C., 92, 316
Subramaniam, Kamala, 153, 317
substitution, 171, 210
suffering, 177, 233, 269, 301, 303
Sulkava, R., 311
Sun Cities, 81, 114
superannuation, 41, 68, 110–113, 176, 247, 278–281, 284–286
Sushruta, 129
Suśruta Saṃhitā, 110, 129–130, 245, 319, 323
suture, 288
Svoboda, Robert E., 324
symbolic, 179, 288; Hegelian, 22
system, bodily, 22

tabloids, 47–53, 304
tamasha, 15–16, 18, 37
Tambe family, 10, 202–206, 282
Tambiah, Stanley, 281, 324
tapas, 155
Tapeshwara, and family, 243
Tarunachandra, 145
Taussig, Michael, 270, 324
technobiological artifact, 84
technology, symbolic use of, 20, 32
television, 128, 302
tension, 194–195, 207–208, 233
testamentary capacity, 24–25
Thakur, 226–228, 232, 236, 252–253
Tharu, Susie, 105, 317
theodicy, 53, 63, 242, 269, 301
Thewlis, Malford, 69, 314
thick analysis, xvi
Thirty-Plus, 136, 220
36-Hour Day, The, 54–55, 58
Thomas, Eugene, 205
"303" (tonic), 135
Tiffany, William J., 314
Tikri village, 145
time, 168, 170, 270, 285–286, 288–289, 293; collapse of, 58–59; as violence, 32, 54

Times of India, 174, 195, 199, 266
tīrtha, 39, 115
Tiwari the lawyer, 24–25
tonic, 131–138, 145, 168, 198, 217–218, 220, 240, 246–247
total institution, 116, 296
totality, 32, 115, 120, 154, 231, 288–289
totalization, 7, 79, 89
touristic, 9, 14, 39, 292–293, 296
Townsend, Peter, 100, 317
toxemia, 23, 76
transactional, 22, 137, 144, 170, 220, 231–233, 244–245, 270, 281; deficit, 230, 247, 302; flow, 275; refusal, 201, 214, 266, 269. *See also* gift; self, relational/transactional
transmigration, 213
Trawick, Margaret, 154, 320
"trope of ambiguity," 71
tropical medicine, 21–22
Turner, Victor, 16, 56, 284, 310, 313, 321
Tytler, Jadgish, 174

Uberoi, J. P. S., 49, 322
Unani, 40
uncanny, 268–270
uncle, 136, 175, 206, 212, 243, 271; *tau*, 157–158, 203
undernutrition, 245
United Nations, 38, 266
United States, 62, 109–111, 200, 218, 292, 294–295, 303–305; fieldwork, 6, 48–50, 53–61, 70, 117; history of old age in, 62–64, 69, 73–74, 76–79, 81–84, 101; policy debate in, 71, 94; West of, 53, 58–60, 304
University of Kentucky study, 85
unmatching, 171, 173, 175, 177, 212
Untouchable, 204, 237. *See also* Chamar
urbanization, 17, 89
Uttar Pradesh, 10, 35, 281–282
utopia, gerontological, 91, 97

Vaishya, 226
vānaprastha (forest-dwelling stage), 113–115, 196, 202–203, 205, 214, 237, 251, 275, 277. *See also* ashram, Vanaprastha
Van der Veen, Klaas W., 317
Varanasi (Banaras, Benares, Kashi), 1–4, 9, 14, 24, 31, 34–37, 39–43, 105, 115, 121, 127–129, 131, 133–139, 150, 154–155, 159–160, 166–168, 174, 179, 186, 188–200, 203–206, 208–211, 216–217, 222–228, 236–237, 245,
252, 254, 258–260, 263–268, 270–273, 277–278, 282, 284–285, 291–293, 295, 297, 300, 302–304, 307–308, 310, 313, 320, 322
Varuna, 223, 257–258
vasana, 143
Vasant College, 206, 264, 303
vasodilator, 69, 80, 218
Vatuk, Sylvia, 124–125, 140, 170, 175–176, 181, 184, 200, 240, 248, 312, 318, 320–321
vāyu, 153, 181, 245
Vedanta, 142–143
Vedas, 135, 142–143, 187–188, 203, 206, 226, 245
Venkoba Rao, A. K., 216, 218, 311–312, 321
victimhood, 33, 47, 50, 53–54, 56, 59, 61, 69; "other victim," 51, 53–54, 56, 69, 201, 294, 296, 304
vidanga kalpa, 129, 132
Vijaya Kumar, S., 316
Vikramacarita, 146, 319
Vinayashila, 112, 145, 219, 288
violence, 54, 268
Vipat, and family, 237–242
Vishwanath, and family, 241–243, 323
Visvanathan, Shiv, 310
Vivekananda, Swami, 93
voice, xv, 47, 54, 58–59, 73–74, 78, 124, 149–151, 153–158, 170, 174–181, 183, 188, 194, 202, 210, 221, 223, 230, 237–238, 240–241, 244–246, 248–250, 255, 265, 267–269, 271–279, 282–283, 285, 293, 300

Wadia, Noshir H., 311–312
Walford, Roy, 110–112, 129, 153, 317
Walker, Barbara, 315
wandering, 51–53, 61, 202, 210, 303
Warthin, Aldred, 68, 78, 314
weakener/weakened, 232, 236, 243, 252, 255
weakness (*kamzorī*), 37, 78, 130, 134–135, 138, 161, 182, 190, 194, 198, 207, 213, 217, 220, 223, 227–238, 240, 243–244, 247, 249, 251–252, 255, 269, 300–302, 322; of brain/mind (*dimāg*), 10, 37, 147, 196, 200, 205, 210, 212, 216, 233–235, 238–239, 241, 244, 248; of hands and feet (*hāth pair*), 124–125, 176, 212, 245; of memory, 215
Weber, Max, 281
Weiner, Dora, 64–65, 314
welfare, 4, 48, 116–117, 178
West, 8–9, 17, 19, 37–38, 93, 98, 104–106, 129, 135, 178, 184, 190, 223, 241, 285, 305
Westernization, 17, 89

Weyer, Johannes, 72–74, 78, 315

White, David, 266, 324

widow, 40, 77–79, 81, 113–114, 116–120, 185, 205–208, 239–240, 243, 264–268, 270, 272–274, 278, 283; *kāśīvāsī*, 206, 250–252, 264–265, 273, 275, 277

Wig, N. N., 311

wisdom, 123, 212

witchcraft, 22, 72–74, 78–79, 81, 85–86, 258–261, 265, 268–274, 283. See also *ḍaīn; cuṟail*

Wolfenstein, Martha, 315

Women's Coordinating Council (WCC), 116–118

Woodward, Kathleen, 321

World Assembly on Aging, 93–95, 99, 184, 316

World Health Organization (WHO), 28

World Parliament of Religions, 93

"worldly ascetic," 236

world system, 48, 100, 219

Yadav, Laloo Prasad, 283

Yayati, 166–170, 179

Yesavage, J. A., 322

Yogavasiṣṭha, 144

yogi/yoga, 110, 113, 142, 145, 185, 236, 285

Young, Allan, 301, 325

Zagreb, 7, 15–19, 31–33, 38, 48, 87, 199, 305, 310

Zandu, 134, 137, 159

Zimmermann, Francis, 245, 317–319, 323

Compositor:	Impressions Book and Journal Services, Inc.
Text:	10/12 Baskerville
Display:	Baskerville
Printer and binder:	Thomson-Shore, Inc.